Action Stations Revisited

Other books by Michael J F Bowyer include

Mosquito (with C Martin Sharp)

2 Group – A Complete History 1936-1945

Air Raid!

Interceptor Fighters

Action Stations Revisited No 1 – Military Airfields of East Anglia

Actions Stations Revisited No 2 – Central England and the London area

Action Stations Revisited No 6 – Military Airfields of the Cotswolds and Central Midlands

Force for Freedom – The USAF in the UK since 1948

The Battle of Britain – Fifty Years On

Aircraft for the Few – The RAF Fighters and Bombers in 1940

The Spitfire Fifty Years On

Aircraft for the Many – A Detailed Survey of the RAF's Aircraft in June 1944

Aircraft for the Royal Air Force

The Stirling Story

Action Stations Revisited

The complete history of Britain's
military airfields:
No. 1 Eastern England

Michael J F Bowyer

Crécy Publishing Limited

First published in 2000 by Crécy Publishing Limited
Second edition 2010
All rights reserved

A CIP record for this book is available from the British Library

ISBN 9 780859 791458

Printed and bound in the UK by MPG Books Ltd

Crécy Publishing Limited
1a Ringway Trading Estate, Shadowmoss Road, Manchester M22 5LH
www.crecy.co.uk

CONTENTS

INTRODUCTION AND ACKNOWLEDGEMENTS

In passing

This, the third major revision of *Action Stations*, updates what has, for thirty years, been highly popular at home and abroad. It appears because, since the appearance of *Action Stations Revisited* in 2000, the RAF, like so much else, has undergone fundamental change. New types of aircraft – or 'platforms' as they are now quaintly known – are replacing Cold War warriors, and main military airfields serve as home bases for supporting engagements of the latest threats.

Action Stations first appeared in 1979 when the Cold War dominated international relations. How long ago that seems. Tornado had yet to enter service, a Falklands War was unexpected and no bombing mission had been launched from the UK since May 1945. Personal computers were still a rare novelty like their accompanying daisywheel printers. Laptops, inkjets, lasers, mobile phones, digital cameras, CDs, the 'Web', UAVs and much else were all for the future.

Many highly regarded personalities have, since 2000, become treasured memories. Foremost among the unquestionably great is that irreplaceable and justly famous East Anglian, Sir Arthur Marshall, who in 2008 became the first person to be awarded aviation pioneer status by the Royal Aeronautical Society. His passing at the age of 103 in January 2007 brought to a close the era of great aviation achievement. He always rated as his most important contribution his 1940 plan for much faster output of RAF pilots by choosing the best of the new pilots and training them to become instructors, thereby increasing pilot output at a most critical time. Marshall Aerospace, for which Sir Arthur was then a test pilot, was entrusted with making the Mosquito into a superlative night-fighter by marrying it to scanning radar, and overhauled Typhoons to keep the front line supplied from D-Day to VE-Day. Well known is the speed by which his company designed and developed in-flight refuelling equipment for the RAF Hercules at the time of the Falklands campaign. Lesser known is Sir Arthur's scheme to achieve rapid getaway by the Valiant V-force. Sir Arthur was honoured and remembered by more than 900 people in a never-to-be-forgotten memorial service held in cavernous No 17, 'the big hangar' at Cambridge. It was, without any doubt, a sad and very special milestone in aviation history.

Quite different was the loss of someone much admired on both sides of 'the pond', the USAAF's Best Friend, dear Roger Freeman. No one, anywhere, has done more to keep alive and revered the memory of the men and 'airplanes' of what he christened 'The Mighty Eighth'. From 1947 Roger was a close friend, ever seizing the moment to direct his grand sense of humour towards me (much to my pleasure) and to place me in 'disadvantageous' situations, which, I can now reveal, were (fortunately) carefully and mutually devised. There must be millions of people who miss Roger, a delightful companion, very popular writer, fine raconteur. Immediately following his memorial service in Dedham church, the B-17 'Sally B' roared across low, singing his praises. Moments later a P-51 did a high-speed, whistling climb into the wild blue yonder. Either Roger's spirit was aboard the Mustang or it was climbing to be nearer to it.

Farewell also had to be taken of Bruce Robertson, who became well known in the 1950s for the books he wrote for Harleyford. Leaders they were in their field, and 'Robbie' was greatly thrilled when he persuaded the Air Ministry to release details and drawings of the Lancasters used for the dams raid in 1943 so that they could be featured in his Lancaster book. All subsequent 'dambuster' epics stemmed from that magic morning at Woodford, which has come to give a second meaning to 617 Squadron's motto, 'Après moi le deluge'. After a stint as Editor of *The Recognition Journal*, he later edited *Air Clues*. He was particularly interested in the 1914-1918 air war, of which he held encyclopaedic knowledge. All who had the privilege of knowing and working with him found Bruce highly likeable, a person of great charm with a grand sense of humour. On the day of his retirement

"TAKE - OFF : 1945"

Just remembering Roger Freeeman, his skills, his friendship with so many.

from the MoD his love of Californian wine was celebrated by the appearance in Main Building of many of the unusual and significantly shaped bottles then in use. All were filled with yellow water!

Gone, too, is David Dean, who in 1978 produced the superb pace-making diagrams used in *Action Stations 1*. David was a highly professional, very self-demanding draughtsman involved in the defence industry. He teamed with me in the 1950s as my illustrator, like another close artistic companion, George Burn, who passed away in 2008. Marshall pilot-trained in 1945, he tuned his skill to handling Horsas and Hamilcars, and was so proud to have served in the Glider Pilot Regiment. At his passing the Regiment's Colour was suitably deployed. How he would have loved that! George holds a special place in publishing for he introduced to the aviation press, and extended, the mechanical tint Zippatone, forerunner of Letratone. George pioneered its use in books at the time when photo lithography was changing everything – and especially non-professional newsletters. At last it was possible to include 'photos' and elaborate drawings in publications wherever appropriate and without the considerable expense of plate-making.

Many more well-known and influential personalities from the war years – professional and amateur – have recently passed on, among them Charles Cain, who replaced Peter Masefield (later Sir), of BEA fame, as Editor of *The Aeroplane Spotter*. The effect of 'The Spotter' upon aviation was enormous because not only did it encourage widespread wartime interest, but also launched many into a career in aviation. It set very high standards of accuracy, illustration, quality and stylish presentation. Everything aeronautical in print since the mid-1940s reflects the attainment levels set by 'Charlie' and 'The Spotter'. It was also he who introduced many aviation enthusiasts to the magic of photo lithography.

As this revision of *Action Stations* was under way news came of the sudden departure of another outstanding aviation enthusiast, Ray Sturtivant. His meticulous recording and skilled presentation display a level of attainment, which should be emulated by everyone with academic calling. I first corresponded with him in 1948 when another of world class standard, that top-echelon organisation Air-Britain, was formed. Between them Ray and 'AB' established a standard superb. When Ray's interest in military aviation began, gathering material and photographs was fraught with problems due to misguided 'security' and total inaccessibility of official files. When many records became 'open' after thirty years, Ray performed a special service by seeking in particular those relating to the Fleet Air Arm. Thank you, Ray, for all the fascination you brought into our lives.

Tribute must also be paid to Eric Watts, who for many years maintained Air-Britain's photograph collection. Eric, a true 'Page's' man, was an aviation fan throughout his life. How he delighted in extolling the virtues of the Victor while regarding the Vulcan with less enthusiasm. He presented me with a picture of a 7 Squadron Lincoln used later in *Action Stations*. 'How did you acquire it?' I asked him. His sardonic reply: 'I shot it through an open toilet window, Bowyer. A young lad like you needs to learn to show initiative.'

Very many people have, over the decades, contributed to *Action Stations 1* and its derivatives. Indeed, there can surely be few enthusiasts from the 1940-1960 era who have not at some time weighed in with information and photographs. For the content of this latest volume thanks are particularly due, in alphabetical order, to Stanley Barraclough, Keith Braybrooke, Tommy Cushing, Fred Donaldson Jr and Snr, Chris Jakes and The Cambridgeshire Collection, Ian MacIntegart, Graham Murfitt, who has contributed fine photographs, George Pennick, who has done likewise and been ever ready to provide much help, the late John Rawlings, the late Bruce Robertson, Andy Thomas, Eric Watts and Alan Wright. My grateful thanks are in particular due to Andy Jackson who, when my main computer was being 'difficult', tackled it with great skill and persistence to make it behave!

Many organisations have given help, among them BAe Systems, Marshall Aerospace, the 100th Bomb Group Museum at Thorpe Abbotts, the 390th BG Museum Parham, the Imperial War Museum Duxford, the Ministry of Defence and of course the Royal Air Force and its Museum, National Archives (ex-PRO) and the USAF.

Before closing this Introduction let us spare thoughts for those, mostly elderly and some with well-known names, who are encountering the problems that ageing brings. If you are a young reader, give them a thought because they, and many recently taken from us, laid the foundations of the pleasures derived when flying, photographing, observing, scribbling away, reading or just experiencing the thrill of aviation. In so doing you will be affording them a well-earned and appreciated memorial.

Michael J. F. Bowyer

Cambridge, February 2010

GLOSSARY

271/297	Eg 271 aircraft attacked the target out of 297 despatched
A&AEE	Aeroplane & Armament Experimental Establishment
A&IEU	Armament & Instrument Experimental Unit
AA	Anti-aircraft
AACU	Anti-Aircraft Co-operation Unit
AAR	Air-to-air refuelling
AATT Flight	Anti-Aircraft and Target Towing Flight
ACHU	Aircrew Holding Unit
ADGB	Air Defence of Great Britain (previously Fighter Command)
AEF	Air Experience Flight
AFDS	Air Fighting Development Squadron
AFDU	Air Fighting Development Unit
AFRC	Air Force Reserve Command
AFS	Advanced Flying School
AI	Airborne Interception (radar)
ANG	Air National Guard
ANS	Air Navigation School
Anti-diver	patrol to shoot down V-1 flying bombs
AOC (-in-C)	Air Officer Commanding (-in-Chief)
AOP	Air Observation Post
APC	Armament Practice Camp
APS	Armament Practice Station
ASH	Narrow beam radar allowing low-level operations
ASP	Aircraft Servicing Platform
ASR	Air-Sea Rescue
AWDS	All-Weather Development Squadron
AWFCS	All-Weather Fighter Combat Squadron
B&G flight	Bombing & Gunnery Flight
Baedeker raid	German reprisal attack delivered upon historic city
BAT Flight	Blind Approach Training Flight
BBMF	Battle of Britain Memorial Flight
BDTF	Bomber Defence Training Flight
BDU	Bombing Development Unit
BG	Bomb Group (USAAF)
BLEU	Blind Landing Experimental Unit
BSDU	Bomber Support Development Unit
CAACU	Civilian Anti-Aircraft Co-operation Unit
Calvert **Bar** landing light system	A system of bars and intervening lights leading to the runway threshold
Carpet operation	Supply dropping sortie to Resistance forces

CCRC	Combat Crew Replacement Center
CFS	Central Flying School
Circus	Operation escorted by fighters to entice enemy response
CONUS	USAF supply organisation (ie. Continental United States)
CSE	Central Signals Establishment
Darkie system	Method of homing at night on radio bearings
Day Ranger	Operation to engage air and ground targets within a wide but specified area, by day
DFCS	Day Fighter Combat School
Distil operation	Fighter operation to shoot down enemy aircraft minesweeping, usually off Denmark
Drem lighting	System of outer markers and approach lights installed at many airfields in the early years of the war
E&RFTS	Elementary & Reserve Flying Training School
EBTS (Coastal Command)	Elementary and Basic Training School
ECM	Electronic Counter Measures
EFTS	Elementary Flying Training School
EM	Enlisted Men (USAAF)
ETO	European Theatre of Operations
Exercise *Spartan*	Exercise to establish methods of making entire airfield formation mobile
Fg Off	Flying Officer
FG	Fighter Group
FIDO	Fog Investigation and Dispersal Operation
Fighter Night	Fighter patrol over area where anti-aircraft gunners were ordered not to fire, sometimes restricted to certain altitudes
Firebash sorties	Sorties by Mosquitoes of 100 Group with the aircraft delivering incendiary or napalm loads on German airfields
FTS	Flying Training School
Gee	Medium-range radio aid to navigation, equipment employing ground transmitters and airborne receiver
GP (bomb)	General Purpose high explosive bomb
GRU	General Reconnaissance Unit
GSU	Group Support Unit
H2S	Airborne radar navigation target location aid
HE (bomb)	High explosive bomb
IRBM	Intermediate Range Ballistic Missile
LAC	Leading Aircraftman
Lagoon	Shipping reconnaissance operation off the Dutch coast
LCN	Method of identifying the weight characteristics of a runway
LFS	Lancaster Finishing School
Lindholme gear	Equipment dropped from air-sea rescue aircraft to crew ditched in the sea, developed at Lindholme
LNSF	Light Night Striking Force – Mosquitoes of 8 Group
Lorenz system	Blind beam approach radio beacon system
MAEE	Marine Aircraft Experimental Establishment

Mahmoud	Sortie by night fighter to specific point over enemy territory to engage his night fighters in that area
Mandrel	Airborne radar jammer device used by 100 Group
MAP	Ministry of Aircraft Production
MCU	Mosquito Conversion Unit
MoS	Ministry of Supply
MR squadron	Medium Reconnaissance squadron
MU	Maintenance Unit
Night Ranger	Operation to enemy air and ground targets within a within specified area, by night
Oboe	Ground-controlled radio aid to blind bombing in which one beam indicated track to be followed another at the bomb release point
OCU	Operational Conversion Unit
OLUK	Operating Location United Kingdom
Operation *Aphrodite*	Use of an aircraft as radio-controlled bomber
Operation *Channel Stop*	Attempt to close the English Channel to the passage of enemy shipping
Operation *Haddock*	Code name for force of Wellingtons sent to the south of France in 1940 to bomb Italy
Operation *Manna*	Delivery of food and supplies to Holland by air May 1945
Operation *Musketeer*	Code name for Suez operation 1956
Operation *Starkey*	Large scale feint invasion of the Pas de Calais in 1943 mounted to assess reaction and bring his fighters into action
Operation *Torch*	Invasion of North Africa in November 1942
Operation *Varsity*	Airborne support for Rhine crossing March 1945
Operation *Exodus*	Ferrying of displaced persons
ORTU	Operational Refresher Training Unit
ORP	Operational Readiness Platform
OUT	Operational Training Unit
(P)AFU	Pilots Advanced Flying Unit
PAMPA	Long-range weather reporting sortie
PFF	Pathfinder Force
PFFNTU	Pathfinder Force Navigational Training Unit
Pirat	Luftwaffe daylight bomber attacking targets of opportunity
POL depot	Petrol, Oil and Lubricants depot
POW	Prisoner of war
Prata	Weather reconnaissance flight
PRU	Photographic Reconnaissance Unit
PSP runway	Pierced Steel Planking runway
Pundit light/letters	Letters or lights displayed giving the airfield identity
Q-site	A site flashing lights to represent a mock airfield to attract enemy attention at night
Ramrod	Bomber raid escorted by fighters and aimed at destruction of a specified target
RCAF	Royal Canadian Air Force
RCM /Squadron /Flight	Radio Counter Measures Squadron Flight
RDF	Radio Direction Finding

RFS	Reserve Flying School
Rhombus	Weather reporting flight
Rhubarb	Low-level strike operation mounted in cloudy conditions
RIC	Reconnaissance Intelligence Centre
RLG	Relief Landing Ground
Roadstead	Fighter operation mounted to stop the passage of enemy shipping
Rodeo	Fighter sweep
Rover	Coastal Command armed patrol to search for enemy shipping
RTC	Recruit Training Centre
SAC	US Strategic Air Command
Sashlite bulb	Photo-flash bulb used for training and experimental purposes
SBC	Small Bomb Container
Serrate sortie	Operation to locate and destroy enemy night fighters and combined with night bomber raids
SHQ	Station Headquarters
SLG	Satellite Landing Ground
SOE operations	Operations under the control of the Special Operations Executive
SRW	Strategic Reconnaissance Wing
Sunray	Overseas training flight for bomber crews
SWO	Station Warrant Officer
TAF	Tactical Air Force
TAMU	Transport Aircraft Maintenance Unit
TAW	Tactical Airlift Wing (USAF)
TDY	Temporary Duty Overseas (USAF)
TFW	Tactical Fighter Wing
THUM	Weather reporting flight (temperature and humidity)
TRS	Tactical Reconnaissance Squadron
UAS	University Air Squadron
UAV	Unmanned Aerial Vehicle
UP	Projector for firing anti-aircraft Z rockets
USAAC	United States Army Air Corps
USAAF	United States Army Air Force (designated thus from 20 June 1941, although the term Army Air Corps remained in common use long after that date)
USAF	Post-war formation from the USAAF, the United States Air Force
USAFE	USAF Europe
Window	Metallised paper strips dropped by bombers to disrupt enemy radar system

THREATS, RESPONSES, IDEAS

Nothing is forever, not even diamonds. Fundamental changes in international relations, altering threats and limited resources have led to a slim, overworked Royal Air Force, a sleek equivalent of its earliest days. After ending its role as a major home defence, deterrent and rapid response force, its main raison d'être has become the provision of air support for the Army. Home defence in the main now means high alert protection from airborne terrorist attack. Eastern England's elaborate airfields have become home bases for expeditionary activities.

THREATS

Following the collapse of the east European Communist monolith that started in 1989, six discernable threats of varying importance evolved. All involved lands by, or relatively close to, the eastern Mediterranean. Fortunately, the feared break-up of Yugoslavia followed by the trouble in Kosovo developed after the demise of the USSR. NATO's provision of force to impose a curb on the activities of warring elements in the Balkans included participation by Coltishall's Jaguar squadrons and Lakenheath's USAF F-15s.

RESPONSES

Iraq's unexpected, unprovoked, foolish invasion of Kuwait, and fear of its extension (surely not feasible) into Saudi Arabia, sensibly encountered worldwide condemnation. It eventually brought a multi-power campaign that freed Kuwait.

By contrast the '9/11' evil assault upon New York's twin towers provoked wrong responses. By 2002 the US President and those around him had decided to avenge that heinous crime by destroying Saddam Hussein's power base. A more logical action should have been a ferocious, sustained assault upon those in Afghanistan and nearby mountain regions responsible for unleashing hideous terror upon New York.

In 1997 the British saddled themselves with an unwise Prime Minister, Tony Blair. Foolishly, he and his unimpressive entourage decided to ally themselves closely with the 2003 internationally disapproved US invasion of Iraq. By misguidedly claiming that intelligence sources had discovered Iraq to be holding weapons capable of great destruction, they attempted to gain the British nation's support for a crazy venture. To have suggested that in less than an hour the Iraqis could prepare and fire large missiles lacked as much credulity as reality. A US official, during an early 2002 transatlantic voyage, conversing with me loudly, boasted that 'next year we are going to invade Iraq, deal with Saddam', adding that we would view the opening rounds with what he termed 'shock and awe'. Hussein was no saint, but he was not responsible for the 9/11 outrage.

Many personnel from eastern airfields, British and American, were sucked into the venture, while few were more logically sent to deal with terrorist activity in Afghanistan. There was ample justification for a punishing campaign in the latter region. In the case of Iraq let there be not the slightest prevarication. That was an illegal, unprovoked attack upon a sovereign state. The assault, with the aforementioned 'shock and awe', killed tens of thousands of Iraqi civilians. Incredibly, no post-combat pacification plan and policy for withdrawal from Iraq existed. Strong, specially trained and properly equipped forces were needed, but in both theatres those available had been intended for a far different fight. Harriers and Tornados designed to stem a rapid Soviet thrust across the European Plain instead became weapons platforms committed to backing street battles and attacking small groups of 'dissidents'. Education, freedom, democracy and choice would have been far better commodities to deploy. Minds, not bodies, needed attention. Instead, RAF service men and women from eastern bases were despatched to participate in expeditionary activities. Reduction in RAF total strength gives them unacceptably brief time at home.

After decades of deterring war the Services were, disgracefully, being used to start them. Blair's schemes soon brought not only loss of life. Transportation costs, together with damage to equipment and necessary weapons, incurred high cost. These expensive activities were undertaken as vast numbers of immigrants, many poor and unskilled, were by various means establishing themselves in Britain. Housing and sustaining them, providing health care and education while simultaneously fighting two wars, has become horrendously costly. Britain has insufficient resources, inadequate infrastructure and not enough space for the scale of population expansion seen in recent years. Race and colour are irrelevant, it is a matter of logistics and money, the vast expenditure affecting Britain's armed forces.

One outcome was the rapid destruction of the Jaguar strike force more suitable than most for expeditionary activity and rough field operation. Its demise so soon after update at considerable cost, illustrates bad governmental management.

Arrival of the financial collapse, along with the incredibly inept government, has undermined much of British life and generated alarming prospects for Britain's future and its military forces. British Government needs to make fundamental policy decisions for we are at major crossroads. Although a threat from mainland Europe has faded, the extent and variable nature of the EU could lead to instability and its sole currency might release problems as of yore. The EU's undemocratic and dictatorial core, and the readiness shown recently by some states to 'go it alone' when faced with financial disaster show a need for care. Trouble is likely to come, from traditionally unstable and troublesome states. Iran – for decades a cause for concern – tops the list.

When it comes to priorities, Britain's land forces will have first place with the RAF occupying mainly an Army support role. It would be very unwise to further reduce the home defence fighter force and the RAF's air-to-air refuelling capability. For Britain to lose its nuclear deterrent might be an irrecoverable, regrettable move, although the cost of maintaining Trident is high. Perhaps a less costly submarine launched alternative to Trident might be possible? Enormous, too, is the expense of the planned large attack carriers that the Royal Navy so much desires, and which might be useful in supporting land action far from home. Whether Britain should keep punching high while other comparable nations fail to play a fair part in trouble areas needs consideration.

Answers to such questions undoubtedly relate to the few active remaining military establishments in the eastern region. One thing is certain. Never again must we have a Defence Minister occupying a second office of State, one economical with the truth and certainly never one who, when standing by a Nimrod, enquired politely, 'What's this?' Overseas adventures have not only played havoc with Service and family life, they have undoubtedly damaged morale. Additionally, they have encouraged responsive assaults upon civilised values by fanatical terrorists who need no such encouragement. Resultant government action has greatly eroded freedom that has been in place for hundreds of years and has been defended at great expense from the airfields of Eastern England. Government snooping upon privacy through shoals of often ridiculous, dubious anti-terrorist regulations must bring satisfaction to the despicable creatures prepared to launch awful atrocities. Dreadful as those are, it should also be remembered that more people die daily from falling over in Britain than from terrorism.

IDEAS

Greatly influencing the defence arena is the amazing pace of technological change – incredible its speed during the thirty years since *Action Stations 1* appeared. Writing then was by hand, or aided by a mechanical typewriter. Widespread computerisation, digital this-and-that, sensors, the Internet, sophisticated mobile and astonishing phones able to take photographs and via satellite link to view (possibly with alarm) the state of one's bank account, surely each is the terrorist's best friend. All were way off in 1979. These objects will surely become historically rated as revolutionary. Closed-circuit TV – acceptable when sensibly applied, but never when used to intrude upon harmless personal behaviour – was in its infancy. Attempts were made in the late 1940s to use television to obtain survey pictures over Canada and transmit them live to ground stations. It proved very difficult. Present-day real-time 3D air-to-ground data links would have seemed amazing. That privately owned aircraft would have 'glass cockpits', and be able to find their own way, would have provoked disbelief. That it would be possible to control aircraft by voice command – limited to a degree in a Typhoon – would have seemed ludicrous in the Battle of Britain. To electronically release precision advanced weapons from an unmanned airborne vehicle in any weather, with extreme accuracy and through a protected radio link from a small computer thousands of miles away, would have bordered on an impossible dream even twenty years ago. Such has been the advance of multi-role electronics that all of these developments are in daily use.

The heart of the RAF, its personnel, had fallen numerically from 500,000 at the end of the Second World War to around 40,000 in 2009, a total too small for the heavy demands placed upon them. The number of main active airfields has dramatically fallen. Of 132 airfields featured in *Action Stations Revisited 1*, only nine remain active, two accommodating the USAF. Coningsby, Marham and Waddington are three of the RAF's eleven Main Operating Bases, or front-line UK airfields. Wattisham has taken on a major role as the training, maintenance and operational home base for the Army's Apache attack helicopter. Wyton, to become a major intelligence-gathering centre, retains flying training elements fielding Grob 115E Tutors. More reside at Cranwell whose associated RLG, Barkston Heath, houses Slingsby Fireflies. Sculthorpe sees limited use.

THE CIVILIANS

Cambridge-based Marshall Aerospace looks after the RAF's much worn, intensively employed Hercules fleet, a task commenced in December 1966. It also cares for foreign and civilian C-130s, and supports the RAF's TriStar fleet. Marshall Aerospace had the exacting task of flight-testing the three-spool Rolls-Royce/BMW TP400, the most powerful turboprop engine ever developed outside Eastern Europe. Driving a giant eight-bladed propeller, the completely new power plant has been tested for the politically aggravated, much troubled, long gestating Future Large Aircraft, the Airbus 400M tactical military transport intended to replace the RAF's battered C-130K Hercules fleet. Cambridge Airport's military association is further enhanced by secondment of service personnel.

Marshall Aerospace has established a business aircraft centre and supports the Cessna Citation business jet. For those purposes the only new large hangar erected in Eastern England for many years came into use during October 2008. Flying training – personal and business – is also a major feature of activity at Cambridge.

London Stansted Airport, set in fine countryside some way from London and dominated by Ryanair, hopes and desperately tries to expand. It still needs to attract and keep long-haul operators, and ultimately will probably require a second runway despite damaging the local scene. Publicity shy Norwich Airport, once RAF Horsham St Faith, has limited but useful internal and overseas services backed by friendly passenger facilities. Ten small remnants of Second World War airfields for light aircraft increase the total to twenty-one regularly active aerodromes in the region under review.

ABLE, ADAPTIVE, AGILE

Bomber, Coastal, Fighter, Strike and Training Commands have flown into Memory Lane, replaced by a Royal Air Force that has evolved as able, adaptive and agile. No longer available to deliver a nuclear slam, the Service employs multi-role 'launch platforms' from which to thrust a rapier instead of unleashing a bludgeon.

RAF aircraft of the 1930s Expansion Schemes were designed to carry weapons internally, in keeping with the need for streamlining. External loads left behind with biplane days caused some surprise when carried by Germany's best bomber, the Ju 88, and soon by Me 109s and 110s. In 1941 Hurricanes externally carrying bombs and soon heavy guns and rockets set a new trend in the RAF. By the 1990s, more sophisticated weapons and gadgets as hung externally beneath Marham's Tornados, greatly upgraded their operational capabilities.

Highly portentous is the activity at Waddington, home of No 39 Squadron whose overseas equipment is the MQ-9 Reaper. A small unmanned aerial vehicle (UAV), it is able to quietly loiter for long periods reconnoitring and can, if needs be – even when thousands of miles away from base – strike with amazing accuracy at an unsuspecting foe. Recoverable UAVs are quite slow fliers that cannot change orbit zones quickly, but they will be developed into fast movers and undoubtedly see ever more widespread use. They are attractive because they require neither expensive aircrew, nor large bases.

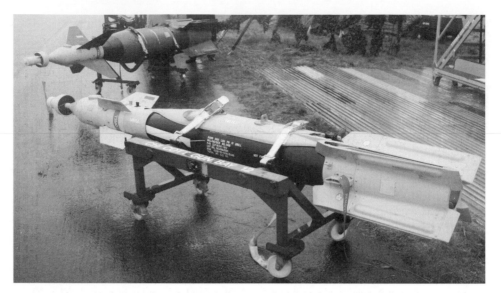

Modern expensive 'bomb' – Paveway IV, 225kg warhead, Global positioning guidance, can be re-programmed in flight.

Tornado GR4A ZG714 alias '124' of XIII Squadron carrying Thermal imaging (TIALD) centre-line pod and two long-range tanks. 'Chaff' dispensers outboard.

What future – if any in the long term – for the impressive, 1934 custom-designed, traditional Permanent Stations with seventy-year old large 'C' Type Aircraft Sheds and adjacent mock-Georgian buildings? Artistically designed, elaborately built, costly to maintain and operate, having lengthy perimeters and large domestic sites, these huge airfields need to be well defended against land assault. There have been improvements to domestic sites, and some have RASs. Efficient, soulless, adapted modern industrial units have been added to some stations and include the engineering facility at Marham, Waddington's Cobb hangar and giant 'Sentry box'. All but gone is the need for huge aeroplane sheds costing much to heat, light and maintain. Such was the overall excellence of design that they still tone remarkably well with their surroundings, and are not outdated in appearance. Will the airfields of the 1930s expansion period one day be regarded as the castles of our age?

Tornado GR 1 XX946 of TWCU Honington before an updated 'Aeroplane Shed Type C'.

With little likelihood of ferocious air attack upon UK air bases in the foreseeable future, the Hardened Aircraft Shelters (HASs) of the 1980s, expensive to construct, costly to use although still useful as at Coningsby and Marham, have been rather outflanked. Favoured now are transportable, easy and rapid to erect Rubberised Aircraft Shelters (RASs), ideal for a mobile air force and useful also at main bases. Moveable weapons stores and fuel dumps have become necessities.

Paired T2 Transportable Sheds, Duxford. Left one modified for tall fin.

Earth banks and sandbags served as WW2 revetments. Reinforced blast walls carefully angled protected dispersed aircraft (here at Coltishall) 1950-1980s.

Hardened Aircraft Shelters (HAS) were developed from the blast wall concept. Reinforced concrete construction.. Those at Bentwaters each held two A-10 Thunderbolt IIs.

Rubberised Aircraft Shelter (RAS). Steel framed, rubberised fabric, portable, easy to erect. Suitable for the Typhoon.

RAS showing protective roll-down front curtain. Ideal for expeditionary activities.

The expeditionary air force is also reliant upon transportable, simple to erect, metal-framed, fabric/rubberised protective tents. Many have a traditional footprint the size of former huts, 16 feet by 24 feet. Within the range are larger variants in which sophisticated activities ranging from battlefield scenarios to perimeter protection are undertaken, aided by sensors, laptops and multi-sized screens. Personnel sit at rudimentary wooden trestle tables equally suitable for church halls. Instead of elaborately protected hardened permanent buildings, tents accommodate briefing and intelligence organisations, mobile field kitchens, messes and, of course, easily erected mobile homes with plastic sheeted floors. More permanent structures, akin to shipping containers, can also be quickly positioned for multifarious purposes. Theoretically, it is now possible, through modern mobility, to quickly establish a sophisticated operating base if space, terrain and surroundings allow.

Traditional 1920s-1930s style brick, slate roofed Barrack Block, Martlesham Heath, still to be seen alongside Ipswich by-pass.

In contrast accommodation 2000s style. Multi-purpose tent, footprint often 16 ft x 24 ft. Useful during 'expeditions'.

Sturdy fabric tents, mixed sizes, for messing, operational activities and general purposes.

Transportable flying control 2000s style complete with radar unit.

Force protection on the ground has taken on much increased importance as a result of possible terrorist action and the deployments to Iraq and Afghanistan. Metal fences surround bases, activity along the perimeter being observed very effectively through electronic means, making assault or attempted penetration by day or night easily detectable. Rapid response using rocket weapons can fast remove a threat. Without the courageous RAF Regiment (HQ Honington, Suffolk) handling force protection, deployment of personnel and enormously expensive hardware and software would be highly vulnerable to terrorists and their like.

Sentinel R1 battlefield surveillance aircraft with a part of ground component alongside.

A BIG CHANGE

When on 1 April 2007 RAF Strike Command merged with Personnel & Training Command Innsworth to form HQ Air Command High Wycombe, a slimmer force structure emerged. It was committed to the UK Permanent Joint HQ at Northwood, apart from the Northern and Southern Quick Reaction Alert (QRA) squadrons at Leuchars in Fife and Coningsby. Current plans call for the Northern QRA force to operate the Tornado F3 until April 2011. The Southern QRA force operates Typhoons from Coningsby's HASs, and each station holds two aircraft at readiness. Since summer 2007 Typhoons have, on numerous occasions, been 'scrambled' to intrude upon roving and rumbling elderly Russian Bears curiously poking their noses towards the UK ADR.

The essence of the layout of the new force is its ability to rapidly achieve air superiority over battle zones, and respond to new tasks. To achieve that, assets were split between two new Groups. With 12,000 personnel, No 1 Group Air Combat holds the fast jet offensive and defensive squadrons. Air transport, air-to-air refuelling, air-sea rescue, casevac, disaster relief, ISTAR, airfield protection and civil contingency activities are the prerogative of Combat Support No 2 Group, which absorbed the 2005 No 3 Group intelligence set-up. Aircraft are mostly grouped by type at RAF stations, for both operational and economical reasons. Coningsby presently houses all the Typhoons, Marham shares the Tornado GR4 force with Lossiemouth, while Waddington holds intelligence, surveillance, targeting, attack and reconnaissance (ISTAR) squadrons. Detachments to war zones mean that many personnel and aircraft are away for much of the time, particularly those of No 2 Group.

Type J hangar, Coningsby, modified for tall fin aircraft.

Following agreement reached on 1 April 2003, and contracted for a minimum of ten years, HQ Elementary Flying Training in July 2003 became No 1 Elementary Flying Training School, part of No 22 (Training) Group, bearing a title of yesteryear. Ascent (a joint Lockheed-Martin and VT Group consortium) has since been awarded a contract within a Private Finance Initiative (PFI) scheme to operate elementary RAF aircrew training as part of the Military Flying Training Service. The Light Aircraft Flying Task, also a PFI and let to the Bombardier Service Division in 1990, is now managed by VT Aerospace. They supply civilian-registered Grob 115E Tutors to elementary training schools, UASs and AEFs. Babcock Defence Services agreed, through a six-year contract, to provide Slingsby T67M-260 Fireflies for use at the Defence Elementary Flying Training School, Barkston Heath, where No 703 Naval Air Squadron and No 674 Squadron Army Air Corps provide initial flying training.

A mobility introduction of 1 April 2006 was based upon a 1942 idea for forty 'Airfield HQ' organisations, the first of which, No 121 Airfield, formed in February 1943. Squadrons with like roles were brought together, necessary personnel and support facilities were drawn from various sources and the organisations earmarked for rapid transfer to France once a beachhead was secured. From hastily prepared landing grounds, squadrons would respond more easily to provide close support and air cover for the Army.

In similar style, and following the proven need in recent times to quickly transfer home-based squadrons to combat zones, an Expeditionary Air Wing (EAW) has been established at nine Main Operating Bases. Some 600 air and ground personnel and equipment are earmarked to establish a fully functioning Deployed Operating Base. They form a complete, rapidly deployable and sufficiently self-supporting organisation. Personnel drawn upon – not necessarily from the EAW main base – become acquainted with each other so that, when responding to rapid deployment, they can quickly become a team.

Three EAWs have been established in the eastern region. No 34 EAW at Waddington perpetuates the identity of the 1944 No 34 Wing, which, flying reconnaissance Mosquitoes and Wellington XIIIs, concentrated upon collecting tactical intelligence by day and night prior to, and following, the 1944 Normandy landings. No 121 EAW at Coningsby carries the identity number of the first wartime 'Airfield HQ', which comprised squadrons of ground-attack Hawker Typhoons and supporting organisations. Now it is concerned with Eurofighter Typhoon. No 138 EAW Marham, organised to deploy and support with Tornado GR4 squadrons, takes its identity from 'No 138 Airfield', which, in 1944, included Mitchell bomber and Mosquito fighter-bomber squadrons of No 2 Group 2TAF. Additional to these is Honington's Joint NBC Regiment including RAF Regiment, Army and Royal Marine personnel, whose skills relate to chemical, bacteriological and nuclear warfare. Although EAW home airfields present no obvious evidence of the organisations within, these are an essential feature of the modern RAF's structure. Squadron organisations remain, although in combat zones they draw upon aircraft already in position rather than bringing along from home bases the aircraft flown by them there. Squadron and unit identity markings carried by aircraft no longer confirm their assignment.

Throughout the Armed Services there is an ever-increasing percentage of women, many holding considerable responsibilities. In the RAF they fly and maintain aircraft and hold important status. In the tough Afghanistan environment they face the same harsh conditions, dangers and risks as their male counterparts. Casualties are, sadly, inevitable, and particularly from enemy improvised explosive devices. For service men and women those are an inbuilt risk, something little understood by civilians.

That 'health and safety' has been able to sneak into the armed services shows an unrealistic appreciation of the ethos of Service life that remains so very different from that led by civilians. Status differences between ranks, particularly in combat zones, have undoubtedly been softened for the better, and rules compartmenting men and women have been adapted sensibly, making service life more acceptable and equitable.

When the 1930s new stations opened, RAF dress remained a variation of early-20th-century Army dress, with puttees and peak caps being the order of the day. The change to Working Blue, Best Blue and forage cap for non-commissioned ranks came as war approached. Camouflage-patterned working dress is now the norm for almost all ranks. Parades are few, overseas deployments many, and working hours can be very variable.

If, like me, you experienced RAF life in the 1940s, the current living style would, for many, have been unknown. A private room for most, an armchair, a telly, en-suite facilities and a mess bill – oh, and a bedside reading lamp … what *would* the old SWO say? Maybe you've missed out on him, and his 'discip sergeant'? Well, you can't have everything. You can, though, and in a very short time, enjoy an overview of aerodrome development by trying the following tour.

COME TOUR WITH ME

A Fighter Command review estimated that about four million operational flights – mainly by four-engined bombers – were made over Cambridgeshire in 1944, mainly at between 1,000 and 18,000 feet. A further two million involved an amazing array of aircraft types. A likely total for current times is 500,000 movements annually, including high-flying, contrailing airliners in transit mainly to North America. Thus, the sky is empty compared with former times.

Few if any areas of the world offer a more comprehensive view of airfield design, purpose, use and development than Cambridgeshire. If looking at airfields is new to you, then it is easy to undertake from Cambridge a tour of a little over 50 miles chronologically embracing basic types spanning almost a century. Come with me, a life-long 'local', and tour my homeland!

Ideally, you should be on a bicycle – you can stop at will, have no parking problem, enjoy fresh air (plentiful in flat eastern areas) and pause at places of aeronautical interest. Cycling is now very hazardous, especially on main and country highways. So it had better be by car, and preferably on a fine summer day when the blue panoply above East Anglia is huge, wide open, and beautifully flecked with billowing cumulus so ideal for Gransden's sailplanes. With Ordnance Survey LandRanger Map No 154 so that you can appreciate just where you are, and of course a camera and notebook, let's start out from Cambridge's Madingley Road Park & Ride site.

The city may have witnessed more fascinating air activity than anywhere comparable. In wartime its sky saw passage of an astonishing array of unusual birds – the RAF's lone Ford Tri-motor, Wellington jet testbed, the Halifax III prototype, Do 215, Fw 200, SV4C, a Ju 86R, the F.9/40 Meteor prototype on its first cross-country, the twin-tailed Wellington II, Heston Phoenix and a Bermuda, just to mention a mere few. By contrast daily aircraft movements over the city now average between 50 and 150, mostly produced by light and business aircraft, civilian helicopters, occasional C-130s and high-fliers contrailing north-westerly. Military flying, once so obvious, has all but faded. Contrailing airliners can be considerable in number, their trails merging to generate evening and morning clouds reminiscent of 1940 days when, after intense fighting in the south, battle clouds rolled across the evening sky. In recent years there has been a direction reversal of the surface wind from south-west to north-east. Rainfall has been less, but thick gloomy clouds have all too often settled across East Anglia, sometimes staying for weeks. Fortunately, most main runways were laid on a NE/SW orientation, and flight patterns have needed adjustment. Much is made of 'global warming', but climate fluctuation – a better description – has been occurring for thousands of years irrespective of present-day unacceptably high pollution levels and their causes. It is important to separate the meteorological aspects from the political and financial slants!

While, sadly for such an aeronautically rich city, Cambridge has no aviation-orientated centre, it does have Magnificent Marshall Aerospace. Many great aeronautical personages have, or have had, links with them, and others with the University and city. Foremost, of course, is the late Sir Arthur Marshall. Top figures in aviation used to visit the Barnwell aerodrome where Sir Alan Cobham's Flying *Circus* delighted the locals. RAF fighter ace Johnnie Johnson learned to fly at the present Cambridge airport. Highly successful personages within industry and the services have also had links with the University. Frank Whittle, the jet-engine pioneer, who studied in the Department of Engineering in the mid-1930s, lodged in a Trumpington Road house. He used to visit us together with his RAF pilot friend, fellow student Leslie Dan, who was later an Air Staff weapons expert before heading the Irvin UK parachute company. We had no idea what Frank Whittle was up to, or how well known he would become. I remember him as a quiet visitor, telling my mother how much he enjoyed her scones and usually wearing one red and one blue sock – 'squadron colours', he memorably educated me.

Now let's start the tour by turning right on leaving the Park & Ride. To the left, just before the M11 South turn-off, is the first place of interest, a white-painted two-storey building. Between 1941 and 1946 it served as the office and gatehouse for SEBRO, the Short Brothers Repair Organisation, which repaired and rebuilt many broken Stirlings ferried in with difficulty on 60-foot RAF lorries commonly called 'Queen Marys'. At this entrance the workforce emotionally greeted the shattered famous Stirling 'MacRoberts Reply'. In a clutch of five T2 hangars, now gone, Stirling parts were repaired then wedded to a fuselage to become a 'new' aircraft, retaining that fuselage serial number. Components were conveyed along the route we are using to Bourn airfield for reassembly, flight test and delivery. That white building is now the University's Schofield Centre, and contains a centrifuge used for earthquake research.

Right, at the top of the hill ahead, lies the huge American Cemetery, resting place of thousands – mainly aircrew – and almost all killed between 1942 and 1945. There is an impressive chapel and a wall of remembrance listing those missing without trace, some from airfields we shall pass. One well-known is Glenn Miller, the band leader.

At the roundabout we'll take the first exit and head for Hardwick, reached after taking the first left turn. Park near the church. A short walk on the pathway alongside leads to private farmland, beyond which lies our first aerodrome site. Being private land we can walk no further.

The Hardwick field used during the early days of military flying.

What memories it holds, for from here over a few days in 1912, at what looks like a most unlikely spot, famed pioneers helped to fashion tactics the RFC would soon employ in war. The Army Grand Manoeuvres of 1912 were the biggest yet held, troop numbers greater than the BEF sent to France in 1914. They assembled on 14-15 September 1912 forming two Armies. Supposition was that the 'Red' Army that landed on the Norfolk coast between Wells and Hunstanton had penetrated inland towards London. The 'Blue' Army, mainly in Cambridgeshire, faced them. Each was at two-infantry-division strength, had a cavalry division and included territorials, some of them cyclists. 'Red' Army had 22,500 men, 9,000 horses, 100 guns and 68 machine-guns. 'Blue' had more men but fewer horses.

Each Army was allocated a Flight of seven aircraft (RFC and naval) and one airship. General Sir John French (commander of the BEF, 1914-15) decreed that any aeroplane flying below 2,000 feet over troops would be declared shot down by machine-gun fire! Nothing much was known about the aeroplane versus the soldier.

Movement of the newly formed Royal Flying Corps had begun on 9 September, the 'Reds' establishing their HQ near Thetford (where during the First World War there was to be a major RFC training depot), while the 'Blues' moved to the grass field ahead, a meadow at Hardwick where, a year previously, the Royal Engineers had encamped.

Famous Commander C. R. Samson, flying a naval Short Tractor Biplane S41 (serial number 10) set out from Sheerness on 5 September for Hardwick. With engine trouble he force-landed near Whittlesford (close to Duxford). Next day an S45 set out but also had to force-land en route. Even more disastrous was an attempt to bring along a Deperdussin Monoplane of No 3 Squadron; it broke up in mid-air. As a result no monoplanes participated in the manoeuvres.

On 10 September there was a Cavalry Division warm-up exercise. 'White' Force advanced towards Cambridge from Long Melford while 'Brown' Force took up defensive positions along the narrow River Granta. Four aircraft were positioned at Worsted Lodge, 3 miles north of Linton, giving each side two aircraft to make observation flights. A Maurice Longhorn from CFS Upavon arrived carrying Major Hugh Trenchard to view the activity, and there were two naval Short biplanes. Another was BE 3 No 203 fitted with wireless telephony (W/T) equipment. They used an advanced landing ground at Babraham, just south of Cambridge. The Short Tractor S45 (No 5) force-landed near Cherry Hinton waterworks, and motor transport took it to Hardwick for repair, showing the need for such support.

Aeroplanes and airships were a rare, exotic sight for a local population soon on the scene. More overwhelming was the swarm of troops that came to Cambridge on 13 and 14 September, during the evening of which Colonel Cody in his famous aeroplane made a dusk arrival at Hardwick. Locals complained that his noisy contraption upset their horses.

Next day the airships headed east. The 'Blue' Army's *Delta* carrying W/T encountered trouble over London and took no part in the exercise, her place being taken by Beta II, which had no W/T. *Gamma* flew to the 'Blue' airship camp at Kneesworth, close to Bassingbourn, Beta II then joining the 'Reds'.

The main event started at 06.00hrs on the 16th. Setting out early, *Gamma* drifted over Cambridge with a troublesome engine, then hovered over a huge array of tents on Midsummer Common. It settled on a clear patch near the River Cam and attempts were made to check the 45hp Clerget engine. My mother, living close by, told me how she and a huge crowd, many still in nightclothes, raced to the scene to catch a glimpse of this amazing arrival. Such was the crowd that the airship and attendants were hemmed in. They lightened the craft then soldiers led it like a dog to Jesus College grounds where it slipped over iron fencing to safety. There it soon won the help of a young Arthur Marshall, who related in his memoirs *The Marshall Story* (Haynes) how he carried cans of petrol and oil to the airship from Marshall's garage in Jesus Lane.

At the time the exercise began two aircraft set off from Hardwick to seek 'Red' Army positions. It was hazy, crews finding it difficult to assess the situation. For one of them action was short, engine trouble forcing a landing near Barton Mills, where the crew were captured. Not far from Horseheath (where Sir Arthur Marshall later lived) came the famous episode when an angry senior cavalry officer complained that the aeroplanes were frightening his horses and thus had no value in warfare.

King George V reached the battleground on the 17th. He was told that observation from the aircraft revealed a main troop engagement along a front from Gog Magog to Haverhill. No 3 Squadron, through its commander, Sir Robert Brooke-Popham, gave HM a report on the position of 'Red' troops, which made it easier to curb their advance.

Next day the King came here, to Hardwick, in a smart Maudsley car, probably travelling over where we are standing. At 10.00hrs he met and congratulated Colonel Cody, and then Commander Samson after he landed. The Royal party left before Geoffrey de Havilland arrived in a BE2. They had gone to Horseheath where the 'Red' thrust was being held at the close of the exercise. As he headed home on the 19th, the King passed a W/T station established at Whittlesford, which had been working with airship *Gamma*. The most important policy-making event was discussed that day at Trinity College, Cambridge, it being clear to everyone that the aeroplane did indeed have a great part to play in war, especially as a scout and reconnaissance tool of the Army. One might fairly say that the close Army-RAF operations in Afghanistan draw upon those flights from Hardwick and also Thetford.

A logical question is 'What part in the 1914-1918 war did Hardwick play?' The answer is 'nil'. It was merely a convenient meadow briefly used for flying. In the early 1920s light aircraft in civilian hands used Hardwick, whose aerodrome days featured just once more.

Based nearby on Bourn airfield in 1943 was No 97 Squadron. Like others nearby, the Squadron took part in the 16/17 December 1943 Berlin raid described later. Dense fog over Eastern England faced returning bombers and Flying Officer Thackway and crew of Lancaster OF-Z attempted to land at Bourn. Approaching in line with the main runway, but too far east, they crashed on the field before us, becoming the last aircraft to land there. The event is detailed in Jennie Gray's book *Fire by Night*.

The distant hawthorn hedge on the southern side of the field is apparently a descendent of one there in 1912. A low portion, over which it is claimed the early aeroplanes took to the sky, is a retained feature.

Now it is time to view a fully built, albeit late First World War, aerodrome. That, of course, is Duxford, a 225-acre site developed into a typical RAF fighter station of the 1920s and early 1930s.

It is easily reached by returning to the M11 and taking the southern carriageway. The motorway passes close to New Farm, Newton, on the right just before Whittlesford. On 6 June 1940 a Ju 88 (an early visit of one over the UK at night) dropped the first incendiaries to fall in the No 12 ARP/Civil Defence Region. Hoards of important officials viewed the field, collected bomb tails, counted holes and obviously enjoyed a nice picnic among strange East Anglian folk. Over to the left is the spot where I took to a ditch as a Ju 88 roared low overhead below rain clouds as its gunner blazed away. But now it's time to filter off at the A505 junction, take the left-hand lane, turn right and follow the slip road to park at Duxford.

Normally one would visit AirSpace, but we're here to have a quick look at Duxford's late-First World War and 1920s unique, fascinating buildings. This collection is the best remaining. Originally only two Aircraft Sheds were scheduled with a third to serve as an Aircraft Repair Shed. Instead, construction of three paired General Service Sheds (later renamed Aircraft Sheds in place of the term providing for varied use) began late 1917. Completed post-war, they are of wood, concrete and brick construction, the curved roofing affording ample drainage being supported internally by so-called Belfast Truss spans. Wooden concertina doors remain in use.

Walking from the public entrance, follow the road behind the brick Aircraft Gun Firing Butts, an early wartime addition that entertained such rare items as the second prototype Whirlwind fighter bearing a hefty cannon in the nose. The old firing range was at the far western end of the site. Notice to the right the line of bungalow-type buildings constructed of brick, stone-dashed and slate-roofed. At their eastern end was the camp boiler system, then came oil and dope stores and barrack stores. 'Blenheim Palace' occupies some – the name derives from this being where Duxford's famous Blenheim-cum-Bolingbroke was restored. At the end of the line stood Station Main Stores. Behind these buildings, and still very much intact, is the 1917-designed Motor Transport Section (MT) complete with yard and garages. Notice to the left before reaching the main entry road the tablet commemorating the July 1935 RAF Jubilee Fly Past, which HM King George V reviewed at Duxford.

Ahead to the right is the one-time Station Head Quarters (ex-Station Offices) building and now the IWM Head Quarters at Duxford. To a 1922 design, it was modified in 1933 as the date above the entrance testifies. Basically little changed from its original form, the building retains its bell tower, the bell being tolled in the event of fire to summon the fire picket. Facing SHQ is the 1922 Guardhouse, later called the Main Guardroom. Behind its right-hand office was 'the cooler' for wrongdoers. Notice the building's somewhat imperial portico, a remnant of Empire days. At the start of the 1920s Duxford held a flying training school, which trained many personnel for overseas service. As a result of the 1922 Defence Review Duxford was chosen to accommodate two fighter squadrons and a fighter operational training squadron. The latter, No 19, was soon upgraded into a front-line squadron.

Behind SHQ, and protective earth and sandbag mounds, is the 1930-40-style Operations Room. It has been laid out to represent the situation of Duxford/Fowlmere squadrons at around 08.30hrs on 31 August 1940 as Dornier 17s of II/KG2 attempted to bomb Duxford. Notice the plotting table, the state boards and the distinctive wall clocks.

Walk along the road westerly and pass small buildings – a parachute store, post office, navigation room – then face garages of the Fire Section, still similarly used. Beyond a long-gone fire practice pit originally stood a line of eight canvas Bessonneau hangars used until the main sheds were ready.

Turn left at the last hangar, Building 78, which in pre-war days was home for the yellow Avro Tutors of the Cambridge UAS and in early wartime housed Blenheim If strike and escort fighters of No 222 Squadron. Walk along the front of the hangars on the pre-war narrow metalled 'road' serving as a taxiway to the end of the sheds; it also covered the spaces between them, and surrounded the western and eastern ends. On the large space halfway along stood a single 170ft by 100ft Aircraft Repair Shed, which in its early days was used both as a vehicle store and gymnasium. To its rear were the Main Stores, before they moved to the building next to the Guard House.

The existing somewhat modified control tower of 1941 style was in use by early 1942. Its first-floor front room and balcony are much as they were originally, and to the end of Duxford's Service days. Prior to having the tower, a small wooden hut served as the watch office, where pilots went for weather information and to explain their flight plans, etc.

Let's pause by the tower recalling bygone days. Biplane fighters would rest on the grass between flying, while Zwicky bowsers refuelled them. Soon they would bump and sing their way across the turf, then sort of jump into the wild blue yonder to dance around in teasing mock combat. Along the front of the Aircraft Sheds were Squadron and Flight offices, small equipment stores and dope stores. On the outbreak of war in 1939 three Spitfires squadrons dispersed to either end of the field, with No 611 Squadron dispersing in the south-west corner of the small landing ground and near College Farm. During 1940 Cierva C-30A Rota autogiros, Blenheim IVs and Hornet Moths of No 74 Wing began dispersing along the southern perimeter.

On 7 September 1940 fires consuming much of London's docks could easily be seen tinting the distant southern sky with tones of red and yellow. Evenings during that summer often saw a steady increase in high cloud cover produced by merging contrails drifting over from the fighting south.

At the start of 1941 all changed with the arrival of the Air Fighting Development Unit, which occupied the duo of eastern sheds, and dispersed its ever-varying fleet of fascinating aircraft along the easterly perimeter of the airfield and around its hangars. The Naval Air Fighting Development Unit (alias No 787 Squadron) positioned its motley array of aircraft in the south-eastern corner of the airfield. Operational squadrons dispersed along the western edge and used 'Hangar 78'. In 1941 Hurricanes of No 310 (Czech) Squadron dispersed along the western edge of Duxford. They were replaced by No 601 (County of London) Squadron in mid-summer, which came to convert to Bell Airacobras. When Hurricanes of No 56 Squadron arrived, No 601 moved to the southern perimeter of the field. Seemingly massive, quite secret Hawker Typhoons began re-equipping No 56 in August 1941 and sat surprisingly close to the western hawthorn hedge along the main road. Splendid easy viewing.

We have walked around the Technical Site and gazed across the landing ground. Now look across the A505. Almost opposite Main Gate, the 1934-style impressive Officers' Mess remains basically unchanged and internally laid out as it was when built. Originally the Mess was to be built well back with a prestigious road linking it with what is now the A505, but in 1918 plans resulted in the initial Mess being built where the present one is sited. On the left of the Domestic Site entry road was the Sergeants' Mess. That area is fenced off for safety reasons, but it is possible to have a tour. Large two-storey 1933-style barrack blocks remain alongside the parade ground, to the north of which remains the Airmen's Mess with the NAAFI above. To the right, where cars are parked on show days, huts to accommodate mainly officers were positioned near the grass sports areas.

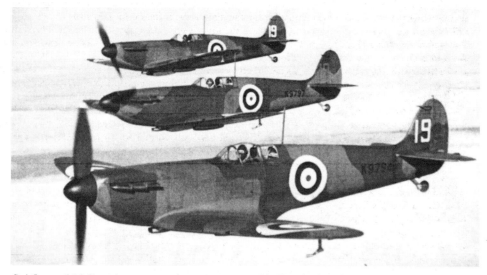

Spitfire and 19 Squadron are surely synonymous with 'Duxford'.

To view the next main stage in RAF aerodrome design we'll take the A505 westerly, turning off at the sign marked Thriplow. Very soon on the right, on the 35-foot hilltop, can be seen a collection of buildings occupying the site from where, on 31 August 1940, 3-inch AA guns of the 78th Heavy AA Battery engaged and helped drive off the attempted Dornier raid.

In Thriplow village we turn left for Fowlmere, passing a field where Manchester QR-J belly-landed in June 1941. It did so because its engines stopped! Wartime Fowlmere, Duxford's satellite, was by the B1368. Our route takes us through Shepreth, around which fell some of the HEs and marker incendiaries dropped on 31 August 1940. Almost 100 bombs straddled either side of the railway line to Royston as a London-bound train passed through. For many years roads around Meldreth and

Whaddon were lined with securely fastened Nissen huts packed with emergency food supplies. At Kneesworth crossroads, we'll turn right along Ermine Street (A1198) where Roman legions trod. In a few moments we pass on the left where the airship was sited for the 1912 manoeuvres before reaching a typical Permanent RAF Station of 1934 design. Since 1968 it has been in Army hands.

First in view are ample playing fields – strong emphasis on PT and games has always been a main feature of RAF life – and distantly stands a typical 1934-style Officers' Mess. An early expansion period station, Bassingbourn was built to a high specification. Easily seen are hipped-roof barrack blocks. Left, just inside the main entrance – the layout of which is rather unusual – is the memorial to the 91st Bomb Group, USAAF. Centrally stood Changi jail's wooden gateway in memory of many Cambridgeshire Regiment soldiers brutally treated in Japanese hands. Beyond is the ex-Station HQ. Visible are assorted standard red-brick, hip-roofed buildings. A Canberra resting among them recalls Bassingbourn's role as the world's first jet bomber operational training base. Three of four 'C' Type hangars remain bearing various modifications. They were built on a curve due to the shape of the landing ground and also to make it difficult to bomb them all during one run. The pre-war control tower stood between the central hangars, the East Anglian Aviation Society mid-wartime tower near the hangars now serving as a memorial to Bassingbourn's RAF and USAAF personnel. Visiting is by prior permission, and security very strict. USAF presence in 1950 brought in B-29s, B-50s and attracted C-124 Globemasters. Just imagine one of those slipping in across this main road, as two did on 18 January 1951. Much of the concrete peri-track remains, also the large ASP and parts of two runways. Trees by the road obscure the view, whereas soon, distantly ahead on the right, magnificent Wimpole Hall comes into view. Giant elms once lined the avenue from here to the Hall providing, on moonlit nights, a fine route in to Bassingbourn for Ju 88C night intruders. One placed a huge bomb close to the standard tall water tower (now gone), leaving a gigantic crater close to the domestic quarters. We passed a few MQ houses opposite the main gate, this being a split site.

Canberra T4 WT480 by one of Bassingbourn's C Type Hangars, 8 May 1969.

A familiar sight over Cambridge 1952 to 1969, Canberras of No 231 OCU here making a final 16-ship fly past over southern Cambridge on 20 May 1969, WE192 nearest.

On either side of that avenue B-17s of the 91st Bomb Group dispersed between the trees. To answer an operational call they paraded across the road – their route remains – to join others, some from dispersals among the turkeys of Howe's Farm, which stood close to where Canberras dispersed in the 1950s and '60s. To stand by the low hawthorn hedge bordering the wartime airfield as more than thirty very low-flying B-17s landed back from 'ops' was unforgettable. Some would stream smoke, leak fuel and display battle scars. 'Memphis Belle', 'Jack the Ripper', 'The Sad Sack', 'General Ike' and so many more would thunder over where the legions trod. Only by meeting the men leaving the bombers could the terrible psychological toll that daylight raids forced upon them be appreciated. Many would have watched the horrific incinerating end of dear friends, and lots cried. From 'the Forts' would be taken many seriously wounded, while sometimes unrecognisable bodies could be seen in blood-stained turrets. Yes, war is ghastly – it always will be.

Let's press on, passing Croydon on the left where, on the hill, there was a practice bombing range in Bassingbourn's early days. The East Anglian Aviation Society superbly restored a Dragon Rapide near Croydon.

We'll turn right at Caxton Gibbet roundabout, joining the new A428 dual carriageway that continues to Felixstowe. On the right lies the 1940-44 Caxton Gibbet Relief Landing Ground. A large meadow, it saw pre-war use by the Cambridge University Gliding Club. To cope with intense flying by 22 EFTS Cambridge, Caxton was requisitioned and controlled by Marshall Flying School. It came into use for Tiger Moth circuit flying, soon playing an important part when night-flying training was introduced. Its flare path was soon discovered by Ju 88 marauders, which attacked circling Tiger Moths, presumably mistaking them for Bassingbourn Wellingtons. In 1944 huts by the then A45 road accommodated personnel from RAF Bourn, who well decorated the interiors. Sadly, they have gone.

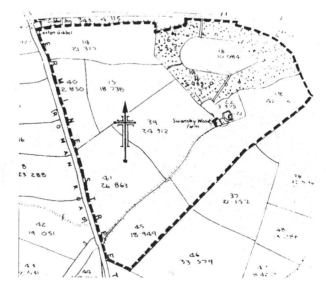

Caxton Gibbet boundary and terrain.

Half a mile beyond the Cambourne intersection lies the one-time satellite for Oakington, RAF Bourn, first occupied in February 1941. As well as accommodating Wellingtons of 101 Squadron it was used by 7 Squadron Stirlings, and later by XV Squadron, which introduced the Mk III to operations. By then this Built Satellite type (it was one of the first bomber bases in the area to be built with runways) had acquired full self-accounting Station status. *Oboe*-equipped Mossies of three-Flight 105 Squadron moved in from Marham and operated at very high intensity to the end of hostilities. The westbound carriageway follows the line of the peri-track linking two runways, and passes over the spot where a Lancaster was burned out on 17 December 1943. Present-day flying takes place from the south-western corner. On 7 September 1945 the huge Shetland flying boat passed over the road at this point at a mere 50 feet.

*Bourn's western end viewed
from a XV Squadron Stirling
April 1943 (Brian Harris).*

We're now in line with Hardwick as we turn left at the second roundabout to pass through Dry Drayton, then cross the A14 dual carriageway, heading for Oakington and taking the Cottenham road. Oakington held the first RAF four-engined bombers used in the Second World War. Just before reaching the crossing point for the crazy misguided bus, to the left is the area where coke-coated dispersal pads were laid for some of the first Stirlings, oft-pictured N3641, MG-D, among them. You could touch the secret bombers – more than once I did so – by taking advantage of an unguarded entrance. Of Oakington's buildings nothing is visible, so instead we'll view a station of similar construction, Waterbeach. Also a 1939 austerity airfield, it came into use later than Oakington – at the start of 1941.

On reaching Cottenham we need to turn right, follow the road left by the green opposite The College, quickly fork right and make for Landbeach. Turn left at the T-junction towards Goose Farm, then join the A10 by turning right – with great care – to come alongside Waterbeach aerodrome. Runways remain hidden by the long mound alongside the very ancient waterway and also the perimeter track. Wellington 1cs of 99 Squadron were once dispersed by the A10, such as LN-K R1472, which sat in the corner by the traffic light junction and in 1943 was superseded by Lancaster II JI-C. The troublesome trio of Wellington IIs able to carry 4,000lb 'cookies' dispersed in the south-east corner. After the war came Liberator transports superseded by Yorks of 51 Squadron. Turn left at the traffic lights into Waterbeach village and the curved-top 'J' Type hangars and wartime tower are visible, as well as a T2 hangar added long after. The smart structure on the left is Stirling House, home for Defence Estates before its Wyton move. Near the Army barracks main entrance can be seen a Hunter, reminder of the fighter squadron days. Flat-roof buildings are a reminder of a need to build fast.

We have now glimpsed the six main, basic types of military airfields of the period 1912-60, and have just one more aerodrome to see, travelling via Clayhithe and Horningsea.

Waterbeach – wartime bomber base but for far longer a fighter station.

A short ride will take us to Cambridge Airport, home of Marshall Aerospace, one of the few remaining aerospace players bearing the founder's name. Through 70 years, with little more than a few hours break, Cambridge Airport has been active. That, alone, marks it as outstanding. Before reaching Marshalls' we'll pass the City Cemetery. Opposite, by Newmarket Road, was No 54 MU Salvage Centre. Opened alongside Barnwell Bridge, it moved on to a meadow here in late September 1939, first attracting wreckage of a camouflaged Vickers Vildebeest and soon a T2 Hangar. Thereafter, '54 MU' acquired treasures galore including parts of a He 115 which exploded on Sheringham's shore in December 1939 and wooden remnants of Felixstowe's Fokker T8-W floatplanes.

In 1944 two new huge sub-sites opened, one alongside Teversham Lane on the eastern boundary of the airport. The other straddled the Newmarket Road – Coldham's Lane ring road. Both were metal recycling centres, nothing is new. Handley Page Hereford fuselages ended their days there, also a B-26 makers plate and a Stirling 'undercarriage up down' notice. Fragments of both now lodge with me.

From Coldham's Lane comes a fine view across the 438 acre Marshall's regional airport who's Public Use Licence allows flights by public transports to Boeing 757/ Airbus 320 size. The landing ground was much extended in the mid -1950s, fields having previously separated it from this road. A He 111 left craters in August 1940, but more spectacular was a 1945 landing just short of the airfield boundary by giant Hamilcar glider (NX816) after its tow line broke. The 23/05 runway built in 1953 was later extended to its current 6,447 foot length.

Hangars, custom-built and now covering 1.24 million square feet of the 800 acre MA site, where 1,800 are employed, have played a very important part in the Marshall story. Dominant is No 17 the largest such building in Europe which was erected to accommodate wide-bodied jets, and can hold three 747s. Arrival and departure of the latter demanded highly skilled airmanship. 747-400s of BA started coming in 2001 for reconfiguration, refurbishment and fitment of video screens to passenger seats.

Airport Way, another main public road, skirts the airfield's eastern perimeter giving clear views of flying. A road from Teversham ran close to the rifle range buildings to join Newmarket Road before runway lengthening led to road diversion and Airport Way.

Thanks to Marshall Aeropsace, through Terry Holloway, FRAeS, the Group Support Executive, we are being treated to a guided tour of the airfield complex on a very hot, cloudless 30 June, 2009. The private family group of companies employing 3,900 has an annual turnover of around £700m. Government and private contracts mean that access is understandably very restricted.

We are entering by way of the pristine, elegant Company head quarters building whose interior is much oak lined. Little changed since its mid-1930s birth, this shapely building is as purely white as it was in prewar days.

No 1 Hangar is just to the east, beyond the Cambridge Aero Club office and general aviation reception centre. Cambridge Aero Club are flying several of their five Cessna 172's. They have an Extra 200 for aerobatic practice. Formed in 1929, this is one of the oldest flying clubs in the UK. Pilot training has always been important at Marshalls. Others including Air Service Training of Oxford use the runway approach aids for training and Cranfield-based Cabair's Diamond Stars have been a common sight.

Initially No 1 Hangar's roof was marked 'CAMBRIDGE' to aid pilots without radio. In 2008 it had a major facelift, and was joined to an unusual looking new hangar by insertion of the fine Marshall Business Aviation Centre, which handles executive travel, corporate travelling and biz-jet maintenance. 'No 1' came into use in autumn 1937 as the lair of 22 E&RFTS whose military aircraft mingled with de Havilland, Miles and Percival treats, a gorgeous Stinson Reliant G-AFRS and Cierva autogiros.

Let's move to the apron. Cambridge Airport has attracted an astonishing assortment of aircraft types, certainly over 500 and it continues to do so. Here's the evidence. A Duxford-based P-51 Mustang is emerging from 'No 1', Marshall's executive Piper Aztec G-BATN soon to have a new paint scheme stands where, from January 1946, M.38s, Proctors, and of course the local Tiger Moth population, came to refuel from the lonely, aged petrol pump by the duty crew hut at the hangar's corner.

Traffic associated with racing and bloodstock dealing at Newmarket has long been a feature, and evidenced by the beautiful Boeing 737-800 of Dubai Air Wing here today. Race-goers used to come in Rapides, Consuls, Geminis and Proctors. Miles Aerovans were first to bring one or two horses, Bristol 170s followed, and nowadays horses come, like their owners, in 737s, 757s or BAe 146s of TNT.

Unusual in shape is the small hangar on one-time grass erected to protect Aeromega Helicopters' small Robinsons used for flying training. Vicky, our guide, points out that this small hangar is like a prototype for the larger, Canadian-designed, similarly shaped and semi-permanent example attached to Marshall Business Aviation Centre opened in October 2008.

All within is exceedingly tasteful, and thus in tune with so much at Marshall Aerospace. There are offices, an executive suite, hospitality lounge from which one can look through this huge, very fine quality glass window onto a very special, private world. A clutch of Citations, immaculate in themselves, rest on a spotless, white floor! The bright view of biz-jets receiving tender care is breathtaking.

In a hallway a glass case contains precious memories and possessions of two famous Marshall pilots, Herbert 'Taps' Tapping and Leslie Worsdell. The former was one of the first post-war charter pilots who, on 8/9 February 1944, flying a Mosquito of 157 Squadron, came across a giant Bv 222 six-engine flying boat about to splash down on Lake Biscarosse. He 'assisted it spectacularly', he told me, with a tinge of sorrow. For decades Leslie Worsdell was Chief Test Pilot. In wartime, he courageously led Malta-based No 86 Beaufort torpedo-bomber squadron. Not surprisingly, their medals testify to courage and skill.

From the apron the 1940 built twin-blister hangar which has been the home of the Cambridge Private Flying Group since the 1950s, can be seen. This is the lair of the revered 'Tigers', G-AOEI and G-AHIZ, resident since 1958 and very active ever since.

Beyond, in the engine test bay commonly called 'the mound', are two Lockheed Martin C-130s. Marshall Aerospace (MA) is prime contractor of Integrated Operational Support Contracts for RAF C-130s and TriStars, Sister Design Authority for the UK C-130K and Conversion Design Authority for RAF TriStar tankers. MA is thus intensively deeply involved in maintaining the RAF transport force, as we shall notice. Their aircraft are diminishing numerically, disturbingly, due to demanding intensive use in rough, tough desert conditions and in Afghanistan.

ZH866, clearly a much-worked overall-green C.Mk 4, is engine running. The distinctive band encircling the fuselage, and areas of similar colour on the fuselage underside are of a special, protective material to minimise stone damage from rough terrain. MA applies that protection and, during major servicing fits other specialised items such as the Directed Infra Red Countermeasures System in the DIRCM turret, for guided missile diversion.

Passing along the runway is C-130 G-988, one of two ex-US Navy airframes, purchased by the Netherlands Government from desert storage and brought here by road in poor state four years ago. Rebuilding typifies Marshall skill. We shall pass 8741/G-741, the second still being prepared in Hangar 16, also an Austrian Air Force C-130 and two Royal Swedish Air Force (RSAF) examples. Swedish 'Hercs' regularly come for attention.

As many as two dozen light aircraft often rest on the grass, activity which began when Ipswich airport closed. The gathering frequently changes, today's collection including two Moonies and assorted Cessnas. Light aircraft also make use of No 1 Hangar.

Passing the customs pad we come close to a Jetstream 31 of Highland Airways. On most days one conveys BAE Systems personnel to and from Blackpool. It is an apt reminder that MA is not just a major maintenance contractor, as Marshall Solutions provides specialised engineering and aviation solutions within Defence and Aerospace industries. Test Services use a hangar containing a C-130K fuselage and a C-130J wing for fatigue testing. MA has an Aircraft Design office, staffed by 400, sited alongside the huge motor business north of Newmarket Road. Their work has resulted in special fuel tanks for the Boeing 747-400ER and the 777-200LR. They have designed the Auxiliary Fuel System for the US Navy P-8A Multi Mission Maritime Aircraft, recently won a contract to design and manufacture nacelles for the new Hondajet and have been involved in many major projects.

No 2 Hangar, completed in 1939, was the main wartime centre for Marshall CRO whose workforce totalled over 12,000 personnel. The Duty Pilot office at its south-east corner developed into the flying control tower whose 2001, 120 foot high replacement provides an amazing all round view.

Inside, 'No 2' presents an unexpected scene. Skillfully positioned on the floor are many components needed to make an RAF C-130J. MA played a considerable part in the J's development, test flying its engine and special propeller. After five years of tough service the Js are in need of thorough checks. Re-assembly follows in high roofed No 10 hangar. ZH874 is in advanced condition, and others are in adjacent No 12 Hangar. A very large curtain blanks off the paint bay where, in 1967, the first RAF Hercules to come (XV177) became the first such aircraft to have long-

Aerial view of the modifications joining No 1 Hangar to the new Business Aviation Centre and new hangar with apron.

Interior view of the new business aircraft hangar containing two Cessna Citations on a pristine floor.

Outside Cambridge No 1 Hangar, Piper Aztec G-BATN, company executive transport.
All photographs on this and the following page were take 30 June 2009.

P-51D 'Miss Velma' from Duxford, emerging from No 1 after attention. Business Centre beyond.

The new hangar and
Business Centre.

Boeing 737-800 A6-BRJ,Dubai Air Wing, typical but still rare Cambridge visitor. Photographed 30 June 2009.

Pilatus PC XII N12AG, a business aircraft using Cambridge. Behind, No 2 Hangar, old control tower at right end. Photographed 30 June 2009.

A frequent caller, Jetstream 31 G-EIGG of Highland Airways.

lasting polyurethane paint applied. That occasioned much interest, the finished application needing to be baked. Intended to last for 25 years, it was soon replaced with difficulty to make way for a different paint scheme. Few all-grey 'Hercs' remain, most now wearing dark green overall and have featured black, green or grey protective zones. Outside, alongside the tall tower, rests '846', one of three Royal Swedish Air Force C-130Hs here today.

Walking through well-organised No 16 Hangar, previously the business aircraft hangar where Gulfstreams galore and Global Express were handled, we pass a modified T2 and exit to the vast No 17 hangar. Here, more RAF 'Hercs' are being worked upon, and two very special aircraft. Dominant is white TriStar ZD949 to which MA is applying fly-by-wire and glass cockpit technology. An amazing transformation, it has demanded an exceedingly clever conversion. Completion is expected in March 2010.

The other is one-time 'Snoopy', XV208, the meteorological research Mk 2 Hercules. Marshall Aerospace purchased it for use as a risk reduction flying test bed for the huge EPI TP-400D 10,000shp, three-spool turboprop engine intended for the long awaited 'FLA', the Airbus A400M. So mighty is the engine that bracing struts link its nacelle with the fuselage. Usually operated by a crew of 12, a range of instruments and screens in the spartan interior answer the test needs of Airbus, a Rolls-Royce consortium and Marshall. Its massive propeller with a 38 inch diameter boss has eight vicious looking blades quite closely set, and is one of the biggest ever. Its ground clearance is about two feet. Ground test running started in May 2008, it first flew on 17 December, and to date has flown for around 30 hours.

Here our tour ends, in the cavernous building where, one May day, the memorial service for Sir Arthur Marshall was held. Millions of memories must have raced around, for Sir Arthur and the Marshall family have contributed much to Cambridge life. Hospitals, schools, a range of organisations and many people have benefited from their endeavours. The world aviation community has certainly been enriched.

Encouraging acquisition of skills and qualifications by young people has long been a major feature too. Aircraft engineers, after acquiring NVQ 3, are encouraged to advance to degree level, former apprentices now holding senior posts within the company. Annually, 15 university sandwich courses in engineering are on offer. The level of loyalty Marshalls' inspires has led to three awards for 60 years service, 29 for 50 years, 217 for forty and 620 for 30 years of service.

Hyper conscientious, highly self-demanding, Sir Arthur was an international figure whose like is rare. You and I would probably associate him with aircraft but he said to me 'I like cars as well, you know!' He would have been thrilled by the company's centenary year.

Whenever I, as an outsider leave 'Marvellous Marshalls', I do so in the knowledge that I have visited a special place, one so much endowed with excellence and loyalty. Anyone associated with the Company can surely always say, with pride, 'I worked at Marshalls'.

Leslie Worsdell guides 'brown and black' XV177 on to the runway to make the first flight of a Hercules from Cambridge, February 1967.

Marshall operated three de Havilland Rapides for charter work in the late 1940s, G-AGZO, G-AHED and G-AHLM shown.

Rare 1947 bird, Beechcraft 18 ZS-BTH called in from South Africa in 1947.

Tim Mason brings Tristar ZD953 into Cambridge during a test flight.

Main listed features of airfields are applicable to December 1944 unless otherwise stated. Runway lengths are given as prescribed but not to precise lengths, and overruns were often added. The longest runway is listed first, followed by the orientation of usually two subsidiary 4,200ft x 150ft runways. Accommodation figures give an indication of what was available, but off-camp billeting would increase these. Those listed were produced by surveying the type of buildings (standard) in situ.

078 Metheringham, Lincolnshire

079 Methwold, Norfolk

080 Mildenhall, Suffolk

081 Newmarket Heath, Suffolk

082 North Creake, Norfolk

083 North Pickenham, Norfolk

084 North Witham, Lincolnshire

085 Oakington, Cambridgeshire

086 Old Buckenham, Norfolk

087 Oulton, Norfolk

088 Peterborough (Westwood), Unitary Borough of Peterborough

089 Rackheath, Norfolk

090 Rattlesden, Suffolk

091 Raydon, Essex

092 Ridgewell, Essex

093 Rivenhall, Essex

094 Rougham, Suffolk

095 Sculthorpe, Norfolk

096 Seething, Norfolk

097 Shepherd's Grove, Suffolk

098 Shipdham, Norfolk

099 Snailwell, Cambridgeshire

100 Snetterton Heath, Norfolk

101 Somersham, Cambridgeshire

102 Spilsby, Lincolnshire

103 Spitalgate (Grantham), Lincolnshire

104 Stansted, Essex

105 Steeple Morden, Cambridgeshire

106 Stradishall, Suffolk

107 Sudbury (Acton), Suffolk

108 Sutton Bridge, Lincolnshire

109 Swannington, Norfolk

110 Swanton Morley, Norfolk

111 Thorpe Abbotts, Norfolk

112 Tibenham, Norfolk

113 Tuddenham, Suffolk

114 Upwood, Cambridgeshire

115 Waddington, Lincolnshire

116 Warboys, Cambridgeshire

117 Waterbeach, Cambridgeshire

118 Wattisham, Suffolk

119 Watton, Norfolk

120 Wellingore, Lincolnshire

121 Wendling, Norfolk

122 Westley, (Bury St Edmunds) Suffolk

123 West Raynham, Norfolk

124 Wethersfield, Essex

125 Weybourne, Norfolk

126 Witchford, Cambridgeshire

127 Woodbridge, Suffolk

128 Woodhall Spa, Lincolnshire

129 Woolfox Lodge, Rutland

130 Wormingford, Essex

131 Wratting Common, Cambridgeshire

132 Wyton, Cambridgeshire

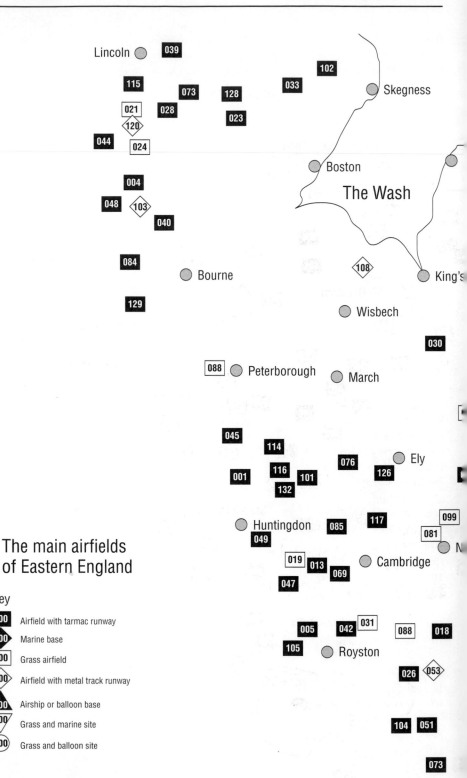

The main airfields
of Eastern England

Key

- **000** Airfield with tarmac runway
- **◆000◆** Marine base
- [000] Grass airfield
- **◇000◇** Airfield with metal track runway
- **▲000▲** Airship or balloon base
- **▽000▽** Grass and marine site
- **(000)** Grass and balloon site

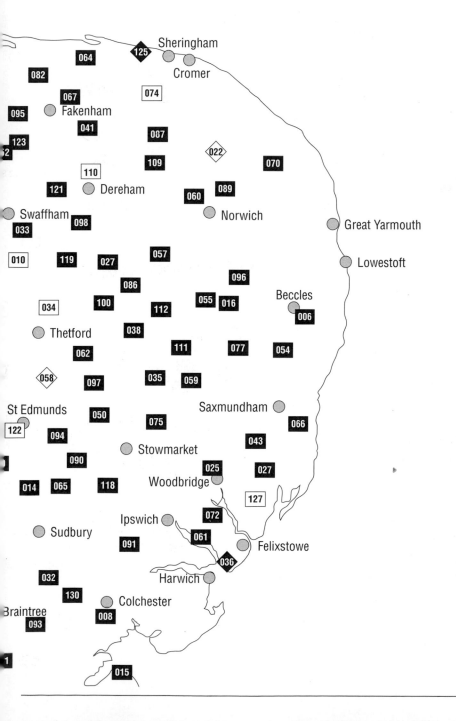

North Sea

Sheringham
125
064
Cromer
082
067
074
095 Fakenham
041
123
087
22   022
109   070
110
121   Dereham
060   089
Swaffham   098   Norwich
033
010   119   027   057
096
086
100   112   055 016   Beccles
034   006
Thetford   038
062   111   077   054
58   097   035   059
St Edmunds   Saxmundham
050
122   094   075   066
043
090   Stowmarket
025
014 065   118   027
Woodbridge
127
Ipswich   072
Sudbury   061
091   Felixstowe
036
032   Harwich
130
Braintree   008   Colchester
093

015

Great Yarmouth
Lowestoft

THE AIRFIELDS

ALCONBURY, Cambridgeshire

52°22N/00°3W 165ft asl; TL295795. 5 miles NW of Huntingdon

It was 5 June. On the grass and between the hangars they sprawled, over 600 paratroopers mainly of the US 82nd and 101st Airborne Divisions whose briefed DZ – close to St Mère Eglise – they regarded with foreboding. At 1045 hrs they emplaned and at precisely 1100 hrs the props that would tow their aircraft into action began turning. Ten minutes later and the first of the large transports edged forward, brakes squealing, propellers tightly grasping the warm air of summer. Very soon all thirteen machines were in line nose to tail along Alconbury's unusually wide taxiway and proclaiming a wide array of engine notes which mingled with masses of smoke. At 1130 hrs the first aircraft lurched forward as lift off started. Within ten minutes all were heading for Normandy, but on this occasion it was not to war.

The Lockheed C-130s drawn from Rhein-Main's 435th Airlift Wing, the 2nd and 41st Airlift Squadrons of the 23rd AW, Pope AFB and a lone French example of Et 61 Orleans were setting off in 1994 to peacefully commemorate the airborne landings on D-Day fifty years before. Alconbury will surely never again experience anything so impressive, so extensive and so noisy. Already it was entering its death throes, a superb airfield soon to be all but cast aside with what may come to be seen as insufficient common sense. World events as the century ends point to the possibility of exceedingly dangerous international situations which cannot be readily countered with advanced weapons. If numbers ever again have a part to play then sufficient airfields must remain available one of which could have been Alconbury.

Compared with its original state Alconbury in 1994 was a colossus whose main runway stretched for almost two miles while the memorably personalised hardened shelters at the western end of the field housed only memories of Phantoms. To the north were larger caverns each securely fenced, and built to protect Lockheed TR-1 battlefield 'spy planes'. Nearby stretched a perimeter track of almost runway proportions which allowed US special operations crews aboard C-130s to practice night landings after all base lights were extinguished and cockpit curtains drawn. On 5 June 1994 it was, instead, packed with grey 'Charlie 130s' some snarling through vicious shark's teeth nose art. The Cold War was over, Alconbury's end was nigh and I reckoned that seeing this activity would be a good way to say farewell to an airfield I had known almost since its birth. Driving home I recalled that day in 1938 when a companion in school told me that his Dad had seen Fairey Battles on a meadow near Huntingdon. What a ridiculous story, I thought, yet it happened to be true.

In pre-war days aircraft returned to their hangars at the end of each working day – until fear of air attack promoted the idea of dispersal around airfield perimeters in wartime. With perhaps forty and even more aircraft on one aerodrome considerable risks remained, especially as 1930s landing grounds were usually quite small. A simple appealing scheme surfaced whereby aircraft would be flown to large meadows for dispersal, and for trials a grass field on Alconbury Hill was selected.

The land was acquired early in 1938 and on 17-18 May, Battles of 63 Squadron, Upwood, sampled it and were picketed in the open on 'the Hill'. Their crews and ground supporters were accommodated under canvas. The squadron chosen was earmarked for No 1 Group Advanced Air Striking Force which, in the event of war, would move to rudimentary airfields in France to carry out short range bombing raids in Germany or support the BEF by attacking battlefield and Rhineland targets. On trial was the satellite landing ground (SLG) and dispersal system, and Alconbury was the RAF's first such site. More were soon chosen for other operational stations.

When hostilities started the site immediately became active, control of what was initially called Alconbury Hill being switched to No 2 Group because Upwood's Battle squadrons were transferred to operational training. It now became Wyton's SLG where its Blenheims spasmodically dispersed until Norway was invaded. Then the squadrons went to high alert and in the late afternoon of 14 April 1940 XV Squadron moved completely to Alconbury and awaited orders, personnel returning nightly to Wyton.

Not until the German invasion of the Low Countries on 10 May was an order to operate given. At mid-morning Alconbury launched two Blenheims to reconnoitre the state of river bridges in the battle area, and at 1415 hrs another nine left to attack Waalhaven airfield south of Rotterdam. An unpleasant welcome greeted the Blenheims, serious battle damage making it 12 May before XV Squadron was ready for another foray.

History should be a core curriculum subject for all politicians in order that past errors maybe be studied along with the manner by which many events evolve and often all but repeat themselves – and often in the same places. Such has happened at Maastricht in the Netherlands where, twice in the 20th century, action vital to the survival of British freedom has not been taken. In 1940 it was absolutely essential to halt the Wehrmacht's advance by destroying bridges over the Maas in and near the town, and among those ordered to achieve that were thirty-six men aboard twelve Blenheims of Alconbury's XV Squadron.

The outcome of this effort was disastrous. Anti-aircraft fire blasted the formation apart allowing Bf 109s to sweep in and pick off the singletons. The despair, anguish, terrible reality when only half of the force returned – one of which crashed – can barely be imagined. A massacre had occurred while Maastricht's bridges largely survived leaving remnants of a proud squadron to be comforted (but not, let it be said, counselled) and absorbed by Wyton's No 40 Squadron.

Undaunted, No XV rapidly re-established themselves at Wyton, returned to Alconbury and on 18 May set out to continue the fight displaying the enormous courage so powerfully featured by all 2 Group squadrons which fought so valiantly throughout the 1940 summer. Something of what that involved may be found in *2 Group RAF* (Crécy Publishing, 1992).

By that time some squadrons were entirely based at satellites, for a new notion was in vogue. By concentrating night flying at the lit primitive site, enemy bombing would cause less damage and disruption than at a lit permanent aerodrome.

On 1 November 1940, XV at Alconbury and 40 Squadron at Wyton, along with their bases, were transferred to No 3 (Bomber) Group. Bomber Command's strategic targets lay beyond the Blenheim's range and its offensive load was small. Some Blenheim squadrons were rearmed with Wellington 1cs and switched to Main Force night operations. Alconbury's Blenheim crews already had night operational experience having participated in attacks on barges massing in the Channel ports for the invasion of Britain.

No XV Squadron's Wellingtons first went into action, from Alconbury, on 22 December, 1940. In February 1941 after mounting eleven raids, XV Squadron was replaced by 40 Squadron, the former moving to Wyton to rearm and become the second Stirling squadron. Alconbury which had steadily increased in size was now further transformed by the commencement of runway construction. A perimeter track and hard dispersal pads were also laid to allow the heavy Stirlings of XV Squadron to use the airfield which, still Wyton's satellite, was changing into a Built satellite.

Although Alconbury had plenty of winter mud, its surface was not as bad as Oakington's churned up by the heavy Stirlings sharing the station with No 3 PRU. Needing a firmer surface for its Spitfires, Oakington on 30 January 1941 began operational flying from Alconbury. The most meritorious sortie took place on 14 March when Squadron Leader P B B Ogilvie in Spitfire Type C X4712 left Alconbury at 0945 hrs took on twenty gallons of fuel at Horsham St Faith, then flew to Berlin which he reached at 1225 hrs thereby becoming the first Allied airman to fly over the city in daylight. It was a stupendous achievement especially as, when he landed back at Alconbury at 1440 hrs with twenty gallons of fuel left he was returning with twenty-five superb photographs of the city.

The Spitfire interlude was but brief. Alconbury's main operational occupants until November 1941 were 40 Squadron's Wellington 1cs, usually totalling sixteen. Then, much of 40 Squadron began moving overseas. Its Wellingtons had, by 26 November 1941, flown 713 operational sorties. A total of twenty-three aircraft had failed to return and a further five crashed.

Throughout that operational period there were many action packed moments. On 2/3 September 1941 for instance, with Frankfurt the target, R1030 'R-Robert' had an engine failure when over the North Sea. To the moment of ditching Sergeant Robertson, the wireless operator, bravely stayed at his post sending SOS messages requesting help until the impact. A trawler hearing the calls managed to rescue four of the crew, but sadly Pilot Officer Fitch, who had so skilfully ditched the 'Wimpey', and the wireless operator were both drowned.

On dark nights homing was never easy, radio aids being quite sparse. Sergeant Jenner and crew reached and bombed Berlin on 18 March 1941, but as if that task was not worrying enough they became lost over England during their nine-hour flight. Eventually R1331 – also an 'R-Robert' – crashed into a hill near distant Combe Martin, Devon. Sergeant Griffin, the rear gunner, baled out too low and was killed, but the others miraculously survived.

A remaining echelon of 40 Squadron continued to operate from Alconbury between 27 November and 14 February 1942 on which day it was renumbered 156 Squadron after it had flown sixty-nine sorties during nineteen operations. The final sorties were flown by the detachment on 12 February 1942 and carried out by five crews seeking the German capital ships escaping from Brest. Among them was F/O Barr aboard DV507. Front gun problems caused him to abort in the Lowestoft exit area and, as he turned south to clear it, local AA guns opened fire damaging the aircraft. To escape he flew very low and made an emergency landing at Lakenheath. Next day many of the remaining personnel of 40 Squadron moved overseas leaving their aircraft behind to form the basis of the new squadron. Five days later the new squadron received its first Hercules-powered Wellington III, and first operated two examples on 25 March. One was X3339 flown by Flight Lieutenant Wells whose aircraft was attacked near Eindhoven by a Ju 88 which seriously damaged the bomber. A few Mk Ics remained on strength throughout 156's stay at Alconbury. Wellington squadrons in 1941 were established at sixteen aircraft until March 1941 when each squadron had two reserves added. Actual strength usually remained close to these figures.

From Alconbury No 156 Squadron participated in the three 1942 'Thousand Plan' raids. For the first on 30/31 May on Cologne it despatched sixteen aircraft and lost two. On the Essen raid it fielded eight Mk Ics and five Mk IIIs, and had twenty crews operating against Bremen on 25/26 June. On 16 April it had commenced mining. Two hazardous daylight *Moling* sorties over north-west Germany were flown, but mainly the squadron was now concentrating on a new role of dropping flares and incendiaries during rudimentary target marking operations. Considerable effort was needed to keep pace with weapon demands, three flares being bundled for carrying on standard racks and set to ignite as required. Thousands of such bundles were needed for this embryo pathfinder force.

Instances of extreme courage abounded. On 23 July 1942 Flight Sergeant T E Case had suddenly to take evasive action when another Wellington closed upon him. His violent manoeuvre caused some incendiaries to burst into flames, and Warrant Officer McLennan saved the aircraft by picking up burning bombs and pushing them along with ammunition through the aircraft's fabric skin even though he had no gloves on his hands.

Between its formation and 6/7 August 1942, No 156 Squadron managed sixty-two operations, flew 386 sorties and lost fourteen aircraft. In August 1942 the Pathfinder Force formed within No 3 Group and 156 Squadron moved from Wyton's satellite to its parent on 5 August then on 7 August to Wyton's new SLG, nearby Warboys, which had entered 3 Group on 5 August. The squadron in the process also became part of The Pathfinder Force within 3 Group. The reason for the move? The Americans were coming to Alconbury for which reason on 12 August the station was transferred to No 8 (Substitution) Group.

Americans began arriving late August 1942 and to a much changed Alconbury which now featured two 'T' Type hangars, a control tower, strengthened hardstandings and an array of domestic sites outside the airfield. Great excitement greeted the arrival on 7 September of a highly distinctive new aircraft shape, the first of the US 8th AAFs B-24D Liberators to be based in Britain. The 93rd Bomb Group was moving in and by darkness next day eighteen B-24s had reached Alconbury. Three days later there were thirty-four B-24s on the airfield and their crews were dangerously raring to go into action. That was clear when one chatted to them and it was obvious that they had no idea of the risks and horrors involved, and certainly knew nothing of the torture endured by their Alconbury predecessors. Luckily the B-24s needed plentiful attention, thirteen of them being unserviceable by 29 September.

After a month of intensive flying, impressive formation work-up and much toning down of international markings by painting the star emblem grey, the drab green and dark grey B-24s and the 93rd BG were ready for action. On 8 October they entered the battle arena.

They were part of *Circus* 224, in which 108 US bombers were billed for their largest operation yet. Whether anyone told the crews they were acting as bait for German fighters remains unknown. Five formations of 8th AF bombers had been ordered to bomb Target Z 183, the Fives-Lille steel works, with B-17s of the 301st Bomb Group leading followed by twelve drawn from the 11th CCRG and twenty-four B-17s of the 306th. Then twenty-four B-24s of the 93rd followed while in the rear were twenty-four B-17s of the experienced 97th Bomb Group.

Take-off from Alconbury came at around 0830 hrs, on a crisp, sunny autumn morning. It was indeed exciting to watch the B-24s being nudged into their battle formation over the Cambridge area and against a sky soon crossed by seemingly countless vapour trails. Once assembled the bomber force headed for Felixstowe where the five formations assumed battle stations before swinging southerly to meet two Canadian squadrons of Spitfire IXs, Nos 401 and 402 from Kenley. Three squadrons of USAAF P-38 Lightnings (Nos 27, 71 and 94) homed in five miles east of Dunkirk while further east was an unusual sight, a formation of *Moonshine* Defiants of 515 Squadron which had earlier milled around over East Anglia attempting in vain to confuse enemy radar and screen the attackers.

Heading directly for Fives-Lille the bombers met more RAF Spitfire squadrons, Nos 64, 122, 306 and 611 briefed to provide target support. To protect the inexperienced 93rd and 306th Bomb Groups there were three more squadrons of Spitfires and to discourage any 'bouncing' were high flying Spitfire VIs of 124 and 616 Squadrons.

All of those formed the main component of the operation further protected by three major diversion sweeps. The Main Diversion comprised eight Spitfire squadrons (Nos 132, 302, 308, 315, 331, 332, 411, 485) protecting some of the Defiants. More of the latter providing the second diversion were protected by Spitfires of Nos 303, 310, 312, 313 and 316 Squadron. Three B-17s flew the third diversion in which Spitfire Vs of Nos 334, 335 and 336 US Squadrons (Debden-based) took part with other Spitfires of Nos 131, 164, 165, 403, 412, 416 Squadrons. Allied airmen taking part included American, Australian, British, Canadian, Czech and Polish.

Not surprisingly German reaction was fierce, a B-24 and three B-17s being shot down and ten B-24s damaged. Although sixty-six bomber crews attacked, bombing accuracy was poor and only nine bombs exploded within a quarter of a mile of the target. Many homes were destroyed. When the 9pm BBC news bulletin revealed the American claims of forty-eight enemy fighters being shot down and thirty-eight probably so, they were generally rated unacceptable. By next day the officially announced claims had risen to fifty-four – twenty-seven and twenty-seven damaged. Post-war research suggests that only one German fighter was destroyed – by the second target support force. The initial claims were in no way a propaganda dream, the figures were based upon what gunners aboard the bombers, and the fighter pilots, genuinely believed to be so. In the ferocious battle much exaggerated claims were easy to place. The Defiants – not mentioned at the time – suffered equipment failure in both formations. One thing the Liberator crews readily admitted – combat was no joyride.

B-24 spares at Alconbury were in very short supply, the aircraft needing so many modifications that on 5 November, for instance, eighteen out of thirty-three were unserviceable. Nevertheless, operations had continued with La Pallice, Brest, St Nazaire and Lorient as targets before a new task was presented. Convoys sailing for North-West Africa and operation *Torch* needed air cover so the 93rd BG and some of its long range Liberators were detached to North Africa in December 1942.

Remaining B-24s left for Hardwick on 6 December. During January 1943 the 327th Bomb Squadron, 92nd Bomb Group, an operational training unit, arrived from Bovingdon bringing mostly B-17Es retaining the unusual mid-1942 camouflage worn by RAF day bombers. The 325th followed, the 92nd resuming operations on 1 May 1943. It was the 327th that received twelve YB-40 heavily armed, overweight B-17s for operational trials, abandoned after fourteen missions. The 95th Bomb Group was held at Alconbury from 5 April 1943 to 19 June, when it left for Horsham St Faith. The 92nd Bomb Group moved to Podington on 15 September 1943.

The 95th Bomb Group passed through in summer and on 19 June Alconbury became Station 102, US 8th Air Force. The 92nd left for Podington and newer B-17s in mid-September 1943 leaving behind an Alconbury which now had as well as three runways – 24/06 of 5,765ft and two of 4,200ft – a total of fifty loop hardstandings. Accommodation for over 400 officers and nearly 2,500 other ranks was available. Some advance from its 1938 days!

An extensive area on Alconbury's eastern edge held the 35th Air Depot Group (35th Depot Repair Squadron) Abbots Ripton. There 3,000 men undertook repair and servicing of 1st Air Division B-17s. The unit's Noorduyn UC-64A is claimed to be that in which Glenn Miller died on 15 December 1944.

B-17E 19022 Alabama Exterminator II of the 92nd BG at Alconbury in summer 1943 retains July 1942 colouring (USAF).

On 20 August 1943 the 482nd Bomb Group formed to develop *H2S*, H2X and APS-15A equipment, then use it for bomb aiming through cloud. Two of its squadrons – the 6th and 814th – flew nose-turreted B-24s intended as lead ships for the 2nd Air Division. In September the 812th (later supplemented with the 813th) flew in with a dozen B-17s fitted with US radar. By mid-1944 B-17s entirely equipped the Group. Preceding bomber formations, the 482nd first operated as target markers on 27 September 1943 leading the 1st and 3rd Air Divisions to Emden. During the 'Big Week' of 20-25 February 1944 they spearheaded raids on factories in Gotha, Schweinfurt and Brunswick.

B-24s available when the 22nd Anti-Submarine Squadron disbanded reached Alconbury in November 1943 for the 36th and 406th Bomb Squadrons transferred to Watton in December of that year. Too heavy for its muddy surface, they returned to Alconbury in January. For their *Carpetbagger* special drops to Resistance forces in Europe, Alconbury was too 'exposed'. They moved to Harrington between 25 March and 1 May 1944.

In March 1944 the 482nd changed to being all-B-17 equipped on coming off operations to organize a school at Alconbury to train pathfinder crews for each 8th AF bomb group. The Group also produced radarscope photographs of enemy territory, tested radar equipment and guided *H2S* into service. For this purpose they also flew a few Mosquito PR XVIs which dispersed in the south-west corner of the field along with a Dominie, Norseman and Cessna Bobcat used for communications.

RB-66B-DL 40528 of the 10th TRW holding during final pre-take-off checks at Alconbury.

On 6 June 1944, with forty-nine B-17Gs serviceable and nine needing attention, the Group led attacks on surface traffic behind the beachhead. By then it had become the 482nd BG(Heavy). A mixture of trials, training and some operations continued to the end of the war, the 482nd leaving for America in May-June 1945.

February 1945 saw the arrival of B-24s and a handful of special P-38s of the 36th Bomb Squadron, the only 8th AF electronic warfare squadron. Their role was listening to, and jamming, German VHF radio transmissions. The 36th stayed until 15 October 1945.

On 15 April 1945 the 435th Air Service Group (H) had taken over Alconbury. From Harrington, B-24 transports of the 857th Bomb Squadron, 492nd Bomb Group, arrived on 11 June and remained until de-activation on 6 August. The 652nd Bomb Squadron using B-17s for weather reconnaissance came from Watton on 11 June 1945 and was at Alconbury until 25 October. For company it had HQ 1st Air Division, which vacated Brampton Grange on 20 September 1945. The 1st and the 435th ASG inactivated on 31 October 1945.

Alconbury then rapidly quietened and the RAF's 264 MU moved into the Abbot's Ripton area on 26 November 1945 bringing a bomb disposal unit which stayed into 1946. There was also a general equipment MU which stayed until closure on 30 September 1948 when the station was placed on Care and Maintenance. Alconbury was being retained under Plan F but for an uncertain purpose.

Old airfields have a rejuvenation habit and Alconbury certainly proved the point. It seemed an unlikely candidate for re-opening but on 24 August 1951 it was declared a 'USAF Primary Installation'. The USAF had asked for an 11,000ft runway but finally the US Congress agreed to fund one 9,000ft long and to modernize the airfield over a two-year period. Republic F-84s were to move in from Manston in the event of war, otherwise Alconbury would serve as a USAF Air Depot.

On 1 June 1953 the Americans returned. Their 7523rd Air Base Squadron USAFE set things rolling and on 1 January 1954 became the 7523rd Support Squadron which evolved into the 7560th ABS on 7 November 1954 who ran the site as the 7560th Air Base Group from 21 March 1955 to August 1959. In 1954 overruns were laid extending the asphalt runway 12/30 to its ultimate 10,046ft.

Alconbury in 1955 was once more a satellite station, this time of Sculthorpe from where, on 15 September 1955, B-45A jet bombers of the 86th Bomb Squadron (Tactical), 47th Bomb Wing, arrived. During May 1958 they converted to Douglas B-66Bs, used until the unit left on 5 August 1959. From May 1957 they had shared the base with C-47s, C-54s and SA-16s of the 42nd Troop Carrier Squadron(M) until de-activated on 8 December 1957. Between May and August 1959 WB-50Ds of the 53rd Weather Squadron operated from the station observing more than just rain clouds.

Departure of the 86th resulted from the implementation of *Red Richard*, the re-arrangement of USAFE units arising from the unwillingness of the French to allow them to remain upon its territory. In manner reminiscent of the August 1942 movements the 10th Tactical Reconnaissance Wing HQ came from Spangdahlem to Alconbury on 25 August 1959 bringing two squadrons, the 1st and 30th equipped with RB-66s. A generous backup team included C-47s, T-33s, T-39s and L-20/U-6s.

A dramatic change came about between May and August 1965 when the 1st TRS re-armed with McDonnell RF-4C Phantom IIs and by 1966 the second squadron also had them. Reinforcement came on 15 August 1966, when RF-4Cs of the 32nd TRS, 26th TRW at Toul/Rosieres, joined the 10th TRW. Each Alconbury squadron had an establishment of eighteen aircraft. Autumn 1966 saw another arrival: Detachment 1, 40th Air Rescue & Recovery Wing which, until its demise late summer 1972, operated a couple of curiosities, Kaman HH-43F Husky twin intermeshing rotor rescue and fire-fighting helicopters.

From January 1970 the now camouflaged Phantoms exhibited squadron markings, the 1st identifying itself with blue fin tips and tail letters 'AR'. The 30th used red and 'AS', the 32nd yellow and 'AT'. In August-September 1972 all switched to having 'AR' only on their tails as a result of a central servicing policy. Switching to detachable camera pods on US tactical aircraft rather than having dedicated fighter-reconnaissance aircraft resulted in a phased withdrawal of the RF-4s. First to go, on 1 January 1976 was the 32nd TRS which on 28 February 1976 was followed by the 30th TRS.

Their places were taken by the specialised 527th Tactical Fighter Training Aggressor Squadron on 1 April 1976 to provide 'dissimilar air combat training'. Although the first of twenty assigned Northrop F-5E Tiger II fighters were air freighted in aboard a C-5 on 21 May 1976, it was January 1977 before the squadron was declared fully functioning. Thereafter detachments from NATO and Stateside units trained in mock combat with the squadron whose aircraft wore the colours of potential foes. On 14

Snowy RF-4C Phantom at Alconbury in early 1967.

August 1967 westerly view from Alconbury tower over dispersed 10th TRW RF-4Cs.

RF-4C 68-561 'Grim Reaper' on 26 August 1987 shortly before making the 10th's final Phantom operational flight.

Camouflaged RF-4C Phantom 64-1009 009/AS of the 30th TRS.

Further view from the tower on 12 October 1990.

April 1983 the squadron was renamed the 527th Aggressor Squadron. By then an extensive array of hardened shelters had been built at the western end of the airfield to protect the RF-4 fleet.

During August 1976 the 10th TRW became parent of three Wethersfield-based formations, the 66th Combat Support Squadron, 819th Civil Engineering Squadron Heavy Repair, and 2166th Communications Squadron. Wethersfield was serving as a dispersal airfield for Alconbury, some of whose war material was stored there. Such association continued until 3 July 1990 when tenure ceased.

On 12 February 1983 a most spectacular form arrived, the first of Alconbury's spooky all-black Lockheed TR-1, battlefield surveillance version of the notorious U-2. The 95th Recon Sqn, 17th Recon Wing under SAC control had formed on 1 October 1982 to operate fifteen of these ultra-high fliers for which in 1986 the north side perimeter track was widened in 1986, five prefabricated 'Ready Sheds' were erected and thirteen extra-wide hardened aircraft shelters with associated large

A westerly view of Alconbury's HASs. 12 October 1990.

concrete aprons were laid. Alconbury's shorter subsidiary runway was subsequently resurfaced because of their tricky crosswind handling on take-off and landing. The single-seat sailplane-like machine, almost inaudible, carried super-sophisticated radar and sensors allowing high resolution surveillance and scanning at altitudes up to thirteen miles. With continuous day/night all-weather capability it could carry out battlefield surveillance from a safe distance. An astonishing structure was the so-called 'Magic Mountain', now subject to a preservation order. A huge mound in the south-east corner of the site, and reminiscent of a Stone Age burial barrow, it rose above a 60-foot-deep, very extensive, massively reinforced concrete bunker officially called the Avionics, Photographic Interpretation Centre. It was reckoned able to survive any strike other than a nuclear direct hit. Optimistically, road traffic used a one-way system – including an exit route!

Alconbury now had a varied battlefield role carried out by widely differing aircraft – until 29 August 1987. 'All change' started on 26 August 1987 when the last RF-4 sortie by the 1st TRS was flown and three days later the squadron disbanded and the Phantom's roar was silenced.

TR-1/U-2 aircraft resided in specialised hardened shelters.

U-2 creeping by the incomplete 'magic mountain' topping the electronic warfare bunker.

On 20 August 1987 the 10th TRW became the 10th Tactical Fighter Wing for two squadrons holding a total of thirty-six Fairchild A-10As soon to leave Bentwaters and become part of the 10th. Re-organisation for the new task took awhile, the first A-10 not arriving until 4 January 1988 and for general handling, etc. Two more arrived on 15 April heralding the move of the 509th Tactical Fighter Squadron (grey fin band) from the 81st TFW. The latter was so richly supplied with Fairchild A-10A tank-busters that it made sense to share them between two Wings. The second squadron, No 511 (black fin band), began arriving on 1 July 1988 upon which day both the 509th and 511th TFSs were activated to operate the A-10. Last flights by F-5s of the 527th AS were made on 22 June and on 14 July 1988 the squadron moved to Bentwaters leaving behind its F-5s for overseas disposal. On 15 September 1988 the arrival of the 36th A-10 signalled completion of the changeover.

Between April and November 1989 the A-10As flew from Wyton while runway repair took place at Alconbury. In late 1990 more important movements involved three TR-1As despatched to Taif AB, Saudi Arabia, among the first aircraft to deploy to theatre for *Desert Storm*, the first Gulf War. They

TR-1A (later redesignated U-2) 01094 of the 95th RS, 17 TRW, landing at Alconbury in summer 1990.

were followed on 27 December 1990 by twenty-three A-10s of the 511th TFS sent to Damman/King Fahd International Airport, where they became part of the 354th TFW home base Myrtle Beach AFB, South Carolina. Not until 8 June 1991 did the 511th TFS return, soon followed by the TR-1As. Although the 17th TRW was downgraded, the 95th RS did not close until 15 September 1993. It was reactivated on 1 July 1994 as the 95th RS at Mildenhall and as part of the 55th Operations Group.

With the Cold War having melted, the Gulf conflict ended for the time being, the demise of the 10th TRW followed. In October 1991 the first six A-10s to leave headed for South Carolina. The 509th TFS flew its last training flight on 16 December 1991, the 511th on 27 March 1992. The last A-10As quit the base on 30 March 1992, by which time only four TR-1s (renamed U-2R in December 1991) remained. The 95th RS was de-activated on 15 September 1993 such U-2s as seen at the base subsequently being of the 9th SRW on OLUK.

Alconbury's use as a major US air base had not yet finished for on 1 December 1992 the 39th Special Operations Wing began moving in from Woodbridge. Promptly reformed as the 352nd Special Operations Group, the newcomers included the 321st Special Tactics Squadron and the 352nd Special Operations Maintenance Squadron. These backed the 7th Special Operations Squadron (SOS) operating MC-130Es, soon replaced by MC-130H Combat Talon IIs, the 21st SOS flying MH-53J Pave Low III helicopters and the 67th SOS Combat Shadow using C-130s for helicopter in-flight refuelling and general support. The 7th SOS was trained to carry out infiltration and retrieval duties from hostile environments. In December 1992 the 39th SOW was downgraded into being the 352nd Special Operations Group whose role was officially described as 'infiltration, exfiltration, re-supply and in-flight refuelling of Special Forces aircraft'. The base was now run by the 10th Air Base Wing, USAFE.

From 31 March 1993 Alconbury was administered by the 10th Air Base Wing, a revamped 10th TRW renamed on 1 October 1994 as the 710th Air Base Wing, USAFE, which functioned until deactivation on 12 July 1995. Alconbury was subsequently administered from Molesworth, by the 423rd Air Base Squadron.

On 1 September 1994 the 352nd SOG began leaving for Mildenhall, aircraft movement starting in November and Group movement being completed on 17 February 1995. The last three U-2Rs at the OLUK of the 9th SRW left for Fairford on 15 March 1995, and on 31 March Alconbury's runway closed to flying. The last aircraft to leave was an MH-53J, which whirred away on 14 April 1995. Alconbury airfield was returned to the MoD on 30 September 1995. The US

Alconbury's final special event – 5 June 1994. Paratroopers about to emplane in C-130s for the D-Day 50th Anniversary drop near Ranville, Normandy.

C-130E-LM 64-570 of the 41st ALS soars by Alconbury's sports stadium 5 June 1994.

423rd Base Squadron (later Group) still looks after the base support area, providing domestic accommodation for Molesworth's Joint Intelligence Analysis Centre. The ex-airfield area was run at first by Alconbury Developments Ltd and in November 2009 was sold to developer Urban & Civic for £27m. Freight depot ideas have been replaced with plans for high tech industry and a frighteningly large housing scheme.

Main features:

Runways: 240° 2,000 yards x 50 yards, 180°, 300°, concrete and asphalt. *Hangars:* two T2. *Hardstandings:* fifty loop type. *Accommodation:* 421 officers, 2,473 enlisted men.

1950 modifications: NW/SE runway became a taxiway and seven main dispersal areas were designated. A new perimeter track the entire length of the main runway was added on its southern side. Major runway extension to the east. Northern half of the SW/NE runway retained.

By 1965 it comprised one main runway, one subsidiary, two technical areas, one domestic area, two married quarters areas. The LCG Group III 12/30 main 300ft wide runway is 9,009ft long asphalt surfaced and 10,046ft long including overshoots, of LCG Group III. It was fitted with Bak 13/14 rotary hydraulic arresting gear. Alconbury features an assortment of hangars and two large nose docks.

Places of interest nearby:

Pathfinder House in Huntingdon, part of the local government HQ complex, was the site of HQ 2 Group and later HQ 8 (Pathfinder) Group, Bomber Command. By Huntingdon's river Ouse, Portholme Meadow was where the first flight in the area took place by a Bleriot monoplane on 19 April 1910. Portholme Aviation, started in 1915, built seaplanes and later Sopwith Camels and Snipes. Further towards Cambridge was Conington airfield used in the late 1920s by the Suffolk and Eastern Counties Aero Club. In November 1928, Cambridge Aero Club started here and twice a week Blackburn Bluebird II or III biplanes carried passengers to and from Ipswich for fifty shillings. The airfield was closed when Cambridge aerodrome opened in March 1929.

ANDREWS FIELD (previously Great Saling – officially renamed on 21 May 1943), Essex

51°52N/00°26E 290ft asl; TL695245. 3 miles W of Braintree

Andrews Field remains the only US air base in Britain to be named in American style. It also held the distinction of being the first constructed in England by the US Army. Initially called Great Saling, it was re-named in memory of Lieutenant-General F M Andrews killed in a flying accident in Iceland. Andrew's Field holds further distinctions for it was not only the first East Anglian base for a jet fighter squadron, it was also the first from which jets flew operationally. Thus, it is a far more distinguished airfield than might generally be thought. Fortunately it has survived. With a 2,600ft grass 09/27 runway it is home for light aircraft.

Great Saling was one of the first East Anglian sites to receive Americans – serving with the 819th Aviation Engineer Battalion – who first set foot here on 4 July 1942, a most apt day for the initiation of any American venture. They worked fast at their new enterprise, the 8th Bomber Command party replacing the RAF 4th Substitution Wing on 19 April and the airfield opening (as Andrews Field) on 24 April 1943. From 13 May the US 96th Bomb Group lodged here and until 12 June when they proceeded to Snetterton Heath, their permanent base. Their place was immediately taken by B-26B Marauders of the 322nd Bomb Group, US 8th AF, which arrived on 12 June 1943 from Rattlesden and Rougham for hitherto they used two bases.

Re-positioning followed the proven unsuitability of the Marauder for low-level operations. New policy decreed that the B-26s based in Essex would fly medium altitude saturation bombing raids in groups of eighteen aircraft. They would transfer to the US IXth AF once it was functioning.

Considerable training needed meant that the Group was not ready to resume operations until 17 July 1943. Airfields became the first and most suitable targets, but bombing of rail installations and shipyards was another main activity against which most opposition came from predicted anti-aircraft fire.

On 16 October 1943 the Group was transferred to the fledgling IXth AF. The end of 1943 brought a switch to intensive operations against flying-bomb sites. Many missions at this time were part of extensive multi-part *Ramrod* operations embracing RAF and US fighter-bomber raids for which huge armadas mainly comprising RAF fighters gave protection by means of broad inter-locked sweeps over France and the Low Countries. Usually the B-26s operated in multiples totalling seventy-two aircraft.

In March 1944 the 322nd switched to supporting the invasion build-up by bombing of bridges, railways and tactical targets.

Intensively involved on 6 June 1944 the B-26s attacked coastal defences and gun batteries and during ensuing days switched attention to fuel and ammunition dumps, bridges, railway junctions and troop defiles while the Allies were consolidating the Normandy bridgehead. Next, the 322nd supported the US break-out at St-Lô, then provided field support to advancing forces.

So rapid was the August progress across Europe that the B-26s and other tactical bombers needed to move to France in order to be able to operate effectively. In September 1944 the 322nd joined the exodus and took up residence at Beauvais/Tille.

Since February 1944 the 1st Pathfinder Squadron (Provisional) had been based here, a specialist unit which on D-Day flew six B-26 missions against vital targets in Normandy. They left for Beauvais/Tille on 24 September 1944.

By then the air war had so much changed that RAF Bomber Command could as readily operate by day as by night, something the USAAF never achieved. Vacated US bomber bases in south-east England were ideal for RAF fighters covering the Lancaster and Halifax daylight raids into Germany and the RAF occupied Andrews Field. On 1 October 1944 the station became part of No 11 Group as a Forward Airfield in the North Weald Sector, receiving escort fighters and in strength. Indeed, more RAF Mustangs were based here than at any other station.

First to arrive – on 10 October – were 129 and 315 Squadrons which, on 15 October 1944, supported eighteen Lancasters attempting to breach the famous – and rather curious – Sorpe Dam. Three days later one squadron encountered an Me 163 rocket fighter near Arnhem. Busily participating in *Ramrods*, they had been joined on 14 October by Nos 19, 65, 122 Squadrons supplemented on 24 October with 316 Squadron. All were using Mustang IIIs and for a time around 100 RAF Mustang IIIs were here.

To lessen the strain re-arrangement of the squadrons soon took place, Nos 315 and 316 leaving for Coltishall on 24 October on which date No 129 moved to Bentwaters. No 309 (Polish) Mustang Squadron arrived on 12 December. Mid-January 1945 saw the exchange of 315 and 316 Squadrons with 65 Squadron which replaced them at Peterhead. No 19 Squadron joined them on 13 February 1945.

On 28 February a new sound was heard over the airfield when the first of seventeen Meteor III jet fighters of 616 Squadron arrived from Colerne for anti-V-1 (alias anti-Diver) patrols, and to combat any German jet activity over Essex. No 616 left for Gilze-Rijen on 31 March, by which time the Germans had launched the last of their long-range flying-bombs across Essex towards London challenged by the Mustangs at Andrews Field. *Ramrod* operations still occupied the Mustangs and on 15 March No 315 Squadron was among those which escorted Lancasters of 617 Squadron and their Mosquito markers attacking the Bielefeld viaduct with 22,000lb 'Grand Slam' DP bombs. With 303 (Polish) Squadron, which arrived at this time bringing to Andrews Field its first P-51D Mustang IVs, '315' participated in the Lancaster raid on Hitler's eyrie at Berchtesgaden. A replacement detachment of Meteors from 504 Squadron resided here in April in case the Luftwaffe mounted last-minute attacks.

High scoring Mustang III FB355 PK-H of No 315 (Polish) Squadron based here 1945.

Mustangs remained after the war when the station was taken into the busy North Weald Sector. Air-sea rescue cover off Essex was provided by a handful of Walrus/Sea Otter amphibians of 276 Squadron based here between 8 June and 23 August 1945. On 6 May No 65 Squadron returned for a brief stay which ended with its departure for Bentwaters on 15 May 1945. Next day No 303 Squadron moved out to Coltishall but returned on 19 August. No 315 moved to Coltishall on 8 August from where No 303 Squadron arrived on 19 August. The last two Polish squadrons here were thus 316, which left for Wick on 28 November 1945, and 303 Squadron, which moved to Turnhouse the same day.

Andrews Field fell silent and on 23 February 1946 Fighter Command offered the airfield to the Air Ministry to decide its future status. Fighter Command on 4 May 1946 left and Technical Training Command took control before care and maintenance was imposed and agricultural airfield status followed. In October 1952 interest arose in giving it a temporary military future in USAF hands and connected with Wethersfield although replacement was already under consideration and rejuvenation was abandoned.

In 1972 a 3,000-foot grass strip for light aircraft was prepared along the original main runway line. A clubhouse and flying control were added for Andrewsfield Flying Club. The airfield, from where Andrewsfield Aviation Ltd operates, was licensed by the CAA in 1976, light aircraft making good use of this popular, busy venue. Of the wartime airfield little more than the T2 hangars and a few Nissen huts remain. American presence is recalled by two nearby memorials, to the 819th AEB and the 322nd BG.

Andrews Field April 2008. Popular, flourishing light aviation centre (George Pennick).

Main features (December 1944):
Runways: 270° 6,000ft x 150ft, 020°, 330°, concrete with tar and wood chip surface.
Hangars: two T2. *Hardstandings:* fifty loop type. *Accommodation:* RAF: 200 officers, 352 SNCOs, 1,939 ORs; WAAF: 16 SNCOs and 240 ORs.

ATTLEBRIDGE, Norfolk

52°41/01°06E 200ft asl; TG105148. Turn S off A1067 at Morton, airfield ½ mile SW of Weston Longville

They were making their first bombing raid on their homeland, on the Dornier factory at Flushing, these Dutchmen of 320 Squadron. Intense was the flak greeting and, as the formation turned for the return to Attlebridge, 'C-Charlie' was hit. Gradually the Mitchell fell behind and was ditched mid-afternoon. Proficient in their dinghy drill and with intrepidity they sailed away from the sinking bomber. Luckily a couple of Mustang pilots spotted them then circled radioing for help. An ASR Walrus amphibian from Coltishall soon appeared, Spitfire escorted. It landed, picked up the Dutchmen and took them back to Norfolk. Such dramas were part of the pace in 1943.

Attlebridge had opened as a grass field Unbuilt Satellite of Swanton Morley in June 1941 and Blenheims of 105 Squadron then dispersed there. July 1941 saw No 88 Squadron's arrival at Swanton Morley from Northern Ireland and in August they gradually moved into Attlebridge. No 88 was an unusual squadron for half was in England flying Blenheim IVs while the remainder in Ireland was trying out the Boston for 2 Group use. When this element arrived in England it also moved to Swanton Morley there to fully arm with Boston IIIs.

Meanwhile their companions had been declared fully operational on Blenheims and went into action from Attlebridge during August 1941 playing a part in 2 Group's hazardous anti-shipping campaign. Following a couple of low-level raids on Rotterdam docks the squadron was detached to Manston for three weeks for a share in the *Channel Stop* campaign directed against German merchant ships supplying French ports. Operations took place in the face of fearsome onslaughts by German fighters which took a heavy toll of British bombers.

Back at Attlebridge, 88 Squadron undertook further dangerous anti-shipping raids and their last Blenheim operation, on 26 October 1941 was as fierce as any. A 4,000 ton motor vessel had been located off the Hague with four other merchant ships and all guarded by three flak ships. Squadron Leader Barr led the formation to the convoy against which a very low level attack was billed. Barr's task was to photograph the attack. Pilot Officer Rowlinson roared in at masthead height, dropped his four 250lb bombs and very quickly fire from the flak ships set ablaze his port engine. His aircraft was soon in the sea. It was hardly encouraging for the others each of which carried out one fast enormously courageous pass each against one ship before they raced for home.

Compared with the Blenheim the Boston was utter luxury. Finely appointed, streamlined and so attractive to view and with a shoulder wing, it was ideal for low-level work and Bostons began arriving for 88 Squadron at Attlebridge in November 1941. The nosewheel undercarriage took some getting used to so to practice well away from battle they moved, in January 1942, to Long Kesh in Ulster for tactical work-up at what became the site of the notorious prison.

Barely had they re-settled at Attlebridge when the two German battle cruisers and the *Prinz Eugen* made their Channel dash. Quickly bombed-up, 88 Squadron took its Bostons somewhat prematurely into fruitless action. Now committed to battle, they flew a few anti-shipping sorties before attempting a low-level raid on the Matford factory at Poissy near Paris. It was unsuccessful for, as they left their take-off point, Thorney Island, troubles overtook them.

Thereafter, Attlebridge's Bostons were out most days but usually participating in fighter-escorted *Circus* operations, attacking Continental targets. When the clouds were low 88 squadron mounted some fast, low-level attacks on power stations – hazardous, lonely ventures. Come August and they participated in the Dieppe raid. After more *Circus* operations they moved to Oulton on 30 September 1942. It had been a busy year for Attlebridge.

They had moved to make way for Americans of the 319th Bomb Group being held here for operation *Torch*, the North-West Africa landings. With them came at least twenty-five examples of another new and very shapely aeroplane, early examples of the Martin B-26A/B Marauder. Far from battle-ready the bombers left in late November for Africa amid considerable secrecy.

Attlebridge continued to accommodate Americans while the airfield was raised to Wartime Class A Standard and runways were laid. By March 1943 the RAF's 2 Group was also expanding, its new squadrons needing to be accommodated while the USAAF clamoured for airfields. No 320 Royal Netherlands Navy Squadron was currently at Methwold, but when 3 Group won Feltwell, whose Venturas were nudged into Methwold, 320 took up residence at 'new' Attlebridge.

Yet again it was the base for a new type for 320 was in the process of learning to use the still temperamental North American Mitchell whose gun turret was being very troublesome. Hope was that it would be useful for low-level bombing but for that it was unsuitable, and in May 320 Squadron was ordered to stop low flying over Norfolk to make way for B-24s practising for their Ploesti raid. A very frustrated No 320 Squadron was allowed, in June 1943, to undertake some deep air-sea rescue sweeps. The Dutch Prime Minister visited them on 29 July to raise their spirits, but next day they fell when a Mitchell went missing from an ASR sortie.

The squadron's first bombing operation using Mitchells was flown from Attlebridge on 17 August 1943 when six crews attacked marshalling yards at Calais. On the 19th they bombed Poix airfield and on the 20th came the Flushing raid. Then a pause as 320 Squadron moved to Dunsfold via Lasham on 2 September to be closer to their area of action. Attlebridge lay quiet again, its runways closed for extension and the airfield for much modification. There had briefly been other occupants, Typhoons of 247 Squadron here for a week in August.

Work completed, the Americans returned on a big scale in March 1944 in B-24Hs of the 466th Bomb Group, 2nd Bomb Division. Work-up was rapid, the need urgent, and they celebrated their readiness on 22 March 1944 by making Berlin their first target.

The morning of D-Day found them bombing gun emplacements on the Normandy shore and for a time their targets were behind the enemy front as they aided the break-out from St-Lô. During July 1944 the 784th Squadron began a pathfinder role. When in September 1944 the advancing US Army was short of fuel the 466th ferried supplies to France. Since July the 784th Squadron had engaged in pathfinder duties.

Targets for the Liberators were spread widely across Europe and included marshalling yards at Liege and Saarbrucken, airfields such as St Trond and Chartres, aviation targets at Kempton and Eisenach, fuel targets and factories in Brunswick and Hamburg. They helped stem the German advance in the Ardennes offensive and bombed Nordhorn airfield in support of the Rhine crossing. Their 232nd and final operation flown on 25 April 1945 was directed against a transformer station aiding German railways at Traunsten.

Early July 1945 saw the Americans quickly complete their exodus and sail home aboard the Queen Mary. Attlebridge was transferred to RAF Maintenance Command on 15 July 1945 and 231 MU opened an ammunition store for fighters here. On 27 January 1948, 94 MU took over and remained here until 2 October 1956. The site was disposed of on 15 March 1959.

From the air three runways, perimeter track and some dispersal pans suggest that the airfield – encircled by public roads – is active until one notices on the runways the broiler houses in which Bernard Matthews raises turkeys. Precious little – if any – flying takes place by the feathered occupants, but a helicopter sometimes flits by. A memorial window in the local church serves as a tribute to those who served here.

Main features (December 1944):
Runways: 270° 6,000ft x 150ft, 220°, 140°, concrete. *Hangars:* two T2.
Hardstandings: fifty loop type. *Accommodation:* 421 US officers, 2,473 enlisted men.

BARKSTON HEATH, Lincolnshire

52°57N/00°33W 366ft asl; SK968415. NE of Grantham of B6403, 2 miles S of Ancaster

Barkston doesn't have a landing ground, it has one of the world's finest lawns in keeping with its master's pristine image. It must surely be the world's best kept, smartest airfield. One might go even further and claim that no RAF Station Warrant Officer could ever have asked for more! On a summer morn with the Slingsby Fireflies gently dancing hither and thither the vista is unique. Whatever would the rough and ready Roman soldiers make of it could they return to tramp along their Ermine Street which still passes along the airfield's eastern perimeter?

Built on what was actually Barkston Heath, the primitive landing ground was first used for flying in 1937 as an RLG for Cranwell. Rapid expansion put great pressure on existing training schools and in the area around the College a number of similar sites were acquired. During wartime and until November 1942 it was used by Oxfords employed in the training of flying instructors at Cranwell SFTS.

Control of the airfield passed from Flying Training to Bomber Command in March 1943 for it had been selected for upgrading into a standard wartime RAF bomber type station with the intention of accommodating here a heavy conversion unit, an off-shoot of No 1660 HCU Swinderby, to train crews for the airborne forces squadrons. Special sheds were accordingly erected for gliders. However, airfields with good approaches and fine weather patterns were also required by fast emerging front line RAF, and US transport forces needed to support an invasion of Europe. Barkston, within that category, was passed to the US 9th AF Troop Carrier Command and re-opened on 11 January 1944 under American control and with Sub-Stations at Folkingham and North Witham.

Barkston's layout was somewhat unusual apart from the standard triple runway pattern. Two T2s and a B1 hangar on the main site were supplemented by four T2s on the opposite side of Ermine Street.

On 18 February 1944 the 61st Troop Carrier Group officially moved in from Sciacca, Sicily, its four Troop Carrier Squadrons – Nos 14, 15, 53 and 59 – flying a mixture of C-47s and C-53s, the latter being dedicated paratroop transports. Many of the aircraft retained tan coloured upper surfaces, a reminder that operating from Kairouan, Tunisia, they had participated in the assault on Sicily where, since September 1943, they had been based.

As soon as the Group was up to strength intensive training commenced. Large formations of low flying Skytrains and Skytroopers, their navigation lights on, toured Eastern England at dusk preparing for the dropping of paratroops on Normandy. Although that was their primary role they also trained in glider towing by sometimes trailing Waco CG-4As. A few of their aircraft featured glider snatch equipment and formation leaders had distinctive radomes also below the fuselage.

On 1 and 2 June 1944 many paratroopers arrived at Barkston where on 5 June Group strength totalled eighty-five aircraft all of which were serviceable! At 2352 hrs mainly C-47s and some C-53s began setting off for their part in D-Day. Take off was extremely rapid and within six minutes seventy-two were away carrying 1,167 men of the 507th Parachute Infantry Regiment for DZ 'T' near St Mere Eglise. Only one aircraft failed to return and six were damaged, among them that of Colonel Mitchell, the Group Commander, who sustained shrapnel injuries to his right hand.

The Group operated again early on 7 June when a re-supply mission was flown which resulted in three aircraft coming down in the English Channel and twenty having flak damage. Transfer of personnel and supplies occupied the Group once air strips were available in Normandy. In late August training started for the next big airborne assault, operation *Market*. At 1121 hrs on Sunday 17 September, the seventy-two aircraft earmarked for use began taking off lifting and loaded in all with 1,268 paratroopers. In addition 432 packages were aboard many being slung on external centre-section racks. All was for dropping on DZ 'X' close to near Heelsum. The sight of C-47s and 53s streaming fairly low over the Fens towards Aldeburgh remains unforgettable.

Next day the 61st despatched forty aircraft each towing one Waco CG4A glider. Loads aboard the latter included troops, guns, Jeeps, and various items of equipment along with ammunition needed to support the ill-starred venture. This time four aircraft failed to return.

After participating in *Market* the Group resumed intensive supply flights to airfields in France, and carried out casualty evacuation by bringing back wounded to the clutch of specially designated airfields. The 61st also used specially modified aircraft for the transportation of fuel to aid the rapid Allied advance across Europe.

To increase the value of their activity the 61st TCG moved to Abbeville, France, in mid-March 1945. They were replaced by another US 9th AF formation, the 349th TCG, whose four squadrons, Nos 23, 312, 313 and 314, flew a mixture of C-47s, C-53s and most impressively the larger, very curvaceous Curtiss C-46 Commandos. The sight of those passing low over the road must remain unforgettable for any who witnessed it. First Commandos to come, on 30 March 1945 belonged to the 312th TCS and they were followed by the others on 3 April. The C-46s were sometimes to be seen towing two Waco CG-4As. Equally memorable was to see a Commando towing a Waco CG-13A only a few of which saw European service. The stay of the C-46s was brief, the Group leaving for Roye/Amy, France, on 18 April although a few of the aircraft made a brief re-appearance at Barkston in May when they came to assist in the movement of Allied forces to Norway.

What a sight! Three Curtiss C-46 Commandos of the 23rd Squadron, 349th Troop Carrier Group. Anyone seen a photograph of one of their CG-13A?

By mid-May the USAAF had given up its tenure of the station which was returned to the RAF on 1 June 1945. On 1 September it was transferred to No 22 Group, Technical Training Command and became an RAF Regiment depot parented by RAF Belton Park before in Autumn 1946 it was reduced to care & maintenance.

Strength reduction left the station devoid of activity until limited RAF expansion saw it re-open in February 1949 as a satellite-cum-RLG for The Royal Air Force College Cranwell. Circuit and general flying training began, and later the airfield was available for the use of 3 FTS Cranwell. In the late 1980s Bloodhound II missiles of D Flight, 85 Squadron were based here.

In 1994 Barkston Heath became the home of the Joint Elementary Flying Training School operated by Hunting and providing basic flying training for the RAF, RN and Army using civilian-registered Slingsby T.67M 260 Firefly Mk II two-seater trainers. Babcock Defence Services was in July 2003 awarded a six-year contract to supply and operate them, as part of the Defence Elementary Flying Training School (DEFTS). In July 2003 HQ EFT at Cranwell, which oversees activity at Barkston Heath, became No 1 EFTS. No 703 Naval Aviation Squadron trains Royal Navy pilots here while No 674 Squadron caters for Army Air Corps pilots. Although most domestic accommodation has gone, new buildings, needed for pilot training, have been added. Most hangars remain, and some stored the remains of cattle destroyed during the BSE crisis.

Yellow and black Slingsby 260 Firefly G-BNSR at Barkston Heath being operated under the Hunting Contract Service.

Main features:

December 1944: *Runways:* 250° 6,000ft x 150ft, 290°, 190°, concrete with wood chip surface. *Hangars:* two T2 on airfield and four T2 opposite, one B1, four Glider Type. *Hardstandings:* forty-eight loop type mainly on NW perimeter and two circular. *Accommodation:* establishment for RAF bomber station: RAF; 136 officers, 410 SNCOs, 1,279 ORs; WAAF: 10 officers, 10 SNCOs, 450 ORs.

1980s and 90s: *Runways available:* 06/24 6,007ft and 11/29 4,206ft. Both asphalt.

BASSINGBOURN, Cambridgeshire

52°05N/00°03W 78ft asl; TL335458. By the A1198 4 miles N of Royston, Hertfordshire

B ritish combat aircraft have never been noted for comfort. During take-off strapped in an ejector seat beneath a tiny window too high to provide any view, I had no idea of speed or position as the Canberra climbed away. Just a few minutes after leaving Bassingbourn I quit the navigator's seat to peer out from the cockpit. 'North London?' I enquired. 'We've left that behind, we're running in for the turn off at Southend' was the response. In a 'Lanc' or Lincoln one would have had ample time to recognise familiar landmarks but in their successor even the best known passed before one could be sure of them. An angular Canberra may appear to be rather sluggish and to be outshone by more shiny aeroplanes. Forget it, so spectacular was its world beating performance when it entered service in 1951 that HQ Bomber Command arranged a large scale conference to brief those with a need to know about the aircraft's amazing performance, its all round excellence, outstanding capability and great potential. At around 50,000ft it would cruise at 500mph carrying a 6,000lb load for as far as 2,000 miles. When the Hunter came into service it was often hard pushed to intercept an incoming Canberra 'raid' in time to 'save' the nation. Not only could that performance be improved, the load for the Mk 6 soon became nuclear, and extended range was intended to permit sorties into China from Far East bases.

For fifteen years Canberras roamed Bassingbourn's sky. Even beyond Newmarket they could daily be seen starting the long talk down to the airfield while others were touring the UK or much of Europe and practising very high flying or 'LABS' toss bombing. Nor was it only the RAF which was training, every air force which used the Canberra had its personnel Bassingbourn trained in order to obtain the maximum from the ubiquitous aircraft.

For all that world beating excellence the US 8th AAF strangely seems still to hold first prize in the Bassingbourn popularity stakes, although the Americans – large in hearts, considerable in numbers – were here for only a short portion of Bassingbourn's aviation history. That in no way diminishes their courageous exploits over two and a half years, its importance just needs to be viewed in historical perspective.

Although the station opened in March 1938 it was not the first flying ground in the area. At Kneesworth, close to RAF Bassingbourn of later times, mooring masts were erected during the large scale Army manoeuvres of September 1912, for the blimps *Gamma* and *Delta*.

Thereafter there seems to have been no more air activity until a Magister and an Avro Tutor preceded by a few days the arrival, beginning on 2 May 1938, of two dozen Hawker Hinds shared by 104 and 108 Squadrons. Their presence was brief for the first Blenheim I bombers replaced them – initially in 104 Squadron between 10 and 31 May and in 108 Squadron between 10 and 24 June 1938. Each squadron held twelve Blenheims and four in reserve.

Both 2 Group squadrons arrived before the station's four white washed concrete and brick 'C' Type Aircraft Sheds were complete, let alone the many other mock-Georgian buildings many of which remained, little altered, to the end of Bassingbourn's flying days. In appearance the station, building of which began in 1937, was of standard attractive looking design for a Permanent expansion period light/medium bomber split site aerodrome. There had been suggestions for naming it Whaddon, but confusion with Watton ruled that out.

Many saplings, now large trees, were planted within the camp not just for camouflage but also to ensure that the extensive enterprise did as little as possible to spoil an area close by in which magnificent trees were a prominent feature. In 1939 large brown nets were slung over the hangars, which were camouflage painted when war came.

In May 1939, twenty-three Avro Ansons arrived to supplement the Blenheims being used to provide the RAF Volunteer Reserve aircrew with experience of operational aircraft. That was in keeping with the

Bristol Blenheim 1 L1203 of No 108 Squadron outside now demolished No 4 Hangar, Bassingbourn. (Bob Wilsdon)

station's new role, the training of aircrew for 2 Group's Blenheim squadrons for which purpose, on 17-18 September 1939, both Blenheim squadrons moved to Bicester leaving their Ansons behind.

Replacement came from Honington on 24 September 1939 in the form of Wellington Is of 215 Squadron serving 3 Group as an operational training unit. There had been concern about the airfield's surface for some time, and the heavier bombers converted part of the field into a quagmire so that drainage work was needed before the winter set in. Once that was completed, early December 1939 saw three Flights of Battle bombers of 35 Squadron arrive from Cranfield allowing attention to a similar problem there. The latter squadron trained aircrew for the Advanced Air Striking Force in France, and left for Upwood at the start of February 1940. Camouflage and dispersal of Bassingbourn's Ansons which wore bomber colours was, from the start of the war, between trees bordering a broad avenue leading toward Wimpole Hall. Traffic on the Old North Road halted to let aircraft cross via a track still obvious.

Under an extensive new plan No 215 Squadron and Bassingbourn SHQ combined in April 1940 (the effective date being 17 April) to become 'No 11 OTU Bassingbourn' administered by No 6 Group. To give experience of operational flying, leaflet dropping over France using the Wellingtons commenced on 21/22 July and continued spasmodically while the main task remained establishment and general training of crews for 3 Group squadrons. Bassingbourn was very 'open' so unusual security check points were placed on the Old North Road at either end of its passage by the landing ground to prevent unwanted viewing of the steadily increasing amount of Wellington activity. A highlight came on 5 November when Whitleys of 10 and 78 Squadrons refuelled here before setting off for a target in Italy.

Bombs fell on the station a number of times. In August 1940 eleven men were killed and fifteen injured when the barrack block on the southern side of the parade ground received a direct hit. After a raid on 16 January 1941 a crater 20ft deep and 50ft across could be seen fairly close to the main road and not far from the impressive typical 90ft high water tower demolished, incidentally, in 1998.

Accent on training from airfields in Cambridgeshire has long been considerable and important. In the case of 11 OTU the enemy soon recognised that fact by directing numerous intruders against Bassingbourn, the most spectacular occurring on 22 July 1941.

Bassingbourn being an easterly bomber Operational Training Unit was the nearest within easy strike by an enemy rightly assuming crews under training to be easy prey. On the night in question moonlit Wellingtons were flying the usual round of circuits and bumps, or setting off on cross-country journeys from both Bassingbourn and its satellite, when in from the Wash crept Lt Heinz Volker flying Ju 88C2 W Nr.842, R4+BL of NJG 2 operating out of Gilze Rijen in the Netherlands. Wellington R1334 had just taken off from Bassingbourn when the '88 closed and to the west of the airfield its pilot opened fire. The Wellington swerved as the German aircraft turned. They collided, there was a tremendous explosion, a brilliant flash, visible for miles around and for eleven men the end must have been instantaneous. Mangled wreckage fell near Ashwell station.

That was not the first intrusion to end in disaster for on 10 April 1941 Wellington I, L4253, was brought down near Ashwell. A fortnight later another Wellington attacked by a Ju 88C crashed on a dispersal pan. On 7 May yet one more was shot down, this time during landing approach, and in August NJG2 engaged a Wellington near Barrington not far from Lord's Bridge bomb dump.

The Wellington Ia was gradually introduced to 215 Squadron from March 1940 and Mk Ics to the OTU from July 1940. Unit strength rose from twenty-four aircraft to ultimately fifty-four Wellingtons and eleven Ansons supplemented by two Lysander target towers for air-to-air gunnery practice. The last two Mk Is left in July 1942 and the last of the comparatively few Mk Ia not until February 1943.

Runway construction commenced in December 1941 causing much of 11 OTU to move temporarily to Steeple Morden satellite (which came into use late in 1940) and to Tempsford. It was at this time that No 1446 Ferry Training Flight was established here to train Wellington crews to deliver that type overseas. The unit moved to Moreton-in-Marsh on 18 May. On 24 April 1942 Bassingbourn's main concrete runway had opened allowing the return of 11 OTU in time for the 1,000 bomber raids. A dozen Wellingtons set off for the Cologne raid and eleven for Essen on 1/2 June. Against Bremen another dozen were despatched on 25/26 June and two did not return. No 11 OTU also took part in *Grand National* Main Force operations, attacking Düsseldorf on 31 July and Bremen on 13/14 September. No 11 OTU Bassingbourn had become part of 91 Group when No 6 Group was renumbered on 11 May.

In September rumour mongers announced that the Americans were coming. Their belief may have stemmed from a chance landing on 3 August by the first USAAF aircraft to call here, C-47 41-7820 from Chelveston. Unrecognised by Grantchester's heavy gun battery and failing to fire the colour of the day it was promptly set upon as a result of which the crew hastily sought sanctuary at Bassingbourn from where 11 OTU began departing for Westcott on 25 September. More auspicious was the arrival, on 14 October 1942, of the 91st Bomb Group, USAAF which brought from Kimbolton some of the first B-17Fs in Britain.

B-17F-75-BO 42-29837 'LG A' of the 324th BS, 91st BG. On 7 June 1943 it replaced Memphis Belle, became Lady Luck and served until March 1944 when B-17Gs replaced remaining B-17Fs (USAF).

For nationals used to comfort, Bassingbourn and its historic facade much pleased them and they named it 'The Country Club'. Soon the 91st was learning to fly in battle formation and contrailing high above Cambridge. On 7 November 1942 when the Group held thirty-four of the 232 B-17s in the UK, fourteen of them set out with the 93rd, 301st and 306 Bomb Groups on their first mission with Brest's U-boat facilities targeted. Submarine pens, shipyards, docks and harbours were their main targets at this period during which the 91st took part in the first raid on Germany carried out on 27 January 1943 when Wilhelmshaven's navy yard was the target. A Distinguished Unit Citation was awarded for the unit's attack on Hamm, the first by the USAAF on the Ruhr and flown on 4 March 1943 when the weather was bad, the fighting tough and four B-17s never returned. That reduced existing strength to twenty-seven aircraft. A gradual build up resulted in the Group having forty-six aircraft by 13 May. From mid-1943 targets were in particular aircraft factories, airfields, chemical works, oil installations and long distance penetrations were made to Berlin, Oranienburg, Peenemunde and Schweinfurt where an important ball bearing factory was situated. Of the 671 B-17s serving in UK-based Groups on 24 July 1943, forty-five were at Bassingbourn.

The very mention of Schweinfurt at Bassingbourn always evoked a silent response, and with good cause for ten of the B-17s despatched on the 17 August 1943 raid failed to return. Of the total thirty-six B-17s missing eleven were of the 381st BG Ridgewell, with the 91st suffering almost as harshly. Bomber Mission 84 began badly, departure being delayed by mist. In all 230 B-17s set off for the panacea target deep in Germany and with Colonel Warzbach and the 91st leading. A year to the day since the 8th Air Force had commenced B-17 operations in Europe, it was mid-morning and far later than usual when only eighteen of the intended twenty-four B-17s of the 91st eventually formed up over Cambridgeshire. When the 91st returned they were within a mixed unit gaggle of thirty-six with nine more trailing behind two of which could be seen with engines out of action. They had, during almost the entire time over enemy territory, been assaulted by fighters which had concentrated upon the leaders.

Late that evening I recorded in my diary that 'B-17s have come home late in chaotic formation'. Little wonder, Schweinfurt for the 91st had been a ghastly experience. At base the count showed eleven B-17s damaged, one beyond repair. Far worse, ninety-seven men were missing and unaccounted for in addition to one dead and another seriously wounded.

By next morning it was widely known by those living around the base that the 91st had suffered badly. Bassingbourn's dispersals provided a sorry sight, only three B-17s being visible. The remainder were either missing or in the hangars being repaired. Equally astonishing, though, was the speed with which replacements arrived allowing resumption of operations on 19th. It was, however, some time before the 91st again operated in strength. On 14 October the revived 91st headed again for Schweinfurt and this time only one of the eleven participants was shot down.

Many of the 'Forts' were displaying affectionate names including 'Jack the Ripper' 41-24490, 'Stric Nine' 42-29475, 'Oklahoma Okie' 42-29921 and best known of all 'Memphis Belle' 41-24485 (now to be seen in Memphis, Tennessee) star of the wartime film of that name and the first B-17 to complete twenty-five missions. 'Nine-O-Nine' 42-31909 flew 140 sorties, more than any other in the 8th AF. Of the eleven YB-40 heavily armed over-weight 'escort bombers' in use in August 1943 three served in the 91st which from June 1943 displayed its prime status by wearing 'A in a triangle' on its aircraft which from July 1944 could be identified easily by their red tails.

On 11 January 1944 the 91st joined the many Groups starting a period of concentrated bombing of aircraft factories in central Germany. Of the 1,216 B-17s serving in front line 8th AF Groups on D-Day forty-four were with the 91st BG. They bombed gun emplacements and enemy troop concentrations in Normandy. German troops were attacked to aid the breakthrough at St-Lô on 24-25 July and near Caen in August. During the later Rhine crossing operation the 91st attacked airfields, bridges and rail routes leading to the battle area. The strength of the Group was maintained close to forty-five aircraft to the end of hostilities, the 91st remaining in the forefront of the 8th AF BC campaign often leading the 1st Air Division into battle. Pilsen was bombed by the 91st during its 340th and final mission flown on 25 April 1945. During the course of 9,591 sorties from which 197 B-17s never returned, 22,142 tons of bombs were dropped. Gunners claimed to shoot down 420 enemy aircraft, probably destroyed 127 and damaged 238 which claims were the highest of any 8th AF Group. Its own losses which exceeded 600 men were also the highest in the 8th AF.

The first B-17s began heading back to the USA on 27 May, the speed with which the Americans hurried home after VE-Day being amazing. Gone within days were their delectable peaches and ice cream and the piles of peanut butter looking like mini termite mounds. Gone, too, the *Dodge* trucks and cheery cowboys while for quite a few local ladies there was an abrupt, unannounced termination of exciting love lives and for some a worrying legacy. The last Americans are recorded as leaving on 23 June then on 26 June 1945 it was all change with the return of the far less exotic RAF. No 47 Group Transport Command took control on 1 July and on 7 July it was declared open for Liberator arrivals.

North American accents lingered for the personnel of Nos 422 and 423 (Canadian) Squadrons after giving up their Sunderlands lodged here before sailing for home conventionally. Next it was Australians manning No 466 Squadron and they spent August to October here, and without aircraft. Of more importance was the August 1945 arrival of No 102 Squadron and their transport Liberators mostly adorned with Coastal Command colours. Rapidly switched to transport duties, Liberators had been selected to ferry personnel to and from the Far East, and with internal modifications complete commenced trooping flights in October 1945. That role continued until February when, on 15th, No 102 Squadron moved to Upwood.

Next day Bassingbourn acquired a more upmarket status when No 24 (Commonwealth) Squadron flying mainly Dakotas left its ancestral Hendon home and moved in. Bassingbourn was more suitable for heavy aircraft carrying out considerable amounts of flying than an airfield within a much built-up area of London. Evidence of this came between 16 and 26 February when a United Nations delegation attended a radar and radio aids demonstration, Bassingbourn being one of the first airfields to feature a Ground Controlled Approach system.

With the move completed by 25 February, transportation of VIPs, senior officers and government officials was resumed. During March 1946 the main task was conveying up to fourteen passengers each time in Dakotas plying between Blackbushe and Prestwick. Fourteen VIPs were carried during April, among them Mr Aneurin Bevan conveyed from Cornwall to Northolt on 1 April in famous Dakota KP208. Mr Ernest Bevin, the Foreign Secretary, on 28th flew from Le Bourget to Northolt in KP248. During May, Field Marshal Smuts journeyed in KP208 from Northolt to Gatow and Air Chief Marshal Sir John Slessor in KN386. Bassingbourn's aircraft generally worked to and from Northolt.

To operate fast courier, long-range services No 1359 (VIP) Flight, equipped with luxuriously appointed Lancastrians and Yorks had arrived from Lyneham in February. In March 1946 two of the Lancastrians made record flights to New Zealand, and from 3 June, No 1359 Flight and 24 Squadron began operating as one. They merged on 1 July as 24 Squadron whose establishment changed to twelve Dakota 3s and 4s, five Yorks and five Lancastrian IIs. Among the VIP aircraft were Yorks MW100, MW101 and Field Marshal Montgomery's LV633 containing a huge leather chair for his personal comfort.

It was MW100 which, after carrying General Sir Arthur Cunningham to Lydda on 25 July 1946, achieved a record-breaking 2,660 mile non-stop flight from Habbaniya to Lyneham. Most of the flights were still by Dakota, but on 14 July MW101 carried Air Vice-Marshal Cochrane on his tour of Mediterranean bases, and in August General Alexander was flown overseas in MW100. On 4 August Lancastrian VM701 set off carrying Lieutenant General Sir A C D Wiart on a three-and-a-half month tour of China during which it became one of the first aircraft to fly non-stop from Calcutta to Nanking. In China it was joined by VM727 which, between 29 September and 20 December, conveyed Sir Leslie Boyce and a trade mission. Christmas mail was flown to Australia and New Zealand in York MW128 and in January 1947 Lord and Lady Mountbatten travelled to Zurich in one of Bassingbourn's Dakotas. Many long distance flights, now daily events and still not necessarily comfortable, were simply feats of tortuous endurance in the late 1940s.

Four Lancastrian crews were selected to operate a return London-Moscow courier service during the 1947 March-April Foreign Ministers' Conference. One aircraft left London at 0300 hrs GMT and another Moscow/Vnukovo at 2300 hrs GMT every day (except Sunday) between 11 March and 29 April. Other memorable flights that year were to Dorval, Gander and in September-October to Central and South Africa in connection with the Royal Tour. Similar special flights continued throughout 1948 although some of the aircraft participated in the Berlin Airlift flying directly from Bassingbourn to Gatow. There was accordingly a general reduction in VIP flying and indeed activity at Bassingbourn.

On 23 March 1946 Airspeed Oxfords of No 1552 Radio Aids Training Flight moved in to provide special training and stayed until 26 October. Oxfords of 1555 RAT Flight replaced them on 31 October and remained only until 24 March 1947 for the training they offered could be given by other means.

In a general reduction and shake-up of Transport Command No 24 Squadron was re-deployed to Waterbeach on 8 June 1949 and replaced by Yorks of Nos 40, 51 and 59 Squadrons which became operationally effective at their new station on 25 June. Overall control of Bassingbourn now lay with 38 Group, the tactical portion of Transport Command. Nevertheless, the squadrons each contributed to the station's five monthly services within Transport Command's scheduled trunk network which included flights to Ceylon, Nairobi and sometimes special flights between Manston, Gütersloh and Celle. During 1950 further reduction came when No 40 Squadron ceased operations on 20 February and officially disbanded on 15 March. By May a typical month's work for 51 Squadron called for passenger-cum-freight runs to Nairobi, one passenger and two freight services to Singapore and one special flight routed as needed. Both 51 and 59 Squadrons disbanded at the end of October 1950, route flying by Yorks having ceased on 16 October.

For Bassingbourn there had already been a most unexpected change – the Yanks were back, and so soon! The Korean conflict caused a profound shock wave which buffeted Eastern England. It

1951 Bassingbourn resident, RB-50B 47-124 of the 38th SRS, 55th SRW.

resulted, on 25 August 1950, in the Americans returning to Bassingbourn where in April 1944 they had thrilled to the sight of a solitary huge camouflaged B-29 Superfortress – the first to visit Britain. Now, the 353rd Bomb Squadron, 301st Bomb Group, had brought along some fifteen B-29s. Dispersals were once more fully guarded by machine-guns and the Somerset Light Infantry.

A further influx into Britain of two more Bomb Groups produced the question of where to base them. The result was that small numbers of bombers were temporarily to be dispersed – useful protection against air attack, but causing logistics problems. Bassingbourn – almost empty and with its runway suitable for large bombers only when lightly laden – was been chosen to accommodate the 353rd BS of B-29s dispersed from Lakenheath.

Meanwhile, Bassingbourn's future under post war Air Force Plan G had been determined. It would be a base for three squadrons of what were then called Canberra B22 light marker aircraft and also hold a Medium Bomber OCU, all confirmed in December 1950 after Bomber Command repossessed the station on 1 November 1950. In February 1951 an amended plan called for two Mosquito B35 marker squadrons to arrive from Hemswell in December 1951 with the possibility of keeping one, re-arming one with Canberra B22s and still opening here the Medium Bomber OCU training Lincoln and Washington crews.

Then came a new plan calling for the run down of the four remaining Lincoln squadrons and the Lincoln training element along with 230 OCU Scampton all of which would close in December 1951. A new 230 OCU would then open at Topcliffe as the Light Bomber OCU to train aircrew for so-called Canberra PR31s and Meteor PR10s.

Meanwhile the 1950 stay of the US lodgers, the 301st BG, had been extended due to the serious international situation. To see to their overall needs the 7516th Air Support Squadron was established on 11 December 1950 and on 27 January 1951 came under USAFE control. February 1951 saw Stansted become Bassingbourn's Standby Airfield and in March 1951 work began on improving the runway and making Bassingbourn generally more suitable for two B-29/50 squadrons. The 7516th ASS was replaced on 16 May 1951 by the 3913th Air Support Squadron (SAC) which looked after American interests until the unit disbanded in April 1953.

When the first Group rotation came in January 1951 it resulted in the arrival of ten highly secret spooky-looking RB-50Bs of the 38th Squadron, 55th Strategic Reconnaissance Wing which stayed until May 1951. Unusually marked in Arctic trim, bristling with radomes and aerials and carrying long-range external tanks, loose talk concerning them overheard in local hostelries revealed that these strangers were undertaking spying flights around the northern and western peripheries of eastern Europe to produce 'radar maps'.

Other January 1951 arrivals were fifteen B-50Ds of the 341st Bomb Squadron, 97th Bomb Group (part of the 97th Bomb Wing), the outburst in activity attracting two of the earliest C-I24A Globemaster IIs to visit the UK. Exciting as they all were, the most alluring caller at this time came on 26 April 1951. It was B-17, 48997, bringing visitors from the US Embassy.

While here the 97th BG like its predecessors participated in 'raids' upon Helgoland and practised interception with RAF fighters. Between May and late August 1951 Bassingbourn hosted for 'TDY' B-50Ds of the 96th Bomb Squadron, 2nd Bomb Group, then on 1 September 1951, most of the 3913rd Air Base Squadron left for Standby Stansted. Remaining Americans departed by 1 April 1953.

The intention was now to upgrade Bassingbourn to Very Heavy Bomber standard by closing a minor road and extending the runway with construction to start at the end of August 1951 when the USAF had been scheduled to leave. Washingtons needed a 3,000 yard long high LCN runway which only Marham then possessed, but the cost of that improvement and the short planned service life of the RAF B-29s led to the scheme being abandoned. Instead, the station would leap one step ahead of nearly all bomber bases.

By early autumn 1951 the run up to Bassingbourn's most unique status was well underway. RAF Bomber Command was equipping with Canberras by having Meteor T7s of the Jet Conversion Flight visit squadrons scheduled to re-arm and give pilots basic training in flying jets. That was only a temporary measure. Late 1951 Bassingbourn received twelve Mosquito T3s, five PR34s, two Mosquito VIs, six Meteor T7s and four strategic reconnaissance PR10s of 237 OCU. On 1 December 1951 No 231 OCU re-formed, re-established itself, strength further increasing when on 13 February 1952 the RAF's light bomber training unit, No 204 Advanced Flying School, arrived from Swinderby bringing along more Mosquito 3s and 6s. From these two newcomers on 29 February 1952 was formed 'D' Squadron. No 231 OCU was now also responsible for producing PR Mosquito squadron crews.

Great was the thrill when on 14 January 1952 WD957 arrived, the first Canberra B2 jet bomber for No 231 OCU, the world's first jet bomber operational training unit. WD966 and WD981 arrived in mid-February and Canberra training courses commenced on 27 May 1952. By June there were fourteen Canberras at Bassingbourn. A year later the full strength of twenty-six Canberras was reached and in July 1953 Bassingbourn's first dual-control Canberra T4 arrived. Seven Canberra PR3s were received in November 1953 but it was June 1955 before the Meteor PR10 strategic reconnaissance aircraft were retired. To cope with the jets the station had been given a facelift including additional taxiways, a new control tower on the western side and most noticeably a large aircraft servicing platform built well out on the field. The latter was mainly used by the trainers, some bombers settling on the north-eastern dispersals.

Canberra PR3
WF927 of 231
OCU May 1969.
(Alan Wright)

Because of the intensity of Canberra bomber crew training, the PR element of 231 OCU was in April 1955 moved first to Merryfield then to Weston Zoyland soon after. It became 237 OCU on 23 October 1956 and transferred to Wyton in 1958 where on 21 February it disbanded. Crews and aircraft moved immediately to become the PR section of 231 OCU Bassingbourn.

In December 1958, 231 OCU was given a wartime operational role. Hardly surprising, for its existence put it in the forefront of the introduction of the latest bombing techniques among them LABS, the Low Approach Bombing System by which nuclear stores could be tossed on to a tactical target leaving the aircraft to turn fast and race away. Training for that task commenced at Bassingbourn in 1959, and in April 1960 low-level PR flying was introduced into the syllabus. Originally under 1 Group, 231 OCU was administered by 3 Group between 1 March 1965 and 1 November 1967 before reverting to 1 Group when No 3 Group disbanded. Also on the station between 1963 and 1969 was the Joint School of Photographic Interpretation.

A distinguished aeroplane joined 231 OCU on 19 December 1962. This was Canberra PR 3 WE139 which, flown by Flight Lieutenants R L E Burton and D H Cannon, had made the 12,270 mile flight from London to New Zealand in twenty-three hours during the Air Race. The aircraft was at Bassingbourn until April 1969 then it was taken to Henlow and now resides in the RAF Museum, Hendon.

The visitor to Bassingbourn in June 1967 might hardly have believed his eyes for six Canberras were painted in Russian markings for a part in the film 'Billion Dollar Brain'. It led to Israeli claims that the British were colluding with its enemies during the Six Day War.

For seventeen years Bassingbourn's Canberras were a very familiar sight in the county's skies, particularly as they turned in near Newmarket on their low, slow GCA approaches which led them from one side of Cambridgeshire to the other. By the late 1960s the need for Canberra crews was diminishing and a reduction in training came about. By February 1967 after fifteen years of Canberra flying, 231 OCU had trained over 2,200 pilots and navigators for the RAF, RN and other air forces, and flown some seventy-five million miles in the course of 163,000 hours of flying.

On 19 May 1969 Bassingbourn's Canberras taxied out in strength for the last time and in a final show of strength sixteen flew by in salute to Bassingbourn as they headed for their new base at Cottesmore leaving a T4, WE195, to be the last RAF aeroplane to take off from Bassingbourn during the RAF's tenancy.

Apart from one more spell of glory on 27/28 May 1978 when an air display was mounted, Bassingbourn's flying days were virtually over although occasionally a light aircraft or Army helicopter calls. The silence was once well broken when the Glen Miller sound was re-created. In a hangar wherein he had once performed, the Syd Lawrence big band spectacularly re-created the Miller sound, thanks to the East Anglian Aviation Society, on a warm June evening in 1974. The ghosts of the B-17s were very clear and as 'Moonlight Serenade' echoed around the great hall I enjoyed memories of that magic moment when I had climbed aboard 'General Ike' on the spot where the music was being re-created.

On 29 August 1969 the RAF ensign was lowered for the last time and the camp passed to the Army's Queen's Division. Recruit training began in January 1970, permanent staff coming from the Regiment's former depots in Kent, Warwickshire and Suffolk. In Command was Lt Col W C Deller who had previously commanded The Royal Anglian Regiment at Bury St Edmunds and who, throughout the time I knew him as a school chum, was as devoted to the Army as I was to the RAF! The first adult Recruit intake formed on 22 January 1970. On 15 July HQ The Queen's Division arrived from Colchester.

Bassingbourn was now providing fourteen-week basic training for soldiers joining a regular battalion of the Queen's Regiment, Royal Regiment of Fusiliers and the Royal Anglian Regiment. Junior bandsmen, Junior Drummers and Junior Infantrymen doing two-year and eighteen-month courses respectively were trained. Between 1970 and 1985 adult recruits of the Royal Army Veterinary Corps, and from 1985 The Royal Pioneer Corps, were also trained here. Bassingbourn remained home for the Depot of the Queen's Division (embracing The Princess of Wales's Royal Regiment, The Royal Regiment of Fusiliers and The Royal Anglian Regiment) as well as giving twenty-one-week recruit training phases.

On 1 January 1993 the Depot became one of five Army Training Regiments carrying out Phase 1 or Basic Training for the Royal Corps of Signals, the Queen's Division of Infantry and from April 1993 the Royal Logistics Corps. Much Army basic training continues.

For some time an unusual gateway faced you upon entering the Barracks. When Britain vacated Singapore the lychgate entrance to the cemetery at Changi Gaol was in 1971 brought back to Britain. Standing outside Regimental HQ it was erected here because so many East Anglians died in Japanese POW camps. To the left of the main entrance is 91st BG Propeller Memorial to the crews of the 197 aircraft missing in action.

Bassingbourn is in good, caring hands and is one of the few of the superbly built pre-war stations where the parade ground still echoes to marching feet. If you're used to the Air Force then at Bassingbourn the different ethos which drives the Army is at once apparent. You notice too that Bassingbourn's structural ambience is slowly fading for the cost of maintaining large buildings with little part to play is so high that the most western hangar has already passed into memory. Hangar No 1 has been given over to vehicles, No 2 is a gymnasium with its doors replaced by walls and No 3 is a kit store. The 90ft bricked water tower which the Luftwaffe only just missed and being now no longer needed has vanished and double glazing, while improving comfort, has taken away some of the feel of barrack block life. There is, of course, the still 'comforting' sound of the RSM!

Only a portion of the main runway remains and dispersal pans and the encircling perimeter track are intact. The post-war control tower looks dejected but not so its earlier counterpart for, since 1974, it has been lovingly cared for by the East Anglian Aviation Society (visits by special appointment only) and serves as a shrine to all airmen who have served on the station. Trees which tried to hide the hangars in wartime have become so large that at ground level they completely hide from view Bassingbourn's remaining hangars. Tall trees border the Old North Road, which passes the camp along the line of Ermine Street upon which Roman soldiers marched from London to York. Well hidden is the one-time landing ground, now an area amply supplied with sports and other entertainment paraphernalia including a dry training ski slope.

Main features (December 1944):
Runways: 254° 6,000ft x 150ft, 308° and 350°, concrete, asphalt topped. *Hangars:* four Type C. *Hardstandings:* fifty-four mixed loop and pan type. *Accommodation:* 443 officers, 2,529 enlisted men.

Places of interest nearby:
Wimpole Park and stately home are worth visiting. The post-war USAF had a hospital in the park. At nearby Croydon, on a hill top, a small bombing and firing range was used by RAF Bassingbourn between 1939 and 1942. Beyond Royston sprawls its attractive Heath with picnic areas. Ashwell, an attractive village around a gurgling spring and the source of the river Cam, has a fascinating local museum.

BECCLES (ELLOUGH), Suffolk

52°52N/01°36E 50-80ft asl; TM461879. 2 miles SE of Beccles on B1127 (crosses site)

'What's your shoe size? Hmm, then you'll need 10s. And here's your wet suit.' Everything was so huge, terribly uncomfortable, and I felt I'd trip at any moment. Strange looking orange-coated upright beetles who'd emptied their pockets passed through a mini-airport lounge, answered the Flight Number call and headed for 'the chopper'.

Safety and security were paramount. Heading out to sea on a fifty mile journey to the Shell North Sea Leman gas compression complex off Great Yarmouth gave ample time to contemplate the harsh environment and obvious dangers we were sampling – on a fine day, fortunately.

Our platform destination was visible from afar, but had bad weather cloaked its tall masts and cranes all would have been very different. Safety rules were paramount on the platform. Just one spark and ... So, not even the click of a camera while on the rig.

After G-AYOY's touchdown there was an uneasy moment when stepping down from the landing platform 120ft above the swirling sea on to a rather steep steel mesh ladder. It demanded a few fearsome steps without a handrail while wearing those giant shoes – for safety! Some of the party were uneasy when gazing at the sea below through the steel net footways designed to ensure water hurled high on stormy (usual) days quickly drained.

Meeting the community manning this outpost of the Empire was fascinating. My lunch companion recalled 'I was sitting here having a meal on a windy day when a rotor blade whizzed by the window. Gave me food for thought. I can tell you – it could have hit us.' It also gave me food for thought because one could be stranded. Joe West, our pilot, and Roger Smith the air host and well-known East Anglian enthusiast, were telling us it was time to return to Beccles.

Of the memories I have retained, one standing the test of time is of seeing the gas under staggering pressure as a muddy coloured liquid being pushed ashore from power supplied by industrial Avon jet engines. Another is of a rig worker cradling a sick sea bird – 'Out here you need sometimes to be on your own, and you have to be ever ready to help others in desperate need', he said to me. It was a lovely, clear autumn day, and as the S.61 settled safely back at Beccles I thought how close disaster must often be in what was a strange almost spooky world just over the horizon and soon to be largely overtaken by automation.

It was a memorable experience showing what a useful and almost unknown important part aeroplanes have come to play in our daily lives. Cooking Christmas Dinner in the gas oven would never be the same again, and all thanks to Beccles which in its heyday was just as commonly called Ellough. Strong emotions were certainly then a daily occurrence, and so were strange events.

While 'The Dam Busters', No 617 Squadron, are widely known., their sister squadron No 618 formed to sink the *Tirpitz* by employing *Highball*, a smaller edition of the Upkeep bombs used against the German dams never hit the headlines. Equipped with Mosquito IVs specially modified at Weybridge by Vickers and at Cambridge by Marshall of Cambridge, each aircraft accommodated two of the spinning mines. Emphasis was placed upon developing the weapons for the Dams raid and the intended simultaneous operation against the *Tirpitz* fell by the wayside. A lot of research and development went into *Highball*, the perfected weapon being held back because its use in daylight would have revealed its operating technique allowing the enemy to produce similar weapons. Targets available to him were particularly numerous in the Pacific Theatre.

No 618 Squadron formed and was reformed, and in August 1944 moved to Beccles where training was undertaken using sashlite bulbs against a target marked on the runway. It would have been impossible for a viewer to discover the technique of releasing *Highball*.

Beccles, built in 1943 for the USAAF, was used by battle damaged aircraft which limped in, the first being B-17 *Herky Jerky II* forced to put down when returning from Munster on 10 October 1943. The base surplus to US need was, in mid-summer 1944, taken over under the substitution plan by RAF Bomber Command. On 14 August No 16 Group, Coastal Command, took over the station and 618 Squadron brought along their Mosquitoes. The Royal Navy had a presence on many of the Command's stations and Beccles was no exception. On 13 September five Swordfishes of 819 Squadron FAA and five Albacores of 119 Squadron RAF arrived for operations that night although only three aircraft operated. Next day the Navy moved out to Swingfield and 119 Squadron soon after.

On 11 October 1944 seventeen Barracudas of 827 Squadron FAA arrived from Crail, Fife, for anti-shipping operations and left for Langham on 28 October, the day before 618 Squadron moved out. Their places were taken by air/sea rescue Warwick ASR1s of 280 Squadron which used both lifeboat-equipped and conventional aircraft. Most of their deep sea searches, which commenced on 1 November 1944, were in support of the US 8th AAF. A detachment of ASR Walruses of 278 Squadron also used the station between March and October 1945.

No 814 Squadron FAA placed a detachment here from Thorney Island and in April 1945 Barracudas of 810 Squadron operated anti-midget submarine patrols from Beccles. Success came to 'L/810 Sqn' on 13 April when a small submarine was sunk. Another was attacked the same day while a third escaped.

No 288 Anti-Aircraft Co-operation Squadron was here for a short time in May 1945. No 810 Squadron moved to Machrihanish on 3 June which left 280 Squadron as sole occupant. When HM King George VI and Queen Elizabeth visited the Channel Islands on 6 June 1945 No 280 Squadron gave ASR cover. Some Warwicks were detached to Tiree during August 1945 to offer rescue facilities for any USAAF crews ditching in the Atlantic when flying home. ASR patrols continued from Beccles into November 1945 although the squadron moved to Langham on 3 November.

A supplement had arrived on 3 September 1945 in the form of 279 Squadron which brought in from Thornaby their Warwicks and Sea Otters. Mosquito FB VIs of 248 and 254 Squadrons detached here the same month came to participate in the Battle of Britain flypast over London on 15 September and on that day operated from North Weald.

No 280 Squadron began the move to Langham on 31 October which left 278 and 279 Squadrons in residence along with No 15 Aircrew Holding Unit. The squadrons left in the middle of the month and 15 ACHU closed on 16 November. The station became non-operational on 30 November 1945 and SHQ closed during December.

In general appearance Beccles was a typical mid-war temporary three-runway bomber airfield with T2 hangars. Its proximity to the coast led in January 1947 to it being earmarked as a potential fighter station under the 1947 Plan F for which reason it survived for over a decade.

Exploration of gas under the North Sea led, in 1965, to British European Helicopters establishing themselves here. They were absorbed by British Airways Helicopters (BAH), which positioned one of its two Sikorsky S-61Ns at Beccles. The other aircraft became Aberdeen-based. Serving Shell, the Beccles-based S-61 operated a 'bus service' to rigs between 40 and 70 nautical miles off shore, the helicopter sometimes calling at as many as fifteen in one sortie. In 1971 BAH positioned a Bell 212 at Beccles after the company acquired a service contract from Philips, also exploring southern North Sea gas. Later that was supplemented with two Sikorsky S-58T helicopters. By then the main passenger terminal for rig flights was North Denes (Great Yarmouth), but its 1,000-foot cloud base minimum for operations was partly the reason Beccles remained in use for Shell's operations. After several financial changes Robert Maxwell of Mirror Group fame acquired the company, which, when he died, was found to be in dire straits. Its employee pension fund had been heavily reduced. Salvaging what they could, a group including staff and reputedly some Canadian helpers on 27 January 1993 established British International Helicopters. Together with Bond

Helicopters, and Bristow operations centred on North Denes Heliport, the new company began serving the extractors of natural gas from the North Sea platforms. Beccles Heliport – soon very busy – was established on the seaward side of wartime Beccles. A landing strip 800ft by 50ft bearing 310 degrees was marked out and five parking areas were designated. Servicing of the fleet of Sikorsky S-61N helicopters was undertaken in a T2 hangar. That remains on the edge of Ellough Industrial Estate, but the heliport has long gone due to much automation of remaining gas platforms. KLM Helicopters took over the southern North Sea support services using Norwich Airport.

Workers head for a Sikorsky S 76 and the gas fields of the southern North Sea.

Sikorsky S.61N G-BEJL about to settle at Beccles heliport.

Sikorsky S61N G-AYOM emerges from the Beccles heliport hangar. (Audrey Bowyer)

As for wartime Beccles, it came alive again after Rainier Forster transferred his aircraft here from Swanton Morley in 1997. Initially he made use of a Portakabin and a caravan, but now Beccles has a professional operations centre. Rainier Flying Club was established. Rain Air offers light aircraft for hire, private parking space is available and there are licensed engineering facilities. A ground school and simulator are run by QFIs, and PPL training is available. Microlights operate under ECO Flight, and Rise Helicopters provide lessons and private charter.

Main features (December 1944):
Runways: 099° 6,000ft x 150ft, 172°, 226°, concrete. *Hangars:* two T2. *Hardstandings:* fifty loop type. *Accommodation:* RAF: 115 officers, 524 SNCOs, 228 ORs; WAAF: 3 officers, 24 ORs.
Beccles Heliport had an 800ft x 50ft landing strip with white side lights and red end lights, aligned on 310°.

BENTWATERS, Suffolk

52°07N/01°26E 80ft asl; TM350530. By the A1152, 5 miles NE of Woodbridge

Bentwaters, which became one of East Anglia's finest military airfields, had played a vital role during the Cold War's final decade as being the main base for the USAF's anti-armoured vehicle force of A-10A Thunderbolt II aircraft. They were scheduled to halt, by any necessary means, any westward thrust by Warsaw Pact land forces pouring through a weak defensive point, then racing across the flat northern European plain to the Channel coast. When the Warsaw Pact's power collapsed, the A-10 role abruptly ended, and its massive strike capability was no longer essential.

Retention being costly, the question arose of how to make use of this custom-built, elaborate NATO-style airfield. With a 10,000-foot runway, adequate maintenance facilities, hardened shelters, ample weapon storage areas, good flying approaches, excellent and plentiful domestic quarters and supporting features, it was seriously considered for use by the RAF Jaguar force. Coltishall would then close. Hardened Aircraft Shelters, costly to use and maintain, were unnecessary for an RAF with an increasing overseas expeditionary role. True, there might sometime be instability in Europe caused by very large-scale population migration, and serious squabbling within the EU. Economic and financial problems, increasing lack of democracy leading to civil unrest could, as previously, result in unwelcome political developments. Yet for all such troubles sophisticated air bases hold little value. Dramatic advances in technology for warfare will surely and increasingly involve unmanned combat aircraft whose sophisticated operation will be from small hardened installations or well-protected temporary and less well-developed installations.

Extensive was the weapons storage area at Bentwaters.

Making use of Bentwaters in a peaceful situation raised classic problems facing such huge developed sites intended for military and non-civilian use. During the American tenure, it possessed fine and all-embracing on-base facilities including a shopping mall, large hospital with superb dentistry section, a theatre and excellent sports hall. RAF families would certainly have found such features excellent, but they would have been more likely to travel off-station and frequently. Then they would have encountered unpopular, tedious, poor links with towns, schools and shopping areas. Restrictive road links, and lack of population centres in the hinterland, also much limited the airfield's viability as a civilian passenger or freight airport. A small section could be, and occasionally is, used by light aircraft. As a major industrial site Bentwaters had an unsuitable surrounding infrastructure. Eventually, and steadily, it has largely reverted to agricultural use, coupling that with light industries and specialised businesses using military buildings, particularly for storage. From time to time public events are held, and there is limited flying. Caroline Grace bases her famous Spitfire here. Bentwaters is otherwise closed to the public for sound reasons, of which safety is one.

It has something few airfields possess, a magnificent woodland extension on its southern side in which dispersals were built not long before closure. That area must surely be retained as a wildlife reserve and become available for general enjoyment of its natural attractiveness although the usual question arises. Who pays the bill? Similar problems arise whenever sophisticated airfields in country settings seem no longer needed.

Construction began in late 1942 of a standard wartime temporary airfield designated for a USAAF bomber group. Originally it was known as Butley being named after a village to the south-east. On 23 January 1943 the name changed to Bentwaters for reasons of clarity, the new title commemorating a farmhouse sited on the main runway's position.

Incomplete Bentwaters opened on a Care & Maintenance basis on 17 April 1944 and was placed in Bomber Command being surplus to US needs. Building slowed and, when almost complete, construction was halted in May 1944. Its coastal situation attracted several emergency landings, the first caller on 20 July being a 96th Bomb Group B-17 which was severely damaged by obstructions placed on the unopened runway. Next came a P-51 of 359th Fighter Group and in October 1944 a B-17 of the 95th Bomb Group homed in.

Runways were made safe to use by 10 October and two weeks later three fuel-short P-51s landed. Well placed for escort fighters, the airfield was on 22 November 1944 declared open, taken over by No 11 Group ADGB, placed in the North Weald Sector and became the last new wartime RAF airfield in Britain to be introduced for operational purposes.

On 11 December 1944 Mustang IIIs of No 129 Squadron arrived and were soon joined by four others and a Spitfire squadron awaiting conversion. These were Nos 118 on the 15th and converting at the time, '165' on the 16th flying Spitfire IXs, '234' on the 17th, '64' on the 28th and

'126' on the 30th. All were soon covering Lancaster and Halifax day raids, their operations beginning on 23 December when four Mustang squadrons helped to escort 150 Lancasters attacking Trier. Many similar operations followed, and Nos 64 and 126 Squadrons gave cover for the famous Mosquito day raid, mounted from Fersfield, on the Gestapo HQ in the Shellhaus, Copenhagen. The final escort operation from Bentwaters was flown on 4 May 1945 to protect Beaufighters attacking U-Boats in the Great Belt off Denmark. Five were damaged.

During May 1945 Nos 129, 165 and 234 Squadrons moved out, the remainder leaving by September. No 65 Squadron flying Spitfire LF XVIs arrived on 15 May 1945 and with No 126 still using Mustang IIIs moved to Hethel early in September 1945 leaving the station to No 234 Squadron and No 2707 Squadron RAF Regiment.

No 124 Squadron's sixteen Meteor IIIs, the station's first jets, arrived from Boxted also in the Essex Sector on 5 October 1945. On 1 April 1946 the squadron was renumbered '56' and remained here until 16 September 1946 when they returned to Boxted . They had been joined at Bentwaters late July 1945 by 234 Squadron flying Spitfire HF IXs which left on 12 February 1946 upon posting to Molesworth and 12 Group for Meteor conversion. Meteor IIIs of 245 Squadron arrived in June 1946 and stayed only until mid-August 1946 when they left for Boxted, Wattisham's satellite, intention being that 56 and 245 would move to the parent station when it reopened.

Bentwaters had become North Weald's main satellite in February 1946. In a fast changing situation it had cared for Martlesham Heath since 15 October 1945 when that station was placed on 'C&M' and from 1 December it similarly parented Bradwell Bay and beginning 8 March 1946 administered RAF Orfordness. Ipswich and Raydon were also looked after, commitments which gradually faded.

Although Plan F called for two 'SRD' squadrons to stay here until October 1951 a change resulted in the replacement of the first line squadrons when on 10 October 1946 No 226 Operational Conversion Unit arrived from Molesworth. They trained pilots for day fighter and fighter-reconnaissance squadrons after initial fighter conversion at 61 OTU (until 1 July 1947 when that unit became 203 AFS). Air-ground firing was carried out using Denghie Flats.

Woodbridge and Bentwaters were separate until 15 March 1948 when Bomber Command abandonment of the former brought it under the care of Bentwaters.

On 26 August 1949 226 OCU began departing for Driffield where it became 203 AFS. Their handful of jets – mainly Meteor 7s – had been using Shepherds Grove. A new 226 OCU was raised on 1 September 1949 from 203 AFS at Stradishall.

Gloster Meteor F4 VW788 of No 226 OCU 18 February 1949.

Bentwaters was inactive from 1 September 1949 until 1 July 1950 when it was assigned for Care & Maintenance.

The US government had been seeking bases in East Anglia where they could position escort fighters in accord with *Plan Galloper*. In September 1950 they were offered Bentwaters. On 16 March 1951 the USAF's 7506th Air Support Group arrived to prepare for twenty-five F-86A Sabre fighters assigned here on 8 July 1951. Although the station had been transferred to the USAF on 16 April, operational administration passed from 12 to 11 Group, RAF Fighter Command for the agreement now was that interceptor and not escort fighters would be based here to help defend bomber bases.

On 5 September 1951, the first F-86A Sabres arrived, the first supersonic fighters in Europe and flown by the 81st Fighter Interceptor Wing. Their first two squadrons made Shepherd's Grove their home, it being the 91st Squadron which, on 26 September 1951, moved their twenty-five F-86As into Bentwaters where the 81st had set up HQ. The 7506th ASG disbanded, their job done, on 16 October 1951. Since 7 September Bentwaters had been part of USAFE and two days later came under 3rd AF control and was attached to the 49th Air Division when that formed. For company the Sabres had Boeing SB-29s of C Flight, 9 Air Rescue Squadron which stayed here until 14 November 1952.

Woodbridge became a domestic satellite of Bentwaters on 26 May 1952, more personnel being expected. That initially came about when the 7554th Tow Target Flight using TB-26 Invaders used Bentwaters between 22 March and 16 December 1952 when they departed for Sculthorpe.

The 91st FIS re-armed with blue-marked F-86Fs withdrew in autumn 1953. The runway was lengthened and gravel overshoots were added at either end. An MA-1A runway barrier was installed at the western end and special shelters to house nuclear weapons were erected on the south-eastern side of the airfield. Re-designation on 1 April 1954 produced the 81st Fighter Bomber Wing. Re-equipment with F-84F Thunderstreaks had already begun.

F-101A-30-MC 54-1461 of 92 Squadron 81st FBW at Bentwaters in 1963.

On 13 December 1954 came another new arrival, the 87th Fighter Interceptor Squadron flying twenty-five F-86D 'Dog Sabre' radar-equipped fighters armed with 'Mighty Mouse' rocket pod weapons. The squadron, part of the 406th FIW based at Manston, operated from here until 8 September 1955.

F-86Ds of the 406th FIW at readiness in 1956 by the side of the main runway at Bentwaters during Exercise Vigilant. FU-044 is a Flight Commander's aircraft. (Peter Hutting)

Bentwaters' strength increased again when on 30 April 1958 No 92 FBS came here from Manston, and took up residence on the east side of Bentwaters opposite the 91st Squadron dispersal area. Another title change transformed the unit into the 81st Tactical Fighter Wing on 8 July 1958 at which time the base became twinned with Woodbridge. Since January 1955 they had been fully equipped with F-84F Thunderstreaks, the first in the UK.

A taste of things to come came with the arrival on 8 August 1958 of seven F-101A Voodoos of the 27th FBW. They had been refuelled by KC-135 tankers (yes, they are that old!) and established a world record for the duration of their formation flight. On 4 December 1958 came delivery of the first five F-101A Voodoos for the 81st and forty-one F-84Fs were soon after transferred to the West German Air Force. The large, impressive Voodoo nuclear armed fighter-bombers with which the 91st and 92nd TFS rearmed between December 1958 and March 1959 had completed 100,000 flying hours by 8 August 1963. Voodoo pilots trained in LABS and Low Angled Drogue Delivery of weapons, and faced flying one-way sorties to increase penetration of Eastern Europe. By then a glimpse of another future had been given when on 14 June 1962 an 'F-110A Phantom II' (the USAF version of the US Navy F-4), paid a short call.

F-101C-MC 54-1461 of 92 Squadron 81st FBW at Bentwaters in 1963.

Alert 'barns' in Phantom times contained aircraft at 15 minutes readiness. Serviceable and fuelled, they often were operationally armed and in times of crisis with nuclear stores.

Aircrew were accommodated alongside the barns in this smart 'hotel'.

Modified Type T2 hangar, on the north side, used for major servicing. The control tower can be seen distantly.

Voodoos began leaving the 81st in July 1965 to make way for the F-4C Phantom II the first of which reached Bentwaters on 4 October 1965, conversion being completion 26 April 1966. The last five F-101s had quit Bentwaters on 3 January 1966. Between August and October 1973 the 91st and 92nd squadrons converted to F-4Ds.

F-4C-24-MC Phantom II 64-852 of the 81st TFW at Bentwaters in 1971. (P. Offen via George Pennick)

The final stage in the USAF's use of the base materialised on 24 August 1978 when three A-10A Thunderbolt II tank busters arrived for ground crew training. It was this time that the hardened aircraft shelters were being built. Main A-10 deliveries began in December 1978, seven A-10As having arrived by the end of the year, which permitted the 92nd TFS to commence rearming. Ultimately many were sometimes on the base, a powerful response to the plentiful tanks possessed by the Warsaw Pact. To cope with so many aircraft the 91st TFS transferred to Woodbridge making way for three more Tactical Fighter Squadrons to form, Nos 509 and 510 both activated on 1 October 1979 and No 511 on 1 January 1980. No 81st TFW thus increased to an unusual six squadrons. Once up and running the 81st detached some eight aircraft weekly (40 percent total strength) to each one of the four Forward Operating Locations in Germany, Det 1 at Sembach, 2 at Leipheim, 3 at Norvenich and 4 at Aalhorn. At Bentwaters by the early 1980s the A-10s occupied HASs on its south side, and like their predecessors the Thunderbolt IIs made good use of a large warm-up pan near Butley church.

Two A-10As on the 'last minute' and arming pan.

To accommodate so many aircraft the base was extended comprehensively to the south by taking in the wooded area into which a main taxiway led and dispersal pads were laid.

To improve the tactical flexibility of the A-10 force the 10th TRW – whose Alconbury based RF-4s had been overtaken by new technology – changed role and aircraft. The 509th TFS transferred to them on 15 April 1988 followed by the 511th on 1 July 1988.

They nudged out the F-5Es of the 527th Aggressor Squadron, which moved to Bentwaters on 14 July 1988. At the turn of the year the 527th began conversion to F-16Cs. A Detachment of those and F-5Es was maintained at Decimomannu, Sardinia. In late 1989 the F-16s began leaving Bentwaters, although the 527th was not inactivated until 30 September 1990.

F-16C 85-479 of the Bentwaters-based 527th Aggressors in August 1988.

Unloved by so many, grisly green A-10s wove their ways in small groups at low levels over much of Britain. This was an amazingly strong anti-tank machine intended to absorb great punishment and administer it from a staggering 6,000 rounds per minute Gatling revolver while dropping bombs. Not surprisingly the Warsaw Pact appears to have collapsed before putting the A-10s to the test! Instead it was Saddam Hussein's army that from late 1991 to the end of 1992 caused the 81st to keep at least eight A-10s at Incirlik to protect the Kurds in northern Iraq, the Woodbridge 78th doing a three month stint followed by the 92nd. On 4 January 1993 the 510th TFS was transferred to the 52nd TFW Spangdahlem AB, Germany.

Will we ever look back nostalgically to the unattrqactive A-10s? Claim was that they could still fly with half a tail and one engine!.

A breezy, sunny day it was, 23 March 1993. About 300 'Brits' just strolled or drove through the once so heavily guarded Bentwaters Main Gate, for the base held nuclear weapons. There was a short speech emphasising that although they loved us, didn't want to leave us, they simply had to go. The 92nd TFS was inactivated on 31 March, the A-10s mainly joining ANG units in the States. The 81st would stay on, but only until 21 May 1993. There were tears as the two last A-10s 655 and 962 started engines and as they taxied out firemen produced a water arch. Exactly at noon they rolled, officially the last USAF aircraft to depart Bentwaters. One pass and it was all over – or was it?

Bentwaters held some splendid open days, During one the US Navy Blue Angels performed mirror flying in Phantoms. What an experience!

How dangerous, that word 'last'. Come September 1994 and Bentwaters breathed a wondrous few gasps thanks to *Hazel Flute*. The RAF's Harrier Force discovered that lovely woodland park on the south side where they slung their nets and decided to hide a few Harriers by a building simulating an urban operating environment and hid their HQ. They also dug a hole in which they placed a giant bag to contain their fuel. They drank tea in a disused ammunition bunker, set up their own bomb dump and a plastic walled hospital, and used only one HAS for the cost of positioning shelter doors back on their rails – they had been lifted out to secure them – was colossal. So was reconnection and the water rate. Electricity they could provide themselves. And for two glorious weeks the birds sang at Bentwaters giving it a 'last' treat.

Acquisition of Bentwaters has brought various prospectors. Chris Parker envisaged an open air leisure complex, but the costs involved were high and removing the runway would cost millions of pounds. The Maharishi Foundation showed interest but gave up when they rated the cost of clearing all 'pollution' would be vastly expensive. Anglia International Air Park for business aircraft providing over 2,000 jobs was proposed. Since closure Bentwaters airfield, now privately owned and known as Bentwaters Parks, has been used for commercial filming. *Dog Borstal* was shot here, as well as Channel 4s *X-Fire* and the TV programme *Space Cadets*. Sequences for *Top Gear* have included stunts filmed on the main runway.

The control tower, originally to pattern 127791 and of 1941 design but much modified since, is now the office of the site owner. On 27 May 2007 Bentwaters 'Cold War Museum', run by the Bentwaters Aviation Society, opened in what had been hardened Building 134, the Wing Command Post. The War Operations Room and 'Battle Cabin' have been restored to active state, and contain exhibitions relating to Bentwaters and Woodbridge. The superb Museum, and indeed the whole airfield site, is only open to the public on Bank Holidays and selected dates. Hope is that public bus tours of the airfield and its infrastructure – much of which remains in very good state – may become available. Details are available on www.bentwaters-as.org.uk

The most noticeable changes involve the domestic site. Large, satisfying-looking buildings including the Officers' Club and shopping mall have fallen prey to developers. In their place have been produced a mixture of dwellings generated by Westbury. The replacement area is variously known as Rendlesham Heath and Woodscombe. Many new houses and flats have been added, producing quite a large new community embracing a few one-time military dwellings. Ample trees attractively supplement an area whose roads from former times remain unaltered.

Bentwaters was special. Maybe it was the idyllic Suffolk setting for much of its countryside is so lovely, provides fresh air so lacking in cities like Cambridge and, far worse, that awful Kensington, the place East Anglians have lately come to hate! Memories are as fragile as they are precious so, with me, spare a few moments to remember how many of us thrilled to the passing Sabres, Voodoos, the noisy F-4s, those glorious air shows and perhaps even wish we hadn't been so unkind to the A-10s. Come back, even you are forgiven!

Main features (December 1944):
Runways: 254° 6,000 ft x 150ft, 018°, 315°, concrete. *Hangars:* two T2. *Hardstandings:* fifty PSP. *Accommodation* (US standard): 421 officers, 2,473 enlisted men.

Post-war: concrete main runway extended to 10,900ft and warm-up pan added at the eastern end. HASs, 'Dutch Barns', ammunition bunkers, additional hangars were added. Major development also resulted in a very elaborate domestic site on the western side of the base. Included was a superb hospital, large shopping mall, theatre and a range of married quarters by tree-lined roads. Some houses are now privately owned.

Places of interest nearby:
Bentwaters is close to Bawdsey Manor of radar development fame, where the Bawdsey Radar Museum Group is aiming to change the Bawdsey Transmitter Block into an exhibition site. The tall towers went decades ago, but remnants of the 85 Squadron Bloodhound missile site on nearby cliffs can be found. Watch for announcements relating to the museum on www.bawdseygroup.co.uk. Also nearby is Orfordness where nuclear triggers and much else were developed. Special visits involving a boat ride are arranged to view what remains on the long bleak spit, a wildlife sanctuary. Orford has a splendid castle keep well worth visiting.

Not far away is Shingle Street, an unusual, spooky place that has figured often in stories of secret trials of anti-invasion weapons and claims of German invasion attempts that quickly spread – and widely – in September-October 1940 after burned bodies were washed ashore.

Very close is Snape Maltings with interesting shops, café and large concert hall particularly commemorating Benjamin Britten. Aldeburgh's First World War flying site has long gone. If you travel this way don't miss Friday Street Farm Shop, one of the best around, which also has a very pleasing café. Venture into Rendlesham Forest after dark and you might be lucky enough to see a UFO, and meet most unusual people like those rumoured to have come in December 1980 and left their marks (still just visible) in the forest. Better take care!

BIRCH, Essex

51°50N/00°47E 140ft asl, TL200925. 5 miles SW Colchester

Nothing is perfect – including sites for wartime airfields. Visit Birch now and you will find a series of large gravel pits marking a very unstable area, so much so that runways subsided not all that long after the base became available for the US 9th AF in 1944.

Although the site was chosen for development in 1942, and provisionally awarded to the US 8th AF in August, it was mid-1943 when the 846th Engineer Battalion, US Army, began constructing the airfield. Most need was for bases at which 9th AF fighter-bombers could lodge prior to moving south before D-Day. Birch therefore passed to the 9th in October 1943. With sufficient airfields by then available to the 9th, it returned the base to 8th AF control early in 1944.

The last airfield built in the UK by the US Army, Birch was a typical mid-war three-runway airfield, with fifty hardstandings, two T2 hangars and dispersed domestic sites. Its baptism of fire came, literally, on the night of 11/12 December 1943 when an intended concentrated raid on Chelmsford was so chaotic that a few bombs fell around Birch.

The base came briefly alive in April 1944 when for a week it temporarily housed the A-20 Havocs and men of the 410th BG.

Its value completely gone after D-Day, Birch was handed to RAF Bomber Command on 31 July 1944, administration being undertaken by RAF Stradishall. The station was declared inactive on 15 December 1944.

With the decision to mount further airborne assaults after June 1944, RAF airborne squadrons needed appropriately positioning in Eastern England. Among the airfields they occupied were some vacated by the US 9th AF. RAF Dakota squadrons of 46 Group were still in southern central England operating in casevac and urgent supply roles. When it was decided to use them in an extensive airborne assault in support of a crossing of the Rhine near Wesel, No 233 Squadron and No 437 (Canadian) Squadron – complete with fifty-six Horsa gliders – temporarily relocated to Birch, arriving on 21 March 1945. The Canadians were fielding nine Dakotas of 'A' Flight, eight of 'B' Flight and seven of 'C' Flight.

Soon after dawn on 23 March 1945 233 Squadron began despatching thirty-two Dakotas at the rate of one a minute, each towing a Horsa. No 437 Squadron's twenty-four Dakotas also each towed a Horsa as both squadrons participated in operation *Varsity*. Following glider release, all but eight 233 Squadron Dakotas returned to their home base, Blakehill Farm. The others were held at Brussels in case re-supply was required, but it was not needed.

The two-dozen Dakotas of No 437 (Canadian) Squadron conveyed 230 men of the 1st Ulster Rifles in Horsas to Landing Zone 'U', where all twenty-four gliders were released into thick haze. Aboard the Horsas – all of which landed safely – were, in addition to the troops, thirteen Jeeps and trailers, six Jeeps towing 6-pounder guns, two ammunition handcarts, two motorbikes and four bicycles

After releasing their gliders, all of the 437 Squadron contingent landed at B75 in case they were needed for a re-supply operation. Instead, they returned to Blakehill Farm on 26 March.

Birch saw no more such activity, and was disposed of in 1946. In addition to the gravel extractors, Birch Airfield Composting Services Ltd plies its trade here.

Main features:
Runways: 260° 6,000ft x 150ft, 200°, 310°, tarmac on concrete. *Hangars:* two T2.
Hardstandings: fifty. *Accommodation:* 421 officers, 2,473 enlisted men.

BIRCHAM NEWTON, Norfolk

52°52N/00°39E 230ft asl; TF790340. On B1153 S of Docking

All airfields begin as building sites. Bircham Newton is different for, after long meritorious service, it became one and launched itself into a new career helping others to create more building sites. Tall tower cranes – one of which you need to climb before you may embark upon a scaffolder's course – along with diggers galore and high scaffolding for plentiful practice, all are featured at what is now the National Construction College, Bircham Newton. Here it is not weapons into plough shares, more a case of bombs into bricks.

Bircham Newton is hallowed aeronautical ground, an action station with a long, varied and significant history for it was here that Lord Trenchard's idea for a strategic bomber element within an independent air force was translated into reality. Although Bomber Command was not born here, it is true that it all but originated at 'Bircham', a very busy station for almost its entire active life. To cope with that it had more large hangars than any other.

Built in 1916 the aerodrome first served as a training station where No 3 Fighter School was established. Fame, however, did not come until the closing weeks of the First World War when the station housed the First Mobilising Unit of No 27 Group formed in August 1918 under Lieutenant Colonel R H Mulock. Preparations to launch long-range bombing attacks on Germany including Berlin commenced here, and on 13 June 1918 No 166 Squadron had formed for the task. With only three Handley Page V/1500 four-engined biplane bombers it proved impossible to mount the campaign and the squadron disbanded on 31 May 1919. A second long-range bomber squadron, No 167 forming at the time of the Armistice, disbanded on 21 May 1919. The plan had not yet run its full course for on 15 June 1919 No 274 Squadron formed out of the other two and flew V/1500s trials until disbandment on 30 January 1920. The four-engined V/1500 was a large aeroplane with a fuselage the length of a Lancaster, 5-foot-diameter tyres and a wing span of 126 feet – greater than any RAF Second World War bomber. Carrying a crew of six and thirty 250lb bombs, it had the range to bomb Berlin.

It was not only heavy bomber squadrons which died at Bircham Newton in the war's aftermath. Among others was No 56 Squadron – McCudden's old squadron – which came in late December 1919 and disbanded on 22 January 1920. Another was No 60 which arrived on 30 December 1919 and disbanded on 22 January 1920. The station, though, had much better prospects including coastal siting.

In the 1922 policy review Bircham Newton was chosen to become a peacetime bomber station which resulted in a building programme leading to construction of an aerodrome similar in layout and appearance to Duxford. Three of its General Service or Double Belfast Truss hangars (which in 1934-6 were supplemented with three Type 'C' Aircraft Sheds) remained until after WWII. Still intact are several 1922 style stone dash and slate single-storey huts of which there were once many similar, an aged water tower and pump house. The 1920s style guardroom is now a shop.

'MONS', a Bircham Newton barrack block of 1922 style and still in use.

Also resulting from the 1922 scheme, No 7 Squadron reformed here on 1 June 1923 as a long-range heavy bomber squadron and equipped with Vickers Vimys. No 7 was enlarged on 5 July when a fourth, or 'D' Flight, was added. They were joined by No 99 Squadron similarly equipped which came from Netheravon and was based here from 31 May 1924. No 99 started re-arming with the large single-engined Avro Aldershot biplane the following August, and SHQ opened at the 'new' Bircham Newton on 12 September 1924.

Vickers Vimy of No 7 Squadron.

No 99 was the only squadron to try the Aldershot whose engine proved so troublesome that at the end of 1925 the squadron starting re-equipping with HP Hyderabads. At the time they were also replacing Vimys in 7 Squadron. Commanded by Charles Portal later Marshal of the Royal Air Force Lord Portal, No 7 left for Worthy Down on 7 April 1927.

Bircham Newton was unusual in that supplementing the heavies since 16 September 1923 had been No 11 Squadron flying DH 9A light day bombers here until May 1924 by which time the squadron had re-armed with Fairey Fawns. Another DH 9A squadron, No 39 which came in January 1928, left for India at the end of that year. Some of No 39s DH 9As were left behind for No 101 Squadron's use when they reformed at Bircham Newton on 21 March 1928. Early 1929 saw this new squadron start to receive Boulton & Paul Sidestrand twin-engined medium bombers the handful of which were built at nearby Norwich. No 101 left in October 1929.

DH 9As of 39 Squadron, Bircham Newton, possibly protecting the King at Sandringham.

First successor to the previously mentioned DH 9A squadrons was No 35 which on 1 March 1929 reformed at Bircham Newton flying DH 9As. They were replaced with Fairey IIIFs then No 35 rearmed with Fairey Gordons in the autumn of 1932. No 207 Squadron commanded by the later Marshal of the Royal Air Force Lord Tedder reformed here on 1 February 1920 with DH 9As, left for Turkey in autumn 1922 and returned on 7 November 1929 also using Fairey IIIFs before re-equipping with Gordons in September 1932.

Formations of Fairey Gordons were a common sight over East Anglia during 1930s exercises and at flying displays. They participated in the RAF Jubilee Review at Mildenhall then on 3 October 1935 No 35 Squadron hurriedly moved to the Middle East, followed by No 207 on the 28th, to reinforce the RAF during the Abyssinian crisis.

At that time RAF Bomber Command was coming alive. On 1 October 1933 the Wessex Bombing Area had split into the Central Area (of which Bircham Newton, 35 and 207 Squadrons were a part) and the Western Area. The Areas amalgamated on 1 May 1936 to form No 3 (Bomber) Group.

After the Gordons left two new squadrons – Nos 21 and 34 equipped with Hawker Hinds - formed to replace them at Bircham on 3 December 1935. They left for Abbotsinch in July 1936 to form the nucleus of 2 Group. No 18 Squadron which had arrived on detachment to Bircham

Boulton Paul Sidestrand of 101 Squadron at Bircham Newton.

Newton in January 1936 flying Hawker Hinds, had parted with its 'C' Flight on 10 February to form the nucleus of 49 Squadron which left the station for Worthy Down during August 1936 followed by its parent on 7 September 1936.

By then Bircham Newton had undergone dramatic change, results of the 1930s RAF expansion being evident everywhere. Policy decreed that this would be a two-squadron Coastal Command station for which three brick-built 'C' Type Aircraft Sheds were being erected to supplement the Belfast Truss wooden sheds. Bircham Newton soon partly resembled a new 1935 style station but retained much of the 1920s domestic accommodation with red-brick barrack blocks bearing names from the 1914-18 war being situated on the technical site alongside the road through the camp. These remain in use for students while alongside can be seen the former airmen's mess and Station Sick Quarters.

Transfer to Coastal Command, the new owner, came on 10 August 1936. Placed in 16 Group it received No 206 Squadron and its Avro Ansons from Manston at the end of July, and on 17 August '220' reformed here attracting more Ansons. On 7 December 1936 'C' Flight, 220 Squadron, was hived off to produce another squadron, No 269 Squadron, which moved out to Abbotsinch at the end of the year.

When the Ansons came the new hangars were incomplete, a commonplace situation, No 220 Squadron not moving into the new No 1 Hangar until 27 July 1937. They left for their war station on 23 August 1939 having been supplemented between June and August of that year by Ansons of 233 Squadron.

By then another activity had been some time underway, one which was to increase in prominence. Anti-aircraft firing ranges near Stiffkey and Weybourne were brought into use on the north Norfolk coast in the summer of 1937 for which reason six Westland Wallace target-towers of 'B' Flight, No 1 Anti-Aircraft Co-operation Unit arrived, towed banner targets for the gunners and were nightly housed in an old hangar. The yellow and black striped Wallaces returned to their base at Biggin Hill in the autumn and the following May those of 'C' Flight came to tow for the summer AA camps and gunners aboard East Anglia's bombers. They stayed until mid-September then, when the Flight returned in 1938, they brought along six impressive Hawker Henley target tugs which this time wintered here. 'D' Flight, similarly equipped, joined them on 28 April 1939 for the seaside summer show.

Commencement of hostilities saw 206 Squadron using Ansons for inshore convoy protection supplemented by No 42 Squadron which brought to its war station on 18 August very aged Vickers Vildebeest torpedo bombers. Fighter Command had recently been allocated a two-Flight lodger right on the station allowing No 1 AACU to remain.

Before the war began Ansons were flying anti-submarine armed patrols and escorting convoys sailing between north Kent and Lincolnshire. Around lunch time on 3 September a 'German submarine' was spotted, but it proved a false sighting. Not so a Do 18 flying-boat which faced an Anson crew on 8 November 1939. That day the first U-boat kill of the war was made by Pilot

Officer Harper and crew of 206 Squadron in Anson K6184. For a brief period Wittering moved Flights of fighters daily to Bircham Newton for the defence of Norfolk, among them Boulton Paul Defiants of No 264 Squadron.

Reconnaissance sorties were also flown by Ansons off the Elbe and Netherlands before, in March 1940, 206 Squadron began to re-arm with Hudsons. Gradually introduced to operations in May 1940, the squadron made a bombing attack that month, on Rotterdam. In June they maintained Battle Flights over the English Channel using all available aircraft to help cover the Dunkirk evacuation. Reconnaissance sorties and attacks by day and night were carried out on Dutch targets and shipping before '206' left for Aldergrove in August 1941.

Hudson T9303 of 206 Squadron departing 'Bircham.'

Much had happened off the East Coast in the first months of war. Concern not only for coastal shipping but also for the safety of the herring fishing fleets operating out of Great Yarmouth and Lowestoft resulted in formation of the Trade Protection Blenheim Flight which became 'D' Flight 233 Squadron in January 1940. On 28 January 1940 they were supplemented by 254 Squadron which arrived to assist. The newcomers absorbed 'D' Flight which became 'B' Flight 254 Squadron also flying Blenheim IV(f) fighters. Heinkel 111s were attacking ships, 254 Squadron inconclusively engaging one on 22 February. Detachments at Lympne also flew convoy escorts, but when Norway was attacked 254 Squadron was on 24 April sent to Hatston and Lossiemouth for a busy operational period. No 235 Squadron replaced '254' at Bircham Newton next day, 42 Squadron and its antiques moving out in mid-April 1940.

Blenheim IV(f)s of 235 Squadron roosting at Bircham Newton's north end with a Bellman hangar poking in.

May 1940s blitzkrieg on the West pulled 235 Squadron immediately into action escorting Coastal Command aircraft over the North Sea and making sweeps off the Netherlands. They also took part in many engagements over the English Channel operating out of advanced bases at Detling and Thorney Island to escort convoys. Other sorties took them to Danish waters. Thus, 235 Squadron found itself exceedingly busy. Add to that plentiful sorties by 206 Squadron's Hudsons and Bircham Newton's occupants were clearly very busy by day and night. To help protect north Norfolk a detachment of Hurricanes from No 229 Squadron was here between June and September 1940.

On 21 November 1940 No 221 Squadron formed equipped with twenty-four maritime Wellington Ic/VIIIs – unusual looking with their Yagi ASV radar aerials – which commenced East Coast patrols on 23 February 1941 before moving out on 2 May 1941 to join their detachment at Limavady. These were not the first Wellingtons based here for No 2 GRU formed on 4 March 1940 with five anti-magnetic mine Mk Is fitted with wide diameter de-gausing rings. They soon left for Manston and low flying 'mine busting' in the Thames Estuary prior to going overseas in June.

Fighter reconnaissance and strike operations by Blenheims and Hudsons were carried out throughout 1941 with a number of squadrons sharing the task. A Blenheim detachment arrived from 59 Squadron on 1 March and stayed until 2 June just after No 200 Squadron reformed on 25 May from part of 206 Squadron and, with long-range Hudson Vs, was preparing to leave in mid-June for West Africa. No 500 Squadron brought along its Blenheims on 30 May for a stay lasting until 2 April 1942. That allowed 235 Squadron to leave for Dyce and Sumburgh on 3 June after having made much use of Docking. On 30 May 1941 long-stay No 206 Squadron left with its Hudsons and moved to St Eval. No 53 Squadron's Hudson Vs replaced them and remained until 19 October 1941 following which came a detachment of 59 Squadron's Hudsons here until 18 December 1941. As well as operating off East Anglia No 500 Squadron kept a detachment at Carew Cheriton to patrol off the French north-west coast and mount shipping strikes. After re-equipping with Hudsons, they flew *Rovers* and made shipping strikes often by night and frequently off the Dutch coast, the main 16 Group area for such action. No 500 was here until 2 April 1942. Hudson and Blenheim squadrons at this time were established at sixteen aircraft with four in reserve.

Throughout 1941 changes had come about in plenty. On 15 June Blenheim IV(f)s of No 248 Squadron arrived and stayed until September 1941 protecting shipping and flying sweeps. Yet another Blenheim squadron, No 608, arrived on 30 June 1941 and in August 1941 switched to Hudsons operated from Bircham Newton until December 1941.

At the start of 1942 the station was mainly operating Hudsons their numbers further increasing when No 407 (Canadian) Squadron arrived on 31 March 1942 followed on 24 April by the Dutch 320 Squadron. Both squadrons participated in the Bremen '1,000 bomber' raid of 25/26 June 1942. No 407 Squadron left on 2 February 1943 and '320' on 15 March 1943. For Bircham Newton 9 March provided a benchmark when the last Hudson strike was despatched.

Throughout the war the station was the main base for units towing targets for Norfolk's anti-aircraft gunnery camps, No 5 HAAPC at Weybourne using 3.7in guns and No 11 LAAPC Stiffkey (usually pronounced 'Stooky') equipped with 40mm Bofors. 'K' Flight, 1 AACU, had arrived with six Henleys on 5 September 1940 and on 27th was joined by 'M' Flight similarly equipped. Both stayed in the area until late 1941 when they settled at Langham. Bircham Newton's complement was soon renewed when Henleys of 1611 and 1612 Flights (formed from 'K' and 'M' Flights) returned in November 1942 and on 1 December 1943 amalgamated as part of 695 Squadron. The latter operated with the Weybourne Range gunners till the war ended, by which time Martinets and Vengeances were also in use.

Bircham Newton was the base for another very important activity, weather reconnaissance. No 403 Meteorological Reconnaissance Flight formed here in November 1940 with three Blenheim IVs and in 1941 received some Hudsons and became 1403 Flight on 1 March 1941. They were joined on 29 October 1941 by 1401 Meteorological Flight which had risen from the pre-war 'Met Flight' at Mildenhall. They generally held five Gloster Gladiators for temperature and humidity flights carried out daily to the end of the war, their biplanes undergoing major overhauls at Marshall of Cambridge works. Hudson IIIs replaced the 'met' Blenheims and Spitfire Vs the Mk IIs and Hurricanes. A lot of the Gladiator high climbs were undertaken from Docking.

The two Meteorological Flights disbanded on 31 July 1942 emerging next day within 521 Squadron holding five Gladiators, four Spitfire Vs, four Spitfire IVs, three Hudsons, and two Blenheim IVs. For dangerous missions they had a pair of Mosquito IVs operated until 521

Squadron disbanded on 13 March 1943 when No 1409 Flight took over the Mosquito role. The Meteorological Flights were reformed and re-established as previously.

Conducting assorted tasks was possible by using Docking and Langham to reduce the pressure. It needed to for on 16 November 1941 a further commitment came when No 279 Air-Sea Rescue Squadron formed and Hudsons were back, their first sortie taking place on 22 January 1942. They undertook ASR search well out to sea and sometimes under fighter watch off the Dutch coast where the number of aircraft ditching was increasingly commensurate with additional operational activity. Improved crew skill in locating airmen at sea led to frequent and sudden detachments. So, whilst targets were being towed, the weather recorded, ASR Hudsons were out searching and on 2 November 1942 they were joined by ASR Ansons on No 280 Squadron. Few stations equalled such diversity.

Coastal Command operated in a totally different manner from other Commands, its aircraft often being detached to distant places sometimes aiding other Groups. Often the point of departure differed from that of return, sorties frequently starting out far from the parent base. No detailed, definitive story of the Command has ever been published mainly because of the complexity of its activities which could only be done justice by being spread through many volumes. The following surely illustrates that.

A typical, eventful operation involving a Bircham Newton crew took place on 29 May 1943. Flying Officer Sherwood and crew, detached to Davidstow Moor, left there at dawn in Bircham Hudson 'K' of 279 Squadron to help in the rescue of twenty-eight survivors from an action 100 miles WSW of Land's End.

On 28 May 1943 a Whitley of 10 OTU had crashed in the sea. Its crew had boarded their dinghy and were spotted by 461 Squadron whose Sunderland crashed as it alighted to rescue them.

Next day another Sunderland of 461 Squadron found two dinghies at the scene, landed and picked up their occupants. Engine trouble prevented the second Sunderland from taking off. K/279 arriving overhead directed a destroyer to take aboard crews of the Sunderlands and the Whitley and also to take in tow the damaged Sunderland. With a skeleton crew, the other Sunderland later took-off. The Hudson returned home after a very successful operation.

This was a busy time for 279 Squadron. On 25/26 July 1943 nine Hudsons set out to find a dinghy reported by the USAAF and others from a ditched Lancaster later reported safe. A half-submerged dinghy was ultimately located and a high-speed launch went to the spot. Reports of additional dinghies turned out to relate to Danish fishing vessels. After continued fruitless searching things began to hot up. Wing Commander Corry DFC, in W/279, was directed towards a dinghy reported sixty-five miles north of Ameland but about thirty-five miles north-east of Cromer he and Flight Lieutenant Penderson instead found a B-17 in the sea. At 1445 hrs W/279 dropped an airborne lifeboat just as the B-17 crew were climbing in their dinghies. Penderson continued searching for the other reported dinghy and dropped his lifeboat to the B-17 crew just before their bomber sank.

Some sixty miles NNE of Cromer two other Hudson crews came upon two dinghies tied together and the eight American airmen aboard began firing Verey cartridges. V/279 dropped Lindholme gear to them and at 1845 hrs two ASR Walrus amphibians arrived to pick up survivors all of whom were brought home safely.

New reports spoke of a ditched RAF bomber around which a Halifax was circling. Hudson U/279 working with an MTB at 1835 hrs was led by the Halifax to five dinghies tied together and carrying US airmen to whom the Hudson dropped its lifeboat. Other aircraft homed in and joy was unbounded when all the Americans climbed aboard, set sail and also started rowing. Three very successful operations had been completed in one day.

In 1943 a BRC steel netting track runway was at last laid but at no time was permanent lighting installed alongside, and only two metal mesh hardstandings were put down. Night flying was always undertaken at Docking, the satellite intensively used by Bircham's squadrons from 1940.

The metal runway was needed for air/sea rescue activity which received a big boost when on 28 June 1943 the first Vickers-Armstrong Warwicks touched down. That type's long gestation period rendered it of little value as a bomber when available, its long range instead being put to use in the air/sea rescue role. June 1943 saw the aircraft introduced into the Warwick Training Unit using both Bircham Newton and especially Docking. Although 279 Squadron tried them it was not equipped until much later.

On 13 October 1943 the Warwick Training Unit became the ASR Training Unit before vacating Bircham Newton on 21 November 1943 leaving 279 Squadron busily operating Hudsons which, since the spring of 1943, had been lifeboat carriers. No 280 ASR Squadron had departed for Thorney Island on 23 September 1943.

Anti-shipping operations were resumed after the arrival on 15 November 1943, both here and at Docking, of 415 (Canadian) Squadron. For night anti-shipping operations off the Dutch coast from Docking they used Wellington GR XIIIs and Fairey Albacore biplanes. Such obsolescent equipment brought friction with the Canadian government although the combination performed very effectively against the small enemy patrol boats potentially very threatening at the time of D-Day.

Much of 1944 found Bircham Newton housing No 279 Squadron ever-active by day and No 415 busy by night from the satellite, and both using Bircham Newton as a maintenance base. No 2 Armament Practice Camp sojourned briefly before moving to Docking on 29 August 1944, the month witnessing the opening of a Coastal Command Preparation Pool at Bircham Newton. Having begun as No 3504 Servicing Unit, its role was the installation of modifications in 16 Group aircraft. Until August 1945 Mosquitoes, Beaufighters, Wellingtons and Albacores for the Command's squadrons were attended to. Mosquito VIs were, for instance, fitted with rocket rails, etc.

Between 6 September and 17 October 1944 Grumman Avengers of No 855 Squadron, FAA, based here carried out night shipping raids from Docking. Nos 819 (FAA) and 119 Squadrons forming 157 Wing flying Swordfishes and Albacores came late September principally to train for anti-submarine night operations to be flown from Belgium. No 119 Squadron left in October and the remainder followed.

No 279 Squadron also moved, one Flight proceeding to Thornaby on 14 October followed by the remainder of the squadron early November. There they at last converted to Warwicks.

Bircham was now quieter. On 27 February 1945 No 819 Squadron returned and paid off on 7 March 1945, then three days later a training Flight for 119 Squadron formed with Swordfishes. No 598 Anti-Aircraft Co-operation Squadron flying Oxfords and Martinets arrived from Peterhead on 12 March 1945, left for Ipswich late April then disbanded.

Cessation of hostilities in Europe soon brought the demise of 119 Squadron's training Flight, and the parent squadron which returned on 22 May disbanded three days later. Between 8 June and 2 September 1945 No 18 Aircrew Holding Unit looked after RCAF personnel awaiting their return home. No 695 Squadron here since 1 December 1943 moved on 11 August 1945 to its permanent post-war station, Horsham St Faith. In their place on 14 August came 1693 Flight from Copenhagen for a brief stay. Between 4 July and 24 September the Coastal Command EBT School was also at Bircham Newton.

Bircham Newton's days of action were over, lack of metalled runways and limited expansion possibilities reducing the station's value. Fighter Command controlled the station between autumn 1945 until October 1946 when 4 Group Transport Command took over. No 15 Air Beam Training Flight's Ansons moved in and stayed until September 1948 along with the Transport Initial Conversion Unit which was here until disbandment in February 1948. In October 1948 the station passed from 38 Group to Technical Training Command whose Officers' Advanced Training School at once arrived from Hornchurch and stayed until disbandment in 1962. Other non-flying units also used Bircham Newton, among them the Junior Command and Staff School which moved to Ternhill and the Administrative Apprentices' Training School which left for Hereford shortly before the station closed on 18 December 1962. A US medical storage facility subsequently supporting Sculthorpe functioned here from 18 June 1963 into 1964.

Although Bircham Newton's demise had come the landing ground had one special service to perform for the RAF. To assess the value of a VTOL combat aircraft the Kestrel Evaluation Squadron formed at West Raynham on 15 October 1964. Rough field trials were in 1965 undertaken here and at North Pickenham by the Harrier's predecessor before the unit closed down on 28 July 1965.

Its soil type being ideal for training purposes, the 225 acre site and buildings were purchased in 1965 for conversion into the Construction Industry Training Centre which opened on 25 April 1967 and has since functioned here under different names.

The three 'C' Type hangars remain along with the mid-1930s 'Fort type' watch office and tower, the Bellman hangars and various buildings from the 1920s through to the 1990s which make Bircham Newton architecturally a most interesting ex-airfield much of which can be seen from the road bisecting it. Remember, though, that the site is a private one. Should you pass by at night watch out for the ghost fervently believed by many to haunt the tennis courts.

Main features:
Runway: Main NW/SE grass run maintained at 2,700ft with possible extension to 6,000ft and supplemented by runs of as much as 5,200ft in other directions. *Hangars* (December 1944): three Belfast Truss, three 'C' Type, three Bellman, ten Blister.

Aerial view of Bircham Newton looking north in CITC times.

Accommodation: RAF: 263 officers, 218 SNCOs, 1,950 ORs; WAAF: 10 officers, 32 SNCOs, 512 ORs.

Places of interest nearby:
RFC Sedgeford opened late 1915 on a site about a mile east of Sedgeford village and on the south side of the main road to Fakenham. One can just make out roads, the site of the main gate and remnants of tarmac bases for hangars which once accommodated The School of Air Fighting. On 1 August 1916, No 64 Squadron formed as its training squadron. Equipped with FE2Bs and Farmans it re-armed with DH5s in June 1917, and departed in October for St Omer and an operational career. No 87 Squadron formed on 14 September 1917 used Avro 504Ks and Pups before leaving for France on 19 December and then SE5As. Also formed here, on 1 November 1917, was No 72 Squadron which on 25 December left for Mesopotamia. No 122 was the replacement, formed on 1 January 1918 as a light bomber squadron which disbanded on 17 August 1918. No 13 Squadron brought its RE8s here on 27 March 1919 and disbanded 31 December 1919. Nearby are Sandringham House and Gardens where a bomb crater remains. Sandringham exudes a strong image of recent Royal history set within rhododendrons at their best in May-June. There is ample parking, picnic space, a restaurant and other usual tourist facilities. In wartime Heacham Beach was the practice camp for Home Guard batteries equipped with 'Z' projectors. Worth visiting are towns and villages by the Wash which have long brought delight to East Anglians of all ages. In his youth Sir Arthur Marshall used to land on Snettisham's sands then park the Gipsy Moth by a beach house for a day by the sea. Things have indeed changed!

BODNEY, Norfolk

52°33N/00°42E 130ft asl; TL850990. On B1108 SE of Hilborough, Norfolk, 4½ miles from Watton

Set to the north of the Watton road, Bodney was never developed like many satellite landing grounds, never much more than a large, almost square grass field edged with a perimeter track from which short spurs led to circular dispersal pads set among trees. Domestic accommodation originally tented later comprised four main sets of assorted temporary buildings grouped to the north-east and south-east of the landing ground and in which up to 1,700 were eventually domiciled. For such a primitive airfield it has a surprisingly action-packed history.

Bodney came to life very early in 1940 as Watton's satellite, activity at both stations being mirrored. Blenheim IVs of 82 Squadron began dispersing here in March 1940, and soon afterwards more arrived in the hands of 21 Squadron likewise Watton-based. Both squadrons used the satellite for operations during the invasion of France and Belgium. In June 1940, 21 Squadron left for Lossiemouth to help oppose any invasion venture from Norway and, operating at extreme range, raided targets there.

Throughout 1941, 82 Squadron (average strength twenty Blenheim IVs) used Bodney for operational purposes, this famous much-battered squadron encountering all the grim tragedies that 2 Group knew so well. Bodney was subjected to intruder forays too usually attracted by its gooseneck flare path lit to guide returning Blenheims. On 11/12 February 1941, when Bodney's Blenheims had been operating against Hanover, Oblt Semrau flying a Ju 88C of I/NJG2 followed home one flown by Squadron Leader Sabine and which, becoming unable to land and short of fuel, was fired upon and forced to crash. He then turned his attention to Sgt Chattaway's Z5877 which he shot down during its final approach to Bodney.

On 12 May 1941, 90 Squadron was ordered to move to Bodney its two Boeing Fortress 1s, the first in squadron hands in Europe. The small airfield's undulating surface was, not surprisingly, unsuitable for the heavy aircraft and after two days of intensive local flying they moved to Great Massingham on 15 May.

As soon as they had left another type unusual on East Anglian airfields arrived. Half of 61 Squadron's Hampden strength was attached to Watton on 13 April 1941 for cloud cover daylight raids under 2 Group control. The first daylight excursion, on the 18th, involved six aircraft which used Bodney as their starting point. Sergeant Metcalf and crew were aboard one of the Hampdens despatched to attack Cherbourg docks where fierce AA fire greeted them. Metcalf was hit in the arm and leg and near Swindon the crew were forced to abandon badly damaged AD825, the only Hampden bomber ever lost in action from a sortie despatched from East Anglia. On 30 April the ten 61 Squadron aircraft returned to 5 Group.

Blenheim IVs still predominated at Bodney, for No 105 Squadron brought twenty here on 21 May 1941. Briefly did they stay for in July No 105 was detached to Malta to participate in the cruel, tortuous Mediterranean anti-shipping crusade carried out by 2 Group with customary bravery.

Throughout 1941, 82 Squadron operated from Bodney. January's night raids within Main Force ended in mid-March when the squadron began exceedingly hazardous low-level operations against shipping off the Low Countries and the German coast. From 17 April to 3 May No 82 was detached to Lossiemouth for similar operations off Norway. Shipping strikes and attacks on ports continued until November 1941 with some crews being sent to Malta in June to help the campaign being waged over the Mediterranean. A few *Circus* operations were flown in the autumn before night operations were resumed in November 1941. Now the squadron found itself thrown into a night intruder campaign against enemy airfields. Bodney and the Blenheim seemed inseparable – until Japan entered the war. There being no modern true substitute for the Blenheim, No 82 Squadron, was taken off operations after they had flown their last two sorties, directed at Schiphol, on 16 February 1942. The squadron bade farewell to its trusty steeds and on 20 March set off for the Far East war.

With its Blenheims soon gone Watton and its satellite Bodney followed a most unlikely course. They became occupied by 21 Group Flying Training Command and were used as 'temporary' bases for a new organisation, No 17 (Pilots) Advanced Flying Unit formed on 29 January 1942 and soon using a host of Master IIs. Many flew from Bodney during the next eighteen months although it was also used for heavier items.

No 21 Squadron back from Malta had, on 4 March 1942, reorganised itself and acquired 'for temporary use' Blenheims which '82' had left behind at Bodney . Then on 25 April 1942 a group of personnel trained to service a new type joined the squadron. They had been learning to maintain the Lockheed Ventura two examples of which – and now the first in squadron hands – arrived on 31 May. The squadron was far from impressed with the bulky, sluggish 'pig' exhibiting many small, irritating snags. Then, to the astonishment of all, another new type for the RAF appeared on July 16, for it was at Bodney where the Mitchell also joined Bomber Command. Apparently the idea was for these new types to be explored for 2 Group use away from operational activity, with Nos 18 and 114 Squadrons billed to re-arm with Mitchells at West Raynham to where the three examples emigrated in early August. Fearing heavy losses if Venturas were committed to day raids, 2 Group insisted that they replace Blenheims in the night intruder role. By mid-August nine Venturas had reached Bodney and twenty-one when the squadron vacated the station on 30 September before operations commenced. Bodney was now left free for Watton's Master multitude numbering not much short of 200. Having No 17(P)AFU situated in a busy operational region was a strange idea and the unit left Watton (and Bodney) for Calveley at the start of May 1943.

Then came a transformation. Much additional temporary living accommodation was erected, and a new control tower was soon in place. The five blister hangars were supplemented by T2s and dispersal areas mostly among fir trees, were much improved. Runways remained grass but PSP matting was laid late 1943 at some hardstandings.

Bodney showing position of replacement control tower.

The reason for all the activity was apparent when in late June US personnel moved in and were joined, from 7 July 1943, by those of the three squadrons (Nos 328, 486 and 487) of the 352nd Fighter Group. During August 1943 they received seventy-five P-47Ds which, crowding out the small field, flew their first mission – withdrawal cover – on 9 September and then participated in the usual round of 8th AF escorts and patrols. During October 1943 they became part of the 67th Fighter Wing and on 25 November were part of the cover for the first 8th AF P-47 fighter-bomber raid, against St Omer/Fort Rouge airfield. In April 1944 the 352nd FG re-armed with P-51B and C Mustangs each squadron maintaining a strength of twenty-five aircraft. Very soon back in the thick of the fight, the 352nd received a Distinguished Unit Citation for its activities on 8 May 1944. Brunswick was the target for B-17s to protect which the 352nd, among the escort, fought until ammunition ran out and fuel ran low. P-51Ds and Ks came into use in summer, their blue noses a ready identity feature.

P-51B 'The Flying Scot II' at Bodney.

Bomber escorts were the order of the day during attacks on factories, submarine pens and V-weapon sites. D-Day saw the Group having seventy-four P-51s available for its Channel support operation. Ground strafing and dive bombing operations followed during the 352nd's support of the St-Lô break-out. In September Bodney's P-51s supported the Arnhem airborne landing.

To help counter the December German Ardennes offensive most of the P-51s moved out quite suddenly to Asch, Belgium, to give cover to 9th AF fighter-bomber operations. It was then that 352nd lost Capt George Preddy, top P-51 scorer who was tragically killed after being brought down near Liege probably by light AA fire. On 28 January 1945 the squadrons were switched to Chievres, Belgium, from where they returned to Bodney on 13-14 April to resume operational flying.

They had missed a night of excitement for on 4 March a Ju 88 dropped two 250kg bombs on the airfield during one of the last bombing raids on a UK aerodrome.

The 352nd flew their final mission on 3 May 1945 and soon after VE Day unit personnel starting leaving for home. Most of the aircraft quit during August but not until 3 November 1945 did the 352nd Fighter Group officially leave Bodney for the USA. RAF personnel had already arrived and on the 8th Bodney passed to No 12 Group and Fighter Command and was briefly Hethel's satellite. Closure came on 26 November 1945 when the station was taken over by the War Office.

Bodney has long remained MoD property for it sits within the Stanford Battle Area. On the south side of the road to Watton adjacent to the Army's Bodney camp is a grass area where a windsock usually flies indicating this to be a landing ground for assorted helicopters. During battle training exercises they frequent the area. In wartime the Bodney area had strong Army associations and near Mundford by the Swaffham road is The 51st Highland Division new memorial and battle training trail.

Main features:
Landing ground: NE/SW runway grass 3,000ft, NW/SE runway grass 2,700ft, E/W runway grass 2,700ft. *Hangars:* two T2, five Blister. *Hardstandings:* twelve small asphalt, fifteen large asphalt. *Accommodation:* 190 USAAF officers and 1,519 enlisted men.

BOREHAM, Essex

51°46N/00°31E 170ft asl; TL740120. 2 miles NW of the A12(T) at Boreham

Built in 1943-44 Boreham had one of the briefest operational careers of any temporary, wartime, three-runway, two T2 bomber base. It became home for the 394th Bomb Group operating B-26s from here between March and July 1944 when the Group left for Holmsley South. They had flown in *Ramrods* to France, Belgium and the Netherlands attacking marshalling yards, airfields, gun emplacements, bridges and V-weapons sites. On D-Day they bombed gun emplacements in the Cherbourg Peninsula, then switched to raiding communications and fuel dumps, strong-points and troop concentrations. Thereafter Boreham remained in US hands. Earmarked for 38 Group RAF, who had no need of the station, it closed to flying in 1945. From late summer 1944 to the end of hostilities Boreham had an interesting role as the UK base from which the USAAF's Air Disarmament unit carried out the disarming of Luftwaffe installations and equipment, investigating enemy booty and keeping anything worth investigation and destroying the remainder. British traffic through the base was from April 1945 handled by a succession of Staging Post, Nos 122, 170, 160 and 94 the latter leaving for Norway early July 1945 and being the last RAF flying unit here. The site was sold by 1947.

Since the 1990s Boreham has seen a resumption of flying. Essex Constabulary, realising that the site was well placed for policing, moved into the wartime control tower. A hangar was built close by to house their Air Support Unit helicopter.

Main features:
Runways: 340° 6,000ft x 150ft, 210°, 270°, concrete and tarmac. *Hangars:* two T2. *Hardstandings:* fifty spectacle type. *Accommodation:* 417 officers, 2,241 enlisted men.

BOTTISHAM, Cambridgeshire

52°12N/00°15E 50ft asl; TL540595. About 2 miles E of Quy interchange; the A14 major road crosses the centre of the former airfield. Three other second-class roads pass along the three sides of the airfield site

Date: 23 March 1942. Time: 1535 hrs. Place: near Midsummer Common, Cambridge. The noise from the racy-looking machine was familiar unlike the shape. Its body was highly streamlined while the wings and tail so incongruously angular looked as if they has been stolen from an Me 109. As it hurried low over the house top flying very fast, I recalled having seen a drawing of something like it in a November 1940 issue of *The Aeroplane* devoted to American aircraft. At last it was here, the delectably elegant Mustang.

Where had it come from? Engine notes confirmed it was Allison powered, indeed, it sounded like a Tomahawk in a hurry – and Tomahawks currently resided at Bottisham. My first chance to check that notion came three days later when I discovered to my delight a group of fourteen North American Mustangs grazing in the north-west corner of Bottisham. Their unusual 'green-brown-sky' colours confirmed that they were being used by Army Co-operation Command and not Fighter Command as might have been expected. Years later I discovered that the first example had reached Bottisham on 15 March, and that 241 Squadron at that time held more than any other. Although others were around by now, Bottisham may reasonably be thought of as the place where the Mustang most populously launched its front-line career, thereby giving this somewhat inconsequential airfield a worthy claim to fame.

My other cherished memory of the station, and at its most primitive, belongs to a hot cloudless July 1940 day. By chance a friend and I were cycling on the road to Newmarket enjoying, as ever, the grand wide vista to the undulating south and discussing what grim moments the weeks ahead would unleash when we decided instead to take the first right turn to Little Wilbraham. To the left a large expanse of grass opened beyond a wheat field. No fence or barbed wire, no airman, yet on the field, widely dispersed rested a clutch of Tiger Moths diverted from their daily flying at 22 EFTS Cambridge. Close inspection revealed that, incredibly, they had 20lb bombs hanging from fuselage racks. The international situation was so serious that these 'Tigers' were part of Training Command's anti-invasion force code named *Banquet Light*. Their task, should any Germans attempt to land on our eastern coastline, would be to dive bomb them at that most vulnerable moment as they stepped ashore – and irrespective of losses. Instructors would fly the aircraft.

Bottisham's all-grass landing ground had been very quickly prepared in Spring 1940 as a satellite for very incomplete Waterbeach, but it never accepted aircraft from that station. Instead the Tiger Moths and a few tents for living quarters tarried until late September 1940 when the main invasion scare receded and the Tiger Moths resumed their use in training pilots so desperately needed. However, until 1943 there remained the fear of German raiding parties landing which would have certainly raised much panic and for which anti-invasion plans remained in situ. Until the summer of 1941 22 EFTS used Bottisham as a Relief Landing Ground for Tiger Moth training.

On 15 July 1941 the station was switched to Army Co-operation Command and the 'Tigers' began using Newmarket as their RLG. To Bottisham came ten Lysanders of 241 Squadron working closely with Eastern Command Army units and often placing detachments at Snailwell.

By August 1941 Bottisham was echoing to a new high-pitched sound for ten Allison-engined Tomahawks had wheeled in to supplement the Lysanders. Whereas the latter performed East Coast patrols and co-operated closely with the Army, the newcomers' task was fighter- reconnaissance. The American Curtiss Tomahawk had been envisaged for such a role in any action needed to defend Uncle Sam's southern borders. The RAF hoped it would be a useful general fighter, but it was too slow and its engine's power faded above 15,000ft. Pairs of P-40 Tomahawks flying low on training 'recce sorties' and often 'beating up' Army convoys became a common sight over Cambridgeshire. Serviceability was poor, there were ground loops and engine troubles abounded. Not surprisingly no offensive operations were undertaken.

The next big change occurred when the Mustang Is arrived. Although fast and manoeuvrable, the performance of the British-inspired Mustang fell away, like the Tomahawk's, at heights above 15,000ft. Below that level it was indeed fast, had an amazing range and handled well although the laminar flow wing section gave it a long take-off run. Like the Tomahawks they had come to replace, the Mustangs had to be relegated to a low-level fighter-reconnaissance role. When I visited on 26 March Bottisham was housing nine Lysanders, six Tomahawks in the markings of 239 Squadron and a Bell Airacobra for which the Command was trying to find a use.

The Mustang's stay was brief for in 241 Squadron's hands they left for Ayr (whence they had come) on 2 May 1942. The other types were ferried away and 652 Squadron moved in on 15 June. Awaiting Auster AOPs, it undertook flying training here using a dozen Tiger Moths whose sojourn was brief for on 21 August they flew away to Westley, near Bury St Edmunds.

By now steel net dispersal pads by the then-A45 side of the field had been laid, and were protected against strafing by earth revetment walls. A couple of Miskins Blister hangars provided cover for maintenance. A few huts used as squadron offices – still standing – later supplemented them. Laying of two all-metal Sommerfeld track runways commenced on 15 October 1941, the first coming into use in July 1942.

Newly formed 168 Squadron, on 13 July 1942, began using Bottisham as a home for its fourteen Tomahawks which had vacated Snailwell because it was needed for Typhoons from Duxford. Considerable excitement came on 23 September when a couple of Whitleys released two Horsa gliders brought in to investigate the feasibility of airlifting 168 Squadron. On 7 November, eight Mustang 1s arrived from Ayr for the squadron. Eleven days later came five Whitleys and Horsas to carry out both a mobility exercise and also to transport 168 Squadron to Odiham for a spell of operational flying.

Following that departure the airfield was placed on Care & Maintenance for extension and very major upgrading. Its metal runways – unusually 300ft wide – were extended, 020/200° to 3,600ft and 090/180° to 4,305ft. Multiple aircraft take-offs were now possible. A 'T2' transportable steel hangar soon supplemented seven Blister hangars, fifteen concrete hardstandings and sixty-eight pierced steel mat dispersals. Domestic sites sufficient to accommodate 190 officers and 1,500 other ranks were built beyond the airfield.

The reason for this extensive and extremely muddy works programme became noisily clear on 3 December 1943 when the unmistakable din of 'razor back' Republic P-47D Thunderbolts disturbed the area. The 361st Fighter Group, USAAF, was arriving, and in very short time reached its full strength comprising three squadrons using around seventy dreary green and grey fighters. Operations began on 21 January 1944, the role being bomber escort and ground strafing. The 361st FG – soon in the thick of the fight – provided an almost daily sight of P-47s scampering off to an awful din before forming into their 'finger four' battle sections.

P-47D 225969 of the 376th FS, 361st FG reputedly photographed on 7 May 1944 during a Berlin raid. (USAF)

During May 1944 the 361st began to receive P-51s – Bs, Cs and some of the first P-51Ds to serve in the 8th AF. At the time of D-Day – when the Mustangs were dispersed along the airfield perimeter, and the main runway crossed that road where I had enjoyed the site of Tiger Moth bombers – some of the 361st FG P-51s had their upper surfaces painted in a superb shade of deep blue and slightly lighter than that used for insignia. That remains my most unexpected memory of the evening of D-Day for a generous American gave me a tour along the perimeter track. Thank goodness I had amply practised 'pocket writing'! Apparently the reason for the blue top surfaces was to camouflage unpainted P-51s and make them less obvious during low level strafing. Olive drab being unavailable, a presumably mixed blue was the next best thing.

Bottisham's Mustangs were extremely busy that summer, operating mainly over France. As soon as the 9th AF quit Hadstock/Little Walden in September 1944 the 361st moved there for it had firm runways and was better equipped and suited for winter flying. Bottisham then fell silent, was placed within Fighter Command's control and became part of the North Weald Sector for administration purposes.

A quartet of Bottisham's 361st FG P-51s.

Between mid-1945 and March 1946 some of the Belgian airmen training at Snailwell to rebuild a new Belgian Air Force were billeted at Bottisham which their Tiger Moths sometimes used. Not for long for Bottisham closed on 1 May 1946, and on 1 October 1958 was sold for agricultural use.

On the blustery afternoon of 14 February 1948, I was passing as bulldozers swung into action reducing to rubble, and within a few minutes, the 1943 control tower. Two gateposts flanking a gap – the one-time main entrance – remain just east of a vehicle compound alongside the old A45. In the north-east corner a collection of buildings named River Farm Smokery include some from the war years. Thousands of vehicles thunder daily cross the centre of the airfield site using the A14 main arterial link with the Port of Felixstowe. How many folk who cross Bottisham have any ideas of its former glory – indeed, have the slightest idea that there was once an historic airfield here? Probably very few!

Main features:
Runways: 020° 3,600ft, 090° 4,305ft both Sommerfeld tracking. NW/SE grass runway 13,420ft. *Hangars:* one T2, seven Blister. *Hardstandings:* fifteen concrete, sixty-eight Pierced Steel Planking. *Accommodation* (temporary) for USAAF: 190 officers, 1,519 enlisted men.

BOURN, Cambridgeshire

52°12N/00°02W 235ft asl; TL345595. On A428 7 miles W of Cambridge

As dusk fell a layer of stratocumulus lying between 1,200ft and 3,000ft with tops rising to 3,500ft completely covered Eastern England. Icing was present near the cloud base and ground visibility was two miles over East Anglia increasing to four miles over Yorkshire. HQ Bomber Command was told that 'These conditions will persist but if cloud base breaks up visibility will quickly deteriorate to less than 2,000 yards.' Such a warning was nothing new, but this time it heralded catastrophe.

Main target for tonight, 16/17 December 1943, was Berlin against which 492 bombers including ninety Lancasters and fifteen Mosquito pathfinders and markers were despatched. No 100 Group in support was sending out two Beaufighters and two Mosquitoes to intrude upon airfields. In addition six 8 Group Mosquitoes flying at 27,000ft would raid the Thyssen steel works in Duisburg, twenty-seven Stirlings and nine Lancasters would bomb V-weapons targets marked by twelve Mosquitoes while thirty-five bombers laid mines. A moderately busy night for the Command.

For most of the route to the 'big city' the clouds were 10/10 and reached 7,000ft over Berlin upon which 117 flares and 159 x 250lb target indicators were dropped some giving an eerie glow through the clouds, others bursting above the stratocumulus. Some 418 crews were reckoned to have bombed the city upon which they are recorded as releasing 334,104 mixed incendiaries along with 788.2 tons of high explosive bombs. Such statistics listed in Tactical Night Report 489 represent likely totals taking into account all possibilities.

Veteran Mosquito B IX GB-H of No 105 Squadron wearing night bomber colouring and dispersed on Bourn's southern edge.

Mosquito B.XX KB458 'CR-U' of 162 Squadron wears symbols recording 54 sorties.

No firm release details came to hand from twenty-five crews missing from the Berlin raid. They comprised six Lancasters of 1 Group, a Lancaster II of 3 Group, eight Lancasters out of 165 despatched by 5 Group, four of 6 Group and six Lancasters out of the ninety despatched by 8 Group whose losses were proportionately the heaviest and worse was to follow.

Around midnight visibility at the bomber bases began to decrease and by 0100 hrs was below one mile. Very soon the 1, 3 and 8 Group airfields were enveloped in thick fog. Some crews arrived back in time to avoid the dire conditions, some were diverted, but with so many aircraft homing and conditions continuing to deteriorate, directing them all to safety became impossible. So bad were the conditions that four aircraft were involved in mid-air collisions.

No 1 Group suffered most, fourteen of its Lancasters crashing including four of 100 Squadron. No 75 Squadron (Mepal) had a Stirling crash, No 6 Group recorded four crashes and 8 Group eleven Lancasters. For Bourn's 97 Squadron the end of the venture was quite appalling for seven of its aircraft crashed.

Twenty-one Lancasters had set off for Berlin and twenty-eight men were killed as the bombers crashed when fuel was no more. Eight crews managed safe landings at Bourn, three at Graveley where the newly installed FIDO was lit. Of the others Flight Sergeant Coates whose Lancaster had been hit by incendiaries falling from another aircraft came home on two engines for the others had been put out of use by flak. He thought he would have to ditch, but managed to bring the crippled Lancaster into Downham. Two Lancasters crashed, near Ely and Wyton, while another was lost without trace. Flying Officer Thackway crashed very near Bourn after approaching parallel but about 800 yards away from its runway. Another two crashed near Graveley and one near Gransden. Squadron Leader Mackenzie's aircraft presented a heart-rending sight for the distorted bomber could be seen lying, a burnt wreck, close to the road to St Neots. The night's disaster was the worst suffered by any East Anglian airfield in such circumstances.

In the small War Cemetery to be found in Cambridge City Cemetery near the airport is a line of airmen's graves. All twenty-two died on the same date in December 1943 – not in battle but on returning from Berlin only to find impenetrable fog. The overall losses that terrible night amounted to twenty-seven aircraft which crashed due to fog, four lost in mid-air collisions and twenty-five missing in action, a grand total of fifty-six.

By late 1943 Bourn was a fully fledged bomber base already home for part of the Command's spearhead. Soon it would house the means of marking and making precision night attacks and the bombers which would lead the air assault on D-Day. That would have seemed highly unlikely when in February 1941 the RAF moved onto Bourn where runways were still being built but little else.

No surviving records confirm when Bourn first resounded to an aircraft arriving, but it was in RAF hands by March 1941. The enemy must have noticed the building for one of Bourn's runways received three bombs from a Ju 88C intruder on 9 April. No aircraft were yet based there but Wellingtons of 101 Squadron and Stirlings of No 7 were certainly using the landing ground in summer 1941. As Oakington's satellite it was a most useful acquisition on account of its three hard runways of which its parent had none.

One of the most memorable 1941 events was the homing to Bourn of two Stirlings back from the large scale daylight raid on Brest carried out on 18 December 1941. The battered form of 'J Johnny' sat at the end of the main runway throughout Christmas 1941.

To reduce pressure on Oakington No 101 Squadron moved to Bourn on 11 February 1942 to complete conversion to Wellington IIIs. Veteran Mk 1c R1780 'B-Beer' operating against Le Havre on 13 March and Lille on the 16th by which time it had completed thirty-five sorties, had flown the squadron's final two sorties using Mk Ics. It then joined nearby 11 OTU, Bassingbourn. Mk IIIs had begun operations on 13 March by raiding Cologne.

Although 500lb and 1,000lb HEs comprised usual loads for Wellingtons, they also delivered bundled flares and frequently nine SBCs each containing eighty 4lb incendiaries. The latter were showered by 101 Squadron upon Lübeck on 28 March, and Rostock on both 23 and 25 April during those notable raids. From Bourn twelve 101 Squadron crews participated in the Cologne '1000 bomber' raid, two failing to return. A detachment of five Wellington Ics from No 23 OTU Pershore also took part from the station and were participants in the '1,000 bomber' raid of 1 June against Essen. To that, 101 Squadron contributed ten aircraft and against Bremen on 25 June six Wellingtons of 101 Squadron were despatched.

May 1942 had seen No 101 Squadron tentatively begin conversion to Stirlings for which No 101 Conversion Flight had formed at Oakington and contributed to the big raids. Instead, as part of August 1942 general shake up, No 101 Squadron moved to Stradishall on the 11th after having from Bourn mounted sixty operations embracing 461 bombing sorties, mining on seven nights and losing seven aircraft during operations.

The Pathfinder Force (later called 8 Group) took over Wyton as its Head Quarters station and as a result 3 Group's XV Squadron's Stirlings were nudged out to Bourn where they arrived on 13 August and from their new home flew the first of their 104 operations and 615 sorties two nights later with Düsseldorf as the target. Bourn had also seen dramatic change for it had become a self accounting 3 Group station within 3 Group and was no longer merely Oakington's satellite.

Bourn's Stirlings took part in autumn's long-distance operations in support of the Western Desert offensive by taking part in harrowing night raids on northern Italy during which the bomber's poor higher altitude performance forced some heavily laden outward flights to be made between alpine peaks.

At the end of 1942 XV Squadron commenced trials with the first Stirling IIIs fitted with superior engines and conventional control lines in place of the much disliked hydraulic type. XV introduced the new variant to operations on 7 February 1943. It proved very disappointing, and Stirling losses remained high.

With the 1943 bombing offensive well underway XV Squadron was ordered to Mildenhall and Bourn took its place in 8 (PFF) Group. After attacking Frankfurt on 10 April the squadron commenced its move, partly travelling in style with the aid of two Horsa gliders towed by Albemarles. During its time at Bourn No XV Squadron lost twenty-six aircraft and some 200 men during operations.

The newcomers brought dramatic change for they were Lancasters of No 97 (Straits Settlement) Squadron, a 5 Group formation loaned to the Pathfinders to perform in a 'back-up' flare dropping marker force. They arrived on 18 April and first operated, against Duisburg, on 26 April. During May a third Flight was added to the squadron boosting its numerical establishment from eighteen to thirty Lancaster I/III.

Lancasters based at Bourn operated intensively and on 13/14 May 1943 took part in the raid on distant Pilsen and then in many other heavy attacks such as those on Wuppertal and Essen. A special raid was mounted on 16 June against Friedrichshafen by four crews detached to Scampton after which they flew on to Maison Blanche, north Africa, in a shuttle operation during which they attacked La Spezia on return. No 97 (The Straits Settlement Squadron), played a back-up marker role in the huge Hamburg raids of July 1943, sent sixteen aircraft to Peenemunde and was very much involved in the Battle of Berlin. As well as flare dropping the Lancasters usually carried considerable loads of HE including 4,000lb bombs and incendiaries in a variety of containers and bundles.

There were many dramatic moments during 97's operations one such involving EE105 'Q-Queenie' which, when returning from the 'Big City' on 23 August, was shot down by an intruder over Norfolk, fortunately now a relatively rare event. No 97 carried out from Bourn seventeen attacks on Berlin by the end of 1943.

Another major change was introduced when on 18 March 1944 'C' Flight was detached to Downham Market to form the nucleus of a new PFF squadron, No 635 Squadron. By that time '97' had added Schweinfurt to its 'targets attacked' list, and again raided Augsburg which for the squadron held bitter memories of its costly daylight venture in April 1942. Bombing emphasis was about to switch to transport targets in France and Belgium when the last Lancaster sortie ended with a return from Aachen on 11/12 April 1944. Bourn's Lancasters had flown 1,158 sorties during ninety-two operations and lost forty-nine of their number.

At midday on 18 April 1944, it was an impressive 'all change' when twenty-one Lancasters set forth for Coningsby where 5 Group welcomed back one of the 'crack' bomber squadrons. Building of runways at Marham and its development into a Very Heavy Bomber airfield had partly been responsible for change, although 97 Squadron had only been loaned to the PFF until it had risen to planned strength.

Nevertheless a new operational base for Marham's Mosquito squadron was needed. Bourn was chosen and late morning of 23 March 1944 witnessed No 105 Mosquito Squadron arrive there in the style learnt in their 2 Group days. Arriving was a squadron with a glittering war record, the premier Mosquito operator whose day raids were legendary. Some of the glamour was lost when they were switched from nuisance to more conventional night bombing, but now *Oboe*-equipped and flying Mk IXs, they were to hold as important a place as any squadron for often they led Bomber Command into action. To accomplish that they wasted no time for, during the evening of the arrival day, they provided the green markers indicating Laon's marshalling yards for the forty-two Halifaxes and twenty-four Stirlings able to attack. No 105's main task during the run-up to the Normandy landings was marking such targets which, being in occupied countries, needed great care. On the night of the invasion they placed their target indicators on gun batteries around Seine Bay for bombers sent to neutralise the defences. The next phase involved day and night operations against V-1 targets and involvement in heavy onslaughts designed to dislodge the enemy army from positions near Caen. Then the Mosquitoes illuminated oil refineries by which time they were using Mosquito XVIs incorporating cabin pressurisation. The squadron's Mosquitoes also carried out bombing raids in their own right, and with exceptional accuracy. Although the squadron was operating with high efficiency things did not go all their own way. As they returned from Orleans and Le Mans on 23 May an Me 410 intruder which disrupted landing for an hour bombed and strafed Bourn damaging two aircraft on the ground. Hardstandings for the thirty Mosquitoes were by the trees on the southern side of the airfield.

By late 1944 the Mosquitoes' operational effectiveness was increased by the use of modified *Oboe* the range of which was extended by the use of continental and relay stations permitting its use deep in Germany. Not only did they aid the ' heavies', 105 Squadron also marked for the Fast Night Striking Force whose Mosquitoes bit hard and often more accurately than the heavy bombers.

On 18 December 1944 a new squadron, No 162, formed at Bourn and was armed with twenty Canadian-built Mosquitoes, XXs but mainly XXVs. They were fitted with *H2S* radar which gave them a long range marking provision useful for the FNSF's Berlin raids. All-Mosquito highly punishing raids had became possible. Furthermore, the aircraft's high speed even permitted it to make twice nightly runs from Bourn to Berlin. Even more important, such operations during which a Mosquito could deliver a 4,000lb bomb were almost without loss. With fifty Mosquitoes on the station Bourn was indeed a busy place, and equipped with the most cost-effective warplane of all time.

A new shape joined the bombers at Bourn in 1945 when Spitfire Vs and Hurricane IIs of 1686 Bomber Defence Training Flight began using the station to provide gunnery and evasive training for 8 Group's crews.

Since 1941 the Short Stirling had remained prominent at Bourn. A collection of T2 hangars on its eastern side housed the erecting shops for the many Stirlings repaired or extensively modified at the Madingley Sebro factory then transported by road to Bourn for assembly, flight test and delivery. During the course of one trial a Short's Chief Test Pilot looped a Stirling made possible because despite their size and limitations Stirlings were by far the most manoeuvrable four-engined bombers. An unusual sight was the half-scale Stirling based here for use by Shorts as a light transport used for flights to and from Stirling bases.

By 1944 Stirling GT4 transports converted from bombers were to be seen here, and Sebro's activity continued to the end of 1945. The 'T' Hangars, all of which remain in place, have of late been used by Vauxhall Motors and Krupp Cornard.

To the end of hostilities Bourn's Mosquitoes were hyperactive, but by August 1945 Bourn had much changed. No 105 Squadron left in June 1945 and No 162 moved to Blackbushe on 10 July to commence high speed mail and courier flights to distant parts of Europe. Sebro had begun overhauling Transport Command Liberators, a task continued almost to the end of 1945.

On 1 January 1946, 3 Group handed the station to 48 Group and on 21 July 1947, it passed to Maintenance Command. Closure came in 1948 but the land was not sold as surplus until April 1961.

Bourn knew many dramatic moments one of which had no tragic overtones. The Sebro workforce had long heard tales of the huge Short Shetland flying-boat and Geoffrey Tyson, Short's Chief Test, was persuaded to demonstrate it. The huge 'silver' machine orbited Cambridge very low, then headed for Bourn's main runway. Tyson, no mean performer, flew it along very, very low and very fast before zooming away in a fantastic performance, the equal of any 'Farnborough' moment.

In 1947 Pest Control of Harston stored in the B1 a handful of unhappy looking Fairey Swordfishes which languished long untouched in the hangar set in fields across the Bourn road. They were intended particularly for spraying of cotton crops and carrying out anti-malaria schemes in Africa. For more local use they were supplemented with Hiller 360s which were based in a new hangar built in the north-eastern corner of the airfield and used during the 1950s. Management Aviation followed them many years later and became Bond helicopters which carved a niche serving North Sea oil and gas rigs. Rotortech was formed at Bourn in 1977 as the maintenance arm of Bond Helicopters and overhauled them in a new workshop and hangar area at Bourn. In 1994 the Bond company was bought by Helikopter Service, a publicly quoted Norwegian-owned concern. December 1998 saw them sell Rotortech to Manu Hathiramani, a previous employee of that company, which remains at Bourn.

Most of wartime RAF Bourn had long gone, but from the south-western part of the airfield, where some Mossies used to disperse, private flying takes place. Use is made of part of the perimeter track and remaining runway. Among the tenants on what is strictly private 'no entry' property has been 'the RFC' – the Rural Flying Corps – at one time operating a Percival Sea Prince. Portions of remaining concrete periodically provide hardstandings for 'Bourn market' traders.

Main features (December 1944):
Runways: 065° 5,775ft x 150ft, 007° 4,800ft x 150ft, 128° 4,200ft x 150ft. *Hangars:* two T2, one B1. *Hardstandings:* thirty-six suitable for heavies. Accommodation (all temporary): RAF 185 officers, 442 SNCOs, 1,200 ORs; WAAF: 4 officers, 10 SNCOs, 220 ORs.

Bourn airfield much intact on 20 April 1956. A428 road to left, Sebro factory at top.

Places of interest nearby:
By the road to Cambridge lies the Cambridge American Cemetery, Madingley, extensive and impressive to visit. Far nearer and behind the Enterprise Cafe is the field TL346595 which, in 1912, served as Hardwick landing ground, one of the first military 'airfields'.

BOXTED, Essex

51°56N/00°56E 157ft asl; TM5305. 5 miles NE of Colchester, W of A12(T)

When the Allies reached Berlin there was a scramble for the spoils of war, the three major contestants grabbing as much of the Reich's archives as remained. Among those eagerly sought were the Luftwaffe's aircraft loss records. The British struck lucky – to a degree – by retrieving the Luftwaffe Quartermaster General's master volumes for the period to the end of 1943, but none was found for the period beyond. It has always been believed that the Russians purloined the remainder. Thus, it has not been possible to compile in the West accurate listing of German losses revealed by these documents for earlier years. Claims made by pilots beyond December 1943 rest, for verification, upon such sources as became available to intelligence organisations.

Nevertheless, it is generally accepted that Boxted's 56th Fighter Group achieved the highest number of combat successes credited to any 8th AF Group during the war. Boxted did not fade away when the Americans left, but was transferred to RAF Fighter Command which busily used the station for almost a year or so. Thus, for all its public anonymity, Boxted certainly has a special claim to fame, and a more complex history than many USAAF East Anglian wartime bases.

Although incomplete, Boxted opened in May 1943 as a typical three-runway two-hangar wartime temporary airfield where, after a week at Snetterton Heath the 386th Bomb Group, 8th AF, arrived on 10 June 1943. Equipped with B-26B Marauders, they commenced operations on 30 July. Principal targets were airfields in France along with marshalling yards and gun positions. Marauders were only briefly at Boxted for they moved to a better site at Great Dunmow late September 1943 and on 16 October were switched to the IXth AF by which time their bombing campaign was becoming effective.

In place of the B-26s came the 354th Fighter Group, IXth AF, which arrived from Greenham Common during the second week of November 1943 and began using some of the first USAAF P-51 Mustangs. These they took into action during December, and found themselves developing deep penetration fighter escort tactics for the P-51. On 11 January 1944 the Group was honoured with the award to Major James H Howard (who died in March 1995) of the Medal of Honour after his courage when alone he defended a bomber formation. Additional to bomber escorts deep into enemy territory the 354th also undertook fighter-bomber missions against airfields, gun positions and railway installations in Belgium, France and the Netherlands. Meanwhile, the 9th AF was gathering its units in the south and during April 1944 the 354th moved out to Lashendon.

On 18 April 1944 P-47D Thunderbolts of the 56th FG moved in from Halesworth, a base then required for 8th AF bombers. With an enviable reputation and a long score list to their credit, among the pilots were two who were outstanding. One was Francis S Gabreski who flew with the 56th between April 1943 and 20 July 1944 when he crash-landed and became a POW. He was the 8th AF's highest scoring pilot being credited with twenty-eight enemy aircraft shot down. His runner-up, Robert S Johnson, whose score of twenty-seven was later adjusted to twenty-eight, also served with the 56th. He flew his last mission in Europe on 8 May 1944, then returned to the USA and later joined Republic Aviation.

P-51B-1-NA 43-12433 AJ-M of the 356th FS, 354th FG, airborne from Boxted (USAF).

Always in the thick of the fight during escorts and ground strafing missions, the 56th managed a dozen fighter-bomber and four fighter missions on 6 and 7 June 1944, losing five P-47s on the 7th, four to AA fire. After D-Day the 56th flew mainly fighter-bomber operations aimed at the destruction of rail targets and bridges. In September 1944 it participated in the Allied airborne landings in the Netherlands. Then, in particular, it escorted B-24s, and on 1 November first encountered an Me 262, whose destruction it shared with the 352nd FG. The 56th was involved in the December Ardennes Battle of the Bulge, by which time it was the last 8th AF Fighter Group flying P-47s. Thunderbolts had been withdrawn from the 353rd FG on 2 October, the 356th on 20 November and the 78th on 29 December 1944.

On 3 January 1945 the 56th started equipping with P-47Ms, the only 8th Group ever to use them. With a more powerful engine and ability to carry a 215-gallon belly-carried fuel tank, the P-47M entered service with the 61st FS. Engine problems beset the new variant until March 1945 when it was employed in low-level attacks on airfields. The aircraft flew protective patrols above Remagen Bridge over the Rhine while the US Army made its famous crossing. Late combat successes included four Me 262s and two Ar 234 jet bombers shot down on 14 March. Near Wittstock on 10 April, 2nd Lt W J Sharbro made the last kill of a Me 262, one belonging to JG 7. The 56th's final mission was flown on 21 April 1945, by which time it was officially credited with 665½ enemy aircraft shot down and 311 destroyed on the ground, at a total cost of 128 P-47s. That made it the second highest scoring 8th AF FG by way of enemy aircraft shot down, the 354th with 701 credited being the top scorer. The 56th remained at Boxted until 9 September 1945 when it moved to Hadstock/Little Walden.

Between May 1944 and mid-January 1945 the 56th had for companions at Boxted an air-sea rescue unit, the 65th Fighter Wing Detachment B, nominally equipped with twenty-five war weary P-47s. Initially they flew as spotter aircraft carrying smoke bombs and two dinghies and later carried a belly long-range tank and a dinghy beneath each mainplane supplemented with markers on belly racks. They left for Halesworth in January 1945.

The RAF retrieved Boxted in September 1945. As soon as North Weald was given up by Transport Command in a cost-cutting exercise Boxted was placed under North Weald control within the Essex Sector of No 11 Group Fighter Command which administered Duxford, Bentwaters and Bradwell Bay. It thus had importance being in The Defended Area of the UK. Primitive wartime airfields would never have been long acceptable in peacetime and at Boxted accommodation was widely dispersed and primeval, heating arrangements in ORs living accommodation comprising a tortoise stove or two in the centre of the hut. Offices and the Operations Sections were little better, and the rough brown linoleum which served as floor covering over concrete or wood gave precious little comfort in cold conditions although it splendidly lent itself to polishing during 'fatigues'. Engineering workshops were equally poor – when they existed – and most maintenance had to be undertaken in the open on dispersal pans. Boxted therefore served the RAF only on an interim basis whilst pre-war permanent stations were renovated and living standards and runways improved.

No 25 Squadron's Mosquito NF30s moved to Boxted on the 11 January 1946 just prior to the closure of Castle Camps that month. On 10 May 1946 Bradwell Bay became a satellite and on 20 May Rivenhall was placed under Boxted's care.

On 28 March Meteor IIIs of 234 Squadron had moved in. Their squadron on 1 September was re-numbered 266 Squadron. No 25 Squadron left for West Malling on 5 September 1946 and No 266 at the start of November 1946. Two other Meteor III squadrons, Nos 222 and 263, made use of Boxted. No 222 was here for a few days in June 1946 when No 263 Squadron arrived and stayed until September 1946. Their arrival coincided with North Weald's switch from Fighter to Reserve Command as an Auxiliary Air Force base. Essex Sector closed and Boxted was transferred to the Metropolitan Sector of 11 Group. Castle Camps remained its satellite on C&M. Meteor IIIs of 56 Squadron nudged out of Bentwaters on 18 September to make way for 226 OCU were here until the start of November, No 695 Squadron, Horsham St Faith, made use of the station during co-operation exercises with the RN Nore Command.

In September-October 1946 the strength of Boxted's aircraft establishment was cut by half and the squadrons were renamed 'Squadron (Cadre)'. Boxted closed to flying on 3 November 1946, partly because of its proximity to Colchester but mainly for other reasons. Although RAF presence faded in 1947 Boxted was retained under Plan F for possible expansion and use for fighters. Although abandoned on 3 February 1948 the site was officially inspected twice weekly and from 1947 to 25 April 1948 No 145 Gliding School's Cadet gliders were flown here by the ATC. Boxted retained Standby Airfield status throughout the 1950s and under Plan G of February 1951 even had as its own Standby Airfields, Andrew's Field and Bradwell Bay. It was disposed of in the late 1950s. Into the 1960s Airspray Ltd operated crop spraying Tiger Moths from the runway. Now it has reverted to agricultural use and is partly covered with orchards.

Boxted Airfield Historical Group, a registered charity since 2008 and formed in 2000 by Richard Turner, has some 140 members worldwide, of which twenty are Boxted US veterans. Using a National Lottery Heritage Grant, a museum is under way, its completion expected in 2010. Relative information can be found at www.boxted-airfield.com.

Main features:
Runways: 220° 2,000 yards x 50 yards, 280°, 340°. *Hangars:* two T2.
Hardstandings: fifty loop. Accommodation (during USAAF tenure): 421 officers and 2,473 enlisted men.

BRADWELL BAY, Essex

51°44N/00°54E 30ft asl; TM000085. To E of end of B1020, E of village

Little remains of this once major yet small and primitive airfield built close to, and alongside, the river Blackwater estuary. Visit the area now and you will certainly not fail to notice its successor, a huge nuclear power station.

Surprisingly, in view of its history, Bradwell Bay aerodrome was not conceived as an operational station. That came about by chance. A pre-war air-to-ground firing range existed on marshland known as Denghie Flats, and indeed remained in use to the early 1950s. To support it, a small landing ground was built for refuelling and other purposes. Such was its valuable position that in 1940 work began to develop it into a satellite landing ground for fighters.

It was not long before work started in upgrading the airfield by laying concrete and tarmac runways, that work commencing during February 1941. Twice that year the runways were lengthened which delayed its operational debut. Maintenance facilities were limited to one Bellman hangar and eventually a dozen Blister hangars were added. Protective revetments for twin-engined fighters and hardstandings were, not surprisingly, necessary at the extremely bleak site.

When RAF Bradwell Bay Station Head Quarters (SHQ) opened on 28 November 1941 it was as an independent RAF station in 11 Group's Hornchurch Sector. Intention had been for Bradwell to become fully operational in January 1942, but winter weather delayed the finishing touches making it unready before April 1942.

First to be based here were Boston III intruders of 418 (Canadian) Squadron which arrived from Debden during mid-morning of 15 April 1942. Late next day Pilot Officer Stabb opened Bradwell's offensive by intruding upon Gilze Rijen. Thereafter, almost nightly, the Bostons sought enemy activity on airfields or the movement of transport on Continental roads and railways, and carried out intruders during the '1,000 bomber' raids. Meanwhile, fighter squadrons continued to refuel here during spells of gunnery training at Denghie Flats.

Bradwell began another phase in its history when on 20 August 1942 Spitfires of 402 Squadron landed to refuel after escorting US B-17 bombers to Amiens during a *Composite Circus*. Similar calls for refuelling brought in many famous fighter squadrons, but it was as a night fighter/intruder base that Bradwell would mainly serve.

In mid-September 1942 came Mosquito IIs of 23 Squadron. By this time 418 Squadron was including leaflet dropping in its repertoire. Bradwell's proximity to the coast was already attracting 'cuckoos', night bombers short of fuel or in damaged state, and three large hardstandings for their use were later added.

Bradwell was by now an extremely busy station, as on the night of 17/18 January 1943. While German aircraft carried out a feeble attack on London, 418 Squadron was calling upon Beauvais, Creil, Chievres, Bretigny and Melun. Two Typhoons of 609 Squadron returning from a night *Rhubarb* landed back after attacking a train, and one of the fighters overturned upon landing. Next to arrive were three Lancasters of 106 Squadron and another of 57 which landed after raiding Berlin. A Hudson called at the end of an anti-shipping sortie. Flying one of seven Mosquitoes of 85 Squadron which also visited that night was Wing Commander Raphael who had just destroyed a Ju 88. By accepting such a variety of aircraft, some combat damaged, Bradwell Bay was playing a role soon to be performed by Woodbridge. No 23 Squadron had left in December 1942 and in its place 264 Squadron was positioning forward detachments here to carry out intruders. No 418 Squadron left on 14 March 1943 and on 13 May Mosquito NF XIIs of No 29 Squadron replaced them the squadron having previously and briefly made use of the airfield.

Just after dawn on 14 May another aspect of the station's value was shown when forty-five P-47s of the 4th FG USAAF landed, refuelled and later set off to cover the return of US bombers from Antwerp. The general absence of German bombers from local skies meant that they had to be sought and on 20/21 May during the only *Ranger* flight from Bradwell that month Flying Officer Crome of 29 Squadron claimed an He 111, his squadron's fiftieth victory. Patrols were also flown that night off Dunkirk, Fw 190 fighter-bomber activity having been forecast. Instead the only major event came when a Mosquito crashed in the sea off Bradwell.

Between March and May 1943, 157's Mosquitoes were also based here, then on 1 June 1943 the station was transferred to the North Weald Sector. With that alteration came a change in the station's role. Two days later the ground crews of 247 Squadron stylishly arrived from Gravesend in Harrow transports. Flying Typhoons the squadron remained until 10 July and was based here to discourage daylight Fw 190 fighter-bomber attacks on the East Anglian coast. Nos 56 and 198 Squadrons took over this commitment in August, and while here made attacks on shipping off the Dutch coast.

There were still a few nights of enemy activity one such being 13 July when three small-scale raids developed in the Newmarket, Colchester, Bradwell and York areas and 29 Squadron chased a raider far out to sea without success. Day fighting predominated as on 25 July, when the Ibsley Wing joined 341 and 485 Squadrons flying from Biggin Hill to cover eighteen B-26C Marauders attacking Ghent. Next day No 165 Squadron and 485 Squadrons likewise flying a fighter escort mission made use of Bradwell.

It was from here that 141 Squadron, based at Wittering, despatched some of its pioneering Beaufighters undertaking bomber support *Serrate* sorties, eight crews setting out on 30 July including famous night fighter pilot Wing Commander Bob Braham. On 12 August it was the turn of the RAF's day fighter top scorer, Wing Commander 'Johnnie' Johnson, to lead the Spitfires of 127 Airfield into Bradwell after escorting home B-17s from Antwerp. Late on 23 August 29 Squadron scrambled against bandits, Squadron Leader Arbon and Flight Lieutenant Goodman each bagging an Me 410 of V/KG2 and bringing 29's score to fifty-six enemy raiders destroyed. Crippled bombers still frequently arrived among them a badly shot about Halifax of 76 Squadron which belly landed on 31 August. No 29 Squadron moved to Ford on 3 September at which time No 488 Squadron was moving in from Drem to replace it and was immediately joined by 605 Squadron. Both were based here until May 1944.

Still the accent remained on day fighter activity, Spitfires flying busily from Bradwell during Operation *Starkey*. the invasion feint mounted in September 1943. On the 5th Nos 402 and 416 Squadrons from Merston operated from here led by Wing Commander Chadburn, also Nos 41 and 91, the only two Spitfire XII squadrons. There was an impressive rendezvous over the airfield as they all formated with Bostons, before the 'beehive' set off for Woensdrecht (Holland). 9 September, the peak day of *Starkey*, proved an anti-climax for, apart from escorting 182 Squadron's Typhoons which bombed St Omer/Fort Rouge airfield, 56 Squadron had an uneventful time. Bradwell was, incidentally, an ideal launching point for daylight photo-reconnaissance sorties flown by Spitfires.

The first success achieved by 488 Squadron since its arrival did not come until 15/16 September when Flight Lieutenant Watts claimed a Do 217 off the French coast. While '488' concentrated on defensive operations, the County of Warwick Squadron, No 605, continued a very productive intruder campaign. No 488 Squadron stood by every night ready for action. On 21 January 1944 it suddenly developed when the Luftwaffe launched operation *Capricorn*, its 'Baby Blitz' on London. On this first night, and despite the enemy's plentiful use of *Düppel*, Flight Lieutenant Hall and Flying Officer Karins bagged a Ju 88 and a Do 217. The squadron's next most profitable night was 24 February when seven crews of 488 operated and a Ju 188 and possibly a Do 217 were claimed. The enemy was unable to sustain *Capricorn* which during March faded into mere nuisance raids. By then the latest RAF fighters were here for Tempests of 3 Squadron arrived on 6 March to work up and stayed until 14 April when they left to commence operations from Newchurch.

The frequency of night activity involving Bradwell was considerable, and its value as a landing ground for aircraft in distress was high. This led it to become unique by being the only fighter station to have FIDO installed to provide for night landings in fog. The line of petrol burners along the main runways was inserted between August and the closing weeks of 1943, the installation saving many aircraft and many lives both of those based here and of many visiting aircraft.

FIDO came into much use as the RAF geared up for its part in the Normandy assault. No 219 Squadron replaced '488' on 1 April. An entirely new activity then emerged from afar when on 21 April No 278 Squadron arrived from distant Sumburgh and immediately placed a detachment at Martlesham. They had come to work up for air/sea rescue duties during the invasion of mainland Europe during which losses at sea were expected to be high. Arriving with Ansons, Spitfire Vs and Walruses they received within days their complement of Warwick ASR1s. More of those along with Hudsons and of other ASR squadrons also staged through Bradwell which still supported fighter daylight operations. Indeed, No 124 Squadron operating Spitfire VII high fliers was based here between 23 April and 26 July 1944. Its prime purpose was to shoot down any high altitude reconnaissance aircraft venturing over the east and south-east of England. In the days immediately preceding D-Day the HF VIIs flew daylight defensive standing patrols and flew high-level sorties over the English Channel during the invasion period.

A new challenge to Bradwell's fighters came on 21 July 1944 when six V-Is passed over the station at night following air launching by He 111s at sea. No 219 Squadron, which had been flying beach-head patrols, was brought in to deal with any more newcomers.

As expected, this was a busy time for No 278 Squadron. On 24 July a Warwick dropped an airborne lifeboat thirty miles south-west of Portland Bill, the crew watching while airmen scrambled aboard. The Bradwell Walruses were also active.

The closing days of August were auspicious for, after so many months succouring passing day fighter squadrons, Bradwell Bay at last received its first own fighter Wing comprising Nos 64, 126 and 611 Spitfire IX squadrons. A dozen Dakotas brought along their ground crews.

On the 31st the Wing went into action by patrolling the Arras area while supporting a Bomber Command operation. No enemy fighters were seen so the Wing profitably indulged in ground strafing, No 126 Squadron swooping upon an airfield near Cambrai. Only as the aircraft pulled away did they realise it was unfortunately a dummy!

September 1944 witnessed the start of almost nightly V-1 traffic heading for London, the weapons being fired at low-level from about fifty miles out to sea. Their course often brought them across the coast in the Bradwell area. British response was to position 501 Squadron here at dusk so that their Tempests could engage the intruders. Such was the V-1 intensity that the squadron moved here on 22 September stayed until 3 March 1945 and obtained many successes. This released 219 Squadron from detachment before Mosquitoes of 68 Squadron (also detached) backed the Tempests in October. To make more room at the packed airfield the Warwick element of 278 Squadron moved to Martlesham Heath on 24 September 1944. Meanwhile the Bradwell Bay Wing Spitfires had been flying many day escorts for Lancasters varying it on 17 September with an anti-flak run over Holland ahead of the Arnhem armada. The following day they escorted Lancasters bombing a Dutch target.

During the disastrous Arnhem campaign the Bradwell Wing undertook ground support sorties. Absence of enemy fighters during Bomber Command day raids led to the removal of 611 Squadron from the Wing on 3 October 1944 but on 12 December, when 64 Squadron was among those escorting Lancasters to Witten (including a group from Wratting Common) they came across fifty Bf 109s near Recklinghausen. Quickly the Spitfire pilots jettisoned their drop tanks and gave chase through the clouds, but it was too late to prevent the enemy from bagging three Lancasters.

At the end of December Bradwell Bay Wing disbanded, only to soon reform when three Czech Spitfire IX squadrons – Nos 310, 312 and 313 – arrived. Remnants of No 278 ASR Squadron left for Thorney Island at the end of January.

With the Allies racing across Europe it made better sense to re-position the Spitfire Wing at Manston to where the Czechs moved on 28 February 1945. Mosquito NF30s of 151 Squadron on 1 March 1945 came in their place, their task was to intercept V-1s and their carriers. After the 'doodle-bugs' stopped coming at the end of the month No 151 was switched to night bomber support, for which they were joined by 456 Squadron in mid-March operating from here until 25 April when they flew their last sorties, four of each squadron undertaking *Night Rangers* in the Munich area while two more of 151 Squadron operated out of Juvincourt.

Squadron reduction was rapid, but not until both had 'shown the flag' over the Channel Islands on 9 May by racing across the islands at 1,000 feet. No 456 Squadron disbanded on 31 May and 151 on 17 May.

On 15 June 1945 the station's history began to turn full circle with the arrival from Hornchurch of No 287 Anti-Aircraft Co-operation Squadron. Beaufighters, Martinets, Oxfords and Spitfires equipped the squadron which left for West Malling on 10 September 1945.

Whilst it is naturally the front-line squadrons that generate most interest a very large number of RAF stations accommodate a variety of ground-based units and in September 1945, for instance, Bradwell was no exception. To be found here were No 5 Fighter Servicing Unit, No 1611 Servicing Wing HQ and No 2727 RAF Regiment Squadron, all under the control of North Weald and 11 Group.

Flying from Bradwell was far from over for soon after the war ended Bradwell Bay became a Sector Airfield serving Denghie Flats as it had done at birth. Between 13 June and 10 July 1945 No 124 Squadron came to make use of the local firing range, and No 19 Squadron's Mustangs arrived from Acklington on 13 August to await space at Molesworth given in early September. The first week of October brought in more Mustangs, Mk IIIs flown by No 309 (Polish) Squadron which was based here until 16 November 1945.

As soon as they had left, the Main Party of 2 APS took their place. The unit was in the process of changing station from Hawkinge, building up at Bradwell and proceeding to Spilsby. It lodged here until Bomber Command vacated the latter airfield at the end of January 1946.

It looked as if the station might have a post-war use for although it became a Care & Maintenance satellite of Bentwaters on 1 December 1945 plans were soon laid for its SHQ to re-open and for Mosquitoes of No 25 Squadron to move in from Castle Camps. No squadron arrived and on 23 February Fighter Command told the Air Ministry that there was no further need for it. On 10 May 1946 Bradwell became a C & M satellite of Boxted. Although apparently redundant now Bradwell's strategic position rated it as valuable and for fifteen years it awaited development being classified as a Category 5 Agricultural Airfield. RAF interest remained quite strong and when in 1953 a farmer erected poles in a runway there was much official concern! Under Plan K of 1954, in which the airfield had been raised to Category 4, there was provision for building eighteen protected dual hardstandings, and to re-open the airfield and position two day fighter squadrons here in 1955. But the station was so derelict that plans for rebuilding were abandoned. That also ended the life of Rivenhall, its intended satellite, both of which were disposed of in 1960 as surplus to needs.

Main features:
Runways: 240° 5,670ft x 150ft and FIDO equipped, 172° 3,000ft x 150ft, 120° 4,200ft x 150ft, tarmac and asphalt surfaced. *Hangars:* one Bellman, twelve Blister. *Hardstandings:* twenty-four protected pens for twin-engined aircraft, twelve open hardstandings, three bomber-type hardstandings. *Accommodation:* RAF: 125 officers, 136 SNCOs and 1,390 ORs; WAAF: 7 officers, 4 SNCOs and 255 ORs.

BUNGAY (FLIXTON), Suffolk

52°25'N/01°25'E 130ft asl; TM325870. 6 miles WSW Beccles, to S of B1062

Unforgettable it remains, linked with a tremendous, deafening din. 0820 hrs it was, on 6 June 1944, the long awaited D-Day. I was about to set off for school when I intercepted a fast increasing rumbling sound heading my way from the south-west. Within moments a B-24 nosed its way very low over the roof of the school opposite my home. A few seconds more and a sky full of Liberators developed, every B-24 literally scurrying home at roof height. It was, for all who witnessed it, a sight never seen on any other occasion – except, maybe, over Ploesti. This time no one was shooting but I was soon busy with binoculars, pencil and paper.

B-24 295059 of the 705th BS, 446th BG, settles on return to Bungay. (via Roger Freeman)

All the bombers were heading home and proudly resplendent in their brightly coloured Group markings. There were so many B-24s that single-handed it was impossible to record all the identity letters although I did my best.

I was very late for school and, inevitably, the headmaster entertained me. Mr A B Mayne was a huge, enormously impressive, very powerful man who many times assured me that unlike him my future would not involve Balliol but have more in common with failure. I therefore, on this occasion, decided to attempt to impress him by throwing in a few Group numbers and bases and a lot of hope. Had I been facing his successor, the much-liked Wing Commander Brindley Newton-John, I might really have achieved something.

'I just had to see them, Sir' I pleaded, to which he replied, 'Calm yourself, boy!' 'Sir, I've been waiting for the invasion for three days!' I honestly told him. At that claim he appeared speechless, probably with errant disbelief, and I concluded that Mr Mayne did not even seem to know that this was D-Day. Yet that it was to take place any day was common knowledge by the start of June 1944.

'Tish', as he was generally known, for once took a surprisingly benevolent view of my antics, let me off and muttered as usual 'I don't know what will become of you.' I had a feeling he didn't care much either. I never pass any one-time Liberator base without thinking of my ineffective attempts to educate him.

After thanking him I told him that for thirty minutes those B-24s back from Normandy had raced overhead, over 200 of them, adding that the leadship was from the 446th Bomb Group, a yellow and black-tailed machine hailing from Bungay and for me ushering unforgettable images from one of mankind's greatest days.

But what of Bungay? Upgrading from being Hardwick's satellite to self accounting bomber airfield stemmed from the need for additional bases to hold the 8th AF bomber force.

In September 1942 it began housing American personnel of the 428th Bomb Squadron, 310th Bomb Group. Hardwick and Bungay acted as a holding camps for the Group which was assigned to serve with the 12th AF in NW Africa. The unit's aircraft were North American B-25Cs which, in USAAF markings, were a rare sight in Britain. By the end of September 1942 nine B-25s had arrived in the UK and all quickly became unserviceable. October saw unit strength gradually rise to thirty-one B-25s held between the two airfields. They left in mid-November 1942 and on 14 December B-24Ds of the 329th Bomb Squadron, 93rd Bomb Group Hardwick, moved in. The Group's other two squadrons had left for North Africa. To maintain morale and provide some raison d'être January 1943 saw them trying their hand at delivering cloud cover solo bombing sorties over Germany thereby joining RAF Bomber Command Wellingtons which had initiated the practice. Soon discovering that cloud runs out when it is most needed, they halted their raids. The 329th joined the B-24s of the 44th Bomb Group to carry out formation bombing raids until mid-June. By then, the remainder of the 93rd Bomb Group had returned to Britain and the 329th left for Hardwick. On 15 June they were detached with the other 93rd squadrons to the Mediterranean Theatre for a part in the Ploesti raid.

Such B-24s as were left behind variously continued using Bungay while major construction work was undertaken which included the erection of two T2 hangars. It was not until the first week of November 1943, which witnessed the arrival of the 446th Bomb Group, that Bungay took its place as a fully active and developed wartime Class A airfield of the 2nd Air Division. Four squadrons of B-24Hs had flown across the Atlantic to Bungay, their ground crews travelling to Britain on the *Queen Mary*.

B-24H-15-FO 42-52583 JU-P of the 707th BS, 446th BG, flying from Bungay on 24 November 1944 (USAF).

The 446th (which later became known as the 'Bungay Buckaroos') went into action on 16 December 1943 as part of the three-Division force bombing Bremen. Subsequent targets included U-boat yards at Kiel, factories at Rostock, Berlin, Munich, marshalling yards at Koblenz, the vehicle factory at Ulm and oil refineries at Hamburg. Their B-24 41-29144 of the 704th BS was the first Liberator to fly 100 operational sorties.

After a share in the dawn assault on D-Day the 446th continued to give interdiction support to the Normandy invasion and aided the St-Lô break-out. They carried out low-level supply dropping at Nijmegen in September 1944, operated during the Ardennes battle and dropped supplies during the March 1945 Rhine crossing. Their final and 273rd operation – flown on 25 April 1945 – involved the bombing of a bridge near Salzburg, Austria.

In June 1945 the B-24s began flying back to America while their companions sailed home- as they had come – on the *Queen Mary*. Although Bungay soon became a satellite for HMS *Europa*, RNAS Halesworth, the main newcomer was No 53 Maintenance Unit which in July 1945 replaced the Americans and established a Sub-Site for bomb storage. No 94 MU on 24 November 1947 replaced them and remained here until 1 January 1950. Although not disposed of until the early 1960s it had already been put to agricultural use. Some of the concrete infra-structure of the airfield remains very much intact.

Main features:
Runways: 050° 6,000ft x 150ft, 000° 4,440ft x 150ft, 100° 4,200ft x 150ft, with concrete, pitch and wood chip surfaces. *Hangars:* two T2. *Hardstandings:* fifty loop type. *Accommodation:* 421 officers, 2,473 enlisted men.

Places of interest nearby:
There is very little to see of wartime Bungay, but very close, behind The Buck Inn by the B1062 west of Bungay town at Flixton, the excellent Norfolk & Suffolk Aviation Museum/East Anglian Aviation Heritage Centre (Telephone 01986 896644) provides splendid fare. Built up over twenty-five years it provides plenty to view. Open most days in summer, even when closed it is still worth visiting for parked in the open are Javelin FAW9 XH892 in 23 Squadron colours, Meteor F8 WF643 and an F-100 42196 in Skyblazers scheme to remind you of, or please you if you missed, their crazy day at Wethersfield!

CAMBRIDGE (TEVERSHAM), Cambridgeshire

52°12N/00°11E 35ft asl; TL484585. By Newmarket Road at city's eastern boundary

For a hundred years Marshall of Cambridge has been one of the most prominent local names. Nowadays it is linked not only with the motor car but also with an international aerospace company, one of the few left in the world known by the name of the family which founded it.

Such association is much reflected locally by the large number of people who have spent their working lives at Marshall Aerospace and hundreds for over forty years. Investing in people has won the company an extremely high sense of loyalty. Apprenticeship, sadly so rare now in industry and elsewhere, is still very much alive at Marshall Aerospace which also trains young people for NVQs while for older people the company has offered year long courses in aviation engineering. Not surprisingly the splendid team which time and again has come along with innovative ideas has always been a strong supporter of local and national charities – including the famous Addenbrooke's hospital to whom a donation was made from the profit arising on the opening day show at the present airfield. Since then changes have been dramatic and now the ILS equipped airfield regularly handles anything from home-builts to Boeing 747s.

It was in 1909 that David Marshall, grandfather of Sir Michael Marshall the present Chief Executive, established a small chauffeur driven car hire business. Catering experience won at Trinity College and in London during the 1914-18 war provided him with business skill. After the war he applied that to a car sales and maintenance business which he established in Jesus Lane close to the Pitt Club and some of his long term customers within the University.

It was not long before the interest in cars of David Marshall's and his son, the late Sir Arthur Marshall, was directed to flying. They had both seen the military blimp *Gamma* operate from Jesus College grounds in 1912, indeed in his book (*The Marshall Story* – PSL), Sir Arthur relates how he excitedly carried supplies to the blimp. His father contributed to the local paper an account of early military flying near Horseheath undertaken in 1912 by the famous fliers operating from a rough field near Hardwick.

Their interest in aviation crystallised in April 1929 when the small aerodrome at Conington closed and a new Cambridge aerodrome opened in Barnwell on a site by Newmarket Road and alongside Coldham's Common. It was reached along a narrow tree-bordered lane which remains. The official opening took place on 9 June 1929 and from October a still strong feature of Marshall enterprise began, pilot flying training. De Havilland DH 60 Moths became a daily sight, some of the earliest being among them including G-AAEH registered to Mr Arthur Marshall on 8 February 1929 and G-EBYZ, the first production DH 60 which had won the 1928 King's Cup Air Race flown by W L Hope averaging 105mph. Sadly the latter was destroyed in a crash near Hauxton on 20 September 1932. The aerodrome was a Mecca for famous pilots civilian and military, and for the local population there came Alan Cobham's Flying Circus which displayed Avro 504s, and of course that strange tri-motor Airspeed Ferry biplane. Visiting aircraft abounded but when M Henri Mignet complete with beret brought along his famous Flying Flea it declined to live up to its name.

To the old site, now Whitehill Estate, came Henri Mignet in 1936 complete with his Flying Flea. No, it didn't fly. (J. Bates)

November 1934 saw the formation of the Cambridge Aero Club and in 1936 the University Aero Club, but by then it had become clear that the airfield was too small and could not be extended. The Air Ministry expressed a desire for civilians to assist in training pilots and in 1935 Marshall acquired a large area of land on the Cambridge boundary where an elaborate aerodrome was then created. It took two years to build by which time the present No 1 Hangar was complete along with an elegant Civil Aviation Centre which has little changed. Its superb wooden panelled interior remains impressively in place. Nearby, the Airport Hotel provided tennis courts as well as refreshment, and was a popular venue when in September 1937 Cambridge Airport opened for flying and the DH 60 fleet moved in along with a Puss Moth. Flying training had resumed when on 21 January 1938 Hawker Hart (T) K6451 arrived to become the first of thousands of RAF aircraft to fly from Cambridge. K6465 flew in on 27 January by which time an amazing love affair had begun for on the previous day two Tiger Moths, K4249 and K4270, settled at their new home. There has never been a day since when a Tiger Moth was not in residence at Cambridge, scarcely a day when one has not flown from here. Likely, it seems, this active marriage of one type to one airfield is unsurpassed.

Metal skeleton of No 1 Hangar at the 1937 start of building development on the new site (Marshall Aerospace).

No 1 stage of building complete, comprising hangar and civil aviation centre (Marshall Aerospace).

Saturday, 8 October 1938, with 22 E&RFTS possessing two Audaxes and six 'Tigers', was grand opening day. Sir Kingsley Wood came in 24 Squadron's DH 86B L7596 to perform the ceremony, and over fifty visiting aircraft were tucked into the north-east corner. The white Monospar Ambulance, Avro Tutors of the CUAS and Edgar Percival performed, the latter aboard a Mew Gull and then in his very new Q6, G-AEYE. Star performers making a public debut were three Spitfires of 19 Squadron of which K9789 and K9795 would fight hard in The Battle of Britain. 'Fastest in the world', the loudspeaker claimed, and as Squadron Leader Cozens and colleagues taxied in, the small crowd rushed forward to greet them and their 'secret' mounts alarming the officials.

On 1 February 1939 No 50 Group took control of the Marshall-operated No 22 E&RFTS, then the Direct Entry Officer's Course was launched, and eight instructors were soon training thirty-two pupils. At weekends RAF Volunteer Reserve pilots learnt to fly using Tiger Moths, Harts, Audaxes, four Hinds and most impressively five Fairey Battles the first two of which (K7618 and K7625) arrived on 20 December 1938 and could be viewed from the public enclosure alongside 'No.1'. They were the first to join a VR school of which No 22 was by far the most efficient.

May 1939 saw Marshall's Flying School receive the first two production DH Moth Minors G-AFNG and G-AFNJ acquired to help train the Civil Air Guard which drew upon four DH 60s (G-AAEH, G-AAVY, G-ABDU and G-ABOY) along with four DH 60Ms including G-AACD, the pre-production demonstrator. The Company's Puss Moth G-ABIZ was in July 1938 replaced by Leopard Moth G-ACRV. Flying instruction cost a guinea an hour on a DH 60, two pounds on the Puss Moth.

By September 1939, 200 VR pilots had commenced training, seventy had their 'wings', fifty had gone solo on a Battle and ninety-five had flown at night aided by the mobile Chance light.

Declaration of war was greeted with an amazing, eerie silence at Cambridge with only the call by a Blenheim breaking the quiet. The Hart variants and DH 60s were soon replaced by many Tiger Moths and twenty-four instructors from Ipswich and Oxford E&RFTSs. The local school became No 22 EFTS on 19 September. The first eight-week wartime flying course started on 6 November by which time Marshall had begun their repair, overhaul and modification business by attending to damaged wooden Oxford trainers. In November metal-skinned Whitleys started arriving for similar attention, that work to exceptionally high standards continuing into 1944.

On 1 January 1940 the flying instructors were drafted into the RAF and in May 1940 pupil population rose from 96 to 104. Course length was cut to seven weeks and the Tiger establishment

No 2 Hangar complete and lonesome, summer 1939 (Marshall Aerospace).

Spring scene 1939. E&RFTS aircraft evident includes two Battles, Tiger Moths and DH 60s (Marshall Aerospace).

was rearranged in two Flights, one of twenty, one of forty. So desperate was the need for pilots that the flying course was reduced in June to six weeks (forty-four hours), Mr Marshall pressing the Air Ministry to increase pilot output.

By then Cambridge had become an operational airfield. Hefty Lysanders of No 2 Squadron, battle scarred in France and now attached to XI Army Corps, sat along the eastern and southern perimeters staying until January 1941. On 29 June 1940 fifteen more, of 16 Squadron, moved in from Redhill and remained until August 1940. From 1 July 1940 pairs of 'Lyssies' set out daily at

Cambridge has always been 'DH orientated'. Tiger Moths – based here since 26th January 1938 – still fly from here which in wartime was the most productive of all EFTSs. DF112, depicted in 1948, now flies from Duxford.

dawn and dusk to patrol the coast line between Wells and Lowestoft seeking German raiding parties expected to land and create bedlam. No 26 Squadron's 'B Flight arrived in August and No 2 Squadron received training in the use of 250lb gas bombs to be used if the Germans achieved a landing in force. Defiant and Blackburn Roc turret fighters for ground strafing were tried out by 2 Squadron before late autumn saw a few precious 20mm Hispano cannon delivered for attachment to Lysander stub wings. No 22 EFTS prepared to repel invaders, two Flights each of five Tiger Moths carrying bombs having, in July 1940, been attached to 2 Corps as the Marshall contribution to *Banquet Light*. By August 1941 the EFTS had available five Flights attached to the 56th Armoured Division out of the UK total of seventy maintained until August 1942.

On 3 July 1940 No 4 Flying Instructors' School opened using Magisters and soon Tiger Moths too as a result of the pressure Mr Arthur Marshall had been applying. For a time it trained instructors for advanced training establishments but in answer to desperate need also trained them for ab initio schools.

While the Lysanders patrolled, the repair business now part of the Civilian Repair Organisation overseen by MAP was ever growing. Additional premises were acquired at Nightingale's Garage near River Lane and more major site development was to come.

The first briefed attempt to bomb Marshall airport took place on 26 August 1940 when a He 111 dropped its load. On 3 September bombs were again aimed at the aerodrome the three 50kg HEs and a few incendiaries falling close to the Lysanders dispersed near Cherry Hinton. On 18 September 239 Squadron reformed and placed six Lysanders here until 22 January 1941. Late September 1940 saw 268 Squadron reform at Bury then another ten Lysanders and crews came to Cambridge for training. Numerically, Lysanders were second only to Tiger Moths roaming the circuit in profusion. To reduce that No 22 EFTS began using RLGs at Bottisham, Newmarket Heath, a field near Lord's Bridge and mainly Caxton Gibbet.

The first and only daylight attack developed on 30 December 1940 when a rare, roaming Do 215 reconnaissance aircraft showed up during a visit of senior Canadian officers. During several passes, it put bullets into three 'Tigers', an Oxford, a Magister and a Lysander while a Spitfire 'passed on the other side'! Not until 9 May, when He 111s of KG 53 attacked the Cambridge railway marshalling yards, did more bombs fall close.

The most effective raid directed at the airport was carried out at 0315 hrs on 10 September 1941 when a Ju 88C of NJG2 made a low run from the north-west and put nine HEs on the landing ground causing superficial damage to several Oxfords.

No 4 FIS received a boost in May 1942 when Master 1s for advanced training courses were posted in, the fifth joining in August by which time the first AW Albemarle had entered the works which now included workshops in T2 hangars on the north side of Newmarket Road. Not until December 1942 did the Albemarle fly, the first of a stream in varying hues and a wide variety of states for various roles.

The Albemarles were outshone on 4 February 1943 when two Mosquito NF IIs impressively raced into the circuit, peeled off and landed. Soon fitted with centimetric radar they left as Mk XIIs and revolutionised night fighting. Later Mosquitoes were modified here into Mk XVIIs featuring American radar. More Mosquito contracts followed, some involving work on *Highball* 'bouncing bomb' Mk IVs. The last Whitley V (EB302) left in immaculate state on 8 June 1944.

The Hawker Typhoon readily identifiable by the raucous scream of its Sabre engine was the other mainstream wartime input. Hundreds came for attention, JR209 which arrived in March 1944 being the first in. Work abruptly ceased a few weeks after hostilities ended. Much CRO work was undertaken in No 2 hangar completed in late Spring 1939. It was there that RAF Dakotas overhauls started in June 1944 a few days after the Normandy landings. Among the Dakotas was the example flown during the Arnhem operation by the famous comedian Flight Lieutenant Jimmy Edwards. When HM King George VI decorated him with the DFC he enquired what had happened to Edwards who astonished the parade by loudly replying 'I burnt my bum, Sir.' HM turned away to stifle his merriment. The arrival of the 'Dak' initiated the continuing Marshall Aerospace association with airliners.

By 1945 the EFTS comprised five Flights, the intensity of activity being astounding. My diary records that on one occasion no less than sixty-six Tiger Moths were in the circuit, and I am sure that was no record. Throughout the war it was 'Tiger Moths, Tiger Moths, Tiger Moths' local people unkindly referring to them as 'Marshall's Messerschmitts'. Nothing could be less true for they helped produce many a famous flier, top scorer 'Johnnie' Johnson for one.

By the end of the war Cambridge held a wide assortment of hangars without which the thousands of aircraft repaired here could never have been processed. Large civilian type hangars, Blisters, T2s, a Bellman and even a large Super Robin, all were here. As well as main tasks Marshall overhauled Gladiators for the Met Flights, Fortress 1s and carried out break-down of the Spitfire Xs. In August 1945 a Hamilcar TK745 was received for conversion to Mk X. When the contract for seventy-five was soon cancelled the huge glider turned itself into fire wood!

An amazing miscellany of aircraft types had called in wartime. Among them was the GAL Owlet, a 1940 all-yellow Heyford, naval Beechcraft Travellers, wartime Anson XIIs, a Hotspur I with Hector, the prototype Firefly, assorted Barracudas, a solitary 149 Squadron Stirling which night landed, a B-17 'LL D' of the 91st BG which crashed in mid-field, P-38s, C-47s, Blenheim Vs, hosts of impressed ex-civil types and on 7 July 1945 the Fw 200C-4 (013) GC+AE used by Gestapo Chief Herr Himmler. A Ju 88G called a few days later.

Miles Aerovans of Air Contractors frequently came in 1947 in connection with the race horse business.

Few Lancasters called, but LL795 came late 1945 for installation of 'Amber', for night flying training.

During the war Marshall CRO handled over 5,000 aircraft and trained over 20,000 pilots at 22 EFTS Cambridge and 29 EFTS Clyffe Pypard. The former had the highest output of any UK EFTS.

Much reduced post-war overhaul work at first centred upon Mosquitoes and Dakotas, the latter including British civil examples and one for UNRAA. A milestone was passed on 1 January 1946 when Lady Bragg flying Tiger Moth G-ACDG made the first post-war private civil flight in Britain. Later during that raw day a Proctor making the first private post-war charter journey stopped briefly at Cambridge. Marshall soon had several civil registered Tiger Moths with which they offered private flying training lessons, while available for charter were two Rapides – later three – and two Proctor Vs. As Dennis Pasco's excellent book *Tested* (Grub Street) relates, Marshall pilots now included some outstanding wartime fliers among them Les Worsdell for so long a leader in the Marshall team. Also here was Herbert Tappin, one of the few pilots to shoot down a giant Bv 222 six-engined flying-boat an example of which so memorably grunted its slow way over Cambridge in summer 1945.

Mosquitoes arrived for attention until the mid-1950s. Famous DZ414 came and, by the end of the war NF 30s like MT487 ZK-L of No 25 Squadron. (John Rawlings).

Mosquito NF30 NT431 which I photographed in July 1948, retained black under surfaces during MU storage, its wartime 100 Group camouflage worn when serving 239 Squadron. Overhauled and delivered to the French Air Force.

Late 1940s brought resumption of military overhauls. Included was Mosquito NF 30 MM742 previously with 406 and 410 Squadrons. After arrival on 22 July 1948, it was overhauled, then joined the French Air Force.

Steady decline of the EFTS ended with its closure on 30 April 1947. At once No 22 Reserve Flying School took its place. Its Tiger Moths were replaced in 1951 with Chipmunks. The RFS closed on 30 April 1954.

Since 1944 the Cambridge University Air Squadron had been flying from here at first using an Oxford and in peacetime Tiger Moths. Among them was a strange sounding Cirrus-engined example, W7950 ex-G-AFSL. January 1950 saw the CUAS become the second RAF unit to have the then exciting Chipmunk which type they operated until March 1975 when Bulldogs replaced them. Like the CUAS, No 5 Air Experience Flight operated Chipmunks and after they were retired the AEF and CUAS jointly used Bulldogs. Training flights using Bulldogs ceased on 6 August, the Bulldogs leaving for Newton on the 12th. The AEF and CUAS moved to Wyton during August 1999 then re-equipped with Grub 115E Tutors.

From 1946 to the early 1960s Tiger Moths including G-AIBN served the civilian flying school.

Post-war years brought civilian light aircraft like M.38ii Messengers. Behind G-AIAJ on 17 May 1948 stands Alan J Wright, author of Ian Allan Civil Aircraft Markings guide.

On 14 September 1946 a Battle of Britain Day Display attracted a jet (a Meteor III) to Cambridge for the first time. Not until 19 March 1947 did one land and stay. It was EE409 of 92 Squadron, Duxford, which put down short of fuel.

International tension brought increased military activity in the works. Marshall overhauled RAF Dakotas participating in the Berlin Airlift while Mosquito work declined as the Company switched to Sea Hornets, Vampire T11s, Venom night-fighters. In the North Works a production assembly line for Venom fighter-bombers was established. Those activities brought expansion of the Marshall Design Office and led to the planning of a feeder airliner in the Dove/Heron class named MA 1. For the RAF's night-fighter force modifications were designed and conversion undertaken of Brigands and Valettas enabling them to carry AI Mk IX used in the Javelin.

Boundary layer airflow research had long interested Cambridge University Engineering Department which used an Anson carrying a pitot comb and aerofoil section slung below its belly. Marshall Aerospace devised a custom-built aeroplane for the task, the ill-fated perforated wing MA 4 based upon Auster VI VF665 and regularly updated. Surface drag removal by suction was envisaged for carrier-based jet fighters.

In 1952 Viscount airliners began arriving for fitting out and modification. An increasing number of operators around the world were soon appreciating the quality and dedication of Marshall workmanship. To enable entry to No 2 Hangar a Viscount needed to be tilted nose-up to allow the tail to clear the entrance.

DF112 currently active at Duxford was RUC-D of the CUAS in 1949.

Pictured in February 1950, Chipmunk WB566 RUC-E of the CUAS, second unit to equip with them.

Arrival from France on 1 May 1949 of the Bristol 170 Freighter F-BCJM was spectacular. So big, so many horses!.

Horses often now come and go in Boeing 757s of DHL.

A need for hangars suitable for such aircraft was vital and with commendable foresight Sir Arthur and the Company saw to it that a large hangar, No 10, was constructed adjacent to No 2. Soon, an extension became No 12, the hangar number sequences having embraced T2s of the North Works.

With ample space on offer the Company received a major boost in 1952 when it secured a contract to undertake work on EE Canberras. A concrete runway essential for them was laid in 1954. Although strong, it was narrow, and when in 1954 the company obtained a prestigious contract to support Valiant V-bombers the runway needed widening.

The new hangars were soon also accommodating Bristol Britannias, Airspeed Ambassadors and, keeping faith with de Havilland, welcoming their superb Comet. Among those were hyper secret R.Mk2s whose special equipment layout was undertaken at Cambridge.

In the late 1950s it was not uncommon to see four white Valiants at The Airport, also early bare metal examples including WP199. Marshall Aerospace adapted that to carry for trials *Blue Steel*, the British nuclear armed stand-off launch missile.

Marshall operated Langham's CAACU attracted visitors away from target towing, like Beaufighter TT 10 RD807 8Q-G.

Mid-1950s and Cambridge has many new buildings including a giant new hangar. Valettas await T4 conversion. Visible are Brigands and Canberras. (Marshall Aerospace)

Rare visitors still abound. Grumman Mallard G-ASCS rested here in February 1969.

Tiger Moth G-AOEI in March 1987 pausing over the line of Teversham Lane.

Work with the deterrent led to consideration of how fast Valiants could 'scramble'. Last minute pre-flight checks such as removal of pitot head covers could delay them so the Marshall team devised solutions, demonstrated them and Bomber Command followed the suggested course.

Construction of Concorde noses in 'No 2' on a specially built floor area was an exacting task demanding fine manufacturing tolerances. State of the art tape-controlled milling machines working over twenty-four hours non-stop carved a Concorde engine nacelle side panel from a block of metal. Marshall also worked upon the design of the Saro F177 rocket fighter, undertook work on the Firestreak missile and fitted a belly pod to a Vulcan for trials of the Tornado's RB199 engine for which programme two Buccaneers were fitted with special instrumentation.

A part of Marshall Aerospace current activity is rooted in the 1960s when rectification, superbly appointing and modifying business executive aircraft commenced. An early contract required orchids (needing high humidity) to impossibly flourish in a BAC-111 and satisfy a well-known shipping magnate. Needless to say, the company answered the need. Backbone of the business aircraft section was the Grumman Gulfstream, beginning with the Ford operated Mk 1 turbo-prop aircraft and later the most advanced variants including the superb Mk V trans-Atlantic high-speed jet and military variants. Cessna Citation jets (used by the Company) from many owners also come for attention. Every Gulfstream had an individualistic internal fit, and all left superbly appointed to the highest possible standards. Business jets used to be handled in No 16 hangar. Many BAe 146s also passed through – some even brought from China – for fitting out and various modifications prior to painting in No 12.

Marshall Aerospace will always be remembered for their association with Lockheed through the C-130 Hercules and TriStar. When in 1964 the RAF ordered sixty-six Hercules transports there was strong lobbying to fit British engines, but instead less dramatic changes were incorporated. Those, and a curious glossy brown and black camouflage coat, were provided at Cambridge. The new long-lasting polyurethane paint required 'baking' after application to ensure durability. The company first tried it using a Vampire T11 once intended for conversion into a 'biz-jet'.

Luxurious Grumman Gulfstreams were long a common sight. HZ-MAL brought race goers for 'The Cambridgeshire'.

The first unpainted C-130K Hercules, XV177, arrived from the USA on Sunday 19 December 1966 and first flew in a strange two-tone brown scheme with glossy black under-surfaces in April 1967. C-130s – mainly RAF but also of other eastern hemisphere operators – still come to Cambridge for type support.

Major tasks involving the RAF Hercules fleet have included eradicating fungi from fuel tanks, renewing main spars, inserting fore and aft fuselage lengthening sections thereby converting almost half the fleet into C Mk 3s, applying revised grey and green paint schemes, keeping the overworked C. Mk 1 tactical fleet flying and most remarkably enabling the Hercules to reach the Falkland Islands.

Their great distance from Ascension, Britain's closest base, left them vulnerable to predators and when on 2 April 1982 the Argentines invaded there was little that could immediately be done to drive out the intruders. As well as a large naval and Army Task Force the RAF sent tankers and bombers to carry out operations from Wideawake on Ascension. To provide a transport back-up Marshall received on 15 April an instruction to design an in-flight refuelling system for the Hercules using V-bomber probe. Intensive design and engineering work resulted in a probe being installed in XV200 only ten days after the start of the ITP, the aircraft making a successful first flight on 28 April. On 5 May, a mere three weeks after work began, XV200 reached Lyneham ready for active service.

On 3 July 2009 C-130H G-988, flew for the first time in 18 years for the RNethAF. Brought from the US desert, the ex-US Navy aircraft acquired a 'glass cockpit'. It was delivered in February 2010.

Since December 1966 Lockheed C-130s have come for attention. Royal Swedish Air Force '848' photographed on 30 June 2009 looks small against the 120 foot tall tower.

Light grey Hercules C4 ZH874 flying over Cambridge features DIRCM turrets and green coloured underbelly protection.

Met Hercules Mk 2 XV208 Snoopy. Later tested the TP-400D turboprop engine for the Airbus A.400M.
It made 18 flights and flew for 55 hours with its last flight being made on 30 September 2009.
Photographed 17 March, 2009.

Speed differential and handling qualities between the Victor tanker and the probed Hercules were extensive. They resulted in Marshall being asked on 30 April to design an AAR version of the Hercules, late afternoon of 1 May seeing XV296 arrive for conversion. That involved installation in the fuselage of large fuel tanks and a hose and drogue feed unit which would trail from a modified cargo door. Again, a first flight – on 8 June – proved very successful although tests at Boscombe Down showed elevator buffeting. Strakes were added to the cargo door and with adjustments complete the first tanker joined the Lyneham Transport Wing on 30 June. Marshall ingenuity and long hours of intensive work spanning a brief period had again paid off and provided Britain with a vital air bridge to the Falklands.

AARs contribution to that campaign was plain for all to see. So was a need for larger transports with AAR facilities. At the 1982 SBAC Show the RAF reviewed acquisition of the KC-10 but instead the path followed once more involved Marshall Aerospace. In February 1983 the Company received a contract to convert into tankers six TriStar airliners about to retire from BA. A further three TriStars would be fitted out for the RAF as passenger transports.

Work immediately started on hangar No 17 able to accommodate the wide bodied airliners. Very large it would be and in size second only to Heathrow's making it one of the largest in Europe. Previous proposals had involved extending the North Works but Boulton & Paul – in a mere eight months – erected No 17 on an area which became known as the South Works.

The first TriStar arrived on 16 February 1983, and as ZD950 and converted into a single point tanker, first flew on 9 July 1985. Each TriStar being slightly different had made the conversion a repeated challenge.

Four of the tankers returned for the fitting of a large cargo door which was a creditable achievement. It led to considerable effort being devoted to marketing civil TriStar freighter conversions and Kalitta led the way. McDonnell Douglas DC-10s and MD-11s have also periodically come for varying reasons, seven of the latter operated by Delta Airlines passing through the works in 1999 for modifications including installation of additional fuel tanks.

A very different activity during not much less than half a century has characterised the Airport's summer scheduled flights linking Cambridge with the Channel Islands. A number of airlines used their fleets of Miles Marathons, Dakotas, DC-4Ms, HP Heralds, Viscounts, Short SD 3-30s, BAe 146s, Dash 7s and Fokker 100s. The runs ended in 1998 because the proximity of Stansted altered the trade.

In 1988 Suckling Airways moved their main base from Ipswich to Cambridge from where Dornier 228s operated daily services to Schiphol. Suckling which for a time also served Manchester gradually expanded introducing larger pressurised Do 328s for additional operations involving Luton and Stansted. Concentrating on business passengers, they presented no-hassle high quality personal service. October 1999 brought an announcement that Suckling had become ScotAirways and were linked with Stagecoach. Their Do 328s come to Cambridge for major overhauls.

During Easter and autumn prestigious world stature university conferences have for many years attracted airliners chartered from various airlines. Since 1946 special charters and privately owned aircraft used by the Newmarket horse racing fraternity have also been frequent visitors. Bristol Freighters, CL-44, 146s 737s and 757s often from Ireland or the Continent come seasonally.

Suckling Airways operated from Cambridge before becoming ScotAir and converting to Do 328s like G-BWIR.

Easter and autumn have long attracted university conference visitors. Unusual was DHC Dash 8 D-BOBY of Hamburg Airlines on the runway end by Coldhams Lane.

Dornier Do 228 G-BUXT of Suckling Airways, October, 1999. Original buildings in view.

Even the massive ANT-124-100 UR-82008 was dwarfed by No 17 Hangar.

In the late 1990s the new C-130J, a re-engined Hercules much computerised and featuring a 'glass cockpit' became a prominent sight at Cambridge. Marshall Aerospace designed suitable ground equipment for RAF use and fitted the boom kit in the fuel line. A stall warning stick shaker was also installed here, along with various equipment items to prepare the factory fresh aircraft for the RAF. Lockheed found the C-130J programme demanding, for although the more powerful GM 2100 engines weigh less they have a different profile, a changed thrust line and drive six-bladed high-tech Dowty propellers all of which considerably altered the aircraft's handling characteristics. Preparing the necessary software was highly demanding, but the new model showed a considerable improvement in performance enhanced by carrying all fuel internally.

Marshall working closely with Lockheed has designed and engineered for the South African Air Force a 'glass cockpit' fitted in three low flight hour C-130Bs.

It was also a South African connection which, on 26 August 1984, brought to Cambridge its largest, heaviest visitor so far, an Antonov An-124 which was delivering a Rooivalk helicopter which it was hoped to sell to the British Army. When the Antonov departed light it steeply roared off into a spectacular and memorable tight steeply ascending turn.

Large as it was, it in no way could equal the thrill of seeing a BA Boeing 747 jumbo jet arrive at Cambridge to where some came direct from Boeing. The practicality of flying such huge aircraft at Cambridge was explored when G-BNLE called on 12 September 1997. From February 1998, 747s came for two or three week stays basically to have video screens installed in the back or by the side of passenger seats and some to have changes made to crew accommodation and toilet facilities. To see as many as three BA 747s outside the large hangar must, for the family and the work force, have been tremendously satisfying.

Another highlight of the '90s was 'Stargazer', the TriStar modified here first to carry below the belly a 40,000lb Pegasus satellite launch rocket then, in 1999, provisioning for the carriage and launch of the X-34 reusable spacecraft. That confirms the company's title, Marshall Aerospace.

What would David Marshall, the company founder, make of the company's amazing achievements? He would surely have concluded that his foresight was well founded. His place was taken by Sir Arthur Marshall who throughout the war and troubled peace, very cleverly led the company from the world of ancient looking biplanes to a place in the Concorde programme, and wisely ensured that suitable hangars to support the company's business were available at the right time. He was aged eighty when he retired, certainly a great figure in British aviation. Now it is Sir Michael Marshall, Chairman and Chief Executive of Marshall Aerospace, Sir Arthur's son, who very skilfully guides the impressive family concern. In October 1999 the company – which embraces a widespread car and specialised varied vehicle business – celebrated their centenary and throughout a weekend of events pride in achievement was everywhere apparent.

Boeing 747s looked huge at Cambridge – but No 17 Hangar still dwarfed them.

Seeing a 747 on Cambridge runway remains unforgettable.

Instrumented here as a weapons target for RAE Llanbedr, Meteor U 16 WK800 being test flown by Tim Mason.

A terrible noise overtook the folk in Sainsbury. Amazingly, a Mildenhall-based MH-53J was using the NDB. An RC-135 once did likewise.

A pristine C Mk 4 yet to enter service paraded at Marshalls' 70th Anniversary in 1999.

TriStar 'Stargazer' modified to carry a Pegasus space rocket seen departing for the US on a snowy morning in 1987.

Marshall Aerospace Cambridge Airport looking south. Foreground 'industrial' buildings are related to Marshall road vehicle business. (Marshall Aerospace)

Sir Arthur Marshall's Memorial Service in No 17 Hangar. XV214 is to the right of the dais. (Marshall Aerospace)

Aerospace is a tough, unforgiving, enormously expensive and still pioneering world. Despite the risks, though, aviation still generates thrills as great as any. If you are ever fortunate enough to visit Marshall Aerospace contemplate upon what can be achieved when you work hard and value the efforts of all those around you. How absolutely fabulous it must have felt to gaze from your window upon a 747 landing on your own aerodrome!

Main features:

Hangars (December 1944): Permanent Civil – No 1 200ft x 100ft, No 2 300ft x 200ft. Wartime civil – one 160ft x 150ft, one 195ft x 95ft. one Super Robin 240ft x 150ft. one Bellman 240ft x 120ft, one permanent hangar 96ft x 87ft. Around perimeter eight Blisters and one Double Blister (remaining). Additional to these were T2s on the North Site.

Hangars (current): Nos 1 and 2 as given, No 10 and No 12 are joined with No 2, No 16 contains a C-130 unit and stores, and the huge No 17, 476ft x 282ft with two 230ft doors includes a wide-body paint shop. One Double Blister unit is used by PFA in SW corner previously the CU Gliding Club HQ. A new hangar attached to the Business Centre opened in 2008.

Sufficient hangar space has been vital to the company since the work here needs to be undertaken internally and in the correct conditions. An indication of the quantity of throughput is shown by these figures for the number of aircraft attended to1998: Gulfstream – 140, C-130 – 59, Citation – 35, 747-400 – 30, TriStar – 27, DC-10 – 4 and one each of the following types – A320, Boeing 727, MD-11 and Sentry. 1999 saw seven MD-11s of Delta Airlines have fuel tank modifications. In March 1999 a typical Gulfstream IV contract was for cabin re-trim and the fitting of two triple divans to fold out as a bed. Meanwhile the design staff were working on the possibility of adapting the Boeing 767 to answer an Air Staff requirement for a new strategic tanker for the RAF.

Runways: asphalt: Main 23/05 6,550ft x 153ft; grass: 23/05 2,983ft x 116ft south-east and parallel to main runway, 35/10 2,316ft x 116ft, 20/02 2,956ft x 116ft. Taxiway B links the perimeter track eastern end to the main runway, taxiway C links it with the customs pad and taxiway D links No 17 apron with the main runway. Three rows each of nine parking slots on grass outside general aviation centre. Special facilities for helicopters. Cambridge Airport is without doubt the most interesting in the area.

Places of interest nearby:

Just inside the city boundary is the City Cemetery in the centre of which is a War Cemetery containing the resting places of many fliers. Opposite the east end of the airfield is one of the city's four park and ride sites. There is little of aeronautical interest in Cambridge whose popularity is based upon attractive college buildings and not its city centre once so appealing but which, so sadly, has little to commend it.

CASTLE CAMPS, Cambridgeshire

52°04N/00°22E 420ft asl; TL630425. 3 miles NW of Steeple Bumpstead, W of Camps Green

How often names mislead and milestone events occur in the most unlikely places. Windswept and bleak, Castle Camps resting surprisingly high at 420ft asl on the East Anglian Heights certainly fell into both categories. Difficult it was just to find Castle Camps airfield in its hey day situated as it was over the brow of a hillock among fields, and accessible only via a lane near the church and which, in wartime, was blocked to unauthorised folk.

Of the airfield from where Stanford Tuck flew as one of 'the Few' there are merely remnants of huts and runway fragments. Remain they do to the squawking of pigs and the rustle of crops in the aforementioned wind which soars across bringing lashing rain from the open west or bitter cold direct from the Arctic to prosperous farmland. Hard to believe that it was at Castle Camps where on 26 January 1942 that the unsurpassed Mosquito night fighter, albeit in dual control form, joined its first RAF squadron.

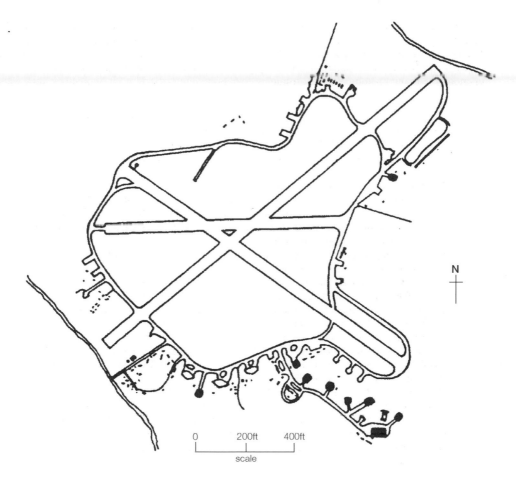

Diagram showing 1944 layout of Castle Camps. Imposing runways on to a basic satellite result in a strange layout. A solitary Bellman hangar is supplemented by eight Over Blister types. Domestic sites are scattered.

Preparation, levelling and grass sowing on the site chosen to be Debden's Unbuilt Satellite known as 'F.1', the first satellite in No 11 (Fighter) Group's Sector F (ie. the Debden Sector), commenced in September 1939. Ready by May 1940, it came into use the following month and served as Debden's satellite until replaced by Great Sampford in 1942.

On 27 June 1940 Hurricanes of Debden's 85 Squadron (whose detached 'A' Flight was at Martlesham Heath) moved its 'B' Flight to F.1 where tented accommodation and little else provided sparse creature comfort. Squadron Leader Peter Townsend was among those who flew from here with the squadron. On 22 July F.1 became the base for all night Sector patrolling for which goose neck flares had to be lit, but it was shipping protection off East Anglia that mainly occupied the squadron. On 13 August No 85 Squadron consolidated itself at Debden 'A' Flight returning from Martlesham and 'B' Flight from Castle Camps.

'Treble One' alias No 111 Squadron based at Croydon was rested at Castle Camps from the front line at the end of 18 August 1940, and next day made a direct swap with No 85 at what was the height of the Battle of Britain. The newcomers, half of them using Castle Camps, were involved in scramble response to enemy activity off the East Coast before exchanging once more with No 85 which returned in full to Castle Camps on 3 September. Two days later the squadron was ordered to exchange bases with No 73 which left Church Fenton on 5 September, established its HQ at Debden and positioned all its Hurricanes at the satellite still very primitive and called 'F.1'. Action overtook them almost immediately for, a mere four hours after arrival on 5 September, they were engaging over the Thames Estuary a raid heading for oil tanks at Thameshaven. The fight to protect those cost 73 Squadron one pilot killed, another wounded, three Hurricanes shot down and three damaged. It was a ferocious introduction to the fight in which German casualties amounted to one He 111 of KG 53 damaged. On the following day 73 Squadron again hurled itself into action from Castle Camps, and over north Kent as well as the Thames Estuary. Pilot Officer Marchand drew first blood from the new station, a Bf 109 of JG 26.

Late afternoon on 7 September when the Luftwaffe launched its first heavy raid on London, No 73 Squadron helping to defend over the Billericay area the approach to London weighed into a formation of Bf 110s claiming three destroyed. Back at Castle Camps rough tents near the aircraft were all the comfort available for weary pilots and hard worked ground crews, who fed in a marquee erected in adjacent woodland alongside which the station's only maintenance hangar was later sited. From their high, exposed position, the personnel had a clear view of the horrendous incineration of London's East End where rivers of burning sugar surged through the mean streets and minute particles of glass surged about in the inferno. As they watched they awaited news of a seaborne invasion expected the next day but which never materialised.

Every day 73 Squadron at Castle Camps was ready for action. At mid-morning on 15 September, now called Battle of Britain Day, they intercepted a raid over Maidstone claiming two Bf 109s. Another they shot down as they flew home low over the Blackwater Estuary. At 1445 hrs the squadron was 'scrambled' again, the only six serviceable Hurricanes coming face to face over Maidstone with 100 German bombers three of which they claimed to damage. On 21 September the squadron began to be reinforced daily by detachments drawn from 257 Squadron, Martlesham, and usually led by Flight Lieutenant Stanford-Tuck. Two days later Debden-based No 17 with 73 and 257 Squadrons operating in a combined formation were 'bounced' over Kent in an encounter which cost 73 Squadron five Hurricanes. Another fierce battle, with Bf 110s, occurred on 27 September.

For much of October Nos 17, 73 and 257 Squadrons either Debden, Castle Camps, Martlesham or North Weald based operated together until the 23rd when No 73 Squadron received the news that it was to move overseas and become a night fighter squadron. They left Castle Camps during the first week of November.

Work now began to upgrade Castle Camps which was extended and enhanced. Three tarmac runways were laid, '06/24' being the longest at 5,850ft x 150ft, '31/13' the next at 4,800ft x 150ft and '10/28' at 3,210ft x 150ft. All were of unusual lengths in order to fit the available area, their central intersection being most unusually very close. A Bellman hangar was erected and eventually eight Over Blisters supplementing sixteen hardstandings each intended to accommodate one twin-engined fighter for which the 'new' version of Castle Camps had been planned. Permanent accommodation still primitive was also built at dispersed sites.

SHQ opened in time for Wing Commander Gordon Slade, later a test pilot for Fairey Aviation, to bring in the RAF's first all-black Mosquito, a dual control T Mk III W4073, on 26 January 1942. Fitting AI radar at No 32 MU delayed arrival of Mosquito II night-fighters and even when on 9 March 1942 two (W4087 and W4098) were at last ferried in they still lacked essential equipment. Night flying proved possible only on 13 March such was their unserviceability. By the end of the month No 157 had fourteen Mosquitoes. To afford Merlin handling experience to the pilots of No 157 Squadron (officially based at Debden, but using the Built Satellite to maintain secrecy), a Merlin-engined Beaufighter II had arrived on 22 February and supplemented the Magister N3880 used for local journeys.

So exotic was the Mosquito fighter that very soon it was wrapped in many amazing stories. One told how a notice in the cockpit reminded the pilot not to exceed 600mph! For all its excellence the 'Mossie' was not a forgiving aeroplane, and there were some unfortunate accidents. Worrying moments also surrounded cowling panels which were repeatedly burnt through by hot exhaust gases. Accommodation and poor workshops at Castle Camps still left much to be desired but the bugs were worked out at this airfield loathed by many of its occupants. Despite its reputation for being damp which played havoc with the aircraft's electrics, its close proximity to de Havilland's Hatfield base was the main reason for its selection for the Mosquito introduction.

Not until 27 April 1942 were crews of 157 Squadron ordered on their first operational night patrols in response to the 'Baedeker raid ' on Norwich, and it was 22 May before the squadron was declared fully operational due to engine manifold problems and a high accident rate. Apart from radar contacts success eluded No 157 until 30 May when Squadron Leader Ashfield flying W4099 chased a Dornier 217E, fired at it off Dover and claimed it as the first enemy aircraft to fall to 157 Squadron. It was not the first credited to a Mosquito, that prize undoubtedly belongs to Wittering's 151 Squadron. Confirmation of these early claims by Mosquito crews are unlikely to be established now. Luftwaffe records indicate that four Do 217s failed to return from operations on 30 May. South coast radar lost trace of Ashfield's quarry, but a Do 217 fitting the activity came down off the Netherlands and seems likely to have been his. No 157 Squadron was very unlucky, for many of their patrols and scrambles brought no reward. Not until 22 August did they have a proven success, when Wing Commander Slade brought down a Do 217E-4 of II/KG2 which crashed at Worlingworth.

The operation build up had resulted in only sixteen patrols from Castle Camps in May, fifty-one at night in June, ninety-seven in July and 132 in August. During autumn some day patrols were flown, but by the end of the year there was so little enemy activity over Britain that in December only twenty-nine sorties were launched and one contact recorded. In January and February 1943 there was almost no German activity in the Sector and that resulted in a very important change, the use of Mosquitoes for night offensive operations in support of Bomber Command in which Castle Camps played a major part.

On 15 March 1943 No 157 Squadron moved to Bradwell Bay to commence night intruders over the Low Countries, and No 605 (County of Warwick) Squadron which had been similarly employing Bostons replaced them. Rearmed with Mosquito IIs the previous month, '605' flew their first Mosquito sorties on 10 March then suddenly they were on 14 March ordered to Castle Camps and moved there next day. In recording that event the squadron's diarist wrote 'See Rome and die, see Castle Camps and pass out'. That expresses the general feeling of the squadron when it arrives at the new base. Actually it's not as bad as that by any means. It's the comparison with Ford that makes the chaps seem browned off. They'll get used to it. Many worse places to be.' From Ford fourteen aircraft arrived on the 15th including an Oxford and a Magister. The squadron wasted no time for the following night two Mosquitoes operated, Wing Commander G L Denholme (DZ684-H) over Soesterberg and Deelen and Squadron Leader C D Tomalin over Gilze Rijen. Primarily, intruders were intended to disrupt German bomber operations against the UK. More worrying was the possibility that their night attacks might be directed against RAF bomber bases. For patrols over the Netherlands, Mosquitoes had far longer loiter duration than Bostons.

No 605s conversion to Mosquitoes soon showed good results for on 15 April Flying Officer R R Smart destroyed two Ju 87s at Avord and damaged three trains. In all seven trains were strafed that month by which time long-range tanks fitted to all the aircraft extended their range as far as Colmar and Bordeaux. During a detachment to Peterhead Squadron Leader Bocock flew a five hour intruder to Stavanger, Norway. A very experienced South African pilot, he was killed when he crashed near Lewes during operational flying on 23 April.

May 1943 found No 605 along with another six Mosquito fighter squadrons active over German night-fighter bases in the Low Countries, Castle Camps being the forward base for such activity. On 23 May, for instance, fourteen 'Ranger' Mosquitoes drawn from seven squadrons took part in intensive bomber support operations and No 605 had six Mosquitoes operating. Success was limited to an enemy aircraft attacked at Vechta by 151 Squadron. Two nights later thirteen visiting Mosquitoes operated from the station, and on 29 May Squadron Leader Linn of 605 Squadron destroyed a Do 217 near St Trond.

During June 605 Squadron without loss flew eighty-five intruders mainly to the Netherlands, carried out two special operations and twelve times flew Distil sorties during which they tried to shoot down Ju 52s attempting to explode British sown magnetic mines.

The Luftwaffe had recently started night nuisance raids using Fw 190 fighter-bombers one of which at around 0300 hrs on 15 June crept along the eastern side of Castle Camps where the Glem Lights were on, turned and dropped a bomb which fell in a field near the 'Marquis of Granby' public house damaging five houses. A second raid in September 1943 was carried out by an Me 410 which dropped a solitary 250kg bomb. It exploded as two Mosquitoes were landing and set fire to another on a dispersal. Compared with 605's activity this was puny for July had seen No 605 carry out eighty-two night sorties and Castle Camps become a satellite of North Weald.

On 3 July Squadron Leader Heath flew to Evreux making the squadron's first operational sortie using a Mosquito Mk VI fighter-bomber. Mosquitoes were at this time being introduced to *Flowers*, more precisely defined night intruder operations against airfields. The squadron also flew *Rangers* widely and deep into Europe, but their greatest contribution was the introduction of the Mosquito to *Serrate* night bomber support operations in which they gave loose cover to Bomber Command night raids.

Their first such operation took place on 31 August in support of a Berlin raid. Four nights later they began *Mahmouds*, operations on the flank of the bomber stream designed to intercept enemy night fighters.

No 605 squadron left Castle Camps on 6 October 1943, after working with Mosquitoes of Nos 9 and 10 Groups. No 456 Squadron was among those, and participated in *Mahmouds* from Castle Camps.

Mosquitoes had not been the station's only residents for on 15 June 1943 a new squadron, No 527, formed there. Its task was calibration of radar at stations in East Anglia and for which a motley collection of Blenheim IVs and Vs, Hurricanes and de Havilland Hornet Moths operating from the north-east corner of the airfield were used. A few Blenheims wore the predominantly white scheme of Coastal Command because they often operated over the North Sea.

Mosquitoes once more dominated the scene when No 410 (Canadian) Squadron brought along seventeen Mosquito NF XIIIs between 28 and 30 December 1943. No 410 was a night home defence squadron positioned to defend the north-eastern approaches to London, and advance intelligence indicated the launch of a major attack on New year's Eve. Instead, the 'baby blitz' materialised on 21 January 1944, No 410 Squadron being in the firing line and putting up eight aircraft. They drew no blood for the air was drenched with *Düppel*, the German equivalent of *Window*, and it much confused the British. Defeating it was far from easy but during another raid, on 28 January, No 410 claimed a Ju 88 and thereafter the success rate steadily rose. A Do 217 was shot down at sea on 3 February, a Ju 88 and a Ju 188 on the 13th, success repeated on the 22nd and again on 14 March. The most spectacular kill was a He 177 shot down at Cole End by Flying Officer S S Huppert in the early hours of 19 April during which month ninety-six night interception sorties were flown. The Canadian squadron which had been undertaking some flying from Hunsdon moved there on 28-29 April 1944 as part of the repositioning of forces to cover the Normandy invasion. By then there had been a number of other noteworthy changes at Castle Camps.

On 28 February 1944 No 527 Squadron left for Snailwell. Next day 91 Squadron's Griffon Spitfires, Mk XIIs and six of the impressive and hefty Spitfire F Mk XIVs replaced them. The second squadron to dabble with the latter, they encountered numerous problems including engine stacks fast burning away and a need for frequent tyre changes due to the weight of the aircraft. The squadron left for Drem on 17 March taking thirteen Mk XIVs and four Mk XIIs. The Spitfires had come at a time when preparations for D-Day were everywhere evident. At Castle Camps No 149 Airfield HQ was established on 1 March 1944 and as part of 85 Group moved forward on 4 April 1944. No 85 Group Communication Flight formed here on 1 May 1944 and left for Heston on 3 June 1944.

In place of the Spitfires came No 486 (New Zealand) Squadron flying Hawker Typhoons. Although trained in January 1944 to fly Tempests these had been switched to No 3 Squadron on 28 February. On 3 April No 486 received a Tempest V with which to recommence conversion to the fast and furious newcomer. At the same time two Typhoons were daily placed at Bradwell Bay on 'readiness'. On 29 April, with conversion and Wing training with No 3 Squadron completed, they quit No 149 Airfield Castle Camps and joined No 150 Airfield Newchurch to where next day they took their sixteen Tempests. The Typhoons they left behind to be allotted away.

Castle Camps lay quiet for a short time. Now a Forward Airfield (Night Fighter) in North Weald Sector it received No 68 Squadron in June 1944 along with their Mosquito NF XVIIs. During July they began to partially re-equip with NF XIXs and first operated them on 26 July. Their task was the destruction of V-1 flying bombs the first of which they had shot down on 9 July. The squadron moved to Coltishall on 27 October 1944 and continued the task.

A five-week sojourn beginning on 8 October was made by Mosquito XIIIs of 151 Squadron, and on 27 October 25 Squadron, Mosquito NF XVII equipped, joined them. Soon after, the latter squadron re-equipped with Mosquito NF XXXs. Bomber support was once more the station's main activity and was enhanced when more XXXs arrived in the hands of 307 (Polish) Squadron which was in residence between the end of January and June 1945. On the 27th of that month 85 Squadron arrived, also with more Mosquito XXX night fighters. On 28 July six of those escorted the Prime Minister's aircraft to the Potsdam Conference.

Mosquito NF 30 VY-Q of No 85 Squadron.

Wind down of the station began in October 1945 and on the 9th No 85 moved out to Tangmere. The nineteen Mosquito XXXs of 25 Squadron left for Boxted (which had been the Castle Camp satellite) in the first week of January 1946, the rear party of Station HQ following on 17 January 1946. Flying at Castle Camps had ended. This was a period of rapid change and complexity within Fighter Command, its Essex Sector with HQ at North Weald controlling Boxted whose satellite was Castle Camps until 7 January when that role ceased. Castle Camps was at once placed on Care & Maintenance and on 1 February, 1946, passed to War Office control for use as a storage depot. Castle Camps was declared surplus to need in July 1948.

Main features:
Runways: 063° 4,850ft x 150ft, 100° 3,210ft x 150ft, 317° 14,800ft x 150ft, tarmac surfaced. *Hangars:* one Bellman, eight Over Blister. *Hardstandings:* sixteen. *Accommodation:* RAF: 68 officers, 101 SNCOs, 1,009 ORs; WAAF: 4 officers, 10 SNCOs, 170 ORs.

CAXTON GIBBET, Cambridgeshire

52°13N/00°05W 200ft asl; TL300605. At junction of A1198 and A428 E of St Neots, 9 miles W of Cambridge

Night flying by Tiger Moths of No 22 EFTS took place at their Caxton Gibbet Relief Landing Ground before any was undertaken, during the war, at Cambridge. In the early hours of 16 July 1941, Tiger Moths R4962 and R4968 were floating around the circuit when Fw Koster's intruding Ju 88C opened fire. Some flashes, the biplanes burst into flames, fell to the ground and when the German pilot reached his base he claimed to have shot down two Blenheims – at Wyton!

The Luftwaffe seemed to have had an obsession with Caxton, although its fairly close proximity to Bassingbourn may have had something to do with repeated attacks on what was only a large meadow with a few tents, goose neck flares, and some Marshall employees to maintain two Flights of Tiger Moths.

The triangular field had been used from 17 May 1935 by the Cambridge University Gliding Club. Among the sights here was their beautiful turquoise blue painted Cambridge Sailplane.

As Sir Arthur Marshall reminds us in his autobiography *The Marshall Story* (PSL), there were so many Tiger Moths at Cambridge that Relief Landing Grounds needed to be opened at Bottisham and Newmarket in September 1940. It was then that wartime use also began of the flying field once Swanley Wood Farm and situated south-east of the Ermine Street/A45 cross roads and by the Caxton Gibbet inn. It now became a valuable Relief Landing Ground for 'circuit and bumping' 22 EFTS Tiger Moths, and relieved pressure on very busy Cambridge Airport.

June 1941, saw 'F' Flight of the EFTS move to Caxton whose basic facilities made it more suitable for night flying than important Cambridge Airport. Despite its small size, larger aircraft occasionally put down, one example being a Wellington of 101 Squadron.

Initial German interest had come in darkness on 25 February 1941 when the Luftwaffe was very active in the region and a Ju 88C circled as Tiger Moths were flying. A second call came on 16 July when the aforementioned Tiger Moths were shot down. During the third, on 6 August 1941, an aircraft called up the control van, flashed the correct 'colour of the day' then dropped ten 50kg bombs which damaged two Tiger Moths. The night of 23/24 August 1941 brought another ten HEs released from about 500ft and this time one of the Marshall team was killed. NJG2 had still not finished with the little airfield for on 3 September another Ju 88 arrived. It circled twice, made two approaches and during the fourth run dropped three HEs and a container of incendiaries which, between them, damaged five Tiger Moths.

After the EFTS left in 1944 huts within Swanley Wood along the northern edge were taken over to accommodate personnel of 105 Squadron then at Bourn. Evidently the squadron had a skilled artist and murals on walls of the huts survived into the 1950s.

A gibbet remains, the inn was seriously damaged by fire in 2008. Of aeronautical associations almost nothing remains. Of course, there's nothing to stop a German Senior citizen – with a good tale to tell – renewing acquaintance with his youthful days.

Main features:
Grass runways: N/S 3,300ft, NW/SE 2,100ft, E/W 1,800ft yards, NW/SE 3,000ft
Hangars: two Over Blister, five Standard Blister. Personnel: seventy-eight ORs only in tents, later in huts.

Places of interest nearby:
Papworth, site of the village settlement 3 miles to the north, famous for its special facilities and accommodation of many tuberculosis suffers, is now widely known for its pioneering heart transplants. Less well known is its production line in a Settlement workshop where twenty-five wooden Grunau Baby gliders were built for post-war ATC use.

CHEDBURGH, Suffolk

52°10/00°37E 410ft asl; TL93567. By the A143, S of the village of Chedburgh

Their uniforms were slightly different, the men very brave. Some had trod many miles along a tortuous route to take part in the fight for freedom. These were the Poles and when our service personnel were demobbed many Poles remained in the Polish squadrons within the RAF. Most were manning fighter squadrons but at Chedburgh it was different. The Poles were to be found in two transport squadrons both eventually equipped with Halifax C VIIIs, a rare commodity indeed. Chedburgh, a typical temporary wartime bomber airfield is, however, probably most readily remembered as a base for Short Stirling bombers.

After opening on 7 September 1942 as a second satellite for Stradishall, the first week of October 1942 saw 214 Squadron move in. From here the Straits Settlement squadron operated until the Stirling was withdrawn from Main Force operations late in 1943. In the summer of 1943 a second squadron formed here, No 620, from 'C' Flight of 214 Squadron, and was declared operational on 17 June 1943. They only stayed until late November when they moved to Leicester East to become part of 38 Group and fly transport Stirlings.

Their replacement on 21 November 1943 was No 1653 Conversion Unit formed at Chedburgh and equipped with thirty-two Stirlings. Mid-summer 1943 had seen HQ No 31 Base, within 3 Group, established at Stradishall to control Stirling training at Chedburgh and Wratting Common, these latter two being the two sub-stations. All Stirling training for 3 Group would now be concentrated at the three stations, although some months passed before the policy became effective.

The intent had been that Chedburgh would be one of two storage sites for Hamilcar gliders but slow production meant that they were directly delivered to Tarrant Rushton, their operational base. That left only No 1653 Conversion Unit which in November 1944 was passed to No 7 Group and soon after left for North Luffenham. Their place was taken by 218 Squadron which arrived on 5 December flying Lancaster Is and IIIs and participated in the 3 Group bomber offensive. At the end of hostilities they dropped much needed food to the Dutch, and flew prisoner of war repatriation flights. Disbandment came at Chedburgh on 10 August 1945.

The first week of September 1945 saw two Polish squadrons arrive, Nos 301 and 304, bringing examples of the rare Warwick III and, in the case of 304 Squadron, some Wellington GR XIVs still wearing Coastal Command colours. Those were used for conversion training while the Warwick IIIs settled down to route flying mainly to the Middle East under Transport Command control. The Warwick had followed almost as difficult a path to success as the Poles during their journeys, and served only as an interim transport until the first Halifax VIIIs arrived for 301 Squadron at the start of 1946.

In their belly panniers they carried freight during runs to India, and had found official favour as 'ideal' transports. In May 1946, 304 Squadron also equipped with them, the two squadrons operating trunk routes overseas until both disbanded in December 1946. The Chedburgh site, having no particular merit, was disposed of in October 1952.

Thereafter it was the usual story with the route to full civilian use being protracted. Chedburgh's hangars are still used for light industrial and agricultural purposes. The one-time airfield is not easy to see, the best view across the site being from the road to Rede leading off the A143 just to the east of the village.

Crop spraying aircraft occasionally operated from here.

In the local church a Roll of Honour for Chedburgh lists 395 personnel killed in action. There is also a memorial near the airfield perimeter.

Main features:
Runways: 231° 6,000ft x 150ft, 173°, 302°, concrete. *Hangars:* two T2, one B1, three for gliders. *Hardstandings:* thirty-six for heavy bombers. *Accommodation:* RAF: 161 officers, 495 SNCOs, 966 ORs; WAAF: 10 officers, 9 SNCOs, 222 ORs.

COLEBY GRANGE, Lincolnshire

53°07N/00°29W 200ft asl; TF005605. S of Lincoln, between the A15 and A607 roads, alongside the B1202, and named after The Grange

By the western side of the A15 shortly before Waddington comes into view from the south a collection of buildings contains one of unmistakable form, the control tower of the wartime grass airfield called Coleby Grange. One might be forgiven, then, for thinking this was a satellite of the Permanent RAF Station. True, a few Manchesters once stayed here but when it came into use in the late 1930s it was as one of Cranwell's relief landing grounds. To make that possible the B1202 road had to be closed and eventually a portion of the perimeter track was constructed along the line of the road. A solitary Blister hangar and seven EO Blister hangars were supplemented in 1941 by one unusual T1 erected in a wooded area on the opposite side of the A15.

Despite its very primitive nature Coleby Grange converted itself almost overnight into an operational SLG when late in May 1940 a detachment of 253 Squadron's Hurricanes arrived from Kirton-in-Lindsey. Defiants of No 264 Squadron from Kirton replaced them in late July and as lodgers they had several short stays here during August 1940.

Coleby Grange nevertheless remained until May 1941 primarily Cranwell's RLG for both pilots flying Oxfords and for aircraft being used to train radio operators. Then the airfield became 'WCII', a second satellite operational landing ground of Digby and controlled by No 12 Fighter Group. Digby's other satellite was Wellingore (WCI).

Digby was now an established home for Canadian fighter squadrons and it was the second of these, No 402 flying Hurricane I and IIas, which arrived at Coleby on 16 May 1941 to initiate another new role for the station. As for the Grange, it served as an ideal stately residence.

No 402 Squadron left on 23 June 1941 making way for No 409 (Canadian) Squadron, a night-fighter squadron which had formed at Digby on 17 June 1941 and on 25 July 1941 moved to

Coleby Grange to complete workup on Defiant 1s.

First operational sorties were flown on 3 August 1941, but it was not until 20 August that the squadron was declared fully operational. By then conversion to Beaufighter IIfs was about to start. The first claim of a raider destroyed, a Do 217, came on 1 November although the re-armed squadron was not declared fully operational until the end of that month.

By then enemy aircraft were quite a scarce commodity although another claim was laid on 8 March 1942 to an He 111 near Grimsby and on 7 April 1942 to a Do 217 off Cromer. In June 1942 faster and more manoeuvrable Beaufighter NF VIfs replaced the Merlin-engined Mk IIs. Four raiders were claimed in July, seven in August – mainly Do 217s. Coleby, despite its primitive nature, had certainly established itself as a night fighter base. As for 409 Squadron they were destined not to see as much action again until D-Day in 1944.

On 22 February 1943 night fighter squadrons were switched. No 409 moved to Acklington to help defend Newcastle and No 410 (Canadian) Squadron flying Mosquito NF IIs moved to Coleby Grange. Hibaldstow now ceased to be the main night fighter station in Lincolnshire leaving Coleby Grange to take over its role. On 18 March Flying Officer Williams shot down a Do 217, the first Mosquito kill from the station. At the end of that month the squadron began flying *Day Rangers*, offensive sorties over north-west Germany from one of which, on 15 April, Warrant Officer Mackenzie returned with portions of a cable embedded in his aircraft and acquired during low flying near Apeldoorn. As well as some twenty Mosquito IIs the squadron held a Magister for local jaunts.

During June they undertook *Instep* operations against German aircraft and ships in the Bay of Biscay area and on 14 June attacked five U-boats. Such offensive operations were undertaken from advanced bases in Cornwall. *Night Rangers*, scrambles, night patrols, bomber support operations, all were flown from Coltishall. On 13 July a Do 217 was destroyed north of the Humber Estuary, the enemy retaliating on 31 August when DD779 during take-off was fired upon by an intruder. On 5 November an Me 410 fell to HJ917 fifteen miles off Dungeness three days before the squadron moved to Hunsdon.

Part of No 288 Squadron, which undertook anti-aircraft co-operation in the 12 Group area from Digby, also used Coleby Grange between 9 and 23 November for their Defiants and Oxfords. They were joined on 17 November 1943 by No 264 Squadron which returned equipped with Mosquito II night fighters. Like their predecessors they used Coltishall as their forward base for night bomber support operations. After a brief stay, they left for Church Fenton on 18 December.

Between 5 February and 1 March 1944 No 68 Squadron Beaufighter VIFs used Coleby then it was the turn of No 307 (Polish) squadron to be based here between 1 March and 6 May 1944. They had recently received Mosquito NF XIIs. The Poles, who thought little of the cramped and inadequate conditions at the station, carried out many night patrols – usually guided by Patrington radar – during 'The Baby Blitz'. On 19/20 March Pilot Officer J Brochocki scored spectacularly by bringing down a Heinkel He 177. No 307's departure to Church Fenton on 6 May 1944 ended many years of Coleby's operational status.

After the Mosquitoes departed, the station resumed its role of RLG for Cranwell. Last unit to be stationed here, between 28 February and 1 June 1945 was Oxford-equipped No 1515 BAT Flight. Between 1 May 1945 and January 1946, 19 FTS Cranwell used Coleby as its RLG and then the airfield – still only with grass and limited facilities – closed to flying.

As in so many cases government control of the site was not surrendered and in 1959 it was resurrected as an operational station possessing power and might undreamed of when it was last active. A guarded enclave was built in 1958-9 within which No 142 Squadron reformed on 22 July 1959. There they held three Thor IRBMs under joint UK/US control as part of the Hemswell Complex. Vulnerable because they were surface based missiles the Thors soon departed and the squadron disbanded on 24 May 1963.

With no foreseeable value Coleby Grange closed later that year and was returned to agricultural use; likewise the T1 hangar across the road.

Main features:
Grass runways: NE/SW 6,000ft, NW/SE 4,200ft, N/S 2,898ft. *Hangars:* one TI, one Blister, seven EO Blister. *Hardstandings:* seven for twin-engined aircraft. *Accommodation:* RAF: 78 officers, 102 SNCOs, 1,066 ORs; WAAF: 2 officers, 1 SNCO, 135 ORs.

COLTISHALL, Norfolk

52°45N/01°21E 57ft asl; TG261330. 9 miles NNE of Norwich on the B1150

On 30 April 2006 the RAF Ensign was lowered for the last time at Coltishall, a station with a glittering history. Through its Main Gate had passed so many of the famous, the great and the mighty: HM King George VI and Queen Elizabeth, numerous Chiefs of the Air Staff, famed fliers including Douglas Bader, 'Cowboy' Blatchford, Bob Braham, Denis Crowley-Milling, V2 dive-bomber and TV star Raymond Baxter, to name but a few. For sixty-six years a host of service men and women, as well as many civilians, served at Coltishall almost continuously in the front line through peacetime and during hot and cold wars. From here the Battle of Britain was fought, the wartime Allied air campaign was supported, V2 launch sites were assaulted, Norwich and the east were defended and Saddam Hussein's supporters were justifiably mauled. Certainly Coltishall's passing – like that of its big cats – brings tears and regrets, but change is as inevitable as night-time follows daylight.

From the moment one reached the Guardroom, Coltishall presented an image of an airfield different from others. SHQ as usual dominated the way ahead, but in an unusually open setting. Flat-roofed buildings predominated, the domestic site was split and the dominant 'C' Type hangars portrayed austerity born of a haste for completion at a lower cost than normal. Construction, like the station, was very function-orientated, an early 'no frills' aviation event.

For an astonishing thirty-two years Coltishall was the Jaguars' lair, home of surely the most successful Anglo-French aeronautical venture. Like their namesake, the Jaguars were a mobile tribe intended to roam for the kill far from their hide. Their protective home and support were found in existing hangars. They had little need for hardened shelters on the station so close to the coast that it would have survived for only a few moments in a full-scale East-West exchange. Ironically, the absence of costly, protective HASs enabled Coltishall to survive as long as it did because the expense of its upkeep, still very considerable, was less than would have been the case had the Jaguar force moved to the attracting Bentwaters.

When WWII began, Duxford and Wittering were responsible for defending the northern half of East Anglia. A government assessment concluded that in East Anglia there was very little worth protecting other than oil tanks at King's Lynn, the 'kipper fleet' and Harwich harbour. AA guns were almost absent, fighters few – until the Luftwaffe began attacking coal carrying coastal shipping and laid pernicious mines. In May 1940 came changes. Construction of a bomber aerodrome at Coltishall for No 2 Group had commenced in February 1939 and resulting from the general situation in May 1940 came the decision to adapt Coltishall for use as a fighter station. Although unfinished, Spitfires of No 66 Squadron began on 29 May to use the aerodrome as a forward base, Sections being here for coastal shipping protection.

Expenditure on elaborate airfields had, by 1939, led to specifications lowering the cost which resulted in some of reduced dimensions with less grandeur. At Coltishall that is apparent in the case of the SHQ design facing as customary the main gate. The four 'C' Type Sheds at Coltishall (instead of a proposed five, but all of eleven-bay bomber type) had their aircraft entrances reduced in height by five feet and were distinctive because of the absence of brick columns and trim at each end. Barrack blocks were completed to a lower specification all of which gave the station a somewhat 'Spartan' look.

Wing Commander W K Beisiegle was in command when Coltishall opened fully operational as a 12 Group station at 0001 hrs on 23 June 1940. Three days earlier the remnants of 242 Squadron had arrived from France and Squadron Leader Douglas R S Bader had been put in command of the squadron.

Although the area around had already been bombed, most of the action was for months to take place off the East Coast where on 10 July 1940 No 66 Squadron (which had moved in on 4 July) drew first blood for Coltishall, a Do 17. Then it was 242 Squadron's turn – they bagged an He 111 on 19 July, another two on the 29th and a Ju 88 on 1 August. At this time No 604 Squadron began placing detachments here for the defence of Norwich.

The enemy soon responded to recent losses and out of the clouds over Coltishall on 19 August an He 111 of KG27 suddenly emerged to drop six bombs on an unfinished hangar. No 66 Squadron would have none of that so scrambled and claimed the uninvited stranger. The Battle of Britain lay largely out of Coltishall's range – until 12 Group's 'Big Wing' was launched in late August.

Then on each day six squadrons assembled in Duxford's sector. When 'scramble!' was ordered, some seventy-two fighters were launched within a few minutes. Suddenly Duxford's sky would be packed with more than twice as many fighters as at any Flying Legends show. Indeed, they really were the making of the legend. They and the amazing sound of so many Merlins needed to be more quickly marshalled than nowadays before heading south to deal with the foe.

Among Duxford's daily callers were No 242 Squadron first committed to battle on 30 August. Heading for Vauxhall's Luton factory, a large formation of escorted Heinkels was attacked between Enfield and Hatfield where seven Bf 110s and three He 111s were claimed by the 12 Group Wing and without loss.

Meanwhile, No 66 Squadron carrying out shipping patrols from Coltishall put a Do 17 in the sea off Happisburgh. No 242 Squadron's Hurricanes went daily to Duxford to deal with the foe engaged over North Weald on 7 September. Pilot Officer Denis Crowley-Milling (later the famous Air Marshal) was shot down near Chelmsford.

No 616 Squadron had arrived at Coltishall on 3 September from Kenley, and was replaced by 74 Squadron on 9 September. The newcomers joined 'Big Wing' operations and on 11 September claimed six enemy aircraft over the London area. No 242 Squadron patrolled over London on 14 September, the day that Douglas Bader was awarded the DSO. Meanwhile, '74' claimed a probable Bf 110 and a Ju 88 off Happisburgh. In the complex fighting the truth about claims would need to await the passage of time. Of one thing there was certainty: the ferocity and hectic fighting involving hundreds of aircraft resulted in 15 September 1940 justifiably becoming known as Battle of Britain Day. It is one that must be remembered by all for many decades into the new millennium for it portrayed all that was magnificent in our 'Finest Hour' and enshrined a magnificent sense of right and the determination to quell evil. On that great day No 242 Squadron first claimed five Do 17s and a Bf 109 and in a later engagement another three Do 17s, an He 111 and two Bf 109s. Three days later further action was concentrated around Hornchurch.

Although 242 Squadron continued to undertake the regular early morning journey to Duxford and returned in the evening, action was limited by the difficulty of positioning the 'Big Wing' advantageously in time and space.

On 20 October 1940, '242' moved to Duxford, and was replaced by 72 Squadron. Seven days later an He 111 made a dusk bombing and strafing attack on Coltishall whose ground defences opened up. They winged the raider which crashed in the sea off Lowestoft.

Matlaske opened in October as Coltishall's satellite allowing dispersed operation of Coltishall's squadrons. Furniture was removed from Matlaske Hall, just in case, and the staircase and fireplaces were boxed in. Air and ground crews were then accommodated without precious features becoming damaged by exuberance.

On 8 November the Luftwaffe again called on Coltishall dropping eleven bombs on the station and damaged the watch office.

By now squadrons were quickly passing through. No 222's Spitfires arrived on 11 November 1940 to replace No 64's which had been here since 15 October. On 29 November 1940 No 72 Squadron moved to Leuchars and on 15 December were replaced by Hurricanes of No 257 (Burma) Squadron. They stayed for eleven months and came to be looked upon as 'Coltishall's own'. By the end of 1940, Coltishall squadrons had claimed eighty-three enemy aircraft shot down.

Action was again centring around shipping raids off East Anglia. *Pirat* intruders, too, were busily using cloudy, rainy days to cloak their annoying overland activity. Coltishall's fighters did their best to halt these small scale yet often very damaging incursions during which gunners aboard the intruders readily opened fire upon civilians and bombed opportune targets, military or civilian. It was difficult to locate them – usually Do 17s or He 111s – as they scudded low and erratically among clouds. Even the Observer Corps found tracking the raiders difficult.

A different form faced the enemy on 20 March 1941 when No 151 Squadron began placing detachments of Defiant turret fighters here for night standbys. For Coltishall this was the opening of a new phase for night fighting was to play a large part in its history for almost the next three decades. Previously, such activity had been carried out over the Sector by aircraft operating out of Wittering.

Nos 222 and 257 Squadrons meanwhile busied themselves in daylight. Squadron Leader Stanford-Tuck of 257 Squadron claimed several enemy aircraft and, on 12 May, Flight Lieutenant 'Cowboy' Blatchford, who became a well-known Coltishall figure, shot down an He 111 off Great Yarmouth. Greater success came to Squadron Leader Stanford-Tuck on 21 June when, off Holland, he engaged three Bf 109s shooting down two. His damaged Hurricane crashed in the sea off the English coast, a trawler fishing him out of the water thirty minutes later.

The RAF did not have it all their own way. On 26 April 1941 an appalling night bombing incident engulfed The Ferry Inn, Horning, and its customers. Among the twenty-two people killed were three Coltishall pilots and a plaque in the bar recalls that horrendous night.

A milestone of a different sort was passed on 22 June 1941 when No 222 Squadron carried out their and Coltishall's first offensive operation over France damaging a Bf 109 in the process. The station's distance from France meant either that landing to refuel was necessary in both directions, or the squadrons needed to operate from advanced bases. Coltishall's fighters at this time usually provided various types of support and protection to Blenheims of 2 Group and Coastal Command when they were attacking targets off or within the coastal fringe of the Netherlands.

When Squadron Leader Stanford-Tuck ceased to command 257 Squadron on 4 July 1941, and was promoted to Wing Commander, his place taken by Squadron Leader 'Cowboy' Blatchford.

Although it has had a very long and active career, Coltishall has never been completely in American hands. The closest it ever came was on 29 July 1941 when the third Eagle Squadron, No 133, formed here.

Once airborne from Coltishall, one's immediate realisation is of how close the North Sea is, the proximity long rendering it an ideal base for air/sea rescue activities. One of the first ASR units, No 5 ASR Flight, formed here in July 1941 and received two Walrus amphibians on 19 July. In October the Flight which also used Lysanders became 278 Squadron, moved to Matlask, then jockeyed between the two airfields until April 1944. No 278 contributed enormously to the ASR service.

By August 1941 the German night offensive against Britain had largely been overtaken by the departure of squadrons to other activities. No 604 Squadron released from its night protection role brought its Beaufighters to Coltishall for interception of mine-laying aircraft and to help stop Ju 88C night intruders from interfering with Bomber Command's operations. This brought to Coltishall that famous night-fighting team, Wing Commander John Cunningham and Pilot Officer C F Rawnsley who, on 22 August made their first kill from here, an He 111 shot down thirty-five miles north-west of Coltishall. Occasionally night raids on British cities usually near the coast still took place, one being directed against Norwich on 16 September 1941.

No 93, another night fighting squadron, had also run out of trade. Their operating method was unique for they were equipped with aerial mine laying Havocs, a detachment of which moved into Coltishall on 7 September. Their activity involved releasing ahead of approaching enemy aircraft a large number of grenades attached to parachutes. In theory some should collide with the foe bringing disaster, but the actuality was different. Mine laying in the area was difficult because so many RAF aircraft were active over East Anglia at night.

Nevertheless, on 16 September 1941, a minelayer was 'scrambled', the consequences of which can only be dubbed incredible. The eighty-three mines sown over south-west Norwich drifted down on to its residents. One landed in the bicycle basket of an airman, another on the roof of a house. Warned of the danger, the occupant astonished a policeman by telling him that they would vacate the bedroom over which the mine rested and move into another. East Anglians are a tough lot! By the end October the detachment had flown twenty-four sorties without success.

No 604 Squadron left on 21 September 1941 and were replaced by Merlin-engined Beaufighter NF IIs of 255 Squadron. The replacement for 257 Squadron was No 137 flying Whirlwinds which soon moved to Matlask. Ludham, Coltishall's second satellite opened on 19 November. To the end of 1941 anti-shipping operations were supported by Coltishall's fighters, night fighters of 151 and 255 Squadron mounted night defence stand-bys and 278 Squadron was on hand for rescue duties.

Coltishall figured prominently in the dash of the *Scharnhorst* and *Gneisenau* through the Channel on 12 February 1942. Fourteen Beauforts of 42 Squadron hurried here from Leuchars and nine took off, six without success releasing their torpedoes towards the ships. Next day Beauforts of 86 Squadron arrived too late to be of use, like more Beauforts of 22 Squadron which stood by at Coltishall on the 15th.

In March 1942, No 2 Group opened a new daylight offensive using Bostons, and Coltishall's Spitfires assisted from advanced bases. Operations from within the clutch of Coltishall airfields – the main station, Ludham and Matlask – were integrated, squadrons moving forward daily from Duxford to replace any sent to other Sectors. Early March 1942 brought in No 68 Squadron commanded by Wing Commander Max Aitken, son of Lord Beaverbrook. Shortly before midnight on 27 April around seventy German bombers opened an hour-long raid on Norwich. Heavy incendiary loads soon incinerated the city centre into which high explosives rained. As a result of the many fires and extensive bombing of residential areas 53 people died, and nearly 200 had serious injuries. Coltishall's squadrons were 'scrambled', 610 Squadron putting up ten Spitfires, No 68 nine Beaufighters and 151 Squadron joining in. There were contacts but no enemy aircraft were claimed.

Two nights later the enemy returned again inflicting serious damage. Coltishall's sorties were once again fruitless. Details of the raids upon Norwich may be found in *Air Raid!* (PSL). When on 30 April the Luftwaffe headed for more northerly targets, 68 Squadron at last found the bombers, claiming two He 111s and a Do 217E.

Some surprise punctuated this period when on 7 May six Defiants joined 278 Squadron. Too bad, for the squadron had no fuel bowser carrying 100-octane fuel, let alone a 24-volt starter!

The Luftwaffe again tried for Norwich on 8 May, but the bombs fell wide on the city outskirts. No 68 Squadron patrolled unsuccessfully, but a Do 217 of KG2 was brought down near Stoke Holy Cross either as a result of hitting a balloon cable or by AA fire. Great Yarmouth came under attack on 29 May and 68 Squadron was more successful. Wing Commander Aitken claimed a Do 217 and a damaged Ju 88. Squadron Leader Howden and Flight Lieutenant Winward between them accounted for a Do 217 and a Ju 88.

Coltishall's proximity to the sea made it ideal for 'cuckoos', bombers damaged or short of fuel and after the Cologne 1,000 bomber raid a Stirling landed with sufficient fuel for a mere five minutes' flying. At first light Coltishall's fighters patrolled in case German aircraft attempted to intrude upon returning bombers.

Norwich was yet again attacked on 26 June and serious fires were started. This time 610 Squadron's Spitfires patrolling at night destroyed a Ju 88, a rare event for fighters without AI radar. No 68 Squadron's turn came on 23 July 1942. Bombs were dropped on Great Yarmouth and King's Lynn and ten Beaufighters responded. Wing Commander Aitken destroyed a Ju 88 and Do 217, Sergeant Truscott a Do 217, Warrant Officer Bebek a Do 217 and Squadron Leader Vesely another Do 217. Max Aitken was awarded the DSO on 27 July.

Autumn 1942 found Duxford overflowing with aircraft and when USAAF P-39 squadrons arrived there pending involvement in operation *Torch*, No 346 Squadron USAAF was temporarily placed at Coltishall decreasing pressure on Duxford. On 28 January 1943 HM King George VI visited 68 and 118 Squadrons and personally awarded 278 Squadron their badge signed by himself, the first time he had handed one over in person.

A reminder of earlier days came on 4 February 1943 when Wing Commander Blatchford assumed the post of Coltishall's Wing Commander Flying. Swordfish and Albacores of 841 Squadron, Fleet Air Arm, were currently operating at night from the station, also small detachments of 515 Squadron. The latter were flying Defiants employing *Moonshine*, an aid developed in an attempt to electronically cloak movement of our night bombers. More momentous was the arrival on 14 June of Beaufighters of 141 Squadron to undertake in great secrecy their first night bomber support *Serrate* operation.

Ventura day escorts by Coltishall's Spitfires included the disastrous operation of 3 May 1943 (see Methwold) when 118 and 504 Squadrons participated from here. Wing Commander Blatchford was shot down during this operation.

Mid-1943 found the station extremely busy, particularly 278 Squadron. On 13 June a searching Walrus found a dinghy with eight men in it. Despite a five-foot sea, the pilot eventually put down but with the Americans aboard, the Walrus could not take off. It was taxied for ten miles in the stormy sea before the precious load could be transferred to a launch.

A bad day for the Coltishall Sector was 6 July. Seven Typhoons led by Wing Commander Rabagliati set on a shipping strike left three small ships in an enemy convoy damaged. Some sixty miles from home the leader reported engine trouble. He climbed, streaming smoke, before crashing in the sea. He was thought to have scrambled clear, but his dinghy was empty. The others orbited before their fuel began to run short. A Walrus escorted by six Spitfires of 118 Squadron set out from Coltishall but the sea was getting rougher, it started raining and thunderstorms were encountered. Some sixty aircraft searched, unsuccessfully, for the Wing Commander and the day's drama was far from over. Coltishall was ordered to 'scramble' four Typhoons to intercept Fw 190s near Great Yarmouth. Instead, the attackers chased the defenders and shot Flight Sergeant Clusas into the sea. A Walrus searched, but in awful weather nothing was seen. Even those were not the last of the bad moments, for a Spitfire which had taken off to escort the Walrus crashed soon after take-off. No 278 Squadron also used

Ansons for search, and when the pilot of a PR Spitfire baled out not far from the coast an Anson crew directed a launch to the steamer *Cagny* which had fished him out of the water.

On 17 July 278 Squadron was again to the fore. An Anson crew sighted two dinghies from a B-17 which had shot down two of four Fw 190s following it home. Two Walruses were 'scrambled' and one landed and picked up the survivors. Again, heavy swell prevented the amphibian from taking off. An Anson directed two launches to the scene, the men were taken aboard and the Walrus was guarded by 118 Squadron Spitfires during its six-hour taxi back to Great Yarmouth harbour.

Better weather on 25 July saw 611 Spitfire Squadron escorting day bombers to Holland where they mixed it with German fighters. Thirty miles off the Dutch coast Squadron Leader Charles, leading 611 Squadron, was shot down, his position orbited by Flight Lieutenant Mansfield. A dozen pilots of 611 keeping guard were relieved by 416 Squadron led by Wing Commander Chadburn who escorted a Walrus to the spot. It alighted, rescuing Charles despite his proximity to the enemy coast.

So busy was Coltishall that Sommerfeld track runways had at last to be laid. Extra D/F stations opened making eleven available to the complex.

When Flying Officer Overton on 20 August flying a Mustang of 613 Squadron and back from a *Lagoon* landed to refuel he brought news of yet another dinghy fifty miles east of Lowestoft, and which he had circled until his fuel ran low. Despite the rough sea, a Walrus alighted and rescued four Dutchmen of 320 Squadron. The port engine of their Mitchell had been damaged necessitating ditching. Prevented from taking off by heavy swell, Flying Officer Sims taxied until he found a sufficiently smooth patch. This was the 100th rescue by 278 Squadron.

Enemy night activity over Britain increased in late summer 1943 with the introduction of high flying Me 410s and Ju 188s. A Beaufighter of 68 Squadron had just landed at Coltishall on 22 August when three bombs fell parallel to the flare path, the first of a string starting in front of the control tower. A similar incident came on 27 September after a Halifax back from Hanover and flying on two engines landed wheels-up at the main runway end. Almost immediately high explosives fell on the airfield, also a load of pernicious butterfly bombs. On 12 October Flight Lieutenant Allen of 68 Squadron chased an Me 410 intruder across Norfolk and as it crossed the coast over Cromer, Flying Officer Boyle in a Mosquito of 151 Squadron (attached to Coltishall) was waiting. He caught up with it just as the raider turned east and, aided by Neatishead Radar, Boyle closed and gave it a short burst. There was an explosion and an engine fire. The Me 410 went down, a mass of flames, some fragments hitting the Mosquito which eventually landed at Church Fenton.

Another noteworthy day was 5 February 1944. No 68 Squadron, here since 8 March 1942, moved out and was now credited with a score of seventy enemy aircraft. No 25 Squadron under Wing Commander Wight-Boycott DSO replaced them as the Luftwaffe's 'Baby Blitz' was underway. Coltishall became involved on 19 March 1944 when raiders entered the 12 Group area. No 25 Squadron went after them producing a night to remember for they destroyed five German bombers. Two Ju 188s were added to their score on 21 March bringing the total to eleven since their arrival. High spirits among the night fighters were further lifted when LACW Swann became 'Miss Coltishall'. Maybe that enticed more intruders to sneak up on Coltishall. About twelve followed our bombers home on 12 April when a 64 Squadron Spitfire landing with navigation lights on was attacked. The pilot feeling a severe shock opened up and climbed to 4,000 feet. With his engine temperature fast rising, Flight Sergeant Maunders rolled over to bale out but instead found his aircraft spinning. He hurled himself out and parachuted down safely.

Two other long-serving squadrons left Coltishall in April 1944, '611' here since 25 September 1943, and '64' here since 1 July 1943 and which departed on the 29th. No 316 (Polish) Squadron moved in during the month which witnessed the movement of 278 Squadron to Bradwell Bay there to receive Warwicks for D-Day support activity.

Coltishall was a departure point for Mosquito fighters setting out on or returning from long-distance *Ranger* flights. On 16 May four crews of 418 Squadron set off and near Lübeck destroyed an He 111. They bagged a Fw 190 near Zingst and over Kubitzer Bay a Heinkel 177. At Stralsund they destroyed a grounded He 111 and blew up a Bucker 131. A further success in Kubitzer Bay was a Do 18, then south of Stralsund they claimed a rare Ju 86. Squadron Leader Cleveland's Mosquito was damaged and he force landed in Sweden.

Coltishall was not much involved with the Normandy landings, but on 8 June reports came in that enemy aircraft had attacked three night-flying B-24s. A Mosquito of 25 Squadron was soon chasing an Me 410 of KG2 which was shot into the sea forty miles east of Southwold.

The first flying bomb alert for the station came on 1 July, Mustangs of 316 Squadron destroying the missile five miles off Lowestoft. These Mustangs were here primarily to give close support to Coastal Command Beaufighters.

Spitfire IXs of 229 Squadron had arrived in the Sector in July 1944 to form part of the screen for the next airborne landings. The arrival of the first V2 rocket at 1630 hrs on 26 September heralded more soon falling around Norwich, and that had Spitfire fighter-bombers on the offensive. There was no way in which a V2 could be shot down but, like the Scuds of *Desert Storm,* they were vulnerable on the ground – if they could be found. Yes, history does almost repeat itself – and often, which is why it should be a core curriculum subject for all.

In an attempt to halt the V2 offensive, Coltishall's Spitfires were to play the most important part. They mounted armed reconnaissance and dive-bombed V2 launch sites found in woodland around Wassenar and in the centre of Den Haag, a duty carried on well into 1945. Among those flying such missions from here was the late Raymond Baxter. Detached Mustangs of 26 Squadron scouted for the Spitfires.

The closing months of the war saw the Poles move in. No 307 Squadron's Mosquito 30s came, as did Mustangs of 303 and 316 Squadrons.

Immediate post-war Mustang IIIs included FZ120 used by 309 (Polish)Squadron from 1 March 1945 to 4 December 1946.

At the end of hostilities the soon all-Polish station held claims to 207 enemy aircraft destroyed, 48 probably destroyed and 100-plus damaged. For this, arguably the most active wartime airfield in East Anglia, the end of the war brought no quiet period. Indeed, great elation on 27 July 1945 greeted Group Captain Douglas Bader when he visited Coltishall. The whole station turned out to see the famous warrior fly a Spitfire again, and for the first time since his capture.

Then followed a period of jockeying as Mosquito, Spitfire and Mustang squadrons used Coltishall until it settled to its peacetime role as a night fighter base. The Polish Resettlement Corps took over Coltishall which became part of the Polish Air Force until January 1947 when Coltishall replaced Horsham as Eastern Sector HQ then forming. On 23 January 1947 Mosquito 36s of 23 and 141 Squadrons moved in for the immediate post war years and 264 Squadron joined them on 13 January 1948. By May 1948 the metal runways were breaking apart and in November 1949 the Wing was temporarily detached to Church Fenton while concrete runways were laid. Return to Coltishall came in September 1950 at which time squadron strength rose to twelve UE each.

No 23 Squadron re-equipped with Vampire NF 10s in the autumn of 1951, and 141 Squadron rearmed with eight Meteor NF 11s between July and September 1951. No 264 Squadron left for Linton-on-Ouse on 24 August 1951.

Venom NF 2s and later 3s replaced the initial jet equipment, 141 Squadron being the first to fly Venom NF 3s. In summer 1952, 23 Squadron's strength rose to twenty-two UE.

In 1957 both squadrons re-equipped with Javelin 4s and formed the first Javelin Wing in Fighter Command. No 141 Squadron was re-numbered 41 Squadron on 16 January 1958 and left in July 1960 after re-equipping with Javelin 8s. No 23 Squadron, still at Coltishall, later received Javelin 7s then 9s, and stayed until March 1963.

During 1958 extensive alterations were made to the station before the arrival, on 1 September 1959, of the Air Fighting Development Squadron of the Central Fighter Establishment which became the first RAF unit to receive Lightnings and on 5 October 1962 left for CFE Binbrook. On 4 January 1960 the Lightning Conversion Squadron, part of CFE, formed and was here until August 1961 when they moved to Middleton-St-George.

Late in the afternoon of 2 August 1960 No 74 Squadron, which had arrived with Hunter 6s in mid-1959, received its first Lightning 1s. They operated from here until February 1964 when they moved to Leuchars. Their place was taken by No 226 OCU which came in from Middleton-St-George on 20 April 1964, their assorted Lightnings wearing the colours of No 145 (Reserve) Squadron. Such was the sophistication of the Lightning that the OCU ran a ground school, gave flying training, included a special course on the weapons system and trained pilots in the special operating techniques needed. On 4 May 1971 they were renumbered 65 (Reserve) Squadron and disbanded on 30 September 1974 their task being taken over elsewhere by the Lightning Training Flight.

'Wow! Can I go along the line?' 'Yes, but be quick they're ready to roll'. Assorted Lightnings of 226 OCU on parade.

Coltishall held ASR helicopters including Sea King HAR 3s of 202 Squadron like XZ594.

The Battle of Britain Flight arrived on 1 April 1963 and became the Battle of Britain Memorial Flight on 1 June 1969 then moved out to Coningsby on 1 March 1970 taking a Hurricane, four Spitfires and the Lancaster.

The Air-sea rescue helicopters first moved in when Horsham St Faith closed. In the 1960s C Flight of 202 Squadron Whirlwinds stood by twenty-four hours a day and at fifteen minutes readiness to carry out short-range rescue. Subsequently Wessex HC2s of E Flight 22 Squadron were here until withdrawl mid-1994.

Lightning T Mk 4 XM974 T-Tiger of 74 Squadron – prowling on home territory.

The present and most long lasting phase in Coltishall's history began in 1974 with the arrival of SEPECAT Jaguar GR1s which formed a UK-based mobile reaction force. Ease of deployment and maintenance at an affordable price characterised the aircraft, the first European fighter-bomber with a navigation attack system and moving map display. Repeated updating took place and improved engines fitted. Jaguars have proven very useful in Peace Support and Peace Enforcement Operations.

No 54 Squadron arrived at Coltishall in early August 1974, No 6 in November 1974 and No 41 in April 1977, the latter concentrating on reconnaissance duties. They and their Jaguars have turned out to be the most operationally active of the post-war occupants. On 11 August 1990, a week after Iraq invaded Kuwait, twelve Jaguars, twenty-four pilots and 300 ground personnel drawn from the three squadrons deployed to Thumrait, Oman, and moved to Muharraq, Bahrain in October as part of operation *Granby*. Between 17 January and 27 February 1991 during *Desert Storm* they flew 615 sorties attacking assorted ground targets and then the Republican Guard. During 915 hours of flying they delivered 750 x 1,000lb HEs, 385 x CBU 887s, 8 x BL755 cluster bombs, fired three Sidewinders and 9,600 rounds of 30mm ammunition. The force returned to Coltishall on 13 March 1991.

Two Jags a-leaping from Coltishall.

On 4 September 1991 No 54 Squadron left Coltishall to take part in operation *Warden* from Incirlik, Turkey, the protection of the Kurds in Iraq north of 36°, other squadrons taking turns until 3 April 1993 when Harriers took over.

Jaguar XZ398 'FA' of 41 Squadron crossing Coltishall's lowered barrier.

In July 1993 nine Jaguars flew to Gioia del Colle, Italy, to form part of a multi-national contingent (operation *Grapple*) to protect the people of Bosnia Herzegovina, the duty continuing until April 1998. They carried out two air strikes and on 22 September 1994 No 41 Squadron – by attacking a tank near Osijek – was the first RAF squadron to drop bombs on mainland Europe since WWII. On 20 November 1994 No 54 Squadron led a bombing attack on Ubdina AB.

In September 1997 the Jaguars resumed their role as part of the NATO Rapid Reaction Force (Air). That has taken them for training many times overseas: to Oman, north Norway and Nevada.

No 54 Squadron flew the last operation *Deliberate Guard* on 4 April 1998. Barely were the Jaguars home from Italy in summer 1998 when in June they were ordered back for flag waving and possible intervention in Kosovo. Such was the suddenness of the order which came on a Friday that obtaining sufficient lire to see crews through at the start meant scouring every likely supplier in Norwich – and in desperation! No call to combat came; but had it done so then maybe the later terrible mess might, just might, have been avoided.

Jaguar of 'GO' 54 Squadron deploys its braking chute on landing.

The three squadrons, each nominally holding thirteen Jaguar GR1A/Bs and one T2/A, were soon receiving updated Jaguars, GR Mk3/3A, re-engined examples with capability enhanced through new avionics, improved systems and superior weapon launch capability. Wet film cameras were replaced with an electro-video pod carried by aircraft of 41 Squadron. That change enabled faster handling and more rapid intelligence gathering from a huge amount of material acquired for investigation in fixed or mobile RICs.

In 1997 overhaul and modification of Coltishall's hangars began and included the removal of asbestos within the roofing. By contrast, several blast walls, built to protect dispersal pans, remained to the end, and by then had become quiet rare items. The two large concrete ORPs, one at each right-hand runway end, also remained like the two sets each of nine dispersal pads and the two ASPs flanking the control tower.

Shooting day! The Jags line their lair having faced sudden, unexpected death.

Half the Jaguar force was brought down when, in March 2005, Nos 16 and 54 Squadrons disbanded, their demise marked on the western ASP, which performed as a parade ground while overhead snarling Jaguars expressed their feelings. As a result they, too, were slaughtered, partially, on 1 April 2006. No 41 Squadron died that day, but No 6 Squadron and its cats escaped to Coningsby. It but remained to carry away the carcases from Coltishall, some ironically to Bentwaters. GR Mk3 XZ112 was the last to fly away.

All items moveable and worth saving were removed. Houses were soon sold while the technical site began fast decaying. Now it is quite overgrown. As for the future, mutterings of 'immigration centre' soon evaporated. Coltishall is to become a prison. Let's hope that the souls of whoever resides there will be improved by the haunting, lasting courage and fine lives of their predecessors. Fancy living on the spot where Lightnings used to thunder away. Wow!

Main features:
Runways (Sommerfeld tracking): 096° 6,000ft x 150ft, 050° 4,800ft x 150ft, 150° 4,200ft x 150ft. *Hangars:* five C Type, six Over Blister, two EO Blister. *Hardstandings:* six single-engine, fourteen twin-engine. *Accommodation:* RAF: 137 officers, 190 SNCOs, 1,876 ORs; WAAF: 9 officers, 8 SNCOs, 488 ORs.

Place of interest nearby:
Coltishall is by the Norfolk Broads. The Bure Valley Railway runs narrow gauge steam-hauled trains between Wroxham and Aylsham (coach available to Blickling Hall in summer). Red Wings Horse Sanctuary, Hill Top Farm, Frettenham by the B1150 is worth a visit. The RAF Air Defence Radar Museum, Neatishead is certainly worth a visit. It is open on the second Saturday of each month, Bank Holiday Mondays and Tuesdays in summer 1000 hrs to 1600 hrs. Follow signs for RAF Neatishead, off A1062 near Horning.

CONINGSBY, Lincolnshire

53°05N/00°10W 20ft asl; TF225565. Just S of Coningsby village, W of the B1192 road. Main entrance on closed road to south of village, BBMF area signposted from village centre

Fate has played strange tricks on Coningsby. It took three years to construct, the proposed RAF station undergoing changes to reduce the overall cost of the building programme. Barely had it opened when the Manchester bomber and its vicissitudes descended on Coningsby. Come the Lancaster and fortune smiled – until the need for runway building put the station of out use at the height of the fight. Then 'The Dam Busters' looked in before Mossie target markers, Washingtons, and of course Canberras – with atomic bombs – found homes here.

Coningsby subsequently became a V-bomber station with all that entailed and then trouble struck again for it was the intended lair of TSR-2. Cancellation of that, let alone the dismantling of the V-Force, provided Coningsby with a problematical future fortuitously countered by the station's excellent sighting. Within the Eastern fighter belt it very suitably sat between Wattisham and Leeming. When the Tornado ADV arrived the station played the part for which it is so well positioned, and its use as the prime base for the Typhoon in not surprising.

Coningsby is one of the few stations built well within the Fens. Although flat, allowing superb open approaches, they inevitably present drainage problems. Surveys of the preferred site here showed less of a problem than expected.

Construction commenced in late 1937 proceeding slowly for new concepts were evolving. Eventually they led to a bomber station basically comprising a grass landing ground and having two of the new largely prefabricated metal Errol 'J' Type hangars prescribed for third generation Permanent Stations. Technical and domestic buildings, many flat roofed, were generally small and built to a lower specification than previously.

Although SHQ Coningsby opened in 5 Group on 4 November 1940, it was not until 23 February 1941 that No 106 Squadron and their Hampdens arrived. Four of those commenced Coningsby's battle career on 1/2 March by setting out to attack Cologne. It was on 10 March that trouble emerged when No 97 Squadron started transferring their Avro Manchesters from Waddington. Although they began bombing raids on 8 April, trouble with Rolls-Royce Vulture engines plagued the aircraft lowering morale and producing very troubled times. Losses were attributed to the engines, not the enemy, and '97' reverted to operating Hampdens between July and August 1941. Miscellaneous organisations here at this time included No 1485 TTF formed here on 30 October 1941 using Lysanders and became No 5 Group TTF on 7 January 1942. It was renamed 1485 TT&GF before leaving on 1 August 1942 by which time it was using Whitleys, Wellingtons and Lysanders. No 1514 BAT Flight functioned here between 22 September 1941 and 2 January 1944.

Meanwhile the Manchester's engine problems were cured, but too late in 1942 by which time in any case the bomber's cleverly conceived airframe was being brilliantly utilised as the basis of the most effective heavy bomber of the war, the Lancaster. In January 1942 No 97 Squadron began rearming with them, bidding farewell to the Manchester during February. Although 106's turn came next, it was June before their last Manchester retreated.

Barely had the changes become effective when No 97 at the start of March began moving to nearby Woodhall Spa so that runway construction could start at Coningsby. But with space a rare commodity No 106 remained, started Lancaster conversion in May and kept Manchesters to the end of June. No 106 despatched fifteen of them to Cologne and again to Essen as their contribution to operation *Millennium*.

Not until 1 October 1942 was No 106 Squadron able to leave for Syerston thereby allowing construction of three conventional concrete runways to begin at Coningsby. They were completed on 1 August 1943. Additional hangars – a B1 and the three T2s all still in use – had been erected in time for re-opening in great style on 30 August 1943 when famous 617 Squadron took up residence under the command of Wing Commander Guy Gibson. Their stay extended to 10 January 1944 by which time their special operations had included an eight aircraft attack on 15 September when the Dortmund-Ems Canal received the first 12,000lb HC bombs to be used. Costly it was for only three Lancasters returned.

Woodhall's No 619 Squadron immediately replaced '617' at Coningsby where, on 1 February 1944, they were joined by Lancasters of No 61 Squadron. Both carried out Main Force operations as ordered by No 5 Group until April 1944 when No 61 returned to Skellingthorpe and No 619 moved to Dunholme Lodge.

Their move made space for Nos 83 and 97 Squadrons to return from loan to No 8 (PFF) Group which ended on 18 April 1944. Acquired backup marking skills made them very useful to No 5 Group with whom they operated until the end of hostilities. Coningsby's last operational sorties were despatched on 25 April 1945 against an oil refinery at Tonsberg in Norway.

Nos 83 and 97 Squadrons remained at Coningsby and transferred to No 1 Group after No 5 Group disbanded on 15 December 1945. During July 1946 both converted to Lincolns and in November moved to Hemswell. They were replaced with Mosquitoes of No 109 Squadron (five B16s and three PR 16s) and the eight B16s of No 139 Squadron, for whom crews were supplied by No 231 OCU, formed on 15 March 1947. No 231 absorbed No 237 OCU and then also trained Mosquito PR crews. In September and July 1948 respectively Mosquito B 35s replaced the Mk 16s in Nos 109 and 139 Squadrons. Although based here until March/April 1950 both squadrons were frequently detached overseas.

Following that departure Coningsby's dispersal pans were strengthened, additional living quarters were built and the runway was improved making it suitable for the next occupants, four squadrons of B-29 Washingtons. On 17 October No 149 Squadron was first to arrive, its aircraft being delivered in November. Next came No XV in February 1951, followed by No 44 (Rhodesian) Squadron in April and by No 57 a year later. Establishment then totalled thirty-two Washingtons.

Outmoded by jet bombers No 149 Squadron began re-arming with Canberra B2s in March 1953. No 44 followed suit in April, the other two in May. In late October 1953 No 40 Squadron joined them and also flew Canberra B2s. The latter moved to Wittering in May 1954, the others to Cottesmore at roughly the same time allowing Coningsby to be reconstructed for the V-Force.

When the station re-opened in late 1956 its main runway, now 200ft wide, had been extended to 9,000ft in length and was supplemented by a widened 6,000ft long subsidiary runway, the normal layout for such a station.

Over the next few years Coningsby housed several squadrons of Canberras while the V-bombers were awaited. First in was No 57 from Honington in mid-November 1956 which disbanded at the end of the following year.

No IX Squadron came in from Binbrook on 2 June 1959 and was joined on 2 July 1959 by No 12 Squadron. Both flew Canberra B6s suitably modified to carry nuclear weapons and were part of the force assigned to SACEUR. On 13 July 1961 both squadrons disbanded.

A Canberra B.Mk 6 of IX Squadron at Coningsby.

On 1 March 1962 IX Squadron reformed followed by 12 Squadron on 1 July and on 1 December 1962 No 35 Squadron joined them. All were equipped with Vulcan B2s able to carry conventional or nuclear weapons. Their stay too was brief for in November 1964 they departed for Cottesmore and Coningsby's long stint as a bomber station ended.

More modification of the station followed for it had been chosen to be the main centre for TSR2. With its cancellation the pace of work slowed and soon it was on Care & Maintenance.

In 1966 Coningsby again became Active for the modern, well-equipped airfield was chosen as the first base for ground attack Phantom FGR2s. Further building work to adapt the station cost of £4.5 million, then Coningsby became part of Air Support Command in December 1967. A new No 5 School of Technical Training opened to train personnel needed to maintain Phantom systems, the first course beginning in December 1967. On 1 August 1968 No 228 OCU opened and the first

Vulcan B2 XM601 of IX Squadron on a Coningsby pad.

Phantom FGR2 arrived at Coningsby. No 5 STT became No 3 Squadron of No 228 OCU. October 1968 saw the first aircrew join 228 OCU which was also responsible for training the Royal Navy's Phantom personnel.

No 6 Squadron, the first to fly Phantom FGR2s, reformed here on 7 May 1969. Based here, it operated them until September 1974 having for company No 54 Squadron which flew Phantoms from Coningsby between 1 September 1969 and 29 March 1974. Completing a trio, No 41 Squadron was here between 1 April 1972 and 31 March 1977.

Phantom FGR2 ground attack aircraft of 6 Squadron (XV408 nearest) on Coningsby's bomber type huge ASP.

Two other squadrons acquired Phantom strike fighters here, No 111, which reformed on 1 June 1974 and moved to Leuchars on 3 November 1977, and No 29, which rearmed with them in late 1974. October 1974 had brought radical change when the station and squadrons transferred from 38 Group, Air Support Command, to 11 Group, Strike Command, and the role altered to air defence within the UKADR. Policy change also awarded OCUs shadow squadron status and a front-line role in wartime. As a result 228 OCU became No 64 (Reserve) Squadron.

On 1 March 1976 the Battle of Britain Memorial Flight arrived, bringing its Lancaster, two Hurricanes and a Spitfire, to which another four were added. For support duties the BBMF relied upon two Chipmunks and a Devon VP981, the last of these two types in RAF service. The Devon was auctioned in 1998 and bought by Air Atlantique, which painted it to represent Dove G-AMJZ for a Gulf Air anniversary. Now it is G-DHDV. In 1993 Dakota IV ZA947, a 1942 C-47 supplied to the RCAF and later operated in Europe as KG661, joined the Flight. Uncertainty over that being its true identity resulted in the new late serial number. The aircraft was added to the BBMF in March 1993 for use as a support aircraft and to aid training for tail-wheel aircraft like the Lancaster. Its initial markings were those carried by the Dakota of 271 Squadron, being flown by Flight Lieutenant David Lord when he was awarded the Victoria Cross for his courageous part in the ill-fated 1944 Arnhem venture. It later acquired the colours of a 267 Squadron aircraft.

PA474, the BBMF Lancaster, resting outside its home.

BBMFs Devon C.1 VP981, long-serving support aircraft now civilianised.

Phantoms were in front-line use when in June 1981 'hardening' of the station commenced. Hardened Aircraft Shelters, sufficient in number to protect the aircraft of two squadrons, were built on the southern side of the airfield. Less obvious steps were taken to protect 1,000 personnel from air attack, and the operations room was hardened too. Between 1 March and 31 October 1984 No 29 and No 64 (R) Squadrons used Waddington while Coningsby's runway was resurfaced in preparation for the next chapter in the station's story.

That commenced in November 1984 when the first air defence Tornado F2 equipped with Foxhunter radar with a range of 100 miles arrived for 229 OCU, which was re-established here on 1 November 1984 to train aircrew. On 1 May 1985 the OCU opened. Eight more Tornados had reached Coningsby by July 1985. The OCU was renamed No 65 (Reserve) Squadron, which saw its F2s replaced by Tornado F3s in 1986.

During 1985 the Tornado Air Intercept Trainer had been installed followed by an Air Combat simulator, and in 1988 by two Mission Simulators. At nearby RAF Woodhall Spa an enclave now held a modern facility allowing for RB 199 engines from Tornados to be fully stripped and overhauled.

Phantoms had been gradually phased out as 29 Squadron became the first front-line squadron to equip with Tornado F3s. No 228 OCU was sustained in connection with the Phantom Aircraft Servicing Flight, XV470 being the last Phantom handled. On 16 October 1987 it made the last flight by a Phantom from Coningsby, in the hands of Air Vice-Marshal D T Bryant OBE, who had flown Coningsby's first Phantom in 1968. No 64 (Reserve) Squadron departed for Leuchars on 22 April 1987 together with its Phantoms. After English Electric Lightnings were withdrawn from No 5 Squadron at Binbrook a new No 5 armed with Tornado F3s formed at Coningsby during February 1988.

A milestone in Tornado fighter history came at the start of August 1990 when No 5 Squadron was deployed to Dharan at the start of the build-up for operation *Desert Storm*, the first Iraq conflict. For three months No 5 and its F3s made available air defence of the Gulf region. They were replaced during December 1990 by 29 Squadron, which, during its three-month spell in Saudi Arabia, flew more than 500 air defence sorties.

Both squadrons were next operationally deployed in expedition style to Gioia del Colle, Italy, to help police no-fly zones over Bosnia during operation *Deny Flight*. Throughout this period Coningsby personnel continued to support the RAF commitment at Mount Pleasant in the Falklands. No 5 Squadron was also deployed to Al Kharg in support of operation *Bolton*. July 1992 saw the Tornado OCU renumbered as No 56 (Reserve) Squadron.

The Strategic Defence Review that followed the end of the 'Cold War' led to a reduction in the number of home defence fighter squadrons. Evidence of this came on 31 October 1998 when No 29 Squadron disbanded, leaving Coningsby to 5 Squadron and its twelve F3s, No 56 (Reserve) Squadron – the F3 Conversion Unit – holding twenty-one aircraft, and the Tornado F3 Operational Evaluation Unit, which had formed on 1 April 1987 and which, from July 1993, was part of the Air Warfare Centre at Waddington. The BBMF also remained at Coningsby. No 5 Squadron disbanded in September 2002 and 56 (Reserve) Squadron relocated to Leuchars in March 2003. Coningsby's runway then underwent improvement, during which period the BBMF lodged at Waddington.

All this was in preparation for a very exciting change. Eurofighter Typhoons would soon be heading this way, and Coningsby would become their main home as well as being the main UK air defence centre. The new phase began with the relocation of No 17 (Reserve) Squadron to Coningsby on 1 April 2005, and it received the first single-seat Typhoon to enter squadron service. No 17 had reformed at Warton on 1 September 2002 as the Typhoon Operational Evaluation Unit (OEU), its task being to bring the Typhoon into RAF service. No 29 (Reserve) Squadron had begun assembling at Warton in September 2003 to become the Typhoon OCU. It was to train engineers as well as pilots, a task developed over eleven months with support from BAE Systems. During June 2005 No 29 (Reserve) Squadron moved to Coningsby where, on 4 November 2005, it 'stood up' as the Operational Conversion Unit to train Typhoon pilots.

Representative Tornado F3s of Coningsby's squadrons on parade.

In addition to housing the two Typhoon organisations, July 2005 found the station as the home of the Fast Jet & Weapons Operational Evaluation Unit (FJWOEU), brought about through the merger of the Strike/Attack OEU previously at Boscombe Down, and which had formed there on 1 April 2004. With it were the Tornado F3 OEU, Air Guided Weapons OEU evaluating *Brimstone* and *Storm Shadow*, the Air-Launched Munitions Engineering & Development Investigation Team, and The Battle of Britain Memorial Flight.

From September 1939 to May 1944 No 3 Squadron used QO to identify themselves. Strangely, long after that item retired, No 3 Squadron's Typhoon F2s like QO-Z ZJ814 and QO-E ZJ923 display them. DC ZJ919 of No XI sits between the pair on Coningsby runway (Graham Murfitt).

Coningsby was by now in the forefront of the Single Living Accommodation Modernisation Programme, with 552 single quarters, each room having en-suite facilities. Those, and good communal areas, have made this a very modern RAF base. Other improvements for all living there were a nursery centre, general community centre, hobby and handicraft clubs, 'The Cedar Bowl' four-lane bowling alley, The Thrift Shop, Sports & Social Club, and a Health & Fitness Centre.

On 31 March 2006 No 3 Squadron arrived from Cottesmore having left behind its Harriers. Next day the FJWOEU, flying Harrier GR 9s and Tornado Mks 3 and 4, became No 41 Squadron, taking the number plate of the famous squadron that had just disbanded at Coltishall. At Coningsby No 3 Squadron rearmed and became the lead front-line operational Typhoon-equipped squadron. Compared with the Tornado F3, the newcomer was much more agile, far more sophisticated, more adaptable and also better suited to the RAF's new role as an available expeditionary force.

The first day of April 2006 had brought evidence of that with the introduction of a 'new' operational concept. Formed was an organisation similar in style to the 1943 'Airfield' introduction. An 'Airfield's' personnel combined to form and support a comprehensive forward force with the ability and mobility to be rapidly repositioned to operate far from base and in its entirety. Coningsby's 2006 variant was entitled No 121 Expeditionary Air Wing and embraced the station's squadrons, support formations and input from other bases as a field force. Also on 1 April 2006 No 6 Squadron, the last flying Jaguars, moved in from Coltishall. During June 2006 five Typhoons (four of 17 (Reserve) Squadron and one from 29 (Reserve) Squadron) were, as a composite qualified weapons instructors' wing, detached to Leuchars for two weeks to participate for the first time in a major defence exercise.

No 6 Squadron's Coningsby stay was shorter than expected for, on 30 April 2007, it flew its last sortie and disbanded on 31 May 2007. The Jaguar had by then seen thirty-three years of RAF service, and No 6 Squadron had existed without a break for an astonishing ninety-three years.

No XI Squadron had, on 29 March 2007, become the second front-line Typhoon squadron to be 'stood up' at Coningsby. The first multi-role Typhoon GR3 squadron, on 6 August it received the first two multi-role examples to enter squadron service.

In June 2007 six Typhoons of 29 Squadron carried out the first deployment of the type to Akrotiri, Cyprus. No 3 Squadron was declared fully operational with effect from 29 June 2007, and on 2 July became responsible for Southern Quick Reaction Alert. On 17 August 2007 it was scrambled for the first time, to intercept a Russian Tu 95 Bear H reconnaissance bomber nosing around the edge of the UKADR. QRA was being shared. Tornado F3s at Leeming and Leuchars protected northern areas. Nos 3 and XI Squadrons subsequently shared QRA South at Coningsby. Disbandment of 25 Squadron at Leeming in March 2008, and that station's change of role, left only two operational RAF fighter stations in the UK.

On 1 July 2008 No XI Squadron was declared as operational in an air-ground role. Weapons to be used were *Paveway 2*, enhanced *Paveway 2* and freefall 1,000lb HE bombs. The aircraft can carry the Litening III designator pod, which can transfer pictures and data to ground troops through their laptops, allowing both forces to chose suitable responses to enemy ground activity.

Fashionable it is to foolishly knock Typhoon, a superb combat aircraft. Landing here is ZJ939 DXI, an FGR Mk 4 of XI Squadron, on 5 November 2008.

Typhoons replaced Coningsby-supported Tornado F3s in the Falklands, during Autumn 2009 and No 6 Squadron will train here in 2010 to use multi-role Typhoons. Coningsby will for the foreseeable future serve as Britain's main home air defence base.

Main features:
Runways: 264° 4,850ft x 150ft, 306° 4,650ft x 150ft, 217° 4,320ft x 150ft concrete and asphalt. *Hangars:* two Type J, three T2, one B1. *Hardstandings:* thirty-six heavy bomber type. *Accommodation:* RAF: officers 122, SNCOs 396, ORs 1,678; WAAF: officers 13, SNCOs 15, ORs 356. Modifications: Numerous changes – particularly for V-Bomber use – have been made during adaptation for changing roles. The mid-1990s runway 08/26 remains at 9,000ft and features Rotary Hydraulic Arresting Gear. The huge ASP and twenty-two special hardstandings were built when the station was used by the V-force. BBMF uses the B1 hangar. HASs were added on the south side during the early 1980s.

Places of interest nearby:
Dominant is the 100ft tower of Tattersall Castle open for viewing and created by Cromwell as a mark of self importance and aspirations and one of the greatest Middle Ages monuments for many miles. Variously open March to May is Springfields near Spalding, a most beautiful huge garden site for bulb lovers.

CRANWELL, Lincolnshire

53°02N/00°29W 218ft asl; TF015490. NW of Sleaford, between A17(T) and B1429 roads

Cranwell is Britain's most demanding 'university'. Not only do its students need to meet high educational requirements, they have to be supremely fit and face a range of aptitude and motivation tests to make certain they possess leadership potential and necessary skills. At pass-out they can as officers look back upon one of the finest military academy courses available in the world.

The station has a long and perhaps unexpected history. For much of WWI it was a naval base. Very unusually it also featured two landing grounds and associated built-up areas bisected by a now tree-lined public road which passes through the very impressive camp site. Many who have learnt their skills. ground or aircrew, have risen to high positions and prominence in the Service and in many other endeavours. As if that is insufficient it was here that Frank Whittle – himself a Cranwell cadet – saw the Gloster Pioneer make its first flight propelled by the engine he invented. Although not the first to fly, it is fair to call it the first successful jet aircraft.

Cranwell originated in November 1915 when around 2,500 acres of farmland were acquired mainly from the Earl of Bristol's estate. Construction began on 28 December 1915 of wooden huts and assorted buildings for personnel who would be here to handle aeroplanes, dirigibles and kite balloons. Featuring two wooden hangars and two flight sheds, the landing ground was sited to the south of the B1429 road where the present much larger airfield is situated. To the north of the road was a second flying field with balloon sheds along its northern perimeter. This site was chosen in 1914 because it was flat, had no dykes and was near coastal ranges and was called Cranwell North. Buildings requisitioned for use by motor transport in WWI can still be seen from the B1429 road. As with many older aerodromes a single track branch railway line linked the camp with the nearest mainline route, in this instance the Grantham-Boston line. Two locomotives plied the line from 1917 to after WWII, the present Main Guardroom occupying the site of the station.

The Royal Naval Air Service Central Training Establishment Cranwell opened under the command of Commodore Godfrey M Paine on 1 April 1916 and later became HMS *Daedalus* because officers and ratings at Cranwell were officially on the strength of the Medway depot ship of that name. A Boys' Training Wing was also established to train ratings as mechanics and riggers. In February 1918 Prince Albert (later Duke of York and HM King George VI) was appointed Officer in Charge Boys and later Officer Commanding No 4 Squadron Boys' Wing before he left Cranwell in August 1918.

Training was provided by Nos 201, 202 and 213 Training Depot Stations renamed Nos 56, 57 and 58 TDS respectively. There was an Airship Training Wing, Aeroplane Repair Section, and a Wireless Operators' School, and in 1917 briefly a US presence, whereas the Electrical and Wireless School opened in May 1916 continued functioning for decades.

RAF Station Cranwell came into being on 1 April 1918, and Lord Trenchard was keen to see that a cadet college was established here to provide basic and flying training for future RAF leaders. Cranwell's future became questionable after the war until in his Parliamentary Bill of 1919 Mr Winston Churchill, Secretary of State for Air, included a proposal for the RAF cadet college at Cranwell. The Churchill-Trenchard Memorandum was approved and Trenchard reckoned Cranwell an ideal site where the cadets would be 'marooned in the wilderness', cut off from 'pastimes they could not organise themselves', and that they would find life 'cheaper, healthier and more wholesome' at Cranwell.

Suggestions approved, the RAF College opened on 5 February 1920 under the command of Air Commodore C A H Longcroft, and was the world's first military Air Academy. In 1922 came the proposals that permanent buildings should replace the wartime huts, but not until 1929 were plans drawn up for money was short and the depression deep. Sir Samuel Hoare was amazed when he saw drawings prepared by the Ministry of Works. He reckoned that they portrayed a pseudo-Gothic version of St Pancras Station influenced by a Scottish Hydro. He therefore decided to take the architect James West to visit Wren's Royal Hospital, Chelsea and West designed the magnificent College Hall Building which dominates Cranwell.

Fearing cancellation Hoare saw to it that a foundation stone was laid on North Airfield before the April 1929 General Election. The stone may now be seen by the main entrance to the College. Funding for the Hall had yet to be secured, but in September 1933 the magnificent building, constructed of rustic and moulded brick with important features faced with Portland Stone, was completed at a total cost of £321,000.

Aerial view of RAF College Cranwell early in the 1920s. (via Bruce Robertson)

Pass-out parade before the glorious Cranwell College Hall buildings during the visit of Harold Macmillan, the Prime Minister, in April 1959.

Formal opening by HRH The Prince of Wales took place on 11 October 1934. The central block, floodlit at night, is connected by narrow corridors leading to the accommodation wings, the total facing extending 800ft. Six Corinthian columns support the central portico which supports a pediment tower and dome, the latter supported by pillars. At the top of the dome at a height of 130ft a beacon rotates like a lighthouse. The impressive wrought iron entrance gates and lanterns set upon their pillars were made in the 1930s by Flight Sergeant Benton, serving at the College.

Entrance through the main door is denied to cadets until they march off the parade ground, and to the tune of Auld Lang Syne. Passing through the doorway marks their transition to commissioned status. Inside the entrance hall is the Queen's Colour, large portraits and standards of disbanded squadrons which hang from the rotunda. On the wall of the stairway leading to it is Gerald Coulson's painting of 617 Squadron sinking the *Tirpitz*. One long corridor known as The Founder's Gallery accommodates paintings of those who famously encouraged the birth of the Service – Lord Trenchard, Field Marshal Smuts and Sir Winston Churchill.

In the beautiful dining-room hang portraits of famous former cadets among them HRH The Prince of Wales, Wing Commander Malcolm VC, Air Marshal Sir Richard Atcherley, three Marshals of the RAF – Sir Dermot Boyle, Sir Andrew Humphrey and Sir Keith Williamson, along with Orde's portrait of Douglas Bader and a painting of Sir Frank Whittle. He is further remembered in a large modern lecture complex at Cranwell. The College Hall inevitably dominates any thoughts of Cranwell, but what of the overall history?

The two flying fields remain, with South Airfield since the 1930s being served from two C-Type Sheds. In the 1950s an apron was added and it has a rather short concrete runway. North Airfield remains grass only and is used by Cranwell Gliding Club and by light aircraft.

In the 1920s pilots trained using a wide variety of aircraft including Avro 504Ks and Ns, Bristol Fighters, DH9As and Sopwith Snipes. The Armstrong Siddeley Atlas was introduced for the training of bomber pilots, the Siskin for those with fighter desires. In the 1930s Avro Tutors, Airspeed Oxfords and Hawker Hart variants replaced them and were used until the war began. Such had been the increase in flying training that use was made of nearby grass areas suitable for use as landing grounds. Temple Bruer was one, another developed into wartime Wellingore.

Long-distance flying was undertaken by Cranwell's Long Range Development Flight established in 1927. Using a modified Hawker Horsley, Lieutenant C R Carr established an unofficial record in May 1927 when he forced landed in the Persian Gulf area at the end of a 3,420 mile flight achieved in thirty-four and a half hours.

Two years later, flying the Fairey Long Range Monoplane K1991, Squadron Leader A G Jones-Williams and Flight Lieutenant N H Jenkins made a flight of 4,130 miles from Cranwell to Karachi taking fifty hours thirty-five minutes. Then in February 1933 Gayford and Nichollettes flew 5,341 miles from Cranwell to Walvis Bay, South Africa in fifty-seven and a half hours – some flight!

As well as fulfilling its officer cadet training function, Cranwell in the 1920s was the home of No 4 (Apprentices) Wing until Halton opened in 1926. Frank Whittle was a Cranwell trained apprentice.

Prominent in Cranwell's history is the Electrical and Wireless School which originated from earlier organisations, arrived on 6 August 1929 and was renamed No 1 E & WS on 1 November 1938. That became No 1 Radio School which, between January 1943 and 9 October 1950, trained air and ground wireless operators. From 10 March 1941 No 8 Radio School supplemented it and continued training students until June 1946. Among the aircraft used by the Wireless School were Westland Wallaces used between 1939 to November 1940. More spectacular in the war were the School's huge, lumbering aged Vickers Valentia biplanes. In use at Cranwell from 1936 to October 1941, they were certainly incongruous with the E.28/39 Pioneer jet which on 15 May 1941 made its first flight in the hands of P E G Sayer. It flew fifteen more times from Cranwell which, on 5 March 1943, saw the first flight of the Gloster F.9/40 Meteor forerunner. More conventional were the Proctors and Dominies used to train radio operators between November 1940 and November 1947. Ansons, too, were used between June 1949 and October 1952.

Throughout its history Cranwell has hosted a wide array of ground units and continues to do so. One was the RAF Hospital which served local airfields between 1922 and 1940. The School of Store Accounting and Storekeeping opened in 1934 then in December 1936 became the Equipment Training School and stayed until June 1941. The Supplies Depot was here from October 1936 to November 1949 and the School of Clerks Accountancy between May 1939 and late January 1941. HQ No 21 Group, Training Command functioned here between February 1938 and July 1944.

Upon the outbreak of war the College closed and immediately re-opened as the RAF College Flying Training School using Airspeed Oxfords.

Throughout the war the emphasis remained on training. By early 1941 the aircraft establishment of the RAF College SFTS was 150 Oxfords. To reduce pressure during circuit flying, relief landing grounds were used at Fulbeck, Wellingore, Coleby Grange, Barkston Heath, Caistor and Spitalgate. The situation was eased when No 2 FIS formed here on 10 September 1940 using Tutors and Oxfords. It developed into No 2 CFS on 14 November 1940 and on 15 June 1941 moved to Church Lawford.

Avro Tutors of RAF College Cranwell 1935.

Modern equivalent of the Avro Tutor, an SAL Bulldog wears the light blue 'Cranwell band'.

In their place came part of a complex organisation, No 3 (Coastal) OTU. Arriving on 29 July 1941 they were only temporarily here and used both Whitleys and Wellingtons to train maritime reconnaissance crews. In June 1943 the OTU left for Haverford West.

During 1940 the airfield was attacked unsuccessfully several times. The sole bomb to hit the College, in August 1941, was a small incendiary which broke a tile. Far more serious damage occurred when on 18 March 1942 Whitley P5052 of No 3 OTU hit the roof and crashed into a lecture room serving as a dormitory, killed its crew of three and started an inferno.

Throughout 1943 the still busy RAF College FTS still held mainly Oxfords supplemented with Master IIs, Tiger Moths, Blenheims and Spitfires. Re-titled 17 SFTS in March 1943 it moved to Spitalgate in May 1945. Over the war years output from the Cranwell aircrew organisations had been enormous and embraced airmen from Commonwealth and many Allied countries. Some idea of the number of personnel at Cranwell can be gauged from the September 1943 Battle of Britain commemoration parade when an estimated 7,000 took part. Listed accommodation in December 1944 totalled 10,766 personnel, 1,837 being WAAFs. The war claimed the lives of 326 Cranwell graduates out of the 931 who served over 600 won decorations. These included Wing Commander H G Malcolm posthumously awarded the Victoria Cross for his attacks on airfields in North Africa.

Come the end of the war and units came and went fast. On 21 July 1945 No 1 Officer Advanced Training School moved from College Hall to Digby after a stay which began in March 1944. No 17 SFTS formed on 20 March 1944 from the College SFTS and flew Masters and Oxfords as well as Tiger Moths moved to Feltwell in April 1947.

That month was special for it witnessed the official reopening of the RAF College. Other 1947 changes brought in the Secretarial Branch Training Establishment and Equipment Officer School both of which moved on during 1948.

October 1950 saw the departure to Locking of No I Radio School so long part of the Cranwell scene, but its apprentices element stayed becoming No 6 Radio School before, on 1 December 1952,that also moved to Locking. Cranwell then became responsible for officer training only. At this time Chipmunks of No 3 Initial Training Wing (later No 3 ITS) provided basic flying training. Cranwell had long relied upon one asphalt East-West runway on the South Airfield but now, to allow the use of Meteor 7s and Vampire T11s, two concrete runways were constructed on the South Airfield and supplemented in 1954 by the runways available at Barkston Heath which remains in use as an RLG.

A major rebuilding programme came underway in 1960 at a cost of over £2 million. Included was a new Sergeants' Mess which opened in 1963, an Airmen's Social Club opened 1964, another Officers' Mess, a large instructional block, a thermodynamics and engineering complex and married quarters. The space now available was sufficient for the RAF Technical College to move here from Henlow.

In 1970 the College's half century was marked by a Royal Visit and the following year His Royal Highness the Prince of Wales underwent a five month flying training course at the end of which he was awarded his Wings by the Chief of the Air Staff.

Dominies have since the 1960s served as navigation trainers. Cranwells' were much modified then painted black overall like XS727 'D' to make them visible – in daylight…

During November 1971 No 22 Group disbanded and Cranwell took control of all the University Air Squadrons. January 1974 brought the College of Air Warfare from Manby along with their Canberras and DH 125 Dominies, and functioned here until 1978.

On 30 May 1975 the Commandant-in-Chief of the College, Her Majesty the Queen, presented a new Colour and in April 1976 the Central Flying School moved to Cranwell when Little Rissington closed. Their stay was short for on 21 November 1977 CFS moved to Leeming. The piston Provost to Meteor 7 or de Havilland Vampire T11 training progression preceded the basing here of Jet Provosts with which the college embarked upon all-through jet training.

In 1978 a fundamental change brought graduate and non-graduate cadets together in a single-gate entry to a twenty-four week course (except for some specialists) which also meant that a wide range of entrants – school leavers and some experienced RAF personnel – found themselves together on the IOTC. There were now three training squadrons each of up too 120 cadets, and six main courses per year. Four weeks would be devoted to basic training, nine to the basics of leadership.

During 1987 the Flying Training School at the College was re-organised. As a result No 3 FTS reformed on 1 February 1989 from the flying element of basic training. On 29 October 1991 Cranwell's last Jet Provost retired and in 1992 the Officer & Aircrew Selection Centre moved in from Biggin Hill.

Other changes of policy first brought the Shorts Tucano to Cranwell then their quite early removal for concentration at Linton-on-Ouse. April 1995 saw Bulldogs of CFS Scampton arrive as their parent joined 3 FTS. Closure of Finningley resulted in No 6 FTS also becoming part of 3 FTS here in August 1995. The ten Dominies, soon upgraded to feature head-up display and other changes, became No 55 (Reserve) Squadron and the eleven Jetstreams functioning as flying classrooms and equipped No 45 (Reserve) Squadron to afford twin propeller engine flying. Until retired the thirteen Bulldogs equipped the RAF College Air Squadron.

Much use was made of Jet Provosts at Cranwell. XW361 21, a Mk 5, sports the red and white paint scheme.

Among larger Cranwell aircraft have been a few Varsity trainers including WF410.

On 1 April 1997 the RAF College Cranwell became part of the Training Group Defence Agency, in turn part of Personnel and Training Command. The 'Agency' head is the AOC-in-C Personnel and Training Command, the Chief Executive being the AOC Training Group, both having their Head Quarters at RAF Innsworth. The AOC and Commandant of the RAF College is also the AOC Commanding 3 FTS, the Directorate of Recruiting, Selection and Initial Officer Training, the Department of Elementary Flying Training (including UASs), the Department of Specialist Ground Training and HQ Air Cadets. Units lodged at the College include HQ CFS, the RAF Aerobatics Team (ie. The Red Arrows), the Air Warfare Centre Cranwell, HQ Provost and Security Services (Central Region) and the Bands of the RAF College and RAF Regiment. The College and parented units (Barkston Heath, Newton, Syerston and Scampton) hold 1,162 Service personnel, 444 civil servants and a 700 strong civilian workforce. Student population numbers 790 with a further 950 based within the sixteen UASs.

The RAF College Cranwell concentrates upon initial officer training aiming to develop strong leaders through cost-effective training and a wide range of experiences connected generally with aerospace.

Extensive is the flying and ground training here. On the North Side area Initial Officer Training takes place. Cranwell Gliding Club, part of the RAF Gliding & Soaring Association, operates from there. Others in occupation are an Air Warfare Centre, Aerosystems Department (specialist training division), the Directorate and Inspectorate of Recruiting, and the Officers and Aircrew Selection Centre. Cranwell South provides home for the flying elements, the Defence College of Aeronautical Engineering, and the Defence College of Logistics & Personnel Administration.

RAF flying training is administered from Cranwell; it has recently been subjected to much change and is now part of a Private Finance Initiative (PFI) scheme. It covers Initial Officer Training for pilots without UAS experience, who undergo Elementary Flying Training on light piston-engined aircraft of JETS. Students from University Air Squadrons will have had basic pilot training. After selection for Fast-jet, Rotary or Multi-engined Training, some students proceed to Basic Advanced Flying Training (BFTS) using Tucanos at Linton-on-Ouse. There they are prepared for Fast-Jet Advanced Flying Training at Valley. Rotary-wing pilots proceed to the Defence Helicopter Flying Training School Shawbury. Multi-engined training begins at Cranwell with a short lead-in course on light piston-engined aircraft followed by training on multi-engined types. After completing those courses pilots are awarded their Wings, then proceed to the appropriate OCU.

Head Quarters No 1 Elementary Flying Training School, resident in Rauceby, has controlled all three Elementary Flying Training Squadrons, CFS Elementary Squadron and the Defence Elementary Training School (DETS), supported by a civilian contract with Babcock plc. DETS uses Firefly T67M 260 aircraft and is based at Barkston Heath. It trains up to 130 Army and Navy student pilots annually.

No 1 EFTS oversees No 703 Naval Air Squadron and 674 Squadron AAC, Army flying grading at Middle Wallop and the RAF Multi-engine lead-in at Cranwell.

Central Flying School (Elementary) Squadron, Cranwell-based since 1995, is part of No 1 Elementary Flying Training School (1 EFTS) and is responsible to HQ CFS for maintenance of flying standards within flying instructor courses. It provides flying instructor courses for the three services and overseas students. The main six-month course embraces ground school and 80 hours flying Grob 115E Tutors provided and maintained by VT Aerospace. Most graduates proceed to posts within the EFT system.

No 1 EFTS Cranwell provides fixed-wing basic elementary flying training for the three services, running a 60-hour basic flying course lasting for about four months. It annually trains about 160 new RAF pilots, who subsequently proceed to fast-jet, rotary or multi-engined courses. Ab-initio navigation training for WSOs is afforded for 55 (Reserve) Squadron.

No 3 Flying Training School comprises Flying Wing and No 55 (Reserve) Squadron. Flying Wing includes No 45 (Reserve) Squadron, which for pilot training uses the Beechcraft King Air B200 twin-engined aircraft that replaced the Jetstream. Using Dominie T2s supplemented by Tutors drawn from No 115 (R) Squadron (the CFS Tutor Squadron), No 55(R) Squadron trains navigators, air engineers, weapons systems operators, air signallers and loadmasters. Incorporated within Flying Wing are No 115 (R) CFS Tutor Squadron, Ground School Squadron, Air Traffic Control Squadron, General Service Training Squadron and the Meteorological Office.

Replacement for Cranwells' long serving Jetstream at Cranwell, the Beech Kingair. G-RAFX depicted.

Cranwell is the home of the renowned Central Flying School headed by a Commandant whose HQ returned from Scampton, and became a lodger at Cranwell in 1995. At that time the CFS Tucano Squadron was transferred to Topcliffe, then to No 1 FTS, Linton-on-Ouse. The CFS Bulldog Squadron, now Tutor Squadron, moved to 3 FTS RAF Cranwell. The CFS Hawk Squadron reformed as two CFS Flights named 19 (Reserve) Squadron and 208 (Reserve) Squadron, which remained at Valley. CFS (Helicopter) Squadron stayed at Shawbury.

Rationalisation of instructor training led to new titles for instructors: Qualified Flying Instructor, Qualified Pilot Navigation Instructor, Qualified Navigation Instructor, Qualified Helicopter Navigation Instructor, Qualified Helicopter Crewman Instructor, Qualified Air Engineer Instructor, Qualified Air Electronics Instructor, and Qualified Weapons Instructor.

Commandant CFS exercises control of the Royal Air Force Aerobatic Team, the Scampton-based Red Arrows. CFS has existed for longer than any other flying training school in the world, and is renowned for flying instructors of the highest standards and the maintenance of the highest possible standards of pure flying and instructing.

RAF flying training has become part of a major Private Finance Initiative (PFI). The VT Group in 1997 won a ten-year light aircraft contract involving delivery and support of ninety-nine Grob Tutors distributed over twelve UK airfields, replacing SAL Bulldogs. As the end of the contracted period approached a new far-embracing contract became available for bids. Three consortia responded : Sterling (Thales and Boeing), Victor Flying Training Services (Bombardier KBR, Siegler Services Flight Safety Services and Northrop Grumman), and Ascent (Lockheed Martin and VT Group).

This new PFI contract for the UK Military Flying Training System was to extend for twenty-five years at an estimated cost of around £6 billion. The requirement called for the training of all new aircrew for the British services extending from selection to readiness to fly operational aircraft.

In November 2006 Ascent became the preferred bidder for the provision of simulator training, a task to commence in April 2007. Contracts were signed in August 2008 with Ascent and also with Victor Flying Training Services (VT), already handling one-third of flying training. The existing agreement relating to Grob Tutors was extended to November 2008 so that training could continue for the three services. Tutors would now also be provided at Boscombe Down for continuation and refresher flying.

With flying training in civilian hands, the MoD would still control overall policy, and set and monitor standards, while CFS would monitor instruction, flying training and output. IFT would embrace initial and common ground school instruction for all trainees for 'the three pipelines' fixed-wing aircraft training for the RAF, RN and Royal Marines, including basic training for fast-jet. Value for money was to be the core reason for the introduction of PFI, which involved transfers from HQ 22 Group.

A five-year contract signed in November 2008 was set at £160m for instruction basic flying training for RAF and UAS pilots, and a ten-year contract for IFT at a rate of 57,000 flying hours per annum.

No small concern arose in August 2008 when the German Grob firm, builder and supporter of the Tutor, was declared bankrupt, and a buyer was sought to maintain support to the IFT formula. Just what effect the financial disasters of 2008/2009 will have upon all PFI provisions remains to be seen.

Cranwell Tower, 2008.

I never pass or visit Cranwell without recalling one quite astonishing experience there. It was April 1959 and Mr Harold Macmillan, Prime Minister, visited the College primarily to smooth out the waves caused by Mr Duncan Sandys 'no more aeroplanes' statement.

The Dining Hall looked magnificent when the great man looking older and shorter than usual took his place at top table. Pure chance placed me opposite to him on a finger table and when the Mess Waiter asked for his choice Mr M motioned him to take other orders first then when he returned the PM said 'I'll have the spaghetti'.

His skill with a fork was astonishing and as he whisked it around he kept staring at me. Like everyone at the top table I had opted for safety and the roast lamb. It was not long before the Hall erupted as Cadets and soon many others were encouraging Mr Macmillan as he used his great political skill to win the day. He had no need for spin doctors, he was one himself – literally!

Main features:
North Airfield: *Runways:* grass, N/S 3,600ft, NE/SW 4,500ft, E/W 2,700ft, SE/NW 2,250ft.
South Airfield: *Runways:* grass E/W 7,500ft, NE/SW 3,300ft, SE/NW 3,600ft. E/W asphalt 3,300ft x 150ft. *Hangars:* Two C Type, eight F Type, four Bellman, five Blister. *Hardstandings:* nil. *Accommodation:* RAF: 465 officers, 744 SNCOs, 7,7720 ORs; WAAF: 37 officers, 78 SNCOs, 1,722 ORs.
1954 update resulted in building of two concrete runways on South Airfield and an apron in front of the C Sheds. ORPs acting as warm-up pads were built on the south side at each end of the main runway. The 09/27 runway (6,831ft) and 01/19 (4,803ft) have Type A barrier nets and arrester systems unsuitable for fast, heavy jets.

DEBACH, Suffolk

52°08N/01°06E 180ft asl; TM240540. S of B1078, 7 miles W of Wickham Market

Built none too well by the US Army in 1943-4, Debach whose operational career spanned only seven months was the last airfield to become occupied as a US 8th AF bomber base and lay within the 3rd BD/AD area. Here, the 493rd Bomb Group began arriving in April 1944 and equipped with B-24s the following month. B-17s replaced them in September 1944.

The last 8th AF bomber group to become operational, the 493rd Group's first mission was flown on 6 June 1944 as part of the assault on Normandy's beaches. It aided the break-out from St-Lô. As well as assisting during September 1944's airborne landings in Holland, participating in the Ardennes offensive and the aerial bombardment which supported the March 1945 Rhine crossing, the Group acted chiefly against industrial targets including an ordnance depot at Magdeburg and the oil plant at Merseburg.

Deterioration of the runways at Debach became so serious that at the end of 1944 the Group temporarily moved to Little Walden whilst repairs took place, and returned to Debach in March 1945.

Resuming their bombing campaign they attacked airfields, bridges and gun batteries. Their last mission was flown on 20 April 1945 when they attacked marshalling yards at Nauen. Return to the USA took place early in August 1945.

After the war Debach became a POW holding camp and later accommodated displaced persons. Parts of two runways remain, also the control tower.

Main features:
Runways: 180° 6,000ft x 150ft, 250°, 310°, concrete and tarmac. *Hangars:* two T2.
Hardstandings: fifty loop type. *Accommodation:* 421 officers, 2,473 enlisted men.

DEBDEN, Essex

51°59N/00°16E 393ft asl; TL565340. 3 miles SE Saffron Walden on A130

For those privileged to be at RAF Debden on 25 April 1975 it was both a sad and significant day, for the occasion marked the formal closure of this historic station.

Broadly speaking, Debden's history can be divided into four distinct periods. It originated as one of the Expansion Scheme stations during the late 1930s, its location largely determined by the chance forced-landing of a Bristol Bulldog in May 1934.

Construction began in 1935 and was still incomplete at the time of its official opening on 22 April 1937, No 87 Squadron having the distinction of being the first unit to be based here, flying its Fury IIs and later Gladiators.

Accommodation was for three squadrons and soon Nos 80 and 73 arrived, also equipped with Gladiators. In November 1937 No 73 Squadron was replaced by 29 Squadron flying Hawker Demon two-seater fighters, but when 80 Squadron was ordered overseas in April 1938 No 85 Squadron was

Gloster Gladiator K7967 of Debden's No 87 Squadron in 1938.

re-born at Debden and it was these three squadrons which saw out the final months of peace, Nos 85 and 87 flying Hurricanes and No 29 flying Blenheims. Before converting to Hurricanes No 87 Squadron won acclaim for aerobatics performed by three Gladiators tied together. They performed in various parts of England and visited France for the air display at Villacoublay on 8 July 1938. Now it was back to France again, for the war was only a week old when Nos 85 and 87 were posted there. They were replaced at Debden by Nos 17 and 504 Squadrons, also flying Hurricanes.

As one of the important Sector stations within 11 Group, the southern half of East Anglia was under the watchful eye of Debden Operations Room. Construction work continued after the commencement of hostilities with runways and additional taxi-strips laid, the defences being strengthened by the addition of AA units.

A satellite airfield at Castle Camps was also prepared, but the squadrons were frequently split to operate Flights from Martlesham Heath, used as a forward base on a rotation basis.

With all three squadrons it was a case of routine patrols and practice interceptions – important, if unspectacular. Temporary detachments were made to other airfields, the Hurricanes being particularly busy during the evacuation from Dunkirk. Likewise, when such remnants of our valiant, decimated squadrons in France returned to Britain, Debden received No 85 Squadron back to re-muster under its new Commanding Officer, Squadron Leader Peter Townsend, to fight the imminent Battle of Britain. The Blenheims of 29 Squadron were on frequent night patrols, working up on the new AI radar. It was on 25 June 1940 that bombs were first dropped at Debden, the raider using as its marker the flarepath which was switched on for a returning Blenheim. Damage was insignificant. Later No 29 Squadron moved to Digby and the tempo for the Hurricanes increased.

Castle Camps satellite became operational in July, but it was August which proved to be the hot month – both in terms of weather and enemy activity. The number of plots at Debden Operation Room increased, indicated from information supplied by RDF stations and the Observer Corps, and interceptions increased rapidly. Both Nos 1 and 85 Squadrons moved south to be replaced by Nos 111 and 601 Squadrons.

On 24 August the Luftwaffe mounted its concentrated effort to eliminate fighter stations. Debden soon figured within this phase of the Battle and suffered its first major attack on 26 August when, in mid-afternoon, a small force of Do 17s bombed the station, damaging the landing ground, buildings and aircraft inflicting casualties. The leading Dornier was shot down nearby, and from its wreckage a map indicating the course to Debden was retrieved and proudly displayed for the rest of the war in the Officers' Mess.

Four days later, Debden received more attention when, early on 31 August, a strong force of Dornier 17s, escorted by Bf 110s, attacked, again causing damage to buildings and aircraft with further casualties. The raiders were engaged by Spitfires of No 19 Squadron from nearby Duxford. Losses were suffered on both sides, but the enemy never again bombed Debden in such strength. Instead, attacks on Britain were now made mainly under cover of darkness and again Debden's squadrons were involved. The Beaufighter was being introduced to operational use and No 25 Squadron arrived in October, working up on this type to intercept the night bomber. No 85 Squadron had also returned to Debden with a mixture of Defiants and Hurricanes for night defence duties, with No 264 Squadron's Defiants replacing 25 Squadron by the end of the year.

So 1940 closed with the Battle of Britain a victory for the immortal 'Few'. Debden can boast of playing a vital part in the action. There was a price to pay, all participating squadrons at Debden losing valuable pilots. One such was Flight Lieutenant 'Dickie' Lee of 85 Squadron, whose skill was legendary at Debden long before the war. Action film required for a comedy starring George Formby involved flying an aircraft *through* No 1 Hangar – duly accomplished by 'Dickie'.

Their Majesties King George VI and Queen Elizabeth were visitors at Debden on 28 January 1941, but on 14 February the station received an unwelcome guest – an He 111 which landed and took off again before the airfield's guns could be used. In the next few months the airfield was busy with pilots undergoing final training on Hurricanes, for No 52 OTU was established here and also included Battles and Masters. The Havoc made its presence felt at Debden too, when No 85 Squadron began conversion, later moving to Hunsdon.

As 1941 progressed, new squadrons were formed at Debden. No 418 (Canadian) Squadron began its career in November, flying Douglas Boston III intruders, and the aesthetic Mosquito made its debut as a night fighter when 157 Squadron formed at Debden, equipping at Castle Camps.

Fighters were now on the offensive rather than the defensive and by the turn of the year the Debden Wing had formed. Thus 1942 could well be called 'Spitfire Year' at Debden, the first nine months' duties being undertaken by various RAF squadrons, operating mainly *Circus* operations. One squadron, No 65, was moved to the new satellite at Great Sampford in April and No 71 'Eagle' Squadron replaced it at Debden. This was a prelude for major change as, in September, the other two 'Eagle' Squadrons came to Debden to be officially transferred to the USAAF. Thus, the 4th Fighter Group was born, and with it the second chapter of Debden's history. The three squadrons, now re-numbered 334, 335 and 336, carried on a similar pattern of operations, still flying Spitfire Vs but with American markings until the spring of 1943. After reluctant conversion to the P-47 Thunderbolt the initial mission with the new type was flown on 10 March – the first kill coming on 13 April. US 8th AF bomber losses were worrying, deeper fighter cover was needed and Debden's P-47s created history on 28 July 1943 by being the first to penetrate German airspace, an achievement made possible by using newly introduced auxiliary fuel tanks.

More success followed and, under the brilliant leadership of Colonel Don Blakeslee, 1944 at Debden was eventful. In February P-51 Mustangs replaced the Thunderbolts and with these Blakeslee led the 4th Fighter Group to Berlin on 4 March – another 'first'. With two underwing tanks the red-nosed Mustangs roamed far over Europe gaining a steadily mounting total of enemy aircraft destroyed. D-Day, 6 June, had the squadrons flying three times, supporting ground operations, but it was on 21 June that Debden spear-headed another 'first' – this time a 'shuttle' escort via Poland and a landing in Russia. From Russia they flew to Italy, providing escort en route, returning to Debden on 5 July, again providing escort. The Group was awarded the Distinguished Unit Citation, the US highest corporate military honour.

In October 1944 a new sound at Debden heralded the arrival of the jet fighter, for No 616 Squadron had sent a detachment of Meteors to develop tactics.

The closing months of the war were not without incident, as on 18 March when a returning Mustang carried two pilots aboard, one landing in enemy territory to rescue his companion. Many dignitaries visited Debden during American tenure, and the station's popularity for parties led to many varied types of visiting aircraft, British and American.

With the cessation of hostilities in Europe, the 4th Fighter Group emerged as the highest overall scoring unit with over 1,000 enemy aircraft destroyed.

The post-war years were with RAF Technical Training Command – firstly as the Empire Radio School. Amongst the varied aircraft used were the two prestigious *Mercuries*, a Halifax and later a Lincoln, both of which made global tours. The station's role continued as the Debden Division of RAF Technical College until 1960, the last types flown here being Varsities and Chipmunks.

P-51Ds of the 4th FG await pre-service modifications at Debden 1944. (Keith Braybrooke Archives)

Throughout the long period 1946 to 1960 Debden was a Standby Airfield for Duxford. The final chapter in its history commenced in 1960 when Debden became the RAF Police Depot, a role fulfilled until 1975. Nostalgia had returned in 1968 when the Battle of Britain Film Unit used the airfield for varying periods and the sight of Spitfires and Hurricanes in circuit revived happy memories of yesteryear. A series of Gala Days was held between 1967 and 1970 and, on 5 June 1973, Princess Margaret conducted a Royal Review at Debden. A tenuous link with the past could be seen when a Gliding School carried out Air Cadet training at weekends but this has ceased.

Following the withdrawal of the RAF, the station became an Army base under its new name of Carver Barracks. Since then there has been much structural change, with only No 3 Hangar remaining of the original number. Several books (American and British) have been written on the life and times at Debden — a sure indication of the affection held for this hallowed ground.

Main features (December 1944):
Runways: 280° 4,800ft x 150ft, 350° 3,900ft x 150ft, tarmac surfaced concrete. *Hangars:* three Type C (225 ft), one Bellman, eleven Blister. *Accommodation:* 190 officers, 1,519 ORs.

DEOPHAM GREEN, Norfolk

52°33N/00°59W 185ft asl; TM030990. 2 miles NE of Great Ellingham, off B1077

Turn off the B1108 at Hingham then right at the crossroads and you will find yourself in the middle of what used to be an airfield. You will also probably discover that you have a wide expanse of cultivated land and a vast East Anglian sky all to yourself. How remote it must have seemed to the Americans.

Perhaps most moving of all, you can still stand on a portion of the main runway nostalgically recalling the sound of a Fortress straining under its bomb load, groaning, bumping along towards Berlin or even Stalin's USSR. Distant Nissen huts crouch on the north side, and there are remnants of other runways and the perimeter track. Tarry awhile: can you imagine you hear voices, has the station come alive even though there is little tangible to grasp? Try harder and you may even think you can hear the B-17s coming home. Deopham is a must if you enjoy dreaming, and for best effect choose a day when cumulus clouds billow and showers produce the sort of magnificent cloudscape that only East Anglia can provide.

Ponder upon what was demanded of American bomber crews who witnessed their friends perish in smoke and fire during horrific daylight ventures. Patently obvious such things were to East Anglians, between 1943 and the uneasy peace, when a low-flying Fortress was all too often seen with large chunks shot away from its structure. Smoke would trail from an engine, and in an inevitable straggler the crew would be making a superhuman effort to overcome the ordeal involved in carrying their critically wounded and those who had, during horrendous moments, been cruelly sacrificed. One could when watching those forlorn formations easily sense the pathos, the tensions, as the bombers staggered home.

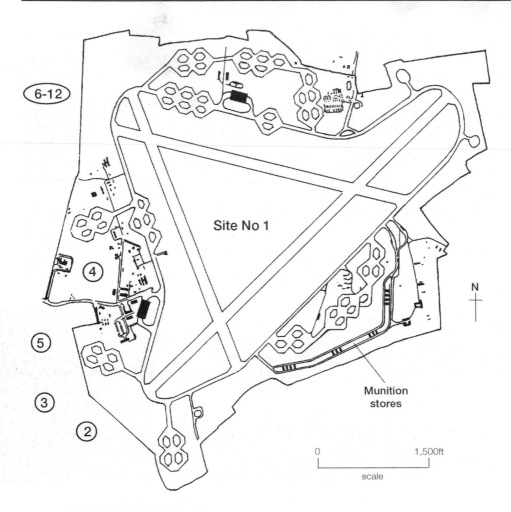

DEOPHAM GREEN

Surrounded by farms and many small fields, Deopham Green was a typical three-runway two-T2 hangar temporary wartime bomber base built for the USAAF. It featured spectacle type hardstandings, one bomber normally parking at the apex of each concrete stand. That allowed easier, faster access and egress necessary when aircraft operated in formation. The airfield was Site No 1, the sewage disposal site was No 2 and sick quarters No 3. The communal site (No 4) comprised a canteen in a Nissen hut as well as temporary brick buildings. No 5 was the mess site while Nos 6 to 12 held domestic accommodation outside Site No 1 boundary.

'Operations' was found in a strong brick building with crew briefing taking place in a temporary brick structure. The typical wartime control tower was linked with No 14 Site (H/F D/F), No 15 H/F transmitting site and the main runway beacon. An oil store could hold up to 3,500 gallons and the standard petrol store 72,000 gallons. All the usual services were to be found mostly in temporary brick buildings. Among them were the bombing trainer section, bombsight store, dinghy shed, parachute store and gas chamber. Main stores occupied a Romney hut and there were in all thirty Nissen huts at Deopham. Earth revetments protected the three 4-bay bomb stores and the incendiary bomb store. There were four small arms ammunition stores.

To be present among them as their engines fell quiet was to experience scenes irremovable from memory. As for the missing, those final terrible moments which encompassed their ending in full view of their comrades was something unspeakable. As for the survivors many would immediately express their elation that another mission was over. Some would be kneeling, heads buried in sweating hands while others were being physically sick at the end of another horrible ordeal which might well be repeated on the morrow. At that prospect many quickly admitted that they were terribly frightened. Foreign by birth, almost British by tongue, and sometimes chided by their very late entry into the conflict, they displayed enormous courage and so far from all that home means. True, their battle claims one viewed with high suspicion and disliked it when their tongues ran away with them. But you could only admire the enormous bravery that many an unlikely hero was called upon to display and admire their panache. Such events and feelings were prevalent at all American bases many with names often little known. Deopham Green is one, an ideal place to pause and remember. If something tangible is needed, there is a memorial to the brave.

It was at the start of 1944 that the 452nd Bomb Group reached Deopham Green bringing the base alive. Operations with B-17Gs commenced on 5 February 1944 with an attack on an aircraft assembly plant near Brunswick. Targets were usually of a strategic nature, the list including an aircraft components factory at Kassel, the ball bearing works at Schweinfurt, synthetic rubber plant at Hanover, oil installations at Bohlen, marshalling yards at Frankfurt, an aircraft assembly plant at Regensburg, etc. Like others the Group also provided tactical support to the Normandy landings and the airborne venture around Arnhem.

B-17G 297222 of the 452nd BG over Deopham. (Imperial War Museum)

On 21 June 1944 the 452nd was among over 1,000 bombers and 1,000 fighters operating against Berlin. Leading the 3rd Air Division, they then carried on eastwards to land at Poltava in the USSR after attacking an oil plant south of the German capital. This twelve-hour flight took them through a harrowing ordeal, and to an end equally distressing for, the following night, the Luftwaffe, having located the landing ground in Russia, despatched a strong force of bombers which delivered a crippling attack on the Fortresses nullifying their intent to assault the enemy during the homeward run. Somehow the Group survived and, undaunted, carried out another shuttle raid through to the USSR on 11 September and bombed Chemnitz on the way.

The style of American courage was well displayed on 9 November 1944 when the 452nd Bomb Group set out for France. This time heavy flak demanded bravery when a B-17 piloted by 1st Lieutenant Donald J Gott and 2nd Lieutenant William E Metzger was crippled beyond recovery. Maybe it took off from the runway on which you can still stand. Three engines were hit and flames spewed to the aft part of the bomber. A serious fire developed and others of the crew were badly wounded. In an effort to save their companions the pilots tried for a landing in friendly territory, and Metzger passed his parachute to a companion. Gott located a suitable landing place on which to put down to save the wounded, even though he had only one engine functioning. But as he came in for the crash landing the aircraft exploded and three of the men aboard, including the two pilots, were killed. To mark their courage both pilots were posthumously awarded the Medal of Honour.

A Distinguished Unit Citation was awarded after the 452nd attacked the jet fighter base at Kaltnekirchen on 7 April 1945, in the face of vigorous fighter defence. Before the war finished the Fortresses from Deopham flew five food drops to the Dutch. The last of 200 bombing raids mounted from here took place on 21 April 1945 when rail yards at Ingoldstadt were bombed.

During June 1945 the Americans began to pull out of Deopham and by August 1945 they had gone. RAF Maintenance Command retrieved the airfield on 9 October 1945 and No 258 NW had a sub-Site here between 15 November 1945 and its closure on 18 November 1946. RAF presence at Deopham Green ended on 1 January 1948 and the site was sold in March 1959.

Main features:
Runways: 240° 6,000ft x 150ft, 110°, 350°, concrete and tarmac surfaces. *Hangars:* two T2. *Hardstandings:* nine loop, one frying pan. *Accommodation:* 421 officers, 2,473 enlisted men.

DIGBY, Lincolnshire

53°06N/00°26W 115ft asl; 10 miles SSE Lincoln

'Yes, we're into aerial farming. No, we don't grow them, we show others how to!' Pass Digby and you will see some excellent specimens grown by expert 'aerialculturalists' of the RAF Aerial Erector School which flourishes here.

Civilian, government and military folk, indeed anyone needing tall aerials can learn the skills needed in erecting those incredible structures.

Digby is one of the RAF's longest serving stations. Originally it was named Scopwick after the nearby village where, in 1917, green pastures were transformed into a landing ground to which aeroplane sheds and living quarters were added. All was needed to cope with an excessive number of aircraft and cadets being trained nearby at HMS *Daedalus*, RNAS Cranwell.

Three 1917 brick and wood Coupled General Service Sheds – commonly called Belfast Truss hangars – were supplemented by a singleton of like design for use, as customary, as an aircraft repair shed. Single storey, pebbly concrete long huts with slate roofs served for 'technical' and domestic purposes. Although completion did not come until the closing days of the war, sufficient had been achieved for the airfield to open independently on 28 March 1918.

First in were not now the expected 'trainers' but Handley Page 0/400 bombers coming to the original 12 Group. Scopwick was then under the control of RFC Major D'Albiac DSO who days later became a Squadron Leader better years hence as Air Marshal Sir John D'Albiac, KCVO, KBE, CB, DSO.

Those 'heavy' bombers were few in number and No 59 Training Depot Station too, which opened here in 15 October 1918, never met its listed establishment. In March 1919 the title changed to No 59 Training Station, the four 'flights', Nos 209, 210 and 213 (formerly Nos 9, 10 and 13 RNAS) and 273 all using Sopwith Camels training RNAS pilots. In the main Scopwick housed BE2es and Brisfits. No 11 Squadron's F2Bs were also here between September and December 1919 and No 25 Squadron came here in December 1919 and officially disbanded on 31 January 1920.

Service re-structuring resulted in the training element becoming No 3 Flying Training School Scopwick on 26 April 1920. Squadron Leader A T Harris AFC, later Marshal of the RAF Sir Arthur Harris, wartime C-in-C Bomber Command, was in command of the 23 Group station which, three months later, changed its name to Digby to avoid confusion with Shotwick Aerodrome, Flint, which was re-titled Sealand. No 3 FTS relying upon Avro 504s and wartime fighters as trainers lasted only until strength reduction brought closure in 1922. Digby was placed on Care & Maintenance.

Meanwhile the 1922 Steele-Bartholomew policy for Home Air Defence set in motion the pattern which lasted into the 1960s. A string of fighter squadrons on stations positioned at about forty mile intervals would extend northerly and westerly from London to protect the Midlands and vital points forward of the belts. North Weald was one, Duxford (a training school) the next in the chain and No 2 FTS left Duxford for Digby at the end of June 1924 bringing along an assortment of Avro 504s, Bristol Fighters and Sopwiths. The new Station Commander from 17 September 1922 was Wing Commander A W Tedder, later Marshal of the RAF Lord Tedder GCB DCL LLD.

Digby was further developed, new buildings giving it the look of a typical station of the 1920s and early 1930s. Vickers Vimys were added to strength in 1926. No 2 FTS disbanded on 15 December 1933 leaving Digby an outstation of Cranwell.

A view across personnel huts at Digby circa 1933. (via Bruce Robertson)

With the international situation deteriorating No 2 Flying Training School re-opened on 1 October 1934 equipped with early versions of the Avro Tutor, Hawker Harts and Furies. A much earlier policy decision to develop Digby as a fighter station being within the aforementioned belt came into play when on 7 September 1937 No 2 FTS left for Brize Norton. The aged aircraft sheds were replaced with two eight-bay 'C' Type Aircraft Sheds. New barrack blocks and a modem technical site were added along with married quarters.

Digby joined 12 Group, Fighter Command and on 9 November No 73 Squadron arrived from Debden bringing Gladiators. They were supplemented on 15 November 1937 with Gauntlets of No 46 Squadron from Kenley. The former began rearming with Hurricanes in July 1938, the latter in February 1939. On 27 August 1939 Hurricanes of No 504 (County of Nottingham) Squadron joined them at Digby, their War Station, and stayed until 9 October 1939.

Gladiator 1s of 73 Squadron parade before a Digby hangar in 1938. (Bruce Robertson Archives)

Digby's first Spitfire squadron, No 611 (County of Lancashire), arrived from Duxford on 10 October 1939 for a long stay – punctuated by detachments and forward placings – which continued until 14 December 1940.

Luftwaffe activity against coastal shipping caused the formation here on 6 October 1939 of No 229 Squadron equipped with Blenheim 1f to perform shipping protection patrols started on 21 December. In January 1940 night flying training and radar trials began followed in March by rearming with Hurricanes and a switch to a day fighter role, the squadron moving to Wittering on 26 June 1940.

A number of squadrons passed through Digby during north-south movements and 17 January 1940 saw the return to stay of No 46 Squadron's Hurricanes.

After Norway was invaded in April they were chosen to support the handful of Gladiators operating there from improvised airfields. The Hurricanes were embarked on HMS *Glorious* in the Clyde which on 14 May sailed with the intention that they would operate from a site near Harstad. That being unsuitable, the carrier returned to Scapa Flow. A second attempt followed and on 26 May ten 46 Squadron Hurricanes flew off. The surface at Skaanland, their destination, being unsuitable, they were ordered to land at Bardufoss about sixty miles away and from where they provided cover over Narvik. To the bad general situation came the German invasion of France causing British forces to be recalled from Norway. No 46 Squadron landed their Hurricanes – none fitted with arrester hooks – on to the carrier HMS Glorious. The German capital warship *Scharnhorst* closed in, sank the carrier and the Hurricanes were lost. Three weeks later some of '46' personnel were back at Digby reforming their squadron. After resuming operations they left for Stapleford Tawney on 1 September 1940.

Meanwhile, between 10 and 23 May No 222 Squadron's Spitfires were at Digby and replacing 111 Squadron's Hurricanes there during the last week of May. Nos 56 and 79 Squadrons, both using Hurricanes, spent the following week at the station. Then it was the turn of No 29 Squadron and their Blenheim 1(f)s.

Digby, a Sector Station, now controlled two Unbuilt satellite landing grounds, Wellingore and Coleby Grange, No 29 Squadron moving to the former in early July and remained in the Digby Sector until April 1941.

No 46 Squadron's place was taken by 151 Squadron's Hurricanes based here between I September until 28 November when they left for Bramcote. No 46 Squadron returned on 14 December for a tenancy lasting until 28 February 1941. Digby's future was then emerging.

On 11 December 1940 a group of Canadian officers arrived and the station's association with the RCAF began. Personnel of No 112 (City of Winnipeg) Squadron, redesignated No 2 Squadron RCAF, were at Digby. Canadian squadrons were allocated RAF squadron numbers in the 400 series.

Flying conditions being far removed from those in Canada, a small flying and operational training unit converted Hurricane and Spitfire pilots flying in a different environment.

Summer 1941 saw many more Canadians arrive. No 411 Squadron formed here on 16 June with eighteen ageing Spitfire Is was rearmed with Mk IIas in July. In October they re-equipped with Mk Vbs before leaving for Hornchurch on 19 November. Next in was No 409 Squadron formed at Digby on 17 June 1941 and equipped with Defiant night-fighters before moving to Coleby on 25 July. Fourth to come alive, on 30 June, was No 412 which used Spitfire IIas and had Mk Vbs before moving to Wellingore in October 1941. From 5 May 1941 No 12 Group's AA Co-operation Flight operated from Digby and its satellites and became 288 Squadron on 18 November 1941.

Belgians were among the personnel of No 609 Squadron which flew Spitfires from Digby between 21 November 1941 and 30 March 1942. Other Spitfire squadrons briefly here were No 601 (25 March to 10 April thence sent overseas), a course followed by No 242 in September.

Most of all it was the Canadian influence that predominated and on 16 September 1942 the station was remained RCAF Digby, the maple leaf within the station badge being a reminder of those times.

No 198 Squadron reformed here on 8 December 1942 and left on 23 January, both 19 and 167 Squadrons being here in May-June 1943. But it was the Canadians who used Digby throughout 1943. No 402 Squadron which arrived on 21 March 1943 to exchange Spitfire IXs for Mk Vbs next month flew diversionary sweeps, escorted B-17 s and flew *Lagoons* off Holland usually from forward bases.

No 416 Squadron which joined the Sector on 29 May 1943 flying Spitfire Vb/Vc came from

Wellingore to Digby on 13 June and stayed until 9 August. As a variation the Belgians were back between 24 August and 1 October when No 350 (Belgian) Squadron's Spitfires were here.

No 402 Squadron replaced them on 2 October. Arriving from Wellingore, they were here until 22 March 1944 left for a spell at APC and departed for Home on 1 May 1944 with 19 Spitfire Vb/Vc. Typhoons of No 438 Squadron had kept them company between 20 November and 18 December 1943.

The 8 February 1944 saw the formation of two more Canadian Spitfire squadrons, Nos 441 and 442, whose Spitfire Vbs were replaced in March with F.IXs. By then No 443 Squadron had joined them, all three moving to Holmsley South as a Wing which became much distinguished during operation *Overlord*. Digby meanwhile had fallen quieter, fast and furious days being over.

Next in was No 527 Squadron which brought along Blenheim IVs, Hornet Moths and Oxfords to engage in coastal radar calibration in the 12 Group area. No 528 Squadron which arrived mid-May 1944 supplemented them and on 1 September merged with No 527 Squadron. No 310 (Czech) Squadron's Spitfires here between 11 July and 28 August 1944 brought a brief reminder of days passed.

May 1945 saw the station revert to being RAF Digby, most Canadians having left, and on 22 July 1945 the station was transferred from Fighter Command to Technical Training Command. No 1 Officers' Advanced Training School moved from Cranwell in August 1945 and stayed until July 1947 when they left for Hornchurch.

Cranwell-based No 19 Flying Training School used Digby as an RLG between January 1946 and 1948. A variety of training units followed. No 2 Initial Training School handled selection of National Service aircrew between October 1950 and mid-August 1951 when the Aircrew Grading School formed from the Aircrew Training Unit and No 2 Grading School. That evolved into being No 1 Grading Unit in June 1952 which selected personnel for aircrew training. On 30 June 1952 it became No 1 Grading Unit. In September 1953 Digby was placed in Care & Maintenance.

The next chapter in the Digby story began on 1 October 1954 when preparations commenced to station No 399 Signals Unit, No 90 Group, here.

Additional buildings, technical and domestic, were built before the unit arrived in January 1955 followed, in July, by No 591 Signals Unit. The Aerial Erectors School set up home in September 1959, No 54 Signals Unit joining them during February 1969.

No 399 Signals Unit became the Joint Service Signals Unit on 15 September 1998. On 1 April 2005 the Unit merged with the remainder of the station, becoming Joint Service Signals Wing Digby.

The Aerial Erector School, part of the Communications Electronics Basic Training Squadron centred at Cosford, has, as its main task, the training of Trade Group 4 RAF aerial erectors. Glance at any radio or radar tower and installation and one can instantly appreciate how demanding the construction and maintenance of such structures must be. Specialised training has to take account of the inherent demands of scaffolding, necessary climbing aptitude, working at height and meeting highly demanding safety rules. The School is one of the few that also offers a specialised course in advanced fibre optics including single and multi-mode fibre systems. Training courses are available to civilians from commercial concerns. With a staff of twenty-one the school currently runs nine courses, maximum class size being twelve. Apprenticeships in communications are available leading to Edexcel and City & Guilds awards. The facilities on offer are continuously updated, workshops and new training facilities having recently been added.

Digby, which has exchanged one its two hangars for assorted aerials, offers a tit-bit – a guided tour of the wartime Operations Room Museum available in summer on Sundays at 1100hrs. You need to arrive on time at the Sports Ground car park on the B1191 between the A15 and Scopwick the latter having a war graves cemetery in Vicarage Lane one mile from Digby. No District Council does more to promote interest in the RAF than North Kesteven associated with this and similar ventures. Others should emulate them for it costs little and provides excellent reminders, and opportunities for awareness, of the cost of freedom.

Main features (December 1944):
Grass runs: NE/SW 4,200ft, N/S 3,700ft, E/W 3,150ft. *Hangars:* two C Type, three Over Blister, four Extra Over Blister. *Hardstandings:* seven for single-engined aircraft. *Accommodation:* RAF: 130 officers, 190 SNCOs, 1,630 ORs; WAAF: 20 officers, 10 SNCOs, 510 ORs.

DOCKING, Norfolk

52°55N/00°39E 210ft asl; TF770380. E of B1153 out of Docking

Unbuilt Satellite airfields little more than giant meadows, contributed much to the war effort and Docking was no exception. Many were upgraded to Built Satellite and then Class A Airfield but some – Docking included – remained large grass fields throughout the war.

A site for an operational satellite for Bircham Newton was selected at Docking in 1939, its preparation resulting in a flying ground believed to have come into use by May 1940 and used then for the dispersal of 235 Squadron's Blenheim IVfs which escorted ships and flew offensive fighter patrols off the Netherlands.

Hudsons of 206 Squadron were also using the airfield by September 1940 principally for protective dispersal and particularly for night flying. Later in 1940, 235 Squadron's twenty Blenheims took up full residence staying until June 1941. A few weeks later 53 Squadron's Blenheims were also briefly at Docking from where they set out to patrol the Dutch coast and protect coastal convoys.

Between July and October 1941 their Hudsons made use of Docking. On 25 December 1941, 221 Squadron arrived in their Wellington VIIIs having come from Iceland to tarry briefly here and at Bircham Newton before leaving in early January for the Middle East. More permanent occupants, from early 1942, were No 1401 Meteorological Reconnaissance Flight. Prominent among gatherers of weather forecast data, they carried out many of their *THUM* sorties from Docking using Gladiator biplanes, Blenheims and Hudsons the latter from May 1942. In July Spitfires joined them. *Rhombus*, *Prata* and *THUM* flights were undertaken differing mainly by way of duration, routing and altitude. The aircraft were maintained at Bircham Newton where the Flight disbanded on 31 July 1942.

Companionship for the 'Met Flight' was provided by 235 Squadron flying twenty Beaufighter 1cs and which returned and used the satellite between 3 May and 16 July 1942. On 15 July No 1525 BAT Flight's Oxfords arrived, training of Bircham Newton's pilots continuing until May 1945.

Mid-February 1943 saw the return of another squadron, No 53 Squadron recently re-equipped with twenty Whitley GR VIIs. At the time Hampden TBR 1s of No 415 (Canadian) Squadron were using the station as an advanced base for anti-shipping operations off Norway which continued until May 1943. No 53 Squadron moved out to the parent station in mid-March and left the complex in late April. They were supplanted at Docking from 2 April 1943 by Wellington Ics of 304 (Polish) Squadron which flew maritime patrols and stayed until 5 June.

By then Bircham Newton was playing a major part in Coastal Command's deep-sea ASR operations and exploring the unwanted Warwick bomber's suitability as a Hudson supplement. To Docking and Bircham Newton had come the first Coastal Command assorted Warwick ASR Mk Is and on 25 June 1943 the Warwick Training Unit formed at Docking to train crews. They moved to Bircham Newton on 3 July 1943 making way for a ferry training element of the unit which gathered and trained crews to deliver Warwicks to overseas ASR squadrons.

Summer 1943 saw daylight training flights from Docking by these Warwick ASR 1s of the Warwick Training Unit depicted in July 1943. (Imperial War Museum)

No 1401 Meteorological Flight reformed on 1 April 1943 and soon partially moved to Docking from where as previously they operated Gladiators, Spitfires and Hudsons. Several Hampdens were here in May when the Flight's strength on 25 July typically stood at four Hampdens, five Gladiators, three Spitfire VIs and two Hudsons. Very active from here in August and September, the Flight moved to Manston.

Whenever space was available at Docking it was filled with detachments from Bircham Newton. No night flying was undertaken at the parent which, unlike Docking, did not possess Drem Mk II lighting. It did, however, offer excellent personnel accommodation and the maintenance facilities of a Permanent Station.

Docking never had metalled hardstandings, only grass runways, a few Blister hangars, with Maycrete and wooden huts being provided for domestic and administrative use. Its position so near the coast also attracted aircraft returning from operations and needing to land as soon as possible.

Even after No 1401 Met Flight had left, weather reconnaissance flights continued to be undertaken from here until after the war. From September 1943, 521 Squadron using Hudsons and Venturas began flying to Wick in north-east Scotland. The aircraft returned the following day. No 519 Squadron, Wick, operated in the reciprocal direction, which resulted in examples of its fourteen rare Ventura Vs being a regular sight at Docking. No 521 Squadron which usually also held a few Gladiators moved to Langham on 30 October 1944.

On 15 November 1943 No 415 (Canadian) Squadron arrived bringing Wellington GR XIIIs maintained at Bircham Newton. With few blockade runners and Beaufighters in short supply, No 415 was rearmed with Wellingtons in October and been given a special role, operation *Deadly*, which involved finding E-boats from thirty-five miles off the coast and guiding surface forces to deal with them. They also dropped flares for Torbeau night operations against enemy shipping. But the Canadians emphatically wanted their crews in bomber squadrons so from March 1944 no more RCAF crews were posted in. There was some talk of forming a replacement squadron, No 210, to carry on their work.

On 1 March 1944 operation *Gilby* began involving reconnaissance along the Dutch coast. Actually '415' had performed very well and most usefully especially around D-Day in the maritime role. Nevertheless, on 2 July 1944 personnel of No 524 Squadron began arriving to take over 415's ten Wellingtons.

The Canadian squadron flew their final night searches from Docking on 20 July, then No 524 took over staying until November 1944 when they moved to Langham where previously they had sent detachments.

Bircham Newton's target towers throughout Docking's life span made frequent use of it although none were based here until No 2 Armament Training Camp used the station in August 1944. No 288 Squadron positioned a small detachment at Docking in March 1945.

Nor was the Royal Navy absent, and from the parent station on 7 September 1944 Avengers of No 855 Squadron arrived for night operations from Docking and made use of its parent station during daylight until mid-October.

Bircham Newton's and Docking's operational days had ended with the removal of 524 Squadron, and Docking then assumed far less importance. No 1693 ASR Training Unit was here in June-July 1945 before 16 Group Coastal Command relinquished use of Docking on 21 September 1945. It was then transferred to 54 Group, Maintenance Command. The site, surplus to need, was in April 1958 sold for agricultural use. Very little evidence remains of an operational, very active wartime satellite airfield.

Main features (December 1944):
Grass runways: NE/SW 5,190ft; E/W 5,200ft, N/S 3,300ft. *Hangars:* eight Blister, one Type Al. *Hardstandings:* nil. *Accommodation:* RAF: 60 officers, 115 SNCOs, 614 ORs; WAAF: 2 officers, 2 SNCOs, 88 ORs.

Places of interest nearby:
Unspoilt Ringstead village is 2½ miles from the very attractive north Norfolk coast. Peddars Way and Icknield Way are near. Note the chalk and brown carrstone houses special to this area. Holme-next-the Sea and Scolt Head wild life sanctuary are close and eight miles away is elegant Holkham Hall.

DOWNHAM MARKET, Norfolk

52°36N/00°24E 123ft asl; TL630045. 2 miles NE of town and E of A10

Bombing raids on Italy from Britain were always difficult, hazardous, unpleasant operations. Whereas today jets cross the Alps with impunity, wartime fliers not only had to face the distance involved but also combat that Alps which formed a formidable barrier. Either they skimmed the summits or threaded their way between them often in darkness, occasionally in moonlight and frequently in atrocious weather.

One difficult raid took place on 12/13 August 1943, participants including Downham Market's Stirlings of 218 Squadron whose target was the Fiat works at Turin. Among the aircraft involved was Stirling III EF452 captained by Flight Sergeant Louis Aaron.

Loading mines aboard a Stirling III of 218 Squadron at Downham. (Gp Capt G.H.Giles)

Over the target machine-gun fire raked his Stirling and put three of his four engines out of action, shattered the windscreen, caused damage to the elevator cables and made two of the three turrets useless. Aaron suffered terribly, for his face and a lung were injured and his right arm was broken. How he survived was miraculous yet Aaron not only clung to life but persisted in continuing to help fly the crippled bomber.

Return across the Alps being clearly out of the question, the crew decided to head for North Africa which entailed a lengthy flight. Aaron's place at the controls was first taken by the bomb aimer, but the gallant skipper, after trying to fly the aircraft again, instead wrote handling instructions for the bomb aimer using his left hand and despite the tremendous pain he was suffering. After five hours' flying Bone airfield was sighted then came the most difficult part of the journey, the landing. Four attempts were made, Aaron assisting as best he could although he was on the point of collapse. The fifth attempt was successful, but nine hours later Aaron died, his death due more to his selfless devotion to his colleagues than to his wounds. Had he rested he might have recovered. He was posthumously awarded the Victoria Cross.

Downham Market airfield, just north of the town on a site now marked by a tall TV booster aerial and a few huts, opened in 1942 as Marham's satellite in place of Barton Bendish, which was unsuitable for Stirlings. On 10 July 1942, just before Marham passed to 2 Group (in August 1942), No 218 Squadron took its Stirlings to lodge at Downham, a Built Satellite upgraded to Airfield War Class A standard and with three customary runways and metal transportable hangars, an airfield previously they had used for dispersal. Operations commenced from the station on 12 July. Downham Market became part of Marham Base structure on 1 December 1942. From Downham the squadron participated in the bombing campaign until its Stirlings moved to Woolfox Lodge on 7 March 1944.

To expand the strength of 3 Group, 'C' Flight 218 Squadron had become 623 Squadron on 10 August 1943 and operated from Downham between 10 August and 4 December 1943, disbandment occurring on 6 December 1943.

Since March 1943 Horsa gliders picketed out in storage had been cared for by No 14 Section, No 2 HGCU. Support facilities were based in three T2 hangars erected specially for the purpose. In March 1944 the Horsas were towed away to contribute to the Normandy invasion.

Nudged out of Chedburgh when Stradishall Base switched to an operational conversion role, No 214 Squadron brought its Stirling IIIs to Downham on 1 December 1943. Their stay was brief for between 17 and 24 January the unit relinquished its aircraft and moved to Sculthorpe to undertake training for special operations in 100 Group.

Downham Market next passed to No 8 Group, the Pathfinders. For the new role a new squadron, No 635, formed here on 20 March from elements of 35 and 97 Squadrons and first operated, against Frankfurt, on 22/23 March 1944.

Like other 8 Group stations, Downham fell into line by having a Mosquito bomber squadron when No 571 formed here on 7 April 1944. Although they did not operate from Downham, a detachment sent to Graveley flew two operations from there before the squadron moved to Oakington, their operational station.

By now 635 Squadron was in the thick of battle and during July 1944 a rare item of equipment joined them, the Lancaster Mk VI. This interim bomber was being used to try out a new armour-plated annular radiator Merlin engine first intended for the Windsor and now scheduled for the Lancaster IV (which became the Lincoln). To 635 Squadron came five of these unusual Lancasters, the squadron trying them out operationally between August and November 1944.

Downham's own Mosquito squadron, No 608, formed on 1 August 1944 and armed with Canadian-built Mosquito XXs. They began operations on 5 August by attacking the Wanne Eickel synthetic oil plant. Thereafter the squadron was busily engaged as part of the LNSF, flying the refused Mk XXV from October 1944. In March 1945 the Mosquito XVI with two-stage Merlins was introduced for operations, this type entirely equipping the squadron before the war ended.

On 28 August 1945 No 608 Squadron disbanded followed by 635 Squadron on 1 September. No 274 MU used part of the station for storage purposes between November 1945 and late 1946. Flying here had ended in April 1946 and Downham declared surplus to need closed on 24 October 1946. The site was sold for civilian use in February 1957. To the east of the wartime airfield a farm strip saw use in the 1970s and 1980s for crop spraying and private flying which involved a variety of light aircraft.

Main features:
Runways: 093° at 5,700ft x 150ft slightly shorter than usual, 034° and 337°, all concrete. *Hangars:* two T2, three T2 for gliders, one Bl. *Hardstandings:* thirty-six frying pan type. *Accommodation:* RAF: 185 officers, 262 SNCOs, 1,272 ORs; WAAF: 8 officers, 8 SNCOs, 310 ORs.

DUXFORD, Cambridgeshire

52°05N/00°08E 97ft asl; TL460460. 7 miles NE of Royston, by the A505

Duxford is legendary. That most iconic of all aeroplanes, the Supermarine Spitfire, entered RAF service here, at an aerodrome that has been active, often hyperactive and with very few short breaks, for more than ninety years. With such a long life it is not surprising that somewhere so special has produced so many memorable moments.

Who, having witnessed it, could ever forget the show-day sight of that South African Airways Boeing 747-400 departing after a pass with a tight upward spiral before disappearing into cloud far above? Equally memorable was the arrival in June 1968 of two 'Heinkel 111s' leading a swarm of 'Me 109s' of the Spanish Air Force, all settling in for a summer of Battle of Britain filming. That event, more than any other, was the catalyst for Duxford's survival and development as a lively world-class museum.

Fewer in total, memorable for content, was another German arrival at 15.30hrs on 12 September 1941 when the well-known Heinkel He 111 AW177 and Ju 88A-6 EE205 flew in from Farnborough escorted by an amazing array of Spitfire IIs and Hurricane IIs. Airborne to greet them was an astonishing group comprising a Fulmar, Skua, the Bf 109E AE479 already there, the ever-exciting Westland Whirlwind first prototype L6844 and, as if that was insufficient, Duxford's latest

Duxford surely means Spitfires, as during 2008 'Flying Legends' show. MH434 leading.

fighter, Hawker Typhoon 1a R7581, here for tactical assessment. On the previous 7 September Duxford's personnel had gazed southerly watching a furious red and yellow sky reflecting the incineration of London's dockland following the first massive bombing of London. As they did so they knew that invasion was expected next dawn. Those 1941 captive Germans – soon joined by a Bf 110 – were to become part of No 1426 (EA) Flight, which performed as a touring circus. One might fairly claim that that afternoon's activity presaged the ever-popular balbo that yearly ends the 'Flying Legends' display.

By 1941 Duxford was entering its most exciting era by hosting the latest aircraft types and new variants joining the RAF and FAA. Here for tactical exploration came the Americans – the Chesapeake dive-bomber, Martlet, Mohawk and Tomahawk fighters, early Boston bomber and the very useful long-range Martin Maryland, a pair of which NAFDU reviewed. Americans were no newcomers, for US engineers had trained here at the end of the 1914-1918 war. When their forces returned in 1943 they did so flying P-47s and later P-51s. It is apt that nowadays within the main annual show there is usually a spectacular P-51 Mustang performance. Naturally, there is a strong Spitfire presentation too.

Although Duxford originated in summer 1917, and much of it was in being by the end of the 1914-1918 war, it was 1919 before its RAF structure was fully in place on the Technical Site – the flying side. The brick and wood three Double General Service Sheds retain much of their original appearance. An additional, lone, central example – which for some time housed a gymnasium – had Station Workshops to its north. A large concrete area now spreads where that hangar stood before it erupted in flames during the mock bombing of Duxford for *The Battle of Britain* film. Workshops were moved in the 1930s into huts still in position behind the hangars near the guardhouse and close to the mixed stores popularly now called 'Blenheim Palace'.

Like Fowlmere, Duxford opened under HQ 26 Wing on 1 March 1918 upon which day Nos 119 and 129 Squadrons moved in. The association with America started on 15 March 1918 when Nos 137 and 159 US Aero Squadron ground engineers arrived for a five-month training stint, then dispersed. Next in was No 123 Squadron RFC from Waddington which, on 1 September 1918, became part of No 35 TDS which had just moved here from Thetford. No 129 Squadron had disbanded on 4 July 1918. Three more US aero engineer squadrons arrived in September 1918, Nos 23, 256 and 268, but they folded as the war ended and had left by mid-November 1918 when No 119 Squadron also retired. Nos 119, 123 and 124 Squadrons RFC had used BE2e, DH6 and DH 9 biplanes. Among post-war residents was No 8 Squadron using Bristol F2Bs at only cadre strength; they came from Sart, France on 11 May 1919 and disbanded on 21 January 1920. Duxford was placed on Care & Maintenance between 1 June 1919 and 30 April 1920. Fowlmere kept watch over the station where 35 TDS had died on 30 September 1919.

Late in 1919 Duxford began awakening and on 1 April 1920 No 2 Flying Training School was established and by June was fully functional with fifteen aircraft including Avro 504s F2Bs and DH 9As under the control of No 3 Group.

The 1922-1923 Steele-Bartholomew Review of the air defence of the United Kingdom resulted in a dramatic change of role for Duxford which was retained in favour of Fowlmere because of

Duxford 1919. GS hangars being constructed, technical site layout largely as now. Bessoneau `hangars at west end where the American Museum stands. (Imperial War Museum)

easier access and the proximity of the railway. Duxford was chosen as a base for the fighter force charged with defending the approach to the Midlands and protecting central East Anglia. A new building programme was initiated, the present IWM Head Quarters being in what was the 1923 (modified in 1933) Station HQ. Accommodation blocks were built in 1923 on the Domestic Site on the opposite side of the main road.

On 1 April 1923 Nos 19 and 29 Squadrons re-formed and equipped with Sopwith Snipes. Initially, they concentrated upon training pilots for other squadrons soon to become established. By the end of 1924 Nos 19 and 29 were rearming with Gloster Grebes. These they operated until March 1928 when Siskin IIIAs were introduced. No 2 FTS finally completed their move to Digby in July 1924

On 1 October 1923 No 111 Squadron had moved in and they too initially used Snipes and Grebes and until 1924 when they re-equipped with Siskin IIIs. 'Treble-One' had a special role as the High Altitude Squadron which, from 1926, was responsible for developing equipment and techniques for high altitude fighting. In September 1926 they received Siskin IIIAs, and in 1927 command of the squadron passed to Squadron Leader Keith R. Park, in 1940 11 Group AOC.

Both Nos 29 and 111 Squadrons vacated Duxford on 1 April 1928 leaving behind No 19 which, in September 1931, re-armed with Bristol Bulldogs Since 1926 the fighters here had been adorned with squadron identity colours to enable rapid recognition during combat. No'19' adopted blue in their marking because of their Cambridge association.

The mid-1930s saw superior barrack blocks replace those around the parade ground, by the north side of which was a new Airmen's Mess and NAAFI. The elegance of the 1930s Georgian-looking Officers' Mess close to the main road is best seen from the Bailey Bridge opened on show days to allow safe crossing of the A505 road. Officer accommodation was originally within long huts sited at the north end of the extensive grass sports field area often now used as a car park. Other buildings of the 1930s included an enlarged Sergeants' Mess together with Married Quarters, which remain, now civilian-occupied, at the west end of the domestic area.

In his book *Spitfire – A Test Pilot's Story* (John Murray 1983) Jeffrey Quill records delivering K9792 to CFS Upavon on 29 July 1938 and next day piloting Spitfire K9789 on its first flight. He states that on 4 August 1938, after the four flights needed to clear that Spitfire, 'I flew it to Duxford and handed it over to Squadron Leader H I Cozens, CO of 19 (Fighter) Squadron'. He recalls the whole station turning out to watch the arrival of the RAF's first squadron Spitfire. His flying instructor

Avro 504N K1049 of the Duxford based University Air Squadron.

at the Grantham school, 'Pingo' Lester, now a Wing Commander and Duxford's Station Commander, walked him to the new Mess. There he felt twinges of sadness at the passing of the old whitewashed single-storey RFC-style building he knew in his days when flying with the Meteorological Flight here.

January 1935 saw 19 Squadron become the first to equip with Gloster Gauntlets and, when 66 Squadron re-formed here on 20 July 1936, they were similarly equipped. During the Munich crisis, Duxford's Gauntlets stood armed, refuelled, conflict seeming imminent. Once the crisis passed, both squadrons reverted to air drill, explored the possibilities of their Spitfires, tried night flying and detached themselves to Sutton Bridge to try out their eight-guns. Everywhere there was camouflage and sandbags as the station faced the inevitable.

Since 1 October 1925 Duxford had been home for the Cambridge University Air Squadron. Their flying had commenced on 19 February 1926 using 'Brisfits' and 504s which were displaced first by the AW Atlas and in 1933 with yellow coated Avro Tutors, conspicuous shapes to the outbreak of war. Cambridge University Engineering Department also used an Atlas and a Hart for experimental purposes.

According to local people and then-resident RAF personnel, Duxford's relationship with the Spitfire began on Saturday 30 July 1938 when one whistled in. Following afternoon tea in the Officers' Mess, the pilot brilliantly displayed the Spitfire, which was then taken into a hangar. Could it have come from CFS Upavon, or A&AEE Martlesham Heath? It is said to have been at Duxford on the following Tuesday among the Gauntlets of 19 Squadron. It would be interesting to hear from anyone

Gauntlet 1s of 19 Squadron – can you hear the wind, wires twanging, the engines roaring? Wonderful dreams!.

then stationed at Duxford who can confirm or deny beyond doubt this potentially special event.

Pre-war Duxford also housed the Meteorological Flight's Bulldogs which in September 1936 was re-equipped with four Gloster Gauntlets before moving to Mildenhall on 2 November 1936.

The Spitfires of Duxford made it a hive of activity in 1939. Hurricane squadrons came to look and learn alongside, and a clutch of Fairey Battles (Merlin-engined) came to help with pilot training.

When hostilities broke out three Spitfire squadrons were here, the third being No 611 (West Lancashire) Auxiliary Air Force Squadron on summer camp. All expected a fight, but when it did not materialise '611' impressively left for Digby on 10 October 1939, their Spitfires breaking the intense security of those days left in a formation inscribing '611'.

Daily detachments of Spitfires were placed at Watton, Duxford's forward airfield. On 20 October huge Ensign airliners impressed into service came to lift the personnel of 19 Squadron for a short, unprofitable stay, at Catterick in the expectation of a big Trafalgar Day onslaught upon shipping. No 66 Squadron, declared a mobile squadron on 25 October, expected to go to Leconfield, but that move was cancelled. During November both squadrons began placing detached Flights at unfinished Horsham St Faith from where on 11 January 1940 a fight at last came. Three Spitfires of 66 Squadron latched onto a Heinkel He 111 attacking shipping off Cromer, badly damaged it and later learned of its crash in Denmark. Duxford's Spitfires had made their first kill. No 66 Squadron eventually moved to Horsham St Faith, on 16 May 1940.

Placing Flights forward provided space for the formation on 5 October 1939 of a new squadron, No 222, equipped from November 1939 with Blenheim I(f) long-range fighters. To this squadron, based in the western hangar, came early in 1940 the famed legless pilot, Squadron Leader D R S Bader who became very much a Duxford figure. In March 1940 222 Squadron received Spitfires.

The suddenness of the May 1940 blitzkrieg caught the squadrons off guard. Defiants of 264 Squadron quickly rushed in to their war station, Duxford, daily moving forward to Horsham St Faith from where they fought their first battles. Duxford's Spitfires operating from Horsham were also involved in action off Holland before on 25 May 19 Squadron was detached to Hornchurch from there to cover the Dunkirk withdrawal. Return to Duxford came on 5 June by which time the seriousness of the general situation was plain for all to see. AA guns protected the station's perimeter which was constantly patrolled to prevent invaders. Even more sandbags were in place, and there were many false alarms. Trouble, big trouble, was brewing. First it was from an incendiary bomb raid which went wide then late on 18 June 19 Squadron scrambled in the dark. That cost them a Spitfire shot down in flames, but in exchange for a He 111 destroyed so unusually at night by a Spitfire.

Two Gladiators at Duxford's 2008 'Flying Memories' show.

The satellite at Fowlmere was now much in use, 19 Squadron dispersing there. During June 1940, 264 Squadron re-established themselves after their terrible combat hammering, and recuperated at Fowlmere. No 19 was chosen to try the cannon-armed Spitfire Ib which, from the start, encountered big trouble when cartridges jammed the guns after firing. The squadron was told to persevere, but when the Battle of Britain began, 19 Squadron's cannon Spitfires were far from ready for action. Fortunately, Duxford lay largely beyond the range of the daylight onslaught. Nevertheless, many patrols and scrambles took place and 19 Squadron fought off the East Coast. On 11 July Czech pilots arrived to form 310 Squadron, the first Czech fighter squadron, for which Hurricanes began to arrive on 18 July. Their operations commenced on 18 August, the newcomers first engaging in battle on the 26th and soon indulging in spectacular fights.

Not until 31 August did Duxford face its most dangerous day – ever. A glorious, hot summer morn was unfolding when around 0810 hrs air raid sirens wailed over much of Essex and around Duxford. Could the Luftwaffe be coming at last to flatten the dear old place? At 0820 hrs Debden's AA guns distantly thundered defiance, then a few minutes later came a most ferocious roar from the mixed batteries at Duxford and Thriplow. There was a colossal explosion ten miles away sufficient to shake the nine-inch concrete walls of our shelter. Recent research in Germany has revealed that a load of 253 SC50 HEs and 100 incendiaries had been simultaneously released from fifteen Do 17Zs of II/KG2, the largest such salvo ever released upon Britain. At the time it seemed certain that Duxford must have become a ruin. But that was not the case, not by any means.

Duxford's operations room laid out to represent the State at 08.30 hrs on 31 August 1940 when Duxford was targeted by Do 17Zs of II/KG2.

Part of the Dornier 17Z force had attacked Debden leaving the rest covered by Bf 110s to wipe out Duxford. They soon met a wall of AA fire of such ferocity that they were driven off track and onto a course leading between Fowlmere and Barrington. In that area they jettisoned their loads, turned about in a wide circle skirting the south of Cambridge and then were engaged by 19 Squadron. Those failing cannon cost the squadron dear, two Spitfires falling in the face of fire from the Dorniers and escorting Bf 110s.

Most of Duxford's Battle of Britain fighting took place well to the south in September 1940 when Leigh Mallory's 'Big Wing' ideas were tried from here. Squadrons from 12 Group stations arrived early each day to turn a Wing scramble into a legendary air show supreme as literally scores of fighters raced away. Often, Douglas Bader would be leading 242 Squadron, Hurricanes ironically far outnumbering Spitfires at their shrine.

No 310 (Czech) Hurricane Squadron was much in the fight during September. The pilots waded into Do 17Zs and Bf 110s over North Weald on the 3rd and again on the 7th, making high claims. On the morning of the 15th No 310 flying in the Wing with 19, 242, 302 and 611 Squadrons in the defence of London faced huge enemy formations. The two Spitfire squadrons went for the fighters leaving the bombers to the Hurricanes. 'A' Flight, 310 Squadron, was unable to engage due to AA fire, but 242 and 'B' Flight, 310 Squadron waded in, engaging the enemy at 22,000ft over Kingston-upon-Thames. The afternoon brought another, more desperate fight for Bf 109s broke up the 'Big Wing' making the squadrons fight on their own with 310 Squadron having to sort themselves out after a climb to 24,000ft. There they faced a huge enemy conglomeration and claimed four raiders for the loss of two Hurricanes, one being that of Squadron Leader A Hess, 'A'

Flight Commander, who safely baled out. Duxford was at this time briefly hosting Poles of No 302 Squadron who claimed eleven bombers during the defence of London on that memorable day. By the end of the 15th Duxford's squadrons were claiming forty-four enemy aircraft, eight more shared and eight probables, but the true total for the day was far less. Confusion had arisen during very complex engagements. It is now unlikely that a totally accurate record of enemy losses during the Battle of Britain will ever be compiled. Not until 27 September did 310 Squadron find itself in the thick of the fight again, and then distantly over Kent. A second Czech squadron, No 312, formed at Duxford in September but soon moved away.

Once the battle had died down Duxford entered a very new phase in its life. Too far from France for offensive operations, its two squadrons – 19 and 310 – were assigned to Sector defence. Joining them from Northolt came the Air Fighting Development Unit to make room for which No 19 Squadron moved to Fowlmere. Apart from Spitfires and Hurricanes used to assess equipment and tactics, AFDU attracted the very latest types of aircraft, sometimes borrowed from squadrons. At the start of 1941 came newly received American types like the Tomahawk and Boston. The Naval Air Fighting Development Unit, alias 787 Squadron, arrived bringing Fulmars, Martlets and Skuas placed on its dispersal area in the south-eastern corner and giving Duxford a cosmopolitan appearance. The procession of many aircraft and types made Duxford as much of an enthusiasts paradise then as it is now, somewhere to enjoy such rare birds as the Maryland, Mohawk, first Halifaxes, a Whirlwind big gun prototype and 'secret' aircraft emerging from official silhouettes into reality.

Next in was the Air Gun Mounting Establishment here between early 1941 and late 1942. That also attracted interesting aircraft, among them Havoc BJ474 with a battery of upward firing guns German-style and, even more exotic, the twin-finned Wellington II L4250 with a 40mm gun in its huge dorsal turret and here from 13 December 1941 to 24 January 1942.

On 26 June 1941, 310's Hurricanes were at last replaced and by more belonging to 56 Squadron which managed some offensive sorties before facing conversion to the new, troublesome hefty Hawker Typhoon. AFDU acquired one in July then in September arrived those for '56'. The next month it was the turn of No 601 (County of London) Squadron to face a problem. They had arrived in mid-August 1941 to take delivery of the Bell Airacobra, a strange aircraft for its engine was behind the pilot, and the cannon fired through the propeller hub. That upset the DR compass so badly that the Airacobra was rejected and 601 hurried away to get Spitfires.

From the southern side of the airfield Blenheim IVs, Hornet Moths and Cierva C30A autogiros of 74 Signals Wing were daily setting forth to calibrate coastal radar equipment. The autogiros which arrived in summer 1940 stayed until late 1942 often roosted at radar stations.

Between 1940 and 1942 Duxford's Cierva C 30a autogiros hovered at coastal stations for radar calibration.

Great excitement surrounded the September 1941 arrival of Heinkel He 111 AW177, a Ju 88A, a Bf 109E and a Bf 110 here for combat evaluation and mainly for demonstration to squadrons. At the end of 1941 they were gathered in No 1426 Enemy Aircraft Flight which dispersed in the airfield's south-west corner where ironically, decades later, part of the *Battle of Britain* film was made. From their corner they presumably shook with fear when one of the first production Mosquito PRU Conversion bombers, W4066, showed itself.

Duxford's main 1942 task was to work the troublesome Sabre-engined Typhoon into operational service for which purpose No 56 Squadron was joined by '266' in January, and followed by '609' in March. Typhoons comprised the Duxford Wing led by Wing Commander John Grandy who in the 1960s became the CAS. The Typhoons went into action in June and, from West Malling, were busy during the Dieppe landings. The following autumn, No 181 Squadron formed at Duxford to try out the 'Bomphoon' before moving to the station's second satellite at Snailwell. The 'Hurribomber', too, had earlier been tried at Duxford where AFDU still busy evaluating newcomers explored the Mitchell, Marauder and Ventura.

In October 1942 the Yanks returned. The 345th Fighter Squadron, 350th Fighter Group, USAAF, became temporary lodgers while others of the Group were temporarily sited at Coltishall and Snailwell. All happily flew an assortment of Bell Airacobras, the motley collection being active briefly before being taken for a part in Operation *Torch* – hence their unusual tan colouring.

In 1943 important trials of the Merlin Mustang AM203 took place and AFDU smarted from a wigging after clipping without authority the wing tips of a Spitfire V thereby turning it into a fine low-altitude fighter. After dressing them down a senior officer went away and ordered mass production of the idea and sort of claimed that it was his own. That came before February and March when AFDU moved to Wittering for the USAAF was about to paddle in 'the Duckpond'.

During the first week of April 1943 Republic P-47C Thunderbolts of the 78th Fighter Group noisily came out of the wild blue yonder in strength, for an unbelievable seventy-five of them were fielded by the three squadrons. The Americans worked up great affection for Duxford some referring to it as 'real antique'!

On 13 April 1943 the '78th' commenced operations, first combat claims (two Fw 190s) being made on 14 May. P-47Ds came into use in June and long-range tanks were first operationally carried on 30 July. That enabled the Thunderbolts to penetrate into Germany escorting bombers, which was a great step forward for the 8th AF. Ground strafing commenced in January 1944, pilots returning with photo coverage of strikes on He 177s and Ju 188s intending to operate against London. Even more spectacular was some of the first air-to-air combat film showing Me 163s and Me 262s being engaged.

P-47s of the 78th FG, MX-S 227339 nearest, MX-W 228367 next in line (USAF).

P-47Ds with teardrop canopies came into use just before D-Day. On that memorable morn the 78th gave beach cover early on. Later the 84th FS dive-bombed Alençon, the 83rd engaged eight Fw 190s near Mayonne and destroyed two and the 82nd and 84th FS flew an evening patrol. On 10 June during the course of four missions the Group claimed five enemy aircraft but nine P-47s did not return and another crashed. Cover was given to Allied troops in Normandy and to the ill-fated Arnhem venture. A PSP runway was laid at Duxford in November-December 1944, during which time the 78th flew from Bassingbourn. Then it was all change as the Group converted to flying P-51D Mustangs which they took into action for the first time on 29 December 1944. April 1945 found long-range Mustangs penetrating as far as Czechoslovakia, the final operation taking place on 25 April when the Group supported the RAF bombing raid on Hitler's Berchtesgaden lair. In the course of 450 operations, 167 US fighters had been lost in action. Pilots of the 78th claimed 338 enemy aircraft destroyed in the air, 358 on the ground, and shared one of each with other Groups.

Most of the Americans left in August 1945 after which Duxford was held on C&M. On 28 November 1945 the decision was taken to re-open it as a one squadron fighter station, briefly as a satellite of Andrews Field. No 165 Squadron moved in, their twelve Spitfire LF9s arriving on 27 January 1946. In one sense the Duxford story had run full circle, and more so when in April 1946 No 91 Squadron moved in with Spitfire 21s. Both Spitfire squadrons took part in the Victory Fly-Past over London on 8 June.

No 165 Squadron on 1 September 1946 changed into being a new 66 Squadron and on 20 November 1946 both squadrons began using Duxford's satellite, Debden, whose hard runways were very useful when the squadrons converted late 1946 and into 1947 to long nacelled, higher powered versions of the Meteor III.

When 91 Squadron returned to Duxford from APS Acklington on 15 February 1947 it did so as 92 Squadron having been re-numbered on 31 January 1947. No 66 Squadron became fully operational on Meteors in March and on 17 April No 56 Squadron, also flying Meteor IIIs, moved in from Wattisham.

Major appraisal of fighter defence needs had been undertaken in January 1947. As a result, the three short-range day fighter squadrons were reduced to cadres and armed at half squadron strength with twenty-four Meteor IIIs. At the end of 1947 the Meteor 4 was in the offing and it was clear that Duxford could not accommodate them because it lacked a permanent hard 2,000 yard runway. In order to convert No 56 Squadron, on 1 February 1948, moved to Thorney Island. Both 66/111 and 92 Squadrons vacated Duxford in mid-May, also to convert the Meteor 4, the first of which reached both 66 Squadron and 92 Squadron on 6 May. While Duxford's metal runway was extended and repaired for temporary use the two squadrons worked up on Meteor 4s at Martlesham Heath and returned to Duxford on 10 June 1948.

Duxford was still unsuitable for fast jets and Plan F of 21 January 1948 called for it to accommodate four Mosquito night fighter squadrons instead. Long-range intruders were billed for Coltishall and Wattisham. Then a further re-appraisal of Duxford showed insufficient support facilities for Mosquito night fighters, so its role was switched with Coltishall's.

Revised 1949 plans called for two Hornet squadrons, Nos 64 and 65 and later a Canberra intruder squadron, to be sited at Duxford – after a 2,000 yard concrete 06/24 runway was laid. On 6 and 7 October 1949 both Meteor squadrons left Duxford for Linton-on-Ouse, after which the station was placed on C&M. Funding for the hard runway was not available until the next year, the contract was let in May 1950 and on 18 September 1950 Messrs W C French began constructing it for completion in May 1951. Stradishall now parented the station.

Terrorist activity in Malaya was so serious that Hornet intruders were all ordered there as ground-attack aircraft. An intended jet intruder, the DH 110 Vixen, being years away, the UK-based long-range intruder force disbanded. Its squadrons were given a short range day interceptor role and re-armed in 1951 with Meteor 8s. When in mid-August 1951 the intended 'intruder' squadrons reached Duxford Nos 64 and 65 were day fighter squadrons.

Until recently, at no time in its existence has the home fighter defence force been so dangerously neglected as it was in the late 1940s and early 1950s. Implications of the USSR's ever-increasing military potential well known through western intelligence gathering was not responded to with conviction until the Korean War. By then, an armada of over 700 TU-4s, the Russian copies of the American B-29, had been produced. Some would soon be able to deliver an atomic bomb. So dangerous did the situation become that before the Meteors returned to incomplete Duxford in 1951 Exercise *Fabulous* was well under way. That involved all squadrons taking turns at standing fully armed, carrying live ammunition

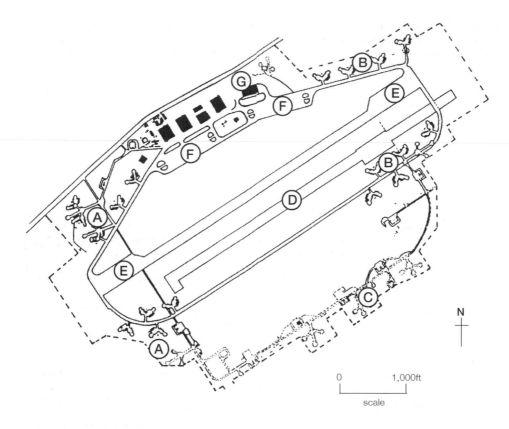

DUXFORD

Extended for the nuclear age, the plan shows Duxford of August 1953. Areas A and B each support a squadron, with blast walls flanking hardstandings. Projected dispersals for a third squadron are shown at the dotted area marked C. D is the second PSP runway and E is the main runway with ORPs at either end. Areas marked F are the ASPs and G an additional metal T2 hangar.

and at instant readiness to intercept, if necessary even destroy, any unidentified aircraft venturing into British air space. Never before in peacetime had such a measure been implemented. By September 1951 the Duxford squadrons were participating in the quick reaction alert scheme which, in varied styles, continued to the end of the Cold War and remains in force.

Among defence concepts explored at this time was Exercise *Hopscotch* in which entire Wings assembled after fast take-offs for which Duxford's PSP runway was very useful. It allowed fighters to scramble simultaneously from two runways. During one trial thirty-two Meteors of the Duxford Wing were away in a mere seventy-five seconds. Apart from special activities and *Fabulous*, the squadrons carried out continuation training and on 2 June 1953 Wing Commander Jimmy Wallace led the Duxford Wing which on that rainy evening of Coronation Day headed seven Wings comprising 144 Meteor 8s and also 24 RCAF Sabres as they saluted the new Queen by flying over Buckingham Palace.

The intention by now was to re-arm 64 and 65 Squadrons with Hunters, then exchange both squadrons with Horsham St Faith's two future squadrons of Swift 7s (Nos 74 and 245) armed with Fairey Fireflash beam-riding missiles intended for daylight operations against Russian TU-4s. The move was dictated by the Hunter's inferior range to that of the Swift. But the Swift proved a distressing failure and after the Duxford squadrons re-armed with Hunters they stayed put.

To bring Duxford in line with other stations fulfilling all-weather capability No 64 Squadron was switched to a night fighter role using Meteor NF12s from August 1956 and by the end of the year also had NF14s. No 65 Squadron received Hunter 6s in January and February 1957, and flew their last operational Meteor F8 sortie on 21 March 1957. Javelin 7s replaced 64's Meteors during September and October 1958, and all could be dispersed on revetments protected since 1954 by blast walls and positioned at the four corners of the airfield. At each end of the runway an ORP and telescramble lines were in place for QRA purposes. Javelin FAW 9s with limited re-heat began replacing 64's Mk 7s in July and August 1960.

A trio of Meteor 8s of 65 Squadron landing in September 1955.

With the V-force now providing the main defence posture, Fighter Command was drastically cut, and No 65 Squadron disbanded on 31 March 1961. No runway extension or necessary update was deemed feasible, Duxford no longer had strategic significance and its aged infrastructure left much to be desired. No 64 Squadron moved to Waterbeach on 28 July 1961.

On 31 July 1961 Air Vice-Marshal R. N. Bateson, leader of 613 Mosquito Squadron's famous 1944 low-level raid on the Gestapo registry in the Hague, in a Meteor T7 made the last take-off from Duxford ceremoniously ending its active days as an RAF station.

General assumption was that flying from Duxford had ceased. Behind the scenes consideration was given to placing Britain's Blue Streak IRBMs, here but the ballistic missile was cancelled.

In 1968 Duxford suddenly came back to life and astonishingly resounded to a multitude of Merlins when it became the main centre for the making of the film *Battle of Britain*. Spitfires and Hurricanes chuckled their way gleefully to their old home. Strange mock-ups of them taxied about, and most incongruously came a fleet of Spanish 'Me Hispano 109s' and 'He 111s' which filled the ASP. Reliance upon Rolls-Royce engines redeemed them making the sight of sixteen 'Me 109s' delectable even if they sounded like Hurricanes.

Such scenes awoke a driving desire that they must never end as enthusiasts from far flocked to view the wonder. A group of young folk banded themselves together, formed the East Anglian Aviation Society and led by David Crow started fighting hard to save Duxford. Somehow it survived, just, and attracted some rare aeroplanes including a B-17 N17. Launching a worthwhile venture let alone keeping it going was a project demanding an enormous amount of money and eventually the Imperial War Museum injected not only money but vital business acumen, also a realistic understanding of what was required and what could be achieved – in stages. Mr Haydon Baillie had based his two Canadair T-33A jet trainers here and a fine Sea Fury, CF-CHB, which added spice to the proceedings. Time-expired aeroplanes found a home, like a Ju 52, a P-51 used by the USAF and RCAF, a Gannet and an ex-51 Squadron Comet. An undoubted high spot was the arrival of a live B-24 Liberator from India and heading for the USA and which provoked enormous interest. It was eclipsed only by a somewhat battered, turret-less B-17G-105-VE, 44-85784 alias F-BGSR/N17TE and G-BEDF. Privately bought by Euroworld from the French, it arrived from Beauvais via Biggin Hill on 15 March 1975 to become that exotic, splendid delight, 'Sally B', which needs as much support – financial and moral – as possible to keep her flying.

The IWMs P-51D, first Museum aircraft here. It was the first renovation, and undertaken by the East Anglian Aviation Society. It then represented 472258 WZ-I 'Big Beautiful Doll' of the 78th FG 1945.

By Duxford's T2 pair, Spitfire XIV MV268 'JE J' marked in tribute to top scorer 'Johnnie' Johnson.

News that the Science Museum wanted to place the first British Concorde at Duxford was greeted with mixed feelings, for it seemed out of place. By then the Museum was attracting considerable support. Cambridgeshire County Council (who until mid-2008 owned the flying ground) became involved and, after some difficult weeks, Duxford was rescued to provide a home for an ever wider array of grounded and flying aeroplanes including a rare airworthy Republic P-47 Thunderbolt, a popular performer in the decade from 1986.

A really lovely sight at a Duxford show, Morane Saulnier MS 230 No 157.

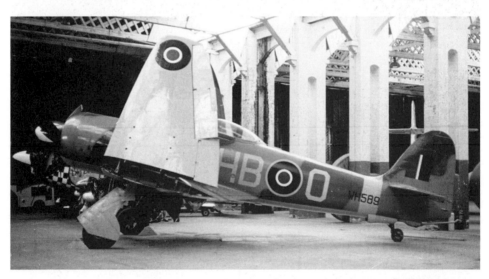

Early museum-era flying resident, Mr Haydon Baillie's Sea Fury FB 11, HB O WH589, in a Duxford hangar.

Mr Baillie's joy, G-OAHB, one of two T-33As.

'Sally B' just after arriving as N17TE at Duxford in 1975.

The IWM B-52 makes an inquisitive pass over Duxford.

The B-52s arrival was quite an event. Prayers, chute out, engines off – yes, we've made it!

Post-service Duxford has evolved along seven routes. First came the filming of *Battle of Britain*, then the brave saving of Duxford by David Crow and his friends in the East Anglian Aviation Society. Next, to the financial rescue came the Imperial War Museum and its collection of aeroplanes and associated items first housed in the 1918-style hangars or left to brave the elements. The prestigious American Air Museum dedicated to US personnel who have served in the UK was opened by HM Queen Elizabeth II on 1 August 1997 at an event attended by George Bush Snr. The IWM's Land Warfare Centre contains a wide assortment of Army items in an impressive building at the far western end of the site. The final major attraction is AirSpace.

Local flying attractions are mainly provided by The Breitling Fighter Collection, whose fine array of aircraft housed in a T2 hangar has long been masterminded by Stephen Gray, a great display pilot by any measure. Ray and Mark Hannah, of the Old Flying Machine Company and both sadly no longer with us, provided superb flying displays at Duxford. The Aircraft Restoration Company, with brilliant pilot John Romain at the helm, operates from an enclave at the eastern end of the airfield. Nearby is the huge AirSpace exhibition centre supported by BAE Systems and dedicated to British and Commonwealth aviation history and engineering. Support has been given by The Duxford Aviation Society and Friends of Duxford.

Great the joy to see once more, a Blenheim – well, Bolingbroke Blenheim IV pretending to be R3821 UX-N of 82 Squadron.

The IWMs B-17G really 44-83735 posing as IY-G of the 401st BG before the large hangar modified into 'AirSpace'.

One of the best things about Duxford is that one can as ever arrive being unsure of what – old or new – awaits on the airfield. Army, Navy and RAF helicopters call and USAF C-130s practice landings here. You might even be lucky enough to catch an amphibious DHC Otter or a Falklands-registered Twin Otter avoiding the Antarctic winter. That the M11 was able to hack its way through the runway is regrettable, but many of the nicest aeroplanes dislike long runways. Duxford attracts visitors from all over the world. It is one of the few aerodromes where you can hide away between ancient buildings and hear wonderful sounds, glimpse wonderful things. You can also dream of great days all gone, detect a whiff of dope and petrol while a Kestrel passes and echoes in a proper hangar. You cannot afford to miss any of this.

For many years The Fighter Collection's rare P-47 delighted in its very convincing 78th FG markings.

Within the American Air Museum resides the immaculate US Navy F-4.

The IWM American Air Museum which plays a major role at Duxford, has its most treasured item an SR-71 Blackbird seen here before the large hangar.

Unexpected Flying Legends treat, one of two Grumman F3F US Navy 'barrel fighters.

Almost traditionally, Stephen Gray played 'the Joker' in his Tigercat during Flying Legends balbo assembly. Shown here soon after arrival at Duxford.

Flying Legends 2008 highlight, the B-17 from the US formating with a P-51.

Two replica Fw 190s on Duxford's eastern ASP bravely visiting the home of the Spitfire during July 2009 Flying Legends display.

Main features:
Grass runways: N/S 4,200ft, NW/SE 4,800ft, NE/SW 6,000ft. *Hangars:* three Double Belfast Truss, one Single Belfast Truss, eight Blister. *Hardstandings:* twenty-six for twin-engined aircraft, forty-seven PSP for fighters. Accommodation (US): 190 officers, 1,519 enlisted men.

Duxford's greatest possession is its unique collection of airfield buildings, some still in use dating from the First World War. The well-known backdrop to the 'WZ' Spitfires in pre-war pictures remains little altered. Bungalow-type workshops of 1917 design and 1918-1919 construction, and Station Head Quarters from the 1922-1923 building programme, remain little changed. The air electronics block survived to serve, until recently, as the main public restaurant. Where one had a cup of tea and a sausage roll, AI radar servicing once took place and, more fascinating, Firestreak missiles were attended to.

Duxford Museum is open daily from 10.00am. Since April 1999 admission for children has been free, in addition to which a free bus connects the Museum to Cambridge railway station and the centre of that city. More than 150 historic aircraft are on show and admission is free to the American Air Museum, named Building of the Year and awarded the 1998 Stirling Prize by the Royal Institute of British Architects. For general information the telephone number is 01223 835000.

EARLS COLNE, Essex

51°55N/00°42E 225ft asl; TL850270. By B1024 S of Earls Colne

'Earls Colne? Which Earls Colne?' That is the question, for in a short time three airfields of that name each a smaller part of the original have existed.

Earls Colne was one of the first bases built by the US Army in Britain. When the wartime site started its military career on 26 August 1942 it was already under the control of the RAF's No 3 (Bomber) Group and administered by Stradishall. Its active life began in May 1943 when the 94th Bomb Group moved in bringing B-17Fs. Their stay was brief because of the decision to gather together at Earls Colne the three B-26 squadrons of the 323rd Bomb Group. On 15 June the 94th BG swapped places with Rougham's Marauder squadron. B-26 operations began from their new base on 16 July 1943 under 8th AF control.

B-26C-45-MO 42-107692 YU-F of the 455th BS, 323 BG (via George Pennick).

Their round of operations was as for other B-26 Groups. Some attacks on airfields, military camps and rail centres in France and the Low Countries were particularly successful especially when large formations employed carpet bombing techniques.

The Group was transferred to 9th AF control on 16 October 1943 and by the end of the year they were committed to attempts to prevent the V-1 campaign by attacking launch sites and supply sources in France. They also were very active in *Ramrod* operations during the pre-*Overlord* phase. Their support of the Normandy invasion was briefly interrupted when, on 21 July, they left Earls Colne for Beaulieu, Hampshire. ADGB (later renamed Fighter Command) then took control of the station.

B-26 passes over Earls Colne (via George Pennick).

B-26B-30-MA 41-31918 RJ-R of the 454th BS, 323rd BG (USAF).

At the end of September 1944 airborne forces Nos 296 and 297 Squadrons of 38 Group arrived. Although both were converting to Halifax G.T.Vs and 296 reached Earls Colne still using Albemarles, both were flying Halifax A.IIIs by January 1945. SOE operations had commenced in December 1944. Horsas were by then being flown in for use from Earls Colne by the squadrons during operation *Varsity*.

Both squadrons were actively engaged after the war transporting troops, freight and mail to and from the Continent, Middle East and India. No 296 Squadron disbanded on 23 January 1946 whereas during March 1946 No 297 moved to Tarrant Rushton.

Late December 1945 Meteors of 74 Squadron and Spitfire XVIs of 124 Squadron of 11 Group were scheduled to be stationed here but instead Earls Colne was in June 1946 placed under Care & Maintenance and held for possible development until the early 1950s.

Disposed of in 1955, Earls Colne was acquired at auction by an investment company. Eric Hobbs purchased it in a 1965 deal, with St Ives Sand & Gravel allowing retention of concrete roadways and a T2 hangar. Available land was used for agriculture, and thousands of trees were planted around the edges of the site. A 10-million-gallon reservoir was established in 1975 for irrigating potato crops.

During 1979 E Hobbs (Farms) Ltd received a farming and wildlife award for conservation, national recognition for creating an environment attractive to wildlife in an area now rich in deciduous and coniferous trees.

The early 1980s saw a shift from agriculture to industry, the T2 hangar becoming a distribution centre. Farm buildings were converted into a retail base for International Harvester in 1981. While the business park flourished during the 1990s, the control tower served as a house until 2003. By 2005 a variety of businesses were on site.

Earls Colne in 2009, a flourishing light aircraft centre (George Pennick).

The former Earls Colne airfield is now home to the Essex Golf & Country Club, which runs an eighteen-hole golf course and has twenty lakes and ponds supplementing the grasslands, while the reservoir supplies water to the golf course and business park. A variety of sports and athletic activities now take place at a site, which includes The Lodge, a forty-two-bed hotel. Adjacent is the Anglia Flight Centre, a CAA-licensed private flying/charter airfield with helicopter facilities, which uses part of the 07/25 runway. A prior permission airfield, with one grass runway 06/24 with an asphalt insert and edged with lighting, Earls Colne is open for flying daily.

Main features (December 1944):
Runways: 192° 6,000ft x 150ft, 252°, 302° concrete with tarmac and wood chips. *Hangars:* two T2. *Hardstandings:* fifty loop type. *Accommodation:* RAF: 208 officers, 501 SNCOs, 1,304 ORs; WAAF: 10 officers, 20 SNCOs, 255 ORs.

Place of interest nearby:
HQ 38 Group was based at nearby Marks Hall between October 1944 and May 1946, aircraft of its Communications Flight using Earls Colne.

EAST KIRKBY, Lincolnshire

53°08N/00°15E 30ft asl; TF345615. SE of the village between A155 and A16

Construction of East Kirkby, situated on the northern edge of The Fens, began in 1942. Although a typical wartime temporary bomber base, it unusually had seven metal transportable hangars and a mixture of hardstandings.

East Kirkby opened in August 1943 was declared completed on 1 September. No 57 Squadron had moved in on 28 August freeing Scampton for runway building to begin there. The 5 Group Lancaster squadron operated from East Kirkby to the end of the war.

On 15 November 1943 'B' Flight 57 Squadron became the basis of a new squadron, No 630, based here until disbandment on 18 July 1945. From 15 April 1944 until 1 November 1945, 55 Base HQ was here with Sub-Stations Spilsby and Strubby under their control. The final operation from East Kirkby took place on 25 April 1945 with Berchtesgaden as the target.

A major accident during bombing up occurred on 17 April 1945. Two 1,000lb MCs exploded while being hauled aboard Lancaster PB360 setting off a chain of explosions. Three airmen were killed and fourteen injured in addition to two civilian casualties. The night's operations were cancelled and by the following morning five Lancasters had been written-off and another fourteen grounded due to various damage states. This was one of the worst accidents of its type in Bomber Command.

No 554 Wing to control Nos 207 and 617 Squadrons of *Tiger Force* formed here on 29 May 1945. Australian No 460 Squadron arrived from Binbrook on 20 July 1945 also for a part in the Far East war which halted and brought about an end to the build up on 17 August. Flying continued at a low key and included tours of Germany to view the effectiveness of the Allied campaign. Some trooping flights within Europe were also flown before No 460 Squadron ceased activity on 22 September. On 10 October the squadron officially disbanded. By the 25th all the squadron personnel had been posted to Gamston awaiting return to Australia.

In Tiger Force colours, one of East Kirkby's Lincoln BII (FE)s of No 57 Squadron.

August saw No 57 Squadron receive three Lincolns for Service Trials but on 25 November 1945 the squadron disbanded then reformed next day at Elsham Wolds. After the departure of 57 Squadron the airfield closed to flying but the site was retained by the Air Ministry. Between 1948 and 1950 a Sub-Site of 93 MU functioned here. In August 1947 the airfield was reactivated and a detachment from 139 Squadron, Coningsby, made use of it until February 1948. In July 1948 it became Inactive and after closing to flying was placed on 'C & M'.

When the USAF needed more airfields in the UK East Kirkby was allocated to them. Considerable improvements were made to basic facilities, then on 17 June 1954 the 3931st Air Base Group (SAC) arrived and stayed until disbanded in 1955. In August 1954 C-47s of the 3917 ABS, 7th AD, SAC, arrived and stayed until 1958 when the airfield was returned to the RAF and declared Inactive. It was disposed of in April 1970.

'Inactive'? No longer for, amazingly, a Lancaster which years ago slipped in to Lavenham lives here in fine health and in a private hangar. On special days it emerges, its Merlins roar with delight and better still it taxies to admiring (and envious) Lancaster lovers along the old familiar peri-track presenting a most wonderful sight.

Main features:
Runways: 200° 6,000ft x 150ft, 263°, 308°, concrete. *Hangars:* six T2, one B1.
Hardstandings: twenty-seven circular, five loop. *Accommodation:* RAF: 196 officers,
428 SNCOs, 1,341 ORs; WAAF: 10 officers, 26 SNCOs, 450 ORs.

EAST WRETHAM, Norfolk

52°28N/00°48E 135ft asl; TL910810. A1075 5 miles NE of Thetford

Seen from the air in 1940 East Wretham, Honington's satellite, was little more than a large square grass meadow giving no hint of its future interesting history. Dispersed Wellingtons began using the Unbuilt SLG in March 1940, but it was as a home for Czech airmen that it came very much into its own. Over 200 came to Britain after gathering on the French west coast, sailing in the *Apapa*, which docked at Liverpool on 9 July. They were taken to Beeston Castle, Cheshire, and next day Air Ministry officials interviewed them and posted many to Innsworth Lane, Gloucestershire, where a grouped formed 311 (Czech) Bomber Squadron. On 17 July the contingent proceeded to Cosford, were enrolled in the RAF and sworn in and the forty-three officers were given British commissions. Wing Commander Griffiths took command and the embryo squadron moved to Honington on 29 July with Wing Commander Toman as the Czech commanding officer.

Teaching the crews to fly Wellington Ics was masterminded by the famous Flight Lieutenant P C Pickard. After three weeks they began flying from the grass satellite making their first operational sorties on 10 September 1940 with Brussels their target.

On 16 September the ground echelon of 311 Squadron moved to the satellite for better dispersal. Accommodation there was very primitive, tents housing the airmen and a brick building the officers. Emphasising the value of dispersal a Do 17Z came out of the clouds and circled just as the ground party arrived. Airfield defences opened up driving the bomber's crew away – to unload eight delayed action bombs at Honington. There a fierce and accurate reception resulted in the raider crashing near Bury St Edmunds.

Three days later the Wellingtons of 311 Squadron proceeded to East Wretham and in the afternoon five returned to Honington in what became normal procedure for night operations, in this instance cancelled. The first operation, after repositioning, took place against Calais on 21 September. To keep the parent station in darkness landings were scheduled for East Wretham on a grass runway edged by Glim flares, but fog descended. Only Flight Lieutenant Ocelca landed damaging his aircraft in the process.

On 23/24 September three crews set off for Berlin, one returning early. The second reached the target but the third, flying KX-E:L7778, forced-landed intact in the Netherlands. On 26 September the Dutch radio gave news of the arrival of the Wellington, whose crew had escaped. An offer amounting to £60 was made to anyone giving news of the crew.

The squadron took part in many 3 Group night raids from Wretham or Honington, incidents typical of the period punctuating the action. Three crews were despatched on 16 December to Mannheim and as the third Wellington (P2577:Q) took off it soon met trouble and circled low. Trying to land it crashed on the Wretham-Wretham Hall road and burst into flames. Pilot Officer Nedved scrambled clear, then, in spite of the exploding bombs, went back to rescue his colleagues. Fire tenders had come fast on the scene to rescue Pilot Officer Taul who was critically injured. Metal lattice frames of crashed Wellingtons, their fabric burnt away, were a common East Anglian sight between 1939 and 1942.

During the winter of 1940-1 enemy intruders were often active in the Wretham area. It is generally believed that this was another station upon which an He 111 landed in darkness and quickly departed. Is there an ex-Luftwaffe pilot or anyone else who can recall these strange tales? More certain were the events of 3 February 1941 when twenty bombs fell, thirteen on the airfield damaging a Wellington.

Another attack came on 3/4 March when 311 Squadron was carrying out night flying. A Ju 88C followed a Wellington into Wretham, dropping ten bombs in the process, and on 8/9 April Fw Hahn flying a Ju 88C shot down 'X-Xray' while the Czechs were making a training flight.

No 311 Squadron's Wellingtons operated from East Wretham bombing a wide variety of targets until 1 May 1942 brought an abrupt change involving a move to Aldergrove and transfer to Coastal Command. Remaining at Wretham was the Czech Training Unit (renamed 1429 Flight on 1 January 1942) holding twelve Wellington 1cs and three Airspeed Oxfords. Bomber Command's call for a contribution to the '1,000 bomber' raids saw the Flight despatch six Wellingtons for the Cologne and Essen attacks and two to Bremen on 25 June 1942. The Flight moved to Woolfox Lodge on 1 July 1942 and in August East Wretham was switched to Care & Maintenance in preparation for upgrading and its transfer to the USAAF.

In November runway construction began at Mildenhall. That meant finding a new home for Wellington IIIs of 115 Squadron so on 21 November they came for a temporary stay at East Wretham which became Mildenhall's third satellite.

October 1942 had seen a few early production Hercules-engined Lancaster IIs flying alongside Mk Is in No 61 Squadron, Syerston. Being prematurely used, they were withdrawn after only thirty-three sorties. Improved Lancaster IIs were instead delivered to 3 Group which had more experience of the Bristol engines powering the Mk II. March 1943 saw them joining No 115 Squadron whose final Wellington III sorties were flown from Wretham on 12 March 1943.

On 24 March 1943, 32 Base HQ opened at Mildenhall and administered East Wretham until 7 August. Among the units it controlled was a detached Flight of No 1657 CU formed on 22 March 1943, supplied with eight Lancaster IIs for crew conversion and named 1678 Conversion Flight on 18 May. On the 23rd approval was given for renaming it 1678 Conversion Unit by which time No 115 Squadron had taken their Lancaster IIs into action, for on 20 March they laid mines and on 22 March raided St Nazaire. The first major raid, against Berlin, followed on March and thereafter the squadron engaged in Main Force operations. During April 1943 the US began pressing for runway laying to begin here but it was 7 August before No 115 Squadron and 1678 CU moved from their temporary base to Little Snoring to make way for the Americans.

Although East Wretham was passed to the USAAF on 1 August 1943 it was mid-October 1943 before the 359th Fighter Group arrived flying P-47D Thunderbolts which commenced operations on 13 December. Re-equipment with P-51s came during April 1944. At first the Group had concentrated on providing escorts covering raids on French airfields, then in May 1944 switched to escorting bombers raiding rail targets in Germany and oil plants in Poland.

They supported the invasion, patrolled over the Channel, escorted bombers to France and made dive-bombing and strafing attacks on the battle area perimeter.

A highlight came on 28 July when the Group made the 8th AF's first sighting of Me 163 rocket fighters. Between July 1944 and February 1945 the 359th concentrated on bomber escort, and for the close protection they gave to B-17s bombing Chemnitz en route for a shuttle raid to Russia on 11 September they were awarded a Distinguished Unit Citation. Participation in the Arnhem operation, the Battle of the Bulge and the Rhine crossing were also undertaken.

On 10 November 1945 the 359th Group was deactivated and East Wretham bade farewell to the Americans. RAF Fighter Command took over the station on 1 November 1945 placing it under Hethel's wing within 12 Group. On 23 February 1946 Fighter Command declared it was no longer needed and on 21 May 1946 Air Ministry placed it in Bomber Command under 1 Group's Methwold.

On 10 July 1946 it was switched to RAF Technical Training Command after which it became a Polish Resettlement Corps camp.

Some of East Wretham was sold in October 1954 although a Bellman hangar and some wartime buildings remain in use for various purposes. The camp lies within the Army's Stanford Battle Area.

Main features (December 1944):
Runways: NE/SW 1,880 yards with PSP laid in 1944, other two runways NNW/SSE and N/S 4,200ft both grass. *Hangars:* two Bellman, six Blister and one steel frame and canvas. *Hardstandings:* twenty-four tarmac, twelve PSP. *Accommodation:* 190 officers, 1,519 enlisted men.

ELLOUGH, Suffolk – see BECCLES

EYE, Suffolk

52°20N/01°08E 150ft asl; TM130750. 1 mile SW Brome on A140, NW of Eye

B-24H 42-94837 THE JINX of the 490th BG on stand 13 on the airfield's south side by the Yaxley–Eye road in early summer 1944. '13' refers to the crew number assigned to Thomas J Keyes. (390th Memorial Museum, Parham)

To have one of the lowest loss rates in 8th AF operations was a welcome distinction brought about partly because the 490th Bomb Group joined the conflict relatively late. The Americans arrived at Eye, built by British and American organisations, in February 1944. The 490th Bomb Group moved in during April, commencing operations on 31 May. It took part in attacks on airfields and supported the Normandy invasion. Rail targets were bombed, vehicle concentrations, bridges, and the Group was active in the Caen area in July 1944. The Liberators flew their fortieth and final operation on 6 August 1944 after which the Group switched to flying B-17s in keeping with other 3rd Air Division units. Gone their 'T in a square' identity in favour of red and white tails with curious '-' or '+' signs ahead of the individual letter on the fin which seemed so unusual at the time.

September found them helping to reduce Brest prior to its capture. Then they switched to the strategic offensive bombing oil plants, tank factories, marshalling yards, aircraft plants and airfields. Berlin, Hamburg, Merseburg, Munster, Kassel, Hanover, Cologne – all were on target manifestos. They took part in the Ardennes offensive in bad weather which had allowed von Rundstedt to make his surprise offensive. Then they switched to further interdiction attacking rail and military targets to support the advance which ended the war. In the closing days of hostilities they dropped food supplies to the Dutch, retrieved prisoners of war and flew refugees and troops back to their home countries. The 490th left Eye in August 1945. It was allowed to run down and Eye is now the scene of light industry and agriculture.

Main features:
Runways: 212° 6,000ft x 150ft, 270°, 328° concrete/screed finish. *Hangars:* two T2.
Hardstandings: fifty spectacle type. *Accommodation:* 421 officers, 2,473 enlisted men.

FELIXSTOWE, Suffolk

51°51N/01°19E; TM280330. Now the Port of Felixstowe, S of town. Car park and good viewing point

Langar Road, 26 July 1938, my diary tells me mentioning 'sheer magic'. Ah yes, I remember it well, that first sighting of the first production silver Sunderland L2158 banking low during circuit and splash in the Orwell. For over forty years the sea and the sky were as one at Felixstowe. Southampton, Scapa, Singapore – even the names came out of the sea like the splendid sights. There was the amazing Sarafand all wings, tails and six pusher-pullers, a Perth grumbling along, the lovely 'swish' and cool note from a passing Empire Boat, that cranked wing, weird Short Knuckleduster – not to mention the semi-modernistic Londons and Stranraers. If you knew pre-war

Felixstowe you, like me, surely swooned at the sight and sound of them all, thrilled to the foam they all delighted in. Possibly all is not quite lost if, like me, you also excite at the sight of colourful merchant ships, and have discovered that now aeroplanes have lost their individuality you might like to try ship photography. It also thrives on a diet of the sort of skill, patience, knowledge you have had to apply to your first love. There is no better place to try it than at Felixstowe, Britain's premier container port and the Haven.

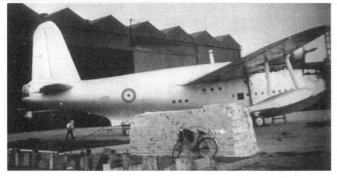

What a beauty! 'My first Sunderland', L2158. Two days after seeing it fly I took a chance and shot it through the fence on 9 July 1938. My first successful photo – thanks to "Mr Snaps"!

Slowly it paraded along the town's seafront. Noisily, majestically, its six Kestrels straining, the Short Sarafand remains unforgettable.

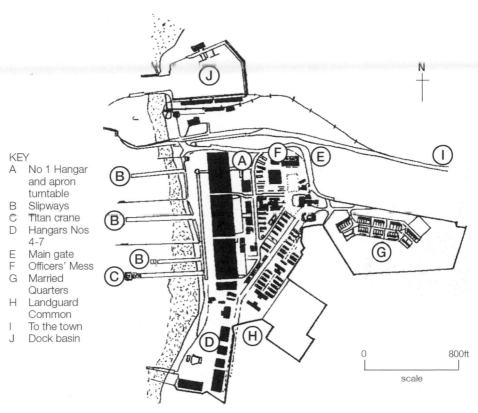

KEY
A   No 1 Hangar
    and apron
    turntable
B   Slipways
C   Titan crane
D   Hangars Nos
    4-7
E   Main gate
F   Officers' Mess
G   Married
    Quarters
H   Landguard
    Common
I   To the town
J   Dock basin

0   800ft
scale

FELIXSTOWE

Most of Felixstowe seaplane station was a product of the early 1920s, like its landplane equivalent at Martlesham whose buildings bore much similarity in appearance. Apart from new married quarters and a 1934-style watch office and tower, the station's structure changed little throughout its existence and by 1938 it looked quite 'ancient'. RAF personnel and squadrons were accommodated as well as civilian and military personnel of the MAEE. Most buildings, tightly packed on the technical site, were built of red brick or concrete/stone dash with tiled roofing. Three 1920s large black-painted metal and corrugated iron clad hangars (No 1 for largest seaplanes) contained workshops. Four smaller, aged hangars were sited near Landguard Common. Two engine test houses were in use. There were four 26,000 gallon petrol tanks and twelve assorted stores. Three slipways were separated by two breakwaters. The Titan crane at the end of the largest pier lifted seaplanes on to, or from, a winch hauled trolley. A track along the apron led to a compass swinging turntable. The 1934-style watch office and tower erected on the apron remains. Usual offices were supplemented by the Pier Master's - a barrack hut for the motorboat crew and a room for drying waders. The hut used by the High Speed Flight for speed measurement purposes remained, there were experimental offices along with the drawing office and a meeting room for pilots. Prominent buildings included the Officer's mess and SHQ near the main entrance close to the parade ground. The airmen's dining room and cookhouse were separate from the NAAFI. New features included five groups of married quarters and a school built alongside Langar Road outside the RAF station's iron perimeter fence. There was a camp cinema, gymnasium, ample games facilities, C of E and OD churches. No 2 hangar remains and the huge apron has been overtaken by the Landguard Container Terminal. Famous fire-damaged 'Little Ships' Hotel and the flour mill can still be glimpsed although they are now within the Port of Felixstowe area. Landguard Fort, for which various development schemes have been promoted, holds a museum devoted to an historic area now a splendid shipping viewpoint.

Seaplanes and Felixstowe first met in 1912 when officialdom decreed that landing rights near Harwich should be obtained. On 3 June Lieutenant Commander Samson flew up from Burntwick Island, Kent, to survey the Haven area with particular interest being given to Shotley and Mistley. Samson favoured somewhere else, the northern beach inland from Landguard Fort. A further visit by C R Samson in a Short S.41 biplane seaplane on 3 October 1912 was followed in April 1913 by an Admiralty announcement that a seaplane station was to be built on the favoured area. Boulton & Paul of Norwich erected three huge sheds, jetties and concrete slipways while the SHQ was established in what was later the North Sea Hotel on the front. On 5 August 1913 the seaplane station opened.

When the 1914-18 war began seaplanes started patrolling from Felixstowe, operations being co-ordinated with flights from other RNAS seaplane bases at Clacton and famous Great Yarmouth. Christmas 1914 saw the intended Cuxhaven raid set out from Harwich involving the seaplanes, and in February 1915 the new aircraft carrier HMS *Ark Royal* sailed from the Haven. Zeppelins also became active in the area and in 1916 German aircraft attacked shipping near the Sunk Light. On 4 July 1917 a formation of eighteen Gothas G.IVs delivered a hit-and-run attack on Felixstowe and Harwich pre-dating Second World War fighter-bomber attacks. After successfully evading detection at sea, the bombers' arrival was announced by their engine sounds off Orfordness at 06.55hrs. They crossed over the coastline at Shingle Street; 5 minutes later they reached Bawdsey, then dropped their bombs between 07.20 and 07.25hrs. The only RFC interception came from DH 4 A7436 of Testing Squadron, Martlesham. Captain John Palethorpe, flying an endurance test, spotted the Gothas strung out in a 5-mile line. He selected a middle one but his gun suffered a stoppage. An enemy bullet passed through the heart of his gunner, Air Mechanic James Jessop, instantly killing him. Palethorpe landed, collected another gunner, but was too late to interfere with the raiders. They killed seventeen, injured thirty and caused £2,065 damage in the area. Most bombs fell in the water, but at the air station one H.12 seaplane was destroyed and another was damaged. AA gunners fired 135 rounds without success.

A second raid took place at 08.10-08.17hrs on 22 July 1917 when damage was caused to the port of Harwich and RNAS installations. Casualties were thirteen killed and twenty-six injured, damage amounting to £2,780. One of the twenty-one Gothas attacking was caught later, by a French-based fighter. A Vickers F.B.14D C4547 crewed by famous Captain (later Sir) Vernon Brown – who in the late 1940s became Chief Inspector of Accidents – and Captain (later Sir and a well-known Professor of Cambridge University) B Melvill Jones was the only home-based aircraft to make contact with the bombers, but without success.

On 6 July 1918 German W.29 floatplanes attacked the RN submarine C.25 near Harwich but by then dramatic change had come about with the formation of the RAF on 1 April 1918. Next summer RAF flying-boat squadrons were forming here equipped with F.2A, F.3 and F.5 boats designed and developed here under the leadership of Wing Commander J C Porte. Also from Felixstowe and Harwich, trials and operations were carried out using lighters towed behind destroyers and carrying fighters. Their purpose was to engage enemy aircraft before they reached Britain's shores. No 230 Squadron formed here in August 1918 and, still flying F.2As and F.3s, moved to Calshot in May 1922.

During that year came the famous 'Geddes cuts', the Strategic Defence Review of those days. No new orders for warplanes would be placed leaving Felixstowe to swim along as best it could without even the long-resident 230 Squadron which moved its F.2As to Calshot.

From misfortune cheer may sometimes come as it did for Felixstowe with the coming of the Marine Aircraft Experimental Unit from the Isle of Grain on 1 April 1924 and its transformation into the Marine Aircraft Experimental Establishment. Now Suffolk held three very important such organisations, here, at Martlesham and at Orfordness.

Northern waters of the Orwell estuary provided good runs and the necessary mix of tidal and weather conditions. For that reason the Flying Boat Development Flight existed here from May 1924 to 1932 when it became part of the MAEE. Before individualistic hangars spread a huge concrete apron from which slipways led into the river. Piers enabled aircraft and boats to be safely secured while other seaplanes were anchored off shore, sometimes to test their weather and waterborne qualities. In 1932 Crane Pier was constructed upon which, in 1934, the giant 50-ton Stothert & Pitt Titan crane was erected. On 1 May 1936 the MAEE left Coastal Area and, as part of RAF major reorganisation, joined No 16 Group, Coastal Command.

A 1955 general view of the apron. Hangars little changed since the 1920s.

Supermarine Scapa S1648 on the apron. (Charles Hall)

Felixstowe often hit the headlines, one much publicised event coming after No 205 Squadron, reformed here on 17 May 1927, became the Far East Flight which in October set off in Southampton IIIs for distant Singapore and a Far East tour. In March 1931 No 210 Squadron also reformed with Southampton IIIs and three months later moved to Pembroke Dock.

In March 1931 No 210 Squadron also reformed with Southampton IIIs and three months later moved to Pembroke Dock. On 1 May 1936 the MAEE left the Coastal Area and joined 16 Group, Coastal Command.

Probably the most important event in the station's history resulted from the formation on 1 October 1926 of the first High Speed Flight to look into increasing the speed of British aircraft. It also involved entering the Schneider Trophy races which led to many famous pilots flying fast seaplanes from Felixstowe. Among them was Flight Lieutenant Boothman who, in the Supermarine S.6B S1595, won the Trophy outright averaging 340.8mph and Flight Lieutenant Stainforth who, in S1596, won the World' Airspeed Record by flying at 407.05mph over a 3km course. All of Britain's high-speed seaplanes knew Felixstowe's waters well.

Viewing of the exciting activity at the MAEE was spoilt by a black-painted metal fence – until low tide provided plentiful gaps between bars. Red brick barracks 1922-style were provided for the RAF although many of the Staff were civilians living in town. In the mid-1930s modern barrack blocks and married quarters were built, along with a 'Fort' type control tower and watch office which still stands along with the central, smallest hangar. Landguard Point and Common were largely restricted military zones to the end of the 1950s.

Pre-war MAEE Felixstowe was always a hive of exotic activity and, despite the sort of secrecy pervading, offered excellent viewing possibilities and photography. Almost every type of British seaplane – and many of the best known older generation aviation writers – came here to glimpse, on the forecourt, such beauties as the Calcutta, Iris, and the massive scaffolding called the Short Sarafand the sight of which off the town prom to the sound of six Kestrels whistling in high pitch as they passed never failed to generate some whoops of joy. All such contraptions passed through the Marine Experimental Aircraft Establishment for assessment and usually attracting desire for improved water handling! Elegant boats by the dozen dipped their bottoms into the choppy, cold water undergoing official performance trials and seaworthiness tests.

No 209 Squadron equipped with Singapore IIIs and based here from 1 May 1935 to 12 August 1939 occasionally undertook a prime time cruise. During their stay the Sunderland appeared the most outstanding of all flying-boats on account of its quite incredible ability to double its all-up weight in its life time. Sunderlands passed through here in 1939 heading for squadrons overseas and rubbing shoulders with an American interloper, a PBY-5 bought for evaluation and, because of it amazing duration was ordered for the RAF as the Catalina. But of all the Felixstowe magic none was surely exceeded than those few times when the Mayo Composite duo, *Maia* and *Mercury*, separated over the Orwell. As for elegance, the prize went to the Short C-Class boats type tested here for Imperial Airways.

July 9 1938 and Sunderlands float - watched over by 'Titan'.

Come the war and Felixstowe's great days ended. Too vulnerable for experimental flying, the Marine Aircraft Experimental Establishment quickly evacuated itself to distant Rhu, near Helensburgh on the Clyde. By then seaplanes were judged as having little to commend them. Arguments directed against them included the difficulty in maintenance when afloat and their vulnerability at anchorages easy to mine. A few days after the war began Felixstowe's huge concrete apron began echoing to the sound of the boots of the recruits of 7 RTC.

Coastal Command retrieved the station on 17 May 1940 and on the 29th Dutch personnel flew in escaping in Fokker floatplanes. By now this was a dangerous zone, at least two Hampdens clouting the cables from barrage balloons secured to barges there to protect Harwich.

In September 1940 a desperate, urgent call reached the secret SOE den in Baker Street telling of four brave Dutchmen whose lives were at risk. Could they be snatched from Holland, and if so how could that be achieved? A few Fokker T8-W Dutch naval floatplanes had escaped in May; what better than to use one to rescue these freedom fighters? A Fokker was therefore resurrected from storage here. Could it undertake a dark night, water landing in enemy territory? Perhaps – if the night was not too dark. A trio of October nights was therefore selected. On the first – the 14th – there was a heavy rain but, late the following day, and in great secrecy, the Fokker left Felixstowe for Vlieland. Visibility was good – except over the chosen lake. No accepting lights were exposed or flashed, so the Fokker landed back on the Stour at 0430 hrs. At midnight on the 16th the crew set out again assuming that they were enveloped in secrecy as they headed towards Lake Tjeuke where the expected 'K' identity code letter was flashed. The floatplane landed, a small boat headed towards the

Fokker and suddenly when it was about 30 yards away someone in the boat opened fire so the seaplane's gunner replied. Searchlights swept the surface of the lake, but the worthy old aircraft escaped and headed straight for Felixstowe where it landed at 0500 hrs. The drama was not quite over for, as it came in for splashdown, trigger-happy Home Guards opened up forcing the crew to make quickly for the shore. Forty bullet holes were found in the T8-W whose tanks had emptied. Years later it was discovered that the Germans had arrested the resistance workers on the second night and on the third arranged an ambush from which the seaplane's crew was lucky to escape.

Felixstowe's hangars remained largely empty until March 1942 when, with less enemy activity generally in the area, Sunderlands, Lerwicks and Londons began coming for major overhauls. Late August 1942 saw the first Catalinas arrive for under-wing attachment of Leigh Light airborne searchlights, work which continued until the end of the war. Almost the only flying-boats seen over East Anglia during the conflict were flying to or from Felixstowe from or to western coast bases. The Norwegian Government stored a Northrop N-3PB here from January 1944.

Aerial view of RAF Felixstowe in October 1945 with the Short Shetland afloat.

In May 1945 the MAEE returned to its favoured home, but without the old status. There was a touch of magic when to the MAEE came captured German flying-boats including a couple of peculiar twin-boomed Bv 138Bs, two Do 24s, briefly some Ju 52W floatplanes and, most impressive of all, the giant Bv 222. Its stay was short, its diesel propelled noisy journey over East Anglia, luckily included Cambridge as it made its absolutely stunning flight to Calshot! A few Sunderland Vs were later used for hull design and water pattern research, the nippy little Saro Shrimp with modified hull and tail also playing a part. The late 1945 arrival of the Shetland was a tonic for the MAEE staff, but its life was dramatically cut short. Early in the morning of 28 January 1946 an air duct overheated while airmen aboard were preparing breakfast. Fire rapidly took hold in the hull and before anything of substance could be done to save it DX166 burnt out and sank at its mooring. A huge pall of smoke drifting out to sea marked the end of British military flying-boat development. A few ex-BOAC Solents retired here for storage and spray tests using two Seafords ended in 1949. RAF association with the MAEE ended on 31 March 1953 but the MAEE did not die until 31 July 1958.

Photographed in August 1946, the last of MAEE Felixstowe's superb Sunderlands, GR5 SZ599 on unit charge 18 June 1946 to 31 January 1951 and used for water spray and hull dynamics research.

The last British new military seaplane type evaluated here was the Short Seaford. 'B' MZ271 here afloat was one of two.

The terrifying floods of February 1953 devastated the whole low lying area and seriously battered the old flying boat base. The building of Landguard Terminal in the 1960s, and a deep water quayside, overtook the apron to which Singapores and many others crept ashore up slipways. For a time old Titan, accustomed to lifting a Scapa or two, continued earning a living by hoisting road tankers aboard coasters. He passed away when his pier needed demolition. The huge black shed, lair of Perths, Singapores and Sunderlands, was dismembered in a mere fortnight during 1986. The Officers' Mess has become an office block while juggernauts accost the parade ground upon which the ghost of the SWO of yesteryear waves his swagger stick offering many a curse!

There had been other post-war activity here where the Metropolitan Sector HQ was established close to Trimingham radar. Felixstowe passed for that reason from 19 Group Coastal Command to 11 Group Fighter Command on 15 February 1949 leaving the MAEE under 41 Group. From 1956 to 1961 a detachment of two Whirlwind HAR 2 helicopters of 'B' Flight, 22 Squadron, was based in the biggest shed in the roof of which, to the end, hung the overhead gantry crane which could carry a giant seaplane.

One seaplane shed remains, in fine health, as is the control tower. Major development at Landguard will leave them stranded far from the water.

There was brief re-acquaintance with boats when the USAF used the waterlane for SA-16 Albatross crew training before the station closed on 20 August 1962. Plane Sailing's Catalina much later looked in.

Felixstowe, so well strategically situated, is Britain's largest container port and one of the world's busiest. Some 100 shipping lines link Felixstowe with 365 ports. Trinity Quay's huge 'portainer' cranes lift metal boxes from the world's largest container ships some grossing over 100,000 tons and which berth not far from where the Mayo Composite used to separate. In 1988 just over 900,000 containers were handled; in 1997 the total was 1,600,735. In 1999 Trinity Terminal, the largest container handling facility in the UK, has the longest continuous quay in the British Isles and featuring seven deep-water berths stretches for 2,084m. Cranes recently installed can cope with the new ultra post-Panamax huge vessels. East of the original apron is a concreted area for vehicles for the Port's two Ro-Ro terminals. The flying-boat base area was now fronted by the four ship to shore crane Landguard Terminal, the UK's first purpose built container port, where large ships often berth. The three quay original dock basin, once the home of MTBs and ASR launches, and often used by tugs was filled in 2009.

In April 1946 my lifelong friend Alan J Wright (probably best known as the author of Ian Allan's annual *Civil Aircraft Markings*) and I made our first post-war spotting jaunt to Felixstowe. We found ourselves swooning over those two Bv 138s close by the now long gone old corrugated iron fence. I had a special desire for in my vandalistic youth, I produced a peephole in that high fence alongside the rear of the big hangar in order to have a good view of a towering, magnificent Blackburn Perth which proved too big to fit my lens! Had my spy-hole survived those years of bitter conflict? Indeed it had and was waiting to be put to good use. Unfortunately, there would never again be any flying boat to view.

Gigantic merchant ships – and also huge cruise ships from Parkeston Quay – pass close to the excellent and very popular John Bradfield Viewing Area and large car park alongside Landguard Terminal. There is also a good shore to watch from and the Languard Fort complex which one day will surely become a major attraction complete with photographs of well remembered days. Often the large ships which pass close seem curiously to look more like models providing the feeling that 'I'll take that one home for the bath'!

After reliving treasured memories one simply had to away to Felixstowe town Front for a proper, traditional lunch in Cordy's Alexandra Cafe, a family business sadly no more yet so long a part of Felixstowe and possibly where more delicious oxtail soup and plaice and chips was sold than anywhere else in the world! Those you could consume whilst viewing a wall picture of what it was like before RAF Felixstowe was there. By 'the prom' Peters produces beachside ices just like they did while one watched the stupendous Sarafand trundling past the man who ever wanted to weigh fat ladies on his big brass scales. Alas, he has passed into history too, just like Mr Snaps, to whom you bravely took your naughty shots. No, not of local bathing beauties, but of secret slipway treasures! Ah, the joys of youth!

Main features (RAF):

Flying: Approach from any direction, adopt left hand circuit over Haven until receipt of green Aldis light from the watch tower. Prevailing wind SW, weather typical for East coast. Fog on average on thirty-seven days. Tender will lead aircraft to one of four RAF Mooring 9 buoys – the rest are for MAEE. Currents up to $2^{1}/_{2}$-knot. Full RAF refuelling facilities. One slipway for RAF use and the 50-ton crane. Additional facilities are for MAEE use. *Accommodation:* RAF: 86 officers, 90 SNCOs, 937 ORs; WAAF: 6 officers, 4 SNCOs, 308 ORs.

FELTWELL, Norfolk

52°28N/00°31E 50ft asl; TL710900. To left of B1112, turn left in Feltwell village

Feltwell is unique having changed from a Permanent Heavy Bomber Station of the 1930s into an American Middle School for USAF Lakenheath's very questioning and most certainly lively children. That makes them a pleasure to teach – and I speak with some experience (and experiences) in mind! Barrack blocks surrounding yesterday's parade ground have become classrooms, one hangar houses a superb gymnasium and the one-time Airmen's Mess is now the library. Remember the sinks where one washed 'the irons'? Gone – a battery of computers occupies that space, and the kitchens have become smart offices.

Ironically, the guardroom remains for in our strange world schools need security as much as bomber bases. That is very sad. The modern main entrance by the south site is dominated by three huge golf balls inside of which each holds a giant radar dish which spends its time looking deep into space perhaps enquiring 'Can you hear me mother? Is there anybody or anything out there?'

Feltwell, overlooking the Fens, originated in 1915 when an RFC aerodrome opened on land just to the south of the present boundary. What at first glance looks like a clutch of old farm buildings includes some of the sheds of the 1914-18 aerodrome which from November 1917 was home to No 7 Training Depot Station which closed on 22 April 1919 leaving its 504s, Camels and Pups stranded. Flying instructors were also trained at Feltwell between July 1918 and March 1920 and mainly on Avro 504Js and Ks.

The first Feltwell 5 July 1918, from south-west. Preparations were underway to build GS hangars (central). Bessoneau hangars top left. (RAF Museum)

Feltwell's position being very good, its flying field and beacon were retained. In 1925 the government negotiated for additional nearby land upon which to build a heavy bomber station. Subsequent redesign took place in 1934, construction getting under way in 1935. The Air Ministry had wanted eleven hangars but eventually five 'C' Type Hangars were erected. Feltwell, a two-squadron station, had a somewhat unusual arrangement of buildings, the aircraft sheds being built around a tighter arc than usual. That served to prevent serious damage should a raider release a stick of bombs upon them. Almost the entire station – technical and domestic areas – was combined with a centre spine road leading directly to the apron. Most buildings being of the early expansion period have sloping roofs, those for accommodation being to the East with the 90ft water tower, main stores, MT yard and other 'tech site' buildings mainly to the West or right and to the rear of the hangars. The 'fort style' pre-war Watch Office and tower was mid-set by the narrow apron.

SHQ Feltwell opened in April 1937 within 3 (Bomber) Group and on 19 April Harrows of 214 Squadron arrived from Scampton. Their 'B' Flight on 26 April detached itself and became 37 Squadron also Harrow-equipped. The RAF's 100 examples of those lanky bombers, primed for potentially disastrous action during the Munich Crisis, were an interim item, both Feltwell squadrons receiving their first Wellington Is on 6 May 1939.

Work-up was hectic and barely complete when on 27 August 1939 No 37 Squadron mobilised and No 214, already a reserve and training squadron, moved to Methwold Unbuilt SLG. The war was only six hours old when six crews of 37 Squadron set out to attack warships off Helgoland, but bad light and approaching darkness stopped play. Although they flew more sweeps over the North Sea, it was 15 December before they set out to attack specified warships but without success. On 22 December they tried once more and this time the enemy, aware of the Wellingtons' undefended beam, had fighters waiting. For eighty miles they pestered the bombers so effectively that only one of the six returned. Soon after, Bomber Command was forced to look to darkness for cover – and that meant much training.

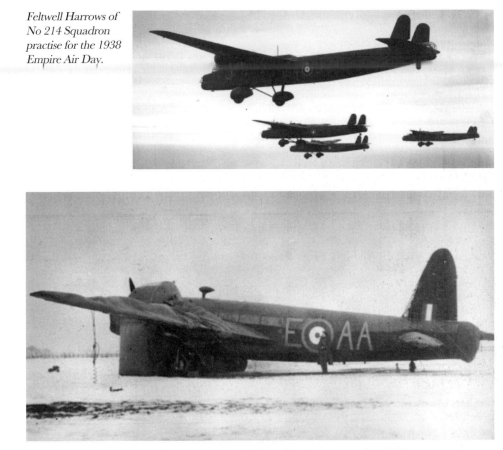

Feltwell Harrows of No 214 Squadron practise for the 1938 Empire Air Day.

Wellington 1c AA-E of No 75 (NZ) Squadron in Feltwell's winter snow of 1940/41.

By early 1940 Australians and New Zealanders were arriving in Britain in some numbers. The RNZAF had pre-war ordered sufficient Wellingtons to form a squadron for which personnel had come to train. Instead of going home they and the aircraft stayed in Europe and on 12 February 1940 the New Zealand Heavy Bomber Flight moved to Feltwell and on 4 April 1940 became No 75 (NZ) Squadron.

As soon as Norway was violated Nos 37 and 75 Squadrons tried to locate the *Scharnhorst*, operated off Norway and bombed the Danish airfield at Aalborg. Late on the afternoon of 30 April 1940 two pairs of Wellington Is from 37 Squadron set off to bomb Stavanger. The first pair dived in and raced away followed by enemy fighters. Then the second two zoomed down to the target and left at sea level pursued by Bf 109s, one of which was claimed. One bomber climbed into cloud chased by Bf 110s which ten times made quarter attacks and persisted in the chase to seventy miles out to sea. Amazingly the Wellington was not hit, but two crews failed to return. Feltwell's Wellingtons were very active during the distant Norwegian campaign until the second front opened.

On the night of 10 May in response to the German attack on the Netherlands Bomber Command launched its night bombing offensive, Feltwell's Wellingtons trying to find and bomb Waalhaven. Thereafter they did their best to help stem the German advance On 11 June six crews in response to Italy's declaration of war were ordered to Salon in France with the intention of raiding Italian targets. The French, fearing reprisals, refused to allow the bombers to operate.

Feltwell's Wellingtons were among those which, during June, dropped phosphorus strips intended to set alight the Black Forest or at best to tempt a German into pocketing a souvenir which would burst into flames and singe his posterior. For the Dutch they had better offerings – small bags of tea and sweets for their children. Merriment on most operations was not a common feature for raids were carried out under DR and straightforward navigation skills were practised in darkness using primitive homing equipment.

There were alarming ground incidents too. L7781 was being bombed-up on 3 August 1940 when a fuse ignited in a photo flash in an aircraft carrying 600 gallons of fuel and six 500lb bombs. Four of the latter exploded, their splinters raining on N2937 which burst into flames.

German bombers were now starting a bombing campaign directed at the 3 Group stations. During the 27 October 1940 raid on Feltwell a shower of incendiaries set ablaze part of the roof of a hangar and an air raid shelter was hit. Such attacks emphasise the point that one aircraft sometimes inflicted as much damage as several.

Boosting Middle East strength, No 37 Squadron left at night for Malta between 8 and 13 November. Their place was taken by 57 Squadron which arrived from Wyton on 18 November and despatched their first Wellington sorties on 13 January 1941. On 23 March 1941 they made their first Berlin raid. Although based at Feltwell, the squadron permanently dispersed its aircraft at Methwold and usually operated from there.

Meanwhile, the enemy had revisited Feltwell dropping a bomb near the ammunition dump on 3 February. A far more bizarre event occurred late on 14 February. As the Wellingtons were returning an unscheduled aircraft joined the circuit and, exposing a very bright landing light, landed on the flare path, turned round then took off. Those present were adamant that it was a Ju 88. A confirmed landing by an He 111 took place at Debden, and an He 111 was reckoned to have landed at Newmarket.

Feltwell was attacked again by flare light on 1/2 March. Five days later a Dornier raced low across the aerodrome strafing as it went. After a raid the following night twenty-two craters dotted the flying ground. Another raid took place a few moments after midnight on 11 May. Incendiaries this time rained down onto the roof of No 1 Hangar which was set on fire. Unexploded high explosives were later found in addition to which there were three craters on the apron to be filled.

Wellington operations continued and in July a DSO was awarded to Flying Officer Pritchard whose badly damaged Wellington skidded to a wheels-up landing. Both squadrons participated in many major raids of the period before January 1942 saw the start re-equipping with Wellington IIIs first taken into action during the 'Channel Dash' of 12 February. Then came participation in the Lübeck and Rostock raids before the two squadrons won the honour of despatching, on 30 May, thirty-seven Wellingtons, the highest number of aircraft operated by any one station for the Cologne '1,000 plane' raid. For the ensuing Essen operation thirty-nine were despatched. As a sideline, 75 Squadron maintained ability to deliver gas attack against an invasion, the only 3 Group squadron currently so trained.

Summer 1942 saw the arrival in Britain in quantity of the Lockheed Vega Ventura, a bomber based on the Hudson and forced upon 2 Group as a Blenheim replacement. In the general shake-up caused by the formation of the pathfinder force and arrival of the USAAF in the UK, No 2 Group took over Feltwell on 15 August, and 75 Squadron moved to Mildenhall. On 4 September, 57 Squadron vacated Methwold and joined 1 Group. Feltwell, long the home of New Zealanders, had the link renewed when No 487 (NZ) Squadron formed here on 15 August 1942. Australians arrived in September to man another new squadron, No 464, formed at Feltwell on 1 September.

Feltwell's landing ground decorated with mock black hedgerows as on 24 July 1942.

464 Squadron arrived autumn 1942 used Venturas, until Spring 1943. Ventura II AE939 depicted.

Both squadrons took four months to work up, and went into action spectacularly on Sunday 6 December. In mid-morning the station launched a fleet of thirty Venturas all carrying incendiaries and bound for the Philips works at Eindhoven. In immaculate formation they crossed Feltwell, crowded with well-wishers, and flew low over the sea to avoid radar detection. Exactly on time they went into the attack, leaving the factory a mass of flames.

Thereafter these unpopular bombers were used for *Circus* and *Ramrod* daylight operations over Occupied territories until April 1943. There was a brief interlude when Dutchmen of 320 Squadron were stationed here and at Methwold, but the big change came when 3 Group, short of stations, on 23 July recaptured Feltwell and Methwold. No 192 (Special Duty) Squadron and the Bombing Development Unit moved in from Gransden. Mosquitoes and Wellington Xs of 192 Squadron soon began snooping on enemy radio transmissions during bomber raids while the BDU continued examining bombers and developing bombing aids, equipment and techniques. Among the unusual aircraft tested were a Vengeance, Liberator and a Marauder – all rare in RAF hands in Britain.

A regular sight since the start of 1942 had been Oxfords of No 1519 BAT Flight and in June 1943 they began to be joined by Horsa gliders resting, awaiting the call to battle. The intention was for No 1473 RCM Flight to join them all on 1 September but it was on the 14th when their sixteen specialised aircraft began arriving for operations. The eight Wellington Xs were backed by two Halifaxes, four Ansons and a very secret Mosquito radio 'spy plane'.

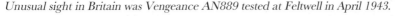

Unusual sight in Britain was Vengeance AN889 tested at Feltwell in April 1943.

Following the July 1943 decision to replace the Stirling bomber in 3 Group through The Ladder Plan, No 3 Lancaster Finishing School was established at Feltwell on 21 November 1943 which caused the departure of 192 Squadron, the BDU and 1473 Flight. Lancaster conversion courses commenced in December but it took until 31 January 1945 for sufficient crews to be trained to allow School closure.

With Feltwell available the BDU returned, from Newmarket, and before the war ended the Lincoln bomber was being tested, a black and white scheme for bombers of *Tiger Force* had been devised and RAF in-flight refuelling trials initiated using the saddle tank Lancaster.

BDU in summer 1945 explored the Lincoln 1 and its suitability for Tiger Force.

After the BDU evolved into the Central Bomber Establishment it moved to Marham. No 1688 BDTF which had arrived on 26 February 1945 with Spitfire Vs and Hurricane IIcs without the cannon in place left for Wyton on 19 March 1946. Feltwell – still a grass airfield whose surface had been badly scarred by heavy bombers – was thoroughly cleaned for post-war use and when ready No 3 Flying Training School arrived on 9 April 1947 with a swarm of Tiger Moths and Harvards. The latter were replaced by Prentices and in 1949 the Tiger Moths withdrew. On 23 September 1954 the first Provost arrived. Prentice replacement started, and subsequently Provosts served until the School closed at the end of April 1958. On 1 May 1958 two groups of Provosts ceremoniously left Feltwell then a farewell beat-up by a Valetta brought flying to an end. No 3 FTS disbanded on 31 May 1958 then the station served for training personnel and between 1964 and 1966 had a signals training role.

There had in 1956-7 been an incongruous presence, Auster AOP6s of 1903 AOP Flight some of which wore desert camouflage. They left in November 1956 only to be replaced by others here between March and November 1957 which, in conventional garb, were operated by No 3 Reconnaissance Flight AAC.

Perhaps unexpectedly, Feltwell's operational days were far from over. During 1957 it had been chosen to be the first HQ base for Thor WMs, the first strategic missile system deployed in the Free world. Feltwell would have four satellites – Mepal, North Pickenham, Shepherd's Grove and Tuddenham. Armed with three Thors, they each eventually became a squadron.

Building of the Thor base on the south side of Feltwell began in June 1958 and was completed in August. Then the associated equipment was added in time for No 77 (Strategic Missile) Squadron, previously known as 'A' Flight, to form on 1 September 1958. The first Thor arrived at Feltwell in November, launch crew training commenced in April 1959 and by July each of the five squadrons held Thors fitted with megaton nuclear warheads.

Expertise acquired at Feltwell was passed to other Thor squadrons, all training being undertaken at Feltwell from 5 June 1961. That embraced crew training, missile servicing, readiness exercises and work within high levels of security. At each site control was in Anglo-American hands. Eventually sixty-five percent of the entire Thor force was always at fifteen minutes readiness, the remainder of the missiles being stored horizontally each in its retractable shelter. Two keys were needed for a launch, one American held activating the nuclear warhead and the RAF key to make the launch. From the turn of the two keys to lift off would have taken fifteen minutes. By May 1960 warheads had been fitted to the sixty missiles, fifty-nine of which were at launch readiness, on the Saturday afternoon of the October 1962 Cuban missile crisis.

The stay of the Thors was brief for being surface stored they were highly vulnerable. No 77 Squadron and the remainder of the Feltwell Complex became non-operational on 1 July 1963 and eventually the Thors returned to the USA where they were used for the space programme.

Feltwell's buildings much hidden by trees planted many decades ago are externally little changed. It is the activity within that makes the station so unique.

Main features:
Grass runways: E/W 5,400ft, NE/SW 4,200ft, NW/SE 3,600ft. *Hangars:* five Type 'C'. *Hardstandings:* twenty circular pans. *Accommodation:* RAF: 117 officers, 157 SNCOs, 1,106 ORs; WAAF: 9 officers, 17 SNCOs, 332 ORs.

FERSFIELD, Suffolk

52°25N/01°23E 175ft asl; T80850. 4 miles NE South Lopham on A1066

Fersfield is well tucked away. Maybe this had something to do with its choice as a base for Operation *Aphrodite* for at Fersfield the USAAF and US Navy worked upon a joint scheme to employ 'war weary' bombers flying under radio control from escorting fighters. Laden with 20,000lb of explosive, aged aircraft could thus be directed against heavily defended precision targets.

Operations were supervised by the 388th BG, Knettishall. After manually controlled take-off the crew would set the fuses then parachute out leaving the bomber under control of another aircraft. The first operation was flown on 4 August with huge V-weapons installations in France targeted. The attacks achieved little except great public alarm when a B-17 crashed at Sudbourne Park, Suffolk. On 12 August Lieutenant Kennedy, brother of President Kennedy, was killed when an aged PB4Y-1 in which he was flying exploded near Blythburgh. Trials were halted, worthwhile suitable targets being few. When word of the Fersfield activity leaked to those living around it caused no mean alarm, especially when it was realised that a lengthy flight path to the coast was involved.

In November 1944 the USAAF departed from the typical two-hangar wartime bomber base and the RAF's No 2 Group Support Unit moved in during mid-December 1944. Fersfield they used for a variety of purposes, and as a holding camp for replacement aircrews. A few operations were flown from here by No 2 GSU Mitchells although that was not their primary role. No 416 RSU which collected the Group's crashed aircraft came here in 1945 and closed on 30 April 1945.

Fersfield's finest hour perhaps surprisingly came in March 1945. To avoid flying over Germany in daylight Mosquito FB VIs of Nos 21, 464 and 487 Squadrons flew to Fersfield from their continental bases. On 21 March 1945 they set out escorted by Mustangs of 64 and 126 Squadrons also operating from Fersfield to carry out their famous last low-level spectacular on the Shellhaus, the Gestapo HQ in Copenhagen.

After the war squadrons of 2 Group came here for armament training conducted by No 2 Group Training Flight. Mitchells of No 180 came in June 1945 and Mosquito VIs of Nos 605, 140 and 613 during July. On 1 August 1945, No 2 Group Disbandment Centre formed from the GSU and supervised wind down of 2 Group squadrons until its closure in December 1945. Fersfield was passed from BAFO to 12 Group, Fighter Command, on 31 December 1945. No longer needed, it was on 23 February 1946 passed to Air Ministry. Its Active state was ended. Assorted buildings remain in use for agricultural purposes.

Main features:
Runways: 066° 6,000ft x 150ft, 186°, 304°, concrete surface. *Hangars:* two T2. *Hardstandings:* fifty spectacle. *Accommodation:* 421 officers, 2,473 enlisted men.

Places of interest nearby:
By the A1066 road west of Diss are Bressingham Steam Museum, Gardens and famous garden centre where the locomotive *Royal Scot* never fails to impress.

FISKERTON, Lincolnshire

53°14N/00°25W 55ft asl; TF0453730. 5 miles E of Lincoln, S of A158 between Reepham and Fiskerton

Construction of Fiskerton began in 1942. Situated a few miles east of Lincoln, it was roughly in the centre of wartime 5 Group area. A typical wartime temporary bomber station with its two T2s and three runways it also acted as a store for Horsa gliders work upon which was undertaken from the B1 hangar. Its main purpose, though, was as a Lancaster base.

Fiskerton opened in January 1943 and between May 1943 and October 1944 was part of 52 Base Scampton. First user of the airfield was No 49 Squadron here from 2 January 1943 to 16 October 1944. During that time they participated in Main Force operations including as specialities the first night 'shuttle-bombing 'raid, the August 1943 attack on Peenemunde and the punishing Nuremberg operation of 30/31 March 1944. Of the sixteen Lancasters despatched that night two failed to return.

Like other bomber bases Fiskerton had its BAT Flight, No 1514 being here between January 1944 and its disbandment on 9 January 1945.

Following the departure of No 49 Squadron the station was placed on Care & Maintenance. Major modifications were begun, Fiskerton having been selected for a FIDO installation.

After completion Fiskerton was a Sub-Station of 15 Base from 7 October 1944 to 20 October 1945. On 11 October 1944 Lancasters of No 576 moved in. Between 1 and 22 November 1944 they had for company a second and newly formed Lancaster squadron, No 150 formed on 1 November from 'C' Flight, 550 Squadron, and here only until Hemswell was able to accommodate them.

As well as Main Force day and night raids No 576 Squadron took part in the assorted end-of-the-war operations – *Manna*, *Dodge* and *Exodus*. The Squadron disbanded on 11 September 1945 and Fiskerton closed to flying on 21 September 1945. From the station No 576 had despatched 2,788 operational sorties from which sixty-seven aircraft had failed to return.

Fiskerton, where at this time 61 MU had a sub-site, was placed on Care & Maintenance on 15 December 1945, a state which lasted into 1946. An enclosure on the site remained government property and a Royal Observer Corps nuclear fall-out reporting and warning centre was established on a small area. This saw the development of not only HQ 15 Group, Royal Observer Corps which moved in from Waddington but also the first purpose-built underground ROC operations centre above which wartime Fiskerton had returned to agricultural use. The underground unit survives, but very little remains of the wartime airfield.

> **Main features:**
> *Runways:* 263° 6,000ft x 150ft, 311°, 054°, concrete and tarmac. *Hangars:* two T2, one B1. *Hardstandings:* thirty-six. *Accommodation:* RAF: 102 officers, 356 SNCOs, 979 ORs; WAAF: 2 officers, 4 SNCOs, 192 ORs.

FLIXTON, Suffolk – see BUNGAY

FOLKINGHAM, Lincolnshire

52°51N/00°26W 240ft asl; TF050300. W of the A15 road between Aslackby and Folkingham

If you think Lincolnshire is dull, flat, unattractive, that image is quickly dispelled by little Folkingham sitting on the beautiful Wolds and looking like a Cotswolds transplant. As for the three-runway two T2 wartime bomber airfield, that was built on a low plateau to the south-east of Grantham near to where in 1940 decoy airfield KQ tried to attract and divert bombs from raiders. Folkingham airfield was laid down in 1943 as a temporary wartime station for No 5 Group.

That was not to be. With insufficient space in southern England to accommodate all the aircraft required for the Normandy invasion, other areas were considered. South Lincolnshire was chosen as a base area for C-47 Troop Carrier Groups of the US 9th AF Folkingham airfield being one.

The base came alive on 5 February 1944, a substitution unit placing it in the hands of the 9th AF 52nd Troop Carrier Wing. Then on 24 February the 313th TC Group began moving in its four squadrons – 29th, 47th, 48th and 49th Squadrons – which between them soon held over 70 C-47s and a handful of C-53s.

During the next few months they practised daylight then night formation flying, paratroop dropping and towing CG-4A Hadrian gliders during the build up period prior to D-Day. Late on 5 June 1944 their eighty-two C-47/C-53 transports bearing the prominent black and white AEAF markings set forth carrying paratroops of the 508th Parachute Infantry and 82nd US Airborne Division which they dropped in the Cherbourg Peninsula. They had been allocated DZ 'N', about three miles south of St Mere Eglise in which the famous incident of the paratrooper impaled upon the church spire took place. The 1,181 paratroopers that the 313th was transporting began their drop just after 0200 hrs on 6 June by which time German forces were alerted and as a result three aircraft were shot down and twenty-one others were damaged.

Next night a re-supply mission was mounted, a force of fifty-two C-47s beginning operation *Freeport* the re-supply drop for the 82nd Airborne Division at 0310 hrs. Thick cloud made the mission difficult and much flak damage was also received. Over the following weeks the 313th flew many supply and support missions to US forces in France making use of advanced landing grounds.

In late August another spell of intensive training was undertaken then at 1130 hrs on Sunday, 17 September 1944, ninety aircraft of the 313th TCG began to take off and head for Arnhem carrying paratroopers of the British 1st Parachute Brigade. Next day, after a delay due to thick autumn mist, forty-two C-47s each towed a CG-4A glider to LZ 'N'. Further re-supply drops followed in which fighters and flak had to be faced.

Following the disastrous airborne campaign, C-47s from Folkingham flew to the Continental airfields almost every day with supplies and returned with wounded troops. Once it was safe, and a suitable airfield had been found, the 313th TCG moved to France, the American units beginning to vacate Folkingham on 23 February 1945. By that time the base had been returned to the RAF was part of Bomber Command and within Barkston Heath Base.

The airfield closed to flying on 20 March its active career ended. It was vacated by the USAAF on 15 April 1945 and on 4 June 1945 transferred to 40 Group, Maintenance Command, RAF. It served as a Sub-Site of 16 MU Stafford until 1948. On 10 August 1945 it passed to 22 Group, Technical Training Command, and the station became home to No 3 RAF Regiment Sub-Depot where members of the RAF Regiment were trained for service overseas. The station served in that role until mid-1946. Unit closure came on 27 June and the station was returned to Maintenance Command in 1947.

A Standby Airfield under each successive Plan it would, in war, have joined Eastern Sector, Fighter Command and have accommodated two RAuxAF fighter squadrons. Active state was resumed in September 1957 for Folkingham had become a designated RLG for Barkston Heath, a state held until August 1959 by which a very different future awaited it.

Revised planning in 1958 resulted in another part of Folkingham coming into active state. During 1959 an enclave was developed as a base for three Thor IRBMs operated by 233 Squadron, the last to arm and which received its third missile on 1 April 1960 thereby completing the entire Thor force. It was a case then of last in last out for, as part of the North Luffenham Complex, Folkingham became non-operational on 15 August 1963. When 233 Squadron disbanded on 23 August 1963 that ended the IRBM era in Bomber Command.

Folkingham, soon disposed of, was in the mid-1960s was used briefly by the British Racing Motor Company under Raymond Mays, both for testing and development of racing cars. Then the site reverted to agriculture. Little remains of the former airfield.

Main features:
Runways: 020° 6,000ft x 150ft, 250°, 310°, tarmac and concrete. *Hangars:* two T2. *Hardstandings:* fifty loop type. Accommodation (RAF, December 1944): 245 officers, 1,053 ORs.

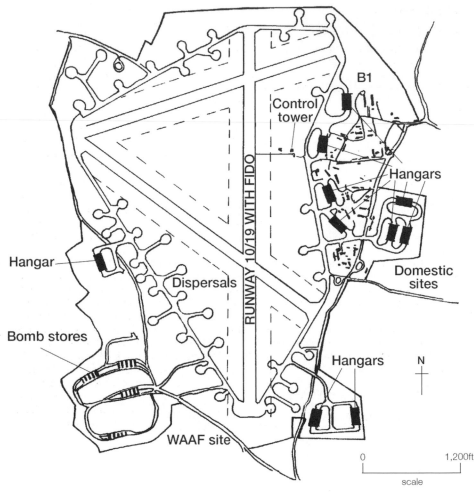

FOULSHAM

No airfields are identical. Indeed Foulsham, planned to hold two bomber squadrons, displayed unusual features the most prominent of which were no less nine Type T2 hangars and a lone Type B1 for glider and MAP use. Construction started – amid many farms, fields and narrow country lanes – in late 1940. Adjacent to the 1940 control tower were the fire tender shed and, before it, the 40ft signals square. Kept alongside was the Chance Light trailer and tractor for use before airfield lighting was installed. In 1941 three runways were confirmed as needed along with thirty-six 'frying pan' circular type hardstandings. Fitting in the hangars and the dispersal pans within the airfield technical site was difficult and resulted in four pans being very close to the extensive bombs store and embracing four HE stores, four incendiary bomb stores, an SBC store, pyrotechnics store and a fuzing building. Six other pans were uncomfortably close to the runway ends. Air attack being likely, air raid shelters and blast shelters were built and in wartime style a main communal site supported domestic quarters at six dispersed sites and in addition a WAAF site. Due to the mid-war increase in camp population, ten Nissen general purpose huts were available (one for the FIDO operation) along with twelve Laing huts used as barrack blocks and another one providing Officers' quarters. Two Romney huts served as barrack equipment and clothing stores. Two crew rest rooms were provided, but a less usual feature was a pigeon loft. By 1945 Foulsham was clearly a major airfield and retained for possible upgrading post-war.

FOULSHAM, Norfolk

52°48N/01°01E 190ft asl; TG631270. E of Foulsham village, off A1067

Mitchells were far too slow and clumsy for use in low-level raids in which No 2 Group specialised. Yet when 98 and 180 Squadrons at long last took the bombers into action on 11 January 1943, they were employed in a roof height attack on Ghent/Terneuzen carried out from Foulsham. Flak was heavy and as the bombers and their unusual escort of Mustang 1s (best at low level) retired, then FW 190s raced in. Three Mitchells out of twelve were shot down.

Foulsham far from complete had nevertheless opened in May 1942 and joined 2 Group the following month. Not until October did the first squadrons move in, Nos 98 and 180 Squadrons which brought along their Mitchells from Great Massingham. Foulsham became the first Mitchell operational station where the squadrons worked up plagued with gun and turret problems. So bad were they that the squadrons had to be withdrawn from participation in the December Philips raid, although 180 Squadron managed ASR patrols on 8 December, the first operational sorties by RAF Mitchells.

The January 1943 raid was probably undertaken for political reasons for turret and gun troubles remained unsolved until May. Training had been hindered too, by the poor state of the typical wartime muddy bomber airfield where accommodation was primitive. That did not prevent thirty-two Horsa gliders from arriving for dispersed storage during summer 1943, and No 2 Glider MU looked after them for a year.

On 5 May 1943 Nos 98 and 180 Squadrons at last became operational on Mitchells. Six crews of 180 Mitchell Squadron set out for Boulogne on 11 May flying in the long practised box formation only to have their attack thwarted by bad weather. That left 98 Squadron to next day successfully raid the same target. On 15 and 16 May they bombed Caen airfield and 180 Squadron also flew the first Mitchell *Circus* on 16 May with Tricqueville as target. Although a swarm of enemy fighters engaged them the Mitchells all returned safely to Foulsham. Thereafter both squadrons flew *Circus* and *Ramrod* operations when the weather permitted. By July there was a general feeling that the Mitchell would be of more use in the Middle East. Indeed, 98 Squadron flew to Honiley in July for range trials. The idea of sending them there was abandoned, operations continued and, by mid-August 1943, 180 Squadron had managed seventeen raids. The first twenty-four-aircraft operation was flown on 12 August after which plans for change came underway. Long hauls to many targets were time and nerve-consuming, and to be better placed for operations running up to D-Day both squadrons moved to Dunsfold on 18-19 August, the aircraft going singly for security reasons.

Mitchells of Nos 98 and 180 Squadrons were here in 1943.

General view of Foulsham, largely intact although only three T2s remain, August 1978.

Vacant Foulsham having far more T2 hangars than usual and the B1s for glider support, was snapped up by 3 Group on 1 September and on the same day No 514, a second Lancaster II squadron for the Group, formed here. Providing crews for 3 Group's Lancaster IIs had brought about the formation of No 1678 Flight which moved to Foulsham on 16 September to train crews for '514' which attained operational status in time to allow operations to commence on 3/4 November 1943 when six Lancasters operated with two going to Düsseldorf and four went mining. Such activity was but a brief interlude for in another general shake up 514 Squadron and the Conversion Flight left for Waterbeach on 23 November.

Space for bombers was at a premium. Necessity also demanded that 3 Group Stirling crews convert as soon as possible to Lancasters for which 3 Group Lancaster Finishing School had been opened at Feltwell even though it was a grass airfield. Intensity of flying there was rated lower than at operational stations, but it did mean that Feltwell must lose its operational status so on 25 November No 192 Squadron left for Foulsham. Highly specialised and with an important role, the squadron was flying Halifaxes, Mosquito IVs and Wellington Xs all fitted out with highly secret listening equipment able to snoop upon German radio and radar transmissions.

On 7 December 1943 the new 100 Group took over Foulsham snatching 192 Squadron in the process. The squadron was enlarged when on 12 December No 1473 Flight, which had been similarly employed, arrived from Little Snoring to become on 1 February 1944 their 'C' Flight. In mid-April 1944 the Special Duty Radar & Radio Development Unit arrived and on I May became the Bomber Support Development Unit which, along with their Mosquitoes, stayed until 23

December 1944. On 27 December 1944 and replacing BSDU Halifax IIIs of 462 (Australian) Squadron arrived from 4 Group, trained in the use of special listening and jamming equipment, and commenced operations on 13 March 1945.

Needing similar intelligence material to that which 192 Squadron was acquiring, the USAAF from August 1944 to early 1945 maintained a small detachment of two-seater P-38s at Foulsham. No 192 Squadron played a vital part in the bomber offensive by operating widely over occupied territory and Germany. Its crews listened to enemy radio chatter and discovered radio frequencies and those of radar equipment. They snooped upon the airborne radar of night fighters, jammed VHF transmissions and achieved RAF control of German fighters. By summer 1944 they were operating by day and night, and the squadron was, on 9 April 1945, the last to fly the Mosquito IV operationally when they jammed enemy R/T.

Both Foulsham squadrons disbanded after the war, No 192 on 22 August 1945 and 462 on 24 September. Then the station slipped into Care &Maintenance under 40 Group. A sub-site of 16 MU functioned here between 10 November 1945 and 31 October 1948 handling various equipment items. Although the RAF soon vacated it, the station was not sold off and in 1954 the US Army opened a special signals unit here handing back the station on 5 October 1955.

Runways, T2 hangars, the perimeter track and the water tower remain among the farm land, and limited flying continued in the 1970s and 1980s when a crop-spraying Piper Pawnee could often be seen making use of what was suitable as it went about its summertime business.

Main features:
Runways: 190° 5,700ft x 150ft equipped with FIDO, 260°, 326°, tar and wood chip surfaces. *Hangars:* nine T2, one B1. *Hardstandings:* thirty-six for heavy bombers. *Accommodation:* RAF: 101 officers, 330 SNCOs, 1,704 ORs; WAAF: 9 officers, 10 SNCOs, 336 ORs.

FOWLMERE, Cambridgeshire

52°05/N 00°03W 100ft asl; TL415440. By B1368 leading south from village

Fowlmere certainly attracts airfields – it has had three. Developed upon an existing landing ground utilising part of Manor Farm, the first aerodrome opened in 1918. Like Duxford, Fowlmere provided a home for US Aero Squadrons, No 165 arriving on 15 March 1918. British squadrons here in 1918 were Nos 124, 125 and 126 all flying DH 6s with the latter two squadrons also using DH 4As and RE 8s. No 31 TDS functioned at Fowlmere from 1 June 1918. On 30 August 1918 No 338 US Aero Squadron arrived and was here until 14 November 1918. Another US Squadron, No 151, was here between 2 September 1918 and disbandment on 28 February 1919. Three RE 8 squadrons arrived at cadre strength in February 1919 and disbanded late that year.

With the 1917 decision to form an Independent Air Force the following year saw a complete revision of aircrew preparation. A score or so of Training Depot Stations like Fowlmere were established to provide basic, advanced and operational flying practice preparatory to operational participation. For such a purpose the Fowlmere site had been chosen for development into a quite elaborate aerodrome. Its extensive building – very similar to some still to be seen at Duxford – included three double and one single Belfast Truss aircraft sheds along with a variety of single storey huts. Those forming the domestic site on the opposite side of the road through the camp were further to one end of the landing ground than Duxford's.

The Armistice of November 1918 meant that many aerodromes would be no longer required and Duxford – having better road and rail links – resulted in Fowlmere being chosen for closure in 1922. By then it was storing hefty Handley Page HP 0/400 bombers. The buildings were demolished in 1923.

A second Fowlmere, at first only a grass Unbuilt Satellite Landing Ground prepared for Duxford's use, and very primitive by comparison with its predecessor, utilised a different site. It came into use in Spring 1940. Perhaps the Germans rapidly acquired knowledge of it for on 5/6 June 1940 they released over 100 incendiaries which burnt brightly in a field at New Farm at nearby Newton. This was the first bombing incident in Cambridgeshire and the load was most probably intended for Duxford fell wide.

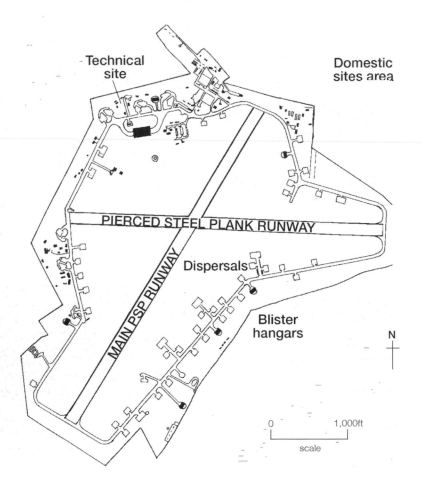

FOWLMERE

Fowlmere exhibits problems encountered in upgrading a small fighter satellite landing ground to a year round operational station incorporating runways and catering for a USAAF Fighter Group. On the opposite side of the road to the WWI station, the 1940 SLG was so small that there was room only for two PSP runways (and some Army Tracking) even with the road closure. Square-shaped PSP track hardstandings for SEFs were mainly south of the runways, hardstandings for twin-engined visitors being sandbag protected. The usual items were to be found including a Nissen hut housing 'Operations.' There was a cine-camera gun room and workshop. A 25 yard aircraft gun range was supplemented by the SAA store. Bomb stores were added allowing the Group to undertake ground attack. The 1941 gas warfare and decontamination centre remained to the end of the war. The typical wartime control tower was linked with three VHF stations. Over Blister and enlarged Over Blister hangars for first line maintenance were supplemented by one twenty-three bay T2 hangar. There were sleeping shelters (brick) for maintenance personnel, a main stores, a 12,000 gallon static water tank, usual bulk petrol tanks and one for 3,500 gallons of oil. The MT shed was a converted 130ft x 40ft Dutch barn. Since 1940 temporary brick buildings and huts had been erected mainly in the north-west corner of the site. By 1944 three Laing barrack huts and Officers' quarters, nine Nissen huts as well as Romney huts were supplementing a variety of small brick huts. The briefing room, dining room and kitchen, SHQ and on-site barracks were all found in Nissen huts. Nine off-camp domestic sites were to be found north of the airfield.

An Airco DH4 at Fowlmere in 1918. (Marshall Aerospace)

The first Fowlmere, from the air, 1919. GS hangars complete, domestic site set differently from Duxford's. (Marshall Aerospace)

This second Fowlmere was originally known as G1 after its Sector Identity, and some of its parent's 19 Squadron Spitfires began dispersing here on 1 July. Apart from tented accommodation and messing arrangements, little else at this time decorated the developed meadow.

Three days later 19 Squadron returned to Duxford thereby making way for Defiants of 264 Squadron. Working into operational state after their recent terrible battle mauling over the English Channel, they detached Sections to Martlesham Heath to carry out patrols over East Coast shipping. Possible use of the Defiant for night fighting was explored from Fowlmere before the squadron left for Kirton-in-Lindsey on 23 July 1940. Two days later, 19 Squadron resumed use of Fowlmere from where they placed Sections at Coltishall for shipping protection duties.

During August 1940 No 19 Squadron was partly dispersed at Fowlmere where some of its troublesome cannon-armed Spitfire Ibs awaited a chance for action. That first came on 19 August, Green Section claiming three Bf 110s. Further fighting came on the 24th when the squadron engaged Bf 109s. Then at breakfast time on 31 August came their greatest challenge so far, the close protection of fighter stations in the area. No 19 Squadron was 'scrambled' to defend Debden.

Two formations totalling thirty-nine Dornier 17Zs of KG2 had crossed Essex, the main force heading for Debden while a smaller group tracked towards Duxford. Bofors guns defending that aerodrome opened up, then Thriplow battery of 3in ex-naval AA guns joined in. That was sufficient to drive the Dorniers on to a north-westerly course which took them over Fowlmere. Thwarted from their intent the bombers unloaded 253 HE bombs and incendiaries in one salvo. Several HEs exploded on Fowlmere, the rest along the sides of the main railway line to Royston, some exploding on the flanks of a passing train.

Escorted by Bf 110s, the whole force turned about and was then engaged south-east of Cambridge by Fowlmere's Spitfires. Their cannon had been placed on their sides in order to fit in the thin wing and very soon after opening fire spent cartridges jammed the breech mechanism. Therefore in the first week of September 1940 eight-gun Spitfires replaced the cannon variety. No 19 Squadron now joined the 12 Group 'Big Wing', usually operating from Fowlmere to reduce pressure on Duxford where the other squadrons assembled.

Nevertheless, '19' was still part of the parent station to where it returned in November 1940. It was not just '19' that used Fowlmere, Hurricanes of Duxford's Czech-manned 310 Squadron also made use of the satellite now renamed WA1. On 6 February 1941, 19 Squadron moved back because new units at Duxford needed additional space.

Standbys, interception and sector patrols, reinforcement flights into 11 Group territory to hold sway while its squadrons operated over France, these were daily events for the squadron that been defending Cambridgeshire and adjacent areas.

Fowlmere was too far from the Continent to allow its use as a starting point for offensive operations. Not until May 1941 was No 19 involved in cross-Channel activity, the first participation in a fighter sweep from an advanced base taking place on 21 May. Enemy reaction to sweeps and *Circus* operations was spasmodic and it was 23 June before Fowlmere's Spitfires tangled with Bf 109s two of which were claimed as destroyed. Action soon became more intense, 19 Squadron engaging more Bf 109s near St Omer on 27 June.

Offensive operations continued throughout July then on 12 August the squadron had an early call. They were to provide withdrawal cover for 2 Group Blenheims which had ventured to Cologne in daylight. Fierce combat developed off Schouwen as the fighters tried to protect the Blenheims. Four days later 19 Squadron bade farewell to Fowlmere and Duxford when they moved to Matlaske, Coltishall's satellite.

Hurricane IIbs of No 133, the third America Eagle squadron, which arrived at Duxford in August, moved to Fowlmere on 3 October and by way of Wittering, left on the 8th for Eglinton, Northern Ireland.

A new squadron, No 154 armed with Spitfire IIs, was formed at Fowlmere on 17 November 1941. They first scrambled from Fowlmere in February 1942, and carried out forward patrols from Coltishall and Swanton Morley before moving to Church Stanton on 7 May. In July it was No 174 Squadron's turn to briefly use WA1 where next in was 'Treble One' which arrived with Spitfires on 27 September 1942 and almost immediately went on embarkation leave. Upon returning squadron personnel were given tropical kit, forsook their Spitfires and left to embark for North Africa.

Auster 1s of 655 Squadron were the next occupants. They came from Gatwick in February and left in March 1943 making way for more fighters. Fowlmere's part in Exercise *Spartan* immediately followed, the station helping to formulate, develop and test mobility techniques being prepared for the tactical air force which was soon to be hived off from Fighter Command. This trial which included the idea of gathering squadrons into complete 'airfields' which would move forward as one unit from advanced landing grounds following the Allied invasion of France. For this reason No 411 (Canadian) Squadron's Spitfire Vs came to Fowlmere for a brief stay in March 1943.

Then it was back to a short, portentous operational phase when, on 19 March, 2 Squadron's Mustang Is came from Bottisham. Ten days later the Mustang squadron commenced flying *Lagoon* shipping searches mainly off Texel. The Mustangs operated busily during April, in pairs, before leaving for Sawbridgeworth on the 27th of the month.

Now devoid of aircraft Fowlmere underwent a major facelift and extension. Two Sommerfeld track runways and a T2 hangar were added to the seven Blister hangars already in situ, while dispersed temporary domestic sites were erected in the surrounding area. By March 1944 'the Yanks were coming' to declare Fowlmere as Station 378 USAAF where on 4 April the 339th Fighter Group, US 8th AAF, began arriving along with their P-51B Mustangs.

On 30 April they flew their first operation which involved fifty-one of the P-51s providing forward support for US fighter-bombers attacking targets in France. Next day they flew a diversionary sweep off Belgium then on 7 May helped provide support to 8th AF bombers attacking targets in the Reich. During their first five weeks of operations the 339th flew mainly escort duty and next provided cover for bombers raiding strategic targets. Then they began carrying out strikes of opportunity on ground targets including airfields, and were similarly employed particularly during St-Lô break-out. P-51Ds were by now gradually replacing earlier models. Escort duties to the 8th

AF bombers remained the main role and during one such operation on 10 September they carried out a very effective strike upon Erding airfield. Next day while protecting bombers attacking Munich, the 339th engaged in fierce combat with German fighters before bearing down upon airfield near Karlsruhe. They fought hard during the airborne landings of September 1944, during the tough Ardennes battle in mid-winter and again to assist the Rhine crossing. The 339th's final operational sorties were flown on 21 April 1945 by which time the Group was claiming over 200 enemy aircraft shot down and another 400 destroyed on the ground during their 264 operations. Achieved in one year that was a creditable performance.

The green-nosed P-51s remained a familiar sight for many post-war weeks, but by August 1945 the unit was winding down fast and left for America in October that year.

On 15 October 1945 Fowlmere was handed by the USAAF to 11 Group Fighter Command which on 1 November 1945 declared it a satellite of Castle Camps while also placing it on Care & Maintenance. January 1946 saw it pass to the Ministry of Works for disposal. Military Fowlmere slowly withered away for it was not until 1957 that the site was disposed of.

The third 'Fowlmere', a small privately owned aerodrome for light aircraft, opened in the 1980s and remains active.

Main features:
Runways: 110° 4,200ft x 150ft, 050° 4,800ft x 150ft, both of Sommerfeld Track. Caused the closure of the Fowlmere-Barley road. *Hangars:* one T2, seven Blister. *Hardstandings:* eighty, concrete, off the concrete perimeter track. *Accommodation:* 190 officers, 1,519 enlisted men.

Places of interest nearby:
Remains of the Thriplow heavy gun site, Heydon (now best known as the Wood Green Animal Shelter) whose church in 1940 received a direct hit in the centre, the only one in Cambridgeshire to be bombed.

FRAMLINGHAM (PARHAM), Suffolk

52°11N/01°24E 140ft asl; TM330605. 1 mile SE Great Glenham off B1190, E of Framlingham

Follow the A12 north from Woodbridge and just beyond Farnham, as you approach Glenham Hall, keep a watch for the 'Air Museum' sign and the narrow, tree-lined Great Glenham road to the left. Drive along it and turn right just before reaching Parham to travel along the old runway line and cross the wide open expanse which was 'Framlingham' sometimes called Parham. Stop wishing there were lots of B-17s resting around and follow the narrow road leading to the prominent, finely restored flying control tower and park there.

Make sure you have allowed ample time in which to savour one of the best laid out museums of its type, one packed with fascinating items including the main undercarriage leg of a B-24 and, joy of joys, a real B-24 tail – suitably inscribed. Climb the easy stairs to the control tower's first floor to enjoy more splendid photographs relevant to Framlingham once the home of the 390th Bomb Group – 'J in a square' to spotters of yesteryear. Stand on the tower balcony to take in one of those splendid, expansive views which only East Anglia (and East Africa) can offer. You can easily imagine the sound of a Wright Cyclone whereas you may be able to enjoy real and even more beautiful notes from skylarks. During wartime their song, soothing warm summer evenings as slight breeze ruffled the grass provided a reminder of kinder times. Superb the panorama maybe, but you have better to come because Framlingham's tower has a roof 'cupola' like that at Thorpe Abbotts. Do not miss the chance to savour the even better views it affords.

While gazing from the tower try to imagine the drama which fast unfolded shortly before 0900 hrs on 27 December 1944 when a B-17G, heavily laden with bombs and fuel, struggled unsuccessfully to get airborne. On that icy morn the bomber, possibly due to freezing conditions during take-off, barely managed to gain any height and smashed into the village centre. Within the holocaust the entire crew died but, miraculously, not one of the inhabitants suffered beyond minor injuries even though every house was damaged.

As to the Museum's future on site is a Dorman Long Blister Hangar awaiting erection to house the real Douglas DC-3 N4565L snatched to safety from the burghers of Ipswich. In a vintage Nissen hut is the Museum of British Resistance Organisation – The Auxiliary Units – showing that we East

Parham's Braithwaite water tower in July 1978, basically of 8ft square units. Later used by Anglian Water.

Framlingham tower serving as the museum in August 1999. (Audrey Bowyer)

Anglians are not to be trifled with! You can take tea, too, while enjoying video entertainment so a visit certainly represents excellent value for ... but wait a minute, entry is free so make sure you contribute fairly to the expensive upkeep of the Framlingham Tower Museum – and never venture on to the cultivated land of its owner and benefactor, Mr Peter Kindred.

As to Framlingham's history, it was constructed during 1942-3 as yet another temporary wartime three-runway, two T2 bomber base planned to have thirty-six loop hardstandings which were increased to fifty. That was to allow for forty-five B-17s and five for assorted support aircraft

A 390th BG B-17G 46954 drops food to starving Netherlanders in May 1945. (390th BG Air Museum)

and visitors. The opening party arrived on 19 April 1943. First in were B-17Fs of the 95th Bomb Group ('B in a square') which arrived in mid-May 1943 although the station was not declared complete until 30 June, the runways having been completed on 11 June. Barely was the Group operational when disaster struck.

On 13 June 1943 the 8th AF despatched two forces of bombers, one to Bremen and another – led by the 95th – to Kiel. As the latter started the bomb run German fighters pounced upon the Fortresses destroying ten and causing one to crash into another aircraft so that the loss was almost half the despatched force. Already the 95th had experienced hard fighting and, over a few days, they lost half their aircrew strength. Two days after the catastrophic operation the 95th moved to Horham to re-establish allowing finishing touches to Framlingham.

A month passed, then the 390th Bomb Group arrived bringing more B-17s. On 12 August they flew the first of 320 missions from here and on the 17th, as part of the 4th Combat Wing, 3rd Air Division, twenty Fortresses set off for a part in the first shuttle bombing raid attacking Regensburg before pressing on to North Africa. Brave endeavour indeed so soon after entering operations.

Before long the 390th were participating in the general run of attacks on strategic targets which on 14 October 1943 brought the next highlight when Schweinffurt's ball bearing factory was the aiming point. This was a two-pronged attack with the B-17s of the 3rd Air Division approaching on a westerly track which brought them into contact with enemy fighters later than was the case with the other force. Raid photographs showed the 390th's drop to have been the most accurate, but the big fight lay before them. As they headed homewards, German fighters switched their main onslaught on to the 3rd Air Division, pressing home their attacks even as far as the English Channel. The 390th was fortunate to lose only one of their fifteen aircraft for Mission 115 cost sixty B-17s. For their part the 390th were justifiably awarded a Distinguished Unit Citation.

Thereafter, and often aided by pathfinders, the 390th attacked such targets as the marshalling yards at Frankfurt, oil facilities at Zeltz, factories at Mannheim, naval installations at Bremen and the synthetic oil plant at Merseburg. They gave tactical support to the Normandy invasion and, as the war ended, dropped food supplies to the Netherlanders after having carried out their final bombing raid on 20 April 1945.

August 1945 saw the Americans leave for home and flying ceased at Framlingham. The Polish Settlement Corps established a camp here while the station was administered by RAF Technical Training Command. The airfield's coastal position and proximity to other RAF stations resulted in it being retained but as an Agricultural Airfield. One of the T2s was brought back to work when, between 2 March 1955 and 1967, and surrounded by a strong metal fence, it was used as a storage station by USAF Bentwaters.

If you are near Framlingham then do visit the 390th BG Memorial Air Museum, a very worthwhile expedition. As a reminder of the past there are by the tower plaques recalling the 95th and 390th BGs. There are other ex-airfields in the area too making a tour well worth making – especially if you like letting your imagination loose!

Veteran B-17E 19025 LITTLE JOHN Parham's hack in 1945. The tower behind is now the museum. (390th BG Air Museum)

Main features:
Runways: 280° 6,000ft x 150ft, 173°, 234°, concrete with tar and wood chip surfaces. *Hangars:* two T2. *Hardstandings:* fifty loop type. *Accommodation:* 421 officers, 2,473 enlisted men.

Places of interest nearby:
Apart from Metfield, Leiston, Woodbridge, Halesworth and Horham airfields which are reasonably close, there is dominant Framlingham 12th century castle with thirteen towers, red Tudor chimneys and safe walls offering fine views. Mary I's supporters rallied here after the attempt to put Lady Jane Grey on the throne, and Queen Elizabeth I tucked away recalcitrant priests in the castle. At Saxstead Green the lovely post windmill of 18th Century origin earned its keep by working hard until 1947. For 700 years a windmill has occupied the same position, the present mill being very photogenic.

FULBECK, Lincolnshire

53°03N/00°39W 50ft asl; SK900510. 8 miles W of Newark, W of the A17(T) road

Didn't it do well, for Fulbeck began life not even as a satellite landing ground but just a lowly RLG which blossomed into a base for a hoard of IXth AF transports and US personnel, the vanguard of which arrived on 1 October 1943. They preceded the four squadrons of the 434th Troop Carrier Group which, during mid-October, brought along from the USA a mixture of C-47s and C-53s. Their training programme reached a climax when on 10 December 1943 they were detached to Welford Park for a training exercise with Allied paratroopers and returned on 10 January 1944. Their subsequent stay was brief for, on 3 March, they all moved to Aldermaston.

Fulbeck was not quiet for long because more C-47s and C-53s this time of the 442nd TCG began arriving direct from the USA at the end of the month. An intensive period of training followed for the new arrivals needed to be fully operational by the start of June 1944.

The eve of D-Day saw them committed to operation *Boston*, the 82nd Airborne's part of the action, forty-five transport aircraft setting off for Drop Zone T two miles south-west of St Mere Eglise. At around 0240 hrs, from the C-47s and C-53s, jumped the 1st Battalion, 507th Paratroop Infantry Regiment along with Regiment headquarters. Three aircraft were shot down and twenty-eight variously damaged.

Next day fifty-six aircraft of the 442nd played their part in operation *Memphis*, the re-supply mission for the American 101st Airborne Division. It turned out to be the 442nd's final operation from Fulbeck for on 12 June 1944 they moved to Weston Zoyland, Somerset. By the end of that month most of the Americans had quit Fulbeck which was soon being used by Bomber Command training units.

That phase ceased on 30 August when Fulbeck again became a busy US transport base with the arrival of C-47s and C-53s of the 440th TCG. They came to participate in operation *Comet*, a planned forerunner of the Arnhem venture which was abandoned because Allied ground forces had not yet advanced far enough to make the operation likely to succeed. Accordingly, the 440th returned to its Exeter base only to come back temporarily to Fulbeck on September for a share in operation *Market*. On that memorable, bright Sunday morning of 17 September 1944, no less than ninety aircraft of the 440th TCG, carrying personnel and equipment of the 376th Parachute Field Artillery, left Fulbeck. Over March they entered the huge cavalcade, crossed the southern edge of the Wash then headed for North Foreland over which they set course for their DZ near Nijmegen. Fierce the opposition which brought down some of the Group's aircraft including that of the Group Commander, Colonel Frank Krebs, who managed to make his way back to his unit aided by the Dutch Resistance.

Next day, and again on 23rd, the 440th flew two glider reinforcement operations before returning on 24th to transporting supplies and personnel to and from France. That activity was but brief for the Group soon left Fulbeck. During the first two weeks of October remaining Americans left, then the station permanently returned to the RAF.

All of that major activity was a far cry from that day in late summer 1940 when Fulbeck opened as one of Cranwell's Relief Landing Grounds and for use by its Airspeed Oxfords until May 1942. Oxfords of No 11 FTS had also made use of Fulbeck in September and October 1941 and in 1942. On 27 October 1942, No 1485 Bombing and Gunnery Flight moved in brought along eight Manchesters and stayed to mid-December. With them was the Air Bomber Training Flight which in March 1943 joined the 'BGF'. Fulbeck was one of the first stations to receive Horsa gliders for storage, fourteen of which were delivered here by air during March 1943. By the end of June twenty-nine gliders had arrived, the full quota of thirty-two being in place by mid-July. Here they stayed, watched over by No 2 HGMU. Fulbeck had three T2s for glider maintenance. Here until April 1944, glider tugs then called to tow them to operational bases.

During 1943 the airfield had been extensively developed, the three concrete and tarmac runways and hardstandings raising it to temporary wartime Class A airfield standard.

Fulbeck was taken over by the RAF's No 5 (Bomber) Group. On 17 October 1944, No 49 Squadron, flying Lancaster Mk Is and IIIs moved in from Fiskerton to carry out Main Force operations. Among the raids in which they participated was an attack on German naval ships in Gdynia and the bombing support given to the Rhine crossing in March 1945. On 22 April 1945 No 49 Squadron moved to Syerston.

For company the squadron briefly had No 189 Squadron which, after reforming on 15 October 1944 at Bardney, arrived at Fulbeck on 2 November 1944. No 189 operated alongside a highly experienced companion. It was from Fulbeck while flying with 189 Squadron that Lancaster EE136, named 'Spirit of Russia' flew its 109th and last sortie. No 189's final operational mission took place on 25/26 April 1945 when fourteen Lancasters participated in the raid on an oil refinery at Vallo, Norway. During its brief wartime bomber career. No 189 Squadron flew 652 bombing sorties, 647 of them from Fulbeck. The squadron also took part in operation *Manna* and later ferried British troops home from Italy. No 189 Squadron moved to Metheringham on 15 October 1945.

In that year a number of other units had been stationed here. One was the Automatic Gun Laying Turret Training Flight, but in the main they were non-flying units. No 4 Equipment Disposal Depot formed on 1 June and on the 14th became part of 255 MU which opened here that day and stayed until 30 November 1948 when it amalgamated with No 93 MU which, an explosive storage unit, remained until 30 April 1956 when the airfield became Active for use as one of Cranwell's RLGs.

Traces of this airfield with an unusual career remain, but resumption of flying from Fulbeck seems unlikely.

Main features:
Runways: 233° 6,000ft x 150ft, 297°, 007°. *Hangars:* two T2 and three T2 for glider maintenance. *Hardstandings:* fifty. *Accommodation:* RAF: 517 officers, 33 SNCOs, 2,285 ORs. No WAAF accommodation. The large establishment had come about because two RAF bomber squadrons were based here late 1944 in accommodation built for the USAAF.

GLATTON, Cambridgeshire

52°27N/00°15W 20ft asl; TL185870. Off A1, 11 miles N of Huntingdon, by B660 near Conington

Travel along the wartime A1 in early 1944 and you could not miss seeing the gleaming B-17s of the 457th for initially all were in unpainted metal finish. Another unusual feature was the absence of squadron identity letters, coloured spinners being instead relied upon. Not until about late July 1944 did any aircraft carry the rich blue diagonal fin band supporting the 'U in a triangle' Group identity marking. Glatton, constructed by the 809th US Army engineers in 1943 and completed with two T2 hangars had an unusual layout. In the centre of the usual three runway intersection sat Rose Court Farm still functioning while surrounded by the men and machines of war. Farming on US bases was far from unknown of course.

Glatton came alive when B-17Gs of the 457th Bomb Group, 1st Air Division, moved in during the last week of January 1944. They flew their first mission on 21 February 1944, during the 'Big Week' when targets included Gutersloh and Lippstadt airfields. On 24 February they attacked Schweinfurt, and next day penetrated deeply to Augsburg. Doubtless they viewed with awe the brief call on 12 March of B-29 43-6963, the first to come to Britain and too heavy for full-load UK operations.

Intensive fighting ensued, so much so that on the eve of D-Day the 457th had only thirty-two aircraft serviceable and twenty-two unserviceable, the third worst state in the 1st Air Division. During June 1944 they participated in softening up operations prior to the Normandy landings and bombed defences in the Cherbourg Peninsula. During June 1944 they also attacked airfields, roads and railways before reverting to strategic targets in July. On 22 June twenty-four crews attacked a tactical target near Rouen. Piloting 'Skunk Hollow', B-17 42-31620, Lt Frank Morrell brought his flak-damaged Fortress home on three engines. One was on fire as he approached Glatton, and with no brakes effective the bomber swung off the runway heading for parked aircraft. The wing of one was clipped before 231620 crashed into another. Morrell and crew were indeed lucky to escape. Two B-17s near the ensuing fire were taxied away by 1st Lt Eugene Tangherlini and Master Sergeant Mayer, both of whom were awarded a Bronze Star medal. Such raids continued until the final operation, the 237th, on 20 April 1945. By then they had flown 7,086 sorties and lost eighty-three B-17s in action. The Group then participated in Operation *Exodus*, repatriation of POWs from France and Austria, before the B-17s left for home between 19 and 23 May 1945.

On 5 July Glatton passed from the 1st Air Division Substitution Unit (which occupied or cleared vacant US bases after the Group left) to 3 Group, RAF Bomber Command, to be prepared for the trooping of personnel to the Middle East. Plans called for up to 20,000 personnel to pass through the station each month, and late in August 1945 Liberators and Lancasters, mainly Upwood-based, began using the station for the task, but at less than the forecast rate. By the end of December, only 1,149 personnel had been flown out and 174 in, with No 70 Transit Camp accommodating them. Quite a number of Liberators were brought from the Mediterranean Theatre and held here before Glatton passed to Care & Maintenance on 30 April 1946 and closed soon after. In the post-war period, between 10 July 1945 and 15 September 1947 when the unit disbanded, No 273 MU made use of Glatton as a satellite site. The airfield was declared surplus to need in July 1948.

*B-17G
'Mission
Maid' of the
457th BG at
Glatton on 1
January 1945
after its
75th mission.
(USAF)*

B-17G of the 457th BG during
operations.

Great excitement, greeted the first B-29 to come here and at Bassingbourn April 1944.

Now CAA-licensed and known as Peterborough Business Airport, it is privately operated by Aerolease Ltd, which provides aircraft servicing facilities. Portable cabins brought into use in the 1970s were supplemented with a control tower in 1995. The sole licensed runway 10/28 is 3,238 feet long and asphalt-surfaced, whereas the wartime concrete runway 16/34 is unlicensed. In 2000 the local flying club changed hands and became Flying Club Conington. MFH Helicopters offer hire and pilot training. Fly CB Peterborough offers high-quality microlight flying training using all-metal, low-wing EV-97 Eurostars designed and built by the Czech Republic company Evektor-Aerotechnik. The 450kg aircraft, factory-built and delivered ready to fly, are relatively cheap to learn to fly and easy to handle.

Main features:
Runways: 140° 6,000ft x 150ft, 160°, 235°, tarmac and wood chip surfaces.
Hangars: two T2. *Hardstandings:* fifty loop type. *Accommodation:* 421 officers and 2,473 enlisted men.

In passing
South-east of Huntingdon is another village named Conington where, in November 1928, an offshoot of The Suffolk & Eastern Counties Aero Club was established. The parent, founded in 1925, operated from Hadleigh, and by 1928 had three Blackburn Bluebirds, examples of the first production side-by-side two-seater biplane. Two of them were often seen at Conington. Frequent movements between there and Hadleigh led to a service carrying, for 30 shillings single and 50 shillings return, one passenger on the so-called Ipswich-Cambridge Airway. Operated on Monday and Thursday, it was supplemented with a Tuesday service from Hadleigh to Grantham, there connecting with the 'Flying Scotsman' rail service to Edinburgh. Cambridge Aero Club formed at Conington, which closed in March 1929 following the Club's movement to Marshall Aerospace Barnwell aerodrome. In 1931 Suffolk Aero Club was reorganised at Ipswich aerodrome. Two Robinson Redwings replaced the Bluebirds, one of which was used by a new club from a field near Colchester.

GOSFIELD, Essex

51°57N/00°35E 285ft asl; TL770315. W of A1017 at Gosfield

The cheek of it! On the very day that Gosfield opened in autumn 1943 an enemy raider aimed a stick of bombs across the airfield. Such raids, usually by Me 410s or Ju 188s and directed against East Anglian airfields, had little more than nuisance value. Only two bombs landed on the site. Next time it was different for, when on 10/11 December 1943 the Luftwaffe launched an attack on Chelmsford, the marker force made a mistake. Despite the obvious Gosfield Lake flares were dropped in error over Gosfield. That resulted in sixty-five HEs including twenty-six 500kg bombs being dropped on the area by Ju 88s and Do 217s but with some cost to the foe for Flying Officer R. Schultz of 410 Squadron flying Mosquito DZ292 shot down off Clacton three confirmed Do 217M-1s of I/KG2.

Although the US 9th AAF moved into at Gosfield on 22 October 1943, their P-47 equipped 365th Fighter Group did not arrive until late December and commenced tactical operations over France during February 1944. That included fighter support for the B-26 Groups as well as strafing and dive-bombing before the 365th moved to Beaulieu, Hampshire, in March 1944. In their place came the 397th Bomb Group which spent ten days here in April 1944 before proceeding to Rivenhall.

The next arrival was the 410th Bomb Group which brought along A-20s. Intention had been that they should be based at Birch but its unsuitable state brought about their move to Gosfield. The intention was to use A-20s as battlefield close support bombers operating at medium levels and carrying out saturation tactical attacks directed at ground troops. That was not the ideal way to employ the nimble A-20 although with an unnecessary dorsal turret it had become too heavy for its best role. The 9th AF flew them in formations of twelve and multiples of that number, or in boxes of six stepped up in 2 Group fashion operations commencing in May 1944. French and Belgian targets were attacked during medium level runs prior to the invasion. Coastal defences, V-sites and marshalling yards were often targets when the A-20s were slotted into extensive *Ramrod* operations, taking part with B-26s and RAF Bostons and Mitchells, supported by fighter-bomber onslaughts and heavily fighter-escorted.

Then came medium-level tactical raids in direct support of Allied forces in France with attacks on reinforcements, railways, bridges and roads all designed to assist the Allied break-outs from Caen and St-Lô. Such activities continued ahead of the advance until, by September 1944, the ground forces were beyond the effective range of British-based A-20s.

The 410th then took their aircraft to Coulommiers, France, leaving Gosfield – like other 9th AF bases – clear of aircraft. RAF Bomber Command then took control of Gosfield. Some such vacated stations were soon housing squadrons of the RAF's 38 Group. Indeed, there were more than needed, but some were unsuitable for large numbers of heavy aircraft and none had full glider provision.

In January 1945 Gosfield was utilised as an overflow station for Wethersfield's Stirlings and also as a base for Martinets of No 1677 Target Towing Flight. It had, however, already been earmarked as an advanced base for any further major airborne assaults.

Colonel Hughey's A-20G 43-10131 7X-P of the 645th BS, 410th BG at Gosfield. (via Ian Mactaggart)

No 46 Group's Dakota squadrons occupied with freight and casevac services to France and UK based were positioned well back from the front. Required for operation *Varsity*, the airborne assault in support of the Rhine crossing, three Dakota squadrons – Nos 271, 512 and 575 – were briefly based at Gosfield from where a swarm of them operated on 24 March 1945 carrying paratroopers for their airdrop. Afterwards the three squadrons left Gosfield almost immediately and the airfield's operational career had ended. Nos 436 to 439 AC Flights under 11 Group Fighter Command were here in September 1945 before the airfield became inactive later that year. The 410th BG is remembered by a local memorial made in Colorado Springs.

Main features:
Runways: 317° 6,000ft x 150ft, 019°, 084°, concrete with a sixty percent wood chip surface. *Hangars:* two T2. *Hardstandings:* fifty spectacle type. Accommodation (USAAF): 417 officers, 2,241 enlisted men.

GRANSDEN LODGE, Cambridgeshire

52°11N 00°07W 248ft asl; TL293555. SE of Little Gransden on B946 W of A14

The exceptional 405 (Vancouver) Squadron operated for two years from Gransden Lodge as one of the few Canadian squadrons to be based in Cambridgeshire – but only just. Indeed, Gransden Lodge straddling the county boundary was officially addressed as being in Bedfordshire.

A well dispersed wartime bomber station, it was unusually set amidst fields and well away from roads. Its two T2 hangars were supplemented by a B1 which housed the Mosquito squadron. Gransden had less accommodation than many similar stations – 86 officers, nearly 200 NCOs and some 800 airmen. Quarters were available for nearly 300 WAAFs.

It opened as a three-runway satellite of Tempsford early in 1942, and No 1418 Flight arrived on 8 April from the parent station to make first use of Gransden. The Wireless Investigation Flight, detached from 109 Squadron, joined them and became 1474 Flight on 4 July 1942. Both units flew Wellingtons, the former conducting trials of *Gee*, the navigation aid. No 1474 Flight became 192 Squadron on 4 January 1943 shortly after receiving Wellington Xs and a few Mosquito IVs. No 1418 Flight which conducted trials of bombers and on 20 July 1942 was absorbed by the Bombing Development Unit whose establishment comprised four heavy bombers (two Stirlings and two Halifaxes), six Wellington IIIs and a Proctor. Technical trials were conducted by BDU, including a lot of development, work relating to *H2S* radar and radar warning devices for bomber defence against fighter attack. This unit and 192 Squadron moved to Feltwell early in April 1943, Gransden then switching from No 3 to 8 Group and in the process became, on 15 April, a second satellite of Oakington.

On 19 April the Pathfinder Navigation Training Unit opened at Gransden equipped with Halifax IIs and moved to Upwood and Warboys between 11 and 19 June 1943. The transfer was brought about because in April 1943 twenty Halifax IIs of No 405 (Canadian) Squadron had arrived here to join the Pathfinder Force.

Their first operation from Gransden, against Duisburg, was flown on 26 April. On 2 August 1943 the squadron – still only a two Flight squadron – began to fly Lancaster I/IIIs on operations and from the start of September flew them exclusively. Mid-1944 saw the introduction of Canadian-built Lancaster BXs, one of them, KB700 called 'Ruhr Express' flying fifty sorties from Gransden.

Runway work at Bourn resulted in 'B' Flight, 97 Squadron, lodging at Gransden and operating from there during August-September 1943, after which the station was left to the Canadians who intensively operated in the Pathfinder 'backer-up' role to the end of hostilities. No 1517 BAT Flight also used Gransden in 1943.

On 25 October 1944, 142 Squadron re-formed here with twenty Mosquito XXVs as part of the LNSF, and operated with amazing efficiency. Although they flew 1,221 sorties during 169 operations – 61 of them against Berlin – only two aircraft failed to return. Another three were destroyed in crashes and two written off as a result of battle damage.

As the Far East war was ending the squadron became first to receive the longer range Mosquito B Mk 35 bomber intended for service there. Their stay was short for No 142 disbanded on 28 September 1945. No 692 Squadron armed with Mosquito B16s, and which moved in from Graveley on 4 June 1945, replaced No 405 which had left for Linton-on-Ouse on 26 May. No 692 Squadron disbanded on 20 September 1945.

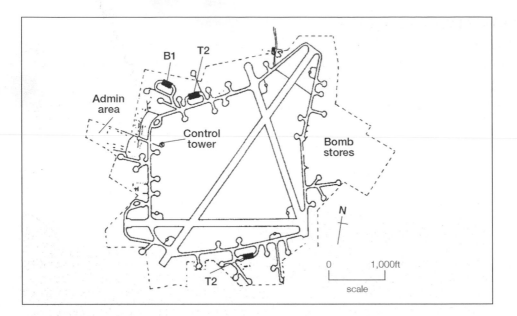

Dramatic change ensued when 47 Group of Transport Command took over the station in November. In December 1945 came Liberator troop transports, thirteen Mk VI, nine Mk VIII and one Mk V all being of No 53 Squadron. Short was the squadron's stay, most personnel leaving on 10 February 1946. The last Liberator returned from trooping on 20 February 1946, and the squadron disbanded on 1 March 1946. Gransden Lodge was retained Inactive under Wyton control. Plan F of January 1947 called for it to be reinstated as a bomber station and made ready for use by March 1954. The station's main runway was accordingly maintained into the 1950s for emergency use. There had also been USAF interest in establishing a tactical air transport base for which Fairchild C-82/119 aircraft were considered. A survey was undertaken in October 1952 to assess its suitability for development for medium bombers. Against any major development was the possibility of a water supply problem and interest switched to Chipping Norton and Podington. Instead, it was a detachment of No 7510 USAF Hospital which made use of Gransden between the mid-1950s and 10 May 1957 when they returned the base to British control.

A portion of the site is now home of the Cambridge Gliding Club which moved from Duxford to Gransden on 12 October 1991. This must not be confused with another small airfield close by on land never part of wartime Gransden Lodge. This is the base of Mark Jefferies, famous for his acrobatic displays, and a centre of the flourishing provision of ex-East European Yak trainers.

Main features:
Runways: 036° 6,000ft x 150ft, 351°, 100°, concrete. *Hangars:* two T2, one B1. *Hardstandings:* thirty-six. *Accommodation:* RAF: 86 Officers, 196 SNCOs, 829 ORs; WAAF: 7 officers, 6 SNCOs, 262 ORs.

GRANTHAM (SEE SPITALGATE), Lincolnshire

52°54N/00°36W 415ft asl; SK935351. On SW side of Grantham, just off the A52

Grantham was the original name of Spitalgate and later there was another station bearing the name. Between October 1937 and November 1943 HQ No 5 Group, Bomber Command was accommodated in a large house known as St Vincents which also took the name RAF Grantham. When 5 Group moved to Morton Hall the premises became HQ US 9th AF Troop Carrier Command which was here from 2 December 1943 to the end of hostilities. St Vincents was sold in 1977 to Grantham Borough Council which has offices there.

GRAVELEY, Cambridgeshire

52°15N/00°11W 177ft asl; TL238645. W of Graveley village off A14, 4 miles S of Huntingdon

Incredible it remains that such a small aeroplane as the Mosquito could carry a 4,000lb 'cookie', representing a fifth of its loaded weight. Carry that load Mosquitoes did, and many times from Graveley whence this amazing load was first delivered to the foe. De Havilland suggested during April 1943 modifying the Mosquito's bomb bay to accommodate a 4,000-pounder and seven weeks later a trial installation was complete. No 627 Squadron was chosen to pioneer the aircraft, but on 2 February 1944 the first two modified Mk IVs arrived instead at Graveley for 692 Squadron specially formed on 1 January 1944 to carry the load as part of 8 Group's Light Night Striking Force.

4,000lb 'cookies' ready for loading into Mosquitoes of 692 Squadron near a B1 hangar. (BAe)

On 23 February three Mosquitoes set off for Düsseldorf, each carrying a 4,000lb bomb. Thenceforth the Mosquito could crush as well as sting, and with exceptional accuracy. By night and day they operated, and often when the rest of Bomber Command was grounded. Graveley had FIDO which 8 Group made good use of when fog descended, and by the end of hostilities No 692 Squadron had despatched 3,148 sorties and lost only sixteen Mosquitoes.

Mosquito pioneering is not Graveley's only claim to fame for this was the first operational airfield to be equipped with FIDO, the petrol burning installation for fog dispersal which lined the main runway. First tested on 19 February 1943 by Air Commodore Don Bennett, it was not until 19 November that FIDO proved its operational value when four 35 Squadron Halifaxes made use of it. On 16/17 December 1943 when Bourn's Lancasters desperately needed help on return, there was not only fog on Graveley's runway – which FIDO could shift – but deep dense cloud above making airfield identification difficult. Although the station was not operating that night the burners were lit and one aircraft landed safely. Another encountered major landing problems and crashed into the Graveley bomb dump without exploding the contents. Too much had been asked of FIDO at that stage. Gradual improvements meant that, by day and night, it proved its worth by bringing safety to around 200 crews. The roar from the lines of burners, the smell, the brilliance of the costly flames they produced, all combined to generate a vision of Hades as I discovered when FIDO was periodically lit during my time at Manston.

Graveley based Halifax B II srs 1a TL-L HR926 of 35 Squadron.

Graveley, opened in 3 Group as a satellite of Tempsford, came into use when 161 (Special Duties) Squadron arrived at the parent from Stradishall/Newmarket on 1 March 1942. 'A' Flight used special Lysanders and 'B' Flight had five Whitley Vs. It was the latter which briefly used Graveley before the squadron consolidated at Tempsford in April 1942.

On 4 August 1942 Graveley passed to the control of the Pathfinder Force. Oxfords of No 1504 BAT Flight nudged out of Wyton stayed only until 14 August. Next day from Linton-on-Ouse and 4 Group came Halifax IIs of 35 Squadron which, as part of the Pathfinder Force, spent four years here. Wyton lost Alconbury to the Americans and on 12 August took in exchange control of Graveley.

The principal task for 35 Squadron was to mark and back-up with flares or incendiaries the Pathfinder Force leaders, ten aircraft commencing such activity on 18/19 August over Flensburg. The three such raids that month involving twenty-six sorties cost the squadron three aircraft.

On 5 October Squadron Leader J C Keny, 'A' Flight Commander in W1047:B, failed to return, and the same night a Halifax flying south of Cambridge suffered a spectacular lightning strike which temporarily blinded a crew member. The Cologne raid of 15 October during which 250lb 'Pink Pansy' incendiaries were dropped was also costly with four aircraft missing. Ten nights later the first raid from Graveley directed upon Italy (Milan) took place, part of Bomber Command's support to the war in the Western Desert. Three raids were launched against Turin in December. No 35 Squadron carried out twenty-nine raids from Graveley in 1942, despatched 237 Halifaxes and lost 8.

Berlin was first attacked from Graveley on 16/17 January 1943 but at this time most raids were against submarine lairs including Lorient. In March 1943 the squadron – operating 'Z' aircraft (without nose turrets) – three times raided Berlin. Twice in April La Spezia was raided which involved nine-hour flights. Another long haul on 16/17th was to Pilsen's Skoda works, an operation repeated on 13/14 May by which time a number of Halifax Mk II Srs 1A aircraft with clear noses were in use.

Memorable indeed was 4/5 May when six Halifaxes set off for Dortmund. Their almost simultaneous return caused confusion in the circuit. Flight Sergeant J A Cobb in DT489:Y crashing on approach with all aboard dying except for the rear gunner. Sergeant J J Williams had run out of fuel, and the crew baled out of W7887:E which crashed at Culverston. Five of nineteen Halifaxes despatched to Krefeld on 21/22 June failed to return in addition to BB368 which Flight Lieutenant D H Milne was forced to ditch off Cromer. In June Station HQ opened at Graveley, which separated it from Wyton.

No 35 Squadron received a boost when a third or 'C' Flight was added raising its establishment to twenty-four aircraft plus six reserves. On 24 July actual strength typically amounted to thirty-three Halifaxes, many being involved when four times 35 Squadron took part in the horrific raids upon Hamburg. On 16 August 1943, twenty-two Halifaxes were among the force attacking Turin, and next night ten crews participated in the Peenemunde operation.

On 31 August Squadron Leader Bill Surtees failed to return from a Berlin raid, his aircraft HR878:J crashing in the IJsselmeer. Some twenty years later he was taken by Gerrit Zwanenburg, the Royal Netherlands Air Force wreck recovery team leader, to the very spot where his aircraft had crashed – by then a wheat field in a polder. Items found in good condition included the fire axe which Surtees had used to get out of the sinking bomber, and which he was now given. The event was featured in the film *One of Our Aircraft is No Longer Missing*.

Although the squadron continued to fly mainly Mk IIs they received their first Halifax III, HX232, on 4 October. Had it come a few hours sooner it would have experienced German bombs one of which exploded on a runway and two others just outside the airfield boundary. At this time 'butterfly' bombs were being dropped in the area.

Operations from Britain against distant targets were at the time regarded with awe by a population many of whom had barely strayed from their birthplace. Mixed feelings greeted the news that on 11/12 November 1943, a nine-hour journey had taken our bombers to the pre-war hyper-luxury resort of Cannes on the 'French Riviera'. Two Halifaxes were shot down and Pilot Officer J R P Andrews ditched his aircraft off very distant Sardinia. On 20 December twenty-one aircraft were despatched to Frankfurt and as Squadron Leader J Sale DSO circled prior to landing a target indicator still aboard exploded in the bomb bay. Sale ordered his crew out and five left the aircraft, the mid-upper gunner being unable to do so for his parachute had been burnt. With skill and courage Sale managed to land the burning aircraft and taxi it off the runway. The two occupants were 200 yards away when HX325:J exploded.

On 1/2 March 1944 No 35 Squadron flew their last Halifax operation using eighteen aircraft against Stuttgart. On 6 March the squadron's first Lancaster, ND643, arrived from Wyton. Bourn's

97 Squadron donated some of theirs allowing operations to commence on 15 March when twelve attacked Stuttgart. Having Lancasters meant that 35 Squadron could at last drop 4,000lb 'cookies'. Graveley's Halifaxes had mounted 159 attacks losing sixty-three aircraft in the course of 1,736 sorties showing a loss rate of 3.6 percent – lower than many squadrons.

Graveley's first 'transport plan' raid took place on 9 April 1944, and when Laon was the target on the 22nd, Wing Commander S P Daniels acted as Master Bomber in ND697:T and Squadron Leader E K Creswell his Deputy in ND755:B. Again, in May 1944, 35 Squadron provided the Master Bomber during operations against railway installations in Lens, Trappes, Bourg Leopold and Montdidier. In the early hours of 6 June the Lancasters attacked heavy guns at Maissy and Longues. Eleven times in June 1944 the master of ceremonies was provided by 35 Squadron, and for a significant raid on the 25th when the squadron made their first Lancaster day raid with Motorgueil the target. Thereafter day raids were interspersed with night operations. Squadron Leaders Creswell and Chigny acted as Master and Deputy Master Bombers for the Villeneuve raid of 4 July, and two days later Wing Commander P H Cribbins directed the Siracourt attack and Flight Lieutenant H J Hoover the bombing of Mimoyecques. Late the following evening Daniels and Creswell controlled the massive bombing assault on German land forces near Caen prior to an assault by land forces.

Throughout summer similar operations continued before '35' played a part in the reduction of Calais and Le Havre. By November day raids to Germany were frequent and then, on the evening of the 21st, 35 Squadron for the first time despatched two *Oboe*-equipped Lancasters for an attack on Wesel. Another unusual raid was that of 4 December when in daylight eighteen Lancasters attempted to destroy the Heinsbach River Dam.

Ever-present with so many, large aircraft operating sometimes in cloud was the possibility of a collision which, for 35 Squadron, came about on 23 December 1944. Ten Lancasters set off for the Gremburg marshalling yards near Cologne and over the sea there was a tremendous explosion when PB678:F and PB683:H collided killing all their occupants. Both the *Oboe* lead aircraft, PB367:Z and PB372:X, were seriously damaged by flak, also PB685:J. Undaunted, '35' set off for Cologne next day and this time ME336:S crashed shortly after take-off. By the end of 1944 the Lancasters had flown 1,657 sorties during 158 attacks which cost eighteen aircraft, but the loss rate had fallen to 1.1 percent.

Lancaster of 35 Squadron landing at Graveley where FIDO has been lit.

Many 1945 operations were directed against fuel installations. There were still deep penetrations, to Magdeburg, Chemnitz and Dresden in which attack ten crews took part. The last bombing operation came on 25 April when eight Lancasters attacked guns on Wangerooge, then came operation *Manna*. From Graveley Lancasters flew 2,272 bombing sorties in the course of 222 operations at a cost of twenty-four aircraft lost in action.

Mosquito of 692 Squadron had been intensively engaged in the fight (as is recorded in *Mosquito*, Crécy Publishing, 1967, 1995) and visited Berlin no less than 111 times. Since June 1944 the special Mk IVs had been replaced by B16s whose final raid, on Kiel, took place on 2 May. The squadron moved to Gransden Lodge on 4 June 1945 making room for 227 Squadron and their Lancasters which joined 35 Squadron in preparation for *Tiger Force* which was not needed. Instead, No 227 Squadron disbanded on 5 September which allowed 115 Squadron to bring twenty assorted Mk I and III Lancasters from Witchford. No 35 Squadron was now established at sixteen Mk I (FE), but possessed only nine and also had fifteen assorted Mk I/IIIs.

Graveley was selected for retention and development into a post-war permanent bomber station. Spring 1946 saw 35 Squadron equip with very smart black-and-white new Lancaster B I (FE)s originally intended for *Tiger Force* and now replacing older Lancasters in 3 Group. Summer was spent improving formation flying and in July-August No 35 (Madras) Squadron undertook a prestigious tour of the USA during which the sixteen Lancasters had, by the time of return on 29 August 1946 flown 300,000 miles between them and visited seventeen airfields. The squadron's subsequent time at Graveley was brief, for the station closed in September following a policy change. Both squadrons took their Lancasters to Stradishall.

Graveley was far from finished. Under Plan F of January 1947 it was prescribed for use as a transport base and for ten years was held on Care & Maintenance. When No 206 AFS (renamed 5 FTS) opened at Oakington in the mid-1950s Graveley was activated and became the RLG for their Vampires and Meteors. The last aircraft to make use of it did so on 16 July 1964. Graveley closed to flying on 1 December 1968 and was quite quickly disposed of.

Main features:
Runways: 269° 6,000ft x 150ft, 209°, 330°, concrete. *Hangars:* three T2, one B1. *Hardstandings:* thirty-six. *Accommodation:* RAF: 159 officers, 386 NCOs, 1,755 ORs; WAAF: 7 officers, 20 SNCOs, 272 ORs.

GREAT ASHFIELD, Suffolk

52°15N/00°56E 200ft asl; TM010665. 2½ miles NE Elmswell, N of A14

Great Ashfield opened in March 1943, the intention being that a Flight of 1665 Conversion Unit would form here in April 1943 as nucleus of this new unit. It would remain until the rest of the unit formed here or elsewhere, then depart. In the event 1665 CU did not form here, although the first aircraft to touch down on the runways were Stirlings, but of 1651 CU. These were making use of the airfield in May 1943 until, following a change of plan, the USAAF arrived in early June 1943.

The occupants between then and August 1945 were B-17s of the 385th Bomb Group ('G in a square'), 3rd Air Division, the Group commencing operations on 17 July 1943 by raiding Germany. A month later they participated in the shuttle raid which bombed Regensburg.

Thereafter the Group's targets lay in Germany, France, Holland, Belgium, Norway and Poland. A number of raids were made on Berlin, and other targets included an aircraft factory at Oschersleben, Marienburg, an electronics factory at Stuttgart, airfields at Beauvais and Chartres, an oil refinery at Ludwigshafen and rail targets at Munich and Oranienburg. The B-17s attacked coastal targets prior to D-Day and choke points on the day of the invasion. They aided the St-Lô break-out and took part in repelling the Ardennes offensive.

The Group's second Distinguished Unit Citation was awarded for an operation on 12 May 1944 when, leading the 4th Combat Wing through heavy fighter opposition, they proceeded to bomb an aircraft repair plant at Zwickau where the aim proved to be very accurate. Coming home the B-17s endured further enemy attacks.

The Group held one distinction for it was the only B-17 Group to lose an aircraft to German bombs dropped upon a USAAF airfield in Britain. An Me 410 intruder bombed Great Ashfield on 22/23 May 1944 scoring a hit on a hangar inside which the B-17 was destroyed.

B-17s of the 385th Bomb Group flew their last operational mission on 20 April 1945 managing a total of 8,264 sorties before setting off for the USA during the last two weeks of June 1945 followed by the ground echelon at the start of August. After Great Ashfield was returned to the RAF it became Inactive and on 14 July 1947 HQ No 94 MU opened in No 40 Group, Maintenance Command, its task the storing of bombs for 3 Group. Many sub-sites in the area were controlled from here. The airfield closed in March 1957 and was sold for agricultural purposes in 1959-60. Parts of the runways remain, and a memorial to the 385th can be found in Great Ashfield church. A minor road circles the one-time airfield site which has recently been used for truck rallies.

Main features:
Runways: 068° 6,000ft x 150ft, 360°, 132°, concrete. *Hangars:* two T2.
Hardstandings: seventeen spectacle type, thirty-three frying pan type.
Accommodation: 421 officers, 2,473 enlisted men.

GREAT DUNMOW, Essex

51°53N/00°18E 325ft asl; TL590255. By Little Easton village

Under supervision of RAF Stradishall, US Army personnel arrived on 4 July 1942 to build an airfield known as Great Easton. Completed on 1 July 1943, one of its memorable features was the host of B-26 Marauders stored alongside roads leading to the airfield, many apparently being held here for other bases.

The first operational unit here was the 386th Bomb Group which arrived from Boxted on 24 September 1943 and started operating before 16 October when the base passed to the US 9th AF. The B-26s operated within *Ramrods* usually involving the RAF. A *Ramrod* might comprise as many as six parts. Part one was often a Typhoon fighter-bomber operation to silence AA guns and fighter response, or directed at radar stations. Other parts might involve RAF Boston and Mitchell formations pattern bombing a particular target such as a bridge, airfield, V-1 site or sites. The B-26s would comprise one or more parts, their basic formation consisting of eighteen aircraft often flying in groups of thirty-six allowing B-26 formations to comprise 72 or 108 aircraft. With such numbers involved the operational careers of Marauder bases were similar. To November 1943 targets were mixed – harbours, airfields, some industrial sites. Then attention switched to V-1 or *Noball* sites and supply depots.

In February 1944 airfields became prime items followed by coastal targets in the period closer to D-Day. During the Normandy campaign B-26s gave close battlefield support, then turned their attention to bridges over the Seine and Loire in order to make enemy retreat difficult. POL (petrol, oil, lubricant) depots in particular were next bombed along with a variety of supply, support and communications targets. The B-26 Groups took part in the Falaise battle before in lending a hand in reducing Brest during September. Next came the big upheaval, the move to France positioning them nearer the land battles. All this was as true of Dunmow's B-26s as of others, the 386th leaving for Beaumont-sur-Olse on 2 October 1944. The station then passed to Fighter Command for administrative purposes.

B-26 HELLS ANGELS awaiting bombs bought through war bonds. Great Dunmow 26 August 1944. (USAF/via Roger Freeman)

Just as the Marauders were needed nearer the battlegrounds, so it was with the transport and supply squadrons of the RAF's 38 Group. Being clustered in the south Midlands had placed them at a disadvantage during the Arnhem airlift and subsequently when damaged aircraft – of which there were many – had to be nursed home for repair far across England. As soon as the terrible wounds of Arnhem were licked clean the Stirling squadrons moved to Essex, to await the next venture. This repositioning brought 190 Squadron to Great Dunmow (never Great Easton to the RAF and now a Fighter Command station) on 14 October 1944 and No 620 a few days later. Both equipped with Stirling Great IVs, these squadrons were largely operationally unemployed apart from undertaking supply dropping missions.

To maintain their operational status the squadrons suddenly found themselves undertaking bombing training, for there was no reason why a Stirling IV could not carry bombs instead of containers. In February 1945 they began night bombing of towns fairly close to the front line thus maintaining an army support role, but lack of sophisticated radar bombing aids limited their achievements.

When they were not operating they were training in the expected airborne forces tasks which in February involved long cross-country flights towing Horsas, the long trains being buffeted in the disturbed air as the assembly generated an indelible image for many an East Anglian.

Such activity presaged the last big airborne venture, operation *Varsity*, in which 38 Group and the US 9th AF assisted, the crossing of the Rhine near Wesel. Every available aircraft and glider was involved, most stations despatching about sixty combinations on as beautiful, clear and sunny warm March day as ever could be.

During the Arnhem operation the transports had traversed southern East Anglia whereas this time the force assembled over the area, then swung into ordered positions with extensive US formations which consisted of C-47s towing CG-4As and while C-46 Commandos towed more of the latter some were hauling the larger CG-13s. The combined armada formed a procession that took an hour to pass over the coast.

Losses were minimal and little direct re-supply was required. Instead, the transport squadrons undertook drops to diminishing Resistance forces and at the end of hostilities transported Allied occupation forces to Norway. From Dunmow the passengers included a group of nurses badly needed there. The whole operation was difficult for the weather was bad snowstorms in Norway bringing several serious disasters.

Dunmow's squadrons then resumed training using a few Horsas, delivered mail to overseas forces and generally made themselves useful by carrying personnel. In June 1945 both Nos 190 and 620 Squadrons re-equipped with Halifax A VIIs. The former left for Tarrant Rushton late November 1945 whereas No 620 Squadron at about the same time was posted to Palestine.

Then placed on Care & Maintenance, the station was maintained in excellent condition for some years. In the mid-1950s the USAF had a storage depot here. A public road utilised the perimeter track affording an excellent view of the airfield area which, although sold for agricultural use in April 1958, retains the general appearance of a one-time aerodrome.

Main features:
Runways: 150° 6,000ft x 150ft, 110°, 040°, concrete and wood chips. *Hangars:* two T2. *Hardstandings:* fifty spectacle type. *Accommodation:* RAF: 187 officers, 513 SNCOs, 1,533 ORs; WAAF: 12 SNCOs and 308 ORs.

GREAT MASSINGHAM, Norfolk

52°46N/00°40E 295ft asl; TF805235. E of Great Massingham, by road to Rudham

'This afternoon, Blenheims of Bomber Command attacked the German naval base at Helgoland. From this operation, one of our aircraft is missing.' So often one heard such simple comment on the BBC's evening news bulletin. Without first-hand experience of such an operation one could scarcely imagine just what was involved, but the crews of Massingham's 107 Squadron knew only too well.

Newly arrived at this bleak airfield set alongside one of Norfolk's most idyllic villages, 107 Squadron sent out twelve crews to bomb Heligoland on 13 May 1941. Approaching at sea level, they attacked from 300ft in line abreast, avoiding enemy fire until their withdrawal. Low-level operations were fraught with risk and Sergeant Chainey, on his first operation with 107, momentarily flew too low. His port propeller touched the sea and was ripped off, nevertheless he made it back to base.

Boston IIIs of 107 Squadron, 2 Group, which flew many operations from here.

.   On 21 May the squadron was again ordered to Helgoland. That a high degree of tenseness gripped the crews we may be certain as the Blenheims roared off in threes from the grass airfield. Visibility was up to fifteen miles in the target area and the enemy, ready for the return match, greeted the raiders with a barrage of gunfire. Almost half the force of nine was hit and the observer with Sergeant Kenneth Wolstenholme – well known later as a television sports commentator – was killed outright. Moments after, Sergeant Ratcliffe's Blenheim, its starboard engine burning, smashed into the sea. The squadron had gone into the attack at 40-60ft, dropped four tons of bombs and gained some satisfaction from seeing German football players scatter in all directions. Direct hits were claimed on some guns on the west side of the island, but such operations, so typical of 2 Group's, whilst having little effect on the outcome of the war, kept the enemy on his toes and his forces in place and dispersed.

Great Massingham came into use, for 2 Group, in the summer of 1940 as West Raynham's satellite to where No 18 Squadron moved on 9 September 1940. From here the squadron flew cloud cover day raids and night intruders against enemy airfields. Great Massingham at this time was an Unbuilt Satellite, a grass field with blister hangars and wooden huts supplemented, as at so many such airfields, with tented accommodation. On 2 April 1941 the squadron moved to the equally primitive airfield at Oulton, satellite of Horsham St Faith.

Their place was on 11 May 1941 taken by 107 Squadron and their Blenheims an intensive operational phase following comprising mainly day operations against shipping and fringe targets. Most of the squadron was sent to Malta in September to undertake anti-shipping operations no less hazardous than previously.

Hardly had 107 Squadron settled at Massingham when on 15 May 1941 a new, large shape arrived. No 90 Squadron based at West Raynham dispersed its Fortress Is here, unready for action until late June.

At the start of 1942, 107 Squadron returned now flying Boston IIIs. The squadron's first operation came on 8 March when, in what became traditional style, six Bostons led by Squadron Leader Lynn formed up in two stepped boxes of three and, fighter-protected, made a medium-level raid on Abbeville's marshalling yards. Such raids, and night intruding during the Bremen '1,000 bomber' raid on 25 June, typified the effort with 107 Squadron mounting escorted day operations to the end of June 1942. The squadron had a special role in that it was trained for gas spray operations.

General view across the airfield, Boston IIIs of 107 Squadron in foreground. In Summer 1942.

July witnessed some very low-level attacks by single Bostons on power stations before in mid-August the squadron was briefly detached to Ford for a part in the Dieppe raid during which they bombed guns and AFVS. There was a brief reminder of times past when in August 1942 West Raynham once more accommodated 18 Squadron working up with Blenheim VDs, the ultimate variant to make use of Massingham's grass during training. On 13 September No 180 Squadron reformed at West Raynham and positioned some of its Mitchells here for flying training. Meanwhile, 107 Squadron continued fighter-escorted day operations into late autumn 1942 and on 6 December twelve crews participated from here in that 2 Group spectacular, the raid on the Philips works at Eindhoven.

Circuses and *Ramrods* flown by Boston IIIAs (which replaced the Mk IIIs sent to north Africa) characterised 1943 activity along with continued training for possible gas spraying. Immediately ahead of 487's disastrous Amsterdam raid of 3 May, 107 Squadron attacked the steel works at IJmuiden. The main concern during such raids was the risk of being hit by flak, for enemy fighters rarely reached the bombers because they were screened by large formations of fighters.

During May 1943 storage of Horsa gliders began under the watchful eyes of No 1 HGMU. A total of twenty-seven was set in April of which fifteen were here by mid-May. Establishment was increased to thirty-two during June but by the 23rd only twenty Horsas had been towed here and during July all were flown out.

Low-level solo Boston operations requiring skill and courage were again mounted against power stations in July 1943, and on 8 August a large-scale low attack was delivered on the Rennes naval stores in an all-Boston operation for which the aircraft was ideal. So low in attacking was 'Dicky' England, their intrepid commanding officer, that he flew home a cable picked up in France streaming from his aircraft. On 20 August 107 Squadron flew out of Massingham for the last time as they departed for Hartford Bridge, Hampshire.

Frenchmen manning Bostons of 342 Squadron had arrived at Massingham on 19 July 1943, and operated from here until 6 September when they followed 107 Squadron to Hartford Bridge (later known as Blackbushe). This left behind only elements of No 1482 B&G Flight 2 Group's fighter affiliation and gunnery training unit which came from West Raynham on 19 May 1943 and stayed until 17 September when they returned to the parent station. Among the Flight's aircraft were a few Mitchells.

As soon as the Bostons left in September 1943 the airfield had a facelift during which its future changed dramatically for on 1 December 1943 it was transferred to the new No 100 Bomber Support Group. The airfield was extended, better accommodation was added, runways were laid and completed on 9 February 1944. Great Massingham reopened on 17 April 1944. No 1694 Target Towing Flight (later Bomber Defence Training Flight) arrived from West Raynham followed on 22 May by No 1692 Bomber Support Training Flight (later called the Bomber Support Training Unit) using *Serrate* equipped Beaufighters and Mosquitoes, which came from Little Snoring.

With the Normandy invasion about to begin 169 Squadron arrived with Mosquito II night fighters. Within days the squadron was switching to the FB Mk VI for fighter-bomber operations under 100 Group. They at once proved a very efficient unit and on 20 July 1944 were responsible for 100 Group's 100th claim in combat. The squadron participated in the intensive night bomber support campaign to the end of the war, re-equipping with Mosquito 19 night fighters in January 1945 but retaining some Mk VI fighter-bombers for special purposes. At the end of the war these included dropping napalm bombs on German airfields. Recently they had concentrated on low-level night strikes.

The fighting over, 1692 Bomber Support Training Unit disbanded on 15 June 1945 and 169 Squadron on 10 August. Massingham passed to 12 Group on 25 August 1945 and when in October the Central Fighter Establishment moved into West Raynham, Great Massingham became its satellite in which role it served until December 1946. Plan F called for its retention for possible development into a fighter station. Over the following four years it remained available for the use of West Raynham having GCA installed, and in February 1951 was classed as a Standby Airfield within Plan G. Although portions of it were in April 1958 released for agricultural use a part of Great Massingham between 8 July 1957 and June 1962 housed a Detachment of the 605th Communications Squadron USAF, and between June 1962 and 30 June 1964 Det. 1979 Communications Squadron USAF after which it was returned to British control for disposal. Its continued use had resulted in it having the appearance of an airfield long after closure.

Main features:
Runways: 100° 6,000ft x 150ft, 040°, 150°, concrete. *Hangars:* four T2, one Bl. *Hardstandings:* twenty-one spectacle, fifteen pan type. *Accommodation:* RAF: 91 officers, 260 SNCOs, 846 ORs; WAAF: 6 officers, 8 SNCOs, 112 ORs.

GREAT SALING, Essex – see ANDREWS FIELD

GREAT SAMPFORD, Essex

51°59N/00°21E 342ft asl; TL615350. W of village, off B1053, near Wimbish Green

17 April 1942 was a bright, breezy day. Soon after 11.30am, eleven Spitfire Vbs of 65 Squadron took off from Sampford, joined 'Treble One' Squadron up from Debden, formated with 71 (Eagle) Squadron over Bradwell and flew to Manston. There they rendezvoused with six Bostons which bombed Calais. It was an uneventful operation like so many of 65's whilst they were at Debden's new satellite. The return was somewhat surprising for, once in Sampford's circuit and following Squadron Leader H T Gilbert, the formation inverted their Spitfires and lowered their undercarriages, an amazing sight!

Great Sampford had only just come into use. On the 4 April laying of the first metal Sommerfeld runway had commenced, 400 men putting down 1,000 yards of tracking in a creditable twelve hours. No 65 Squadron moved in from Debden in the early evening of 14 April at the end of an operational flight.

Thereafter operations came at a fair pace, usually devoid of combat. *Ramrod* 26 of 25 April brought a taste of fighting for, as six Bostons were bombing Dunkirk, about forty Fw 190s bore down out of the sun. Spitfires of 65 Squadron drove them off and later that day they caught sight of more '190s', but there was no engagement. *Circus* 142, flown on 27 April, was more memorable. Over St Omer a fierce fight involving fifty or sixty Fw 190s developed during which two '190s' collided. Pilot Officer T A Burk, a Rhodesian, claimed two Fw 190s shot down. As he fought his way home, and Flight Lieutenant Bartley damaged another over the Channel.

In May trouble developed involving the runway's top layer at an intersection needing soil removal. Flying continued mainly from Debden with 65 Squadron flying sweeps and escorts throughout the month.

Most eventful of 65's operations during its Great Sampford stay occurred on 1 June when Wing Commander J A Gordon was leading eleven Spitfires during *Circus* 177. South of Bruges a dozen or so enemy aircraft were spotted and the Debden Wing confronted them. The enemy raced off so 65 Squadron turned for home. As they neared the French coast they were bounced and within minutes Wing Commander Gordon was calling 'm'aidez'. Like him, Sergeant Parak too was shot down. Over the coast an Fw 190 shot down Pilot Officer Richards, who was picked up 2½ hours later by a naval launch. Sergeant Kopecek, a Czech, fired upon by anti-aircraft guns, was wounded and landed at Manston. The performance of the Fw 190 was more than a match for the Spitfire Vb.

Between 15 and 22 June 1942 Great Sampford lay quiet, '65' being at Martlesham during a tactical exercise. Then the battle resumed with *Rodeos*, *Ramrods* and *Circuses* until 30 June when the squadron flew to Hawkinge on another exercise and the ground crews followed south in two Handley Page 'Sparrows'. Returning to Sampford on 7 July, the squadron was ordered to prepare for overseas, but the order was countermanded and on 20 July they resumed operations by participating next day in a mass *Rhubarb* mounted by the Debden Wing. It turned out to be the squadron's last fling from Sampford, and when they moved out to Gravesend their place was taken by Spitfire VIs of 616 Squadron which stayed until 23 September.

Immediately in came No 133 (Eagle) Squadron arriving from Biggin Hill. On 29 September they joined a parade at Debden and on that auspicious day along with the other two Eagle squadrons became part of the USAAF's 4th Fighter Group in which 133 Squadron became No 336 (Pursuit) Squadron. On 2 October they left Great Sampford for Gravesend returning on the 19th then at the end of the month the squadron moved into Debden. The 335th Squadron came from Martlesham, and replaced them with their fifteen Spitfires on 6 November and stayed until 1 December when they, too, went to Debden. Detachments of American personnel remained at Sampford which periodically handled Spitfires. During February 1943 the 4th Fighter Group received their first P-47 Thunderbolts and these occasionally visited the airfield or were dispersed here. By March 1943 it was being used only for emergency landings for the P-47s were heavy aircraft needing more space than Great Sampford offered.

Its days as an operational station over, the RAF Regiment Battle School took over the camp in mid-1943. During the run-up to D-Day Great Sampford was used for landing practice by Horsa gliders. Flying days ended, it closed at the end of August 1944 but its use by the RAF continued when it was placed in Balloon Command to support balloons used against V-1 assaults. By the end of hostilities it was in 22 Group, Maintenance Command, which declared the site surplus on 28 March 1946.

Main features:
Runways: 230° 4,800ft, 127° 3,150ft – both Sommerfeld tracking. No lighting provided. *Hangars:* four Over Blister. *Accommodation:* RAF: 34 officers, 106 SNCOs, 669 ORs; WAAF: 5 SNCOs, 60 ORs.

HALESWORTH, Suffolk

52°21N/01°32E 120ft asl; TM405798. 2 miles NE Halesworth, off A144. Minor road to Upper Holton runs along perimeter track

It was 29 March 1945 when the huge white and blue US Navy amphibian circled low over Cambridge. Occasionally a Catalina flying-boat plying to and from Felixstowe crossed East Anglia but the amphibian version had not until now appeared. Later I discovered its lair to be Halesworth where, in January 1945, the USAAF began stationing a few OA-10A amphibians for deep sea ASR purposes. Lucky, indeed, was the inland viewer to glimpse such a rare, exotic sight.

Halesworth opened for American use on 31 May 1943 with Knettishall and Sculthorpe as satellites. Early in July the 56th Fighter Group, already a high scoring fighting unit, arrived from Horsham St Faith where they had been ousted by B-24s. For ten months the P-47 pilots fought valiantly over Europe, mainly providing bomber escort. During the latter period of their Halesworth stay the 56th learnt the value of low-level attacks on airfields. In mid-April 1944 the Group left for Boxted.

To Halesworth at the start of May came green and white-tailed B-24s of the 489th Bomb Group which flew their first mission on 30 May 1944 against a pre-invasion target. Tough actions followed fast and on 5 June 1944 the courage of Lieutenant Colonel Leon R Vance Jnr won him the Medal of Honor. The Deputy Group Commander, he was seriously wounded and his right foot was almost severed when the bomber was hit. Nevertheless he flew on bringing the Liberator back to the English coast over which most of the crew baled out. Vance believed one man was still aboard so he carefully ditched the crippled B-24 to save him. Vance was rescued and survived despite his horrific wounds.

Next morning the 489th took part in the dawn assault on Normandy's defences then turned to raiding airfields, railways, V-1 sites, bridges and rail targets. July 1944 saw the Group switch to the strategic offensive by bombing factories, oil refineries and marshalling yards. Ludwigshaven, Magdeburg, Brunswick, Saarbrucken – all had been attacked by November 1944 when the 489th Group ceased operations and returned to the USA before moving to the Pacific Theatre.

In January 1945 the 5th Emergency Rescue Squadron arrived from Boxted flying those rare OA-10As and 'war weary' P-47s carrying dinghies and smoke markers with which to mark crews found at sea. It was customary for USAAF units to hold 'war weary' aircraft, the letters 'WW' being carried on the tails of such aircraft alongside the serial numbers.

In March the squadron began to receive a few B-17s carrying an airborne lifeboat slung under their bellies and operated these aircraft to the end of hostilities. The first successful drop was to a crew off Denmark on 31 March 1945. Additionally, Halesworth housed the 496th Fighter Training Group which arrived here from Goxhill where, since 1942, pilots went for indoctrination in European theatre conditions. The two squadrons flew P-51s here from February to June 1945.

Halesworth was taken over that month by the RAF then on 5 August was handed over to the Royal Navy and became HMS *Sparrowhawk*. In November 1945 No 798 Squadron Fleet Air Arm arrived, their Barracudas and Oxfords being used for advanced flying training. The squadron was joined a few weeks later by 762 Squadron whose Oxfords, Beauforts and Mosquitoes provided twin-engined conversion training, the squadron having been an earlier off-shoot of 798 which left in January 1946. No 762 Squadron moved to Ford in February 1946 and soon after the 'ship' closed to flying. It is now the site of a turkey farm.

A stone memorial on the site commemorates the 489th and includes an airfield layout plan. Kneelers made by the 489th BG veterans' wives can be found in St Peter's Church, Holton.

Main features:
Runways: 240° 6,000ft x 150ft, 190°, 290°, tar and wood chip surface on concrete. *Hangars:* two T2. *Hardstandings:* fifty loop type. *Accommodation:* 433 officers, 2,529 enlisted men.

HARDWICK, Norfolk

52°28N/01°18E 170ft asl; TM250900. 4½ miles NW Harleston, 5½ miles W of Bungay

Hardwick was B-24 territory, and best known as the home of the 93rd, one of the most prominent 2nd Bomb Division Groups. However, it was not always like that for when it entered the American world in September 1942 the occupants were unusual. Prime US contribution to the European war was the 8th AAF here to mount a US-style strategic bombing campaign and suddenly it was all change.

B-24D Liberator 41-23722 BOOMERANG of the 328th BS, 93rd BG operated with the Group in the Middle East, from North Africa and England in 1942/43. (USAF)

Most of the early arrivals in Britain were transferred to a new organisation, the 12th AF, to participate in operation *Torch*, the invasion of north-west Africa. The USAAF was, after all, born of the US Army which still regarded it as a battlefield support force.

Required for the African campaign were tactical bombers and getting those there involved either shipping them to west Africa, or flying them in trans-Atlantic island-hopping batches. A third choice was adopted – they would fly to Britain, then move south when African bases became available. This brought to Britain the 310th Bomb Group and its B-25 Mitchells, the first USAAF examples and almost the only ones ever seen in wartime Britain. Two squadrons took up residence at Hardwick while the third, the 428th, used Bungay, the satellite.

Arrival started on 13 September 1942 and by the end of the month nine green-grey B-25s had reached Britain, thirty-one by 13 November.

Late November 1942 saw the B-25s depart in three groups, and before all the allocated aircraft had arrived for bad weather held back many on route to Britain. Not only was unserviceability high, the bombers were constantly being worked upon to ensure safe flying to their battle zone whence the last examples departed early January 1943. One had to be very lucky to see an airborne B-25.

Even before the B-25Cs had left, Hardwick's better known residents had moved. Making the short trip from Alconbury, these were the thirty-four B-24Ds of the 93rd Bomb Group which arrived stylishly on 6 December 1942. During their Alconbury stay they had acquired much toned down national identity markings, yellow tail individual letters and serials being their only additional trim. They had moved because of a Command decision to assemble a Wing of B-17 Groups in the Bedfordshire-Huntingdonshire-Northamptonshire area and establish a second in Norfolk armed with B-24 Liberators. Expansion led to both Wings being raised to Division status, another reminder of the 'Army' influence.

Almost immediately Hardwick's B-24s seemed to vanish. They too had gone to North Africa to carry out raids upon shipping and land communications. A few B-24s remained at Hardwick for special flights involving the use of the *Gee* navigational aid.

Inadequate technical support and difficult desert operating conditions caused the overseas detachments to return to Hardwick in late February-early March, thirty-six B-24s being at the base on 8 March of which only ten were serviceable. Bombing operations from the home base resumed on 18 March, and in May some crews undertook night flying training whilst others continued operations against Continental targets. East Anglia's sky was now acquiring many more long white vapour trails as the Liberators flew to and for using established East coast exit points. Attacks upon engine repair works, power plants and harbours were all well underway when suddenly Liberator formations began roaring over town and country literally almost at roof top height and supremely spectacular. In June 1943 they suddenly disappeared once more for they had again chosen the sunshine. This time it was to support the Allied Sicilian landings although that was not the main reason for that low-flying practice often led by the first B-24 leadship wearing overall an amazing coat of black and orange 'lightning flashes'.

The 93rd's main intent had been well disguised. On 1 August 1943 the reason became clear when they took part in one of the great adventures of the war, the attack on Rumania's Ploesti oil field. This called for one-pass very accurate low-level attacks, no easy task, and for the 93rd the operation went badly wrong. Following others the Group discovered that they were running up on the wrong target. Opposition was intense and disaster struck hard when the lead ship of the 93rd encountered serious trouble. Its two pilots, Lieutenant Colonel Addison E Baker and Major John L Jerstad, pressed on when an abortive sortie might have saved their lives. Instead, they attacked the target presented to them only to crash in the target area. For their example each was awarded a Medal of Honor.

The Group, which returned to Hardwick in mid-August, flew two raids before they were detached yet again to the Mediterranean Theatre. This time it was to support the Fifth Army landing at Salerno, Italy. They returned to Britain during October 1943. Although on 28 September 1943 they still held nine B-24Ds they were about to re-arm with B-24H and J nose turreted models.

The 93rd operated from Hardwick for the rest of the war and carried out 396 operations (49 from Africa), more than any other 8th AF Bomb Group. Their operational pattern was as for many others and involved attacks upon targets widely spaced across Europe, participation in the lead up to and support of the invasion, the St-Lô break-out, Arnhem and the Rhine crossing. When American land forces became short of fuel in the summer of 1944 the 93rd hauled petrol cans to France, an unenviable task for certain.

Of Hardwick, a typical wartime temporary bomber base, little remains, but runways are evident. The RAF took over the airfield in June 1945 and on 22 September 1945 it joined the Coltishall Sector within 12 Group. March 1946 found it as Horsham St Faith's satellite and in the Norfolk Sector, but by the end of the year it was an uncommitted station under Intermediate Plan F. Nevertheless it was a retained airfield not completely disposed of until June 1962.

One might suppose that the tail of a B-24 suitably mounted might mark this veritable home of America's best heavy bomber, the Liberator. Instead, one is left only to remember such sights, to stare and maybe have to imagine – easier and more satisfying if memory goes back long enough! Yet all is far from lost for private flying has, of late, come under way using a Harvard in the markings of the 100th BG with a P-51 due some time to join it.

Main features:
Runways: 020° 6,000ft x 150ft, 080°, 140° concrete and tarmac. *Hangars:* three T2. *Hardstandings:* fifty loop type. *Accommodation:* 443 officers, 2,529 enlisted men.

HARLAXTON, Lincolnshire

52°53N/00°39W 425ft asl; SK902325. 2 miles S of Grantham

Quite common, they were, over a wide area too, the yellow under-surfaced Blenheim Vs. No designation seems to have been promulgated for them and in their time they were colloquially named Blenheim T. Mk Va. Most had their turrets removed, carried white individual identities and congregated in a large colony at Harlaxton which had functioned as a busy WWI airfield. Like its occupants, it was unusual in that it featured a triangular shaped grass surface landing ground whose apex pointed north. Temporary buildings and no less than eighteen Blister hangars had replaced the old and irreparable of previous days.

Harlaxton, built as an RFC training camp for the RFC, initially featured small wooden 1916-style hangars and wooden huts for staff and trainees. First users were newly formed No 44 Reserve Squadron (re-named No 44 Training Squadron in May 1917). They arrived on 13 November 1916, and brought along Avro 504s, DH 4s, and RE7s. Harlaxton's training career now began.

In 1917 a number of training units passed through. From a Flight of 54 Training Squadron (TS), No 3 Training Depot Station (TDS) formed here on 22 August 1917. On 22 September 1917 No 26 TS (ex-44 Squadron) arrived and stayed until February 1918. November 1917 saw the arrival of No 20 TS which, along with No 53 TS, and which moved in on 6 December 1917, amalgamated on 15 August 1918 to form No 40 Training Depot Station which also embraced No 64 TS which had arrived on 12 December 1917. As a result of training re-organisation in 1918 stations became known as Training Depot Stations, Harlaxton becoming designated No 40 TDS which functioned until disbandment on 8 May 1919. By then the station had seen a wide assortment of aircraft including DH4s, 5s and 6s, a variety of Avro 504s, RE8s. The site was soon given over to agriculture.

Review of the site in the 1930s led to it being rejected for major development. Instead, it was prepared in 1939 for use as a Relief Landing Ground for 12 FTS Grantham/Spitalgate which started using it soon after war began. Ansons and Battle trainers, Harts and Oxfords, all droned around the circuit.

On 1 April 1942 with much flying training taking place overseas, 12 FTS became 12 (P)AFU with much of the flying involving Oxfords. In 1943 Blenheim Is, IVs and unwanted Vs were introduced. During the autumn these heavier aircraft badly damaged the grass landing grounds here and at Spitalgate and a temporary home had to be found for 12 (P)AFU.

Once the grass areas had dried out and been repaired 12 (P)AFU returned to Spitalgate with their Oxfords, Blenheims and Ansons, and made use of Harlaxton until February 1945. Their successor, No 17 SFTS Cranwell, used it between May 1945 and June 1947 for Harvards and Oxfords. Precious little remains of the site just north of Little Ponton and near Grantham bypass.

Main features:
Runways: NNW/SSE 1,300 yards, WSW/ENE 1,300 yards, SW/NE 1,300 yards, grass. Modified Mk II lighting system. *Hangars:* fourteen 69ft Blister type, four 65ft Blister type. *Hardstandings:* nil. *Accommodation:* 1 officer, 16 SNCOs, 219 ORs. Administrative and technical sites along the western edge of aerodrome.

HETHEL, Norfolk

52°33N/01°10E 160ft asl; TL150000. 4 miles SE of Wymondham, NE of Wreningham

Charles Noel has good cause to remember Hethel. He was a gunner aboard B-50D 48-286 of the 342nd Bomb Sqn, 97th Bomb Group, and flown by 1st Lieutenant James P Young when it left Biggs AFB, El Paso, Texas on the night of 5 March 1951. They flew to Gander from where, despite slight fuel leaks, they departed on 7 March. After passing the point of no return No 3 engine began losing oil and fuel leaks became worse. By the time they reached England, their destination (Lakenheath) was fog bound forcing them to seek an alternative for landing. With fuel state very low they decided to make an emergency landing and in poor light, put down on what turned out to be a closed airfield. They missed the runway and as a result the port horizontal stabiliser struck the control tower causing damage to both items. '286' slithered to a halt, but the crew were uninjured. Although front line flying at Hethel ceased in 1946 it was still in better state than most because of its post-war standby classification.

Americans were not the only foreigners to use Hethel. Although they fought so courageously during WWII, the Poles were dealt cruel blows when peace descended. They found it impossible to return to the country they adored, for had they done so most would have suffered mercilessly. Many Poles elected to stay in the RAF or remain in Britain. Two Mustang squadrons, Polish-manned, were stationed at Hethel while the future of their personnel was decided.

Construction of Hethel began late 1941 and although far from complete it housed the ground echelon, USAAF 20th Bomb Group (Medium), but for only ten days, 12-21 November 1942. They subsequently joined their B-26 Marauders which had flown direct to north-west Africa. A few Americans remained at Hethel running their Station 114 while it was completed for heavy bombers.

On 11 June 1943 the 389th Bomb Group arrived, the third in Europe flying B-24Ds. The Group – trained for high-level bombing – had barely settled in when they began practising low-level attack. Quite suddenly and secretly the B-24s quit East Anglia for Benghazi on 3 July and on 9 July began bombing targets in Sicily, Italy and Crete. Operational culmination came on 1 August 1943 when they were one of the three Groups which undertook the hazardous long distance, low-level attack on Rumania's Ploesti oil fields. This brought to 2nd Lieutenant Lloyd H Hughes a Medal of Honor for, although his B-24 was seriously battered and petrol streamed forth, he pressed on to bomb as ordered. Before he was able to land the aircraft it crashed, his high courage being suitably rewarded.

On 13 August the 389th again struck deeply this time at Austria's Wienar Neustadt Messerschmitt factory. They returned to Britain on 25 August 1943 and flew their first operation from Hethel on 7 September 1943 as Operation *Starkey* was unfolding. Barely had they settled in when once more the 389th and its B-24Ds were, on 19 September, sent back to Tunisia to support the Salerno landing. Neither needed or suitable for the prime task, they carried out raids on Italy, Corsica and again on Wienar Neustadt.

When the 389th returned to Hethel on 3 October it was for permanence and re-arming with better defended B-24H/J Liberators of which they held thirty-seven by 26 October. Then began a long, intensive campaign of day bombing that continued until 21 April 1945 and from which over 100 B-24s failed to return. Operational tasks included raids on Berlin, bombing tactical targets during the Normandy landings and break-out at St-Lô, supply dropping during the Nijmegen landing and again during the Rhine assault. At the time of the D-Day landings Group strength stood at fifty-eight B-24s. When the very last landing from operations was made the 389th had flown 351 operations (307 from the UK). On 30 May 1945 the long trek home began.

B-24J-25-CF 42-99982 of the 566th BS, 389th BG airborne from Hethel. (USAF)

Many stations vacated by the Americans were quickly run down, but not Hethel which passed to Fighter Command on 25 June 1945. It had been chosen as a base for some of the RAF's five-squadron strong long-range fighter force.

First to arrive, from Bentwaters on 5 September 1945, was No 126 Squadron flying Mustang IIIs and a few IVs. Next day came Spitfire XVIs of 65 Squadron, and No 12 Group was running the show. Post-war cuts soon surfaced and the intended force fell to four squadron level with No 126 Squadron's disbandment on 10 March 1946, their remnants staying till late April.

Further contraction led to No 65 Squadron moving to Horsham St Faith on 15 March to re-arm with Hornets once their serious handling problems were cured.

With both squadrons gone, the Polish Resettlement Corps squadrons replaced them with Mustang IVs in 303 and Mk IIIs in No 316 Polish Squadrons. They also brought along a few Harvards for conversion flying. Their mid-March arrival coincided with times of considerable change, Hethel's two satellites (East Wretham and Fersfield) having been placed on C&M. Late March 1946 saw a plan for Hethel to be an active permanent post-war station. For the present the two Polish squadrons would remain, with Hethel being part of the Eastern Sector 12 Group. November 1946 saw first the decision to re-establish the station to accommodate five short-range day fighter squadrons. That was soon countermanded – it would close under Sector re-organisation.

Hethel was home for RAF Mustangs including Mk IIIs of No 126 Squadron.

Gradually the Poles were dispersed or left the Service, and both squadrons disbanded on 11 December 1946. Hethel was placed on C&M on 6 January 1947. On 10 March 1947 HQ Eastern Sector was re-established at Coltishall which had also been in Polish hands and with them now gone Hethel was left to be to run down during 1947. By the middle of that year it was serving as a Personnel Transit Centre, then Technical Training Command possessed it. Next year, although Inactive, it was listed as a Standby Airfield remaining so within Plan G of February 1951. For that reason it was many years before it was declared surplus.

In 1964 Lotus Cars established a base here where use of two runways has proven ideal for high speed testing.

Main features:
Runways: 240° 6,000ft, 300°, 350°, concrete partially completed with wood chips and tarmac. *Hangars:* three T2. *Hardstandings:* fifty loop type. Personnel (US): 443 officers, 2,529 enlisted men.

HONINGTON, Suffolk

52°20N/00°46E 174ft asl; TL890755. 3 miles E of A134 S of Thetford

Maintaining the V-Force transcended all else. Those RAF stations selected as V-bomber bases underwent very extensive modifications in respect of operational, technical and domestic requirements. A concrete ORP able to hold four bombers upon which they sat angled for rapid getaway was built to left or right of a runway at least 9,000ft long. Taxiways leading to it needed to be widened, and strengthened for a loaded Vulcan 2 or Victor weighed around 320,000lb. Dispersed hardstandings in many cases needed similar attention although plans to build a huge hardened shelter for each bomber were dropped. The bombers were intended to be on their way before an attack could be made upon them making shelters superfluous. Major servicing could be undertaken in existing hangars.

The great increase in personnel numbers required similar attention. Accommodation was needed for crews on alert state, and new briefing areas and electronics centres were constructed, along with an extremely secure compound in which nuclear weapons could be safely stored. Improved and increased accommodation was provided for all ranks, single or married. At Honington the fine extension to the restaurant in the Officers' Mess was necessary when so many were stationed here.

Those days which lasted for less than a decade have been supplanted by a much slimmed down air force geared to tactical and 'peacekeeping' instead of strategic operations. Modern wars are likely to be too short for long term effects to have much bearing on a campaign unlike yesteryear and as evidenced by Honington's first offensive operation.

It began mid-afternoon on 4 September 1939, the day after war broke out. Six Wellingtons and crews of IX Squadron set off from Honington to participate in the first bombing raid of the war, an attack on warships off Brunsbüttel. Leading was Squadron Leader Lamb, whose section was met by nine Bf 109s which shot down his two wing men. This was a beginning and an end being the only time when pre-war Wellington Is with fixed turrets operated from Honington.

Honington was one of the first Permanent RAF Stations to be built under Expansion Scheme 'A' announced in July 1934, and its finish was more elaborate than later such stations. Land for the aerodrome was purchased from the Duke of Grafton and local farmers. Additions included Hall Farm, Fakenham (300 acres), Hall Farm Honington, Rymer Farm and Troston Farm. Land preparation began in 1934, building construction in 1935. Assigned to No 3 Group, SHQ Honington opened on 3 May 1937. The first squadrons in were Nos 77 and 102, which arrived on 7 July 1937. The former temporarily used Audaxes before rearming with Wellesleys in November. No 102, which transferred to Driffield on 11 July 1938, flew Heyfords. No 77 moved out on 25 July 1938, both squadrons having departed to join the new No 4 Group and rearm with Whitleys. On 11 July 1938 No 75 Squadron replaced them and brought along Harrows, more of which arrived on 25 July in the hands of 215 Squadron.

Handley Page Harrow K6987 of No 75 Squadron, Honington, alongside Wellington 1 L4231 NH-P of No 38 Squadron Marham. Photographed at Debden's 1939 Empire Air Day. (Keith Braybrooke Archives)

No 75 Squadron's role changed when on 1 March 1939 it became a 3 Group Pool Squadron, an operational training formation whose Harrows were now supplemented with Anson navigation and bombing trainers. In mid-July 1939 No 75 Squadron moved to Stradishall in an exchange with No IX Squadron, which brought to Honington the first of very many Wellingtons. No IX, which remained here until departure commenced on 7 August 1942, finally cleared the station in September 1942. No 215 Squadron had begun equipping with Wellingtons in July 1939 and, as a second Pool Squadron, departed for Bassingbourn during the last week of September 1939.

No IX Squadron's Wellington operations were a microcosm of Bomber Command's war effort. Flying Mk 1as, the first of which was received on 6 September 1939, the squadron commenced North Sea shipping sweeps on 9 November and took part in December's most disastrous action. On 18 December 1939 – the day after the last Wellington 1 left the squadron – nine of its Wellingtons were part of a twenty-four-strong formation despatched to seek German warships off Wilhelmshaven. Enemy fighters, alerted by radar, pounced upon the bombers concentrating on beam attacks. Half the entire force was shot down, including six of IX Squadron whose crews claimed two Bf 110s. As a consequence Bomber Command – apart from 2 Group – switched to night operations.

On 8 April 1940 a new No 215 Squadron reformed at Honington and equipped with Wellington 1as. On 22 May it was absorbed by 11 OTU, which, on 17 April 1940, emerged from the Bassingbourn 215 Squadron.

In April 1940 No IX joined 115 Squadron to form a two-week detachment with Coastal Command at Lossiemouth for hectic operations over Scandinavia. Then from Honington they supported maritime operations off Norway until 10 May 1940 when the Germans launched their blitzkrieg in the west. No IX Squadron had received its first Wellington 1c on 2 March 1940, a version on squadron strength until 23 March 1942. During summer 1940 the Wellingtons made night attacks on Germany, which commenced on 15 May with a raid on a Ruhr target.

The extent of the catastrophe in France was evident at Honington when remnants of Nos 103 and 105 Fairey Battle Squadrons arrived here in June-July. Soon after, more newcomers appeared, Czech airmen who came from France via Cosford to fight with the Allies. Most were unable to understand English, and while their own air force had been quite good they had much to learn. They were grouped in a new squadron, No 311 (Czech), formed at Honington on 29 July 1940. To assist, three Anson navigation trainers were used, and they received operational training under famous Flt Lt P C Pickard, a tall Yorkshireman ever to be seen with Ming, his sheepdog. No 311 moved to the stations' satellite airfield, East Wretham, on 16 September 1940. Nos IX and 311 Squadrons, operating alongside, made use of both airfields. On 23 September 1940 three crews of 311 Squadron took off from Honington, as part of a 129-bomber force, to attack Berlin. All three crews were thought to have reached and attacked the city. While returning, Pilot Officer Trofacek's aircraft developed engine trouble, forcing him to crash-land in the Netherlands. Unharmed, the crew escaped, whereas the captured Wellington was soon flying in German hands.

With Italy in the war, night raids involved incredibly long, cold journeys, as in December 1940 when IX Squadron ventured to a target near Venice. In January 1941 Turin was a target. On 31 March 1941 the squadron dropped incendiaries on Emden as markers for the crew of 149 Squadron who were first to drop a 4,000lb bomb.

Mid-March 1941 brought increased potency to Honington with the arrival of two Type 423 Merlin-engined Wellington Mk IIs (W5434 and W5445), each of which, plagued with problems, was able to carry one 4,000lb 'cookie' bomb. The Mk IIs remained in use only until 2 August 1941. The first delivery by IX Squadron was to Cologne on 3 May 1941. Attacks on Germany were interspersed with frequent visits to the *Scharnhorst* and *Gneisenau* in Brest.

On 18 June 1941 IX Squadron became the first to receive a Hercules-powered Wellington III (X3222). The Commanding Officer, Wing Commander K M W Wasse – demonstrating this version's superior take-off to another pilot – gave a 'thumb's up'. His companion misunderstood and retracted the undercarriage too soon, and the new bomber, instead of getting airborne, ended its run awkwardly posing in a corner of the airfield. The Mk III was first operated on 12 September 1941, the new version thereafter coming into general use. At the end of the year operations tailed off while the Wellingtons were fitted with *Gee*, following which came a period of intensive training.

Wellington 1c of IX Squadron at Honington 1941. Black paintwork differed widely between 3 Group's aircraft in 1941.

Well aware of Honington's importance and usage, the enemy directed at least sixteen attacks upon it, far more than most airfields received. The first occurred on 7/8 June 1940 when a Heinkel He 111 dropped ten bombs, which impacted to the west. On 18/19 June an He 111 dropped a salvo of bombs 1 mile from the station, while another Heinkel, 5J+AM, which tried to attack several bomber bases, was shot down by the combined fire from a Duxford Spitfire and a Blenheim of 23 Squadron.

During the 1940-1941 period of assaults the Army ground defenders claimed three enemy raiders, a remarkably high total. The closest bombs so far fell at 05.08hrs on 10 July 1940, two HE bombs overshooting to explode in a nearby cornfield. A Do 17Z of II/KG3, whose crew was also trying to bomb Honington, was chased away then shot down near Winterton by Spitfires of 66 Squadron.

Far more effective were two cloud-cover attacks on 19 August 1940. One bomb exploded on the parade ground, killing eight men and damaging the Airmen's Mess. Later that day a Barrack Block, Building 76, received a hit, causing more casualties, and E Hangar was hit too. At 15.55hrs on 16 September, as Wellingtons of 311 Squadron were arriving to prepare for their first night operation, a Do 17Z bombed the station. A sharp attack developed on 27 October 1940, a cold and damp afternoon when, from Dorniers scudding among low clouds, thirty-six bombs fell on or near to the station. This time E Hangar was set on fire, a Wellington was destroyed, two were damaged and three airmen were killed.

On 8 November, as two Wellingtons were landing, a Ju 88 machine-gunned buildings. Ignoring orders not to do so, Private Sudbury, manning a station defence machine-gun, opened fire, getting a shot into the heart of the 88's pilot. The bomber crashed near D Hangar. Sudbury was reprimanded, but later awarded a Military Medal for his part in the raider's downfall.

Spasmodic day and night attacks continued into 1941, a Czech and three other men being killed when on 5 January a Do 17Z delivered a low attack at 10.35hrs. Two days later Honington was twice bombed in daylight, HEs falling near Station Sick Quarters, on SHQ and close to the Guardroom. Most spectacular of all was a raid around dusk on 10 February. Roaming the area were nineteen Do 17Zs of III/KG2, their crews briefed to attack 3 Group bomber bases at the time when their Wellingtons were known to be setting out on operations. U5+BN bombed Honington at 18.55hrs and its crew, seeing fires, called in their companions. Between them the raiders dropped forty-one HEs, setting heathland ablaze, yet the attack was far from very damaging.

Bombs fell in nearby woodland at 11.43hrs on 11 February, from a Do 17Z of II/KG2. On 18 February He 111 A1+CM, roaming over West Suffolk, dropped bombs that damaged two Wellingtons and put the aerodrome temporarily out of use. During its departure the raider ran into a salvo of parachute and cable rocket weapons fired from Watton. Wires ensnared its wings and ailerons, bringing it to ground in one of the few such successful encounters. The last bombs known to have fallen on the airfield came from a Ju 88C night intruder on 8/9 May 1941. Although German night-fighters operated around the station in March and April 1945, they did not attack.

Between 5 and 12 January 1942 Wellingtons and crews of No 214 Squadron were here for *Gee* training, and soon the bomber offensive took on much increased momentum and effectiveness. Concentrated operations began in March 1942, IX Squadron participating in heavy onslaughts upon Essen, Lubeck and Rostock. For May's Cologne 'thousand bomber' raid, fourteen IX Squadron Wellingtons operated from Honington, two failing to return. In the Essen *Millennium* operation fourteen again participated, and sixteen during the Bremen raid of 25 June. That was the largest number of Wellingtons ever despatched by the squadron on one raid. Operations, some including the dropping of 4,000lb bombs from Mk III Wellingtons fitted with Type 423 gear, continued until August 1942 when the last of 2,458 Wellington sorties from Honington was flown. On 8 August No IX moved out of 3 Group and into 5 Group at Waddington, there to re-equip with Lancasters. The last Wellington III left Honington on 22 August.

As at many East Anglian bomber bases, blind approach training was undertaken. On 1 January 1941 No 5 Blind Approach Training Flight formed here, and became No 1505 BAT Flight in September. Oxfords also served with No 1513 Flight, formed at Honington on 21 September 1941.

Soon it was 'all change', for the Yanks were coming. On 14 September 1942 the first of them moved in, an advance party of the 9th Air Depot. The original intention was to use Honington as a depot for US fighters. Instead, it opened as a major modification and overhaul depot for bombers, particularly B-17s of the 3rd Air Division. By 1 January 1943 1,890 US personnel were on the base, which officially passed from the RAF to the USAAF on 29 April 1943. On 6 September 1943 it became the 1st Strategic Air Depot to where damaged B-17s were flown on return from operations if their undercarriage would not lower, making a crash-landing inevitable. These aircraft were then repaired. It was easier to fly them in than to bring them here by road. Some 400 had crash-landed by 29 June 1944. Modifications undertaken included installation of a .50-inch machine-gun in the noses of the Fortresses.

Important as all the tasks were, a greater need was the provision of stronger fighter cover for day-raiding US bombers. A 6,000ft steel mat runway was laid over the existing main grass runway, and taxiways were provided to link seventy-five new hardstands. Nine blister hangars were erected, along with other temporary buildings. Honington had tripled in area by the time the 364th Fighter Group brought along its P-38J Lightnings on 10 February 1944. Employed in a long-range escort role, the Group first operated on 3 March 1944. Losses were heavy as much due to technical problems as combat. A force of thirty-two P-38s of the 364th gave withdrawal support to B-24s participating in the 6 March 1944 Berlin operation, the most costly of all 8th AF raids. Only one Honington P-38 was, however, lost.

P-38s of the 383rd FS, 364th FG Honington in open combat formation. (via Roger Freeman)

On 15 April 1944 the Lightnings, as part of a 616-aircraft force, undertook their first strafing of German airfields. It cost the Group seven aircraft out of a total of thirty-two lost. Such operations continued into summer, and after the Group provided top cover for Allied ships assembling off the Isle of Wight on 5 June for the D-Day landings.

The last P-38 operation was flown on 29 July 1944 and already P-51Ds had arrived for the Group. Ground strafing missions continued, as well as bomber support. Also based here were P-51Ds of the 1st Scouting Force of the 3rd Air Division. Their task was to fly ahead of bomber formations to report on weather conditions and German fighter activity.

To the end of 1944 both units fought and patrolled, the 364th on 27 December 1944 earning a DUC. On 31 December, during a Hamburg bombing raid, its fighters were credited with almost half the German aircraft shot down that day. Honington's fighters were active during the Battle of the Bulge and the Rhine crossing. Their last combat came on 19 April when they shot down four Fw 190s. On 25 April 1945 they flew their final mission, the 342nd flown, during which they claimed 449½ enemy aircraft for a loss of 134.

The 364th remained until autumn, gradually disposing of its aircraft. Remaining personnel departed for the USA aboard the *Queen Mary* on 4 November 1945 and the Group was de-activated on 10 November. US forces retained Honington until 26 February 1946 when General Emil Kiel passed the station's keys to Air Marshal Sir James Robb, and so the RAF retrieved Honington. It took place at the time of Sir Winston Churchill's dramatic Fulton speech in which he spoke of 'an iron curtain' descending across Europe.

Transport Command took control of the station on 28 February 1946 and No 1 Transport Aircraft Modification Unit opened on 1 April to support 46 Group. On 15 July 1946 1 TAMU became the Transport Command Major Servicing Unit, supplying spares and equipment to transport bases. To speed delivery, a detachment of 77 Squadron operated from here in December and was replaced by part of 62 Squadron in January 1948. A 46 Squadron detachment remained until unit disbandment on 31 March 1950. The TAMU played an important part in backing Transport Command's contribution to the Berlin Airlift, and in particular the RAF's Dakota contingent in Germany

Also here was the Transport Command Signals Training Unit formed on 1 April 1946, which functioned until June 1947, during which period 200 signallers were trained. It later reopened for a brief spell.

Honington returned to Bomber Command in 1949. Between 31 March and 1 September 1950 No 94 MU used the site for storage of ammunition and bombs. In June 1954 Barnham Camp was established to become a Special Storage Area handling atomic weapons. In September 1956 No 94 MU moved out to Barnham. During this period the present 9,000ft x 200ft concrete runway was built and replaced the metal runway laid in 1943. Other major changes were also made, producing a larger base.

Now came the first jet bombers, a fleet of Canberra B2s of XV, 44 and 57 Squadrons in February 1955, the Wing being completed when 10 Squadron came from Scampton in May 1955. A chance spotting of an albino pheasant nearby gave the Canberra squadrons a motif appropriate to the area. Copied as a tail badge, each squadron's aircraft carried had the white tail emblem outlined in their chosen colour.

Some of the Canberras were detached to the Middle East in late summer 1956 for operation *Musketeer*. Nos 10 and XV Squadrons each sent eight B2s to Nicosia, two crews from each squadron participating in the 26 October opening bombing raid on Cairo International Airport. Other pairs bombed Almaza and another five Kabrit. A further twenty-six sorties were flown during the conflict.

Build up of the V-Force was then underway and barely had 'Suez' passed when wind down of the Canberra force began. No 57 Squadron left Honington in November 1956, 10 Squadron disbanded in January 1957, XV in April and 44 in July. All were to re-equip with V-bombers.

On 1 November 1956 No 7 Squadron moved in and in December 1956 the first Valiant 'interim' V-bombers reached the station. Honington soon held a major part of the V-Force for No 90 Squadron reformed at the station on 1 January 1957, also to fly Valiants. Further strengthening came when No 199 Squadron reformed on 1 October 1957 to operate Valiants and Canberras as specialised electronic warfare aircraft. No 199 was short lived here for on 15 December 1958 it disbanded, its role and expertise being taken over next day by a new 18 Squadron at Finningley. There was, between 1 January 1958 and mid-1959 a USAF presence here, a detachment 99 Aviation Depot Squadron, SAC, which moved to Hemswell.

Canberra B2 WJ616 of No 199 Squadron.

To complete the Honington V-bomber contingent, No 57 Squadron reformed on 1 January 1959 and 55 Squadron on 1 September 1960. Victor B1a bombers were flown by both. On 1 September 1960, with Wittering now ready for V-bombers, No 7 Squadron moved there.

As at all V-force stations security was viciously tight for nuclear stores were to hand. With the potential foe possessing IRBMs the large British fighter force had been largely replaced by the V-Force making it as vital as a defensive as an attack weapon. Had it ever been launched to attack the V-Force would have been the first element of the Western strategic bomber force to bomb the USSR. It would also have heralded world destruction. High alert postures and many exercises were held.

Switching the main nuclear deterrent task to the Navy, because mobile deep-water submarines could so well disguise themselves, brought about the end of the V-Force. Nevertheless, Nos 55 and 57 Victor Squadrons retained a future, for they were chosen to operate their aircraft in an IFR role after the Valiant was withdrawn from that duty. Both departed to Marham, 55 on 24 May 1965 and 57 on 1 December 1965.

Honington was held on Care and Maintenance between 1965 and 1969. During 1967 it was earmarked as a base for RAF F-111Ks until cancellation on 16 January 1968. Work then started on preparing the station for an alternative, RAF Blackburn Buccaneer maritime attack squadrons. Honington became Active again on 1 January 1969. Not until 1 October 1969 did 12 Squadron form, receiving its first four aircraft that day.

From March 1970 squadrons of the Central Reconnaissance Establishment made use of Honington while Wyton's runway was attended to. That brought in ten Canberra PR 7s of 58 Squadron, eight Valiants of 543 Squadron and ten more assorted Canberras all continuing operations. A second Buccaneer squadron, No XV, reformed here on 1 October 1970 for low-level overland operations, and moved to Laarbruch in January 1971. To supply more crews, No 237 OCU, equipped with Buccaneers and Hunters, opened at Honington in 1 Group on 1 March 1971.

Fiscal stringency dictated that Honington become the shore base for the Navy's 809 Buccaneer Squadron. Crews for more RAF Buccaneer squadrons were soon in training and, in October 1974, 208 Squadron became the second operational Buccaneer squadron at Honington.

It was during this period that an unmistakable sound rent the Suffolk air and started to do so on 1 April 1971 when No 204 Squadron reformed and equipped with early warning Shackleton 2s. Their stay was brief for they disbanded on 28 April, the aircraft then going to Lossiemouth and 8 Squadron.

In April 1978 No 809 Squadron embarked for the last time on HMS *Ark Royal*. A fourth Buccaneer squadron, No 216, formed on 1 July 1979 and equipped with Buccaneer S.2B maritime strike aircraft. January 1980 saw preparations start for the stationing of Tornado Interdictor/Strike General Reconnaissance aircraft at Honington. They came at a time of considerable concern over the future of the Buccaneer force following a crash in North America attributed to metal fatigue. All Buccaneers were grounded for examination between February and August 1980, and some were written off. The force was completely reorganised, 216 Squadron being disbanded in August 1980. Their aircraft were absorbed by 12 Squadron split as 12 (South) at Honington and 12 (North) at Lossiemouth. The former element joined the latter in December 1980.

A works programme for Tornado included building two groups of Hardened Aircraft Shelters (HAS), each one able to accommodate two Tornados. The first of these, a GR Mk 1, arrived on 29 June 1981 for the Tornado Weapons Conversion Unit (TWCU), formed at Honington in 1 Group on 3 August 1981. Training was initiated on 8 January 1982. After learning to operate Tornado GR 1s at TTTE Cottesmore, crews undertook a 13-week weapons training course at TWCU. It included 32 hours of pilot training and 29½ hrs for the navigator. Practised were lay down, dive, loft bombing, strafing profiles and auto terrain following flying involving day and night practice. Included was an air combat phase involving formation simulated attacks and low-level evasion. Instructors were also trained, to carry out standards checks on Tornado squadrons.

A Buccaneer S2 of No 809 Squadron at Honington. Although an unusual siting, Fleet Air Arm aircraft have often used East Anglian bases.

No IX Squadron reformed at its old home on 1 June 1982 and operated from the northern HAS area until 1986 when it moved to Germany. To accommodate more Tornados the Buccaneers all moved to Lossiemouth, No 12 Squadron in October 1982, No 208 Squadron in July 1983, and No 237 OCU in October 1984.

Further change came on 1 January 1984 when the TWCU was re-named No 45 (Reserve) Squadron, and renumbered No XV (Reserve) Squadron on 1 April 1992 before it moved to Lossiemouth.

On 1 January 1990 No 13 Squadron reformed with Tornado GR 1A reconnaissance bombers, which also had nuclear capability. Although with only two-thirds crew strength, the squadron was placed on standby in August 1990. The squadron had a vital low-level night intelligence gathering role, a daylight attack and reconnaissance role, and practised in-flight refuelling and particularly lone TFR night operations for better protection.

Crews were deployed on 15/16 January 1991 – shortly before the start of *Desert Storm* – to work with II Squadron, the reconnaissance Wing at Dharhan holding six Tornados. The threat from Scud missiles, particularly for attacking Israel, was taken very seriously and several launch sites were found during the early nights of the conflict. Operations were centred on eastern Iraq and included operations to identify Iraq Army units. Tornado GR 1As flew lone sorties to the end of the war, No XIII Squadron using TIALD. Four of its aircraft were deployed to Tabak and by the end of the conflict XIII had flown seventy-two TIALD sorties without loss. Some 200 Honington personnel supported them. An advanced imaging system was being phased in when, in February 1994, No 13 moved to Marham. Although the station later hosted Harriers, F-15s, Jaguars and helicopters for exercises or as lodgers while runway repairs were undertaken at their home bases, Honington ceased to be a regularly active flying station. The '24-7' Honington Air Traffic Control Zone ceased to function.

Tornado GR 1a of XIII Squadron shelters within Honington HAS No 45.

Now the station started a new and increasingly important part of its life, as the RAF Regiment HQ Depot. It administered six regular RAFR squadrons (Nos 1, 2, 3, 34, 51 and 63), as well as the Royal Auxiliary Air Force Regiment's squadrons at home and when temporarily serving abroad. Its current role is Force Protection of UK air assets at home and overseas. The 'airmen' – known as 'gunners' – have seen service wherever the RAF has been operationally deployed – Ulster, Belize, Sierra Leone and, of course, Iraq and Afghanistan, where members of the Regiment serving courageously have given their lives while protecting the RAF. Honington is home to about 2,000 civilian and military personnel in addition to others attending training courses.

On 1 April 1999 No 27 Squadron, RAFR, and No 1 Royal Tank Regiment merged here to become the Joint Chemical Biological Radiological Nuclear Regiment, and in so doing formed the first truly dual-service front-line unit. It now has the vital responsibility of manning and managing the Bio Detective Capability force.

No 1 Squadron RAFR at Honington is a high state readiness squadron always with a tough training programme. The Queen's Colour Squadron of the Royal Air Force, part of the RAFR and based in the London area, operates as No 63 Squadron, RAFR, in which guise it has served in Iraq, the Falklands, the Far East and Kuwait.

Now a very important part of the RAF's front line are its auxiliary members, some of whom man No 2623 (East Anglian) Squadron, RAuxAF Regiment, based at Honington. Their Squadron Honorary Air Commodore is Sir Michael Marshall CBE DL FRAeS of Marshall Aerospace. The squadron was formed on 1 July 1979 to provide Station ground defence, and for fifteen years was specifically tasked to prevent Soviet special forces from disrupting flying operations. No 2623 disbanded as a field squadron on 18 April 1994 following cessation of regular flying at Honington. Re-formed on 1 June 1995, it provided centralised training for RAFR field squadrons before that role was taken on by Training Wing, Honington, at the end of 1997. October 1998 saw the unit's mix of regulars and auxiliaries switch to operating Rapier missiles, with which it was declared operational in April 2001. In May 2003 the unit moved to the Falklands to augment 16 Squadron

View of Honington taken during the station's air show on 27 June 1992.

RAFR as Resident Rapier Squadron during 2003. Further role change came in 2004 as a result of the Defence Review, following which it adopted its present Force Protection role. Personnel, with the usual soldiering skills expected of every member of a Regiment Field Squadron, are associated with the Joint CBRN Regiment, and work alongside No 27 Squadron, RAFR.

Flying has not entirely ended at Honington, where RAF Hercules transports and helicopters occasionally call.

Main features (December 1944):
Runways: 280° 6,000ft x 120ft steel matting. Grass: NE/SW and SE/NW both 4,200ft. *Hangars:* five Type C, nine Blister. *Hardstandings:* seventy-five concrete. Accommodation (USAAF): 190 officers, 1,519 enlisted men. Numerous post-war modifications included the lengthened asphalt/concrete main 09/27 runway lengthened to 9,012ft (9,308ft with overruns) and later fitted with RHAG. For FAA use dummy deck markings were applied.

HORHAM, Suffolk

52°18N/01°14E 180ft asl; TM205728. By B1117 at Horham, 8 miles E of Eye

For several weeks after the Japanese attacked Pearl Harbour the 47th Bomb Group patrolled off the west coast of America. Then they trained for overseas duties, the airborne echelon moving to Horham in September 1942. In late October other elements began transfer in ships to French Morocco. By the end of September only eight of the A-20s had reached Horham, but by early November 1942 nineteen were on strength and at the end of the month the 47th's aircraft were flown out to join the main body at Mediouna. Steady improvement of Horham followed.

On 12 May 1943 the 323rd Bomb Group arrived for a short stay lasting until 14 June when Earls Colne accepted them and their fourteen non-operational B-26s. Replacing the 323rd next day came twenty-nine B-17Fs of the 95th Bomb Group, 3rd BD, transferring from incomplete Framlingham. They resumed operations in July 1943 and actively participated in the strategic bombing offensive. On 17 August 1943 twenty-one B-17Fs set forth as part of the Regensburg shuttle bombing raid and for maintaining tight formation in the face of sustained enemy fighter attack resulting in four B-17s being shot down, the Group received a Distinguished Unit Citation. A second such citation was awarded for a similar courageous action on 10 October 1943 when Munster was the target. Fierce enemy response cost five of twenty B-17s.

On 4 March 1944 only thirty B-17s of the 13CBW (including the 95th BG) out of the 238 B-17s of the 3BD which set forth actually bombed Berlin, the remainder being forced back by bad weather. The 95th became the first US 8th AAF Group to bomb Berlin which they did in spite of the snowstorms, dense clouds and severe enemy attack. As a result they were awarded a third DUC. With fifty-three B-17s serviceable and nine unserviceable they were well equipped for their part in the Normandy D-Day assault. On 18 September 1944 they undertook the last *Frantic*, a long flight to drop containers packed with food, ammunition and medical supplies to the Poles during the Warsaw uprising and then landed in the Soviet Union.

After helping in the Ardennes counter-attack and during the Rhine crossing the Group flew their final bombing mission on 20 April 1945, marshalling yards at Oranienburg being the target. They dropped food to the Dutch before conveying liberated POWs and displaced persons from Austria to France and England.

The 95th left for home between June and August 1945, Horham returning to the RAF on 9 October 1945. No 25 MU moved in and stayed until March 1946. No 262 MU which replaced slowly declined in size and faded in October 1948 when the station went to Care & Maintenance. The 1950s saw a portion of the site held in readiness for Bloodhound Mk 1 defensive missiles until the late 1950s. The entire site was, in the early 1960s, sold for civilian use. In memory of the USAAF Horham church contains a stoned shaped like a B-17s fin. On one side is engraved a 'B' (the Group letter), on the other are details of the 95th. Kneelers within the church are suitably embroidered.

Main features:
Runways: 074° 6,000ft x 150ft, 190°, 310°, concrete. *Hangars:* two T2. *Hardstandings:* fifty loop type. *Accommodation:* 443 officers, 2,524 enlisted men.

HORSHAM ST FAITH, Norfolk

52°04N/01°17W 102ft asl; TG220138. E of A140 on leaving N of Norwich

Time: 0400 hrs. Date: 31 May 1942. Racing across Horsham's grass two Merlin engines roar at maximum power and Squadron Leader Oakeshott is soon away. To him goes the distinction of taking the brilliant Mosquito bomber into action for the first time. Target: Cologne, and not long after 1,000 bombers have laid waste to the city. Main Task: a photo run across at 24,000ft ... Impossible, for smoke blots out the area, Instead, four HE bombs are released into the inferno below. Strongly enforced secrecy surrounds his Mosquito and the other seven so far in 105 Squadron's hands. What a prize for any airfield, to be operationally first with the most outstanding bomber of all time, the trend-setter so far ahead of its day.

Construction of a bomber station at Horsham St Faith on the outskirts of Norwich commenced in 1939. Like Coltishall, it had a more austere appearance than earlier Permanent Stations, large 'C' Type Aircraft Sheds for bombers having a somewhat 'incomplete' appearance and lower roofing. Barrack blocks and other buildings had protective flat roofs.

Prior to its completion, 21 Squadron's Blenheims periodically dispersed here in late 1939 for fear of sudden attack on Watton. 'Horsham', generally known thus or as 'St Faiths', then lay dormant until 10 May 1940 when it burst into life as a well-placed fighter station. The effectiveness of the German attack on Holland was met at Duxford by the immediate forward movement of much of 264 Squadron, whose Defiants operated for the first time on 12 May from Horsham where Station HQ opened on 1 June 1940.

In France No 114 Squadron had been quickly decimated, its remnants returning to Wattisham where they tarried until 10 June when Horsham was ready for them. The squadron there renewed its association with Blenheim IVs before heading out to a new home at Oulton, Horsham's satellite. Serving in France with No 114, No 139 Squadron had also been mauled. They re-grouped and re-equipped with Blenheims at Horsham, and for over a year waged war from Horsham making cloud cover raids, and gradually switching – via night intruder sorties – into the 1941 day *Circus* campaign and anti-shipping raids before moving to Oulton on 13 July 1941.

Another Blenheim IV squadron, No 18, replaced them flying similar operations. They delivered a new metal leg to Wing Commander Douglas Bader after he was shot down – to help him escape. In August the squadron was detached to Manston for *Channel Stop* and then went to Malta for a spell of operations. No 18 Squadron moved to Oulton on 5 November 1941. Meanwhile No 139 on 7 September returned to Horsham before moving back to the satellite to re-equip with Hudsons for Far East service. At Horsham a Ferry Training Flight opened in December 1941 and which on 21 January 1942 became No 1444 FTF which functioned here and at Oulton until late June 1942 when they left for Lyneham.

When No 139 left Horsham their place was taken on 9 December 1941 by No 105 Squadron flying Mosquito IVs. At first the Mosquitoes flew high, lone nuisance and bomber reconnaissance sorties. Next, they were employed in small groups as fast low-level strike aircraft, relying upon speed and using their long range to fly dog-legged tracks for increased immunity. From Horsham they raced across the sea to Denmark making famous attacks and at increasingly low altitudes. No 139 reformed on 8 June 1942 to operate Mosquitoes drawing upon '105s' aircraft until sufficient Mosquito IVs became available to them. Simultaneously No 139 trained using Blenheim Vs in case they were needed in north-west Africa. To aid training to operate Mosquitoes No 1655 Mosquito Conversion Unit opened on 30 August. Suddenly, an abrupt change took all the Mosquitoes to Marham when that station passed to 2 Group in September as a result of the general re-arrangement caused by the impending arrival in the UK of the USAAF.

Horsham was one of the first airfields in Britain over which the Stars and Stripes fluttered. In the first week of October 1942 the 319th Bomb Group moved in from Shipdham tarrying only until the 22nd before leaving for north-west Africa.

The airfield was clear of aircraft until early April 1943 when the 56th Fighter Group arrived bringing bulky, noisy P-47Cs, some of the first in Europe. Their operations began with a fighter sweep flown on 8 April 1943, the Group working closely with experienced pilots of Debden's 4th FG, and they flew their first bomber escort from Horsham on 4 May. Similar missions followed before they moved to Halesworth on 9 July 1943 to permit the building of three runways at Horsham.

P-47s of the 4th FG taxi out for joint operations in 1943 with 56th Fighter Group.
(Keith Braybrooke Archives)

The base re-opened in January 1944 and B-24s of the 458th Bomb Group settled in. On 24 and 25 February they began operations by flying diversions, their bombing campaign starting on 2 March 1944. Although they mainly attacked strategic targets the Group took part in raids during the run-up to D-Day, supported the assault and troops ashore and in September delivered fuel to France. As an interesting sideline they had, in May 1944, tried out radio-controlled bombs against tactical targets in France. The B-24s operated intensively until 25 April 1945 when they undertook their 240th operation.

Outskirts of Norwich beyond, B-24s of the 458th BG taxi out at Horsham on 24 December 1944. (USAF)

Brightly coloured lead-ship of the 458th BG, Horsham St Faith.

Return home came fast allowing RAF Fighter Command to take over the station on 19 July 1945. On 8 August No 307 (Polish) Squadron brought along Mosquito NF30s and 695 Squadron arrived two days later to provide target facilities around the Norfolk coast using Spitfire 16s, Oxfords and Vengeance IVs. On 15 August Mustang 3s of 64 Squadron moved in from Bentwaters and on 8 September Spitfires of 118 Squadron arrived. Horsham was now tightly packed.

Apart from the fighters also here were No 11 Group Servicing Unit, No 1004 Air Servicing Wing HQ, and No 4724 Airfield Construction Flight. Horsham in 12 Group was presently in the Coltishall Sector with Hethel and Fersfield, and cared for its satellite Matlaske which from 15 October went to C&M. It was replaced by Hardwick, a base Command favoured and which in February 1946 became part of the Norfolk Sector along with Coltishall, Hethel and Horsham.

Horsham's association with de Havilland increased on 16 February 1946 when the first Hornet 1 for an RAF squadron arrived for No 64. On 14 March No 65 Squadron joined them and took delivery of their first Hornet on 17 June 1946.

A busy time followed as both squadrons with few aircraft learnt the tricky ways of the new fighter. No 118 Squadron, instead of receiving Hornets, was disbanded on 19 March 1946. The

Norfolk Sector became Eastern Sector on 12 July 1946 and in August both Hornet squadrons left for the new long-range fighter base, Linton-on-Ouse. Within a week Meteor IIIs of 74 and 245 Squadrons from Colerne had formed the Horsham Wing completed with the arrival in September 1946 of 263 Squadron and on 15 April 1947 augmented with 257 Squadron. No 695 Squadron still busy in November 1946 saw their Vengeances begin to be progressively replaced with Martinets.

A red letter day 21 December certainly was when the first Meteor IV for a squadron was delivered to Horsham. The New Year soon saw each squadron holding two examples along with six Mk IIIs. Full re-equipment slowly came about. Meanwhile on 6 January 1947 Coltishall became Sector HQ and took control of Horsham St Faith.

Plan F of 21 January 1948 decreed that, in addition to an AAC squadron, Horsham should continue holding four short-range day fighter squadrons, each at eight UE the cadre strength. On 11 February 1949, 695 Squadron was renumbered 34 Squadron and at the time it was getting Beaufighter TT10s. Martinets were phased out in August. Much re-organisation was then taking place, 266 Squadron at Tangmere becoming No 43. No 266 Squadron's number plate was then featured by 245/266 Squadron at Horsham so that if necessary the squadron could easily split bringing '266' alive again.

Horsham was a busy Meteor base in the late 1940s to early 1950s.

During 1950 the Meteor squadrons rearmed with F.Mk 8s, '245' in July and '74' during October. Like their Mk 4s, some of the 8s by the close of that year featured in-flight refuelling probes. Trials with these commenced in May 1951, in-flight refuelling being provided by Lincoln tankers. AAR extended convoy patrol sorties and trials showed that four hour patrols could reasonably be undertaken.

Another re-arrangement of squadron came with the departure to Wattisham of 257 Squadron on 27 October 1950 and of 263 on 22 November. In August 1951 No 2 CAACU Little Snoring took over the Spitfire commitment from 34 Squadron.

December 1951 saw station establishment change to two short-range day and one night fighter squadrons. In consequence No 23 Squadron arrived on 15 January 1952 bringing Mosquito NF 36s to join Nos 74 and 245 still providing the day force with Meteor 8s.

In March 1952 No 34 Squadron disbanded, their Beaufighters joining 2 CAACU at Cambridge whilst awaiting Langham's readiness to accommodate them.

Revised plans meant that both 74 and 245 like other Meteor Squadrons must further increase in size from sixteen UE to each hold twenty-two Mk 8s in the hope that every Soviet bomber could be destroyed before even one could drop an atomic load on the UK. Plan K of January 1954 reinforcing that scheme called for only two SRD squadrons to remain at Horsham having Hethel as the standby station. No 23 Squadron therefore returned to Coltishall on 4 July 1952.

Throughout 1953-5 Meteor 8s of the Horsham Wing played a major part in the air defence of East Anglia, and between December 1954 and March 1957 the 12 Group Modification Centre functioned here backing Meteors and later became the Hunter Modification Centre at North Weald which returned to Horsham when North Weald closed.

Intention was that Supermarine Swift swept-wing fighter would undergo intensive squadron flying in the hands of No 74 Squadron. Very high hopes were pinned upon the Swift whose good duration soon led to 74 Squadron being earmarked for a move to Duxford from where Fireflash armed Swifts would operate. 'Inferior' shorter duration Hunters would instead be based at Horsham St Faith.

Alas, all did not go well for the Swift, and rather than reduce the effectiveness of a coastal placed squadron the equipment already arriving for the Swift in 1953 was moved to Waterbeach where No 56 Squadron would instead have to tackle the problems blighting the aircraft.

In 1954 as at other fighter stations work began to upgrade Horsham St Faith. A large ASP was constructed along with ORPs at the ends of the main runway where telescramble was installed. Two areas of protected dispersals were established, on the north-western and southerly edges of the airfield, and associated buildings for air and ground crews were erected.

In June 1955, 245 Squadron moved to a new Wing at Stradishall. No 23 Squadron flying Venom NF 3s returned to Horsham in October 1956 and 275 ASR Squadron arrived flying Sycamore helicopters. In March 1957, 74 Squadron re-armed with Hunter 4s, replaced by Mk 6s in November 1957. The 'tiger-marked' Hunters moved to Coltishall in June 1959 during runway re-surfacing, then returned in January 1960. Possibly as compensation for not having the Swift No 74 moved to Coltishall in August to be the first to fly Lightnings. No 23 Squadron flying Javelins from April 1957 left the station the following month. No 275 Squadron, which became a Flight of 228 Squadron on 1 September 1959, moved to Coltishall in 1960. That left 12 Group Communications Flight which flew from here between August 1959 and March 1963. During that time their companions were The Battle of Britain Flight based here from 1 November 1961 to 1 April 1963 when they moved to Coltishall. Horsham closed to flying on 1 August 1963, RAF tenure ending on 24 March 1967.Could civilian flying take place from the modernised airfield?

Aerial view of Horsham St Faith in July 1963. ORPs at both ends of main runway, on the technical site side of the runway.

An answer came in 1967 when Norfolk County Council and Norwich City Council bought the airfield together with land adjacent. They had bravely decided to develop Horsham into a regional airport. To help recover the expense they disposed of some land for industrial use. Two large hangars were sold for commercial enterprise, leaving three for aircraft maintenance. The latter were put to good purpose for aircraft renovation and protective coat spraying, the Sprayair business being taken over by Air Livery in November 2007. Former barrack blocks and the Officers' Mess were converted into halls of residence for the University of East Anglia. Demolished in 1993, they have since been replaced by a housing site.

On 30 May 1970 the airfield officially reopened. By initially catering for general light aviation, no operating licence was needed. For phase two a CAA licence was acquired, which extended the airport's use to include private and executive aircraft with a weight limitation of 6,000lb all-up. Occasionally larger aircraft used Norwich.

It was the third phase of development that much enhanced Norwich Airport. Improved facilities rendered it able to support aircraft to an all-up weight of 40,000lb and sometimes heavier. In 1970 Customs approved import and export of freight. Air traffic control was bettered by the introduction of Plessey ACR 430 radar.

It was at this time that Air Anglia was established through the amalgamation of Norfolk Airways, Rig Air and Anglia Air Charter. Holiday charter flights had already operated from Norwich after the now Category C airfield was given full customs facilities. The major advance came in June 1971 when Air Anglia began UK internal services from Norwich, serving Liverpool, Dublin, Manchester, Newcastle, Edinburgh and Aberdeen. Not only was Norwich set in an agricultural environment supplemented by light industries and major commercial enterprises, but North Sea gas and oil exploration also began to bring work to the region. Air Anglia, in responding, established links with Scotland and the Shetlands. Additional was the movement of cattle by air. Norwich also became involved in the internal UK night mail business at an early stage, but the most important forward step was the commencement on 6 December 1971 of scheduled services to Schiphol/Amsterdam, drawing upon three DC-3s. That service too had its origins in North Sea exploration and later led to links with Denmark and Norway.

During October 1971 Air Anglia, with its HQ at Norwich, moved into larger premises and established at the Airport its own maintenance depot, bonded stores and avionics section. Within a fleet of some twenty aircraft, the thirty-five-seater DC-3s were the most important, together with a nine-seater BN-2A Islander and assorted types like the Piper Aztec, Twin Comanche and Cessna 404. The company offered executive charters and in 1974 acquired Fokker F27-100/200 Friendships, which type would eventually number ten. These it used on the seasonal service to Jersey.

In 1979 Air Anglia acquired two Fokker F.28 jet aircraft. Their additional speed made viable an Aberdeen-Edinburgh-Amsterdam service. Another linked Edinburgh with Leeds and Paris. For a Norwich-Birmingham-Newquay run the company used the Piper Navajo. Its Islander was used on an early morning service from Cambridge to Norwich, where it connected with the DC-3 service to Amsterdam. Early evening saw the Islander conveying passengers from an Amsterdam run back to Cambridge. Sometimes a Piper Aztec was used.

By the end of the 1970s Air Anglia was also using Stansted. In January 1980 the company was merged with British Island Airways, Air Wales and Air Westward to form Air UK, which made use of Norwich until its main base became Stansted.

Airports are, of course, expensive and demanding to run. Their fortunes fluctuate with international events and financial swings, which makes them none too ideal for municipalities to operate. For the Norwich owners funding became easier when the 1986 Airports Act came into force, which required airports with a turnover of £1m or more to be run as Limited Companies. Norwich Airport fell into that category and its assets became entitled Norwich Airport Limited. However, the local authority was still unable to borrow money like a typical business would. Reliance had to be placed upon reinvestment of operating profits. That condition did not ease until April 1999 when an Act of Parliament removed the borrowing restriction for profitable local authority-owned regional airports. Norwich could now borrow money for development, the improved financial position enabling investment in four extensions to the terminal building

Following the establishment of Norwich Airport Limited, consideration had been given to the overall mode of operation. As a result all the terminal functions were run to provide a complete service to passengers. Baggage and cargo handling, aircraft maintenance facilities and a travel agency continued as before, but contracts were let for aircraft refuelling, catering, cleaning, car parking, retail shopping and security.

A new control tower was built on the north side of the airfield, radar cover being provided through a Marconi 511 system. Reopened in August 1995, the short 4,215ft subsidiary 04/22 runway had been completely relaid south of the main runway intersection. Its northern section was resurfaced in 1996. It was finally closed in 2006 and subsequently used as a taxiway connecting with the airport's nine aircraft stands. Runway lighting had allowed its limited use for essential night flying while improvement to the main 6,040ft 09/27 runway was undertaken. In February-March 1997 the western concrete end of runway 27 was overlaid with stone mastic asphalt. Continuing maintenance of runways and taxi-tracks was to become even more essential when the airport began to be used by heavy Boeing 757s and 767s.

Further upgrading of Norwich in 1997 saw the opening of a new workshop and improved fire station. On the west side of the airfield a four-hangar complex was built to accommodate light aircraft, and is currently home of the Norfolk Police helicopter and base of the East Anglian Air Ambulance. Flying club operation and light aircraft maintenance has been undertaken in this area.

England and Wales have air ambulance cover. BK-117 G-OEMT of the East Anglian Air Ambulance uses Cambridge, Norwich or Wyton as bases.

Winter 1998-1999 saw a £1.9m major improvement of the terminal to improve comfort and provide better and more extensive restaurant facilities. Faster passenger handling came with an increase from eight to twelve check-in desks and establishment of three gates. A business travellers' section was also opened. With these improvements in place, Norwich Airport relaunched itself in May 1999 as Norwich International.

December 2000 brought the news that National Car Parks had won a twenty-one-year contract to handle parking facilities, and that Securicor/G4S was taking over the running of airport security. October 2001 saw Air BP take over aircraft refuelling.

Cost and ever more complexity needed to run the airport resulted in the Council owners' decision in March 2004 to sell 80.1% of their business to Omniport plc. Norwich City Council and Norfolk County Council retained the remaining 19.9%.

Considerable further improvement by extending the terminal building was approved in September 2005. Costing £4.5m, it was completed in 2006 and embraced a new arrival hall and a 600-seat departure hall for domestic and international passengers. Optimistically, a throughput of one million passengers was forecast for 2010 following the recent arrival of Flybe, initially serving six destinations. The new arrival had come into being in June 2000 when British European was renamed. The shorter Flybe name was adopted in July 2002 for the low-fare airline. Overdue facelifts were also given to catering facilities, and the departure lounge was further improved. No-frills Flybe proved popular, although services to Spain and Portugal were dropped in 2006 because Stansted operators provided such services. More services to France were suggested, but Paris was to remain the sole Flybe French destination.

An important part of the airport's trade still relates to the North Sea gas and oil industry, which explains the continuing regular services to Aberdeen. Long sustained has been the Amsterdam service first run by Air Anglia and later by KLM, which has for many years used Norwich for S-61N helicopter charter flights to offshore rigs. In 2008 KLM Cityhopper flights still served Amsterdam, while SAAB 240s and Jetstreams of Eastern Airways operated services linking with Stornoway, Wick and Norway via Aberdeen, which is also served by bmi Regional.

In 2008-2009 Flybe used nine airports, having in March 2007 completed the acquisition of nearly all of British Airways' regional services, making it a strong operator. At Norwich it has been the major operator, whose scheduled flights have proven particularly attractive to business folk by giving easy access to the Channel Islands, Dublin, Edinburgh, Exeter (Flybe base), Glasgow, Manchester and Paris. Seasonal and charter holiday flights in winter and summer to Corfu, Crete, Cyprus, Majorca, Minorca, Spain, the Canaries and Turkey have been variously operated by Air Europa, Air Malta, First Choice, LTE International, Pegasus, Thomas Cook and Thomsonfly.

The City of Norwich and its environs provide a potential of 250,000 passengers, the county and adjacent areas some 1.5 million. Inevitably, Norwich International competes with Stansted, a 2-hour train ride from Norwich. In 2003 the passenger throughput was 447,000. In 2005 it rose to 545,000 and in 2006 745,000, showing a steady growth pattern before the financial crisis overtook all. Associated aircraft movement totals for the mentioned years were 52,000, 47,000 and 53,000, the latter including the use of larger aircraft. Norwich International's future largely depends upon factors beyond its control.

Main features:

Runways: 230° 6,000ft x 150ft, 280°, 350°, concrete. *Hangars:* five C Type. *Hardstandings:* fifty loop-type for bombers, six stands for fighters. *Accommodation* (USAAF): 443 officers, 2,529 enlisted men.

Places of interest nearby:

City of Norwich Aviation Museum near airport, off the A140 Cromer Road. Mousehold Heath was the site of much activity in the 1914-18 war and near was the first home of Boulton & Paul Aircraft.

IPSWICH, Suffolk

52°01N/01°11E 123ft asl; TM190415. SE of Ipswich town

On 20 October 1928 the Air Ministry, which controlled civil aviation, circulated a document suggesting that 'sooner or later every town of importance will find it necessary to have an airport like it has roads and a railway station'. Ipswich Corporation in 1929 decided to purchase a light-soil, ideal 147-acre site east of the town upon which, for £13,245, it sensibly established an airport. By the 1990s Ipswich found itself strategically situated near Britain's premier container port at Felixstowe, a grand trade centre extensively linked with Europe – indeed, with the entire world. To have in place a well-run businesslike airport close by made good sense. That seems not to have been the view of the local council, which still owned the airport.

In typical local government style, and displaying complete lack of business acumen, foresight and wisdom, Ipswich City Labour Council responded as one has come to expect. Despite very extensive and vociferous local opposition, and even ignoring the outcome of an earlier Public Enquiry – let alone the wishes of those living close to the inoffensive little airport – the Council of Ipswich wielded its axe. Local aviators reckoned the motive stemmed from spite and jealousy directed at what they perceived to be a superior and elitist organisation! Whatever its reason, it ordered the destruction of its delightful, ever-welcoming and highly popular centre for civilian flying. On 31 December 1996 it grounded the jewel in its crown, turning it into long-lasting wasteland before it emerged years later as just another housing estate.

Ipswich Airport was officially opened on 26 June 1930 by HRH the Prince of Wales. It was leased by the Suffolk & Eastern Counties Aeroplane Club based at Hadleigh Aerodrome from where hangars were brought. Those were supplemented by one from Conington, the so-called Cambridge Aerodrome, closed when Marshall's opened its Barnwell site. To succeed, Ipswich Airport needed improvement, which followed after the Whitney Straight Corporation took over the lease on it during February 1936.

A novel activity began on 20 June 1938, an enterprising 15-minute, once-daily, air taxi service to Clacton. Return fare was 9s 6d (something akin to £18 at present values). A more tangible feature was a fine, state-of-the-art terminal building designed by Hening & Chittey and ceremoniously opened on

9 July 1938 by Captain H Balfour, Under Secretary of State for Air, during the Suffolk Air Day. A new hangar, also added, was essential because the civilians were now co-operating in training the Army and Observer Corps. October 1938 saw the Civil Air Guard, a pseudo-military organisation, begin flying from here and encouraging civilians to learn to fly aided by government subsidy. No 45 E&RFTS, an RAF Volunteer Reserve flying school using a few Magisters Audaxes and Hinds, opened at Ipswich on 3 July 1939, and was barely functioning when the start of the war brought its closure.

Although Ipswich had only a grass landing ground with two grass runways each of a little over 1,000 yards, it was chosen in 1939 to be a wartime satellite for Wattisham. On 2 September 1939 Blenheim IVs of 110 Squadron arrived and returned to their base for operations. Through to March 1942 Ipswich served in like manner, Wattisham's Blenheim squadrons – mainly Nos 107 and 110 – making various use of the airfield and flying operationally from Ipswich during February-March 1941. No 1517 Blind Approach Training Flight stationed at Wattisham also made use of Ipswich.

A memorable day in its history was 12 August 1941, the date of 2 Group's brave daylight assault on two power stations near Cologne and deep for a Blenheim daylight penetration. Three Spitfire squadrons (Nos 19, 65 and 266) arrived at Ipswich beforehand and from here, led by a Blenheim of 226 Squadron, they set off to escort the Blenheim squadrons home from the Dutch coast and tangled with enemy fighters in the process. No 2 Group vacated Wattisham in March 1942 and then Ipswich became a satellite of Martlesham Heath. A succession of detachments and dispersals by aircraft of famous fighter squadrons followed, 340 Squadron being based at the station for a few days late July 1942. Each stay, for battle training, was usually short.

To provide towed targets for the fighter pilots a variety of anti-aircraft co-operation organisations were either based here or sent detachments to Ipswich. 'H' Flight, 1 AACU was here at the start of 1942 and later that year detachments came from 1488 Flight Martlesham Heath. With them came a few Lysanders, Henleys and the inevitable Oxford which all such units seemed to possess.

On 1 March 1943 Ipswich was raised to self accounting station status and it became classified as an AACU (Parent). On the 12 March, 1616 Flight and their Henley target tugs arrived from Martlesham, an advance guard of a succession of such units here to tow targets for naval gunners at Harwich. No 3 Anti-Aircraft Target Towing Flight arrived in April 1943 and on 19 June No 1499 Gunnery Flight equipped with Martinets became a lodger until absorption by 1696 Flight on 15 February 1944.

Army Co-operation Command which controlled the target towers disbanded on 1 June 1943 and during that month 3 AATT Flight was absorbed into 1627 Flight which worked with the RAF Regiment.

Summer 1943 also found a detachment of Martlesham's ASR squadron here, and in October a detachment of No 7 Anti-aircraft Co-operation Unit, flew from the station. On 6 November Auster IIIs of 652 Squadron moved in and remained at Ipswich, apart from detachments, until March 1944. When they left a naval servicing unit replaced them.

On 1 December 1943 Nos 1616 and 1627 Flights had merged to form No 679 Squadron and flew Martinets and Oxfords for anti-aircraft and searchlight co-operation duties. Rare in RAF hands were two Barracudas which joined 679 Squadron on 18 March 1944. No 1696 Bomber Defence Training Flight also arrived in March 1944 bringing Hurricanes, Spitfires and more Martinets, and also stayed until April 1945 when they moved to Gransden Lodge and Wyton. Awaiting action in France, No 658 (Air Observation Post) Squadron flew Austers here for a short time prior to D-Day.

To the end of hostilities target facilities for the Navy at Harwich were provided. The Germans helped too for in September 1944 Heinkel 111s began air-launching V-1s over East Anglia. Many crossed the coast around Felixstowe and on 1 September a V-1 fell just outside the aerodrome boundary demolishing a requisitioned house, killed an NCO and injured three more men. On 18 September another landed in a residential area 400 yards from the airfield causing many civilian casualties.

Among rare visitors to Ipswich were Cierva C30a autogiros of 529 Squadron which, in November 1944, used the station as a base for its radar calibration flights along the East Coast to improve V-1 interception by AA guns.

No 679 Squadron's operational commitment passed to 695 Squadron, Bircham Newton, on 30 June 1945 upon disbandment of the former, Ipswich being placed under on Care & Maintenance on 1 August 1945.

RAF days at Ipswich ended on 16 April 1946 although under Plan F of January 1948 there was a suggestion that in Phase III a Reserve Flying School might open here.

When the RAF left, Ipswich was taken over as a works training centre by the Ministry of Labour. Later in 1946 a group of local businessmen bought one of the new Auster Autocrats. Suffolk Aero Club was revived and acquired two Taylorcraft Plus Ds. Private flying became popular at Ipswich.

Great strides followed at Easter 1953 when East Anglian Flying Services took on the lease of Ipswich Airport. On 1 April 1954 the East Anglian Flying Club formed to use a Tiger Moth and a Proctor. More importantly, EAFS was awarded scheduled route licences in 1955 to operate an Ipswich-Channel Islands route via Southend. It also operated flights to the Channel Islands via Rochester, Shoreham and Portsmouth – all via Southend, and all connected with routes to Calais and Ostend, upon which Rapides and Doves were initially employed. A coach-air extension used Le Touquet for the start of travel in France. Ipswich now had air links with continental Europe far superior to those of any similar provincial town.

On 29 October 1962 EAFS, now flying Doves and Herons, became Channel Airways with a twenty-one-year lease on Ipswich. Its operating bases also included Southend and Stansted, and it also flew DC-3s, which, by 1964, needed replacing. Four HS 748s were therefore ordered for delivery in 1965/66 for Ipswich-Southend-Portsmouth-Jersey services. After an HS 748 skidded off wet grass and onto a road at Portsmouth, both that aerodrome and Ipswich were dropped from commercial services, and plans for a quite lavish restaurant and motel at Ipswich were abandoned.

Rapide G-AKRN, Ipswich-based, during a charter call at Newmarket 1947.

Tipsy Nipper G-AFJR at Ipswich on 28 May 1961 (George Pennick).

Prentice G-AOKH visiting Ipswich (George Pennick).

Piper Saratoga SP G-SULL with the homes of friendly neighbours looking on.

Dakota N17, long resident and to the end of Ipswich days.

Channel Airways launched an unusual service in January 1969. Named 'The Scottish Flyer', it involved a Viscount that departed Stansted and called at pick-up points served by Dove or Heron feeder liners as it made its way to Aberdeen. From Ipswich a Heron connected with 'The Flyer' at East Midlands.

Liquidation overtook Channel Airways on 29 February 1972, and on 31 May Lonmet (Aviation) Ltd moved in, setting up the British School of Flying, which had a contract to train ATC cadets awarded flying scholarships. When in 1976 it lost that contract, Flairavia Ltd took on the lease, and on 1 November 1976 the Suffolk Aero Club was reborn. The Horizon Flying Club followed, and by the 1980s Ipswich was the home of three flying schools, a parachuting centre and an aircraft maintenance base. Business and charter flying also took place.

A rather menacing change of control came in 1980. The lease was bought by Ipswich Co-operative Society, which soon announced an ominous plan. It wanted to use part of the site for a large superstore, leaving only one grass runway and a new club house. A public outcry led to a Public Enquiry, which, in February 1983, resulted in a statement proclaiming that the airfield was 'of more than just local importance', and ruled that 'the existing layout must stay'. Ipswich Council then agreed to continue supporting its two-runway airfield, a 1984 Plan confirming the site's use for business and recreational flying, together with related industry and a transport museum in the area. The Co-op sub-leased the site to Harvest Air of Southend in 1985, general improvements following.

Fourteen years after the last scheduled service from Ipswich, a dynamic duo appeared as Suckling Airways, formed and managed by Mr and Mrs Suckling. They turned Ipswich into a rare British grass-surfaced international airport, and introduced an eighteen-seater Dornier Do 228 G-BMMR on routes between Schiphol, Ipswich and Manchester. Suckling set very high standards, even to the extent of home cooking. While BA memorably provided an unhappy ham roll and a date with a stone in it, Suckling's customers, on the short run to Amsterdam, dined on boeuf stroganoff. Not surprisingly, Suckling flew some 12,000 passengers in 1986 and again in 1987 – many enjoying more than one flight with the excellent operator. All his life Roy Suckling had been keen on aviation, confiding to me that he used to enjoy F-100 logging at the end of Wethersfield's runway. A kindred spirit for sure! For two years their service operated.

Perhaps the fare was too fine for councillors' digestive systems, or the airfield surface too muddy and bumpy, or for some other reason, but Suckling departed in March 1988. The company temporarily used Wattisham for services until it found a new home and a kind welcome at Cambridge.

Meanwhile at Ipswich Region Air proposed a concrete runway and a sell-off of much of the site, but that would have placed too much limitation on general aviation. In January 1989 the Council rejected all compromises, and revealed its intent to close the aerodrome and relocate flying at a new greenfield site. In 1990 it commissioned an enquiry into the future use of its possession. So eager were the councillors to rid themselves of their treasure that they gave £1.2 million of other people's money to Region Air when they cancelled the lease. The Council, now with direct control of the airport, announced the closure date as 31 December 1993, despite the fact that business was booming.

Indeed, 1990 proved to be the airport's busiest ever year during which more than 43,000 movements were handled. The restaurant and bar were thriving too. The three flying schools had been supplemented in 1988 by a helicopter school flying Robinson R.22s.

The early 1990s saw rallies, shows, vintage vehicle events and flying by vintage aircraft. Support from those living nearby was almost total, and a poll of Ipswich folk showed 90% wanting their airport kept open. But such desire and a number of petitions were to no avail.

In 1993 businesses were invited to relinquish their protected tenancies in return for guarantees that the airfield would remain open for two more years, something to which they agreed in November 1993.

June 1995 saw Hawk Air's flying taxi business start using Ipswich for charter flying with its twin-engined Cambridge-based aircraft. In October businesses were offered a further one-year of their leasing. September 1996 saw the local air traffic scheme upgraded, runway improvement being scheduled for October.

Suddenly the Council struck again. In late September 1996 it announced that Ipswich Airport would close. The CAA would de-license it with effect from 31 December 1996. A deafening uproar understandably engulfed 'the wise ones', whose tenants were ordered to quit the site by then. When New Year's Day dawned it witnessed the Occupation of Ipswich Airport. Two major protest marches, Westminster lobbying and an Easter Monday rally and families day were held at the airport. Council collaborators tried to break up the latter.

Unable to cope with hefty High Court fees, the Suffolk Aero Club and Ipswich School of Flying moved out. The last of the local Cessna 150s departed on 12 August 1997, the sole remaining aeroplane, being worked upon in a hangar, flying out in January 1998.

The ensuing years saw the airfield sadly decay while the councillors were said to be wondering who would be remembered on future street name boards. Certainly those would not include Cessna Crescent, Merlin Close or Suckling Way. Eventually that dreaded creature, the 'developer', seized the hallowed ground, turning it into the Ravenswood Estate. It is said that if you put an ear to any of its miniscule grass zones you can hear a Blenheim bomber revving up, awaiting the chance to take revenge on behalf of all who loved their dear airport.

Main features:

The very appealing wooden panelled club house, restaurant and offices built pre-war remained until the airport closed. A 1938 official summary of Ipswich listed three hangars, one measuring 90ft wide, 65ft deep and 14ft high and two 32ft square and 10ft high. There was no fixed lighting.

KNETTISHALL, Suffolk

52°22N/00°53E 130ft asl; TL970795. Off the A1066 2 miles W of Garboldisham and 6 miles SE of Thetford. Road crosses site

A year had passed since 8th AF B-17s carried out their first bombing raid on Europe which made 17 August 1943 apt for a celebration. Elaborate was the planned event for it involved the 3rd AD attacking a distant target then flying on to North Africa while the 1st AD attacked Schweinfurt's ball-bearing factory before returning to Britain. Knettishall's Fortresses were to be among the 3rd AD force which, after bombing an aircraft factory at Regensburg, would head for the African sun. Unfortunately, the mist of a lovely summer morn day caused the delay which led to disaster.

Late take-off made assembly over East Anglia more complicated and fuel consuming before the 3rd AD was ready to set off with their Thunderbolt escort. They passed through the exit area between Great Yarmouth and Lowestoft with the 96th from Snetterton leading and the 388th Bomb Group from Knettishall behind them. The other Groups involved – the 390th, 94th, 95th, 385th with the 100th bringing up the rear – were also flying B-17s carrying more fuel than normally.

Had the Schweinfurt force proceeded simultaneously then the enemy fighter force would have been split. Instead, it was able to dole out severe punishment on one raid at a time. Over Belgium German fighters began making persistent attacks, picking off bombers in the rear. The action continued almost to distant Regensburg where bombs were aimed at the Messerschmitt factory soon to start producing Me 262 jets. Seventeen B-17s had been lost by the time the enemy gave up the fight. Surely surprising the foe, the bombers continued on a southerly track, crossed the Alps, and flew to North Africa. After ten hours' flying they landed – with twenty-four of their number missing.

Now came the problem of the return journey for which reliance had to be placed upon limited maintenance facilities. After a week half the remaining aircraft, about sixty bombers, made the journey back, bombing the Atlantic convoy raiders' base at Bordeaux/Merignac. One can surely imagine the joy and relief when arriving back at home bases including Knettishall. For their part in the Regensburg shuttle bombing operation the 388th received a Distinguished Unit Citation another of which the was awarded for a trio of raids – on a rubber factory in Hanover, synthetic oil plant at Brux and a shuttle raid which took them to the USSR.

Although it was not declared fully complete until 15 May 1943 Knettishall opened on 6 January 1943 in 3 Group as a satellite of RAF Honington. In April it became a satellite of Halesworth which was not completed until 31 May. Such was the need that many airfields came into use while contractors were still busy. It was in the third week of June 1943 that the 388th reached the base, operations commencing on 17 July when an aircraft factory at Amsterdam was the target. Thereafter, the 388th was in the thick of battle as they fought through to targets at Kassel, Brunswick, Berlin, La Pallice, Emden and Ludwigshaven. Like others the 388th gave tactical support to the Normandy invasion, the airborne landings in Holland and the advance into Germany. On the way to victory the 388th had also hit Schweinfurt and in May 1945 dropped food to the Dutch. They were also had responsibility for the *Aphrodite* project at nearby Fersfield.

Knettishall, a conventional temporary bomber base, was built on a plateau at the edge of what is now Knettishall Heath Country Park which, with gorse, heather and gnarled Scots pines is a mixed area of sandy acid and chalk soils attracting creatures as diverse as lizards, deer, semi-wild Exmoor ponies and skylarks. There are beautiful walks in the area, with Peddars Way stretching to north Norfolk and the Icknield Way 120 miles to Buckinghamshire. The Little Ouse river runs through this area of striking contrasts.

The best approach to the airfield is from the north, but if you come from the south then you will notice a very prominent memorial to the 388th. From that feature the road to Coney Weston crosses the airfield with many fragments of runway visible. There are a few ruined buildings near a church on the southern side and a T2 hangar in quite good health on the western side. A grass runway is used by light aircraft and you may see a Cessna here and a windsock. The site was released by the Ministry of Defence in February 1957.

Main features:
Runways: 220° 6,000ft x 150ft, 270°, 330°, tar covered concrete with some areas of wood chips. Hangar: one T2. *Hardstandings:* fifty loop type. *Accommodation:* 421 officers, 2,473 enlisted men.

LAKENHEATH, Suffolk

52°24N/00°33E 28ft asl; TL740820. By the A1065 4 miles SW of Brandon

At Lakenheath on the morning of 26 April 1986 frenzied activity and tighter than ever security confirmed that something special was afoot. Incredibly irresponsible local radio stations soon reported this, adding that bombs were being taken to the F-111s. The better informed had, over recent days, noticed pointers at Mildenhall towards something special.

Around 1815 hrs the first of a fleet of F-111s began taking off from Lakenheath just as they did during major practices. That was cover and for much of the evening F-111s were flying high or low over East Anglia. From the departures two dozen F-111s led by the 493rd TFS headed westerly to drink, repeatedly, from a fleet of KC-10s and KC-135s before calling on Colonel Gaddafi and friends. In so doing they were participating in *Eldorado Canyon* and carrying out the first bombing raid delivered from the UK since 1945.

Releasing laser guided bombs at around midnight after diving to 500ft, the F-111s attacked Tripoli's Al Azziziyah Barracks, Tripoli airfield and Sidi Bilal terrorist training camp where bombs exploded in their 'swimming pool'. Not all the GBU-10s hit their targets, for precisely positioning the laser designator was not all that easy. From 178/LN and 390/LN bombs burst close enough to Gaddafi's house to spoil it while the owner was resting in a big tent. Every effort was made to avoid bombs exploding in civilian residential areas. There was a note of irony when the French Embassy was damaged for its management in Paris had refused to allow the F-111s to cross France. That meant that a blow against international terrorism involved a long, tedious flight with repeated in-flight refuelling. A rainy morning did nothing to dissuade sightseers at Lakenheath from welcoming back the F-111s from a historic mission.

Lakenheath is a vast airfield bearing virtually no resemblance to its initial form. Indeed, the Brandon road entrance is positioned where in the 1914-18 war there was a bombing range on extensive rabbit-owned sandy heathland or Breckland (ie. broken land) some of which remains to the east. Military interest in the area remained and in 1941 preparation of a Built Satellite began on the heathland. With good approaches to three runways it was for Mildenhall, a replacement for Newmarket. To fool the foe wood and canvas aircraft mock-ups (lit when the enemy was around or Mildenhall's Wimpeys were homing) were erected where the gun club now is, on the eastern side of the Brandon road which at the time followed a much more westerly track than now.

Lakenheath came into use in Spring 1941 prior to completion and was frequently used by Honington's IX Squadron Wellingtons diverted when returning from night operations. It opened as a Mildenhall satellite in November 1941 and between 24 November 1941 and 12 January 1942 Wellingtons of No 20 OTU Lossiemouth were based here due to the poor state of their home ground.

In January 1942 Stirlings of No 149 Squadron Mildenhall began flying from Lakenheath as the crews trained to handle them through 149 Conversion Flight which continued training them here until October 1942. No 149 Squadron also flew some early Stirling operational sorties from Lakenheath to where they moved in April 1942. Participation in many famous raids included the 'Thousand Plan' series. Gradually they undertook more night minelaying which, demanding low flying over heavily defended waters, was far from safe. Early 1944, by which time Stirlings were being gradually replaced in Bomber Command, found the squadron also undertaking supply drops to the Resistance forces.

Of all the courage exhibited by the Squadron during its Stirling days, none surely eclipsed that of Sergeant R H Middleton, an Australian and one of quite a number who made Lakenheath their wartime home. Middleton was detailed to attack the Fiat works at Turin on 28/29 November 1942. The difficult flight around The Alps consumed fuel rapidly on this dangerous, dark night. Over Turin in the face of intense flak, he flew low to identify the target. Suddenly an exploding shell created a large hole in the wing, then another burst in the cockpit wounding both pilots. A piece of shrapnel hit Middleton in the face blinding him in his right eye. The second pilot was seriously injured too, and the bomber fell out of control before the second pilot managed to right it. Enemy fire was still striking the aircraft and Middleton ordered the second pilot aft for treatment whilst he struggled to cope with BF372 and set course for home, praying they had sufficient fuel. Crossing the French coast the Stirling was hit again and over the Channel, and with scarcely any fuel remaining Middleton ordered the crew to bale out. Five did so, leaving two to assist Middleton. The Stirling crashed in the Channel and all were lost. Middleton, posthumously awarded the Victoria Cross, was buried in Beck Row Cemetery, opposite Mildenhall airfield, where his grave remains.

During 1942 Lakenheath began to be improved. T2 hangars were erected and on 24 March 1943 the station became part of 31 Base Mildenhall. Soon after Horsa gliders began arriving for storage at the southern end of the field. On 20 June 1943 No 199 arrived with Wellington Xs and flew a few sorties. They began flying Stirling IIIs on 5 July, operated them for the first time on 30th, and were declared on 9 August to be fully operational again. The squadron participated in bombing and mining until 1 December 1943 when they were taken off operations to train in the use of *Mandrel*, a radar jamming device. On 1 May 1944 '199' moved to North Creake and into 100 Group, and 149 Squadron moved to Methwold on 15 May 1944.

Quite desolate, Lakenheath comprised just the T2s, a collection of huts and, amazingly, only a few coils of barbed wire to protect it. One could have roamed at will viewing the occupants – until May 1944 when dramatic change overtook the station. Lakenheath had been chosen for development as a Very Heavy Bomber base. Had the war progressed long enough, B-29s or projected huge British bombers or the Lincoln reckoned to need frighteningly long runs might have been based here.

Illogical rumour claimed that Lakenheath was to become a large international airport once the fight was over. Instead, there came for trials in 1945-6 an unusual new device, the Calvert bar lighting landing system developed at RAE Farnborough. Now most airfields feature a spin off from the Lakenheath tests. By 1948 here was the SBA site used by CSE Watton for trials, and Bomber Command Signals School gave training in the use of *H2S* and GH. The only flying involved an Anson calling for the station was on 'C&M'. Suddenly it was all changed when on 5 August 1948 Lakenheath became Active.

When the Berlin Airlift started the Americans were given what they had been requesting, bases in the UK for B-29s. The airfield they wanted was Mildenhall but it required too much uprating. On 3 July Lakenheath was made available for temporary USAF use, became Active on 5 August and at 1000 hrs on 8th Constellation *Clipper Winged Arrow* of Pan Am opened the US 'temporary' occupation which continues unbroken.

Three squadrons, thirty-two B-29 Superfortresses of the 2nd Bomb Group, opened the USAF presence. Over the next eight years over thirty Bomb Groups or Wings temporarily visited Lakenheath usually staying for about ninety days. On 17 January 1949 the 7404 Base Complement formed to handle the visitors and on 28 January was upgraded to ABG level and became an Air Support Wing on 26 September 1951. Control of Lakenheath passed to the Strategic Air Command on 28 April 1951 and was now administered by the 3909 ABG.

B-50As of the 2nd BG Lakenheath, February 1950.

B-29 of the 2nd BW refuelling at Lakenheath, autumn 1948.

B-29s of the 2nd BG left around 17 November 1948 and two days later the 22nd BG was arriving. B-29s rotated through until 20 August 1949 when the 65th Bomb Squadron, 43rd Bomb Group introduced the B-50A supported by three KB-29M tankers, the first in-flight refuelling aircraft based at Lakenheath. Supporting transports at first included DC-4s, C-47s, C-97s and C-74 Globemasters massive in their time and curious looking because of their 'bug eye' twin cockpit canopies. When in summer 1950 Mildenhall started accommodating SAC bombers Lakenheath was used sometimes for dispersed aircraft from other bases. On 17 May1950 B-29s of the 32nd BS began arriving and for the first time an ARS squadron, No 301, was based here. As a result of the Korean crisis they did a double tour some of their B-29s being stripped of guns and equipment to give them greater capability and range. On 28 June 1950 the 301st BG became the 301st BW. It had become policy for the bombers to equip squadrons organised within a Group which now was part of a Wing bearing the same number and embracing all associated units. Strictly it was Bomb Groups which came here usually although sometimes much of a Wing came on TDY.

Summer 1950 saw Lakenheath declared as the US base in the UK with best development potential. In July under Plan *Galloper* consideration was given to making it a base for escort fighters until Manston was chosen. Lakenheath had a 9,000ft x 300ft main runway and two 6,000ft x 300ft subsidiary runways and bombers were sometimes parked on the latter or on the angular or spectacle type hardstandings. New dispersal pads for twelve B-36s were now approved – but the British Government stressed those were only for brief calls. Five hangars had been adapted to provide nose docks

In January 1951 the 93rd Bomb Group became the first to bring B-50Ds and KB-29P boom refuellers to the base. Then, on 15 January 1951, came six extremely noisy, unmistakable giant B-36s of the 7th and 11th BWs, to pay a brief call. At the same time RB-50Bs of the 55th SRW moved in as at Bassingbourn and stayed until 15 May 1951 to undertake production of radar maps of eastern Europe. With them all came some of the first C-124 Globemaster IIs to come to the UK.

On 28 April 1951 Lakenheath became a USAF Air Base with only RAF liaison staff. Another three B-36Ds arrived in June 1951 for 1 July's memorable flypast at the Paris Aero Show. September-October 1951 brought a jet bomber here for the first time, a B-45A of the 91st SRW.

By 1952 there had been extensive changes. The most obvious was re-alignment of the Brandon road re-routed to the east. When the Americans first came the airfield was still open, barbed wire coils providing the only security. Before the arrival of nuclear weapons a 10ft high wire net fence was built encircling the base, no mean achievement. Housing the weapons led to suggestions for building special bunkers to the south-east across the new road and linking them with the airfield via an underpass. Instead, an area in the north-west of the main site was chosen, and heavily protected special bunkers were built along with a laboratory to supervise the sensitive activity.

On 13 April 1953 the first B-47 Stratojets visited Lakenheath, and at a time when the base was being used by reconnaissance RB-36s and RB-50s. August 1953 saw sixteen F-84Gs of the 508th Strategic Fighter Wing testing their suitability for rapid deployment. On 1 January 1954 the base closed for a 'facelift' after which RB-50s resumed their easterly activities.

Far greater secrecy even than that which cloaked their activities on the perimeter of the USSR enveloped a new mystery machine which drifted quietly and gracefully around the neighbourhood. Resembling a jet-propelled sailplane, this was the Lockheed U-2A first flown in Europe from Lakenheath possibly on 11 May 1956. It was so quickly the talk of the area that for security reasons the two U-2s of the so-called '1st Weather Recon Sqn (Provisional)' left late June for Wiesbaden AB. SAC activity had of late been overseen by the 3909th ABG which was replaced in 1956 by the 3910th ABG here until 1 January 1960.

Another phase in USAF activity had started in 1954 when KC-97 tankers were first based here on TDY, and in June 1954 B-47s were deployed here for the first time. B-47B and E Stratojets dominated the scene until 1956 by which time the Americans were positioning their strategic bombers in the Midlands. An outline of TDY rotations to Lakenheath can be found at the end of this item.

Development of ICBMs by the Soviets led to the activation on 20 February 1958 of the 705th Strategic Missile Wing formed to handle the delivery of Thor IRBMs to the RAF. To mastermind the show the SMW moved on 15 March 1958 to the HQ at Ruislip leaving C-124s and C-133s to deliver the rockets here and at Mildenhall.

American forced withdrawal from France saw Lakenheath close in 1959. Special well protected shelters were built each able to accommodate a nuclear armed F-100 and allow it to make an engine start while inside for fast getaway. Removal of the notorious runway hump was made and other 'modifications' were undertaken before the transfer from SAC to USAFE on 1 October 1959 as part of *Red Richard*, the USAF departure from France.

On 5 January 1960 the 48th Tactical Fighter Wing began moving from France to Lakenheath, transfer of their seventy-five F-100Ds being completed on 15 January. Hard to accept, isn't it, that the 48th has been at Lakenheath for half a century.

F-100D-75-NA 63214 of the 48th TFW gets airborne, Lakenheath tower beyond.

The Super Sabres operated from here until 1971 when conversion to F-4Ds began, the 492nd TFS standing down on 1 October 1971 followed by the 493rd on 1 December and the 494th on 1 February 1972. The first F-4D Phantom II arrived on 7 January, the last F-100D departure was on 15 April 1972 but by then only seventeen F-4Ds had arrived and so the squadrons were forced to adopt operational states while much below strength due to slow throughput of the Phantoms. Not until September 1974 was the 494th fully equipped and operational again, followed by the 492nd on 10 December 1974 and the 493rd on 13 January 1975.

F-4D Phantoms of the 493rd TFS dispersed in pre-HAS times, 66-484 nearest.

Short the Phantom stay. In October 1976 it was announced that the F-111Fs of the 366th TFW were to equip the 48th. Conversion would span the period 14 October 1976 to 31 December 1977.

On 1 March 1977 the first three arrived and on 22 April the last F-4D left, by which time the Wing had stood down to rearm. On 1 April the 495th TFS was re-activated to help make good use of the eighty-four F-111Fs due. They were given three roles – nuclear strike, defence suppression and naval support. Each aircraft would be able to carry two nuclear weapons or a 14,000lb external load. June 1977 witnessed the first main delivery and by the end of July 1977 the Wing held ninety-one F-111Fs. So effective was the entire programme that the 494th became operational on 9 July and the 493rd on 1 August. The 495th (with green fin tipped aircraft) concentrated on training and the 492nd became operational much later, on 31 August 1978.

The late 1970s saw dramatic change for on various parts of the airfield construction commenced of hardened aircraft shelters. The Italian firm contracted to build them sub-contracted the work and there were soon problems with the workforce. Italian workers were brought in but not until October 1978 were the problems settled and the British workforce began the task in earnest and also built new aircraft platforms. It was the early 1980s before all the aircraft were being kept in numbered protective shelters many of which were named one, for instance, being 'Captain Ball VC'. By then the 48th was deploying far afield, to Italy, Greece, even Pakistan and Iran, experiencing monthly 'Tacevals', full scale alerts and frequently undertaking hi-lo profile training sorties to Scotland.

The 1986 Libya raid showed that the F-111s (whoever gave then that crazy name Aardvark?) were really in business, and they trained intensively so that when the next call came they were ready. It did not take long for them to respond to the Iraqi invasion of Kuwait for on 25 August 1990 the vanguard, eighteen F-111s, flew to Taif, Saudi Arabia. In all Lakenheath sent sixty-six there for a major role in January 1991's *Desert Storm*, the 48th *Statue of Liberty Wing* being the only complete one deployed to the Gulf. Saddam Hussein's appalling contempt for all was evident from the memorable TV shots of dying seabirds drenched in oil which he ordered to be poured into the Persian Gulf from the Al Almadi power station. On 28 January 1991 it was from F-111F 70-2390 (which like others carried the Libyan raid banner painted on the tail) flown by Capt Brad Seipel of the 493rd TFS that the two GBU-15s were dropped which turned off the tap. During the Gulf Conflict the 48th flew some 2,200 effective sorties mainly dropping 1,000lb and 2,000lb LGBs. They were credited with the destruction of 920 armoured vehicles, 160 bridges, 113 bunkers and damaged 245 aircraft shelters. On 27 February Lt Col Dan White with Capt Tom Hines as his WSO both of the 492nd TFS flying 71-0889 aimed a 4,700lb GBU-28 deep penetration weapon – developed in seventeen days and tested in Nevada – at the main command bunker 100ft below the surface north of Baghdad. Unfortunately, it failed to kill Hussein. All the F-111Fs were safely back at Lakenheath by mid-May 1991.

On 21 February 1992 the first F-15E Strike Eagle arrived and re-equipment had again started with the 492nd and 494th TFS each to have twenty-four examples. Gradually the F-111s departed, the deployment to Incirlik for *Provide Comfort* ending on 28 September 1992 and the last to go (74-178) leaving on 18 December 1992. On 14 December in the large Luria hangar in the middle of the base the 493rd deactivated.

F-15E 331/LN of the 494th TFS, 48th TFW but 10 August 2001.

Early in 1993 the first F-15 squadron was declared operational and in August two F-15Es deployed to *Provide Comfort* to the Kurds were the first Eagles to drop LGBs when attacking a missile site in Iraq. Late 1993 F-15Cs were delivered for a reactivated 493rd TFS. Between 14-20 September 1994 two F-15Cs visited Slupsk Air Base, home of a dozen MiG-23s of the 28th Ftr Regt, Polish Air Force. The F-15s were making the first visit to a former Warsaw Pact Country.

Deployments of F-15s to Turkey preceded the next conflict. In October 1998 fifteen F-15Cs of the 493rd were deployed to Cervia, Italy and in 1999 F-15Es flew to Aviano. Both detachments were busy during the Kosovo campaign. The F-15s operated in 'high threat' areas and flew protective missions for other aircraft. By June 1999 the 494th Expeditionary Fighter Squadron had flown over 1,000 sorties from Aviano and dropped more ordnance than any other USAF squadron since *Desert Storm*. Due to lack of space on Italian airfields F-15Es began operating as needed from Lakenheath.

Participation by the 48th FW in the second Iraq campaign was followed by frequent detachments to the Middle East, while friendship visits were made to other countries. New additions to the base were HH-60G Blackhawk helicopters of the 56th Rescue Squadron, whose role is combat search and rescue. Lakenheath remains the depository for some 110 nuclear weapons.

It is the prime USAF strike base in Europe. The public viewing area remains off the road to Lakenheath village, making it is still possible, despite security, to enjoy and indeed photograph the activity mainly by F-15s and sometimes by visitors. Understandably, wandering along the perimeter fence is strongly 'discouraged'.

Should the Americans ever leave this base the site would be ideal for an eco-town. OK, you'd rather keep the Eagles – me too. But just fancy planting beans on the spot where a B-36 once rested!

Main features:
Original runways: 246° 6,000ft x 150ft, 186° 4,200ft x 150ft, 322° 4,200ft x 150ft. Increased runway lengths completed summer 1945: 246° 9,000ft x 200ft, 186° 6,000ft x 200ft, 322° 6,000ft x 200ft. Ultimate main runway 06/24 9,000ft (9,850ft including overshoot areas) 300ft wide, asphalt and concrete, features BAK-9 and Dual BAK-12 arrester gear. Warm-up pads on either side of runway ends. Only small sections of two subsidiary runways retained and used for parking. Visiting aircraft use a large concrete 'Victor alert' pad. *Hangars* (1945): two T2, three for Horsa support, one B1. Some later extended for US use, nose docks on some. Concrete HASs in use from early 1980s. *Wartime hardstandings:* thirty-six for heavy bombers. For B-36s, twelve Very Heavy Bomber stands were constructed, and some perimeter track widened to 200ft. *Wartime accommodation:* RAF: 144 officers, 513 SNCOs, 1,048 ORs; WAAF: 6 officers, 11 SNCOs, 228 ORs. During US period a large hospital was built and a domestic site was added to the south side of the main camp. Extensive married quarters were constructed on the southern side of the base and many personnel live in private accommodation off base. The distinctive Braithwaite water tower remains, somewhat modified.

Strategic Air Command Squadrons/Groups/Wings rotated through Lakenheath

Unit	Aircraft type	Date
2 BG	B-29 (+ one F-13)	August-November 1948
22 BG	B-29	November 1948-February 1949
372 BS/370 BG	B-29	February-May 1949
830 BS/509 BG	B-29	May-August 1949
65 BS/43 BG	B-50A/KB-29M	August-November 1949
33 BS/22 BG	B-29	November 1949-February 1950
32 BS/301 BG	B-29	May-November 1950
328,330 BS/93 BW	B-50D	July 1950-February 1951
341 BS/97 BW	B-50D	July 1950-February 1951
393BS/509 BW	B-29	February-May 1951
2 ARS/2 BW	KB-29P	May-August 1951
33BS/22 BW	B-29	September-December 1951
329 BS/93 BW	B-50D	December 1951-March 1952
340 BS/97 BW	B-50D	March -May 1952
393 BS/509 BW	B-50D	June -September 1952
2 ARS/2 BW	KB-29P	September-December 1952
43 ARS/43 BW	KB-29P	March-June 1953
?	B-50D	June-November 1953
68 ARS/68 BW	KC-97E & G	June-August 1954
320 ARS/320 BW	KC-97F	June-September 1954
55 SRW	RB-50	July 1954-1956
43 ARS/43 BW	KC-97G	July 1954-1956
40 BW (all)	B-47E	March-June 1955
340 BW (all)	B-47E	September-November 1955
98 BW (all)	B-47E	October-November 1955
509 ARS/509 BW	KC-97G	February-June 1956
307 BW (all)	B-47E	August-October 1956
384 ARS/384 BW	KC-97F & G	February-April 1957

LANGHAM, Norfolk

52°56N/00°58E 140ft asl; TF990420. On BI388 between Binham and Langham

'That's not a dome, *this* is a Dome', said Mr Burton who, putting the finishing touches to its smart black coating (courtesy of the bank balance of Mr Bernard Matthews, the turkey man) added 'It'll last a darned sight long than *that awful thing*!' I could not imagine to what he was alluding, but agreed with him.

Langham's dome, or to be more precise 'Building 35 Dome Teacher' also known as a Dome Synthetic Trainer, is a splendidly spooky one which sits like a visitor from outer space by the edge of a public lane. Follow that as it wends its way among concrete dispersals providing good views of the control tower area. Then take the first right turn and you will cross the airfield and surprisingly long main runway. By then, if you cannot imagine the sound of a Beaufighter or a 'white Wimpey' you should be ashamed of yourself! Mind you, making do with a skylark, possibly a Tiger Moth or a view of the sea and Blakeney Point from the runway – any of those are almost as satisfying. In truth, Langham and the area around are highly satisfying – like 'The Bluebell', a shrine to Langham's past which included many days like 14 May 1944.

'THAT'S not a dome, THIS is a dome!' August 1999.

It's mid-morning and ground crews over there are making last minute adjustments to Beaufighter Xs on the roadside dispersals. Within moments 'liberty buses' arrive dropping off a pilot and observer at each machine whose Hercules engines are soon whistling, raring to go. The Beaufighters – a dozen of 455 (Australian) Squadron armed with rockets, six of 489 (NZ) Squadron carrying torpedoes and another six to silence the flak men, begin trundling out, their engines rumbling as only the Hercules could. Brakes keep squealing until each 'Beau' finds a niche on the peri-track. They hold at the runway threshold for final checks and a burst of engine power. Then, at precisely 1130 hrs the leader joins '253' and rolls. Within ten minutes Langham Strike Wing has formed up and racing impressively away to meet the Mustang escort.

'Jim crow' reconnaissance earlier located four medium-sized merchant vessels off the Dutch coast, accompanied by sixteen escort ships all heavily armed, and nine minesweepers clearing a path free from the night efforts of East Anglia's Stirling minelayers.

Over the very rough sea and flying below the 300ft cloud base the Strike Wing bumps into heavy rain and poor visibility. Although that cloaks them, it makes flying unpleasant and adds to the terrible danger in flying low over water. Nevertheless, the convoy is located, the Beaufighters break for the attack and enter a tremendous hail of fire from escorting flak ships. A torpedo from 489 Squadron whams into a 3,000-tonner left blazing. Another large ship is victimised and appears to be sinking. Meanwhile, 455 Squadron's rockets are slamming into mine-sweepers and escort vessels, some of which suffer considerable damage. Balloons flying at around 250ft have to be watched – one cable clout would bring instant disaster. Tremendous action has been packed into seconds and all is soon over. Langham's 'Beaus' regroup for home shortly before 1330 hrs, but one is nowhere to be seen. 'B Beer' of 489 Squadron vanished after diving into the sea. Six others report trouble from the merciless flak, and 'M Mother' of 455 Squadron will end its sortie by slithering on its belly across Langham. 'C Charlie' and 'B Beer' have had their wings well peppered, and 'X' and 'K' – also of 455 Squadron – have sustained damage but brought their crews safely home. As it taxies to dispersal 'Y Yoke' of 489 Squadron can be seen to have been hit in the wings and nacelles after what has been just another shipping strike from Langham.

And now? As well as the long sheds of the turkey farm and the wartime control tower now a smart office, the most noticeable thing one sees on flying over is the very long runway partly intact, a feature from the 1950s when Langham was Coltishall's designated bolthole should that station be put out of use or contaminated at homing time.

When Langham opened in 1940 it was as an unbuilt primitive landing ground, a second satellite for Bircham Newton which dispersed second-line aircraft here. The arrival in early October 1940 of Henley target-tugs of 'M' and 'K' Flights, No 1 Anti-Aircraft Co-operation Unit, brought Langham alive. They were here to tow targets for the two large AA practice camps nearby, No 5 Heavy AAPC at Weybourne and No 11 Light AAPC Stiffkey. Henleys, which resembled pregnant Hurricanes and had the same outer wings, had been cast aside pre-war in an act of folly. Accent on the strategic bomber left the 300 Henley light/dive-bomber/army support aircraft stranded without a friend. Had they been used against the German Blitzkrieg on France in 1940 the outcome of that offensive might well have been different. Instead, Henleys roosted and brooded in Norfolk towing targets, the fate officials tried to foist even upon the Mosquito.

Langham's independent status came on 16 July 1942 when, still with only Blister hangars, it opened as a full station under Group Captain T H Carr AFC DFC. Next day the first visitors were not RAF, but sailors and detachment of six black Swordfish of 819 Squadron from distant Machrihanish and under the command of Lieutenant Commander Davenport. They had called to carry out night anti-shipping operations under 16 Group, RAF Coastal Command. Three days later they flew to Thorney Island, each to collect a torpedo and via Docking, returned to Langham.

Meantime, 'M' Flight of 1 AACU began equipping with Defiant target tugs, but it was the general arrangement of Bircham Newton's huge commitment that was more important. No 280 Squadron had arrived there on 31 July and on 5 August moved to Langham. Their task was to seek and assist aircrew who had ditched in the North Sea off East Anglia which provided a busy period for 280's Ansons until they returned to Bircham Newton late October.

On 6 August, No 819 Squadron had also left Langham to operate from Bircham Newton to where 'K' and 'M' Flights returned on 3 November 1942 for their re-establishment after respectively becoming Nos 1611 and 1612 AAC Flights on 1 November. No 2 AAPC formed here on 16 February 1943 and on 17 June changed into being 1626 AA Co-operation Flight which worked with the RAF Regiment AAPC. In December 1943 a number of the AAC units were gathered in a new squadron, No 695, based at Bircham Newton.

During 1943 Langham had undergone major alterations which included the laying of three metalled runways. The road which now passes the dome also crosses what was the technical site, and passes between the wartime siting of two 1942 T2s.

View over Langham looking east. A proposed ORP was never built.

When Langham re-opened in 16 Group on 22 February 1944 it was being prepared for a year of forefront operational activity which began in April when two Beaufighter squadrons moved in from Leuchars, Fife. One was No 455 manned mainly by Australians, the other 489 by New Zealanders who had come from half way around the world to ensure with noble effort the freedom of Europeans many of whom had put up a pathetic fight in defending their countries and, in recent years, have treated the ex-Dominions so very badly. Between them the two Dominion squadrons – at considerable cost in lives – formed 16 Group's Langham Strike Wing.

On 19 April the first *Rover* patrols were flown and ships were attacked off the Netherlands. Thereafter it was similar action whenever the trade and weather permitted it. The first big anti-shipping strike came on 6 May, fifteen of 455 Squadron's aircraft, six torpedo carriers from '489' and five anti-flak Beaufighters finding five escort vessels shielding a large convoy of seven merchant ships. Hits were claimed on a number of them but one Beaufighter was shot down. Flight Sergeant R. Walker, more fortunate, made home despite his aircraft having jammed ailerons, hits in the starboard fuel tank and brakes out of use.

Rovers, 'recces' and sea sweeps followed interspersed with a few very large shipping strikes. Often the Langham Wing joined the North Coates Wing producing a formation of around fifty Beaufighters with sizeable RAF fighter support from Norfolk bases. On D-Day a detachment from Langham operated over the Channel out of Manston and gradually the emphasis switched to anti-E-boat operations.

A large scale Strike Wing attack took place on 15 June, in conjunction with the North Coates squadrons, against a ship of around 8,000 tons protected by sixteen escort vessels and balloons. The Beaufighters struck hard, securing two hits with torpedoes on the large vessel. Two damaging attacks were directed against a naval auxiliary, a minesweeper was blown to pieces and a torpedo rammed into the leading merchant ship. On 21 July a similar heavy onslaught left a motor vessel sinking, another damaged by a torpedo, a third blazing and a fourth burning and settling in the water. Two escorts and three other ships were alight when the Beaufighters left. After landing 'X' of 489 Squadron was found to have fifty yards of cable dangling from a wing leading edge and its rudder was damaged. Two aircraft returned each on one engine, and five of '455' had flak damage.

During August 1944 night strikes were attempted with the aid of flares dropped by Wellingtons, the first such attack being delivered off Le Havre. In September 1944 Intelligence sources rather optimistically reckoned that the Langham Wing had sunk thirty-six ships, damaged a further sixty-one and sunk four U-Boats. The last shipping operation, an armed reconnaissance, came on 19 October after which the Beaufighters left for Dallachy to trade off Norway.

Beaufighter TF Xs of the Dallachy Strike Wing assembled on 3 May 1945 at Langham (Andy Thomas).

Their place was taken by 280 ASR Squadron which returned on 6 September and was now flying Warwick Is for operations over the North Sea which took them far beyond the range possible with Ansons.

A more offensive period recommenced when, on 18 October, Wellington GR XIIIs of 524 Squadron arrived from waterlogged Docking for a temporary stay which became a long one. Bombing by flare light, their crews operated at night off the Dutch coast against E-Boats. They were supplemented on 1 November when more of the squadron's Wellingtons arrived as a result of which No 280 Squadron vacated the station. It was then that a detachment of Barracudas belonging to 827 Squadron, Fleet Air Arm, arrived.

A more portentous change occurred when, on 30 October 1944, No 521 Meteorological Reconnaissance Squadron moved in from Bircham Newton bringing Hudsons, Gladiators and Hurricanes for daily sorties.

The Barracudas of 827 Squadron first went into action on 20 November, three crews on a *Rover* attacking two ships. On the 25th the squadron went into action once more, this time against E-Boats and other ships. They flew similar operations before leaving on 13 December. No 612 Squadron then replaced them making Langham home of two Wellington GR squadrons. Armed with GR Mk XIVs fitted with Leigh Lights, the newcomers set a pattern soon followed by No 524 Squadron which, during December, re-armed with the same variant.

No 521 meteorological reconnaissance squadron had come here from Docking at the end of October 1944 and an Armament Practice Camp had been in place during the autumn making Langham a very active station. No 521 employed Hurricanes and Gladiator IIs and during December received a few Fortress IIs for long range flights. A second 'met squadron', No 519, began flying sorties from here as well as Bircham Newton.

Daylight meteorological reconnaissance flights and night operations by Wellingtons remained the order of events in 1945, with 407 Squadron being detached from Chivenor between 14 April and 9 May adding more Wellingtons to Langham's strike force now established at a high total of fifty Mk XIVs and usually holding around forty-five.

Shortly after the war ended a Meteorological Conversion Unit was established here but not before the Wellington squadrons disbanded – No 407, No 524 on 25 May and No 612 on 9 July. By August 1945 only 521 Squadron remained fully active, using mainly Fortress IIIs.

Langham was now the main UK base for weather reporting, its strength recently swollen with the addition of 1402 Flight. New Meteorological Flights now formed here, some before proceeding overseas, and Hurricanes were made available for them in 1946. No 1561 Met Flight reformed on 17 December 1945, used Spitfire PR XIs but disbanded on 11 February 1946. In January 1946 that year the old strike role was resurrected when 254 Squadron flying Beaufighter TF Xs came for a four month stay.

On 1 September 1945 the Coastal Command Fighter Affiliation Unit had formed equipped with Spitfires and Martinets and moved to Chivenor on 6 January 1946. With no immediate post-war use envisaged for Langham it closed to flying on 15 May 1946. A Royal Netherlands Air Force Technical Training School arrived in July then in September 1947 the station was placed on Care & Maintenance its future being related to Army anti-aircraft training on the Norfolk coast which had occasioned its birth. Between 15 June 1952 and 1955 the flying element of the US Army 32nd AA Brigade was based here, other US Army units having a tenancy extending from 23 April 1951 to 1957.

Under Plan K of January 1954 two short-range day fighter squadrons would deploy here after the station was developed to Airfield (War) Standard. Langham's history is confusing for while the Americans were here the station came more alive after its main runway was refurbished and had, as its Standby, Little Snoring. Beaufighter 10s made a surprising return, this time as target towers along with Mosquito TT Mk 35s and Spitfire LF 16s when No 2 Civilian Anti-Aircraft Co-operation Unit, operated here by Marshall's Flying School between 23 March 1953 and 1 November 1958, and latterly using Vampire T 11s under overall control of No 61 Group. After the civilian-manned unit closed Langham served as an Emergency Landing Ground for Sculthorpe. No longer needed after the US left that base, or as a Fighter Command standby 'bolthole', Langham was sold on 3 October 1961 and is in the hands of two agriculturists.

Wartime Langham is still very evident and retains the general 'look' of an airfield site. It is surrounded by beautiful countryside, the line of oak trees by the Binham road providing a picture of what one imagines England should look like. Visit Langham when the cow parsley is flowering high, the sea close by is blue – and call on Pat and Bridget Newman at 'The Bluebell' – for replenishment with an aeronautical flavour!

Main features:
Runways: 253° 6,000ft x 150ft (refurbished and extended in 1952), 202°, 305°, tar surface on concrete. *Hangars:* three T2, four Blister. *Hardstandings:* thirty-six spectacle type. *Accommodation* (1944): RAF: 147 officers, 434 SNCOs, 1,440 ORs; WAAF: 14 officers, 20 SNCOs, 360 ORs.

Places of interest nearby:
With full justification North Norfolk is classed as an Area of Outstanding Natural Beauty. Its coastal zone is particularly attractive in April-June. There are numerous places worth visiting with Langham Glass and rural crafts centre nearest. Binham Priory and the Walsingham Shrines are close, and a boat ride from Morston Quay takes you to Blakeney Point, sea birds and seals. Holkham Hall, home of the Earl of Leicester, is a majestic stately home and Sheringham Park's superb extensive rhododendron collection is reasonably near. From Holt you can sample the horse-drawn bus, the 'Holt Flyer', or try the steam hauled train operated by the North Norfolk Railway to Sheringham sometimes hauled by a B12 – a very East Anglian touch! For the military minded there is the very impressive Muckleborough Collection of sixteen working tanks, RFC and assorted aviation and other exhibits housed under cover in WWII buildings near Weybourne. Easiest access is from the Wells direction. The Collection (tel. 01263 588210) is by the A149 to the west of Weybourne village.

LAVENHAM, Suffolk

52°08N/00°46E 290ft asl; TL895525. 3 miles NW of Lavenham, between the A1141 and A134 NE of Alpheton

Lavenham with its leaning half-timbered houses and early 16th Century Tudor Guildhall to many is the very quintessence of England. If you have an interest in aeronautical things then head for the bar of the Swan Hotel, a lovely aged building in which to contemplate. Therein, along with your very English ale, you can also gaze upon a collection of signatures donated during the war by such famous RAF figures as Sir Basil Embry and Oswald Gayford, of long-distance flying fame, not to mention many other well known in 2 Group and who visited The Swan when stationed at Wattisham during the grimmest days of the war.

Of Lavenham airfield there is still quite a lot to see although since 1980 time and the elements have clearly visited the old airfield. Before you do that call on Lavenham's Tourist Office in Lady Street near the early 16th Century Tudor Guildhall. Ask for details of how to get permission from the farmer who owns Lavenham ex-airfield, and find out when it is convenient to make a visit to a site where, provided you have acted courteously, you will be welcome. You will find useful leaflets, etc. about the airfield and a variety appertaining to similar sites. Alternatively, telephone 01787 248207 giving the make, colour and number of your car and state when you would like to visit the airfield.

To reach it leave the village taking the A1141 main Bury St Edmunds road then, after about three miles, turn left onto a very narrow road sign-posted 'Smithwood Green only'. It leads to the plateau upon which the airfield stands and on to the perimeter track and part of the runway still intact. Follow the 'peri-track' towards the south and you will find the control tower once a private residence. Alongside is the one-time fire station. The area around the tower contains other wartime buildings in mixed states of health, also a large dispersal area. All is in private hands so you must have permission if you wish to take this close look. Never stray onto any private property or enter fields without full permission, for everyone's sake.

Built during 1943-4, Lavenham became active in February 1944. A typical two-hangar three-runway temporary airfield, its first main occupants were B-24s of the 487th Bomb Group, 3rd BD, which began moving in on 5 April 1944. They began operations on 7 May and attacked French airfields before switching to targets in support of the Normandy landings. They supported the British break-out from the bridgehead before ceasing operations in mid-July and converting to B-17Gs (Group identity 'P in a square'). They were declared combat ready on 1 August and were soon attacking troops and fortifications around Brest to assist the way for the Allies to take the port. Next, they supported the airborne invasion of Holland in September.

Ford-built B-24H 252618 of the 487th BG taxies by Lavenham's tower much of which remains. Pity the Lib has gone! (USAF)

So far most operations from Lavenham had a tactical bias, but between August 1944 and March 1945 strategic targets were bombed including oil refineries at Dulmen, Mannheim and Merseburg, factories at Nuremburg, Berlin and Hanover and marshalling yards at Cologne, Hamm and Munster. Like other Groups the 487th also played a part in the Ardennes battle and assisted during the Rhine crossing.

On 24 December 1944 the 487th led an attack on Babenhausen airfield, Fighters engaged the bombers en route and the leader's aircraft carrying Brigadier General Fred Walker-Castle fell away burning. He took over from the First Pilot and ordered to crew to jump. The aircraft's wing soon broke off and Castle, who was killed, posthumously received the Congressional Medal of Honour, and was the highest in rank in the 8th AF to receive the award. His photograph may be seen in Lavenham Guildhall near which is a memorial plaque to the 487th.

Return of the Group to America was completed in August and Lavenham passed to RAF Transport Command on 12 October 1945 and then to Maintenance Command on 31 July 1946. Bomber Command took control of the station on 20 August 1946 for re-opening and expansion were proposed. Instead it became Inactive from 26 October 1948 and was cared for by Stradishall. It was sold in April 1958 after having been earmarked as a possible 'bolthole' airfield for use by fighter squadrons in the area should the main bases be rendered inoperable by enemy attack.

Main features:
Runways: 270° 6,000ft x 150ft, 220°, 310°, concrete. *Hangars:* two T2.
Accommodation: 421 officers, 2,473 enlisted men.

LEISTON, Suffolk

52°13N/01°33E 75ft asl; TM430645. Off B1119 W of Leiston. Turn first left on to road along perimeter track. The road crosses the airfield of which little remains

One thing was essential in order that the US 8th AF could effectively carry out the bombing campaign to very distant targets. That was the long-range fighter – more precisely, the P-51 Mustang. After the British had bought North American's T-6 Harvard trainer pre-war they were convinced its makers could produce a first rate combat aircraft. As a result the Mustang was initiated. Its early form with excellent range handled well, but it was handicapped by its Allison engine whose power output tailed away fast at over 15,000ft. In another inspired British move that most famous of all piston engines, the Rolls-Royce Merlin, was wedded to the P-51. That resulted in one of the finest fighters of all time. Visit Leiston and you are where Merlin Mustangs first operated in the hands of the 8th AF.

Rather surprisingly the first P-51Bs to arrive in Britain were delivered to the 9th AF. The importance of the new P-51 was still not fully apparent when it began trickling into the UK late 1943 at which time the 8th AF, which had taken quite a hammering from German fighters in 1943, was eager to have the newcomer. The question was 'How could they be acquired?' The answer was relatively simple – transfer them from the 9th AF.

Leiston had become active in November 1943 with the arrival on the 29th, and from Goxhill, of a new P-47 Group, the 358th. Already trained, they were able to commence escort duties on 20 December 1943. On 31 January 1944 they were exchanged with the 357th Fighter Group, Raydon, already flying P-51Bs in the 8th AF. The newcomers flew the first P-51B 8th AF mission on 11 February 1944 from Leiston when they carried out a fighter sweep over the Rouen area. Such short-range activity was soon supplemented by deeper penetration flights, escorting bombers to their targets, giving forward support and providing withdrawal cover for B-17s and B-24s. A single-engined fighter able to reach Berlin, engage in combat and fight its way home was no mean invention, and when on 6 March 1944 US heavies first effectively raided the 'Big City' in daylight Leiston's Mustangs provided fighter support. It is perhaps right to recall that the first Allied single-engined aircraft to reach Berlin in daylight and return was a 1941 PR Spitfire of No 3 PRU, Oakington, but the P-51 differed by being a fully armed combat fighter.

P-51B-15-NA of the 367th FS, 357th FG on a Leiston dispersal (Merle Olmsted).

P-51Ds of the 357th FG taxi out for an escort operation in early 1945 (Merle Olmsted).

Mustangs await the order to 'go' (Merle Olmsted).

The value of the P-51B was quickly appreciated, production rapidly increased and P-47s were replaced as soon as possible. Meanwhile the Leiston Group was very busy and even penetrated as far as Leipzig on 29 June. In recognition of all that was entailed during the long duration flight the Group received their first Distinguished Unit Citation.

Over France and the Low Countries P-51s carried out sweeps. During the Normandy landings they flew fighter patrols and soon they were dive-bombing and strafing airfields, marshalling yards, locomotives, ammunition dumps, barges, tugs and later combining such ventures with bomber escorts.

The 357th's second Distinguished Unit Citation was awarded for their part in the 14 January 1945 raid on Derben when the P-51s successfully broke up an onslaught on the bombers they were escorting.

Not surprisingly the 357th ended the war as the second highest scoring Group in the 8th AF and flew their last operational sorties on 25 April 1945. In July 1945 they moved to Neubiberg, Germany. Leiston in October 1945 was returned to the RAF who established No 18 Recruit Centre here. It closed in 1946, the site being sold in the mid-1950s for agricultural use.

Main features:
Runways: 060° 6,000ft x 150ft, 130°, 180°, tarmac and concrete. *Hangars:* two T2, twelve Blister. *Hardstandings:* thirty-eight frying pan type, twelve fighter revetment pens (for twenty-four aircraft), seventeen Pierced Steel Planking dispersals. *Accommodation:* 215 officers, 1,799 enlisted men.

Places of interest nearby:
A stone memorial on the airfield site is dedicated to 'The Yoxford Boys', eighty-two of those pilots losing their lives. A memorial plaque on the old Leiston post office lists the names of those missing 1944-5, and Leiston's long ship museum has a local aviation display. Nearby is the Sizewell Magnox nuclear power station where tours are available and there is a visitor centre.

LITTLE SNORING, Norfolk

52°51N/00°54E 196ft asl; TF960330. 4 miles NE of Fakenham, off A148

Ekwall's 'English Place Names' states that Great and Little Snoring derive from the first wave of Saxon invaders who arrived in 450 AD as the Romans withdrew. They indicate that these were settlements of Snear's people (Snear being a Saxon invader variously nicknamed 'Swift', 'Bright' or 'Alert'), hence these curious parish names.

For the present day surveyor of the Norfolk airfield the attraction may well involve not only the site used for private flying, but also Little Snoring Church. Noteworthy because of its slender round tower also featured by a number of East Anglian churches it stands close to the airfield site (not open to the public) on the Great Snoring Road. Of particular interest are four Memorial Boards listing enemy aircraft claimed as destroyed or damaged and a record of awards and decorations relating to Little Snoring's time in 100 Group.

Please honour the church for its religious purpose, and use it as the ideal place in which to tarry and remember that airfields were places for people, places from where people flew. Thousands set out on their life's last journey from East Anglia so that we may have freedom which we, too, should be prepared at all times to defend as so many did for us.

One such was the late Squadron Leader 'Micky' Martin of Dam Busters fame who served here for six months with 515 Squadron, also Wing Commander Alan 'Sticky' Murphy, that intrepid 23 Squadron intruder pilot who, with Flight Sergeant D Darbon, his navigator, was killed on 2 December 1944 when intruding upon Gütersloh.

A wartime satellite airfield for 3 Group's Foulsham, Little Snoring opened on 7 July 1943 and before its completion on 31 August 1943. With a pressing need for airfields its status was raised during construction. On 5 August 1943, even before the airfield was completed, No 115 Squadron flying Lancaster IIs arrived from East Wretham making way for Americans there. No 1678, a small Conversion Unit which trained Lancaster II crews, moved in at the same time and departed for Foulsham on 16 September 1943. No 1473 Flight arrived from Feltwell on 28 November and left with '1678'.

Operations by 115 Squadron began with fifteen aircraft setting out for Hamburg on 10 August and ended on 26/27 November when twelve aircraft raided Berlin and landed at their new station, Witchford when returning. When they left Little Snoring confident crews crammed their Lancasters with personal belongings, one aircraft carrying seven bicycles to Berlin and back! What must the Germans have made of the contents aboard the wreckage of another, DS680, when they shot it down that night? 'Stupid English, hoping to cycle home!'

During 1943 the policy of siting by Groups in East Anglia was radically reviewed resulting in 3 Group squadrons being centrally placed. Pathfinding 8 Group would be positioned further inland and the new bomber support Group, No 100, formed late 1943, would occupy a clutch of airfields in north Norfolk. Little Snoring was transferred to 100 Group on 7 December 1943 as 169 Squadron was arriving equipped with a few Beaufighter VIs for training under Wing Commander E J Gracie DFC. More soon joined them, and a few Defiant IIs of 1692 Flight which arrived from Drem in December. A few Mosquito IIs were received and training continued allowing crews to gain experience in tactics and use of the specialised radar with which 100 Group Mosquitoes were equipped.

Little Snoring next welcomed No 515 Squadron from Hunsdon. Arriving on 15 December 1943, they brought Merlin-engined Beaufighter IIs which gave a helpful lead in to Mosquito IIs with which they began to equip in February 1944. They also brought along a few black painted Blenheim Vs.

No 515 Squadron had, since 1942, dabbled in the application of radio and radar warfare, and had been responsible for trying out the possibilities of *Mandrel* jamming to screen assembly and advance of bomber streams, British and American, by day and night. Now it would train to operate in the manner of 169 Squadron.

No 169 Squadron commenced operations on 20 January 1944 during a Berlin raid, its task to prevent enemy fighters from attacking our bombers. First combat success for '169' was a Bf 110 credited on 30 January to Squadron Leader J Cooper and Flying Officer R Connally. In February the squadron flew twenty-eight sorties, then fifty-nine in March, during which month 515 Squadron flew its first operations. That squadron had, at this time, a detachment at Bradwell Bay which used some of 605 Squadron's aircraft. It was in one of those which, during the first sortie, the commanding officer, Wing Commander F F Lambert flying with Flight Lieutenant E W M Morgan, downed an He 177. The 100 Group squadrons were, at this time, established at eighteen aircraft per squadron.

During April 1944, 515 Squadron continued to operate from Bradwell until, on 7 April, they operated from Little Snoring for the first time. On 19/20 April 1944 enemy intruders sneaked in among our returning bombers and put Little Snoring out of action by distributing anti-personnel bombs along the runway.

More successes came to 169 Squadron during April when they claimed four enemy aircraft. On 15 May Pilot Officer W H Miller with Pilot Officer F C Bone claimed three German aircraft while engaged in bomber support to mine layers operating over Kiel Bay. The squadron was still using Mosquito IIs.

Under Group Captain R B O'Hoare, a distinguished intruder pilot, the squadrons had begun a very successful night support campaign. Then came an abrupt change for 23 Squadron. The 'No 1' intruder squadron newly returned from the Mediterranean was ordered into 100 Group and had to learn the new style of operations. No 169 Squadron and 1692 Flight both moved to Great Massingham.

Thereafter the fortunes of Little Snoring were akin to those of other 100 Group bomber support Mosquito stations. No 23 Squadron, after a lot of exciting low flying, resumed operations on 5/6 July attacking enemy airfields from very low levels. Their first combat claim was of a Ju 88 damaged on 26 July. Both of Little Snoring's squadrons briefly flew daylight escorts of Lancasters bombing Bordeaux for which they operated from advanced bases. *Day Rangers* were also flown to intrude upon enemy aircraft during their training flights and, in September 1944, 23 Squadron escorted Fortresses trying to discover whether V2s were radio-controlled.

A *Day Ranger* on 29 October 1944 was a red letter day when Flight Lieutenant T L'Amie flying with Flying Officer R A Smith, and Flying Officer T A Groves with Flight Sergeant R B Dockeray destroyed nine enemy aircraft and destroyed five.

At the end of 1944 training in the use of ASH radar began for it was better for low-level attack on airfields. First success with the new equipment came to Squadron Leader C V Bennett DFC with Flight Lieutenant R A Smith on 31 December 1944, a Ju 88 shot down at Ahlhorn. By April 1945 both squadrons were taking part in spoof attacks on German airfields and towns and supplying Master Bombers to control the raids. Towards the end of the war they flew Firebash sorties designed to set ablaze with incendiaries and napalm German airfield installations. The final sorties were flown from Little Snoring on 2/3 May 1945 when Squadron Leader G Griffiths acted as Master Bomber for an attack on Hohn.

Combat claims of enemy aircraft made by 100 Group squadrons flying from here and still open to confirmation are:

	Destroyed	Damaged
169 Squadron	13	1
515 Squadron	44	42
23 Squadron	9	32
Totals	**66**	**75**

On 10 June 1945 No 515 Squadron disbanded followed by No 23 on 25 September. Little Snoring closed to general flying on 25 October after 141 Squadron had been briefly based here between 3 July and disbandment on 7 September.

December 1945 saw No 112 Sub-Site of 274 MU move in, its purpose to look after Mosquitoes until the end of 1946 when the airfield was put under Care & Maintenance. This was not the first time aircraft had been stored here, for thirty Horsas were placed at Little Snoring in 1943-4.

Little Snoring became Active in June 1950. On 20 July 1951 No 2 Civilian Anti-Aircraft Co-operation Unit opened within No 61 Group and was run by Marshall's Flying School. It replaced No 34 Squadron and from here flew mainly Spitfire LF 16s. On 23 March the CAACU moved to Langham from where its Beaufighter TT10s and Vampire T11s flew. Little Snoring acted as their satellite until unit closure on 1 November 1958.

Little Snoring sees limited flying by light aircraft, and for several years hosted the British Aerobatic Championships and competed for the McAully Trophy given in memory of a superb Norfolk acrobatic pilot.

Close to the airfield is Little Snoring church which contains various items applicable to the local squadrons – well worth viewing. Then for lighter entertainment Cushing's nearby Thursford display of yesteryear's fairground rides, steam engines and many impressive organs including a mighty Wurlitzer pleases very many visitors.

A Mosquito FB VI of 515 Squadron, Little Snoring.

Main features:
Runways: 250° 6,000ft x 150ft, 130°, 190°, concrete. *Hangars:* two T2, two hangars provided for gliders, one B1. *Accommodation:* RAF: 155 officers, 362 SNCOs, 1,290 ORs; WAAF: 10 officers, 24 SNCOs, 327 ORs.

LITTLE WALDEN (HADSTOCK), Essex

52°04/00°11E 365ft asl; TL555435. B1052 Saffron Walden-Linton crosses airfield

When driving from Saffron Walden to Linton on the B1052 the location of this former airfield becomes immediately obvious, for hangars and control tower are still very much extant sixty-five years after the cessation of hostilities.

Little Walden began its career when construction commenced in 1943 on a plateau, and it was opened for operational use on 6 March 1944 as Station 165 under the aegis of the US 9th Air Force. Next day operational elements began arriving and comprised four squadrons of the 409th(L) Bomb Group flying A-20G Havocs. The 409th, under Colonel Preston P Pender, was part of the 97th Combat Wing, the other two Groups in the Wing being at Wethersfield and Gosfield.

Douglas A-20G-30-DO 43-9671 7G-B, a 'solid' nose Havoc of the 641st BS, 409th BG Spring 1944 (USAF).

Their first mission was flown on 13 April 1944 and set the pattern for operations for the next few weeks by operating in a tactical role against targets which were part of the pre-D-Day build up. Fierce German resistance was frequently encountered as on 27 May 1944 when the Group suffered heavy casualties in an attack on the marshalling yards at Amiens.

One evening in May a Havoc crashed soon after take-off near the village of Ashdon and Mrs Everitt from that village was tragically killed in attempting to rescue the crew when the aircraft exploded. For this action she was subsequently awarded a posthumous decoration by the USAAF.

On 6 June the Group had fifty-eight aircraft serviceable and another seven unserviceable. Following the Normandy assault their pattern of operations continued, the targets being directly ahead of the advancing armies. This soon caused problems of range, and in September the 409th moved to Bretigny in France and in company with other units of the 9th AF which also moved to newly liberated Continental airfields. Changes at Little Walden followed, the airfield now coming under the control of the 8th AF and on 26 September the yellow-nosed Mustangs of the 361st Fighter Group moved in from Bottisham. The three squadrons which comprised the Group, Nos 374, 375 and 376, continued their operations of escort and ground support until 1 February 1945 when they were detached to France and operated from there until 9 April, when they returned to Little Walden.

During their absence, the base saw a distinct change of type when B-17s of the 493rd Bomb Group arrived from Debach allowing their former home to undergo repairs. So now it was the turn of heavies to roll along Little Walden's runways, participating in the intense daylight operations during the last few months of the war in Europe.

In April, however, with the return of the 361st Fighter Group, Little Walden reverted to its role as a fighter station and saw the war out as such. The famous 56th Fighter Group, 'the Wolfpack', joined the 361st during late summer, both Groups returning home in November. Little Walden closed to flying in January 1946.

The station was then placed in RAF hands and under Duxford's control until it was transferred to 27 Group, Technical Training Command during March 1946. It then came under Debden's control for administration purposes. It passed through the hands of several government agencies before disposal in the mid-1950s. Parts of the main runway remain, also a T2 hangar. The control tower is also still in position in good health and well protected.

Main features:
Runways: 160° 5,700ft x 150ft, 100°, 040°, concrete with wood chips. *Hangars:* two T2.
Hardstandings: fifty spectacle type. *Accommodation:* 421 officers, 2,473 enlisted men.

LORD'S BRIDGE, Cambridgeshire

52°10N/00V01E 75ft asl; TL385545. N of A603, at Comberton-Barton road junction

Highly secret-looking, the weird things at Lord's Bridge were not 'radar dishes' but radio telescopes through which discoveries of pulsars and such stellar wonders took place. Nearby was an area where gas bombs were once stored, for 2 and 3 Groups and Lysanders. Despite those, surrounded by a huge bomb dump too, the authorities in 1942 requisitioned a small grass field nearby for use as a Relief Landing Ground. Bombs were stored at many unlikely places during the war, and even in Nissen huts lining public roads and frequently unguarded!

The RLG users, in fine weather, were trainee pilots of 22 EFTS and instructors training with 4 FIS Cambridge who practised forced landings here. So at Lord's Bridge one was often confronted by a Tiger Moth suddenly rising from behind the high hedge, and sometimes about to pass over the bomb dumps. To be fair, though, the RLG between 1942 and 1944 was generally in use only when others were fully utilised and the wind permitted the safest possible activity.

LUDHAM, Norfolk

52°43N/01°33E 50ft asl; TG395195. 12½ miles NE of Norwich, between Hickling and Barton Broads

HM King George VI and Queen Elizabeth were coming, and as they set out for Ludham airfield a Ju 88 of KG 6 took off from Soesterberg. Its intent was to torment mariners off the East Anglian coast.

The date was 28 January 1943 and just as their Majesties were due to make their afternoon arrival Pilot Officer Code and Sergeant Nash were ordered to intercept that raider. Nine minutes later the two pilots both of 167 Squadron returned, their landing coinciding with the arrival of the Royal party. Code had scored his first victim, that Ju 88, and he was elated. The King made no attempt to conceal his delight at the present his Air Force had given him on a unique occasion.

Ludham opened as Coltishall's second satellite on 10 November 1941 prior to which the site had much earlier been used as a fighter-bomber range. Now it would serve as a 12 Group forward base under Coltishall control. Its proximity to the coast made it ideal for maritime support, escorting bombers raiding the Continent and for scrambles against raiders. In mid-November 1941, 152 Squadron was sending Sections forward to Ludham from Swanton Morley for convoy escort duty and attacks on E-Boats. Then, on 1 December 1941, 19 Squadron moved into Ludham staying until 4 April 1942 and using Spitfire Vs for 12 Group convoy patrols, shipping reconnaissance, *Circuses*, sweeps and *Rodeos*. No 19 was immediately replaced by 610 Squadron from Hutton Cranswick. Staying until September 1942, they quickly drew blood, at dawn on 27 April when they destroyed an all-black Ju 88 of 3./122 snooping off Lowestoft.

Convoy patrols occupied them for much of the time and resulted in a number of engagements. During the Baedeker night raids on Norwich Ludham's Spitfires flew *Fighter Night* patrols, but unsuccessfully. When they were not patrolling, '610' operated over Europe flying *Rhubarbs*, sweeps and escorts. During the Dieppe raid the Ludham squadron moved forward to West Malling and participated with 411 and 485 Squadrons under Wing Commander Jameson.

An unusual event occurred on 12 May. Warrant Officer Matte, a Free Frenchman of 253 Squadron, Hibaldstowe, had been ordered to carry out a Sector reconnaissance. Finding that somewhat unexciting, he scooted off to the Netherlands. There, using his initiative, he shot up a gasometer at the Hague setting it ablaze before strafing a nearby barge. He was greeted on returning from his private *Rhubarb* by 'authorities' who were far from amused.

Three days later Squadron Leader Haywood and Flight Sergeant Maren of 610 Squadron flying off Great Yarmouth came upon a Do 217E which they swiftly attacked. Then Yellow Section had a go. The bomber's port engine burst into flames, parts fell off the tail, the cockpit area was hit and the Dornier sank leaving three bodies in the sea. A Walrus from Coltishall found them, one barely alive. A launch from Yarmouth took the injured man and the other two bodies ashore.

A rarely mentioned aspect of the 31 May 1942 1,000 bomber Cologne raid was the fighter rear cover provided to prevent intruders from attacking during the landing phase. No 610 was one squadron involved at dawn.

On 14 October Spitfires of No 167 Squadron moved in aided by two Harrows for they were arriving from distant Castletown near Wick in the north-east tip of Scotland. The squadron was then the only Dutch fighter squadron and destined for a seven-month active stay at Ludham. Its role, more offensive than defensive, reflected the current employment of Fighter Command. Much of their work related to escorting Venturas of 2 Group making day raids, escorting Coastal Command Beaufighters, giving rear cover to returning US B-17s, flying shipping reconnaissance off the Netherlands and providing escort for ASR Walruses of 278 Squadron. Additionally, they flew *Rhubarbs* over the Continent and during one such operation on 13 December 1942 lost Squadron Leader Lane to a Fw 190. *Rhubarbs* were becoming increasingly dangerous now that the Fw 190 was about in plenty, and the following day these operations were suspended whilst tactics were reviewed before they were resumed on 22 December 1942.

Activity for 167 Squadron reached a memorable peak on 3 May 1943. That morning a sudden sharp raid was made on Lowestoft by Fw 190 fighter-bombers which raked the town and fled before the defenders could attack them. Spitfire Vs were no match for that sort of thing. That episode was bad enough, but what made this day even more memorable took place later. Shortly before 5.00 pm 167 Squadron took off and joined 118 Squadron, the Coltishall Wing being led by the popular Canadian, Wing Commander 'Cowboy' Blatchford. They made rendezvous with Methwold's 487 Squadron Venturas and set course for Holland. Soon after entering Dutch airspace over twenty enemy fighters swooped upon them from ahead, dived below the Spitfires and then set upon the Venturas now separated from their only escort. In vain the Spitfires tried to shield the bombers but each fighter Section was repeatedly 'jumped' upon by groups of enemy fighters. Eventually the whole fighter force was mingling in chaos. All but one of the Venturas were shot down, the Spitfires were badly mauled and 167 Squadron claimed only one combat success.

As a result of that Lowestoft raid Typhoons of No 195 Squadron were brought from Woodvale to Ludham on 13 May. More fighter-bomber strikes followed but there was never sufficient warning for the Typhoons to thwart them. Instead, they too undertook convoy and Beaufighter escorts before being replaced by Spitfire Vbs of 611 Squadron transferred here from Matlaske, Coltishall's other satellite, on 31 July. They came to work up for low-level operations.

On 4 August the fighters left and on 13 August Ludham passed to Air Ministry Works for conversion into a standard temporary wartime airfield for USAAF use. Plans made in May 1944 to extend the runways came to little for, by the time of its completion, the Americans no longer had need of Ludham. It lay virtually unused until August 1944 when the US VIIIth Fighter Command placed it on loan to the Admiralty for possible North Sea operations.

RAF fighters returned on 22 February 1945. No 229 Squadron re-numbered 603 Squadron at Coltishall on 7 January, moved here to resume attacks on V2 launching sites, undertake armed reconnaissance and escort Beaufighters. These tasks they shared with 602 Squadron which on 23 February came from Matlaske bringing Spitfire LF XVIs.

Early in April 1945 a very different sound was heard when No 91 Squadron arrived on the 8th flying the new wing, Griffon 61-engined Spitfire Mk XXIs intended for the Far East war. On 10 April the first operational sorties were flown by the new mark which set off on scrambles, armed reconnaissance and showed a new operational face by seeking midget submarines. The first two sorties along those lines were undertaken on the morning of 26 April by LA 252 and LA 223 and proved to be the most successful for a midget submarine was destroyed. Spitfire XXIs flew their 152nd and final sortie from Ludham on 1 May 1945.

Ludham's No 91 Squadron, the only wartime Spitfire 21 squadron. LA220 depicted. (Andy Thomas).

To help sort out maintenance problems the only two operational Mk XXI squadrons came together here when No 1 Squadron arrived on 14 May. Both stayed until 14 July 1945 after which Ludham fell quiet. It was handed to 60 Group in September 1945 and wound down during the remaining months of 1945. A landing strip using part of a runway currently exists.

Main features (by December 1944):
Runways: 078° 4,200ft x 150ft, 198°, 3,300ft x 150ft, 322°, 3,300ft x 150ft concrete with partial tarmac surface. No permanent lighting. *Hangars:* one T2, four Blister. *Hardstandings:* nine permanent fighter stands, twelve fighter pens, some fifty PSP type for USAAF use. *Accommodation* (US): 190 officers, 1,519 enlisted men.

MARHAM, Norfolk

52°38N/00°33E 72ft asl; TL730685. By A1122 10 miles E of Downham Market

Across the fields there were huge steel frames and just visible between them were parts of a very neat sort of town all in the middle of nowhere. We stopped for a look, cautiously mind you. All was a long way from the Swaffham road which then was little more than a narrow lane. Viewed now from the sane spot Marham sprawls across the vista for it is one of Europe's most expansive airfields where merely crossing the runway is like traversing a large car park.

For more than forty years Marham played a prominent role in Britain's nuclear deterrent force, and was a depository for assorted nuclear weapons. The contributions its Victor tanker crews made to both the Falklands campaign and *Desert Storm* were vital, and its strike and reconnaissance Tornados have for some years been busy in the troubled Near East. Marham is now the RAF's prime strike and reconnaissance station.

It is descended from a First World War version established close to another landing ground, RNAS Narborough. The latter opened in August 1915 as a satellite for the large RNAS station at Great Yarmouth. Being well inland it was transferred from the Navy to the RFC in April 1916. There were then two aerodromes quite close to one another. What, then, of Narborough?

Late May in 1916, 35 Squadron (also resident of RAF Marham in the 1950s) moved in with AW FK3s, BE2c/e and FB5s, and trained for reconnaissance operations prior to departing for France in January 1917. On 1 August 1916 No 59 Squadron formed here, equipped with RE8s, and left for France on 13 February 1917. Thereafter Narborough became a crew training station. No 48 Reserve Squadron, which had formed here on 2 November 1916, took its DH 6s and RE 8s to Waddington later that month. No 50 Reserve Squadron, which arrived from Sedgeford (near Dersingham) on 14 November 1916, was renamed 53 Training Squadron on 31 May 1917. Avro 504s, BE 2cs, DH 6s and RE 8s were now in use. No 64 Training Squadron, which moved in on 14 April 1917, flew Avro 504s, BE 2cs and RE 8s. No 1 Training Squadron formed here on 1 October 1917, equipped with Sopwith Camels, then left for Oxford. There were many unit changes at busy Narborough, where, in December 1917, No 83 Squadron arrived from Wyton to carry out night-bombing training.

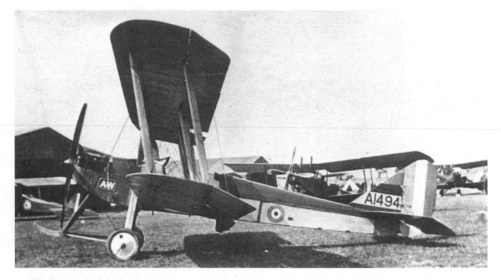

At Narborough (Marham's predecessor) in March-April 1917, Armstrong Whitworth FK 3 A1494, RE8s behind. Used by 50 RS and 65 TS. (Bruce Robertson Archives)

Whereas Narborough was a training station, nearby Marham, an 80-acre landing ground on the eastern part of the present airfield, opened in 1916 and served as an operational night home defence station. September 1916 saw part of No 51 Squadron moving and bringing BE 2c/d, BE 12 and FE 2B fighters for night patrols over northern Norfolk. 'C' Flight 51 Squadron followed, replaced in July 1917 by 'B' Flight. Squadron HQ took up residence soon after. Night interception activity continued while the squadron, using DH 6s and DH 4s, also afforded night-flying training to crews prior to their movement to France. Three new squadrons were sired by No 51, one being No 191 Depot Squadron, born on 6 November 1917. In December that became No 191 (Night) Training Squadron using BE 2d/es, DH 6s and Fe 2bs. It functioned as a dedicated night-flying training squadron, and moved to Upwood in July 1918. No 51 Squadron meanwhile took on charge Avro 504Ks specially modified into single-seater night-fighters. The final months of the war saw Squadron HQ administering a dozen landing grounds. 'C' Flight 51 Squadron left Marham in May 1919 and station closure followed. As with so many landing grounds the site returned to agricultural use – with a proviso that it could be requisitioned, an eventuality that came about in the mid-1930s.

Marham has a name almost synonymous with bombers. With five prominent 'C' Type hangars it opened on 1 April 1937 as a two-squadron heavy bomber station under Wing Commander A P V Daly AFC. At 0930 hrs on 5 May, No 38 Squadron's huge Fairey Hendons sailed in as only Hendons could. November 1938 saw the squadron begin re-arming with Wellingtons, the second squadron to do so. No 115 Squadron, an offshoot of 38, had been inaugurated on 15 June 1937. Equipped with Harrows, they began flying Wellingtons in April 1939. On 1 June No 1 RNZAF Unit began forming also to fly Wellingtons. Early 1937 saw the decision taken for the New Zealanders to receive thirty Wellingtons, of which six would be ready to leave for New Zealand in August 1939. Instead, the unit was put at the disposal of the RAF when the war began and they moved to Harwell.

Upon the outbreak of war some Wellingtons were dispersed at an Unbuilt Satellite at nearby Barton Bendish and soon after there was a spy scare. A man calling himself Flight Lieutenant Weston had been driving around RAF airfields asking about AA defences. He was never found. Dispersals to and from the satellite continued, with the fear of an enemy onslaught on Armistice Day. So far the 'Wimpeys' had only flown armed patrols over the North Sea, then December brought a change. Bright winter weather on the 3rd resulted in twenty-four Wellingtons of 38, 115 and 149 Squadrons setting off for Heligoland. Despite cloud they managed to sink a minesweeper and drop a few bombs on defences. Fighters engaged them and an air gunner of a 38 Squadron aircraft, LAC J Copley, had a bullet lodge in his parachute harness buckle. His return fire destroyed a fighter, and the Wellingtons returned without loss. For Marham crews there were no more raids

The hangar is still there, but the Fairey Hendon has flown away! In case you missed it, it was K5088.

until the night offensive opened in February 1940 and propaganda leaflets were unloaded over Germany by crews mainly undertaking useful training flights.

The invasion of Norway led to Marham launching day and night raids on Stavanger and other targets. A brief resumption of patrols to inhibit enemy minelayers was abruptly halted when the Germans invaded the West. Marham's Wellingtons first attacked inland targets in Germany on 15/16 May claiming to drop bombs on Homberg, Duisburg and Gelsenkirchen.

On 22 June 1940 the air raid warning wailed on the camp, a number of enemy aircraft being in the area. At 0600 hrs bombs fell around the station in the first of a considerable number of small scale attacks. RAF night bombing was now in full swing and on 28 August the Wellingtons made their first flights to Berlin. Channel invasion ports were attacked before the offensive swung back to Germany.

No 38 Squadron was posted to the Middle East in November 1940, their place being taken on 25 November by No 218 (Gold Coast) Squadron which began Wellington operations on 20 December 1940.

Throughout 1941 both squadrons flew many sorties encountering accidents arising from battle damage and facing enemy intruders. On 8/9 April, for instance, Pilot Officer Lambert of 218 Squadron despatched to Kiel encountered flak which hit his port engine making it difficult to stay aloft. Heading for the Frisians all removable equipment was jettisoned, then an enemy fighter picked the aircraft out. The crew flashed their Aldis lamp at it which, to their surprise, flew away. Course was set by guesswork and they headed home at 80mph, then the port engine seized and boost pressure fell on the starboard. They reached England flying on one poor engine and no navigational equipment and made a belly landing at Horsham St Faith. There were many similar hair-raising moments for Marham's crews.

Intruders were a nuisance. On 4 April 1941 a Wellington of '115' was shot down near King's Lynn and the same night bombs fell on a Marham hangar without exploding. May 1941 saw five attacks on the station during which a heavy bomb fell by the Sergeants' Mess and the equipment store was set on fire. On 28 August five aircraft were lost landing back at base, after the Drem Lights and the lit runway were damaged by enemy bombs.

Nine Wellingtons took part in the 24 July daylight raid on Brest and faced flak and fighters in profusion. Operations were carried out continuously throughout 1941 then at the end of the year 115 Squadron began to equip with Wellington IIIs for the 1942 offensive. *Gee* was being fitted into the aircraft and on 6 January 1942 1418 Flight formed to test it using four Wellington IIIs before moving to Tempsford on 1 March. Early in 1942 218 Squadron re-armed with Stirling 1s.

Both Marham squadrons participated in the May/June '1,000-bomber' raids, 218 Squadron having the distinction of carrying the AOC 3 Group, Air Vice-Marshal Baldwin, to Cologne. Marham's crews were in the thick of battle whilst Downham Market airfield was being prepared as a Built Satellite whence 218 Squadron moved in July 1942. No 1483 TT/B&G Flight arrived from Newmarket on 14 July 1942 and returned there on 20 June 1943. In the early war years Marham had housed the 3 Group Fighter Affiliation Training Flight with Battles, etc.

In August 1942 Marham was transferred to 2 Group during a general repositioning of squadrons brought about by forming of the PFF and arrival of the US 8th AF. No 115 Squadron left for Mildenhall and No 105 along with the Mosquito Conversion Unit moved in on 29 September. No 105 was already operating Mosquitoes, but the second squadron to arrive that day, No 139, had to content themselves for the present with Blenheim Vs and Mosquitoes borrowed from '105'. June 1942 had seen 139 Squadron became operational using borrowed Mosquitoes, the two squadrons soon launching that impressive campaign which ultimately resulted in some of the most spectacular raids of the war and one of which was remarkable.

From the grass of the still small airfield Nos 105 and 139 Squadrons waged the most precise and exotic bomber offensive of the entire war. They used to form in Flights – sometimes squadrons – and race across Marham's giant lawn, then fly away faster than any other wartime Allied bombers to penetrate deep into enemy territory in daylight to deliver a painful, accurate bite before returning faster than pursuing fighters. Those amazing little unarmed plywood bombers – which so profoundly influenced and altered all bomber design and RAF operational techniques – wove one of the most exciting tapestries in RAF history. Operating from Marham, they never bettered their morale-boosting performance of 30 January 1943.

It was Hitler's birthday, and 2 Group was determined to give him memorable presents. In the morning Goering would address a Nazi rally in Berlin and, after a sumptuous lunch, Herr Göbbels would belch forth more propaganda. That course of events to be broadcast was seized upon by the RAF. What better background accompaniment than bursting bombs delivered in daylight – twice – by the only aircraft which could achieve that with a high degree of safety and success, Marham's Mosquitoes?

Shortly before 9.00am three crews of 105 Squadron led by Squadron Leader R W Reynolds set off on their dog-legged course for the 'Big City'. Over Holland they flew low to delight its down-trodden people while over Germany they produced a track of fear before zooming to 25,000ft. All went well and exactly at 11.00am bombs fell in long sticks across the city. The Germans had located the raiders but could not intercept them. A confused announcement on German radio, greeted with delight in Britain, spoke of an hour's postponement of the speech. The Mosquitoes returned safely, as Sir Geoffrey de Havilland and Chief Engineer Charles Walker had forecast that they would.

Already three crews of 139 Squadron had left Marham taking another route to Berlin. Just before 1600 hrs they arrived above the city – and as Göbbels was about to start boasting. What anger the Mosquitoes must have provoked! But this time Luftwaffe fighters were ready and Squadron Leader Darling was shot down.

There was a by-product to all this. An accurate measure of Mosquito fuel consumption was achieved from which it was clear the aircraft could easily reach Berlin, knowledge later put to more good use.

On 1 June 1943 the picture fundamentally changed when much of 2 Group was placed under Fighter Command prior to being part of 2TAF. The two Mosquito bomber squadrons were switched to 8 Group, a very unpopular move. For a time they made night nuisance raids keeping Germany awake at night. Bomber Command's management had little time for these specialised aircraft until it was realised that their immunity made them useful for route marking and, as soon as *Oboe* showed its worth, 105's aircraft were fitted with this remarkable bombing aid. No 139 Squadron left in July 1943 and '109' replaced them. Thereafter both squadrons specialised in pathfinding and Main Force night operations which continued until March-April 1944 Their strength had much increased when 109's third Flight opened on 26 October 1943.

As soon as they left work began on a 9,000ft runway 300ft wide making this a station for Very Heavy Bombers. Construction work put Marham out of operational use for the remainder of the war. The MCU had, incidentally, left for Turweston on 1 May 1943, was absorbed by 13 OTU and reconstituted as 1655 MCU base at Marham from 1 July 1943 to 7 March 1944.

Marham reopened late summer 1945. On 25 September the Central Bomber Establishment formed out of the BDU and moved here. It was some months before it was fully functioning using Lancasters to train bombing and gunnery leaders and develop new techniques and to assess new aircraft between February 1946 and 14 April 1949 when CBE moved to Lindholme. Lincolns had been also used along with a few Mosquitoes along with Spitfire XVIs for combat trials. Investigation was carried out into the characteristics of bombs freefall and guided, also of the value of remotely controlled guns.

Early 1947 found four modified Project Ruby USAF B-29s here for trials involving rocket bombs and 12,000lb 'Tallboys', which were dropped on U-boat pens at Farge. In June 1947 nine B-

29s of the 340th BS, 97th Bomb Group, from Smoky Hill, Kansas, came to publicly commemorate the wartime arrival of the 97th in 1942, while giving the RAF an opportunity to assess the B-29 and review its suitability as a Lincoln replacement and interim 'heavy' until new jet bombers were available. Master Airfield Marham, with a long runway and ample concrete stands, strongly appealed to the Americans as an overseas base for their hefty, complex and heavy bombers.

On 23 February 1950, by which time agreement had been made for the RAF to have a fleet of ex-USAAF B-29s, the Bomber Command B-29 Training School opened at Marham, where, in April 1950, the RAF received its first B-29 Washington. On 1 July the Washington Conversion Unit was inaugurated and immediately began training crews for No 35 Squadron and thereafter for Nos XV, 44, 90, 115, 149 and 207 Squadrons. The WCU closed on 1 September 1951 only to reopen in June 1952 and function until March 1953 training additional crews.

In responding to the Korean War the US the 3rd Air Division HQ opened here on 16 July 1948 and for the first time US forces were being stationed in a friendly country in peacetime. Three B-29 Bomb Groups were also despatched to Britain at short notice and lodged where space was available at the few suitable airfields. Two squadrons of the 307th BG (Nos 370 and 371) and their HQ were at Marham between July and November 1948. Seven subsequent Group rotations involving Marham were: 97th BG, 340 BS – November 1948 to February 1949; 307th BG, 370BS – February to May 1949, 509th BG 393 and 715 BS – May to August 1949, 43rd BG 64 BS B-50A, and the first three KB-29M tankers to be based here, – August to November 1949, 22 BG – November 1949 to February 1950, 2nd BG 20 BS B-50A – February to May 1950, 93rd BG 328 BS B-50D – July 1950 to February 1951.

Among them were the 509th BG Gold Plate 'Superforts' able to carry an atomic bomb. Under the 1950 USAF Dispersal Scheme Marham was obliged to accept up to fifteen B-50s yet it was not really possible to operate there more than two full or four half Washington squadrons.

Washingtons of Nos 35, 90, 115 and 207 Squadrons were used only until sufficient Canberras were available. No 115 re-armed with B2s in February 1954, No 207 in March 1954, No 35 in April 1954 and No 90 in November 1954 these forming the Marham Wing.

Marham's striking power spectacularly increased on 15 March 1956 as a result of the arrival of the first Valiant for 214 Squadron, which reformed on 21 January 1956. No 207 Squadron, flying Canberra B2s, disbanded on 27 March, then re-formed on 1 April and started flying Valiants in July. By then Marham had hosted an unusual visit by the Russian leadership duo, Nikita Kruschev and Marshal Bulganin. With them came Mr A N Tupolev, the aircraft designer, and some dubious-looking pals. Standing by Marham's new control tower, Nikita in a frenzied state gesticulated as only he could and finally ominously pointing my way bellowed, 'Vee vill bury zyou!' I felt he really meant it.

Marham then experienced a period of extensive change. On 1 May 1956 No 90 Squadron disbanded, then re-formed at Honington. No 148 Squadron re-formed at Marham on 1 July 1956 and almost immediately was flying Valiants, whose identity was proclaimed only by the squadron badge. No 35 Squadron left for Upwood during July, taking its Canberra B2s.

V-force build-up was slow, likewise the delivery of required bombing aids. Nevertheless, in September-October, as part of the force involved in operation *Musketeer*, the three squadrons contributed sixteen Valiants to the Malta-based V-force detachment involved in attacking Egyptian airfields. Marham's remaining Canberras, of 115 Squadron, operated from Nicosia. The station needed modifications to raise it to Class 1 Medium Bomber standard before it could constantly hold one nuclear-loaded Valiant at high readiness. For fast getaway an ORP with four fingers, each for one Valiant, was laid on the south-eastern end of the main runway.

May 1957 brought agreement for the Valiants to switch from their strategic to a tactical role. The same year the station received its coat of arms featuring a blue bull to denote offensive strength and the motto 'Deter', symbols woven into the station's main gates. On 1 July 1957 No 115 Squadron disbanded, bringing an end to Canberra bomber activity here.

Application of in-flight refuelling gear to all V-bombers had been agreed in 1954, and in December 1957 No 214 Squadron started pioneer trials and the development of a tanker role. It was January 1959 before the first fuel transfer between two Valiants took place. Funding for sixteen Valiant tankers was approved the following April, which allowed for a second Valiant tanker squadron, No 90, Honington-based.

Protection of the V-force from manned aircraft attack was the main task for the home defence fighter force. Further protection was afforded by the Missile Belt. On 1 October 1959 No 242

Squadron was formed, equipped with Bristol Bloodhound Mk 1 missiles and based at Marham. It turned out to be a brief phase, the Squadron disbanding on 30 September 1964, for by then the main threat was from ballistic missiles.

A major change had come on 1 January 1960 when No 207 Squadron was switched to SACEUR control and a tactical role, followed by No 148 on 15 July 1961. One crew would always be held for QRA at 15 minutes. Marham's might increased in 1961 when No 49 Squadron moved in from Wittering bringing more Valiants. The twenty-four-strong Valiant Tactical Bomber Force (TBF) replaced the sixty-four Canberras previously tasked to attack tactical targets, which required limited distance penetration. As a result the Valiants' primary weapon was no longer *Blue Danube*. Now it would be the American 1,900lb Mk 28 atomic bomb, two of which could be carried in a Valiant for release from 40,000ft. To evade the improving Warsaw Pact defences, training using the US Mk 43 nuclear weapon for hi-lo-hi profile operations commenced in April 1963.

While the TBF practised, in-flight refuelling was under way. No 214 Squadron had lost its bomber role in April 1962 in order to become an air-to-air refuelling (AAR) squadron, leaving the offensive role to Nos 49, 148 and 207 Squadrons. Very quickly the value of AAR was proven, especially when record-breaking long-range overseas flights became possible. AAR allowed for easy overseas reinforcement, and enabled fighters to remain in patrol and interception modes for much longer.

With all seemingly going well, tragedy suddenly struck. A Valiant of Wyton's 543 Squadron, during an inspection in Africa, was found to have a crack in its main spar. Buffeting that TBF Valiants endured when low flying, for which they had not been stressed, suggested that they would be ever more vulnerable. On 6 August 1964 serious metal fatigue, and other pointers towards structural problems, were discovered in a Marham Valiant. So serious were they that all Valiants were immediately inspected. Further failings were discovered and flying limitations were imposed.

A replacement tanker type was clearly and urgently needed, desperately sought, and choice fell upon the Victor 1. Valiants were grounded on 26 January 1965, and Nos 214 and 207 Squadrons were disbanded on 28 February, No 148 in April and No 49 on 1 May 1965. Apart from XD818, saved for the RAF Museum, Marham's Valiants were dismembered on the south side of the airfield.

Equipment change ushered in No 55 Squadron with an IE of six Victors at Marham on 24 May 1965. Next month it took on charge its first Victor B(K)1A two-point refueller. In June the Tanker Training Flight (ex-AR Flight) formed to assist Victor conversion, and on 1 December 1965 No 57 Squadron re-formed, using Victor B.1/1As to become the second Victor AAR squadron. Next month it received XA937, the first three-point refuelling Victor tanker. No 214 was resurrected on 1 July 1966 as the third Victor squadron, equipped with three-point tankers. Transfer of Marham from 3 Group to 1 Group took place in April 1968, for the Victors were supporting overseas deployments and working with Lightning and Phantom fighters intercepting Soviet intrusion into the UKADR.

On 6 February 1970 the TTF was upgraded when it became No 232 OCU with responsibility for AAR training. This continued to its disbandment on 4 April 1986. By then much had changed, a major forward step being the arrival, on 7 May 1974 for 232 OCU, of XL233, the first far more capable Victor K2 tanker, which soon replaced the B(K)1As of 55 and 57 Squadrons. Its greater efficiency resulted in force reduction, No 214 Squadron dying on 28 January 1977.

Cutbacks had also engulfed West Raynham, from where, on 5 January 1976, No 100, a target facilities squadron, brought its Canberra B2s, T4s and T17s to Marham. Further Cottesmore Canberras, of No 231 OCU, moved in on 18 February. After No 98 Squadron disbanded at Cottesmore on 27 February, its E Mk 15s were assigned to 100 Squadron, and at the station Canberras were again a common sight over the following four years. Further rationalisation then led to all RAF Canberras being gathered at Wyton, to where No 100 Squadron departed in January 1982, followed by the OCU in July 1982. By then, Marham had played a vital role in an amazing major international event.

The Argentine invasion of the Falkland Islands was quite unexpected. Denting the aggressor's ego meant operating at a vast distance, and it came to highlight as never before the value of AAR. Nine Victor K2s soon flew to Ascension from where they carried out AAR and, as a team, undertook maritime reconnaissance of the Southern Ocean. That task began on 20 April with a 17-hour-long sortie around far distant South Georgia for which special reconnaissance equipment had been fitted to the aircraft.

Victor tankers enabled Harriers and Sea Harriers to be flown, amazingly non-stop, from Cornwall to Ascension, but Marham's tankers became best known for the complex, highly demanding support given to the *Black Buck* Vulcan bombing raids on the Falklands. All was a stunning vindication of AAR and emphasised too how fast the world was 'shrinking'. Norfolk-based aircraft were now operating at almost opposite ends of the globe, and over vast areas of ocean.

Victor deployment to Ascension ended in June 1985 after they had shepherded Phantoms flying to Mount Pleasant, Falklands, in May 1985. Following the distant campaign the Victor tankers settled to supporting fighter activity and assisting in overseas deployments until 30 June 1986, when No 57 Squadron disbanded. The VC-10 tanker was now in service.

Although work had commenced in 1977, it was the 1980s before evidence of forthcoming change became apparent as, on each of two large building sites – one in the south-eastern and the others in the south-western corners of the airfield – a dozen Hardened Aircraft Shelters were erected. They were devised to accommodate two squadrons of Tornado GR 1 bombers; the famed No 617 Squadron ('The Dam Busters') reformed on 1 January 1983, and No 27 Squadron was reborn on 1 May 1983. Both within 1 Group, they were declared to NATO and capable of delivering nuclear weapons. WE177 nuclear bombs stored under certain shelters could be attached to the aircraft while they were sheltering. The number of Tornados much increased when, between March and September 1987, examples flown by Honington's TWCU were here while their home station's runway was attended to. For the same reason a few Nimrod MR2s of St Mawgan-based No 42 Squadron arrived in March 1988 and spent nearly a year at Marham.

With little clear warning came the 2 August 1990 Iraqi invasion of Kuwait. There was no doubting that the invaders would have to be forced out, for they might otherwise attempt a crazy move into Saudi Arabia. Marham was at once alerted for a part in a coalition force to drive the Iraqis from Kuwait. It would take some months to assemble. No 55 Squadron's K2s deployed, on 15 and 16 October, to Muharraq, Bahrain. From there they assisted Tornado and Jaguar work-up before operation *Desert Storm*, during which they provided AAR back-up for many sorties flown against Iraq by coalition forces.

For operation *Granby/Desert Storm* Marham contributed some of its best Tornado airframes and indeed power plants. The aircraft were painted with a special 'washaway desert pink' fluid, and carried identity letters. Although deployed to the Gulf as squadrons, the aircraft were not flown operationally only by their squadron's crews. Such 'sharing', whereby aircraft remain on station while crews are rotated between home station and overseas base, is now the norm.

The first batch of Tornados left Marham for Muharraq in August 1990 to join a composite force drawn from five squadrons. A second group, including 617 Squadron, flew to Tabak, Saudi Arabia, during October, and was in the fight from 16/17 January 1991 when it bombed Baghdad. Subsequently the group often attacked airfields and mainly tactical targets.

On 10 February No 617 was the first to operationally employ the pod-carried Thermal Image & Laser Designator (TIALD) system. Jointly developed by GEC and Ferranti, its development had been hastened in December 1990, for it greatly enhanced attack accuracy.

Gulf activity was very far from over when the *Desert Storm* ceasefire came into effect on 28 February 1991. Although the three Marham squadrons came home in March, autumn 1991 saw the Tornados participating in operation *Jural* and patrolling over southern Iraq.

An important change in Marham's role was under way and was illustrated by the arrival, on 1 December 1991, of No II (AC) Squadron, whose Tornado GR 1A reconnaissance aircraft moved in from Laarbruch as part of the wind-down of RAF Germany. Working with Honington's XIII Squadron, they had flown lone night sorties seeking Iraqi Scud missiles during the recent action. Summer 1992 saw Tornado crews from Marham deployed for a part in operation *Southern Watch* helping enforce the no-fly zone protecting those living in the Euphrates Delta.

After the withdrawal from RAF service of the Buccaneer, Nos 27 and 617 Squadrons replaced them in the maritime role, bringing a move to Lossiemouth, No 27 going in late December 1993 after being renumbered No 12 Squadron in October 1993. No 617 followed during April 1994.

November 1993 had seen No 39 (1 PRU) Squadron arriving with five Canberra PR9s and two T4s. The PR 9s, with an amazing high-flying capability, were to prove of great value as wet film reconnaissance aircraft during Balkan wars and Near East activity.

Honington's No XIII Squadron came to Marham in February 1994, joined II Squadron, and brought along reconnaissance-dedicated Tornado GR 1As. Until 23.59hrs on 31 March 1998 WE177 nuclear bombs were available for use at a scale of one aircraft per squadron. It was at this time that XIII Squadron rearmed with Tornado GR 4as featuring SLIR and Linescan IR, but no longer carried nose cannon.

As for the Victors, they took part in the Queen's Review commemorating the 75th Birthday of the RAF held at Marham on 1 April 1993. No 55 Squadron disbanded on 15 October 1993, its aircraft being somewhat brutally destroyed soon after, on the southern side of Marham where the Valiants died. The final flying departure of a Victor K2 (XH672), which was also the last in-service flight by a V-bomber, took place at 11.48hrs on a dreary 30 November 1993. Lightly laden, the most successful of the V-bombers lifted off steeply for Shawbury, indecently disappearing into low cloud and most unceremoniously ending a momentous phase in the history of the RAF. The strategic heavy bomber role, which had sired it, was no more. The future for the RAF would be mainly as a tactical force supporting the British Army.

As the end of the century approached, Marham was housing two Tornado GR1A/4 squadrons, each nominally holding thirteen aircraft, and No 39 (No 1 PRU) Squadron. Preparations were under way for the arrival of two more Tornado bomber squadrons being withdrawn from Germany. First came No IX, which, in June 1982 and then Honington-based, was the RAF's first Tornado bomber squadron. In 1999 the squadron was the first to rearm with Tornado GR4s, with which it fought in Balkan skies. No IX (Bomber) Squadron arrived at Marham on 17 July 2001, having left Bruggen in Germany a few days before it ceased to be an active RAF airfield. No 31 Squadron followed during August, raising Marham to a four-squadron station, the most potent in the RAF. Hitherto, the reconnaissance squadrons had formed Marham Reconnaissance Wing. Now the title changed to the Marham Wing.

The ill-starred decision to remove Saddam Hussein and his regime resulted in operation *Iraqi Freedom*. Marham's participants included Nos II, IX and 31 Squadrons together with 617 Squadron, which contributed in 2003 to operation *Telic* through the eighteen-strong Tornado GR4/4A Combat Air Wing 1 based at Ali Al Salem. No II Squadron also participated by positioning seven crews at Al Udeid, Qatar, together with elements of 12 and 617 Squadrons. No II Squadron – the oldest fixed-wing flying squadron in the world – again carried out low-level night sorties seeking Iraqi Scud missile activity in its western desert area. No 31 Squadron performed in a 'pathfinder' role and, together with IX Squadron, used ALARM anti-radiation missiles for attacks on Iraqi radars. Since January 1995 No 31 Squadron had been committed to the Suppression of Enemy Air Defences (SEAD), and re-equipped with GR 4s in 1999. The importance of such activity was tragically obvious when a US-operated Patriot missile, fired in error on 23 March 2003, brought down a Tornado of IX Squadron. Since the end of the assault on Iraq, Marham's Tornado squadrons have periodically been detached to the Gulf as part of the ongoing British presence.

. Such activity away from base has had a number of repercussions, not least its most disruptive effect upon the lives of the personnel involved and their families. At a different level it has resulted in reorganisation of the forces involved.

On 11 October 2004 Marham initiated a six-month move to a new status, a complex Depot Support Hub for Tornado GR4 operations embracing Lossiemouth's squadrons too. It was declared in place on 1 April 2005. At that time the small Canberra force was still making a valuable photographic reconnaissance contribution to the needs of ground forces. Its aircraft and equipment well worn, No 39 (1PRU) Squadron was disbanded on 29 July 2006.

Based at Marham in 2009 are four Tornado recon/strike squadrons, making this the RAF's largest operational front-line station. The Cold War has long since passed into history; operations

Tornado GR 4a ZA591/037 of XIII Squadron wearing full squadron markings. March 2007.

Mosquito XVI F556 of the Central Bomber Establishment May 1947.

Tornado GR4A 'Shiny Two' decorated with celebration markings of No 2 Squadron.

now revolve around involvement overseas, for which Marham's GR4 force forms the major element of No 138 Expeditionary Wing.

Being such an important RAF airfield, it is hardly surprising that Marham hosts a wide assortment of organisations in order to sustain its attack, reconnaissance and SEAD role. In the forefront are the Tactical Imagery Intelligence Wing, No 3 Force Protection Wing, the Tactical Armament Squadron, Tornado Maintenance School, and No 2620 (County of Norfolk) Squadron RAuxAF.

Backing the Tornado force are the Operations Wing, Forward Support Wing, Depth Support Wing and Base Support Wing. In depth support are the Tornado Components Squadron (TCS), Tornado Propulsion Squadron (TPS) and Tornado Engineering Squadron (TES). The Forward Support Wing embraces the Technical Intelligence Wing (TIW), No 3 (RAF) Force Protection Wing HQ, Tornado Engineering Development & Investigation Team (TOR (IDS) EDIT), No 93 Expeditionary Armament Squadron, 2620 Squadron RAuxAF, and RAF Holbeach Bombing Range.

Easy it is to regard the RAF as just a combat force. In the case of Marham, involvement during the flooding of Tewkesbury in 2007 is little known. Carrying an amazing Raptor EO/IR system pod, a Tornado GR4, flying very high, secured clear night images of the progress of the flood water and even obtained pictures of window and door arrangements, also opening directions to buildings at risk. Passed to ground services, they enabled rescues to be most effectively performed. One does not normally associate such kind deeds with the Tornado.

Main features:

Runways: 245° 9,000ft x 300ft and subsidiary runways 293° 6,000ft x 300ft, 335° 6,000ft x 300ft, concrete and asphalt. *Hangars:* five Type C. *Hardstandings* (1945): thirty-six heavy bomber pan handle type. *Accommodation:* RAF: 139 officers, 296 SNCOs, 1,893 ORs; WAAF: 10 officers, 16 SNCOs, 318 ORs.

Post-war additions have included two large ASPs and in the 1980s the addition of sets of HASs, one each in the south-west and south-east corners of the airfield each for the use of a Tornado squadron. A special engine workshop has been built by the old apron alongside the operations block.

In passing

At Marham a staff of twenty RAF personnel and ten civilians administer and control RAF Holbeach Bombing Range and Wash Weapons Airspace in which is also sited the Wainfleet range and the Range Control Tower. At Wainfleet gunnery practice takes place, firing being aimed at floating canvas screens on frames placed on a tidal beach. Short- and long-range attacks are carried out at both shallow and steep angles. There are four 150-yard practice bombing targets and three ship targets. Dive attacks can be practised at angles of from 5 to 45 degrees using free and retarded weapons and employing loft and toss techniques; slots of 15 minutes are usually allocated. Run-in can be timed for twenty aircraft at 30-second intervals. Despite the large number of birds to be found over The Wash, only one aircraft in twelve years has been lost to bird strike.

It is possible to view the activity at the ranges from a safe public area at relatively close distance. During the Cold War activity was intense, but that is no longer the case.

MARTLESHAM HEATH, Suffolk

52°03N/01°16E 90ft asl; TM258450. A1093 crosses site

Tesco, Burger King and roller ball chums have, with the aid of a little chef and the local constabulary, tried hard to finish off dear old Martlesham. Here and there its remains bravely stand as bastions pleading with you to heed them, dream a few dreams, imagine you can hear a 'Ginny'. 'A' Shed which knew so many really great things hides its sorrows behind one time saplings while almost rubbing shoulders with a roller king. By the road bisecting the camp site the Main Guardroom remains intact like any self-respecting fortress and is probably disdainful of much around. It will be delighted if you gaze nostalgically at the good assortment of ex-workshops and stores 1920s buildings nearby which are now sales points for electronic marvels (which it cannot understand) or are business premises. Beyond, proudly imperial, stands the former SHQ, its glorious portico pristine white and safe from graffiti merchants courtesy of a high wire mess fence guarding the huge BT presence. A massive concrete block hides their research facility particularly concerned with software development. It keeps watch over the line of the one time main runway – very easy to determine – in fear of Bf 110s returning. By the A14-A12 link road four fine 1922-style red brick tile-roofed barrack blocks remain in good health. Inside, ghosts of fearsome SWOs of yesteryear are reputed to hold nightly soirées while dreaming of Martlesham's ''orrible little men'.

Much of the one-time world's most respected performance and acceptance trials establishment has gone, but sufficient remains to warrant a sight-seeing visit to the flat heathland to the east of Ipswich that offered an ideal site for the Aeroplane Experimental Unit. The aerodrome is believed to have originated as a landing ground for Orfordness experimental station where, on 15 April 1916, No 37 Squadron formed to undertake armament experiments. Martlesham was also possibly intended to be used as a fighter station, No 37 Squadron re-forming on 15 September 1916 as a home defence squadron that soon moved to Essex.

Martlesham was certainly being used by May 1916, for on the 17th a Porte flying boat piloted by its designer, Sqn Cdr John C Porte, took off from Felixstowe with a Bristol Scout attached to its upper wing. Released over The Haven, Flt Lt M J Day safely put down on the Pretyman Estate landing ground, the site upon which Martlesham was established. From there some years previously an attempt to fly a locally built aeroplane is believed to have been made.

Workshops of the 1920s remain by the camp road at the end of which is the one-time Station Head Quarters now within the BT compound. A highly nostalgic road to visit.

At the end of 1916 Major Bertran Hopkinson, Professor of Engineering at Cambridge University, founded an official test centre for prototype aircraft. In November 1915 he had been appointed Director of Aeronautical Equipment. During January 1917 an official ceremony took place at Martlesham to welcome the CFS Testing Squadron, which moved in from Upavon. It possibly merged with a remnant of No 37 Squadron. The move allowed CFS Upavon to concentrate upon flying training, for which reason the armament development element of CFS had moved to Orfordness in June 1916. On 13 October 1917 the Experimental Station Orfordness became the Armament Experimental Station.

On 16 October 1917 Testing Squadron became the origin of the Aeroplane Testing Station. Testing new types of aeroplanes and armament – previously undertaken at Upavon – was now to be carried out here. Captain H T (later Sir Henry) Tizard, appointed Technical Officer, demanded and set in train exceptionally high standards. He undertook much high-altitude testing of aircraft and armament, and had within his team another scientist pilot, F A Lindeman, who later became well-known as Viscount Cherwell. Additional to exploring British and European aircraft designs, captured enemy aircraft were also tested. In December 1918 a Handley Page V/1500 carrying a crew of six departed from Martlesham to make the first through flight to India. Departing at 09.30hrs on the 13th, they reached Delhi on 16 January 1919.

Orfordness, still attached to Martlesham late in the war, became the Experimental Group, which in July 1919 was placed under 3 Group control, and on 16 March 1920 became part of the Armament Experimental Establishment.

In keeping with its increasing importance, the Martlesham organisation was redesignated the Aeroplane Experimental Establishment on 16 March 1920 and was placed within No 3 Group. There was talk of moving, but Martlesham Heath instead passed to No 1 Group on 31 August 1921, and in September 1922 was reorganised into two squadrons flying mainly DH 9As. One would explore aircraft capabilities while the other dealt with armament, for which a range was maintained on Orfordness.

General run-down of the services following the First World War resulted in fewer pilots being available at Martlesham as well as fewer new military aircraft designs. Martlesham therefore took on the role of investigating the characteristics of civilian aircraft, civilian aviation in general, air racing and speed record attempts.

On the night of 5/6 October 1922 a serious fire caused great damage at Martlesham. A hangar and its contents – aircraft and equipment – was completely destroyed. Rebuilding followed, on an extended site, with additional hangars and domestic accommodation transforming the original layout.

On 24 March 1924 a new and informative title was bestowed upon Martlesham Heath, one destined to receive worldwide respect. It became the Aeroplane & Armament Experimental Establishment with the experimental station at Orfordness under its control. Each section then received a separate identity, the Armament Unit becoming XV Squadron and the Aeroplane Unit, No 22 Squadron. Both military and civil aircraft were now to be assessed, for which reason No 22 Squadron was split into three Flights with separate responsibilities. Much of XV Squadron's testing was initially carried out using DH 9s.

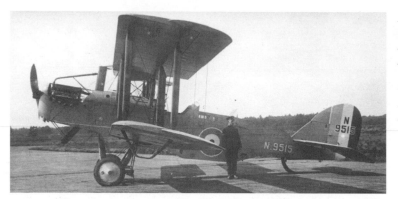

Hosts of aircraft underwent trials at Martlesham, including Westland Walrus N9515 (a DH 9A development).

Another all-important aspect reviewed was aviation safety which figured in Martlesham's testing work for the Parachute Section came under A&AEE until they moved to RAF Henlow.

A very wide array of aircraft – usually prototypes or early production examples – passed through the A&AEE. From the early 1930s the testing tempo fast increased like aircraft performance. The major recession was being overcome mainly by forced rearmament but also by the growing popularity and importance of aviation very evident at Martlesham. In May 1934 the two squadrons disappeared into being armament and performance sections of the A&AEE and the Experimental Co-operation Unit linked them with Orfordness experimental station. Radar development took place with nearby Bawdsey.

On 25 May 1936, Empire Air Day, the station was opened for public viewing. Later that year the Duke and Duchess of York (soon to be King and Queen) visited, also the Prince of Wales. They were able to inspect prototypes of aircraft soon to join the expanding RAF – the Battle, Blenheim, Lysander, Wellesley and especially the Hurricane and Spitfire. To make full use of the aerodrome an operational fighter Squadron, No 64 flying Hawker Demons, arrived on 13 August 1937 and stayed until 18 May 1938 when Church Fenton was able to receive them.

A public road bisecting the camp, and leading from the Woodbridge road to the main Felixstowe road, gave a good view of the general layout of Martlesham. It was still organised into the Performance Testing Section and the Armament Testing Section under Station Headquarters. The three-Flight Performance Test Section occupied the northerly hangars, a large green shed being the base for the testing of twin-engined aircraft. The other two Flights, occupying two other hangars, tested single-engined machines. Of the remaining more southerly hangars, the most northerly was the base for gun testing while a prominent green hangar was the centre for bombing tests. Armament and other needs were attended to in workshops on the eastern side of the road opposite the centre of the hangar line, and some buildings remain. With them were the Main Stores, Pay Accounts Section, the Instrument Shop and Engine Repair Shop. Further along in the Felixstowe direction was the Aircraft Repair Section on the aerodrome side of the road, and to the left the SHQ building, which remains. Beyond were barrack blocks, the Institute and three messes. Martlesham, very mixed in style and age, was unconventional in layout.

Tension created by the Munich crisis of 1938 called for much greater security at RAF stations and especially at Martlesham, whose highly secret activities included links with the nearby Bawdsey 'Radio location' or radar development station whose very tall CH towers were plain for all to see.

Behind the scenes Martlesham delved into the true performance of the Spitfire and Hurricane and looked into the capabilities of new bombers. Top secret work involved such unconventional activities as the laying of aerial minefields and the validity of cannon armament featured by the forthcoming Beaufighter and Whirlwind, prototypes of both being impossible to hide during trials. The alarming take-off problems of the Stirling were discovered and led to major re-design and the unusual undercarriage of what beyond doubt became East Anglia's own wartime bomber.

On 1 September 1939 A&AEE prudently began moving to Boscombe Down, a safer venue, where its soul now resides somewhere within the new trials organisation, Qinetic.

Martlesham's proximity to the coast now came into its own, making it ideal for early interception of raiders at sea. Squadrons at inland stations sent detachments here on a rotation basis. Early arrivals included Nos 17, 29 and 504 Squadrons from Debden, ground personnel being ferried daily in a lumbering Bristol Bombay. No 264 Squadron, first to fly Defiant turret fighter, was the first fully resident wartime unit and worked up to operational status here.

By summer 1940 the tempo had fast increased, Hurricanes of Nos 17, 85 and 151 Squadrons all claiming the destruction of raiders attacking convoys off East Anglia. On the afternoon of 15 August when the Battle of Britain really came underway the airfield itself was sharply attacked by Bf 110 fighter-bombers covered by Bf 109s. Although 17 Squadron gave chase they were unable to catch the raiders. Considerable damage was caused to buildings but casualties were light. Five days later, the station was attacked again little damage being done. Nos 56, 111 and 257 Squadrons, all flying Hurricanes, made use of Martlesham during August and were joined by 25 Squadron Blenheims detached from North Weald.

On 11 November 1940 the Italians made a pathetic attempt to attack Britain. Their target was Harwich harbour (against which they also launched puny night raids) only a short distance from Martlesham. No 257 based here, together with other 11 Group squadrons, treated the visitors with the contempt they deserved and claimed seven destroyed and four damaged without loss. It was without doubt a splendid day for Squadron Leader Stanford-Tuck and his merry men for most merry they did become after recovering wine from an Italian Fiat BR20 bomber brought down on Bromeswell golf course!

Luftwaffe night raids led to No 3 Squadron flying Hurricane IIs operating from Martlesham between 3 April and 3 May 1941 by which time day fighter squadrons were taking part in offensive operations. Hurricanes of 242 Squadron based here between 16 December 1940 and 9 April 1941 set the trend at Martlesham. Convoy protection remained a major feature of life additional to which was the ever increasing air-sea rescue task. It began after No 5 Flight ASR formed here on 14 May 1941. From 22 December 1941 to 22 April 1944 it was undertaken by a detachment from 277 Squadron, Stapleford Tawney, variously consisting of Lysanders, Walruses, Spitfires, Defiants and Sea Otters. The squadron had formed from No 5 Flight. Between May and November 1941 Martlesham hosted a detachment of Lysanders from No 11 Group Anti-Aircraft Co-operation Flight.

Increased offensive operations resulted in frequent squadron changes those flying Spitfires soon becoming the norm. Having a coastal location Martlesham provided a haven for aircraft returning in crippled condition, both bombers and fighters arriving in sorry states. Proximity of the sea afforded squadrons areas for firing practice, supporting tow target aircraft including Henleys and Lysanders often calling at the station. Added punch was given to Martlesham when No 182 Squadron's Typhoons reformed here on 25 August 1942 and stayed until 7 December. By then a significant number of USAAF aircraft were calling. Americans were not new to Martlesham, for Hurricane IIs of No 71 (Eagle) Squadron operated there between 9 April 1941 and 23 June 1941, a second residence following between 14 December 1941 and 2 May 1942.

Proximity to defended coastal areas many times attracted AA target towers to Martlesham including No 1 AACU from whose 'H' Flight No 1616 Flight formed on 1 November 1942 and stayed until 13 March 1943, when they moved to Ipswich from where many such units flew. No 1488 Flight, here from 7 June 1942 to 17 August 1943, when it moved to Rochford, typically maintained an Ipswich detachment.

Autumn 1943 saw runways being laid and general preparations underway for the arrival on 5 October of P-47s belonging to the 356th Fighter Group, 8th Air Force. Their first mission was flown on 15 October.

For two years the 356th FG resided at Martlesham, operating in escort and ground-attack roles. A Distinguished Unit Citation was awarded to the 356th FG in September 1944, then came re-equipment with P-51s in November. RAF's ASR duties at Martlesham had continued alongside the American activity, a detachment from No 278 Squadron being here between 21 April 1944 and 23 September using Ansons, Walruses and Spitfires.

The 356th Group's Mustangs, recognised by their distinctive red nose panel with blue diamonds, flew their last mission on 7 May 1945 by which time they could look back upon a period of brutality for the Group had the 8th AF highest fighter loss rate proportional to enemy aircraft destroyed. The 356th returned to America in October-November 1945. That was not the end of a US presence here for from 10 January 1956 various AFSC units used the base and continuously from 8 July 1956 until about 1967. Indeed, a US facility remained in the area until 27 March 1992.

Martlesham having long been a special RAF Station, it experienced more special uses post-war under Bomber Command. The Blind Landing Experimental Unit formed at Woodbridge on 1 October 1945 as an RAE outpost moved here in July 1946 undertook much vital work with civilian and military fallout having even used an Albemarle as well as Ansons and Varsities under overall RAE supervision. Farnborough was also much in charge of the Bomb Ballistics Unit formed at Woodbridge on 22 May 1944 and which moved here with the BLEU and merged with it on 1 November 1949 when they became the Armament and Instrument Experimental Unit. Not unusual for Martlesham was the immensely varied selection of aircraft they attracted for use at one time, just as in the pre-war days of A&AEE. Transition from propeller to jet was much in evidence as Lincolns (one powered by two Merlins and two Avon jet engines) operated alongside unusual types including the Short B14/16 Sperrin and a rare Avro Ashton Mk 3 WE670. First flown on 4 April 1952, the latter was soon at Martlesham for bombing trials undertaken until the summer of 1953. More familiar types in use at this time were a Valiant, Canberras and Meteors. These were all involved with electrical and ballistics trials in conjunction with the long-established research station on Orfordness, where a landing strip was available. Protected with canvas screens, nuclear bomb cases were often loaded aboard the Sperrin and Valiant for dropping trials supervised by, and filmed by, Orfordness station. The other mainstream development remained instrument flying and was particularly related to bad weather landing procedures. The composite range of aircraft involved varied from the Dakota to the Avro 707 *Delta* wing.

BLEUs Albemarle had additional undercarriage suspension to cope with heavy landings.

Martlesham's links with fighters had been resumed when two Meteor squadrons arrived from Duxford to convert to Mk 4s. In November 1948 the intention had been to base Meteor squadrons here instead of Duxford.

The A&IEU departed in 1957 but already Martlesham had reverted to a previous role with the 1955 arrival of No 22 Squadron for search and rescue operations this time using Whirlwind helicopters. Between 1958 and 1960 No 11 Group Communications Flight was here in support of Group HQ at the station. Another nostalgic note sounded when on 16 May 1958 the Battle of Britain Flight moved in bringing a mixture of Hurricanes and Spitfires. These the station held until the Flight moved to Coltishall on 3 November 1961. While the BBF was here so was HQ 11 Group, between 2 June 1958 and 3 December 1960.

After their departure, activities decreased. Between 1948 and 1 September 1955 No 104 Gliding School functioned here, and now another ATC Gliding School provided weekend flying until 1963. Speculation surrounded Martlesham's future but it was clear that its RAF flying days were over. Shortly after closure on 25 April 1963 commercial interests took control. There was brief use of the airfield by light aircraft.

Avro Ashton WE670 used by BTU for weapons and electrical systems development.

On 16 January 1967 a celebration was held to mark the 50th anniversary of the opening of Martlesham Heath, those in attendance including representatives from many chapters in its history.

There are numerous reminders of the past in the area. Kesgrave RC Church built in 1931 was constructed in memory of Squadron Leader Michael Pop killed in the R101 disaster on 5 October 1930. A model of the R101 over the altar serves as an incense burner, its 'windows' lit by burning oil. Bawdsey Manor (TM 348395) is now in private hands.

In 1968 the Post Office announced that Martlesham with its clear, flat surroundings, would house their research centre, the 1970s seeing their large building come into prominence. Across the road is the Suffolk Police Headquarters. Where Tesco stands the huge Beardmore Inflexible Invincible used to keep a watchful eye. An excellent museum displays Martlesham's great past; opened in the control tower during September 2000, it is certainly worth visiting.

Tesco dominates where until recently stood the Type A main hangar and smaller Hangar (HP) pictured in 1978.

Disdainfully glowering at the Roller King, the 'A' Shed. Amazing to think Britain's nuclear deterrent was partly fashioned here, behind canvas screens!

Main features:
Runways: 300° 5,100ft x 150ft, 220° 4,950ft x 150ft sand-mix hardened runways.
Hangars: One Type A, one General Service and one General Service (repair shop),
three Blister. *Hardstandings:* twenty steel mat type. *Accommodation:* (USAAF) 190
officers, 1,519 enlisted men.

MATCHING, Essex

51°46N/00°14E 275ft asl; TL550110. 1 mile E of Matching Green

A temporary three-runway, two T2, much dispersed wartime airfield built by the US Army,
Matching opened in September 1943. In February and March 1944 HQ 135 Airfield RAF
organised themselves here while, in January and February 1944, B-26s of the 391st Bomb Group,
9th AF, moved in and commenced operations on 15 February. They attacked airfields, marshalling
yards and V-weapons sites operating in large formations over France and the Low Countries. They
bombed coastal defences on 6 and 7 June, and continued their cross-Channel operations to
September 1944 their targets including in particular fuel and ammunition dumps, troop
concentrations and provision of general support to the Allied advance. In common with other 9th
AF Groups the 391st moved out to France leaving Matching for Roye/Amy on 19 September 1944.

Late 1944 the station then in Fighter Command hands was next occupied by 38 Group whose
Operational & Refresher Training Unit moved in during late February 1945. Their task was to afford
practice to 38 Group crews who were being held in readiness to replace any lost in action. They had
operational commitments too, Stirling GTIVs forming the main equipment of ORTU towing
fourteen Horsas as their contribution to operation *Varsity*, the Rhine crossing, in March 1945.

April 1945 saw ORTU equipping with Halifax AIIIs and leaving one Flight using Stirlings. In
mid April No 1677 Target Towing Flight brought in Martinets for gunnery practice. Both units
moved to Wethersfield in mid-October 1945 after which Matching was left to run down.

Main features:
Runways: 200° 6,000ft x 150ft, 270°, 140°, concrete and wood chips. *Hangars:* Two
T2. *Hardstandings:* fifty loop type. *Accommodation:* (USAAF): 417 officers, 2,241
enlisted men.

MATLASKE, Norfolk

52°51N/01°11E 176ft asl; TG158345. E of village

M atlaske (or Matlask), prepared during the summer of 1940 as a satellite for Coltishall, came
into use during October 1940 when 72 Squadron's Spitfires were dispersed there. Matlaske
Hall was requisitioned to provide accommodation for air and ground crews.

Its first major taste of action came on 29 October when five enemy aircraft bombed and strafed
the grass field causing damage and few casualties. Attacks upon East Anglian airfields were
surprisingly few, but on 12 May 1941 incendiaries fell on Matlaske. A few days later Spitfire Vbs of
222 Squadron took up residence to fly sweeps and convoy patrols from here until 1 July when
Hurricane IIbs of 601 (County of London) Squadron under Squadron Leader Gracie replaced
them. They, too, carried out a number of sweeps and escorts sometimes helping to protect Stirling
bombers during their *Circus* participation.

A new type appeared over Matlaske on 13 August 1941, a Bell Airacobra, for 601 Squadron had
been chosen to try out this type. Before that task began the squadron moved to Duxford, their place
being taken the same day (16 August 1941) by 19 Squadron which remained until 1 December 1941.

By then Matlaske housed some of the most talked of, most curious and still fascinating twin-
engined Westland Whirlwind fighters. Only two squadrons ever used them and the second, No 137,
replaced 19 Squadron's Spitfires. The Whirlwinds patrolled over East Coast convoys mainly off
Yarmouth, encountering several enemy aircraft without claiming any. As companions they had a
few Lysanders of Coltishall's 278 Squadron. This ASR squadron, which had formed here (under
Coltishall control) on 1 October 1941 from No 5 ASR Flight (whose two Walruses had been using
Matlaske since July) was now also equipped with three Lysanders, the former equipping 'A' Flight
making use of Matlaske until August 1943.

Never to be forgotten by those involved was 12 February 1942. Soon after noon 137 Squadron was brought to readiness and at 1310 hrs four pilots were ordered to protect British destroyers racing to intercept the *Scharnhorst, Gneisenau* and *Prinz Eugen* daringly passing through the English Channel. In appalling weather the Whirlwind pilots caught sight of the German convoy twenty miles off the Belgian coast and as they dived to investigate about twenty Bf 109s suddenly set about them. A fierce dogfight ensued and just as Flight Sergeant Mercer had a Messerschmitt in his sights his cannon developed a stoppage and another Bf 109 raked his aircraft. Pilot Officer de Houx fired all his ammunition without success. The other two Whirlwinds were shot down. A second detail left Matlaske at 1340 hrs and nothing was heard of them after take-off. Two others, Pilot Officer Bryan and Sergeant Ashton kept watch over the British destroyers for thirty minutes, after which they returned. A sobering day indeed.

Whirlwinds were soon engaged in frequent actions against E-boats operating off the East Coast. During the Baedeker raids on Norwich 137 Squadron flew four *Fighter Night* patrols from Coltishall. It was during this period that a most distressing incident took place. One Whirlwind pilot latched on to what they wrongly concluded to be a Ju 88. It was actually a Blenheim upon which they opened fire. The Whirlwind pilot, soon realising he had shot down a Blenheim in a tragic error, headed out to sea and was not seen again.

First confirmed victory came to the Whirlwinds on 25 June 1942. Pilot Officer McClure and Warrant Officer Smith were on patrol east of Smiths Knoll when they spotted a Ju 88 and two bursts from McClure put the raider into the sea.

While much of Fighter Command was involved in the Dieppe raid of August 1942, 137 Squadron was busy off the East Coast. Flying Officer J M Bryan and Sergeant Roberts scrambled during the morning and fifty miles off Happisburgh destroyed a Do 217 from which the crew baled out as the bomber fell towards the sea burning.

So far 137 Squadron had been mainly involved in defensive action, but on 3 September they took part in their first *Rodeo*. Eleven Whirlwinds with twenty-four Spitfires of 411 and 485 Squadrons mounted a diversion attack on Lille. Hope was that enemy aircraft would engage them, but the Luftwaffe was not so easily attracted. On 17 September the Whirlwinds left for Manston to extend their offensive role.

Earlier months of 1943 had found sections of Coltishall's squadrons dispersing to Matlaske where Lysanders and Martinets of 1489 Gunnery Flight joined them. Activity had increased in August when 266 Squadron's Typhoons were here whilst 137 was at Drem for gunnery training. On 24 August No 56 Squadron's Typhoons replaced 266's, and under Squadron Leader 'Cocky' Dundas stayed until 22 July 1943. These were busy days for '56' with 17 November being typical when three Typhoons flew a *Rhubarb* to Flushing airfield damaging two Bf 109s on the ground. One pilot flew so low that his wing tip hit a German soldier! Daily *Rhubarbs* were now being flown to Belgium and Holland. Between mid-April and June 1943 Martinets of No 12 Group's 1489 TT Flight gave squadrons in the area a chance to improve their aim, soon to be sorely tested.

Thirteen Fw 190s attacked Lowestoft at low-level on 12 May 1943 and six Typhoons were scrambled to engage them. Such fighter-bomber raids flown at very low altitudes to avoid radar detection gave the defences little time to react, and the Typhoons arrived too late. One raider fell to anti-aircraft fire, but bombs hit the town and harbour causing minor damage. A second attack followed during the evening, and again the '190s withdrew before fighters could catch them. In this more damaging raid a gas holder at Lowestoft was set on fire and smaller fires were started. Twenty-three people were killed and twenty-nine seriously wounded.

The British reaction was swift, for next day Typhoons of 245 Squadron were rushed from Gravesend into Matlaske and 195 Squadron came from Woodvale into Ludham, the other station under Coltishall's control. Expensive Sector patrols and standbys were now the order of the day, but with no more attacks the Typhoon squadrons soon resumed offensive operations flying *Rhubarbs* and *Roadsteads*. Spitfire IXs of 611 Squadron spent two weeks here in July 1943 before they were exchanged for 19 Squadron's inferior Mk Vs. No 611 moved out on 31 July 56 Squadron having gone to Manston on 22 July.

Before leaving, 56 Squadron had lost their Commanding Officer during a shipping strike mounted from Ludham. During the evening four Fw 190s attempted to attack Great Yarmouth, but this time the Typhoons reached them in time. In the ensuing battle Flight Sergeant Clusas was shot down in the sea and in atrocious weather a Walrus of 278 Squadron searched for him in vain. Pilot

Officer Libby set out in a Spitfire to escort the Walrus only to have his engine cut soon after take-off causing him to crash in a cornfield.

The fighters left and Matlaske was on 24 August 1943 placed under Care & Maintenance. Some fighter-bomber training took place from the airfield, and between March and April 1944 the 3rd Aviation Engineer Battalion, USAAF, practised its airstrip building task here prior to going to France. Thus, 1944 was a quieter year – until the autumn. Bomber Command now operating in daylight needed plentiful fighter support which was also in demand during the airborne landings in Holland. Tempest Vs of 150 Wing, comprising Nos 3, 56 and 486 (NZ) Squadrons, spent a few days at Matlaske at the end of September 1944 before proceeding to Grimbergen on the 28th. Their place was taken by a Mustang Wing comprising Nos 19, 65 and 122 Squadrons at Matlaske from 28 September to 14 October 1944 when they moved to Andrew's Field.

Matlaske being unsuitable for Mosquitoes was of no use for night operations against V-1s crossing or attacking East Anglia and in which Coltishall played an important part. By October 1944 V-2 rockets were falling in Norfolk and the only effective defence against them was to find and destroy their launch sites. Since these were mobile like the Scuds in *Desert Storm* halting the V-2 assault was no easy task. Into Matlaske in the third week of October 1944 came three squadrons of Spitfire IXs soon replaced by some of the new fighter-bomber LF Mk XVIs fitted with American-built Packard Merlin engines. It was not long before the airfield became waterlogged and 229 Squadron relieved the situation by moving their operations base to Swannington and did not return to Matlaske. No 602 however continued using Matlaske for its V-2 counter attacks until 23 February 1945. That left 453 (RAAF) Squadron to become Matlaske's last for they did not leave until April 1945. The aerodrome was vacated by the RAF in October 1945.

A few buildings and the control tower survive, and one other tangible item from Matlaske's wartime days. This is Spitfire LF16 TB863/G-CDAN, which first operated from Matlaske on 24 March 1945, now resident in New Zealand.

Main features:
Grass runways: 052° 5,500ft, 093° 3,690ft, 125° 14,290ft. 35ft wide concrete perimeter track surrounded the landing ground. *Hardstandings:* twenty-one concrete. No fixed lighting. *Hangars:* one B1, five Blister. *Accommodation* (December 1944): RAF: 108 officers, 105 SNCOs, 2,330 ORs; WAAF: 2 officers, 2 SNCOs, 130 ORs.

MENDLESHAM, Suffolk

52°13N/01°07E 210ft asl; TM120635. By A140 5½ miles NE of Stowmarket

From the air traces remain clear of the unusual runway layout of Mendlesham which resembled an equilateral triangle with a large clear central area. Better known to East Anglians is the tall TV transmitter mast soaring high from the one-time airfield which still has the appearance of an aerodrome.

There is also another reminder of times past for by the A140 is a stone memorial dedicated to those who served here. Erecting such an item at each disused airfield in East Anglia would cost little. Instead of building themselves and their employees grandiose surroundings in which to preach and produce curious schemes, councillors should first honour those who gave their lives or fought to provide them with the freedom by which their chatter may be exercised by building 'the peoples monuments'.

Mendlesham opened for the RAF at the end of 1943. On 19 February 1944 Nos 310, 312 and 313 Czech Spitfire IX squadrons arrived to work up a fighter/dive-bomber role which meant low flying training over East Anglia. One at a time the squadrons were detached to Southend from where they engaged in shallow dive bombing training using Denghie Flats and practice bombs. Otherwise they remained fully operational and took an active part in *Ramrod* operations, giving escort and cover to Mitchells, B-26s and Bostons. No 310 which participated in eight *Ramrods* was the most operationally active, since its training detachment did not come until the end of its stay at Mendlesham. On 26 March the three Spitfire squadrons took part in *Ramrod 689* when a large force of B-26s made a memorable raid on IJmuiden. The squadrons were part of No 134 Airfield whose HQ worked up here alongside them between 18 February and 3 April when they all moved to Appledram and the Americans replaced them.

Late April 1944 the 34th Bomb Group arrived, the oldest such formation to join the 8th AF, and they were based here until July 1945. After active service patrolling off the west coast of America seeking enemy naval activity, the Group served during 1942-3 as a training unit. Changing to a bomber role they re-equipped with B-24s, brought them to Britain and joined the 3rd Air Division.

Their operations commenced on 23 May 1944 when 3rd AD B-24s attacked Etampes. They attacked coastal defences on 6 June then, as they were landing back at dusk on 7 June from an attempted raid on Angers, Me 410s set about the Liberators claiming four. One fell on the airfield, one at Wetheringsett and another at Nedging. A fourth crash landed on Eye airfield. As well as invasion support the 34th raided flying-bomb targets, gun emplacements and, repeatedly, supply lines leading to the front before ceasing operations with B-24s on 24 August.

Re-equipment with B-17s came after their sixty-two B-24s were withdrawn. The Fortresses flew their first mission on 17 September. Tactical targets were mainly under attack until October 1944 when priority changed to strategic items. Now the campaign took them to marshalling yards at Ludwigshaven, Hamm and Osnabrück, oil targets at Bielefeld, Merseburg, Hamburg and Misburg, to factories in Berlin, Dalteln, Hanover and to airfields at Munster, Neumünster and Frankfurt. From March 1945 onwards they concentrated mainly on rail and road communications, and around VE-Day dropped food to the Netherlanders. The 34th returned to the USA in July 1945. The station served as an ammunition store run by 94 MU between April 1950 and August 1952. Militarily inactive from June 1954, Mendlesham is now used by light industrial undertakings sitting amid farmland.

Rare photograph for sure, B-17G 44-8327 Goom-Bah of the 34th BG Mendlesham which arrived in the UK in August 1944. Group aircraft carried unusual markings. (390th Bomb Group Museum)

Main features:
Runways: 010° 6,000ft x 150ft, 160°, 220°, tarmac and concrete. *Hangars:* two T2. *Hardstandings:* forty-eight loop type and two frying pan type. *Accommodation:* 443 officers, 2,529 enlisted men.

MEPAL, Cambridgeshire

52°23N/00°07E 80ft asl; TL449795. 7 miles W of Ely, on A142. Road crosses site

'Where were you when President Kennedy died?' It is said that most people alive at the time can readily answer that question. A far more pertinent one should surely be 'Where were you at 1500 hrs on 27 October, the Saturday afternoon of the 1962 Cuban Missile Crisis?' Shortly before that time a U-2 surveying the rockets already in Cuba was shot down by a SAM triggering an increased alert state which brought the world the closest it has ever been to Armageddon. Overkill to a staggering degree became fifteen minutes away, the high alert involving the three Thor missiles based at Mepal. Yes, it does sound a bizarre situation when a firing from the road to Chatteris could trigger the end of the world. So, 'Do you recall where you were that day, that afternoon, around 1500-1600 hrs?'

The Thors sheltered in sheds within a small and heavily guarded compound on this bleak airfield which opened on 30 July 1943 under Bomber Command control. When Mepal did so within 3 Group the intention remained that it should be a conversion unit as well as the second

Unmistakable angular Thor pads can be seen implanted on Mepal. Sutton-March road crosses the site. March 1965.

station in 33 Base Waterbeach. On 19 April 1943 a request was made to Air Ministry for permission to form a half-strength Stirling conversion unit, No 1665, at Waterbeach. Approval was given for it to open on 1 May and transfer to Mepal soon after.

Whilst Mepal had final touches put to it in the spring of 1943, 1665 CU made use of Great Ashfield, but when the time came to move the unit to Mepal a change of plan resulted in Waterbeach becoming an operational station. Using Mepal for training within an operational Base being illogical, No 1665 HCU was instead moved to Woolfox Lodge on 5 June and Mepal became on 25 June 1943 an operational Sub-Station of Waterbeach able to accommodate twenty-four heavies, ie. a three-flight squadron. Re-arming 3 Group squadrons with Lancasters meant that Newmarket was no longer going to be suitable for operational use. As a result No 75 (RNZAF) Squadron and its Stirling IIIs began moving from Newmarket to Mepal on 26 June 1943, the day after Waterbeach's change of role had been decreed, although that station did not become operational for some months. No 75 was busily operating at this time and although only one runway was complete at Mepal they despatched their first operational sorties from the new home on 3 July, target Cologne. Thereafter the Stirlings took part in many 3 Group operations, flew a large number of mining sorties and in the following winter dropped supplies to the French Resistance.

The squadron re-equipped with Lancaster I/IIIs during March 1944, and despatched them on operations for the first time on 5 April. The last two Stirlings left the squadron on 28 April by which time twenty-six Lancasters were at Mepal. Many Main Force raids followed and at the end of the war 75 Squadron dropped food to the Dutch.

Lancaster of 'C'Flight 75(NZ) Squadron in the snow January 1945.

No 75 Squadron had been chosen to participate in *Tiger Force*, Britain's bomber contribution to the air war against Japan. No 75 (NZ) Squadron would fly the new Avro Lincoln long-range bomber and on 20 July 1945 began moving to Spilsby where they were to convert. Mepal would then transfer to RAF Transport Command along with Oakington and Waterbeach. Those two already in line to become Permanent Peacetime Stations provided sufficient space for the heavy transports so Mepal remained in Bomber Command. That attracted No 44 Squadron's Lancasters along from 5 Group which joined 7 Squadron pushed out of Oakington, both being candidates for *Tiger Force*. The end of hostilities rapidly scotched that idea and No 44 moved to Mildenhall on 25 August. They were replaced at Mepal by 49 Squadron. Nos 7 and 49 remained until July 1946 when both moved to Upwood leaving Mepal to be placed on Care & Maintenance.

Lancasters of 75(NZ) Squadron taxi out to participate in a March 1945 day raid.

Summer 1945 and under wing serials were widely applied to operational aircraft to discourage celebratory low flying. Lancaster AA-P ND974 has them.

Mepal was still in line for Transport Command, the Intermediate Post-war Air Force Plan F on January 1947 listing it as such and ordering it to be held until March 1954. In July 1948 it was given an Inactive status under Upwood's control. Plan G of February 1951 saw Mepal change to becoming a Standby Airfield which status it retained until 1958 when part of the site took on a completely new look. Buildings were placed in the one time centre of the airfield and by the Chatteris road – re-opened after the war – a high security fence guarded at all times was erected around an enclave in which were built three launch pads, also control and domestic associated buildings. for 113 Squadron which, jointly under 3 Group and the USAF, held the Thors here until disbandment came on 10 July 1963. Thors were not the only USAF item here for on 14 February 1952 a storage base opened under the USAF's Air Material Command which returned the site to the RAF on 8 July 1960.

After the Thors left Mepal reverted to agricultural use. Jardins converted a hangar into a corrugated paper factory. The taxi track partly remains, also the control tower and some of the Thor site structures. What is left of Mepal is best viewed from the Chatteris road which crosses it.

Main features:

Runwoys: 259°, 225°, 319°, concrete. *Hangars:* two T2, one B1. *Accommodation:* RAF: 87 Officers, 295 SNCOs, 745 ORs; WAAF: 9 officers, 10 SNCOs, 177 ORs.

METFIELD, Suffolk

52°21N/01°23E 177ft asl; TM312795. Off B1123 6 miles SE Metfield. Carry on and turn left – by-road crosses site

Transport aircraft were rare in eastern skies until 1944. A few 8th and 12th AF's C-47s were evident in summer 1942, and those of the 9th AF became more frequently seen in 1943-4. Additionally, Horsa gliders had been towed by Albemarles and Whitleys for storage on RAF bomber bases, but most of the flying was undertaken by combat organisations – mainly heavy bomber or fighter. At Metfield the activity was very different for this became the base from which the European Division Air Transport, USS TAF maintained direct air links with the USA.

Metfield's runways were completed on 1 June 1943, but the USAAF did not move in until August 1943 when along came the 353rd Fighter Group and their P-47s. Under the watchful eyes of the 56th Fighter Group at nearby Halesworth they began combat flying on 9 August 1943 participating in bomber escorts and sweeps thereafter. During March 1944 tactical trials were undertaken at Metfield which resulted in US fighters supporting bomber operations by strafing enemy bases which was already common RAF practice.

A re-arrangement of P-47 Groups led to the 353rd moving out of Metfield in April 1944, their place being taken by the 491st Bomb Group which had briefly been at North Pickenham. Only the ground elements had assembled there whereas at Metfield they received their B-24s. The Group commenced operations undertaking army support operations on 2 June 1944 and taking part in a prelude to Normandy. After the D-Day period they switched to taking a part in the strategic bombing campaign. On 15 July 1944 a very serious incident occurred when the station's bomb dump exploded.

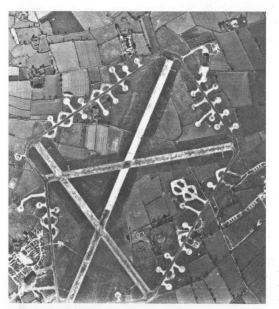

Losses being sustained by the 492nd Bomb Group which replaced the 491st at Pickenham had been heavy. When the Americans needed a major transport supply base in Suffolk they decided to move the 491st to Pickenham, transfer the depleted 492nd to Main duties and use Metfield for this other purpose.

From mid-August 1944 visitors and occupants at this airfield unusually included visiting C-54 Skymasters as well as C-47s and smaller transports. Assorted Liberator variants also flew from here some making hush-hush trips to Sweden.

Runways, frying pan and spectacle hardstandings, all are visible at Metfield in October 1945.

At 0137 hrs on 2 March 1945, during one of the final bursts of intruder activity against the UK, a Ju 88G-6 of 5/NJG 4 joined the Metfield circuit and attacked a B-24 from the lower starboard quarter. The Liberator pilot turned into the attacker without his crew opening fire. Meanwhile, the Ju 88 had been picked up by an RAF Mosquito and, after being attacked, dived into the airfield perimeter.

Although Metfield returned to the RAF later in 1945 it saw no more active use. It now has another claim to fame for Wink's Meadow at its one-time western end is the home of spectacular wild orchids.

Main features:
Runways: 210° 6,000ft x 150ft, 270°, 330°, concrete with wood chips. *Hangars:* two T2. *Hardstandings:* fifty loop type. *Accommodation:* 421 officers, 2,473 enlisted men.

METHERINGHAM, Lincolnshire

53°08N/00°20W 60ft asl; TF105610. SE of Lincoln between B1189 and B1191

Pass through Metheringham village, over the level crossing, follow the B1189 towards Scopwick. Turn left into the road signposted 'Blankney Fen' and almost immediately you will be driving along Metheringham's main runway. Pick up speed on the prescribed road and think satisfyingly of Lancasters. You can also try to imagine what it must have been like to land on the runway with FIDO burning and roaring while providing a sort of Hell on Earth experience at the end of a terrifying long night and an engagement with a Ju 88 night-fighter which has left your dearest friend seriously wounded lying, possibly dying, alongside.

On reaching the commemorative airfield sign – for this is part of Lincolnshire's Kesteven airfield trail – turn off and follow the one-time perimeter track also now a public road. Soon, on the left, you will reach a quite unique squadron memorial in memory of those of No 106 Squadron who left Metheringham and never returned. Tarry, and remember they and so many like them died to provide you with your freedom, and quite possibly even your life.

Metheringham was a typical mid-war temporary three-runway bomber airfield with two T2 hangars. Its construction started in late 1942. As at many such sites, farmers were given only forty-eight hours notice to remove their belongings, their cattle and to quit. The landing ground was prepared here on the open area of sand and gravel area resting slightly above the nearby fenland visible to the east and in strong contrast to rolling country to the west. To the north and east runs Car Dyke, a canal remaining from Roman times. Close by woodland known as Fox Covert and Blankney Wood contains a surprising assortment of trees and shrubs flourishing in assorted soil types.

Metheringham, opened in No 5 Group on 20 October 1943, received on 11 November Lancasters of No 106 Squadron which came from Syerston. Being experienced enabled them, a week later, to despatch eighteen aircraft to bomb Berlin. Thereafter 'Metheringham's own' participated in many of 5 Group's main force operations, and in summer of 1944 commenced daylight raids first in support of the Normandy battlefield targets and then tackled flying-bomb supply depots and sites before resuming strategic bombing.

January 1944 saw work commence on the installation of FIDO burners along the edges of the main runway. Before fully ready for use the burners were lit on 19/20 May 1944 to assist a Lancaster to land as it made an early return only to find fog cloaking the airfield. When necessary 106 Squadron made use of FIDO, especially useful at a station sited near the damp Fens.

A Metheringham 'night to remember' was 26/27 April 1944 when No 106 Squadron set out to bomb that panacea target called Schweinfurt. Lancaster ME669: ZN-O had just unloaded over the target when a night fighter engaged the bomber. Fire broke out in the starboard mainplane close to the fuselage then the adjacent engine burst into flames. Sergeant Jackson, the flight engineer, showed enormous bravery by climbing out of the escape hatch to quell the blaze. With no warning his parachute inadvertently opened into the fuselage. Undaunted he perilously pressed on along the top of the fuselage carrying a fire extinguisher. Other crew members holding his 'chute let out its rigging lines as needed. Suddenly, Jackson slipped, grasped an air-intake on the wing leading edge and within a few moments his face and hands were badly burnt.

He fell away luckily with his parachute and although it was partly on fire, it billowed sufficiently to at least allow him to achieve a heavy but life saving landing in which his ankle was broken. Suffering excruciating pain, he managed to drag himself to a nearby village where he was taken prisoner. For the next ten months he was in hospital in terrible agony. His story was unknown until after the war when his selfless devotion, suffering and amazing courage were recognised with the award of the Victoria Cross. Tragically, and despite his brave deeds, 'O-Orange' crashed. Of the crew, Flying Officer Mifflin, the pilot, and Johnson died in the aircraft. Others – Toft, Higgins, Sandelands and Smith – parachuted out and became prisoners of war.

Every sortie by every crew in Bomber Command demanded varying levels of courage and fortitude. It requires little imagination to understand the emotions experienced when crews cloaked in frightening darkness witnessed other bombers carrying their young friends fell in fireballs from which escape was barely possible. By the end of the war fifty-seven Lancasters had failed to return from the operations despatched from Metheringham. The final wartime operation from there took place on 25/26 April 1945 when fourteen Lancasters set out to attack the Vallo oil refinery in Norway.

After the war, as preparations advanced for *Tiger Force* to bomb Japan, two other Lancaster squadrons joined No 106 to train for their part. On 15 June 1945, No 467 Australian Squadron arrived, but hostilities ceased before the 'Tigers' were in place, and the squadron disbanded on 30 September 1945. The other newcomer was Bardney's No 189 Squadron transferred in mid-October during the post-war run down and disbanded here on 20 November 1945.

At the end of February 1946 Metheringham closed to flying after which it was retained Inactive under Waddington's supervision until, assessed as having no post-war value, it was returned to agricultural use. Its presence is recalled by memorabilia and photographs to be found in the Metheringham Airfield Visitor Centre, a building on the one-time domestic site and now part of Westmoor Farm, Martin Moor, Metheringham, open at weekends late March – October and on Bank Holidays.

Main features:
Runways: 015° 6,000ft x 150ft, 246°, 128°, concrete. *Hangars:* two T2. *Hardstandings:* thirty-six loop type. *Accommodation:* RAF: 91 officers, 200 SNCOs, 561 ORs; WAAF: 10 officers, 16 SNCOs, 316 ORs.

Place of interest nearby:
The North Kesteven Trail takes in Coleby Grange, Metheringham and Skellingthorpe. For details contact the Tourist Information Centre, Corre Street, Sleaford, NG31 7TW (Tel: 01529 414294).

METHWOLD, Norfolk

52°30N/00°33E 75ft asl; TL735935. By B1106 5 miles north of Brandon

Just another Ventura *Circus* it was, an attempt to attract enemy attention whilst Bostons attacked the huge steel works at IJmuiden's river estuary. At 1643 hrs on 3 May 1943 the chosen twelve of No 487 (New Zealand) Squadron set off from Methwold to bomb Amsterdam's power station and give the Dutch Resistance a boost. One soon returned with mechanical trouble but the others pressed on. Calamity; their Spitfire support had arrived off Flushing before planned rendezvous time and, by ill fortune, stirred a hornet's nest. The German Governor of Holland was visiting Haarlem, and the Germans feared he might be the target. A collection of skilled Luftwaffe pilots, already assembled at Schiphol to give him cover, was also alerted.

At 1735 hrs the Venturas crossed the Dutch coast at 12,000ft and within moments were ambushed by the Luftwaffe. One bomber, seriously damaged, made for home while the remainder were gradually picked off. Squadron Leader L H Trent leading pressed on, bombed the target and was then shot down. His courage was not fully realised until after the war and then, back from POW camp, he was awarded the Victoria Cross, the second to go to a Feltwell clutch airman.

Methwold had been prepared before the war as Feltwell's satellite, one of the first such stations, a Harrow in peacetime being the first aircraft to land here. After mobilisation No 37 Squadron dispersed their Wellington 1as on the Spartan site from September 1939. Wellingtons then became a common sight on the grass field which was surrounded on two sides by trees. Late September 1939 No 214 Squadron was exchanged with No 37 and remained here until February 1940, leaving 37 and 75 Squadrons to take their place dispersing to Methwold and undertaking operations out of Feltwell. In November 1940 after 57 Squadron reached Feltwell the squadron began using Methwold for night operational flying.

By 1942 the squadron was flying Wellington IIIs from the Unbuilt Satellite, activity which continued until September 1942 when the squadron moved north and Methwold passed from 3 to 2 Group. On 30 September No 21 Squadron arrived. At the time it was working up with its Venturas and on 3 November took them into action for the first time. The squadron also set out from here for their part in the December Eindhoven raid, thereafter flying *Circus* operations and *Ramrods*. No 3 Group recovered Feltwell on 23 April 1943 and 21 Squadron moved to Oulton making way at Methwold for Feltwell's two Ventura squadrons, Nos 464 and 487. They brought to Methwold the accents of Australians and New Zealanders and continued day bombing operations.

Lockheed Vega Venturas of No 21 Squadron at Methwold in 1942.

Wellington III Z1657 of 57 Squadron at Methwold. (John Holmes, BEM, via S Barraclough)

A difficult problem was meanwhile being resolved. Production of Horsa gliders was embarrassingly fast raising the question of storage prior to use in forthcoming airborne assaults. The answer was to disperse them in groups – initially comprising up to twenty-seven and, from June, thirty-two – on bomber airfields. By the end of April 1943 nine had been air-towed to Methwold. By chance I was on the station when the first Horsas arrived. Hordes turned out to watch as the first two gliders cast off from their Albemarle tug ropes and amazed the onlookers with their astonishingly steep glide paths. Then the aircrews raced over for a close look before setting off to bomb Ostend.

No 2 Heavy Glider Maintenance Unit at Snailwell controlled the storage. By August 1943 thirty-two Horsas were picketed with their control surfaces removed to avoid gale damage. No 21 Heavy Glider Maintenance Section kept them in good state while Methwold thrilled to the news that the two Ventura squadrons were to leave for Sculthorpe and there re-arm with Mosquitoes. Everyone was pleased that 'the pig' was leaving, and the last Ventura operational sorties – air/sea rescue flights – were flown from here on 15 July 1943 and the squadrons had moved to Sculthorpe by the 22nd.

On 23 July 1943 Feltwell and Methwold were again united within 3 Group. Methwold was now to have a major facelift and to become a fully fledged operational airfield with the three usual runways but with five T2 hangars. While Wimpey built the runways using ballast carried in by Lea Valley around the clock, Bower Electrical Engineers put in Drem lighting. While the work was underway the RAF Regiment held a battle course for aircrew resting between tours. Re-building was completed on 31 January 1944. In March 1944 the Horsas were prepared for action then towed away, some being later used in the Arnhem landings.

Methwold's upgrading and availability was linked with that of 32 Base Mildenhall which controlled Lakenheath too, a station which closed to flying in May 1944 for extension and modification into a Heavy Bomber Station for B-29s some of which the RAF hoped to acquire. On 15 May No 149 Squadron completed their move to Methwold and resumed Stirling III operations on 20 May with mine laying.

Famous Stirling III 'K' EF411 of 149 Squadron, Methwold.

On 4 August 1944 they were joined by No 218 Squadron's Lancaster I/IIIs. It fell to 149 Squadron on 8 September 1944 to fly from Methwold the final Bomber Command bombing raid using Stirlings the target being Le Havre. Thereafter both squadrons, Lancaster equipped, operated by day and night in 3 Group's offensive until 4 December 1944 when 218 Squadron moved to Chedburgh. The change had come about because in December 149 Squadron was raised to three-Flight strength.

Post-war wind-down reduced the strength of 149 squadron, which was joined by a reduced 207 Squadron on October 1945. This was a step towards a new bomber force – primarily with an anti-shipping role for 3 Group, a reminder of their initial wartime activity. Late April 1946 both squadrons moved to Tuddenham there to re-equip with a new version of the Lancaster, the B1 (FE). Methwold was placed under Care & Maintenance in September 1946. The station was transferred to Flying Training Command control on 7 December 1946 and again became Feltwell's satellite and relief landing ground for circuit flying by No 3 FTS until June 1954. In 1955 some aircraft of CSE Watton made use of Methwold while their station's runways were attended to.

A visit to Methwold brings T Type hangars into view, and to the east of the B1106 among the trees are remnants of living quarters and the Officers' Mess. Assorted hangar-like buildings by the road mark the position of a T2 while the landing ground area is intensively farmed. Several houses have been built on the site. Those Horsas were picketed in the north-eastern corner.

Main features:
Runways: 237° 6,000ft x 150ft, 294°, 168°, concrete. *Hangars:* five T2. *Hardstandings:* thirty-five loop type, one pan-type. *Accommodation:* RAF: 164 officers, 608 SNCOs, 578 ORs; WAAF: 2 officers, 4 SNCOs, 60 ORs.

MILDENHALL, Suffolk

52°21N/00°28E 28ft asl; TL685768. By A1101 NW out of Mildenhall town

Row upon row they stood in fan-like pattern, squadrons of biplanes, Harts, Bulldogs, Furies and a few Wallaces – 356 in all were there to worship the King. HM King George V, 'the Sailor King' was celebrating his Silver Jubilee Review by reviewing his air force at Mildenhall on 6 July 1935. About half the field – very much smaller than now – was covered by colourful aeroplanes set against a backdrop of menacing looking dark green biplanes. Bombers, naturally, because Mildenhall was *the* No 1 bomber base where, in a few months time, Bomber Command would all but be born.

With all those aircraft on the field – much of the Metropolitan Air Force – floodlights beamed upon them for the fire risks and security were high especially at night. After the King toured the lines he was whisked off to Duxford in a magnificent apple green 'Roller'. By the time it had conveyed him to Duxford all the aircraft were ready for take-off. Upon the firing of a Verey cartridge, engines burst into life. Radio was still a novelty and as for air traffic control – forget such trivia. A gorgeous sound they produced, and soon they were bumping across the new lawn. From what I saw during a practice I can only liken it to departure time at an upmarket PFA rally! Soon they were taking off in squadron swarms, an hour passing before all were airborne and slotting into their places in a long train led by the Heyfords and 'Ginnys' with Furies providing the guard's van and all buzzing along to pass Duxford's Royal Plinth. The memorable event is recalled by a memorial on the front of Building 562, Mildenhall's old SHQ.

Mildenhall's Main Gate, SHQ on the left. Much changed since 1934, and now No 2 Gate. (Cambridgeshire Collection) (B on plan overleaf)

Station HQ shortly after completion remains in use in a similar role. (Cambridgeshire Collection) (C on plan overleaf)

Glance around the present base and incongruities are everywhere. There are 'A' and 'C' Type hangars, buildings of 1920's design, a very modern passenger terminal, recent barrack blocks resembling US condominiums and across the field the Butler 'barns'. A curious collection for sure. Mildenhall was built in 1933-5 when the 1930's expansion was under way so, why so many 1920's buildings?

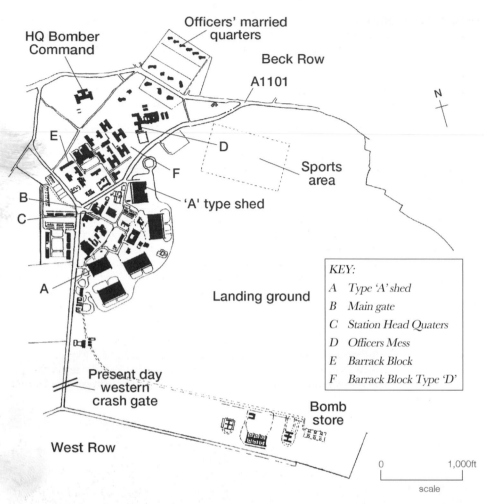

HQ Bomber Command

Officers' married quarters

Beck Row

A1101

N

E

D

F

Sports area

B

C

'A' type shed

A

Landing ground

KEY:
A   Type 'A' shed
B   Main gate
C   Station Head Quaters
D   Officers Mess
E   Barrack Block
F   Barrack Block Type 'D'

Present day western crash gate

Bomb store

West Row

0   1,000ft

scale

MILDENHALL

Design began in 1922 of a split site station known as Beck Row and intended as a base for bombers to counter threats from militant France. Proposed buildings relied upon red bricks, and their roofs were of slates making them similar to those at Felixstowe and Martlesham. Improvement in international affairs put the aerodrome plan in abeyance until 1932 when re-planning took place of a bomber station still known as Beck Row and from 1933 onwards as Mildenhall. Intended initially for Heyfords but primarily for a new bomber generation, construction began in 1933 of a station embracing buildings designed between 1922 and that year. Prominent were two 1929 'A' Type metal framed aircraft sheds with annexes holding Flight Offices and changing rooms. Three very early 1934/35 non-hipped red-brick and steel thirteen-bay Type 'C' sheds supplemented them. All remain in use. At the main entrance stood the 1929 designed guard house facing what was the 1925 designed Station Commander's office and the operations block later known as Station Headquarters. Operations techniques were still quite primitive, aid being provided by the W/T R/T transmitting station and the direction finding station for homing. Three Type 'D' barrack blocks each accommodated four SNCOs and seventy-two airmen and were supplemented by one Type 'B' for four NCOs and fifty-six airmen and another of the type for civilians on camp. As RAF expansion came under way four more barrack huts each for an NCO and eighteen airmen were added. A Sergeants' mess was built for sixty-nine men. Messing arrangements included a dining room for 343 airmen – with the barber's shop close by! To supply all needs a 100,000 gallon reservoir 1930 type was provided and a small water tower built. The Officers' Mess was distinctly more prestigious and retains to this day its imperial style. It was built to a 1932 design to accommodate seventy-four officers. After entry via two very unassuming doors the dining room containing superb chandeliers was to the right, the huge ante-room being to the left. Throughout – as now – it was beautifully panelled with wood. A broad staircase ascended centrally beneath which remains the bar. All quarters within the building also retain the wooden panelling and are largely furnished in keeping with a bygone age making what is now the Officers' Club a most nostalgic treasure.

At the time of opening Mildenhall contained the HQ of the new Bomber Command for which a more modern building was erected on open ground on the north part of the camp near the Littleport Road. In recent years it has housed HQ 3rd AF USAFE. At the same time married quarters were increased with Airmen occupying 1932 type and Sergeants 1933 style. Married quarters of Groups III, IV and V – all new 1933 designs – were added as the station grew.

In 1939 with other functioning bomber stations, Mildenhall had the facelift within Scheme 'L' under which it went to war. New barrack blocks Type 'P' and 'R' brought levels of comfort and luxury few had hitherto experienced – central heating, baths, hot running water in tiled ablution rooms, a comfortable lounge. A new combined dining room and NAAFI was built, married quarters were greatly improved and a grocery shop and general store were added. Sports facilities were much enlarged, with games fields sited where the AMC Terminal stands. Operational improvements included new bomb stores and a machine-gun range. A gas decontamination centre was built, also a new ambulance garage and, ominously, a mortuary. Mildenhall in the 1930s was proclaimed Britain's Number One bomber base.

Times have changed – Mildenhall is now the American forces' 'gateway' to Britain, with many passengers a year passing through. A new terminal opened in June 1999 includes access for the disabled, British immigration officers checking all arrivals, a cyber cafe, nursery, family room and a travel agent. As a sign of our troubled times, blast protection measures make the building less vulnerable to terrorist outrages.

The 1922-designed Officers' Mess in 1934. Now the Officers' Club. (Cambridgeshire Collection) (D on plan opposite)

Type 'C' hangar frame, Type 'A' complete and water tower, seen from the A1101 at Beck Row. Somewhat changed now! (Cambridgeshire Collection)

It's all the fault of the French, our traditional foe, who in the 1920's were throwing their weight about mainly because Germany was not being punished as harshly as they wanted. Such was the friction that the British Government reviewed home defence and decided on building a new bomber base and chose a site by Beck Row. Planning proceeded fast but by 1926 the immediate 'crisis' had passed so building of the aerodrome and 'camp' did not proceed. Plans were periodically updated but not until 1933 was the order given to construct Beck Row bomber station, and with ample publicity.

When it opened on 16 October 1934 under the command of Wing Commander F. J. Linnell (who at the height of the war was Controller of Research and Development at MAP), it already looked antique when compared with other new stations then underway. The main entrance, SHQ, the Officers' Mess even then seemed like Army buildings from times past and puttied airmen clearly ready to go back to the trenches neatly toned in. They were protected from the local natives with a tall, spiked metal black fence which, at either end, dissolved into a low hawthorn hedge. The road leading to the current west end crash gate was the old road joining West Row to the camp through which it passed – until the 1943 runway extension closed it. If there was no flying it was still possible to cycle across to Beck Row ... if you were careful.

Around opening time a very incomplete RAF station hit the headlines when some sixty widely assorted civilian aircraft, British and foreign, arrived to participate in the 'MacRobertson Air Race' to Melbourne, Australia, the greatest air race of all time, marking the centenary of the State of Victoria. Australian philanthropist Sir McPherson Robertson offered a prize of £15,000 and a gold cup for each winner of the two-element contest, a speed race and a handicap race in which entries were graded according to size, load and engine power.

Incomplete Mildenhall was placed at the disposal of the Royal Aero Club for sixteen days in October 1934 to serve as the starting point for the race. Many unusual and spectacular aircraft were entered, including KLM's Douglas DC-2, PH-AJU 'Uiver', the first of its type exported. Also here was a Boeing 247, another state-of-the-art, twin-engined, all-metal airliner.

Britain had no suitable aircraft for the race so de Havilland designed one for the speed section. Its conception was described to me by C C Walker, Chief Engineer of de Havilland, who recalled that the decision to participate was taken over breakfast with Richard Clarkson and (Sir) Geoffrey de Havilland. The design, sketched that morning on a cigarette packet, embraced the very latest ideas – split trailing-edge wing flaps, retractable undercarriage, variable pitch propellers and two 230hp Gipsy Six R specially designed engines. High aspect ratio, long and thin tapered wings would afford good range, while to attain a cruising speed of 200mph the aircraft would depend upon exceptionally clean lines. An amazing maximum range of 2,925 miles was attainable at 220mph. Three examples, to be built in great secrecy, would be offered for sale in time for the race nine months hence. The DH 88 Comet racer was to become, without doubt, one of the most exotic aeroplanes of all time.

HM King George V and Queen Mary were among 70,000 spectators at and around Mildenhall on 20 October 1934 to watch the 06.30hrs departure of the first of the final participants drawn from among the sixty-three aircraft that had originally entered. From positions in two lines, the start of the race took place in darkness and slight drizzle. Famous fliers were taking part, among them Jim and Amy Mollison in Comet G-ACSP 'Black Magic', and Owen Cathcart-Jones with Ken Waller aboard the green Comet G-ACSR entered by racing motorist Bernard Rubin. Flying the third, the superbly finished all-red G-ACSS, which had been ordered by A O Edwards, managing director of Grosvenor House Hotel, and which made its first flight on 9 October, were Charles Scott and Tom Campbell Black. By the end of the first day the latter pair had reached Baghdad, a superb achievement. The Mollisons had to retire from the race after taking on the wrong type of fuel en route. Scott and Black were buffeted so much that by the time they reached Darwin, Australia, their aircraft's cockpit was drenched with their blood. They won the speed race by completing their journey in 70 hours 54 minutes. G-ACSR came in fourth.

The first RAF aircraft to move in to Mildenhall could hardly have been more different for into Britain's most modern, most prestigious bomber station on 14 November 1934 came nine Heyfords of 99 Squadron. When it wasn't staging air races and a Royal Review, Mildenhall was also immersing itself in 'Expansion', the buzz-word of those times and typified when, in September 1935, 99 Squadron detached its 'B' Flight to become 38 Squadron, also Heyford-equipped. Late 1936 the squadron received Fairey Hendons – under-powered anachronisms with incredibly deep wing sections in which their bombs were carried. Huge, thick trousers hiding their legs succeeded in reducing their speed. A turret was wrongly positioned in the nose, while the rear gunner shivered in the breeze and tried to manoeuvre the gun on a Scarff ring. Yet the Hendon was quite a handsome machine which when passing provided ample time in which to admire it.

Most famous Mildenhall item, the DH 88 Comet racer flying over Mildenhall on 25 May 1989 after lengthy, costly restoration.

Menacing line? Heyfords parading for the July 1935 Jubilee Review. Oh! for a walk with a Kodachrome…Best I could manage (just) was to scribble down a few numbers!

In January 1937 came a major step forward when HQ 3 Group was raised at Mildenhall and stayed until the war began when it moved to Exning House. Next to arise was HQ 4 Group formed here on 1 April 1937 followed by 5 Group in July. No wonder the Germans considered Mildenhall as *the* British bomber station and attracted Herr Milch who came to see it for himself

On 12 April 1937 No 99 Squadron again gave birth, 'B' Flight this time becoming 149 Squadron, also Heyford-equipped. On 5 May 1937 the Hendons flew away to Marham making space for 211 Squadron to form, on 14 June 1937, before filling a slot at Grantham on 2 September.

Type 'A' Aircraft Shed at Mildenhall soon after completion in 1935. (Cambridgeshire Collection) (A on plan)

North Sea bombing range practice - Heyford style.

During the Munich crisis in 1938 the Heyfords stood fuelled, were loaded with 250lb bombs in those curious cells between the spats and awaited what would surely have been suicide missions. Better times were almost to hand, great excitement greeting the arrival on 10 October 1938 of the first Wellington I for 99 Squadron. It looked very elegant, so modern, seemed so fast, and on 18 January 1939 No 149 Squadron which had looked on enviously began to re-arm with them. Soon they were flying around East Anglia in formation and made some long distance trips into France allowing training and fuel consumption assessments to proceed during that worrying summer.

Mobilisation for the squadrons came on 27 August 1939 and on Friday 1 September, when Poland was violated, 99 Squadron quickly moved to Newmarket Heath, the war station. Around Mildenhall's perimeter 149 Squadron's Wellingtons dispersed, bombs at hand. On the Sunday afternoon after war was declared the airfield ostensibly was a scene of silence, belying plentiful activity behind the scenes. Surprisingly it was not until 1825 hrs before three crews of 149 Squadron took off, and too late, for poor weather nullified their sortie against the German Fleet and they were lucky to find their way back to land at Honington in darkness.

No 149 Squadron stood by and at 1345 hrs next day was warned to be ready for take-off to attack the enemy fleet at the entrance to Brunsbüttel. Shortly before 1500 hrs eight Wellingtons took off, but bad weather again wrecked the operation, five crews aborting. Of the remainder one mistook the Elbe for the Kiel Canal, one dropped bombs near Esbjerg and the third received hits in a fuel tank. The crew nursed it back to Honington.

Refined Wellington Ias with power-operated turrets had reached Mildenhall. No 149 Squadron worked up with them, then came North Sea sweeps flown on a rotational basis by 3 Group crews. Also at Mildenhall were Gauntlets and Gladiators of the Meteorological Flight which came from Duxford in April 1939. November 1940 saw them become 401 Flight which left for Bircham Newton on 29 October.

February 1940 saw 149 Squadron participating in night armed reconnaissance flights over Germany and experiencing the difficulty of night operations. When Norway was invaded the station was brought to high state of readiness, further increased when on 10 May the Blitzkrieg broke and '149' began night bombing. When Italy entered the war 149 Squadron was ordered to Salon, France. French intransigence made operations against Italy well nigh impossible, and 149 Squadron managed only a few sorties.

Gauntlet K7801 of the 'Met Flight'.

Colgate Darden's Douglas DC-2 pretending to be PH-AJU arriving at Mildenhall.

Dejected and home again, 149 Squadron threw themselves into the night bomber offensive, conducted intensively from Mildenhall to the end of 1942. In 1940 its Wellington Ias starred in the film *The Lion has Wings* and acquired more lasting fame when the film *Target for Tonight* was made here, featuring Wing Commander P C Pickard and P2517 'F for Freddie'. The machine selected was as obscure as any, and there is nothing to confirm that it ever flew even one bombing sortie.

Wellington lc P2517 QJ-F of 'Target for Tonight' fame. Delivered to 37 Squadron Feltwell 9 January 1940, it passed to '149' on 18 November 1940. If the squadron ORB is correct it never operated with '149'before passing to 3 Group TT Flight on 7 September 1941. Soon 2794M at No 4 STT, this most 'famous' Wimpey was struck off charge on 31 December 1945. Depicted parked where the USAF 'Alert' pan was established.

More portentous for the enemy was the night of 31 March 1941 when a Wellington II of '149' became the first RAF bomber to drop a 4,000-pounder on Germany. Only one could be carried in the Wellington, for which the centre doors had to be removed from the bomb cells. Only six Wellington IIs suitably modified were yet in use, two going each to IX, 99 and 149 Squadrons. For the rest the mount remained the trusty Wellington Ic in use since summer 1940, reliable and popular but by 1941 becoming out-dated.

In October 1941 Stirlings were introduced into '149' and carried out their first bombing raid on 30 November 1941. Such flying took place from Lakenheath, now Mildenhall's satellite and which had metalled runways. For that reason 149 Squadron moved there in April 1942.

No 419 (Canadian) Squadron formed at Mildenhall on 15 December 1941 with Wellington IIIs, began operations on 11 January 1942. They left for Leeming on 14 August 1942, after a busy bombing campaign, and were replaced next day by No 75 (New Zealand) Squadron which operated from here until November 1942. In the summer of 1942 No 1503 BAT Flight's Oxfords provided blind approach training and were replaced by 1505 BAT Flight on 5 September, this unit moving to Upper Heyford on 17 December 1942. Another arrival had been 115 Squadron whose Wellington IIIs took up residence on 24 September when 2 Group nudged them out of Marham. No 1403 Meteorological Flight reformed at Mildenhall in November 1942 before going overseas.

Mildenhall still a grass aerodrome closed on 7 November for runway building which caused 115 Squadron to leave the station. Three runways were laid in the customary pattern, and to mark re-opening, an impressive formation of Stirlings heralded the arrival of XV Squadron on 15 April 1943. XV detached their 'C' Flight to form 622 Squadron on 10 August and both squadrons carried out Main Force operations. December 1943 saw them both convert to Lancaster I/IIIs which operated from here by day and night to the end of hostilities. Among them was R5508 LS:C. of XV Squadron, the Lancaster in which Squadron Leader J D Nettleton won the Victoria Cross during the 1942 daylight Augsburg raid. Its dispersal was near where the USAF's MAC terminal stands.

Stirling IIIs of XV Squadron, LS-M central.

Aerial view of Mildenhall from the east in summer 1942.

Between December 1942 and the end of the war Mildenhall was HQ 32 Base which controlled Sub-Stations Lakenheath, Newmarket and Tuddenham (completed 1 October 1943 to replace Lakenheath in June 1944) and the first such organisation to form. Over 8,000 bombing sorties were despatched from Mildenhall during the war, 23,000 tons of bombs were dropped but more than 200 aircraft failed to return.

No 622 Squadron disbanded on 15 August 1945 and was replaced at once by 44 Squadron, here until August 1946. Their task was to work out snags with the Lincoln while No XV Squadron using some Lancaster B1 (Special), which 617 Squadron had operated dropped large bombs for trials on U-Boat pens at Farge and on Helgoland.

In February 1949 four squadrons of Lancaster BI(FE)s each at six UE moved to Mildenhall from stations that were closing or needed for other purposes. They were Nos 35, 115, 149 and 207 all with a maritime attack role and which, later that year, re-armed with Lincolns. That bomber was already obsolescent so in February-March 1950 the four squadrons disbanded. Their crews were mainly posted to Marham to train for forthcoming B-29 Washingtons gap filling until greatly superior Canberras and V-bombers were available.

When in 1948 the USAF moved into Lakenheath the initial intention had been for them to use Mildenhall, but it was unsuitable for B-29s. The station was upgraded and, prompted by the Korean War, on 11 July 1950 re-opened as an Active airfield. Remaining Lincolns left for Marham or Upwood leaving behind No 2 Regional Band, HQ 3 Group, the Command Flight and Signals School.

On 15 July the 329th BS, 93rd Bomb Group flew in their B-50Ds. The USAF tenure has continued ever since. The 7514th ABS took control of the base and into place went coils of barbed wire which encircled the entire field. AA guns of the British 7 AA Bde protected the perimeter. So serious was the situation that some of the bombers arrived carrying 'unarmed' nuclear bombs – hence the high security precautions.

Early 1951 saw the runway being lengthened and in February 1951 B-29s of the 509th Bomb Group (which had dropped the atomic bombs on Japan) arrived for a three month stay. The term 'Bomb Group' defined the flying part of a Bomb Wing that being the collective term for the whole unit of which the Group was a part. Both terms were in general use.

The 2nd BG replaced the '509th' in May 1951 and later the 22nd. On 1 October 1951 Strategic Air Command took control of the base to where Wings rotated during TDY. August 1953 saw KC-97E tankers based here for the first time and thereafter Mildenhall became a base for similar aircraft. Late in 1957 B-47s were first based here. Groups temporarily here from 1951 were:

No 2 BG, 49th BS, (B-50D) May-August 1951
No 22 BG, 2nd BS,(B-29) September-December 1951
No 97 BG, 324th BS (B-50D), March-May 1952
No 509 BG, 393rd BS (B-50D)
No 55 SRW, 38th SRS (RB-50B, D) radar reconnaissance squadron, June-September 1953
306 ARS KC-97E supporting the first B-47B TDY in the UK
305 ARS KC-97G June-November 1953
22 ARS KC-97F December 1953-March 1954
303 ARS KC-97G March-June 1954
380 ARS KC-97F April-July 1957
40 ARS KC-97G July-October 1957.

Between 1958 and August 1959 B-47s with JATO bottles in place were stationed here for brief periods during *Reflex Alert* posture.

Already there had been a major change for at the start of 1959 Mildenhall began to take Burtonwood's place as the USAF's gateway to the UK. Generally poor weather and runway subsidence problems at Burtonwood, also its distance from other USAF bases, led to Mildenhall becoming its replacement where the first C-124C Globemaster II touched down in January and the first C-133 on the 31st. On 1 March 1959 MATS opened their then quite simple terminal and subsequently C-124s, C-133s, C-121s, C-47s, C-118s became increasingly common. Between August and March 1960 WB-50Ds of the 53rd WS also resided here.

C-124C-DL '0-2085', a type prominent in the 1960s.

What would the Wellingtons have thought of B-2 'Spirit of Alaska' stealthily arriving for a Fete?

In 1961 the base assisted ANG units brought to Europe because of the Berlin crisis which also attracted ANG KC-97s. In 1962 HQ US Third Air Division (which became the Third Air Force) moved to Mildenhall. The US Naval Air Facility (200 FASRON) arrived from West Malling on 1 May 1964 and used C-45s and C-117Ds for European communications flying.

With the *Reflex* B-47s gone and C-118 regular trans-Atlantic services ended, Mildenhall was under utilised. Consideration was given to placing an F-105 squadron here. Instead, it became the European C-130 base. When the French asked the US forces to leave their territory the 7513rd Tactical Group (which became the 513rd Combat Support Group) formed on 1 June 1965 at Mildenhall, to pave the way for C-130s leaving France or coming for two-month deployments in two sets known either as Alpha or Bravo squadrons now parented by the 513th TCW from 15 April 1966.

On 19 October 1965 C-141A Starlifter (40634) became the first of many to call here. Equally to be a common sight, November 1965 saw the arrival of the first EC-135 *Silk Purse Control* aircraft, four of which took turns at flying eight-hour shifts listening for East European and other voices. The unit became the 10th ACCS on 1 January 1970.

On 8 June 1966 came the first of the C-130 rotations supplied by the 317th and 516th TCWs. Then on 1 July the 513th TCW became the 513rd TAW. While at Mildenhall C-130s and crews were assigned to the 435th Tactical Airlift Group, a Military Airlift Command unit.

Summer 1968 saw a short stay by sixteen ANG/AFRES C-124Cs whereas 1969 held a less worthy event when Sgt Paul Meyer stole C-130E 37789 of the 36 TAS. Said to be of 'disturbed mind' the non-pilot crashed the Hercules into the Channel on 23 May 1969. At the end of that year Mildenhall took over Upper Heyford's role as the UK support base for RC-135 ELINT operations which role it still performs.

On 16 January 1970 Mildenhall became the UK base to which KC-135 tankers were to the present time deployed for European operations. Upper Heyford also relinquished that role because space was needed to house the 20th TFW's F-111s.

Another familiar Mildenhall sight made its debut on 20 December 1970 when for the first time a C-5 Galaxy (80219) called. There were also 'farewells' for in May 1971 the last C-133 and C-47 flights departed. But on 9 September there was a new, stunning sight to view, the SR-71A Blackbird 17972 which had flown from New York to Farnborough in 1 hour 54 minutes and 56.4 seconds, and which then landed at Mildenhall. Some record flight! In the mid-1970s U-2s were also about.

Mildenhall's future was now obvious – it would concentrate on transports, supporting a tanker fleet and provide a secure base for 'special' flights which summarises its present role. The C-130 rotation strength gradually wound down and was much reduced after January 1976, only about eight aircraft coming to be available for support duties military and civilian. Similarly employed in the late 1970s and early 1980s were European-based Short C-23A Sherpas which regularly visited.

US Navy presence at Mildenhall has been lengthy. This C-131 14011 was a frequent 1980s visitor.

The European Tanker Task Force in the 1970s and 1980s drew upon Strategic Air Command units from Mildenhall controlled by Detachment 1, 306th Strategic Wing. In 1977 some 2,100 KC-135 sorties were despatched for in-flight refuelling, and since the 1970s there have normally been fourteen to sixteen KC-135 tankers here some making short duty calls from US bases. Regulars, Air National Guard and Air Force Reserve, all have been involved and very few KC-135s have never visited Mildenhall.

On 21 April 1980 – yes, that long ago – the first stretched C-141B visited and on 5 September 1986 a C-5B Galaxy first came by which time there had been two spectacular events.

By the start of the 1980s Detachment 4, a 9th SRW SR-71A was usually nesting surrounded by very high secrecy in its Butler barn. In April 1984 the British Government announced that it had agreed to two SR-71s being based here from where they viewed in particular USSR naval activity in Murmansk and elsewhere. Up to eight KC-135Q special AAR aircraft supported them, an activity that ran to January 1990.

The other major event unfolded in 1986. During 11 April tanker aircraft began arriving at the base in considerable numbers. Clearly, the USA was going to retaliate for recent anti-American terrorist activity. Around 1800 hrs on 14 April the tankers began setting out. In all seventeen KC-10s and ten KC-135s were despatched to support F-111s raiding targets in Libya. This was the first combat action launched from Mildenhall since 1945. The same year saw the first arrival of the KC-135R, a quieter and smokeless version of Mildenhall's most common sight.

A daily sight in the 1980s, UC-12M 16-3840 of the US Navy Air Facility.

A little-known event of the 1980s deserves mention. In December 1983 a Douglas DC-2 owned by Colgate Darden, and displaying the registration PH-AJU worn by the 1934 air race entrant, spent a few days at Mildenhall. It departed on 18 December on the first leg of a sponsored flight to Melbourne and, after a nine-day stop at Singapore, reached its destination in February 1984.

An occupant of Mildenhall sometimes seen locally exercising off-base was the RAF Regiment's No 66 Squadron, one of three USAF airfield-protection squadrons.

Summer 1990 saw many transports and tankers stage through on their way to the Gulf then in Spring 1991 came the return. As they passed through homeward bound many of the aircraft had acquired very colourful nose art. In July 1991 some tankers went back to the Gulf for *Ivory Justice*, the AAR support of *Provide Comfort* aircraft.

To provide permanently based tankers for the European theatre, the 100th Air Refuelling Wing was activated on 13 January 1992. Within it the 100th ARS formed on 1 April 1992 and was renamed the 351st ARS on 23 May 1992. Tail trim on its fourteen or so KC-135Rs included a 'D in a square' as carried by B-17s of the 100th BG during wartime.

In July 1990 the last *Silk Purse* sortie was flown and on 21 January 1992 EC-135H 10286 brought to an end the long stay of these aircraft when it left for the USA.

The final stage in the new line up at Mildenhall began in September 1994 when the 352nd SOG started to move here from Alconbury bringing HC-130s and MH-53Js the latter being replaced in 1999 with MH-53Ms.

Surely its amazing how the KC-135s have survived. From Mildenhall they have given wonderful service, and participated extensively in four major campaigns. KC-135Rs of the 100th ARS – 71499 shown here - have operated from here since April 1992.

Starlifters have long gone, but KC-135s, including those of the 100th ARW, are soldiering on. Many are over fifty years old and often face threats of upgrading. Since 1996 the number of transports, steadily falling, has included C-17 Globemaster IIIs. When a US President visits Europe, more exotic transports, helicopters and 'specialised aeroplanes' call at Mildenhall – together with an E-4.

In the 1980s about 100,000 passengers passed yearly through the base, some in the chartered airliners. Assorted freight regularly arrives. In 1994 movements totalled some 25,000 from the 100th ARW based here.

RAF Mildenhall covers over 1,000 acres, has a 9,240ft runway and the base population averages about 2,740 US military personnel, 100 Department of the Air Force civilians and 330 British employees. Nearly 5,000 dependants live off base.

Of the sights at Mildenhall, none would more amaze the pilots of the Heyfords than the SR-71 Blackbirds – unless it be the public enclosure where one could buy an ice cream then sit comfortably while watching spy flights depart.

Reconnaissance Boeings like RC-135V 64-131 of the 55th SRW and quite aged never lose their 'spooky' look.

Some special operations MC-130s have DIRCM turrets fitted a la RAF 'Hercs' shown here have operated from Mildenhall since April 1992. (Graham Murfitt).

Special ops MC-130s change their coats according to their theatrical needs, 40476 displaying a two-tone grey finish.

C-17 Globemaster III 10189 of the 437th/315th AW, a type regularly calling at Mildenhall (Graham Murfitt).

Take-off was so noisy that it could not be disguised. Every SR-71 spying mission seemed to turn into an air show. 17964 lands fast back from an operational sortie.

Spectacular for sure, the long span B-57 Canberra development N926NA periodically flown from Mildenhall for NASA and other agencies interested in high flying and other pastimes (Graham Murfitt).

For a vast number of folk 'Mildenhall' evokes one thing – 'the air fete'. Hope was for a two-day crowd of half a million. The total certainly reached 480,000. As soon as one fete ended work started on the next under the Air Fete Director, Roger Hoeflin (previously the voice of Old Warden). By Christmas invitations to attend were sent for an event with ever more political overtones. At the last big show two Chinese officials spent the afternoon trying to persuade me to get approval for their Chinese Air Force to appear! I pointed out that it was not in my power, and that there could be a few problems. I did not tell them that I had tried to attract a Shin Meiwa Japanese amphibian and, repeatedly, a Portuguese P-3. The latter looked possible until it was confirmed that there was no 'operational reason' for one to patrol our waters. In most cases aircraft came during training flights.

Times were changing, and costs rising dramatically – not least insurance. The end of the show, never universally popular with the Americans, came at 3 o'clock one Friday afternoon when the fete millions had loved was abandoned in the state we had come to thrill to it. In any case, it would never have survived much longer because of air force cut-backs. The effect of '9/11' on the show is too horrendous to briefly think about. Instead of sorrows, let's recall magic moments while thanking Roger for producing what was without doubt one of the greats of all time.

Main features (December 1944):
Runways: 113° 6,000ft x 50ft, 040°, 150°, concrete. *Hangars:* three Type C, two Type A, two T2 for Horsas. *Hardstandings:* thirty-six heavy bomber. *Accommodation:* RAF: 189 officers, 61 SNCOs, 1,816 ORs; WAAF: 15 officers, 11 SNCOs, 327 ORs.

Place of interest nearby:
In Beck Row cemetery, in the village main street, can be seen the grave of Sergeant Middleton VC and other RAF aircrew who died as a result of operations from Mildenhall. Near the lychgate an American pilot died when his F-84 hurtled along the street, on fire, after clipping a parked B-50 when carrying out authorised low flying.

NEWMARKET HEATH (ROWLEY MILE), Suffolk

52°14N/00°22E 96ft asl; TL615625. Heath lies W of the town

Strange thing, secrecy. Its existence – like heavily guarded things – inevitably encourages and enhances suspicion and enquiry. Development of jet propulsion in great secrecy was no exception, although the subject was impossible to hide when the airframe carrying the engine was concerned. News that a heavily guarded B1 hangar on Newmarket Heath contained a 'jet' spread very fast, especially after a strange, low key, blow-torch like sound was reported. Not for many days, though.

Truth was that under very concealing wraps the first Gloster F.9/40 DG202/G, basis for the Meteor, had been brought to Newmarket by road, assembled and, not long after dawn on 10 July 1942, in the hands of Jerry Sayer, made its first fast taxi run. Newmarket had been chosen because it offered the longest take-off run in Britain – essential if the brakes found it difficult to slow the aircraft.

The aeroplane – much heavier although not all that much bigger than a Spitfire – needed two of the heavy W2 engines because each produced low thrust. Sayer tried a second run, and although the engines were unsuitable for sustained flight he managed to get the aeroplane off the ground for a few seconds. Britain's first jet fighter had flown, sort of, and from Newmarket Heath.

I can still hear the distinct whine that came from the Heath when the jet engines ran – and picture the F.9/40 as it finally left for the Cotswolds. WHAT a sight! (Gloster/BAe)

On 11 and 13 July he made more fast early morning runs before the aircraft was locked away and soon collecting dust. For a variety of complex reasons it was March 1943 before flight test engines reached Newmarket by which time DG202/G had much deteriorated.

Another Gloster F.9/40 DG206/G fitted with de Havilland H1 engines first flew from Cranwell on 5 March 1943. Then it was brought to Newmarket by road and on 17 April made a seven-minute flight. Rumours raced around the locality of propeller-less, strange sounding strange craft models of which were soon within many a local collection! Four more flights were made by Michael Daunt before DG206/G made the first UK jet fighter cross-country flight to the new test centre, Barford St John, on 28 May 1943. Newmarket's part in the wartime jet engine saga was complete.

Newmarket Heath was a strange, very open place to have chosen for such highly secret endeavour, the existence of which thereby became very much public knowledge. But then barely had the first wartime aircraft landed on the Heath than crowds were viewing them, as I soon discovered.

It was 3 September 1939, time 1600 hrs, and the war five hours old. Braving the expected Luftwaffe onslaught Dad and me took a short tour of the local airfields. By the road leading into Newmarket many folk out for a Sunday stroll were on the Heath. Parked cars suggested something unusual so ours joined them. Just over the grass brow rested the centre of attraction – a squadron of Wellington Is sheltering behind rolls of hastily placed barbed wire with real, live bombs on trolleys. There was no flying, this was Sunday and everything closed on a 1930s Sunday – except, perhaps, an ice-cream cart. The aircraft's squadron identity letters, 'LN' I had not hitherto seen. A hazardous quick squint through opera glasses revealed a few 'Wimpeys' still wearing serial numbers, and a home check showed that they had recently served with 99 Squadron. For me it was a fascinating first acquaintance with RAF Newmarket Heath or, as many official documents called it, RAF Rowley Mile.

Few racing along the A14 which skirts the Heath realise they pass a place of great pathos linked with portentous developments. One of the former concerned a Stirling mine-layer and crew who ended their days in one of the mightiest explosions ever heard in the area. The bomber, R9245, taking off from the 2,500 yard grass runway with 250 yard overruns at either end, the longest runway in the country, was bound for the mouth of the Gironde. Heavily laden, it lifted off a fraction too late. A main wheel clipped the top of the Devil's Dyke and an oil tank was pierced. An engine seized, the bomber spun in, and its two mines exploded.

Newmarket Heath's turf, trodden by so many famous horses and source of many broken dreams, has long reverberated to the hooves of famous racehorses. One of the greatest, 'The Godolphin Arabian', the first Arabian stallion, was laid to rest in what is now lovely Wandlebury just south of Cambridge, and is immortalised in a beautiful but somewhat embroidered story called *King of the Wind* (Constable) by Marguerite Henry. Well worth a read as you sit on the Dyke wishing a 'Wimpey' or a Stirling would pass, just once, but with no battle intent.

Gazing across the Heath in wartime to distant Ely Cathedral set against a vast blue backdrop and huge puffy clouds that only East Anglia and East Africa provide belied the fact that nightmarish things came this way. On pre-war race days there had been great pageantry when the titled and wealthy flew in as they still do. Indeed, HRH the Prince of Wales landed here on his way to the July 1935 Jubilee Review, Mildenhall.

Two days before the war began Wellingtons of 99 Squadron dispersed here from Mildenhall, Newmarket being its satellite. Crews and ground personnel were accommodated in the old Grandstand replaced in 1999-2000 by the Millennium Grandstand. Hopefully, rats that enjoyed the stables in 1939-40 will never return.

A few days later the bombers were scattered inland, to Upper Heyford and Elmdon, and to fully protect them from air attack. They soon returned and on 9 September No 99 received their first refined Wellington Ia, N2870, fitted with Nash & Thompson turrets and a retractable dustbin turret. No operations were flown using Mk Is, the first operation being by Ias. This, a North Sea shipping sweep, took place on 30 September. Taking off at 1515 hrs meant a night return which, at this time, had to be to Mildenhall. Another operation came on 8 October involving a similar procedure.

There was no combat until 14 December 1939. At 1143 hrs a dozen Wellingtons took off to bomb in daylight German warships off Helgoland. Messerschmitt Bf 110s of ZG76, alerted by radar of which the British knew nothing, homed in and discovered the Wellingtons highly vulnerable to beam attacks. Five were shot down and a sixth crashed before reaching home. Another overshot into a dense hedgerow, the crew having to be cut from the wreckage, and one from a portion of the geodetic structure into which he was horrendously impaled. This significant operation prompted Bomber Command to turn to night bombing, and led to its heavies ultimately having beam and ventral gun protection.

The switch to night operations was first evident here on 11 January 1940 when a leaflet dropping flight was despatched to Hamburg. Night operational reconnaissance flights followed, then the German invasion of Scandinavia resulted in a bomber response from Newmarket commencing on 17/18 April with a raid on distant Stavanger. Bombing was now the order of the day and on 10/11 May at the end of the day when the German assault on the West began the Wellingtons started raiding continental targets at night. Throughout 1940 they operated, and participated in the 30 August retaliatory raid on Berlin. From the Heath '99' operated from a Glim light flarepath and were not the only 'Wimpeys' to do so. Others, carrying additional petrol tanks in the fuselage, and flown by ferry crews under the control of No 3 Group Training Flight, at dusk set out to cross France for Malta and thence Egypt. In so doing the Wellingtons were flying at their very maximum endurance. These little known frequent journeys through heavily defended territory, in pitch darkness, demanded great courage.

The first bombs directed at Newmarket Heath fell wide on 18/19 June 1940. In the following autumn several dusk attacks took place once the enemy had detected the bombers' take-off time. A number of cloud cover raids also took place and at 1100 hrs on 3 February 1941 nine HEs damaged two Wellingtons and a visiting Whitley. The most pernicious attempted raid took place at mid-afternoon on a grey Tuesday market day, 18 February 1941. Wartime Newmarket was always packed with troops as on that day. A Dornier Do 17Z of II/KG2 ducked out of the clouds over the Norwich road and then soldiers opened fire. Possibly in a panic reaction the crew flying exceptionally low along the north side of the main street released their load before reaching the Heath then climbed into low cloud. A line of high explosive bombs bashed into the shops along almost the entire northern side of the main street wrecking the White Hart Hotel and killing civilians in the old post office. For many days the street was littered inches deep with broken glass, and until the rain came pavements could be seen to be soaked with blood. No final casualty total was decided upon, many walking injured making their own way home. Although 114 people received treatment, a reliable estimate suggested 300 had various injuries. For witnesses the abiding memory was of the entire main street, end to end, strewn with hundreds of bodies lying stunned by blast. When you visit Newmarket note the assorted replacement buildings on the north side of the main street. This incident was among the worst in wartime Britain.

Oh, the bitter cold of that second wartime winter. Wellington 1c T2888 of 99 Squadron wrapped up on the snowy Heath. (N Didwell, via Andy Thomas)

Three weeks later 99 Squadron moved to Waterbeach and Newmarket then became a satellite of Stradishall. Stirlings of 'A' Flight, 7 Squadron, from water-logged Oakington temporarily replaced the Wellingtons. On 9 April Stirlings set out from here for their first attack on Berlin. Two were forced to abort and the third was shot down. The heavy aircraft badly damaged the grass and chalk surface and were back at Oakington by 13 April. No 3 Group Gunnery Flight's Wellingtons and lighter types took their place in May 1941.

Great secrecy surrounded the arrival of Whitleys of 1419 (Special Duties) Flight under Stradishall's control. Stories locally circulated linking them with 'cloak and dagger' tasks which involved the dropping of agents even in distant Poland. On 25 August 1941 the Flight became No 138 Squadron. During their stay the Whitleys involved shuffled between Newmarket and Stradishall before their move to Tempsford in mid-March 1942. The 3 Group Gunnery Flight renamed No 1483 Flight left for Marham on 14 July 1942 after having contributed Wellingtons to the first two '1,000 bomber' raids.

Far more novel events were now secretly involving the station, the aforementioned first prototype 'Meteor' being not the only speciality. Another was the second prototype, 110ft wing span tank-carrying Hamilcar glider towed here by its AFEE Halifax tug in late July. Newmarket's long run was ideal for load carrying trials, abruptly ended when the glider's undercarriage was damaged in a heavy landing, but they might have stopped for another reason. At 1330 hrs on 30 August 1942 just after the large combination had ascended a warning was received that a Ju 86R 'stratosphere' bomber was approaching from Clacton. The tug pilot, understandably alarmed at being caught in a compromising situation, was ordered to release the glider and leave the cumbersome Hamilcar to also land – luckily both in safety. The raider passed by, its lone calling card missing by half a mile a small factory in Arbury Road, Cambridge. Newmarket (and Chedburgh) were, incidentally, chosen as storage sites for Hamilcars but none were ready in time before D-Day.

A Hamilcar prototype tank-carrying glider did landing trials here in August 1942.

Operational flying resumed after Newmarket Heath returned to Mildenhall control and Wellington IIIs of No 75 (NZ) Squadron arrived on 1 November 1942. At the time the squadron's crews were converting to Stirlings at Oakington, their first example coming on charge at Newmarket on 16 October and the first operational sorties using them taking place on 20 November. Newmarket formally became part of 32 Base Mildenhall in December 1942, No 75 Squadron was based here until 29 June 1943 and operated within Main Force. Next day No 1483 Gunnery Training Flight returned bringing along eleven Wellington Xs and nine Martinets. Spitfires of the AFDU were often seen here, assisting in bomber defence training.

Newmarket, a Sub-Station of 32 Base Mildenhall until the end of its Bomber Command links in 1945, housed other secret activities this time undertaken by the Bombing Development Unit. Nudged out of Feltwell to make way for 3 Group's Lancaster conversion 'ladder scheme', the BDU arrived on 13 September 1943 then conducted trials of new bombing aids, developed medium altitude mine laying safe from light AA fire and helped crews to extract maximum use from *H2S* and other radar devices and radio aids. It was here, too, that the final form of belly defence for Halifaxes and Stirlings was developed. The BDU returned to Feltwell in late March 1945.

Adjustments to 1483 Flight saw its establishment change to six Spitfire Vs, twelve Hurricanes and eight Martinets before on 11 March 1944 becoming No 1688 Bomber Defence Training Flight and which moved to Feltwell on 26 February 1945. A Flight of 3 Lancaster Finishing School used Newmarket briefly in 1945 before, on 1 March, No 54 Maintenance Unit active in the area since October 1939 took up residence until January 1948.

Flying ceased in February 1945 and by summer the RAF was no longer on the Heath. Long since abandoned, too, had been the autumn 1940 idea that Side Hill (TL668628) to the East of the town might be a suitable site for military glider pilot training.

The end of the war brought a pause in activity at Newmarket until 1946 when race-goers began flying in from Europe, the operation handled by International Air Radio. Of the exotic aircraft which delivered them, pride of place must be shared by the immaculate Grumman Mallard amphibian of M Boussac and a delectable Lockheed 12. If you visit Newmarket on a race day you will probably see a clutch of light aircraft and helicopters there for the sport of kings. Apt, for in 1942 the King's Flight metamorphosed into No 161 (Special Duties) Squadron later famed for SOE operations from Tempsford. The RAF presence on the Heath ended in July 1948 when it was declared surplus to need ...or did it?

Race-goers in 1947 included famous Lockheed 12A c/n 1277. It is believed to have been LA621 and G-AGVZ. Seen here as NC8820 it may be NC18906 currently active in the USA.

Immaculate blue-grey-yellow Grumman Mallard NC2966 of M.Boussac visiting the 'Cesarawitch' on 15 October 1947. It made several visits in 1947.

In writing about aviation it is also risky to use the words 'ended' or 'last time' and just when it seemed certain that military flying had ceased at Newmarket came the unexpected. A 1950s Meteor night-fighter pilot, finding the weather at base too bad for homing, soon also had a very low fuel state. On his own initiative he sensibly decided to take his Meteor to the aircraft's parental home and landed on Newmarket Heath. From there he safely departed – discreetly – after refuelling had taken place. Not a lot of people found out about it – fortunately!

Charter firms mushroomed in the late 1940s, among them Sivewright Airways whose Gemini G-AKGD came several times.

Main features (December 1944):
Runways: E/W 7,500ft, SE/NW 5,400ft, NE/SW 4,800ft, all grass on chalk base. No permanent obstructions on approaches, Mk II lighting. *Hangars:* three T2, three B1, two Blister, one Double Blister. *Hardstandings:* twenty-four circular hardened surface. *Accommodation* (mainly off camp): RAF: 105 officers, 230 SNCOs, 818 ORs; WAAF: 3 officers, 3 SNCOs, 138 ORs.

NORTH CREAKE, Norfolk

52°54/00°49E 240ft asl; TF895385. E of village by Walsingham-Wells road

Opened mid-war, North Creake was created on a site previously Docking's decoy, and to accommodate RAF bomber squadrons forced out of existing stations as the American forces increased in number. Development of North Creake as a Sub-Station of Foulsham started late 1942.

The runways were declared complete on 1 November 1943, and the station was passed to the RAF on 23 November 1943. Temporarily administered by 3 Group, it was passed to 100 Group control on 7 December 1943 and on 31 December was declared fully complete and ready for business.

At that time the Windsor was still a possible future type for Bomber Command as well as the more realistic, heavier Lincoln. Although they knew little about it Bomber Command was also very keen to acquire Boeing B-29s possibly licence built in Britain by English Electric. There was the certainty that these heavy bombers would require runways longer than 2,000 yards and, soon after it opened, a decision was taken to lengthen those at North Creake. Therefore the station was placed on Care & Maintenance pending the construction of extensions. Instead of aircraft at the station a signals unit settled in.

At the same time a decision was taken to raise Lakenheath to the new Very Heavy Bomber station category. Too many changes in the run-up to D-Day being questionable items, extension of North Creake was postponed, and it re-opened in April 1944 to receive Lakenheath's 199 Squadron at the start of May 1944. That placed North Creake in a noteworthy position as the home of the first squadron to operate *Mandrel* radar confusing equipment operationally introduced on 5/6 June 1944. Thereafter North Creake's Stirling IIIs, orbiting in pairs while slowly advancing preceded many Main Force attacks. Often, they also dropped *Window* to further confuse the defenders.

With thirty-six dispersal pads and three hangars available the three Flight squadron could easily be accommodated – and so could two squadrons. Therefore, on 7 September 1944, No 199s 'C' Flight was detached and next day became the nucleus of No 171, a new Stirling RCM squadron. Using *Window* they commenced duties on 15 September 1944 but before the end of the month they converted to Halifax IIIs and were soon assisting the positioning of the *Mandrel* screen. No 199 Squadron also converted to Halifax IIIs but not until March 1945. Thus, they were the last squadron in Bomber Command to fly Stirlings operationally, the last sorties being flown on 14 March. By then both squadrons were also dropping bombs as well as *Window*. Final operational sorties were flown on 2 May 1945, 171 Squadron disbanded on 27 July and 199 Squadron folded two days later.

North Creake went to Care & Maintenance on 30 September 1945. No 111 Storage Sub-Site of 274 MU opened on 12 October 1945 and handled the storage and reduction of Mosquitoes. The unit closed in September 1947 . Blue Storage currently answers commercial and industrial storage needs.

Main features:
Runways: 240° 6,000ft x 150ft, 310°, 190°, concrete. *Hangars:* two T2, one B1. *Hardstandings:* thirty-six loop type. *Accommodation:* RAF: 108 officers, 255 SNCOs, 985 ORs; WAAF: 8 officers, 16 SNCOs, 312 ORs.

NORTH PICKENHAM, Norfolk

52°37N/00°44E 190ft asl; TL850070. By B1077 NW from South Pickenham. Road also along N side by ex-Thor site

For North Pickenham's 491st Bomb Group a more horrendous day than 26 November 1944 would be hard to imagine. Their target – one of a number being raided by B-24s of the 2nd BD – was an oil installation at Misburg. Some 500 enemy fighters are thought to have responded to the 8th AF attacks that day and a high proportion homed in on the Liberators. So ferocious was their onslaught that fifteen B-24s of the 491st, almost half those despatched, were brought down in the Hanover area. Despite the vicious interception the Group had pressed on to bomb the target, for which effort it was awarded a Distinguished Unit Citation. On that terrible day 120 faces familiar at the dawn were, at the homecoming, nowhere to be seen.

There is perhaps an irony there for North Pickenham, throughout its career, seemed to have a particular fascination for Americans into whose hands it passed on making its debut at the close of 1943. On 1 January 1944 the 491st Bomb Group set sail for Britain but with few personnel and little equipment. The air echelon – still training in the USA – arrived in the UK during May 1944 but by then Group HQ, established at Pickenham, had in March 1944 transferred to Metfield.

Their place at North Pickenham was taken from 18 April by the 492nd Bomb Group whose B-24s flew their initial operation on 11 May. Attacks were concentrated upon Germany and with a high loss rate. Indeed, two aircraft crashed while returning from the first operation. At the start of June 1944 the Group switched to bombing airfields and V-1 sites in France during the invasion prelude. Early on the morning of D-Day Pickenham's Liberators helped pound coastal defences, then flew interdiction sorties to aid troops holding the bridge-head. In mid-June 1944 strategic attacks on Germany were resumed, but interrupted when bombing support was needed to assist the break-out from St-Lô on 25 July. Such activity continued into August 1944 when a sudden operational change came about. The Allies wished to make more use of the Resistance Movement in Europe, and air supply forces were limited. The lion's share of this work was being undertaken by 3 Group, RAF Bomber Command using Stirling bombers and two Main duty squadrons at Tempsford. Stirling bomber squadrons had recently been reduced in number and by August 1944 none was available for supply duty. It was then that the Americans made a contribution by switching the 492nd Bomb Group – less personnel and equipment – to Harrington, in Northamptonshire, from where special duty operations were soon being flown.

General view of North Pickenham, Thor stands distant. August 1978.

A B-24J of the 854th BS, 491st BG.

Space available at Pickenham was filled on 15 August when the 491st returned from Metfield allowing that base to become a trans-Atlantic transport centre for the 8th AF.

On 18 September the 491st supply dropped supporting the airborne forces in Holland. During the winter German Ardennes offensive the B-24s attacked enemy fortifications, supply lines, and later during the Rhine crossing bombed an airfield to prevent opposition.

After the Americans left in July 1945, North Pickenham became in July 1946 a Sub-Site for 258 MU at Shipdham and handled barrack furniture and equipment. Rated as suitable for development to Very Heavy Bomber status it was transferred to Bomber Command in October 1948. Its strategic position ahead of the main defence line made it unacceptable to the Americans so it was returned to Maintenance Command a year later. In June 1953 the USAF Air Material Command established an ammunition store here run by the 59th Ammunition Supply Group and 7559 Supply Squadron (Ammunition).

Its military operational days were far from over for late in 1958 Bomber Command again took control, North Pickenham having been chosen as one of Feltwell's four satellites each of which would have a Flight holding three Thor IRBMs. 'E' Flight reformed here on 22 July 1959 and within a self contained enclave had three launch pads, a control centre, ground equipment along with accommodation and messing blocks. On 1 September 1959 the Flight became No 220 Squadron within the Feltwell Operations Wing. The Thors being operated from facilities all above ground vulnerable to attack, agreement was reached on 31 May 1962 to phase out the Thors in 1963 and return them to the USA. Those which formed part of the Feltwell complex stood down on 1 July 1963 and the missiles were returned to the USA for rocket research launches. The Thor site at Pickenham closed in October 1963. A brief resumption of activity on North Pickenham airfield took place between October 1964 and November 1965 when Kestrels of the Evaluation Squadron at West Raynham undertook some flying here.

In 2006 Green Energy Ltd opened North Pickenham Wind Farm. Its wind turbines generate up to 14.4 mega watts.

Main features:
Runways: 240° 5,700ft x 150ft, 190°, 320°, tarmac and concrete. *Hangars:* two T2. *Hardstandings:* fifty concrete. *Accommodation:* 421 officers, 2,473 enlisted men.

NORTH WITHAM, Lincolnshire

52°47N/00°36W 390ft asl; SK945225. S of Grantham, W of the A1 road

Temporary, yes. Three runways and the usual two T2s? Yes; but there the similarity with many other wartime stations ends. North Witham was unusually supplied with six US-built temporary and pre-fabricated Butler 'Barns' more associated in British folklore (but in different form) with Mildenhall's SR-71s.

Late 1943 saw movement of transport units from the Mediterranean Theatre to Britain and the 9th AF. They were coming to airlift US Army's paratroops and their advanced force in the *Overlord* assault, then provide backup. Airfield completion for the new force did not keep pace with the extensive build-up and that led to Groups occupying such airfields as became available. Some were in Lincolnshire instead of southern England.

At the start of January 1944, the 9th Air Service Command had been assigned six airfields for use as Tactical Air Depots equivalent to RAF Maintenance Units, and the 1st Tactical Air Depot was established at North Witham. A weapons dump at a small RAF station known as No 100 MU South Witham had opened in March 1942.

North Witham airfield was completed late 1943, RAF personnel of the 9th Troop Carrier Command Substitution Unit moving in on 14 December to prepare the airfield for opening next day. That unit, and the 8th AF Substitution Unit arranged transfer of RAF bases to the USAAF.

On 31 December 1943 US personnel began arriving from the 9th AF base at Cottesmore. The main element comprising 75 officers and 1,256 enlisted men of the 33rd and 85th Air Depot Groups (ADG) arrived at the end of the month. On 16 February the 85th Air Depot Group became the 29th ADG.

Their important task was the preparation of C-47s and C-53s for operational Troop Carrier Groups. They provided spares, undertook major repairs and gave the type of support for the aircraft impossible to provide at operational airfields.

March 1944 saw the arrival of the 9th AF Pathfinder School which resulted in some Air Depot personnel being accommodated in tented accommodation erected at the northern end of the airfield. With eighty-six RAF personnel and almost 3,600 Americans on camp built to accommodate about 2,000, there was clearly overcrowding. That also applied to hangar space and it was at this time that the six Butler metal pre-fabricated hangars were erected in the depot area just north of a solitary T2. The other of that type stood within the area used by the Pathfinder School.

That unit trained small groups of Pathfinder paratroops to act as an advance party preceding the US airborne troops by setting up responder beacons to guide the main force to the drop zones. The unit also trained aircrew in their use of other radio and radar aids.

At 2130 hrs on 5 June 1944 take-off began of twenty C-47s of the 9th Troop Carrier Command Pathfinder Group carrying some 200 men who were to drop first then indicate drop zones for the 82nd and 101st Airborne Divisions making the main paradrop. Around 0015 hrs the Pathfinders landed in the Cherbourg Peninsula, only one aircraft failing to return.

Over the weeks following the School – later renamed the Pathfinder Group Provisional – trained a detachment of the 1st Independent Polish Airborne Brigade before moving away from North Witham.

The Air Depot Units began transferring to the Continent in December 1944, administration of the station then passing to Barkston Heath RAF Base of Bomber Command in the belief that a bomber HCU might make use of the station. On 7 May 1945 the airfield was instead placed under C&M under 40 Group, RAF Maintenance Command. A few days later No 100 MU began storing bombs here – and in profusion.

No 259 MU took control of the airfield on 1 July for use as a stores centre. Between September 1945 and June 1946 it was also occupied by No 4 Personnel and Despatch Unit which categorised personnel returning from overseas for release.

No 259 MU left in May 1946 and No 100 late 1948. North Witham was retained as an Inactive Airfield which was not sold for civilian use until February 1960. Much of the site passed into Forestry Commission hands with Twyford Forest covering some parts of the one time airfield. A few buildings including a T2 hangar remain within an industrial site.

Main features:
Runways: 020° 6,000ft x 150ft, 240°, 300°, concrete. *Hangars:* two T2, six Butler pre-fabricated. *Hardstandings:* fifty spectacle type. *Accommodation:* RAF: 87 officers, 296 SNCOs, 1,296 ORs; WAAF: 10 officers, 5 SNCOs, 260 ORs.

NORWICH INTERNATIONAL AIRPORT, Norfolk – see HORSHAM ST FAITH

OAKINGTON, Cambridgeshire

52°16N/00°04E 39ft asl; TL412665. 2 miles N of A14, 6 miles NW of Cambridge

'**I**t's a Stirling!', and the sight of our first four-engined bomber was sheer magic. Gawky, incredible legs dangling, the aeroplane proudly displayed its Short mainplanes as it banked over Jesus Green providing proof that there really were Stirlings – at least one – almost on my doorstep. But it meant much more for the Luftwaffe had just destroyed the heart of Coventry. Were we soon going to return the gesture? It wasn't long before the owners' motto slipped out. 'Per Andium per Noctem' – which meant 7 Squadron was the 'proud' owner. Well, not exactly proud because the all-electric wonder was none too well, very temperamental and demanding like many who feel important. Stirling and 7 Squadron will forever be synonymous with Oakington where, from 1941 to the end of the war, the squadron fought by night and day and so valiantly using first Stirlings and then Lancasters during the second half of the war.

Oakington will forever be remembered as the home of East Anglia's own – the Short Stirling and, of course, 7 Squadron.

As long ago as 1910 unsuccessful attempts were made to fly the Grose Monoplane from Oakington, and at nearby Rampton the RFC had one of their many landing grounds. Initial choice for a 1930s bomber station was an area of very flat ground to the east of Rampton immediately north of the ancient line of the A10 leading to Ely and by the village. Drainage problems led to the choice of the developed site where building of RAF Oakington began in 1939, hence the two then fashionable Type 'J' metal hangars whose curved metal panel pre-fabricated roofs were designed to speed construction and improve drainage. They were in direct contrast with the many flat roofed brick and concrete technical and domestic buildings built on one site and not split like many in the 1930s. Gone the graciousness of the pseudo Georgian style and replaced by a collection of functional constructions easier and faster to complete. A standard feature was the parapet surrounding the roof edge into which eighteen inches or so of sand could be tipped to reduce the effect of firebombs and strafing on such large structures.

Such was the desperate need for new aerodromes that unfinished Oakington opened in 2 Group, Bomber Command, on 1 July 1940, Wing Commander L B Duggen taking command at a time when many personnel had to be accommodated in tents. No 218 Squadron's Blenheim IVs moved in on 14 July 1940, dispersed on the south side and commenced daylight operations on 19 August with attacks aimed at Dutch airfields to assist Fighter Command's desperate battle.

Oakington's first very memorable event came on 19 September. Blenheims were delivering mock attacks on the airfield for its army defenders when suddenly a 'Blenheim' made an unscheduled approach and belly landed. Overhead two Hurricanes of 17 Squadron zoomed for the new arrival was their prize, Ju 88A 7A+FM, Werk Nr 0362, of 4(F)/121 and packed with cameras. It had developed engine trouble and was caught spying by the Hurricane duo. Leutnant Helmut Knab and his companions were captured before they could burn their aircraft and their useful equipment was 'confiscated'.

Ironically, the next major movement inwards also involved cameras for on 16 November 1940 a new organisation, No 3 Photographic Reconnaissance Unit formed here under 3 Group Bomber

Command, its role to carry out damage assessment sorties. Spitfires specially modified for the role arrived painted in strange colours including the later customary grey-blue but also white, and with pink examples intended to tone with evening skies at high altitudes.

They first operated on 29 November 1940, and to Cologne. Thereafter 3 PRU flew many sorties and later acquired a few Wellingtons for night photography aided by high-powered flash bulbs. Fascinating as these things were, it was the arrival of 7 Squadron on 29 October 1940 that proved to be the most exciting.

'No 7' took some weeks to move in from Leeming, 218 Squadron leaving late November to make way. Stirling production had been damaged by air attack and in November the squadron held only two of the RAF's first WWII four-engined troublesome bombers. Unfortunately their interim engines delivered highest output at a mere 10,000ft while many problems came from irritating small faults generating a protracted teething period. Chagrin came when the squadron discovered that the Stirling wing span had been reduced in the project stage to allow simultaneous indoor servicing of six examples to keep down weight and cost. Clipping the wings partly caused the low ceiling but also resulted in the hefty bomber being very manoeuvrable – once it was airborne. Achieving that was aggravated first by its long fuselage, barely adequate tail fin area but mostly by slow responding fluid controlled Exactor throttles. Landing, too, could be very difficult especially in crosswinds when rapid engine response would be needed.

Oakington was the centre of another storm. MAP's Lord Beaverbrook in November 1940 told the Air Ministry that new heavy bombers needed concrete runways 4,500ft in length, but the few existing were only 3,000ft long. With Oakington principally in mind, he stated that ground movement by heavy aircraft in winter conditions would cause unsettled turf on new airfields to be churned into mud and ruined. He also suggested laying tarmac runways in place of concrete. Review of the situation resulted in the Air Ministry (AM) deciding that runways should be on the scale of one of 4,200ft and two of 3,300ft at each new operational airfield and satellite.

MAP asked why grass surfaced Oakington was chosen for Stirlings. The AM choice followed consideration of weather, approaches, geography and advice that soil and drainage features were satisfactory. It was believed that by autumn 1941 turf would have settled enough to permit full scale operations. Stirlings had initially been fed to 4 Group, the long-range Whitley bomber Group. But Stirlings had Bristol radials which powered 3 Group's Wellingtons whereas Whitleys had Merlins, so Bomber Command transferred the Stirlings to 3 Group.

It transpired that the Command did not favour metalled runways because they meant queuing to take-off thereby increasing vulnerability to intruder attack. Also, runways would be difficult to camouflage. Not until 4 January 1941 did Bomber Command accept the need or admit any desire for runways.

Only nine airfields in Britain had them pre-war. The only reason for having any was fear of hard wear on unstable surfaces, and even in February 1941 Bomber Command only wanted the runways laid at Stradishall. Yet new airfields immediately benefited from them for they provided instant hard surfaces. Grass took many months to establish, and involved continuous labour for upkeep.

Change followed fast. By April 1941 one hundred new airfields were being built with runways, and another twenty having them provided. Fifty more airfields with runways were being planned with twenty about to be started.

Bomber Command listed Oakington as seventh for runways which brought a flurry of important visitors to the station. Most came by road because the airfield's surface put it unserviceable!

Lightly loaded Stirlings frequently took off to bomb up and operate from Wyton. That could not continue because conditions there were getting as bad as at Oakington and became worse when XV Squadron began receiving Stirlings. Grass surface airfields were unsuitable for heavy aircraft.

January 1941 found Oakington's turned into a sea of mud when ice thawed, a slippery morass when water froze – and it snowed often. So cold was it that rum was issued to 'approved personnel'. Occasionally a Stirling made a flight, to the delight of the locals, and on 19 February 1941 long before the aircraft was really ready to fight, three Stirlings carried out the first raid, against Rotterdam's oil tanks.

Oakington acquired an incomplete satellite at Bourn where on 7 February personnel were sent to commence ground duties. Equipment had already arrived at Oakington for the handling of standard 2,000lb bombs, the largest the Stirling could carry, but the airfield was been declared unsuitable even for PR Spitfires on 22 January which resulted in operations being switched to Alconbury. PR Wellingtons flew their first night sorties from Newmarket on 5 and 6 February.

On 25 February the fiftieth Spitfire sortie was flown. No 3 PRU usually held about six Spitfires and flew a large number of sorties with them before disbanding late July 1941. Oakington's Stirlings were then hitting the headlines, particularly with daylight raids. Yet throughout 1941 Stirlings – virtually hand built mainly as a result of the initial intent to build only 100 and strong as battleships – remained a rare commodity.

On 30 May 1942 word passed among villagers at Oakington that 1,000 bombers would operate that night against Cologne. It seemed highly implausible but proved to be true and 7 Squadron made their biggest effort yet. In addition to their nineteen Stirlings twelve Wellingtons of 101 Squadron operated from Bourn under Oakington's control. That squadron had moved to Oakington in June 1941 flying Wellington Ics and transferred to Bourn on 11 February 1942. No 23 OTU placed five Wellington Ics at both stations for the '1,000 bomber' raids and of the station's force of forty-one aircraft, thirty-three claimed successful attacks.

Major change came in August 1942, when 7 Squadron switched to pathfinding. Flare loads mixed with high explosive and back-up primary markers were increasingly carried. A gradual switch to flare/target indicators and larger incendiary loads came, particularly during the Battle of the Ruhr in summer 1943. On 11 May 1943, 7 Squadron began rearming with Lancasters which took over completely on 12 August 1943. No 7 Squadron, a three-Flight squadron, made a great contribution to the bomber offensive, was very active during the Battle of Berlin, and mounted a heavy, sustained campaign.

Early in 1943 Bellman hangars were erected. Their purpose was to provide homes for the PNTU formed here on 21 March 1943 but soon moved and, starting to form the same day, No 1409 Meteorological Flight using eight Mosquito IVs taken from No 521 Squadron. Their task was to seek weather patterns for Bomber Command operations, PAMPA flights beginning on 2 April. May 1943 saw them start using Mosquito IXs and by the time they moved to Wyton on 8 January 1944 '1409' was fully equipped with that version.

They had been joined by a new Mosquito IV bomber squadron, No 627 Squadron, an off-shoot of 139 Squadron formed on 12 November 1943 at Oakington to fly night nuisance operations. These began on 24 November when DZ615 bombed Berlin, the target for nearly 100 of the 291 sorties flown by the squadron from Oakington for a loss of only three aircraft. Four of the Mosquito IVs were each capable of carrying a 4,000lb bomb. In mid-April 1944 the squadron moved to Woodhall Spa to join 5 Group as a specialised marker squadron.

On 24 April 1944 571 Squadron's Mosquito IX/XVIs completed arrival from Downham Market and later that day two attacked Düsseldorf. Operating mainly at night in 8 Group's LNSF '571' despatched 2,520 sorties, the last on 26 April 1945 with Grossenbrode as target. Only nine Mosquitoes failed to return from their entire operations. Oakington's combination of Lancasters and Mosquitoes was an example of the most efficient and effective bomber team the Allies ever possessed.

No 571 Squadron left for Warboys on 20 July and on 24 July 1945 No 7 Squadron moved to Mepal. Next day Transport Command and 47 Group seized Oakington and the first Liberator VI of 206 Squadron arrived from Leuchars on 30 July still wearing Coastal Command colours. Liberators were soon pouring into mid-Anglian bases to commence trooping flights to India and the Far East. So rapid were the changeovers that on the day after the first arrivals at Oakington two Liberators set out on training flights to India, and even before their squadron had completely moved in from Leuchars. No 86 Squadron's Liberators began arriving on 1 August, both squadrons using Oakington as the base for their thirty-three mixed Liberator GRVI/VIII rapidly fitted out to carry passengers in considerable discomfort on seats dispersed within the aircraft. A major commitment was to airlift Indian troops back to their homeland and bring back British troops for demobilisation. These flights lasted into 1946, both squadrons disbanding on 25 April 1946.

At the start of May 1946 twenty Avro Yorks of 242 Squadron, participants in trunk route services mainly to the Far East, moved in. At the end of November 1947 the squadron left for Abingdon from where, in August 1947, 238 Squadron had brought eight Dakota IVs to Oakington. On 24 November 1947 Nos 27 and 30 Medium Range Transport Squadrons re-formed here, each also holding eight Dakotas, and 46 Squadron joined them. The four squadrons were supplemented by the remainder of the 46 Group tactical air transport force based at Waterbeach. At Oakington there were a few Horsas for glider towing practise.

July 1948's commencement of the Berlin Air Lift caused the despatch of most of the Dakotas to Germany. No 238 Squadron re-numbered 10 Squadron on 5 November 1948 spent much of 1949 at Lübeck from where it returned in September to disband at Oakington on 20 February 1950. No 18 Squadron was also briefly at Oakington in 1949 before settling at Waterbeach in October. No 46 Squadron disbanded here on 20 February 1950 and 27 Squadron departed in June.

Planners had provisionally earmarked Oakington as a training base for BAFO light bomber crews. Instead, February 1950 saw the arrival of 24 (Commonwealth) Squadron from Waterbeach. Dakotas and Yorks equipped this squadron whose first business sortie from Oakington was to Zurich, via Northolt, by Dakota KJ994 on 25 February. The transportation of VIPs remained the task until the last week of November 1950 when '24s' twin-engined aircraft were transferred to 30 Squadron. The remainder of the squadron left for Lyneham on the 27th, its VIP role ending when they converted to Hastings transports.

November 1950 brought a watershed for Oakington passed from Transport Command to 23 Group, Training Command. They moved No 1 Flying Training School and their Harvards to the station creating a noisy stay extending to 29 October 1951. No 206 Advanced Flying School then took over, their Main Party arriving from North Luffenham and the defunct 102 FRS on 7 November, the day when 206 AFS became effective. The first course opened on 5 December. Students commenced by flying Meteor T7s then progressed to refurbished Meteor IIIs, virtually the last of their breed still active. Intensity of activity became high both here and at the RLG, Graveley. One day in January 1953 produced an amazing 612 movements, although the daily average was about 200 'rollers' at Oakington and 100 at Graveley. Oakington was indeed a busy place.

No 206 AFS wound down during May 1954, but there was little evidence of change at Oakington for on 1 June 1954 the unit's remains were absorbed by a new No 5 Flying Training School under 25 Group and using Meteor T7s also Vampire 5s and 9s. These latter types were no newcomers to Oakington because it had often served as a staging post for groups of Vampires heading for 2TAF in Germany. September 1959 saw the replacement of the T7s by Vampire T11s as the Provost-Vampire training programme for new pilots was brought fully into play. Within a few weeks the T7s returned – the T11s were too small for long-legged pilots!

It could be argued that Oakington's days ended as they begun, to the sound of Bristol radials touring the circuit. During March 1962 Varsities came into use as No 5 FTS switched to training pilots for multi-engined aircraft. Intensity of flying remained high with the engines of Varsities running non-stop from 0800 hrs to 1700 hrs. But by the mid-1970s the Varsity was an aged affair inadequate for flying along airways, an essential training item within the course. Late summer 1974 saw the introduction of Jetstream T1s, but their stay was brief for on 31 December 1974 No 5 FTS was disbanded, its task passing to No 6 FTS Finningley.

The last official RAF flight from Oakington was made by Wessex XT606 on 7 May 1975, but flying here was far from over. The camp passed to the Army and accommodated troops returning to Britain as a result of the pull-backs from overseas. First in were the Green Jackets, then early in 1976 came Scouts and Gazelle helicopters of 657 Squadron Army Air Corps. In 1984 – by which time the 2nd Battalion The Queen's Regiment was here – 657 Squadron's Scout element was replaced with Lynx helicopters armed with TOW missiles, for their prime role was anti-tank. Whilst the helicopters were at Oakington, the squadron personnel took their share of garrison duty in the Falklands and Beavers became the most likely fixed-wing machines to use Oakington. Gradually the main and only remaining runway was shortened almost to nothing, and patches of trees and bushes were planted on the landing ground as much for ecological purposes as for infantry training.

Each day Varsity engines started early. Serviceable chosen aircraft had their engines run continuously to the end of the day's flying. Beyond the 5 FTS line up, a glimpse of hangar and tower.

Evening scene, beneath a magnificent sky.

The Army Air Corps was replaced by the 1st Battalion The Royal Anglian Regiment. From time to time RAF Hercules transport, carried out low-level supply drops but that was permanently ended when, with almost no ceremony, Oakington Barracks closed at the end of May 1999. The future of the site was uncertain until the Home Office announced that part of the domestic area was, in 2000, to become an Immigration Reception Centre. There was ample local opposition on grounds of security.

Far more dismay erupted when it was announced that Oakington was, for neither a particular nor sound reason, to become the site of a new town named Northstowe. Later it was claimed that this would be an 'eco-town', but misconception had overcome government minds, including that of the Prime Minister. Towns, hamlets and villages in this part of Britain were centuries ago thoughtfully and logically sited with their distances apart equating that easily covered by walking from one to another during daylight – some 7 miles one way allowing return, or 15 miles for one-way travel. The proposed new town conforms to no logic. Not surprisingly, local opposition remains because of a fear that it will surely engulf the villages of Oakington and Long Stanton, whose populations do not wish to be swallowed. A greater problem will occur when thousands of cars from the new town spill onto the notoriously hazardous, and ever more busy, A14. Thousands of people have appealed for improvements to that major road. By the time it takes place it is unlikely to satisfy anyone due to the greatly increased trade that a much expanded Port of Felixstowe will eventually generate.

Alongside the eastern perimeter of the one-time Oakington aerodrome a monstrous blight has been inflicted upon the landscape. In place of the railway line, upon which trains used to provide aircraft enthusiasts and spies with a splendid view of the secret early Stirlings for a small outlay, there has come a hideous blot on the flat flood-prone landscape, visible even from space! Again facing much opposition, it is ever increasing in cost, displaying repeated delay and causing widespread disruption during construction. This ridiculous, concrete monstrosity for 'guided buses', which become just buses when they leave the track, is intended to link the Huntingdon area with Cambridge. The longest in the world so far, it will not remove heavy traffic from the A14. It may not serve Northstowe (the proposed new town), for the ill-positioned town is also much delayed.

Main features (December 1944):
Runways: 230°, 6,000ft (extended mid-war to 6,500ft) x 150 ft, 275°, 190°, tarmac on concrete. *Hangars:* two J Type, two T2, one B1. *Hardstandings:* thirty-six heavy bomber type mainly on western and southern sides of airfield. *Accommodation:* RAF: 181 officers, 306 SNCOs, 1,104 ORs; WAAF: 12 officers, 23 SNCOs, 315 ORs. *Note:* 1950s modifications included major extension of the control tower, and

building a long office block facing a concrete aircraft servicing area close to the B1 hangar in the north-west corner of the airfield. Alterations in fuel storage first involved tanks for jet fuel and later for prop-jet fuel. Oakington was unusual in layout for after acceptance at the main gate entry continued along the side of the playing fields with the domestic accommodation to the left.

OLD BUCKENHAM, Norfolk

52°30N/01°03E 195ft asl; TG085940. 2 miles NE of village, off B1077 S of Wymondham

Here, tragedy was inextricably mixed with glamour. Horrific moments there were when a B-24 set down carrying its awfully wounded only to incur an undercarriage malfunction producing that terrifying moment when the bomber slid along the runway in a shower of sparks before suddenly erupting, with terrifying speed, in a fireball soon belching dense clouds of impenetrable black smoke concealing death.

Ambulances and fire crews frantically raced straight to the scene, hopeful but very uncertain of retrieving survivors some already suffering from terrible wounds. Such spectacles remain impossible to forget. American courage displayed during and as a result of day raids was considerable. The glamorised view of the 8th AF generated in later years is diluted for those who witnessed the scenes so often surrounding blood drenched interiors of the aircraft producing sensations almost beyond one's worst imagination. War is not glamorous, not a game played to the sound of Glen Miller's band, not a means of improving one's image and furthering one's political career.

The fun, the ample charm and the sort of Hollywood style belong to a very different scenario, an attempt to forget for awhile the sight of a plunging B-24, crew aboard, and that awful spectre of a mid-air explosion. It was in off-duty moments that the glamour peeped through. Beyond that there was none. The Americans seemed such attractive personalities who looked good, lived well, travelled fast. None portrayed that image of the 8th better than the late James Stewart, a popular film star who, in 1944, was Group Executive Officer at Old Buckenham. He didn't seem associated with the carnage, more with the officer in his 'pinks' at a time when the USAAF was still much an Army organisation which dressed its men like soldiers. But he, too, witnessed terrible events.

Old Buckenham had two Transportable Type 2 hangars and triple runways free of obstructions and orientated, as much as possible, to avoid local dwellings. It was a typical temporary wartime airfield positioned well within 2nd Bomb Division territory. 'Temporary' it was in theory, for the removal of vast areas of thick concrete remains a task still incomplete.

From the third week of December 1943 it served as home for B-24s – initially Hs and Js -of the 453rd Bomb Group based here to the end of the war. Remnants of runway and perimeter remain.

Over 250 operations were flown from Old Buckenham by the 453rd, whose first was against Tours airfield on 5 February 1944. The pattern of operations was as for other B-24 Groups, opening shots being aimed at strategic targets followed by those more directly related to the invasion and airborne assault support. More strategic raids followed then finally came attacks upon communications targets. Noteworthy raids involved attacks upon the Dulmen fuel depot, rail yards at Hamm, I G Farben chemical works at Leverküsen, Gelsenkirchen's synthetic oil refinery, the aircraft assembly plant at Gotha and specialised targets including the viaduct at Altenbeken. From Old Buckenham fuel supplies were flown to France in the summer of 1944, along with food, medical supplies and blankets, for which purpose the capacious fuselage of the B-24 was useful. The last and 259th mission took place on 12 April 1945, for the Group was chosen to serve in the Pacific.

During May and June 1945 the 453rd left for America, leaving Old Buckenham to run down. Experiencing one of these airfields resting silent in that sunny summer of 1945 was an eerie experience. One wished once more to thrill from the pounding noise of hundreds of engines running and the sight of the bombers formating in the orange dawn. What a pity such magic moments could not come without their terrifying attendant sorrows.

A major post-war problem facing the Allied forces was munitions disposal, and particularly of smaller calibre ammunition. Maintenance Units HQs in East Anglia established outposts known as Sub Sites to cope with the task. No 231 MU functioned at Old Buckenham between May 1945 and January 1948 when the station became a Sub-Site of 94 MU still handling ammunition. Closure came in March 1950 but with storage facilities remaining the site re-opened on 1 September 1956 and functioned until closure on 1 February 1958.

Much concrete marks Old Buckenham where the sound of America remains resonant. Since the 1980s in a new small private hangar the renovation of Stearman PT-17 biplanes to a very high standard of finish has been undertaken, flight testing generating that gorgeous American radial engine sound. Other light aircraft also fly from here. Wartime days are not forgotten for a 453rd memorial stone commemorating 259 missions flown and fifty-eight aircraft lost stands not far from the hangar. If you visit, please respect it – and remember that the active area is strictly private. The village hall has a memorial room dedicated to the 453rd BG.

Main features:
Runways: 075° 6,000ft x 150ft, 027°, 130°, none suitable for extension; concrete partially surfaced with wood chips. *Hangars:* two T2. *Hardstandings:* fifty concrete. *Accommodation:* 421 officers, 2,473 enlisted men.

OULTON, Norfolk

52°48N/1°11E 157ft asl; TG155270. At Oulton Street, on Cawston road

It was during Oulton's time as an Unbuilt Satellite that it was the starting point for some outstanding adventures. One took place on 4 April 1943 after reconnaissance photographs revealed a 490ft-long oil tanker in well-defended Brest. Blockade runners were often targets for day bomber operations, and No 21 Squadron, just arrived at the station was briefed to make an attack. Twelve Venturas set out from Oulton led by Flight Lieutenant Dennis and headed for an advanced base. After refuelling they took off and set course for Brest screened by 10 Group Spitfire squadrons.

The Lockheed Vega Ventura based upon an airliner design was too slow and lacking manoeuvrability and was quite unsuitable for daylight bombing operations. As the bombers approached the target a swarm of Fw 190s ambushed the *Ramrod* and a fierce battle ensued enhanced by heavy anti-aircraft fire which always welcomed the RAF to Brest. A Ventura fell away leaving the others to press on. Their bombs fell alongside the ship, a large explosion was seen and then the bombers turned for home.

The 190s had held off over the docks but now they pounced again. British fighters were positioned too high to protect the bombers and as the Venturas headed home one dropped away blazing and was soon in the water. Although evasive action was sound the clumsy Venturas could not readily escape, many shots entered their skinning. Forty miles from the Lizard another crashed into the sea, and a fourth, flown by Pilot Officer Hicks, came down off Portreath. Luckily his crew was rescued. Eight Venturas reached Oulton that evening after a typical operation of the period.

The airfield opened as Horsham's grass field satellite on 31 July 1940. First in came No 114 Squadron which during August launched lone sortie cloud cover day raids mainly directed at airfields and which included some PR duties. Attacks upon barges in the Channel ports followed, also roving commission flights. By night, using a hand-lit flarepath the winter of 1940-1 saw the squadron participating in night Main Force raids on industrial targets and they were difficult for crews to carry out.

At the start of 1941 the squadron sent a detachment to Hornchurch and on 10 January 1941 it fell to No 114 to be the main bomber 'bait' in *Circus No 1*. Several more *Circus*es were flown before February saw the squadron participating in 2 Group's anti-shipping campaign under Coastal Command. For that reason the squadron moved to Thornaby on 2 March 1941.

They were replaced at the start of April by 18 Squadron similarly using Blenheim IVs, who flew their first sortie from Oulton, an anti-shipping raid, on 7 April. Operations continued until the squadron left in mid-July 1941. In November they returned and stayed a month whilst some crews were in Malta.

An unusual change came on 9 December 1941 when No 139 Squadron arrived. Long a Blenheim-equipped 2 Group squadron, No 139 was chosen in desperation to reinforce the RAF in the Far East and with Hudson IIIs. Crews to fly them trained here for which No 1428 Hudson Conversion Flight formed on 29 December 1941. Then the squadron sailed for the Far East during February 1942. The Hudson Flight disbanded on 29 May 1942 with its Ferry Training Section becoming 1444 Flight with its HQ at Horsham St Faith before disbanding on 20 June 1942.

Oulton entertained lodgers between 7 July and 19 September 1942, No 236 Squadron using the still primitive site for their Beaufighter Ics controlled by 16 Group Coastal Command.

In September the station became Swanton Morley's satellite and on 30 September No 88 Squadron's Boston IIIs settled and stayed until March 1943. No 88 was a high-spirited squadron, whose crews were billeted stylishly in the desirable surroundings of Blickling Hall. Its precious treasures had been tucked out of sight and parts boarded up to prevent damage during boisterous moments. Legend has it that Anne Boleyn spent some time here and the squadron commander was most satisfied to occupy her supposed bedroom in the hope that her ghost might entertain him! Go to Blickling Hall now and you will see the beautiful dining room much as the officers knew and cherished it – apart from paintings now on the wall.

No 88 Squadron took a major part in 2 Group's *Circus* and *Ramrod* operations by day. The highlight was the 6 December 1942 low-level raid upon the Philips factories at Eindhoven led by Group Captain Pelly-Fry. An account of the operation can be read in his biography, *Heavenly Days* (Crécy Publishing, 1994). The Boston squadrons in East Anglia suffered a major blow when their aircraft were suddenly taken away for use in North Africa. This put the squadron out of action until June 1943 when re-equipment with Mk IIIAs was complete. Meanwhile No 88 had on 31 March moved to Swanton Morley, the parent station.

They were replaced by 21 Squadron which completed their move to Oulton on 2 April 1943 and next day first operated from here against Brest. Similar day raids followed on targets in France and Holland. With effect from 1 June 1943 the squadron was regarded as a Mitchell squadron and a few were received for conversion training. Nevertheless Ventura operations continued the last taking place on 31 August. No 21 then took their Venturas to Sculthorpe and bade farewell to the Horsas stored here.

On 10 September 1943 the station passed to 3 Group and on the 15th became designated an Unbuilt Second Satellite for Foulsham but not for long. Oulton now underwent upgrade to Class 'A' wartime bomber airfield standard having triple runways added, T2 hangars and sufficient accommodation built. It was declared completed on 29 February 1944 and came under the control of No 100 Group.

Re-opened on 16 May 1944 it immediately became the home of No 214 Squadron, flying Fortress IIs. They were soon joined by '1699', the Fortress Training Flight, and No 803 RCM Squadron, USAAF. Both operational squadrons flew *Mandrel* and *Carpet* operations the American, after becoming the 36th Bomb Squadron (Heavy), leaving on 13 August having commenced operations on 3 June. No 1699 evolved into becoming No 1699 (Bomber Support) Conversion Unit on 24 October 1944 and was equipped with Fortresses and Liberator VIs the former unusually bearing their identity letters in bright yellow. The unit disbanded on 29 June 1945.

As soon as the Americans had left in August 1944 their place was taken by a new RAF RCM squadron, No 223, reformed here on 23 August and equipped with Liberator B VIs. The immediate task for those and 214 Squadron's Fortress IIs and IIIs was to seek for evidence that V2s were being radio-controlled, operations under Spitfire cover flown in daylight. To the end of the war both squadrons flew RCM operations, 223 Squadron receiving some Fortress IIIs in April 1945 before disbandment at Oulton on 29 July 1945. No 214 Squadron moved to the Middle East for re-equipment with Lancaster bombers and the run-down of Oulton began. It passed to Maintenance Command on 3 October 1945 and on 30 October became No 119 Sub-Storage Site to 274 MU Swannington. Mosquitoes were stored here until the unit closed on 28 October 1947. Oulton closed soon after.

Main features:
Runways: 120° 6,000ft x 150ft, 070°, 170°, concrete. *Hangars:* two T2. *Hardstandings:* thirty-six spectacle type. *Accommodation:* RAF:104 officers, 233 SNCOs, 937 ORs; WAAF: 6 officers, 9 SNCOs, 196 ORs.

Places of interest nearby:
Blickling Hall is to be found by the B1354 a mile west of Aylsham. An early-17th-century grand home, it served for a while as Oulton's Officers' Mess.

PETERBOROUGH (WESTWOOD), Cambridgeshire

52°35N/00°16W 58ft asl; TF165002. 2miles NW of the city

Peterborough is not generally thought of as having an RAF station. A short time spent there in wartime would have quickly dispelled that notion for the sky often was packed with training aircraft flying from Westwood. Earlier there was also a production source of little Aeroncas.

Westwood began its RAF career as No 1 Aircraft Storage Unit which opened on 2 August 1932 and for which an 'A' Type Aircraft Shed was provided along with mainly single storey buildings. The Officers' Mess has survived along with some other buildings and the suitably decorated main gates. In February 1935 the ASU departed, the airfield was extended and more 1920s style buildings were erected. 'RAF Peterborough (Westwood)' to give it the official title emerged modified for Service pilot training purposes in the autumn of 1935. Of the landing ground by the main East Coast rail route to Scotland almost nothing remains What might have developed into a useful regional airport was sited too close to the Peterborough city and has been engulfed by industrial undertakings. Peterborough now has two so-called small 'airports' – Conington and Sibson – miles away from the thriving, expanding city.

Improvement sufficiently complete, No 7 (Service) Flying Training School (SFTS), an advanced flying school came into being here on 2 December 1935 and took on charge seventeen Hawker Hart (T)s (K4983-4999) posted in the previous month. February 1936 brought reinforcements by way of Avro Tutors, Hawker Furies and Hawker Audaxes. More Harts joined them two months later and soon the advanced training for pilots was generating a considerable amount of flying a further extension of which followed when the first twin-engined Airspeed Oxford flew in on 17 January to supplement the single-engined trainers.

Major upheaval struck between May and July 1939 when the school's overall strength was cut by half as it switched to training FAA pilots whose flying course was reduced in length from six to four months at the outbreak of war. Further amendment came during October 1939 when Oxfords were withdrawn in a switch to flying training limited to single-engined aircraft. Nominal strength was amended to twenty-four Hart (T)s and eight Audaxes placed in the Initial Training Squadron with a further twenty-four Audaxes and eight Hart (T)s in the Advanced Training Squadron.

January 1940 brought a completely different shape when unit establishment was altered to include twenty-nine Battle Trainers and leaving thirty-four Hart (T)s and twenty-one Audaxes. As well as a desperate need for fighter pilots, summer saw 7 SFTS holding in readiness twelve Harts for dive-bombing duty within Plan 'Banquet' (the attack on enemy invaders should they step ashore) for which their operational base would have been Stradishall.

Such was the tempo of circuit flying that 7 SFTS was forced in July 1940 to use a new Relief Landing Ground established at Sibson – little more than a large field with a few tents – and particularly valuable for night flying training. Such policy was short lived for the School in August was ordered to prepare for a move to Canada, one of seven units ordered to undertake the Atlantic crossing. The first echelon left on 29 August 1940 to join No 31 SFTS, the last moving out in January 1941.

Peterborough's role then changed to that of providing initial flying training for which reason it first passed to 50 Group on 20 December 1940 and then No 13 EFTS moved in from White Waltham by 11 January 1941. With them came a swarm of Tiger Moths. Brief was their stay for on 31 May 72 'Tigers' flew to Booker there to form the basis of 21 EFTS.

Station buildings had by now much increased in number, five Bellman hangars prominent in the south-eastern corner being supplemented by six blister hangars. Each of the latter spanned 65ft, three had been joined to form an unusual Treble Blister and two to form a Double Blister. In the south-eastern corner were temporary wooden huts for domestic and general administration purposes. No hard runways were ever laid; instead there were four grass runways.

The day after 13 EFTS moved out Peterborough's new administrators, No 21 Group, formed No 25 (Polish) EFTS which also used Sibson. Again the stay was short and, with only fifty-seven 'Tigers' in hand, the Poles left for Hucknall in mid-July 1941. Yet another Tiger Moth school then moved in – No 17 EFTS which came from North Luffenham on 15 July 1941 and remained until disbandment on 1 June 1942.

These movements reflected frequent changes in operational needs and training policy. The influence of the Dominion and Empire Air Training Scheme became very evident when 17 EFTS's immediate replacement came with the birth, on 1 June 1942, of 7 (Pilots') Advanced Flying Unit. Miles Master I and II-equipped, its task was to provide acclimatisation flying in European conditions for pilots trained in sunny overseas climes, and to provide pilot refresher flying courses. Rapidly it expanded, indeed so fast that two Flights were permanently to be based at Sibson. By April 1943, 7 (P)AFU was holding as many as 130 Masters (mainly Mk IIs) and four Ansons. The pupil population similarly fast increased, from 90 to 211 pilots. As a result a further two Flights then formed, and to answer the need for night fighter pilots and because there were no night flying facilities at Peterborough, night flying was undertaken at King's Cliffe with effect from 25 June 1943. Using three stations allowed a constant pupil population of 150 to be flying, but the luxury was brief for King's Cliffe was required for operational use and 7 (P) AFU had to vacate the station in July 1943.

A Flight of some fifteen Hurricanes was added to the unit in March 1944, at which time command passed to the well-known Wing Commander J M Foxley-Norris.

The use of Sibson RLG had largely faded when on 8 August 1944, Sutton Bridge became Peterborough's satellite and from where since June 1944 the unit had been night flying. No 7 (P) AFU was now yet again reorganised, into two Advanced Flights, a Gunnery Flight and two Battle Flights. At Sutton Bridge twenty-two Oxfords arrived during September 1944 for another version of 7 (P) AFU, soon fully fledged and still under Peterborough's control. Eight Hurricanes were promptly taken from Peterborough to Sutton Bridge while the decision was taken to retire all 95 Masters on roll and replace them with Harvards mainly in the spring of 1945.

At Peterborough a new 7 SFTS was reborn out of 7 (P)AFU on 21 December 1944, and Sibson RLG was given up. The training pattern now called for one-third of the pilots to pass out as single-engined trained and included some for the newly forming French Air Force. Courses by the spring were provided using forty-seven Oxfords, twenty-nine Harvards and four Ansons. No 1 French Course comprising thirty-two pilots passed out in February while the Masters were still in use. Harvards came into use during May 1945 at which time a few aged Spitfire IIs briefly supplemented them.

In June 1945, with Sutton Bridge being relied upon and Wittering in use for night flying, the last Master on strength (AZ497) was ready to leave. Pilot training continued using Oxfords and Harvards until 4 April 1946 when the main party of 7 SFTS left for Kirton-in-Lindsey to amalgamate with 5 SFTS. Peterborough became quiet and was retained on Care & Maintenance.

Following that its end might easily have come. Instead, Westwood had one more, unusual part to play. Trials had in 1934 been carried out in the London area to consider the conveyance of mail by autogiros operating between major post offices upon the roofs of which the aircraft could land. The war ended trials which were resumed after hostilities ceased. A much superior rotary wing Westland S.51 helicopter carried out some 115 mile mail runs from Yeovil, and because of its reliability British European Airways decided to carry out further trials using another S.51. They based it at Peterborough where a Bell 47B3 – too small to carry much load – was used for training.

The first trial run was carried out from Westwood on 12 May 1948, a regular mail service being initiated on 1 June. Its circular route took it in daylight to King's Lynn, along the coast to Cromer then to Norwich. From there a more southerly route was followed during the return journey and throughout intermediate stops were made. On the initial run the S.51 left Peterborough at 0955 hrs carrying 13,000 letters and touched down at Great Yarmouth at 1249 hrs. The return journey began at 1748 hrs, touch down at Peterborough coming at 1930 hrs after a journey of 272 miles. A similar route was flown ninety-five times (only five were cancelled) before trials ended on 25 September 1948. Although the S.51 had proven reliable it was costly to operate.

That was not the end of the investigation. Between 17 October 1949 and 15 April 1950 a night service was tried direct to Norwich and back, 164 flights being undertaken. Night flying was also undertaken at Downham Market, and at a time when helicopter night flying was in its infancy and being explored along with blind flying and suitable navigation aids. From Peterborough a grand total of 283 S.51 flights were made in the course of which 95,000lb of mail was carried.

Costly, enterprising, was BEAs flirtation with mail carrying helicopters. Sikorsky S.51 G-AJOV operated from here.

Limited post-war use of Westwood by light fixed wing civilian aircraft had also been undertaken but the decision to greatly expand the size of Peterborough city caused light industry to overwhelm the airfield site in the early 1950s. That was the price the airfield paid for being too convenient and close to Peterborough.

Main features:
Grass runways: NNE/SW 3,600ft, NE/SW 3,060ft, ENE/WSW 2,340ft, SSE/NNW 2,340ft. No permanent lighting. *Hangars:* one Type 'A', five Bellman, one 65ft Treble Blister, two 65ft Double Blister, one 65ft Single Blister. *Accommodation* (temporary): RAF: 98 officers, 152 SNCOs, 590 ORs; WAAF: 5 officers, 8 SNCOs, 202 ORs.

Places of local interest:
Peterborough Cathedral, built 1118-1238 as a Benedictine Abbey, is a reminder of the city's long history. King Henry VIII made the Abbey a cathedral where Catharine of Aragon is buried. Peterborough was for long a major railway centre on the LNER route along which lovely steam engines brought such delight as they thundered through to York and Scotland. The 7½-mile Nene Valley Railway now operates some impressive engines on its track to Wansford. At Horsey Toll between 1940 and 1945 Morrisons Ltd, part of the CRO, undertook major repair of many Hurricanes some of which used the adjacent short landing strip.

RACKHEATH, Norfolk

52°40N/23°23E 100ft asl; TG285145. E of Norwich

Rackheath was yet another standard three-runway two-T2 hangar, temporary wartime bomber airfield built during 1943 and first occupied at the end of that year. In February-March 1944 the 467th Bomb Group arrived, their move being completed on 11 March. Using B-24Hs and Js they first operated, against Bourges airfield, on 10 April 1944. Subsequent targets included the docks at Kiel, a chemical factory at Bonn, textile works at Stuttgart, an aircraft factory at Brunswick, a steel works at Osnabrück and a power station at Hamm.

Me 410 intruders attacked Rackheath during late evening 22 April 1944 as Liberators circled back from Hamm prior to landing. Two B-24s were shot down and the airfield strafed.

The 467th was among those which attacked shore installations and bridges near Cherbourg on D-Day and on 25 July, after some interdiction missions, attacked troops and supply concentrations at Montreuil to assist the thrust from St-Lô. The Group supplied fuel to mechanised US forces in France during September and gave bomber support during the airborne invasion of the Netherlands and also during the Ardennes offensive. After supporting the Rhine crossing they concentrated on communications targets. Their 212th and final mission came on 25 April 1945. Rackheath's Group has three special claims to fame – its bombing accuracy rated as the best in the 8th AF, their possession of B-24H 'Witchcraft' which managed 130 combat missions – the most by any 8th AF Liberator and in Colonel Albert H Shower a commanding officer who was the only one in charge throughout any Group's entire UK stay.

B-24J 42-52534 'Witchcraft' of the 790th BS, 467th BG (USAF).

Once the RAF returned to Rackheath 231 MU opened, on 15 July 1945. On 27 January 1948 that was absorbed by 94 MU Great Ashfield which had a Sub-Site here until September 1954. Plan F proposed that Rackheath should accommodate a Reserve Flying School for Norwich within Phase III of the development of the Peacetime Air Force. In February 1951 under Plan G Rackheath was changed to becoming a Standby Airfield. Little, apart from the control tower, remains of Rackheath whose technical site is occupied by light industry and landing area has returned to agricultural use.

Main features:
Runways: 210° 6,000ft x 150ft, 320° and 260°, all concrete. *Hangars:* two T2. *Hardstandings:* fifty spectacle, concrete. *Accommodation:* 421 officers, 2,473 enlisted men.

RATTLESDEN, Suffolk

52°10N/00°52E 300ft asl; TL965555. Make for Felsham, airfield to SE. Main runway remains prominent, remnants of others remain

Unless you know the area you will discover Rattlesden only with some difficulty, positioned as it is in the middle of farmland and accessed by country lanes. When you arrive you will probably be surprised to see a long, well kept runway whose state dates from the 1950s/60s when Rattlesden was a bolthole for Wattisham's Hunters and even Lightnings. Fortunately it was never needed. Drive around the southern side and you pass the area where an enclave was built for the Bloodhound ramjet missiles of No 266 Squadron based here from 1 December 1959 to their stand down on 30 June 1964. Continue around the landing ground area from where light aircraft and gliders still operate and you will find, on the right, a superb memorial area erected to the USAAF personnel who flew from Rattlesden and knew tough fighting.

For nearly a year the 447th Bomb Group, 3rd AD had been very active from Rattlesden and 2 November 1944 brought a display of heroism and selfless devotion of one man for another during a raid on Merseburg. Among those flying was 2nd Lieutenant Robert E Femoyer, a B-17 navigator. Flak was hurled against his aircraft and Femoyer was seriously wounded. Staying at his station refusing sedation, for two hours he continued navigating the bomber during its homeward run. He died soon after being lifted from the battered bomber. His courage won him a posthumous Medal of Honor. The homecoming at all US 8th AF bases often brought such events as the injured were taken from their smashed, quite frail machines.

Rattlesden was allotted to the USAAF on 1 October 1942 and on 1 December 1942 the first Americans belonging to Nos 451 and 452 Bomb Squadrons began arriving. They were here to fly some of the first B-26B Marauders to operate from Britain, and which were delivered in February-March 1943. With the 450th BS at Rougham, they formed the 322nd Bomb Group which became consolidated in April 1943 and formed an entity at Andrews Field to where the three squadrons all moved on 12 June 1943.

At the very end of November 1943 the 447th Bomb Group ('K in a square') arrived at Rattlesden from the USA and, using B-17Gs, entered the battle arena on 24 December 1943 by making a raid on V-1 sites in France. Thereafter it took part in the 3rd AD's battle programme and on 19 April 1944 was despatched to Berlin. Station keeping by the 3rd Air Division that day was bad. Straggling, as ever, brought a heavy battering from enemy fighters, the 447th losing eleven of its aircraft, their heaviest loss ever sustained in one raid and at a time when the 8th AF bombing offensive was at a peak. The 447th sustained further heavy losses on 12 May when seven B-17s failed to return from distant Leipzig.

Between December 1943 and May 1944 the Group was primarily engaged in preparations for the invasion by attacking submarine pens, naval units, German industrial targets, ports and V-1 sites, as well as airfields and marshalling yards. June 1944 found them giving direct support to the Normandy invasion, then the break-out at St-Lô. They assisted in the liberation of Brest in September 1944 and made supply drops to the French Resistance. They gave general support to the airborne landings of September before, in October, resuming their part in the strategic air offensive, concentrating on oil targets until December 1944 when they took a part in the Ardennes battle by bombing marshalling yards, rail bridges and communications centres in the battle zone. Then the Group resumed operations against oil, transport and communications targets to the close of hostilities.

The 447th quit Rattlesden in August 1945 and the station was returned to the RAF on 10 October 1945. The Ministry of Food established a supply depot here before closure on 15 August 1946. The site, however, remained in official hands and was sold off in 1966.

Main features:
Runways: 243° 6,000ft x 150ft, 177°, 310° tarmac over concrete, *Hangars:* two T2. *Hardstandings:* fifty loop type. *Accommodation:* 421 officers, 2,473 enlisted men.

RAYDON, Suffolk

52°00N/01°00E 170ft asl; TM395065. Raydon-Hintlesham road crosses part of site, E of village

Part of Raydon, built by the US Army, has disappeared within an industrial area making it seem very unlikely that some of the first P-51Bs for the USAAF in Europe came here. They did so at the end of 1943 and with the 357th Fighter Group, 9th AF, moved in on 30 November 1943. Raydon's first Group, they were the second to have P-51s.

Compared with the hefty Thunderbolt and its Harvard symphony, the sleek P-51 Mustang – which became so effective only after the fitting of a British engine – presented an image of speed and nimbleness. It exuded the sound of a Spitfire IX mingled with a more powerful version of the Allison which powered Mustang Is used by the RAF. The 8th AF was very eager to obtain still scarce Merlin-engined P-51s so the 357th transferred to Leiston on 31 January 1944 before they had flown any missions and became the first 8th AF Group flying Mustangs. In their place came the 358th Fighter Group flying P-47s and Raydon became the home of the tough Thunderbolt.

The 358th, which had already flown operations, was now part of the 9th AF and from Raydon flew escort missions for locally based B-26 Groups. However, policy decreed that 9th AF fighters should be based in the south of England prior to the invasion for which reason the 358th moved to High Haldon early in April 1944.

The vacuum was quickly filled by the 353rd Fighter Group's P-47s posted to Raydon from Metfield in mid-April 1944. They had achieved notoriety by pioneering low-level strafing and bombing in direct support of 8th AF bomber missions. Their fighter-bomber activities reached fever pitch after the Group moved to Raydon, and also when they provided close support around the invasion period. They were again very busy during the September airborne landings in Holland, and for their persistence particularly in attacking ground defences during the days of re-supply between 18 and 23 September were awarded a Distinguished Unit Citation.

During October 1944 they converted to using P-51s and continued rendering very valuable support to the bombers high above by attacking enemy fighters on the ground. One useful ploy they explored was preventing German fighters from refuelling and thus ensuring the enemy had a rough time throughout any operation.

P-47C of the 353rd FG.

P-47D 276141 ARKANSAS TRAVELER of the 350th FS, 353rd FG, Raydon just before D-Day 1944. (USAF)

By the end of hostilities the 353rd FG had flown 447 missions, the last on 24 April 1945. They had lost 137 aircraft during operations and were credited with 414 enemy aircraft destroyed on the ground and 330 in the air. The Group gradually ran down finally departing from Raydon on 10 October 1945. Between October and December the 652nd Weather Squadron maintained an American presence. Raydon was taken over by the RAF at the end of 1945 but not disposed of until summer 1958. Two T2 hangars remain and an air show periodically takes place on part of the old airfield.

Main features:
Runways: 270° 6,000ft x 150ft, 170°, 230°, concrete. *Hangars:* two T2. *Hardstandings:* fifty loop type. *Accommodation:* 364 officers, 2,478 enlisted men.

RIDGEWELL, Essex

52°02N/00°33E 260ft asl; TM740415. 2 miles SE of Ashen

Newly formed and Stirling equipped, 90 Squadron on 29 December 1942 left Bottesford for Ridgewell, Stradishall's recently completed Built Satellite as it came off Care & Maintenance. By this time the new airfield was virtually a typical mid-war temporary bomber base.

As the first Stirling to arrive touched down it bounced and careered into a ditch. The crew was safe, but the remainder of the squadron turned back to the safety of the old homestead. It was an inauspicious opening for Ridgewell.

Next day 'No 90' tried again, and with full success. They flew their first three sorties, minelaying, on 8 January 1943 and were soon slotted into the 3 Group offensive at the time directed mainly at French west coast ports. On 3/4 February they made their first Main Force raid, nine Stirlings being despatched to Hamburg. Next night five undertook a taxing and perilous run to Turin and on 1/2 March 1943 carried our their first raid on Berlin.

It was 5/6 March 1943 that witnessed the start of the 1943 mighty bombing offensive against the Ruhr when Essen was the target and 90 Squadron again contributed seven aircraft. From then onwards the squadron attacked a variety of Main Force targets, interspersing their raids with mining operations. But already the new Stirling IIIs inadequate low operational ceiling was bringing fearsome experiences for the crews. Courageous, indeed, was Sergeant William Davine during a Duisburg raid. Terribly wounded during the bomber's first run up to target, he continued giving instructions for a second run after which the crew nursed him and the battered bomber home. On the same night Pilot Officer Gordon William Young's Stirling was attacked four times by fighters and he still made home. Pilot Officer F Shippard's Stirling too, was attacked, by a fighter fifteen miles off the enemy coast. By holding the control column between his knees he thwarted BF473's persistent desire to climb and also made home.

Operational effectiveness increased first with the addition of a third Flight on 18 April 1943 and further when Ridgewell became part of 31 Base Stradishall on 26 April. At the end of May 1943, 90 Squadron moved to West Wickham. Then 31 Base relinquished control and the 4th Bomb Wing Substitution Unit, USAAF, moved in and the station was placed under Care & Maintenance.

B-17Fs of the 381st Bomb Group arrived in early June 1943, their first operation taking place on 23 June with Antwerp as target. This was the first of 296 B-17 raids from Ridgewell over the course of which 131 aircraft never returned. Most sobering mission was that directed against Schweinfurt on 17 August 1943 when the 381st loss of eleven aircraft was the highest loss sustained by any participant Group.

B-17F-25-DL 42-3078 WINNSOM WINN of the 534th BS, 381st BG, on 31 August 1943. It arrived here 15 June 1943 as the Group moved in. Missing in action 7 January 1944 (USAF).

B-17Gs of the 381st BG taxi out leaving the 534th BS area and pass through the 533rd BS dispersal area. (USAF)

Twice the Group's fortitude was awarded a Distinguished Unit Citation, on the first occasion after they fought their way to Bremen through flak and fighters on 8 October 1943, the second for their part in the 1st Air Division's operations on 11 January 1944. Their target list was long – Le Mans, Munster, Offenburg, Kiel, St Nazaire, Kassel, Leipzig and the nitrate plant at Heoya in Norway. Like other Groups, the 381st supported the build up to D-Day and aided US troops as they battled their way across Europe. Their final mission took place on 25 April 1945, and like many of this period, involved bombing transport targets.

The 381st left the UK with alacrity, almost all having gone by the end of May 1945. On 15 July 1945 Ridgewell passed to RAF Maintenance Command, No 94 MU being here from 10 September 1946 to 31 March 1957 with MU HQ here from 1 September 1956. Between March 1960 and 1967 Ridgewell was used as a USAF off-base storage annexe to Wethersfield. Essex Gliding Club now operates from here between April and October.

Runways have gone, but two hangars remain on an expanse of farmland. The Ashen-Yeldham road built on the line of the perimeter track crosses the western part of the old airfield giving a good general view of the site. Near Ashen is an obvious dispersal area where it is still easy to imagine a B-17 resting.

Main features:
Runways: 100° 6,000ft x 150ft, 060°, 170°, wood chips on concrete. *Hangars:* two T2. *Hardstandings:* fifty loop type. *Accommodation:* 421 officers, 2,473 enlisted men.

RIVENHALL, Essex

51°51N/00°38E 168ft asl; TM820210. N of village

Rivenhall opened late in 1943 as a typical temporary three-runway, two-T2, wartime airfield under control of the US 9th AF. The 363rd Fighter Group which arrived in January 1944 received P-51s here and commenced operations on 23 February 1944. It performed bomber escorts gradually switching to a fighter-bomber/ground-attack role and including dive-bombing in its repertoire. The Group moved to Staplehurst in April 1944, their place being taken by the 397th Bomb Group in mid-April 1944 and in time for a part in pre-invasion preparation raids. They operated in a support role on D-Day, attacking strong-points and defended areas. They supported ground forces, attacked POL depots and defended areas. To impede enemy retreat they had a particular task – reducing bridges across the Loire. Of eighty-six operations their Marauders flew from Rivenhall, thirty-two were against bridges.

The Group advanced to Hurn on 5 August 1944. On 1 October No 38 Group RAF, took over the station, Nos 295 and 570 Squadrons moving in on 7 October bringing Stirling GTIVs. Licking their Arnhem sores and acquiring more Horsa gliders, they were soon preparing for the next airborne venture on a Fighter Command station where they were lodger squadrons. They participated in impressive large-scale exercises and at night continued supply drops to the Resistance forces in Europe.

Some sixty Horsas were towed out of Rivenhall carrying troops taking part in the Rhine crossing operation in March 1945. In May 1945, the squadrons helped to airlift to Norway the Allied occupation force.

A few Miles Martinets of No 1677 Target Towing Flight were here between 10 October and 28 December 1944, but it was Stirling IVs which dominated the scene. Parts of 295 Squadron left the station in December 1945 and in January 1946 the remains of both squadrons disbanded.

Rivenhall then became a camp for displaced persons. In 1956 Marconi took over part of the site. Two hangars and some buildings remain, also parts of the main runway.

Main features:
Runways: 280° 6,000ft x 150ft, 220°, 340°, concrete and tarmac. *Hangars:* two T2. *Hardstandings:* fifty spectacle type. Accommodation (USAAF): 236 officers, 1,686 enlisted men.

ROUGHAM (BURY ST EDMUNDS), Suffolk

52°14N/00°46E 205ft asl; TM890642. E of Bury St Edmunds by A14

'There are Marauders at Rougham'. The news spread fast, but they weren't there long and must have fled when they heard me coming! All there was to be closely seen was an equally rare creature, an A-20C which had previously been an RAF machine. Its tail poked across the barbed wire on the perimeter of the Ipswich road by a large tree which remains. Already some B-17s for the 94th Bomb Group had arrived, and some were wearing 'DF' identity letters more at home on Bassingbourn's Forts. Apparently, Roger Freeman told me, these were 'foggy codes' designed to fox the enemy, a little used ruse. Although generally known as Rougham, it was later re-named Bury St Edmunds.

Rougham opened in August 1942 and although on 1 December 1942 the 450th BS, 322 BG, 8th AF, moved in it took months for the Group to be established. For awhile some A-20Bs and miscellaneous B-26Bs could be seen here. Two other squadrons had arrived at Rattlesden the same day as the 450th. Of these the 451st moved to Rougham on 22 March 1943 and the 452nd on 22 May.

Not until March 1943 did their Martin B-26B Marauders arrive. This was a quite large, heavy, not very manoeuvrable aeroplane. Its high wing loading meant a long take-off run, which the new version's span extension did not cure. In addition, the engines were temperamental. Amazingly, the Americans decided to use B-26s as low-level bombers against European targets. Royal Air Force observers were incredulous, for their handling of the aircraft suggested that, like the Mitchell, it was only suitable for fighter escorted medium level operations and to carry out saturation bombing.

A chance to try the Marauder was brushed aside by the RAF's 2 Group, which suggested the Boston was a much better aeroplane. All British advice went unheeded and as a result East Anglians were treated to some spectacular very low flying by seemingly quite fast, large noisy aeroplanes. Well do I remember a Sunday afternoon in April 1943 when three B-26s raced so low over Wilbraham Fen that one could read the fin serials with ease – and they had to be low for that to happen.

By early May the 450th and 452nd Squadrons were ready for battle – or so they thought – and chosen as their first target was IJmuiden's prominent power station at the mouth of the Maas, a fringe target in a heavily defended zone. On 14 May the Marauders raced low across the North Sea in a vain attempt to avoid radar detection. Enemy reception was intense, and although they gave of their best the aiming was bad. All twelve B-26s sustained flak damage.

High Command, displeased with this poor result, disastrously ordered the 322nd to strike again, at once, at the same target. On 17 May the Marauders set off, with a second target at Haarlem listed for half the force. Half an hour later a solitary B-26 returned to Rougham then landed. Having aborted the crew returned trying to avoid alerting the enemy. It later transpired that the other B-26s made landfall at the wrong point and crossed in over a most heavily defended area, and were seen over Amsterdam encountering its strong defences. Little wonder that these and enemy fighters brought down the entire bomber force.

One can barely imagine the desperation that must have swept through those remaining at Rougham. RAF warnings concerning the B-26 had not been heeded additional to which raid planning, the vital importance of navigation and sufficient crew training had clearly not been fully undertaken. In consequence the 322nd moved to Great Saling on 12 June to work-up a different role.

They were replaced on 13 June 1943 by B-17s of the 94th Bomb Group (later identity 'A in a square') who moved in when they were returning from a raid on Kiel. They had been engaged not long before by a formation of Ju 88 fighters awaiting them off the East coast and there lost seven of their aircraft. Undaunted, they resumed next day and eventually flew a total of 324 missions. With the 385th and 447th Bomb Groups they formed the 94th Combat Wing. Twice the 94th were awarded a Distinguished Unit Citation, the first for their part in the Regensburg shuttle raid of 17 August 1943. The second was given for a raid on an aircraft spares factory at Brunswick on 11 January 1944. Winter weather was reducing the number of high-level raids, but when a spell of fine weather seemed likely a maximum effort was ordered against aircraft factories in the Brunswick area. Optimism exceeded reality for, as the bombers approached their targets, weather turned very bad. The 94th pressed on encountering savage enemy reaction as a result of which seven Rougham B-17s were lost in action.

The 94th ranged widely in making its attacks, raiding the ball bearing works at Eberhausen, oil installations at Merseburg, shipyards at Kiel etc, as well as bombing tactical targets and V-weapon sites.

Unlike most USAAF Groups, the 94th did not immediately return to America. Instead, they carried out a widespread leaflet-dropping campaign to inform displaced persons of means of assistance. It was mid-December before the 94th headed for the USA.

B-17s airborne from Rougham.

Rougham was passed to the RAF on 20 December 1945 and to Bomber Command on 11 September 1946. Of no post-war value it was abandoned in 1948. Thereafter spasmodic flying by light aircraft has taken place.

The cluster of buildings by the A14, and at the main entrance to the one-time base, now constitute part of the Rougham Industrial Estate. The Nissen hut that served as the guardroom remains. The 1941-style control tower has been renovated to serve as Rougham Tower Museum and is a Grade II listed building. Rougham Estate Farms operate the adjacent flying ground, which has two 18m-wide grass runways, the longer one 09/27 of around 900m and 03/21 of 400m. During summer months flying displays are held at Rougham, as well as classic car shows, ploughing competitions, large model aircraft flying and other events.

Main features:
Runways: 275° 6,000ft x 150ft, 160°, 220°, concrete with tarmac and/or wood chip surface. *Hangars:* two T2. *Hardstandings:* fifty loop type. *Accommodation:* 443 officers, 2,529 enlisted men.

Places of interest nearby:
In the very attractive Abbey Gardens at Bury St Edmunds is the Old English Rose Garden dedicated to all who served with the 94th BG during the war. Close by is St Edmundsbury Cathedral in which are laid up Standards of RAF squadrons, Bury St Edmunds having most affinity with RAF Honington.

ROWLEY MILE, Suffolk – see NEWMARKET HEATH

SCULTHORPE, Norfolk

52°50N/00°45E 200ft asl; TF860315. 5 miles W of Fakenham, at junction of A148/B1454

'No, we don't run buses from King's Lynn to Scunthorpe'. 'No, I said Sculthorpe.' 'Never heard of it', the bus lady replied, and in truth when the Americans moved in Sculthorpe was quite a remote place hard as that may be to now accept.

Yet such was the rate of 'progress' that by 1954 even the Russians had heard of it, or so it would seem, because the Base Ops Officer took me for a tour and impressively stated 'This is the base the enemy most fears.' As far as one could see, along the disused runway they sat, wing tip to wing tip, a line of North American B-45 jet bombers their 'nukes' close by. Hiding sheepishly among them were the RB-45s which had overflown parts of the USSR but now showed not the slightest trace of such goings on. When I boldly asked 'Which ones did they use?' – for the British marked examples had aroused interest – he didn't bat an eyelid and replied 'I'll show you – BE-037, that's one.'

Soon, we were quite near fearsome looking warriors armed to the teeth and who at other times would be equally at home cuddling the local ladies instead of guarding what 'he' kept calling 'the nukes'. This was Sculthorpe in the deep winter of the Cold War, when the base swarmed with American things good and bad.

Nothing stays the same. When I last visited Sculthorpe it was unlikely to frighten anyone – unless one of the cows recently present decided to be nasty. The same old buildings poked up from the grass or sat on concrete areas surrounded by what cows appear to do best. 'No, we don't need the tower, we're controlling the flying from that small tent. Have a coffee. Yes, this is the Mess'. Sculthorpe was now Harrier exercise territory. No long lines of shiny Yankee bombers. Instead, grey grimy Harriers from Germany were hiding under nets and from even a few feet blending with the farmland that is still called Sculthorpe. Americans come, occasionally, in transports of some sort, and British Chinooks and Pumas, Gazelle and Lynx helicopters, none seem able to resist an occasional call for old time's sake.

Sculthorpe in the 1940s was truly far from anywhere yet it was to here that SAC in 1948 brought its 'Lucky Lady 11' the round-the-world marathon non-stop in-flight refuelled B-50A. At the time it was regarded as an incredible feat.

Sculthorpe was completed on 31 May 1943 as a typical mid-war bomber station into which the RAF had moved during January 1943. First aircraft in were thirty-two Horsa gliders for open storage in East Anglia. In May 1943 the station ceased to be a satellite of West Raynham, became fully occupied on 8 June 1943 and now had. Group Captain P C Pickard as Station Commander, Sculthorpe became fully occupied on 6 June and No 342 Free French Squadron moved in bringing a collection of Boston IIIs with a few Douglas Havocs for training. July 1943 witnessed their departure.

Dynamic Basil Embry came to 2 Group in mid-1943 with experience of the Mosquito as a night fighter which convinced him of its superlative qualities. He argued for a fighter-bomber variant doing much to promote its development and wanted 2 Group to operate only Mosquitoes. In that he largely succeeded.

On 20/21 July 1943 Nos 464 and 487 Squadrons moved to Sculthorpe where they were soon training with Mosquito FB VIs – an essential, argued Embry, for invasion support, and especially at night. On 27 September, 21 Squadron joined the others at Sculthorpe.

By October all three Mosquito VI squadrons entered battle spectacularly, in Mosquito style. Using Exeter as forward base they followed carefully selected routes taking them deep into France to attack power stations. With them naturally flew Sir Basil. Group Commanders rarely flew on operations, but Sir Basil Embry was highly individualistic, in a top class of his own, and he disguised himself as 'Wg Cdr Smith'. With him was David Atcherley, one of the great Atcherley twins. What a combination with which to inspire the whole world!

Sculthorpe's Mosquitoes were assigned to No 140 Airfield intended to operate as one unit, and which was planned to be able to transport itself rapidly to any other station. That was an idea tested during that most important Exercise *Starkey*.

Soon the No 140 Airfield squadrons were busily raiding targets in France. Then came the discovery of just how advanced the building of flying-bomb sites had become and in December Sculthorpe's Mosquitoes began attacking them. The weather turned sour making the long haul from

Sculthorpe to France unacceptable. Therefore, on 31 December 1943, the three squadrons attacked the Le Ploy site and moved into Hunsdon on the way home.

Sculthorpe being sited within the 100 Group area was then passed to them. On 17 January 1944 No 214 Squadron began arriving from Downham Market and received a few B-17s from the US 8th AAF. Two days after the squadron's arrival a radio counter-measures detachment of the 8th Air Force arrived, under Colonel G A Scott, also equipped with B-17Fs. It was some time before the fitting of radio devices for counter-measure tasks was completed.

Not until 20/21 April 1944 did 214 Squadron venture into action, during raids on two French marshalling yards. Operations – were on a small scale – were barely underway when the jammer squadrons left for Oulton in May 1944. Sculthorpe then closed for conversion into a Very Heavy Bomber airfield which put it out of use for the remainder of the war.

Re-opening came in December 1948 under Group Captain Parker, and it was placed on Care & Maintenance. The USAF considered East Anglia too vulnerable to attack, wanting defence in depth to protect its bombers and in October 1948 the British offered four airfields. 'Exposed' Sculthorpe (a substitute for Scampton and Waddington) was one. Although the Americans wanted escort fighters based there under Plan *Speedway* (ie. fighter reinforcement), they decided to use it for SAC bombers until Midland bases were available. On 17 January 1949 the 7502 Base Complement Squadron arrived to prepare the way.

Sculthorpe's 8,950 foot runway being available, and arrangements for personnel complete, three B-29s of the 92nd Bomb Group started moving in on 7 February 1949. They stayed until 18 May, flew back to Spokane and later participated in the Korean War. Three squadrons of 98th BG B-29s replaced them and stayed until 15 August 1949. On 22nd came the first B-50As (and three KB-29M tankers) which belonged to the 63rd Squadron, 43rd Bomb Group. Among them was 46-010, 'Lucky Lady II' which had taken ninety-four hours and one minute to fly around the world. Refuelled four times using the British-developed probe and drogue in-flight refuelling system, its track covered 23,452 miles.

By way of replacement in November 1949 came B-29s of the 19th BS, 22 BG and ten RB-29s of the 23rd Strategic Recon Squadron, 5th Strategic Recon. Group which operated off the Iron Curtain until February 1950. They were the first unit based here to carry out such activity and during their deployment HM Government agreed to the permanent stationing in the UK of US forces during peacetime. On 28 January 1950 the '7502' was upgraded as an air Base Group, on 26 September 1950 became the 7502 Air Supply Wing and on 16 May 1951 was inactivated.

B-50As and KB-29Ms of the 49th BS, 2nd BG formed the next deployment and on 17 May 1950 two B-29/KB-50M squadrons, the 352nd and 353rd of the 301st BG took their turn during which came the outbreak of the Korean war which doubled the length of their stay. For a time they shared Sculthorpe with nine RB-29s of the 72nd SRS, 5th SRW. B-50Ds of the 97th took over from the 301st during a period of complex movement using available space, and stayed until February 1951. In January 1951 Sculthorpe had passed into American hands under a complicated leasing agreement which left only four RAF officers here.

Arrival of B-50A 'Lucky Lady II' at Sculthorpe in August 1949. Between 26 February and 2 March 1949 46-010 had covered 23,452 miles in 94 hours non-stop. Four times in-flight refuelled it used British devised equipment!

Sculthorpe's use for clandestine activity was much enhanced when, in May 1951, a detachment of 91st SRG placed a clutch of RB-45C reconnaissance jets at Sculthorpe, and which remained a feature of life here until 1955. RAF crewed RB-45Cs in strange British markings twice from Sculthorpe carried out deep flights into the USSR to photograph ICBM sites and other targets. The first, roughly a ten hour twenty minute sortie by three aircraft flown south-easterly across the USSR after AAR north of Denmark, took place during darkness in April 1952. Using a 35mm camera, photographs were taken of the radarscope showing ground features. A second overfly by three 'RAF Special Duties Flight' RB-45s took place in April 1954.

SACs 3911 Air Base Group moved in on 16 May and stayed until 5 June 1952 when they disbanded. The last SAC bomber deployment here, involving the 22nd BG, extended from September to November 1951. Meanwhile a detachment of the 9th Air Rescue Squadron (MATS) arrived on 30 July 1951 flying SA-16s and lifeboat carrying SB-29s, the latter to cope with for possible Atlantic disasters. The unit disbanded on 14 November 1952 and immediately reformed as the 567th Air Rescue Squadron here until 12 November when they moved to Prestwick.

On 31 May 1952 the Americans achieved their desire. Permanent stationing of US forces on bases in stable Britain began and they have remained here. The 49th Air Division opened its HQ at Sculthorpe on 5 June 1952 upon which day the first of Sculthorpe's permanent aircraft residents arrived from Barksdale AFB, La, North American B-45A Tornado four-engined jet bombers of the 84th and 85th Squadrons, 47th Bomb Group (Light). The 49th AD's support aircraft included C-47s, C-119s and L-5s.

B-45A 7078 of the 47th BG on Sculthorpe's subsidiary runway in 1954. Armed with nuclear weapons the B-45s were a major part of NATO's power.

A third squadron for the 47th BG, the 422nd, arrived on 20 December 1953 and was on 23 March 1954 renumbered 85 BS. On 8 February 1955 the 47 BG(L) became the 47 Bomb Wing(Light) and on 20 September 1955 the 86th BS transferred to Alconbury.

RB-45Cs of the 19th Tactical Reconnaissance Squadron (Night Photo Jet), 66th TRW (HQ Sembach), arrived on 11 May 1954.

An unusual arrival on 16 December 1952 was the 7554th Tow Target Flight flying TB-26B Invader target tugs and L-5 Sentinels which supported US Army elements using North Norfolk coastal gunnery ranges. For use there radio-controlled drones were brought to Britain and operated by personnel from Sculthorpe. On 24 June 1954 the unit became the 5th Tow Target Squadron here until 1957. A second overfly by 'RAF Special Duties Flight' RB-45Cs took place on 29/30 April 1954. Three aircraft operated in darkness, one crew taking a northern route into the USSR, one flying centrally and the other pursuing a southern track.

Fascinating as their aircraft were they were nowhere near as spectacular as the colossal RB-36s which periodically undertook from Sculthorpe spying missions in high northern latitudes.

The 19th TRS remained until 10 January 1959 when they left for Spangdahlem. The 86th Bomb Squadron was detached to Alconbury between 15 September 1955 and 5 August 1959.

Sculthorpe since May 1952 had been home for the 49th Air Division which controlled the whole UK permanently based tactical force. They had for support purposes a fleet of C-119 Packets, C-47s, L-20s and T-33s. For most of its time in the UK the entire 47th Bomb Group/ Wing was Sculthorpe based and nominally flew seventy-five B-45s with a nuclear strike role, a force to make any foe uneasy.

North American
B-45A 47-053 of
the 85th BS, 47
BW.

The Americans first publicly displayed their strength at Sculthorpe on 29 May 1954. Attendance was poor, few folk visiting air displays much before the late 1950s mainly due to lack of personal transport. On this occasion those who did were able to sit on the runway during the flying display, surely a unique, exhilarating and hazardous event! For use on the North Norfolk ranges in the 1950s radio-controlled drones were brought to Britain and operated by personnel from Sculthorpe.

It was in January 1958 that RB-66s began replacing RB-45Cs in the 19th Squadron, and before the 47th received B-66s. KB-29P boom tankers had arrived in January 1956, greatly extending the range of the forces here. They were replaced in January 1957 by KB-50Ds, which in April 1958 began to be supplanted by KB-50J jet-assisted tankers. These drogue refuellers were the forerunners of the present European Tanker Force, and the last seven left for America on 22 March 1964.

On 22 June 1962 the 47th Bomb Wing had been deactivated ending Sculthorpe's offensive posture but not the US tenancy for, to the end of the Cold War, it was a Standby Base. Super Mystères and F-100s of the French Air Force funded from the Mutual Defence Aid Pact were stored here.

In January 1967 the US again took control of Sculthorpe for general storage. In April 1967 it was declared a Dispersed Operating Base subsequently a Standby Dispersal Base manned by the 7519th Combat Support Squadron for the 48th TFW for which reason the runway was resurfaced

KB-29P 0-484007 of Sculthorpe's 420th ARS about to refuel F-84Fs of the Bushmasters over southern England in February 1958. (Fred Donaldson)

B/RB-66s like 4421 replaced the B/RB-45s at Sculthorpe.

in 1968. Since then it has seen periodical use by C-130s, C-141s and in 1979 by Marham's aircraft based here while their runway was resurfaced. British and US helicopters have also made use of it for exercises. It remains available for military use once the cows have retreated – as the Harrier deployment of 1996 showed and sundry helicopters confirm.

Main features:

Runways: Built to standard wartime bomber airfield lengths but increased in length and width in 1944-5 to 243° 9,000ft x 300ft, 131° 6,000ft x 300ft, 182° 6,000ft x 300ft, concrete. *Hangars:* four T2 (two initially intended for gliders, modified for docking in US tenure) and one B1. *Hardstandings:* thirty-six heavy bomber type. *Accommodation:* RAF (1945): 139 officers, 434 SNCOs, 1,200 ORs; WAAF: 9 officers, 22 SNCOs, 378 ORs.

SEETHING, Norfolk

52°30N/01°24E 130ft asl; TG320995. Off A146, SW of Loddon

Seething is one of the few airfields built during the war expressly for the Americans and still active although the 'field' is but a shadow of its former self. The memory of its wartime occupants is kept alive by the excellent 'memorial museum' in the tower and well worth visiting. From there one can rightly conclude that this was a typical mid-war two T2, three runway temporary bomber base with living quarters away to the south and a technical site close to one of the hangars.

Although opened in June 1943 Seething did not receive the 448th Bomb Group and its B-24H Liberators until the start of December 1943. Their stay extended to July 1945 during which period they undertook 262 missions the first on 22 December 1943 when Osnabrück was the target and two B-24s did not return. Before the war ended they lost another ninety-nine during the course of over 6,700 sorties.

Targets ranged widely including the synthetic oil plant at Politz, aircraft engine factory at Rostock, marshalling yards at Cologne, the I G Farben works at Ludwigshaven, U-Boat building facilities at Kiel, a ball bearing plant in Berlin, the aircraft factory at Gotha, airfield at Hanau and the V-1 factory at Fallersleben.

Like other 2nd Air Division Groups the 448th took an active part in the run-up to D-Day and supported the landing on Normandy's shore. In September 1944 they dropped supplies from low level to American airborne forces dropped around Nijmegen. Similarly, they undertook supply drops at Wesel during the Rhine crossing. Thereafter the assorted B-24s bombed road and rail communication making their last raid on 25 April 1945 with the Salzburg's marshalling yards as target.

Return to the USA began in early July 1945 after which RAF Maintenance Command took over the airfield. It was then used for ammunition storage by 53 MU (15 July 1945 to 24 November 1947 and again from 1 January 1950 to 22 October 1956), and next by 94 MU between 24 November 1947 and 1 January 1950. In 1946, rated as having no future value for flying, it was eventually sold for agricultural use.

Founded in July 1960, the Waveney Flying Group leased from a farmer part of the former Seething for flying purposes. It took four months to clear the site sufficiently for flying. Doing the work themselves, the members aimed then to make flying available for all who desired to participate. Soon a Miles M 38ii then a Tiger Moth and Rallye were in use. A second-hand prefabricated building served as a clubhouse and a hangar were erected. A fuel installation was constructed and water laid on in 1965.

In 1986 Wingtask Ltd was established to operate the airfield and the Waveney Flying Group leased the field, which is usually open for flying at weekend from 09.00 to 17.00hrs.

Renovation of the wartime control tower took place and it was later leased to the Tower Association for use as a museum, now open on Sundays between May and October.

Following gale damage, a new clubhouse was built in 1987, two new hangars were erected, each including a turntable, and the 06/24 2,625ft asphalt runway was resurfaced.

In 2000 the first hangar was replaced with another able to hold six aircraft and also fitted with a turntable. A new control tower was also built and in 2001 adapted to embrace a classroom and briefing room. The restyled building was opened on 16 June 2001 by Wg Cdr Ken Wallis MBE.

Main features:
Runways: 070° 6,000ft x 150ft, 010°, 300°, concrete. *Hangars:* two T2. *Hardstandings:* fifty-one. *Accommodation:* 421 officers, 2,473 enlisted men.

SHEPHERD'S GROVE, Suffolk

52°19N/00°55E 200ft asl; TM990730. By the A143 NE of Ixworth

During, and immediately after the war, Shepherd's Grove meant Stirlings. Named after a nearby wood, it was built in 1943 as a temporary wartime bomber base for USAAF use. Instead, it opened under 3 Group RAF on 3 April 1944 as a Built Satellite (of Class A standard) of Stradishall. From 14 May 1944 to 5 October 1944 Stirlings of 1657 Conversion Unit were based here.

When Stradishall became operational late 1944, Shepherd's Grove was transferred to 38 Group, Transport Command, and given its own SHQ. Nos 196 and 299 Stirling GTIV squadrons moved in during the last week of January 1945 to continue their SOE supply drops but primarily to train for future airborne operations. On 24 March 1945 they towed Horsa gliders out of Shepherd's Grove for their part in the Rhine Crossing. At the time No 1677 Target Towing Flight Martinets were in residence being based here from 28 January 1945 to 18 April 1945.

Stirling V ZO-F of No 196 Squadron at Shepherd's Grove.

Both Stirling IV squadrons remained after the war and flew passengers, mail and stores overseas. Between January and March 1946, 196 Squadron provided more passenger comfort by using a few Stirling Vs. No 299 Squadron disbanded on 15 February 1946 and No 299 on 16

March 1946, Shepherd's Grove passing to 60 Group in May 1946 and becoming a satellite of Watton, the Radio Warfare Establishment which on 1 September 1946 was renamed the Central Signals Establishment. Under Plan F uncertainty presided over its future commitment, but CSE dispersed Ansons XIXs and Lancasters at Shepherd's Grove until in February 1950 flying ceased and the station was placed on Care & Maintenance.

At this time USAF was pressing to have escort fighters permanently based in the UK to support B-29 operations. That need much increased when in July 1950 the Korean War started. Plan *Galloper* was quickly devised to cover movement to Britain, by late November 1950, of up to four fighter escort Wings. For the desired F-86 Wing an airfield with a 2,000 yard runway was needed. Suitable for such runway extension, Bentwaters, Wethersfield and Shepherds Grove were offered in August 1950 after the American's first choice, East Fortune, was seen to need too much updating. Interim bases – Bassingbourn, Lakenheath and Sculthorpe – were put on offer. By November it was agreed that Manston should become the main fighter base supplemented by the three interim homes. Work would meanwhile begin to upgrade Bentwaters, Wethersfield and Shepherds Grove. Controlled by 42 Group, Maintenance Command, Shepherds Grove was passed to 11 Group, Fighter Command, on 12 February 1951. USAF presence began on 16 March 1951 with the arrival of 7519 Air Base Squadron here to prepare for the F-86 Squadrons.

F86A 49-196 of the 81st FIW shortly after arrival in the UK.

Shepherd's Grove hit the headlines when, on 27 August 1951, No 116 Fighter Interceptor Squadron (FIS), National Air Guard, 81st Fighter-Interceptor Wing flew in stylishly, their leader leaping from his F-86A Sabre as if he had just undertaken a joy ride instead of a lengthy single-seat Atlantic crossing. On 5 September 1951 these first swept wing fighters to be based in Britain were joined by those of the 92nd FIS. A third squadron flew into Bentwaters, these being the first foreign units assigned to the post-war air defence of Britain and under RAF Fighter Command control. On 1 November 1952 the 116th Squadron became the 78th FIS, USAF.

On 1 March 1954 the 81st was assigned to the 49th Air Division, a tactical formation with HQ at Sculthorpe. All three F-86A/F squadrons changed role on 1 April 1954 when the 81 Fighter-Bomber Wing emerged from the 81 FIW with air defence now a secondary task. Re-equipment followed, the 81st being non-operational from 22 April 1954 to 8 February 1955 while they learnt to operate the Republic F-84F Thunderstreak fighter-bomber. Also to be mastered was the spectacular use of rocket-assisted take-off gear and even more so the use of nuclear bombs. January saw the last Sabres leave and on 8 February 1955 came re-designation as Fighter-Bomber Squadrons. Dispersal followed leading to the 92nd FBS moving to Manston on 28 March 1955. That left only the twenty-five F-84Fs of the 78th FBS at heavily guarded Shepherd's Grove.

A Flight Commander's F-84F Thunderstreak of the 92nd FIS, 81st FIW at Shepherd's Grove.

Because of the Wing's importance to NATO the 7519th on 27 January 1956 was upgraded to Support Group level. Between 9 August 1955 and 27 April 1956 the 77th FBS lodged with their F-100s while repairs to Wethersfield's runway took place. Shepherd's Grove's turn began came between 31 May 1956 and 3 May 1957 while the 78th was away at Sculthorpe. On 1 July 1956 they ceased being part of the disbanding 49th AD and now came under Third Air Force, USAFE. On 8 July 1958 the 81st was re-designated the 81st Tactical Fighter Wing.

At the start of 1957 the decision had been taken to station British – US jointly operated Thor intermediate range ballistic missiles in Britain. Four complexes each comprising five squadrons each armed with three missiles would form the basic operating structure run by the RAF. Well dispersed along the eastern side of England the missiles would be surface sheltered each having its own launch pad within a strongly guarded enclave. Siting would be on airfields embracing those categorised Agricultural, Inactive or Standby. Shepherd's Grove was chosen in mid-1958 as one of the Feltwell Complex sites and to make way the 78th moved to Woodbridge on 22 December 1958.

Building began immediately, the RAF repossessing Shepherds Grove on 1 April 1959. No 3 Group assumed overall control, making the station a satellite of Feltwell. 'B' Flight, 77 Squadron, was assigned to Shepherd's Grove on 22 July 1959 and, with the missiles arriving, became 82 Squadron on 1 September 1959. By late May 1960 each missile had its nuclear warhead fitted, launch time being set at just below fifteen minutes. Many exercises were undertaken leading to readiness times being reduced, but being surface stored made the Thors vulnerable to attack. Due to that, at midnight on 30 June 1963 the third complex (ie. Feltwell) became non-operational and the missiles were withdrawn.

Between 1961 and 1966 a variety of USAF support organisations used Shepherd's Grove. Housing on the base was long used for families of those based at Lakenheath and Mildenhall. Shepherds Grove Mushrooms used part of the site where now heavy goods vehicle and fork lift drivers are trained. The USAF has long had a housing annexe area.

Main features (December 1944):
Runways: 010° 6,000ft x 150ft, 080°, 140°, concrete. *Hangars:* two T2. *Hardstandings:* forty-nine spectacle, one frying pan type. *Accommodation* (RAF): 172 officers, 368 SNCOs, 1,676 ORs; WAAF: 12 officers, 25 SNCOs, 507 ORs.

SHIPDHAM, Norfolk

52°37N/00°56E 215ft asl; TM985075. Off A1075, S of Shipdham village

Old airfields rarely die, very few vanish completely, despite the antics of the developers, and some, like Shipdham ('Shippam' to the locals), come, go, then return. Fortunate its survival, for it holds special historical status as the wartime home of the 44th Bomb Group, which operated Consolidated B-24s for longer than any other in the US 8th AAF and, perhaps logically, sustained the highest B-24 Group losses.

Work started on the airfield in 1941. By midsummer 1942, with three runways and three contemporary T2 hangars, wartime Shipdham was all but ready to receive the Americans, who arrived within the 319th Bomb Group (Medium) on 12 September 1942. They then awaited the arrival of the first Martin B-26 Marauders heading for Europe, which they had been earmarked to operate within the 12th AF. Instead, the Group, without aircraft, was transferred to Horsham St Faith during the first week of October.

Meanwhile, personnel of the 44th Bomb Group had, on 4 September, boarded RMS *Queen Mary*, which berthed in the UK on 11 September. The new arrivals made for Cheddington from where they advanced to Shipdham on 10 October to become the second 8th AF Group flying B-24D Liberators from a base in Britain. Eager, perhaps too impatient, to operate, and with twenty-seven B-24s on strength, the Group went into action for the first time on 7 November 1942. Seven aircraft flew a diversion directed at coastal guns on Cap de la Hague, Normandy, while the 8th AF Main Force attacked U-boat pens at Brest. Two days later five 44th B-24s made the Group's first bombing raid when, as part of the forty-seven-strong Main Force, they dropped 500lb GPs on St Nazaire. Although small numbers of B-24s participated in feints or abortive missions, not until 20 December 1942 – with Romily-sur-Seine airfield as the target – did they carry out bombing. A dozen of the twenty-one employed bombed the target zone.

Although technical problems plagued the aircraft, there was nothing fundamentally wrong with the early B-24s. They were, however, committed to a European high-level, daylight bombing role before they were entirely suitable. Distinctively designed with a high aspect ratio Davis wing to help increase its range, and powered by Pratt & Whitney Twin Wasps (the B-17s had Wright Cyclones), the B-24 was a somewhat specialised answer to French and British requirements for a deep penetration bomber. In Britain's case it was envisaged as a night-bomber relying on moderate speed to compensate for its limited self-defence. The B-24's combat range – superior to that of the B-17 – was not essential in north-west Europe, and all too often unserviceability was a problem.

Early B-24 operations were, for the crews, very trying. In the main, small formations undertook diversions carrying no offensive loads. Potentially the first major B-24 operation came on 27 January 1943, but the twenty-seven B-24s involved, drawn from the two Groups, aborted due to poor weather. On 9 February they encountered such intense cold, -40°C, that they had to turn back before even reaching the Dutch coast. A small-scale raid on Dunkirk by both Groups on 15 February cost the 44th two aircraft. Not until 27 February 1943 was the first really effective operation carried out, fourteen out of fifteen B-24s attacking U-boat pens at Brest. Most operations so far related to attacking, or more often providing diversions, during U-boat related raids. By 8 March the 44th had lost thirteen of its original twenty-seven aircraft. In March 1943 a fourth bomb squadron, the 506th, with eight aircraft on strength, joined the 'Flying Eightballs' (as the Group was known). The task now was to make a good design into a potent weapon in European skies.

The 93rd Bomb Group had been detached to North Africa from December 1942 to February 1943, which left the 44th to work out B-24 snags. As the British had discovered, it was difficult to mix bomber types in one daylight mission, differences in performance and defensive fields of fire showing that it was best for the 44th's B-24s to tag along on their own behind the B-17s. As the Liberators arrived the defenders would be well tuned for action , something they proved on 27 January 1943 when, as part of the force intending to bomb Germany for the first time, they lost two of their number.

Early operations demanded much courage, the 44th being awarded a Distinguished Unit Citation for its operation of 14 May 1943. Carrying incendiaries, it followed B-17s to attack Kiel. Running in, it became very apparent that the B-24s lacked the massed defensive firepower of B-17 Groups. Although they made a brave, desperate attempt to bomb the target, the twenty-one-aircraft formation was forced apart by German fighters, which shot down five B-24s.

June 1943 saw the 44th taken off operations. The Group's turbo-supercharged engines, intended to improve high-altitude performance, were now of far less value, when the B-24s began practising very low-level flying over East Anglia. Indeed, some thundered over so low that they shook many a house by flying little above roof-top height.

On 15 June 1943 the 44th flew from Shipdham to Benina Main in Libya. From there the unit flew ten missions including an attack on Rome delivered on 19 July. Support to the invasion of Sicily followed before the prime reason for it being overseas, and for all that low-flying training, was revealed. The 44th was to be part of the 178 B-24 force that, on 1 August 1943, attacked the Ploesti oilfields.

With Colonel Leon Johnson leading, the Group contributed thirty-seven aircraft. Heavy flak and fighter opposition resulted in the loss of eleven aircraft of the total of fifty-four that failed to return. Johnson was awarded the Congressional Medal of Honor for courageous leadership, and the Group received its second Distinguished Unit Citation. Before returning to Shipdham on 25 August, the 44th bombed targets in Austria and Italy and dropped supplies to Allied forces in Sicily.

Operations from Shipdham were resumed on 7 September when, teamed with the new B-24 Group, the 389th, a small-scale anti-shipping attack was undertaken off the Netherlands. On the 9th they raided St Omer, and on 15 September bombed Chartres airfield. With the B-24 build-up in the UK so slow, it made better sense to make good use of them for long-range missions in the Mediterranean theatre. The 44th therefore flew to Oudna, Tunisia, on 19 September, mainly to support the Allied invasion of Italy. On 1 October twenty-five B-24s attacked the Messerschmitt factory at distant Weiner-Neustadt, Austria. Opposition was stiff, and eight B-24s failed to return. On 4 October the Group returned to Shipdham.

Still relatively few in number, B-24s entering service were of a new type with nose, tail, dorsal and ventral turrets as well as side port guns. Although very much better defended, there was a downside. Being heavier than their predecessors, additional weight reduced operational altitude and rendered the B-24H and J vulnerable to anti-aircraft fire. The changeover and need to establish operational crews meant relatively small-scale and fewer operations compared with those carried out by B-17 Groups. Feints, diversions and small-scale fringe target attacks were again the norm. The first major mission for the 44th since returning, and involving the new versions, took place on 3 November when 539/566 8th AAF bombers attacked Wilhelmshaven. Four B-24 Groups participated, despatching 117 aircraft, twenty-eight of them from Shipdham. No Liberators were lost.

On 5 November four B-24 Groups raided Munster and again losses were low, three B-24s out of 118 operating together with eleven pathfinders. Only four more times in 1943 did the B-24s participate in major operations, the deepest penetration being to Ludwigshafen on 30 December. Of the ninety-four B-24s operating, twenty-four were drawn from the 44th. In all, six B-24s failed to return, including one from Shipdham.

By this time the B-24H was the main version in use. Numbers of aircraft available were also increasing, the initial nine aircraft per squadron rising to twelve, then fifteen. By D-Day it had reached twenty.

The 44th bombed many targets in France and the Low Countries during the run-up to D-Day, and also attacked targets associated with the flying-bomb build-up. Its first 1944 B-24 major operation had taken place on 24 February when 213/239 B-24s attacked Gotha, a target well into Germany, which cost thirty-three Liberators including two from the 44th. Berlin was first attacked by 198/226 B-24s drawn from the nine Liberator Groups, which lost sixteen of their number, but none from the 44th. Berlin was raided again two days later and Brunswick on the 15th before two attacks on Friedrichshafen, on the 16th and 18th. The second of those cost twenty-four B-24s, among them six aircraft of the 44th, which, seriously damaged, force-landed in Switzerland. On 29 April twenty-five B-24s (including two of the 44th) of the 212/233 despatched did not return. Concentration was now on tactical rather than strategic targets, and relevant to the D-Day landings. Particularly involved were rail targets and airfields, although on 12 May Shipdham's B-24s attacked the synthetic oil refinery at Zeitz. When 354/369 B-24s targeted airfields in western Germany there were thirteen B-24 Groups operating that day, and only two aircraft failed to return.

At dawn on 6 June 1944 the 44th flew the first of its three missions during the day when it was among 418/543 B-24s bombing the landing beaches ahead of the US assault. Only one B-24 never made home, two more from a second raid, on Argentan. After attacking Caen, 125/300 Liberators bombed German forces in the area inland of the US beachhead. Return from the day's first raid was at extremely low level, offering East Anglians a never-to-be-forgotten spectacle. At around 08.30hrs hundreds of B-24s streamed over the flat lands in a broad swathe heading for their Norfolk bases.

Although the 44th was within the force bombing Berlin on 21 June, it mainly operated intensively that summer in support of the Allied advance, bombing airfields and tactical targets. In mid-September it dropped supplies to Allied troops during the ill-fated airborne forces venture. An indication of the ultimate size of the 2nd Air Division B-24 force was apparent on 24 December 1944 when, on the first fine weather day during the Battle of the Bulge, 634 B-24s were within the largest force of bombers ever despatched by the 8th AAF, 1,884/2,046. Airfields and communications targets in western Germany were targeted in support of the Allied troops engaged in the Battle.

Oil, rail and road targets and airfields all attracted attention in 1945, and support was given by the 44th to the crossing of the Rhine. The final operation for the 44th came on 24 March 1945, by which time it had been flying B-24s longer than any other Group in the 8th AAF. The four squadrons, Nos 66, 67, 68 and 506, had flown 325 missions from Shipdham, from where they began leaving for home on 22 May 1945. Aboard most B-24s making the transatlantic flight home were twenty men jubilantly heading for Bradley Field, CT. By mid-June the Americans had vacated Shipdham, many aboard RMS *Queen Mary* between 15 and 20 June, when she berthed in New York.

Shipdham then became a transit camp for German POWs, after which No 262 MU functioned here between 18 November 1946 and 31 December 1947, disposing of assorted RAF items. Thereafter the airfield was classified as Standby/Inactive. Part was officially disposed of in 1957, the remainder in 1962-63, all for agricultural use.

In September 1969, for possible use as a base for North Sea oil and gas operations, parts of the site were purchased from the farming community. Arrow Air Services Ltd was formed to undertake air charter and engineering work. A large hangar and office building 120ft long and 95ft wide was completed by April 1970 and the site re-opened for flying in June. The first charter flight took place on 16 June using Piper Twin Comanche G-AXRW. More Pipers were acquired before the charter operation moved to Horsham St Faith early in 1973.

At Shipdham much of Arrow's aircraft engineering initially involved de Havilland types, including overhaul of Rapides. Among them were the well-known G-AGTM, G-AIYR and G-AKIF. Arrow's activity aroused much interest when the company acquired from India a large consignment of dismantled Tiger Moths, together with many spares. The first was assembled and registered in February 1981, but most went into long-term storage. March 1984 saw the opening of a new clubhouse for local private flying, catered for by the Shipdham Aero Club Ltd.

By the 1990s Shipdham, as is still the case, was handling a wide assortment of light aircraft for general use, at that time for crop-spraying. On the southern perimeter of the site – where the unusual control tower (pattern 518/40) shell stands – there are nearby industrial units. Parts of the airfield are in decayed state, but Shipdham is still active and very recognisable as a wartime bomber base. It is best seen from the Dereham road, across which is it so easy to imagine a B-24 landing on the main runway. A small museum open at weekends is devoted to the Liberator days.

In the post-war hangar ex-Indian Tiger Moths fuselages were stacked.

Overhauled here were several Rapides, G-AIYR among them.

Main features:
Runways: 090 6,000ft x 150ft, 210/030 tarmac-surfaced. *Hangars:* three T2.
Hardstandings: fifty, concrete. *Accommodation:* 443 officers, 2,529 enlisted men.

SNAILWELL, Cambridgeshire

52°16N/00°28E 70ft asl; TL650668. Off A142, to right, just N of Newmarket

Snailwell, very much to be remembered as an Army Co-operation station, came into use in March 1941. Lysanders of 268 Squadron on 1 April 1941 moved in from Westley which was too small for Tomahawks with which 268 Squadron began re-equipping in May. As a second Unbuilt Satellite of Duxford intended for squadrons of No 22 Group which held army co-operation squadrons before they were placed in a Command of their own, its official opening date was 1 May 1941 when the station was transferred to Army Co-operation Command hands. Three months later, and still loosely affiliated to Duxford, Station HQ opened and Snailwell at last functioned independently. Throughout 1941 Snailwell continued echoing to the tinny note of Lysanders and high pitched call of Tomahawks as many exercises were mounted. Low level flying, practice gun spotting and many reconnaissance were undertaken over the eastern area.

Snailwell, designed for 'spotting', was a busy army co-operation base. No 268 Squadron operated Mustangs from here.

Prior to 14 February 1942, 268 Squadron engaged in just one day's operational flying. Then came detachments to Ibsley, Hampshire, from where the Tomahawks flew *Channel Patrols* protected by 501 Squadron's Spitfires.

That detachment heralded a major change in Snailwell's use further emphasised when in March 1942 Typhoons of 56 Squadron arrived from Duxford. Within a few days they were joined by Mustangs 1s here to replace 268 Squadron's Tomahawks. That allowed the squadrons to start flying *Lagoons* two of which were flown between IJmuiden and Texel on 29 June. They involved searching for enemy shipping between Texel and the Hook, many such sorties being subsequently flown from here. Nevertheless No 268 Squadron also maintained its prime role of fighter reconnaissance for the Army by being attached to 2 Corps, Eastern Command.

The Typhoons under the leadership of Squadron Leader 'Cocky' Dundas were by now practising low-level *Rhubarbs*. From 29 May, detached Flights of 56 Squadron drawing upon their training were placed at Manston and West Hampnett in an attempt to engage low-flying German fighter-bombers.

On 20 June 1942 '56' set out from Duxford for their part in the first Typhoon Wing sweep over the Boulogne-Mardyck area then landed back at Snailwell. More such operations followed then, on 19 August, 56 Squadron detached to West Malling participated in the Dieppe operation and faced Fw 190s for the first time. On 24 August the squadron moved out to Matlaske.

An off-shoot of 268 Squadron, No 168 reformed here on 15 June 1942 and equipped with Tomahawks used Bottisham whose units worked closely with Snailwell's. Whirlwinds of 137 Squadron – briefly here in March 1942 for Army support training at Stanford Battle Area – returned to Snailwell and in September the Squadron Commander first sampled the Whirlwind as a fighter-bomber. On 12 September '137' moved to Manston.

Blenheim Vd interdictor bombers of 614 Squadron then came for a brief spell before on 16 October P-39 Airacobras of the 347th Fighter Squadron, 350th Fighter Group, 12th Air Force arrived here. Striking in their desert camouflage and yellow outline to national insignia the P-39s were here until 8 December when they departed for King's Cliffe. Two days later their place was taken by the first 'Bomphoon' squadron, No 181, whose 'A' Flight left for Ludham to commence operations in February 1943. During March the remainder were active in exercise *Spartan* then the complete squadron moved to Manston on 24 March 1943.

Snailwell by then had become a very active station, 268's Mustang Is flying almost daily *Lagoons* when the weather allowed or the need dictated. A diversion came on 11 January 1943 when the squadron supported the first RAF Mitchell raid. A Fw 190 was destroyed for the loss of a Mustang. Another memorable operation involving seven Mustangs took place on 12 February. SS barracks at Amersfoort were strafed and a Do 217 landing at Soesterberg was brought down. More Mustang 1s – of 170 Squadron – moved here on 25 March their ground crews being ferried in from Andover aboard Horsa gliders. No 170 Squadron remaining an army support squadron was attached to the locally based Guard's Armoured Division before a posting to Odiham on 26 June 1943. Shortly before '170' arrived No 2 Heavy Glider MU HQ was established at Snailwell. No gliders were held here, the MU being responsible for maintaining Horsas stored at twenty-four bomber bases. It closed on 15 March 1944.

Early in May 1943, 309 (Polish) Squadron began arriving to learn the *Lagoon* role before using Mustang Is to take over from 268 Squadron which moved out on 31 May. Between 28 June and October 1943 No 309 was operationally very active. Drawing upon the Mustang's long range they flew an eight-aircraft *Distil* operation off Denmark on 4 October seeking unsuccessfully minesweeping Ju 52s. Operating alongside 309 between 14 July and 8 October 1943 was 613 Squadron whose Mustangs began *Lagoons* in mid-July. Operating almost daily, their role was threefold: searching for enemy shipping, some PR and ASR Walrus escorts, all undertaken under 12 Group, which took control of Snailwell on the disbandment of Army Co-operation Command at the end of May 1943. No 613 Squadron completed their move away in mid-November and 309 Squadron resumed *Lagoons* which continued until January 1944.

No 1426 Enemy Aircraft Flight's selection of German aircraft operated from here from July 1943, the well known He 111 AW177 flying from Snailwell when it crashed on the runway at Polebrook on 10 November 1943. That autumn also saw detachments of 12 Group's 116 and 288 Squadrons using the station for radar calibration and AA support duties.

No 417 Repair & Salvage Unit formed here on 1 January 1944 and on 1 March left for Lasham and an important role in the invasion. More abrupt change had occurred on 8 February

1944 when No 309 Squadron flew their final *Lagoon* and at once began re-arming with Hurricane II/IVs before moving to Drem on 23 April. No 527 Squadron flying six Blenheim IVs, eight Hurricanes and four DH Hornet Moths had moved in from Castle Camps on 28 February 1944 and stayed until late April flying calibration sorties. Then the station was relieved of active aircraft.

On 7 May the 41st Base Complement Squadron, USAAF, moved in, the 33rd and 41st MR Squadrons arriving soon. They handled a few A-20Gs in summer. The Americans stayed until autumn, but the RAF closed its SHQ on 15 July.

When Newmarket Heath closed the 3 Group Communications Flight in February 1945 moved to Snailwell and was there until 21 March 1946.

More activity resulted when in October 1944 the RAF (Belgian) Initial Training School functioning under RAF Technical Training Command moved into Snailwell and used Westley as its satellite. Its purpose was to train air and ground crews for the post-war Belgian Air Force. Tiger Moths and Master IIs were received in February 1945 when flying training commenced. Personnel were accommodated both at this station and at Bottisham where Tiger Moths were flown in the training of pilots for the embryo air force. They left for Belgium in March 1946. At Snailwell remained a Halifax VI, two Lancasters, a Tempest V and a Beaufighter VIf, all for use by the technical training section which closed in August 1946. Activity here ceased in October 1946.

Snailwell then faded away, what little there ever was of it. The aircraft were usually seen hiding among a line of trees which stretched from the ostentatious main gate on the Norwich road across to the village. Accommodation was by the tree lined road. The blister hangar illustrated in *Action Stations 1* was removed in the late 1980s. At the north-east end of the line of trees a farm strip has existed, used by a Cessna.

Main features:
Runways: NNE/SSW 4,290ft, ENE/WSW 5,040ft, ESE/WNW 4,260ft – all grass.
Hangars: one Bellman, ten Blister. *Hardstandings:* twelve for twin-engined aircraft, two 50ft frying-pan type. *Accommodation:* 68 officers, 90 SNCOs, 940 ORs. WAAF accommodation off camp.

SNETTERTON HEATH, Norfolk

52°28N/00°57 150ft asl; TM005895. On A11(T), 7 miles SW of Attleborough

As the exotic cars race around the circuit on a fine summer's day it is worth remembering wartime Snetterton was a typical temporary wartime two-hangar bomber airfield. Furthermore that the 96th Bomb Group based here had the highest loss rate of any unit in the 8th AF. From Snetterton 3rd Air Division B-17s participated in shuttle raids on German targets which, due to their distance from Britain, meant flying on to Russia or the Mediterranean carrying out another attack when coming home. Some operations involved alpine crossings and landing at Italian bases. From those they raided Romania during exceptionally long and exhausting missions.

B-17G-85-BO 43-38282 'SWEENEY BRAT' after serving with 862 BS, 493 BG Debach joined the 338th BS, 96th BG on 8 August 1944. Returned to the USA 6 July 1945 and was broken up 13 December 1945. (George Pennick).

Plenty of Snetterton remains in use for the perimeter tracks form the basis of the race circuit. There are, too, the T2 hangars. At first acquaintance Snetterton would appear as an unusual split site. The explanation is that four T2s were erected to the north of the A11 to form the main buildings of Air Depot to be known as Eccles. It was never completed whereas to accommodate the B-17 Group dispersals additional to the original thirty-six were built before the 96th moved in.

Construction of Snetterton Heath began in autumn 1942. It opened in June 1943 when it was incomplete, the 386th Bomb Group moving in on 3 June. Although they moved to Boxted on 10 June the Group continued making use of Snetterton while working up on B-26s. Meanwhile the 96th had assembled at Great Saling and began moving in to Snetterton on 12 June 1943 after having commenced operations on 14 May 1943.

Their targets included ports, factories, rail installations and for their part in the Regensburg raid of 17 August 1943 the Group received a Distinguished Unit Citation. A second DUC was awarded after the 96th led the 45th Combat Wing on 19 April 1944 when they penetrated through dense cloud and AA fire to reach Poland.

The 96th's target listing is as wide as any. Included are the airfield at Augsburg where the Messerschmitt factory was sited, Bordeaux which was the lair of the anti-shipping raiders; marshalling yards at Kiel, Hamm, Brunswick and Gdynia, aircraft factories at Chemnitz, Hanover and Diosgyor; oil refineries at Merseburg and Brux and chemical works at Wiesbaden, Neukirchen and the great I G Farben complex at Leverküsen.

The Group supported the Normandy landings and the St-Lô break-out, dropped supplies to the maquis in France and in 1945 attacked communications targets behind the front line. At the end of the European war the 96th dropped food to the Dutch and in a transport role moved personnel to Morocco, France, Germany and Ireland. They stayed in Britain longer than most and did not leave until December 1945.

Subsequently placed on Care & Maintenance it was also a Sub-Site between 20 December 1945 and 30 November 1948 of No 262 MU which made use of the hangars on the north side of the main road. For a long time Snetterton was maintained in excellent condition, and was one of the tidiest wartime temporary airfields remaining in East Anglia. The RAF quit in the late 1940s and the site was privately bought in 1952. Quidenham Church nearby contains a memorial to the 96th Bomb Group.

Main features:
Runways: 230° 6,000ft x 150ft, 180°, 270°, concrete and wood chips. *Hangars:* two T2. *Hardstandings:* fifty loop type. *Accommodation:* 443 officers, 2,529 enlisted men.

SOMERSHAM, Cambridgeshire

52°22N/00°03W 80ft asl; TL330770. S of village

Near Somersham was Wyton's Q-Site. Apparently, and with enemy activity slight after mid-1941, Somersham was used by Lysander and Hudson pilots of Tempsford's special duty squadrons to practise short run night landings for their job was the landing and pick-up of agents from continental fields. Little wonder that it was, and remains, cloaked in secrecy. Few such flights were made here.

SPILSBY, Lincolnshire

53°09/00°10E 33ft asl; TF450650. Just over 2 miles E of Spilsby, N of B1195 road

Spilsby completed ready for use on 15 May 1943 was part of 55 Base. Seemingly a typical three-runway temporary wartime bomber station it had runways of unusual lengths – 7,590ft, 6,000ft and 4,290ft with the longest having feasible extension to 9,000ft.

A No 5 Group station, its first squadron was Lancaster equipped No 207 Squadron which arrived from Langar on 12 October 1943. They commenced operations from here and participated in many Main Force operations.

They were joined at the end of September 1944 by Lancasters of No 44 Squadron. Spilsby was now accommodating two of the best known Lancasters squadrons which operated intensively to the end of hostilities. They flew their final bombing sorties on 25 April 1945 when eight Lancasters of No 44 Squadron and ten of No 207 Squadron took part in bombing Hitler's eyrie above Berchtesgaden.

July 1945 saw No 44 Squadron move to Mepal. In their place came No 75 (New Zealand) Squadron to make use of the long runway during Lincoln trials and squadron conversion. The New Zealand squadron was expecting to operate them in the Far East war when it unexpectedly ended. The squadron disbanded on 15 October 1945.

No 207 Squadron moved to Methwold, Suffolk, on 30 October 1945. Their replacement was No 2 Armament Practice Station which formed on 1 December 1945 to afford facilities for 12 Group and local bomber stations. No 2 APS closed on 1 August 1946 then Spilsby was placed on Care and Maintenance. It was retained Inactive supervised by Coningsby.

Spilsby was on 15 June 1955 allocated for USAF use. A detachment of the 7536 Material Sqn (AMC), USAF, used it for storage purposes between 5 July 1956 and 25 May 1957. On 11 March 1958 it was returned to UK control and again closed down.

A hangar remains as do a few small assorted buildings in poor condition.

Main features:
Runways: 110° 6,000ft x 150ft with possibility of ready expansion to 9,000ft, 164° 6,000ft basic x 150ft but use restricted to 4,200ft, 050° 4,200ft x 150ft. *Hangars:* two T2, one B1. *Hardstandings:* fifteen frying pan type and nineteen loop type. *Accommodation:* RAF: 112 officers, 372 SNCOs, 1,026 ORs; WAAF: 12 officers, 20 SNCOs, 140 ORs.

SPITALGATE (ex-GRANTHAM, renamed in 1944), Lincolnshire

52°54N/00°36W 415ft asl; SK940345. E of Grantham adjacent to A52 road

Spitalgate (also known as Spittlegate) and initially called Grantham originated in 1916 on high ground near Grantham town. It has had an exceptionally long life and, not surprisingly, many buildings to the end of the station's career looked attractively antique. Now in Army hands they remain so.

With 1915-style wooden hangars the aerodrome opened in November 1916 as Grantham, a training station where No 24 Wing RFC, set up shop on 24 March 1917 and stayed until April 1918. In April 1917 No 11 Training (alias Reserve) Squadron arrived with BE2s and stayed until 15 September 1917 along with No 49 TS, the other local squadron.

Replacing them came three others, Nos 15, 20 and 37 which all arrived around 15 September 1917. Their aircraft included Avro 504s, BE2s, DH6s, FK3s and RE8s. No 20 TS left for Harlaxton on 27 November leaving the others using Avro 504Ks, FE2s and FK8s to become No 39 Training Depot Station on 15 August 1918 itself renamed 39 Training School on 14 March 1919.

Remaining active after hostilities, slimmed down squadrons (cadres) held against future expansion were based here. No 70 Squadron with Sopwith Camels and Snipes arrived in February 1919 and was followed in August by 29 Squadron and in September by No 43. Both were disbanded here by the end of the year, No 70 Squadron following suit in January 1920.

Grantham was retained, No 39 TS becoming No 6 Flying Training School on 26 April 1920 but before it was equipped the unit in May 1921 moved to Manston.

Now came a period of complete change as the station changed into an operational base. On 4 February 1922 No 100 Squadron (Cadre) using DH9As arrived from southern Ireland following the establishment of the Irish Free State. Its strength increased when a fourth or 'D' Flight equipped with Vickers Vimy bombers was added. On 8 February 1923 No 39 Squadron – also at cadre strength – arrived with DH9A day-bombers and was soon upgraded here to squadron level. No 100 Squadron re-armed with Fairey Fawns in May 1924 and during the 1926 General Strike distributed mail and copies of Winston Churchill's 'British Gazette'. From September 1926 No 100 Squadron flew Hawker Horsley bombers.

Grantham's training days had not ended for on 2 April 1928, No 3 Flying Training School returned with an assortment including AW Atlases, Avro 504Ns, F2Bs and Siskins. The station's future was confirmed when within the 1922 plans RAF Grantham was to be upgraded. Included was the building of permanent hangars, a technical site and domestic buildings. Modern for its time, Grantham became one of the RAF's most active aerodromes. HQ No 23 Group reformed here on 12 April 1926 to control all training establishments but on 14 August moved to St Vincents, a large house in Grantham town which eventually led to the aerodrome's name change.

Brief resumption of operational status came in August 1926 when Horsleys and No 100 Squadron returned only to leave for Bicester in January 1928. No 39, still flying DH9As, left for

Bircham Newton on 21 January 1928. Grantham was in essence, and would remain, a training station. True, in summer 1937 No 3 FTS moved out to make way for a resumption of operations under the new No 5 Group, Bomber Command. That resulted at the end of August 1937 in the arrival of two Hawker Hind equipped squadrons, Nos 113 and 211, both of which left for Egypt on 30 April 1938. They were replaced late September by a Fairey Battle squadron, No 106, here only until 14 October 1938 when they returned to Thornaby.

Spitalgate then reverted to a training role with the opening here in October 1938 of No 12 SFTS. At the outbreak of war in September 1939 the School became No 12 FTS equipped with Hawker Hart variants and Oxfords. Aircraft and personnel numbers quickly increased and by November 1939 the aircraft establishment totalled 105 aircraft. Additional to these were a handful allotted to HQ No 5 Group Communications Flight here since 1938. They included an Avro Tutor, Oxford and Magisters, replaced later by Percival Proctors, the Flight staying until 14 November 1943.

By summer 1940 Fairey Battles including some twin-cockpit Battle (T) examples had replaced the biplanes. August 1940 saw the School standing by for possible transfer to Canada but in October the idea was abandoned. Instead, the training programme expanded. Personnel establishment now exceeded 2,500 to cope with which a large Nissen hut encampment was built.

On 1 April 1942 No 12 SFTS was renamed 12 (Pilots) Advanced Flying Unit which acclimatised pilots to fly in the European environment. Now the unit was re-equipped with Blenheim Vs – sometimes called Mk Vc – advanced trainers. With turrets removed and bombing gear too, in their trainer colours they were a familiar sight over Eastern England. The unit's task was to train pilots to fly twin-engined operational aircraft such as Mosquitoes. No 1536 Beam Approach Training Flight moved in March 1943 and until May 1945 provided instrument landing training.

Bristol Blenheim V trainer AZ900 '42' of No 12 (P) AFU seen at Spitalgate.

By November 1943 both grass landing grounds, here and at Harlaxton, were in very bad condition with their turf breaking apart as a result of so much continuous use. So bad was the state that most aircraft were moved to airfields in Cheshire and Lancashire and a few Blenheims to Balderton. At the start of 1944 two steel Sommerfeld runways were laid allowing the aircraft to return. On 29 March 1944 the station was officially renamed Spitalgate. At the time 12 (P)AFU held fifty-seven Blenheim Vs, thirty Oxfords and a handful of Ansons. During runway laying the original hangars on the western boundary were supplemented and now the site held five Bellman metal hangars, two special hangars, seven 69ft Blisters and a single 65ft Blister. The airfield's most active days had passed and on 8 February 1945, 12 (P) AFU moved to Hixon and Cranage. Next month No 17 SFTS arrived from Cranwell and now only Oxfords remained at the airfield. These the school continued using until 1947 when it was renamed No 1 FTS and re-equipped with Harvards.

Although Spitalgate saw post-war use, the removal of No 1 FTS during February 1948 deprived Spitalgate of a flying unit. Thereafter the station housed various ground formations the first of which was the RAF Officer Cadet Training Unit which took up residence in June 1948 and stayed until March 1954. Over that period Prentices of No 7 FTS Cottesmore used Spitalgate as their RLG. Other units based here included the Mess Staff School within the period September 1949 to August 1957, and HQ No 24 Group, TTC between March 1954 and its disbandment in August 1957. The station also hosted the RAF School of Education and the Central Library 1955-8, the Secretarial Officers' School in 1959 and HQ 3 Police District, renamed HQ Provost and Security Services.

Spitalgate became the WRAF Depot in 1960, all airwomen undertaking basic training at the station until the Depot moved to Hereford in March 1974. Allocated for USAF use on 16 November 1961 a detachment from the 2166 Communications Sqn (AFSC) made use of Spitalgate between 1962 and 1967. In the 1970s the Central Gliding School used the airfield until 1975. Spitalgate was then transferred to the Army who renamed it Grantham. The Royal Corps of Transport took over the camp. It remains in their hands, its appearance not all that much changed from quite distant days.

Main features:
Runways: Sommerfeld Tracking for 290° 3,480ft long, 230° 3,900ft long. Grass runway NE/SW 4,500ft. *Hangars:* five Bellman, five permanent 172ft x 84ft wide x 22ft high, one permanent 177ft long x 102ft wide x 28ft high, seven 69ft base opening Blister and one 65ft base opening Blister. *Accommodation* (December 1944): RAF: 255 officers, 318 SNCOs, 939 ORs; WAAF: 15 officers, 6 SNCOs, 448 ORs.

STANSTED, Essex

51°52N/00°31E asl; TL535230. SE of Stansted Mountfitchet village, E of M11

'Stand on that line. Don't smile. Take off your specs – and stand still.' That's what greeted me, a British citizen for 75 years, at Stansted. 'I'm never flying again.'

'But is it really flying that you hate?'

'Well, no, I suppose it's crowded airports and people insulting you, pestering you, with their security. Not long ago I stood in a queue of more than 300 people, many wearing heavy shoes or trainers. Suddenly, one of these security people swooped upon a lonely, very elderly lady, demanding that she remove her delicate sandals for inspection. Everyone else watched in disbelief, and especially those wearing bulky trainers, for she had great difficulty in removing her shoes. One made me take off my trouser belt in case it had a knife in it. Others just watched, probably hoping… It was so ridiculous. The amazing thing is that one can enter airport terminals without any security check. That is surely foolish. Just imagine the carnage that could so easily be caused by some zealot.'

So often one hears such sentiments expressed by rational people whose concerns are more with flight safety, particularly when turnround times are so brief. Government spying and prying and policemen dangerously waving their toys all help to make airports unpleasant places. Terrorists must be gloating at the discomfort caused. There is, of course, a constant need for vigilance to prevent terrorist atrocities. That needs also to be directed at protecting motorway bridges, gas pipes and electricity power lines, reservoirs, every school. Attacks upon such soft targets would yield extensive problems, yet security is indeed limited. Ensuring that every aircraft is 100% fit to fly is far more important than the terrorist threat.

What, then, of Stansted Airport? It basically has three features, a large lonesome terminal building, a circular railway and three piers to which it conveys passengers. One might logically expect a strict security check of everyone entering the terminal here and at every airport. There is none. After entering the unsecured terminal one finds a marked absence of luggage trolleys, and many folk dragging baggage to check-in desks. After that procedure, one passes through security checks before entering a large shopping area. Then it is time to take the train to the departure pier shown on the data displays. The finger-like piers have large glass windows giving a good view for the few who have any interest in what will be conveying them! Boarding aircraft has an excellent luxury – it can involve actually walking on the apron and, if nothing else, savouring fresh air.

Stansted Airport generates the usual outcries from those living around about the noise and the general activity. Few were there before its airport life began in 1946. That promotes the question of why anyone not in tune with the airport would want to live close by, even in the surrounding attractive territory?

Stansted's basic problem is its geographical position, which is one of the reasons why it has failed to become a hub airport and why it has not collected and kept long-haul operators. Although passenger numbers have hugely increased – except in recent financial-problem times – they have done so largely because of the presence of low-fare, no-frills, short-journey Ryanair and, to a lesser extent, EasyJet. Road and rail links with London are good, but they lead into a major traffic complex on the eastern side of the capital, to the ever-packed M25 or to Liverpool Street station, from where onward travel is rarely enjoyable. Leave Stansted on a northbound train and one travels on a demoralising, circuitous, cross-country route, eventually closing in on another airport! Why, you may ask, did Stansted Airport come about?

On 4 July 1942 the 817th US Engineering Air Battalion arrived to build a 1,919-acre airfield on fine, undulating farmland alongside Stansted Mountfitchet. Almost a year later an Air Depot opened here, its use resulting in double the usual pair of T2 hangars. By October 1943 Stansted was functioning with the customary three runways. To its western side came many a B-26 Marauder to be fitted out for action with the 9th AF.

Significant change came in the form of the 9th AF 344th Bomb Group, equipped with B-26s, which began moving in on 9 February 1944. Commencing bombing operations on 6 March 1944, they were soon attacking airfields, V-1 sites, rail installations, submarine shelters, coastal defences and tactical targets in France, Belgium and the Netherlands. In May the Group bombed important bridges, and on D-Day the coastal guns of Cherbourg. It then supported the drive to seize the Cotentin Peninsula, and bombed enemy positions to assist the British advance near Caen. For its 24-26 July operations in support of the advance on St-Lô, the Group was awarded a Distinguished Unit Citation. It then hindered the German retreat through the Falaise Gap, and raided defences at Brest before moving out of Stansted on 30 September to Cormeilles-en-Vexin in France.

With the 30th Air Depot Group left in control, assorted USAAF aircraft types passed through Stansted. When hostilities ceased in May 1945 the base became a general transit centre for men and machines until 12 August 1945 when the USAAF moved out. German POWs awaiting repatriation, some 400 in number, came here to help clean the site. On 26 November 1945 No 263 MU (which handled assorted equipment) opened its Head Quarters here and controlled two sub-sites, at Hitcham and Triston. The RAF renamed the main station Stansted Mountfitchet.

Conversion into an airport took form on 14 December 1946 when civilian use of the airfield was initiated. Soon on site was Dr Graham Humby's enterprise, London Aero & Motor Services (LAMS), complete with six Handley Page Halifax C.VIIIs, incongruous initially in overseas wartime fading camouflage. LAMS was born to operate freight services primarily for the conveyance of soft fruit and perishable goods between the UK and France and Italy. It was a novel idea, but Halifaxes were very costly to operate, trade seasonable, and the enterprise folded in July 1948. Summer 1947 had seen Kearsley Airways open a charter business using three Dakotas and a Proctor, to attract trade from north of London. Failure to find enough business brought closure partly, it was thought, due to Stansted's location.

RAF activity continued until 1 October 1947, when Hitcham became the main base of 263 MU. Stansted then became a sub-site, steadily run down until closure on 30 November 1948. RAF presence ended.

Government interest in Stansted's potential for development into an airport seemed certain when, on 31 December 1948, the Ministry of Civil Aviation Flying Unit moved in with its Avro XIXs, Consuls and a Dove. In mind was the development of Stansted as London's principal charter and freight airfield in place of Croydon. It would also serve as the main civilian diversion airfield. In April 1949 it formally passed from Air Ministry to MCA control.

Before the airfield could be exploited came the Berlin Airlift, then the Korean War. The US Government desperately pleaded with the British to make more UK airfields available to the USAF and, aware of the practicality of lengthening its main runway, expressed interest in operating large jet reconnaissance aircraft from an improved Stansted. The Americans approached the Secretary of State for Air with suggestions including a 10,000ft x 200ft runway with an LCN of 100, supplemented with eleven hardstandings. There must surely have been crafty government satisfaction with those ideas.

Dark blue overall, Halifax VIII G-AIWP of LAMS June 1947.

From Stansted on 26 August 1951 the very secret Handley-Page 88, the aerodynamic testbed for the Victor bomber, made its first and only flight, for it crashed. The same month Aviation Traders transferred Carvair conversion production from Southend to Stansted, from where the first example flew in the summer of 1952.

Runway and associated development agreed on 9 October 1952, Stansted was allocated for USAF use, and occupied by the 7522 Air Base Squadron (ABS) between 10 November 1952 and 1 September 1953. Then a detachment of the 7532nd took over and stayed until 1 January 1954, when it was renamed the 7532nd Support Squadron. Strategic Air Command's 3913rd ABS was here from 1952 to 1955, then moved to Mildenhall. It was replaced by the 3930th, which disbanded on 1 October 1958. Meanwhile, the 803rd US Aviation Engineering Battalion had, between 1 July 1953 and 8 December 1956, built the 10,000ft runway and associated track and hardstandings.

Stansted's possible use as a major civilian airport had all the while remained the British intent, even though a 1953 White Paper dismissed the idea because it was 'the wrong side of London' and access was poor. It was rated as suitable for use only until Gatwick was fully functioning. The new long runway would be an asset, but passenger handling would be in Nissen huts!

During runway construction, a new and parallel taxiway served as a runway, allowing flying to continue. Prominent were chartered Avro Yorks conveying troops to the Mediterranean area. In 1955 there were 10,731 aircraft movements, and in 1956 44,734 passengers passed through the airport, aircraft movements totalling 15,026.

Stansted following post-war development for USAF reconnaissance aircraft. Note the old runway parallel to the main runway.

US engineers withdrew in April 1957. Advances in strategic intelligence gathering led to the Americans informing the British in mid-1958 that they only wished to use the airport in the event of war, and still only for long-range strategic reconnaissance. US interest declined, its forces finally departing on 14 November 1958. Between 1954 and 1957 Stansted had also served as a War Station/bolt-hole for North Weald's fighters. With the V-force in place and Fighter Command much reduced in strength, the Air Ministry in November 1958 decided that it, too, no longer needed Stansted, irrespective of its long runway.

A new reason for its survival fortuitously emerged. Airwork would now use it to refurbish MDAP-supplied F-86 Sabre fighters discarded by the RAF for issue to other NATO forces. A considerable number of RAF Percival Prentice trainers also arrived, awaiting disposal or civilian buyers. With them languished a collection of Avro Tudor airliners. Charter flights by Yorks of Skyways and Scottish Air Lines continued.

Tudor 2 G-AGRY withdrawn from use 9 September 1954, photographed April 1956 and broken up July 1958.

In November 1960 the Ministry of Aviation Fire Service Training School moved in from Pengam Moors, Cardiff, establishing itself in the south-western corner. It used the wartime US church as its main lecture room while attracting unusual aircraft upon which to practise its trade.

Trooping flights continued until 1964, by which time civilian charter flights to America and Canada were being flown by CPA, Capitol Airlines and KLM using Boeing 707s and DC-8s. In 1963-64 105,157 passengers were carried, and aircraft movements rose to 27,139. Some of those were training flights by BEA, BOAC and foreign airlines, which in number exceeded other types of flying. Decline came in 1964 when BEA training was transferred to Malta and Trident training to Shannon. British United Airways lost its trooping contract in 1964, flights ceasing at the end of the year. Movements nevertheless increased and in 1964-65 totalled 36,378, and by then serious enquiry into Stansted's civilian potential was under way.

Its future seems always to be under consideration. A 1961 Government White Paper had recommended that it should be one of Britain's four major airports, and in July 1964 came the revelation that, after studying seventeen sites, a committee had decided that Stansted would be an ideal third London airport. That immediately brought forth local public outcry. More consideration then resulted in an announcement – presumably for political reasons – that Stansted would not after all be developed! It wasn't long before the government responded further by announcing that, irrespective of local wishes, Stansted would, after all, be developed. In 1966 the government placed it under the control of the British Airports Authority (BAA). Charter/IT flights would, it was argued, be cheaper to operate from here. That would reduce increasing congestion at Gatwick and Heathrow, freeing space for scheduled services.

Local opposition, ever more ferocious, led to yet another enquiry, this time by a six-man team under Mr Justice Roskill, launched in 1968. Examination of the entire idea took two years to complete. Over a period of ten months the team cut to four the number of contenders for a new London airport, and Stansted was not even a semi-finalist. Preference, revealed in 1971, was for Wing, a wartime OTU in Buckinghamshire. The Essex-loving government, instead of accepting that idea, announced that an entirely new airport would be built on Foulness, and that work was to start as soon as possible. A long-used weapons range needed clearing, but a bigger handicap was an outburst of opposition from friends of the site's natural inhabitants.

Stansted's local development had meanwhile edged slowly and quietly forward. In 1969 a terminal building replaced its Nissen huts, after Channel Airways in 1968 had moved its main base here from Southend, where its BAC 1-11 jets had been upsetting local ears. The move to Stansted was important, for it introduced scheduled services that connected Stansted with Rimini and Jersey. Comets also used Stansted, the terminal becoming especially busy when flights to Scandinavia started to supplement charters to the USA. The high level of activity was short-lived for in February 1972 Channel Airways collapsed. Lloyd International, which was using the airport for Britannias and Boeing 707 freighters, also folded.

Stansted looked once more to be heading for obscurity, but survival was still a friend. In July 1974 came the announcement that the government's £642m Foulness (alias Maplin Sands) scheme was being halted, ostensibly because of increasing fuel costs and general recession. There was, it said, no need after all for a third London airport.

Again, holiday inclusive tours (ITs) and charters by Aviaco, Trans European and Spantax air lines would save the airport. Scheduled flights were very few, Jersey being served once a week – on Sunday. By 1979 internal services were increasing, operated particularly by Air Anglia. Other London airports were also experiencing increased traffic, leaving BAA to claim that the expansion of Stansted was essential. The result? An about-turn and another government advisory committee.

The committee's incredible suggestion was that the Amsterdam/Schiphol hub should also serve as London's third airport! Already, it argued, eighteen UK destinations were linked with Schiphol. So ferocious was the backlash, from BAA and the unions, that Whitehall's cowards fled in full retreat. At the end of 1979 they announced, firmly, that Stansted had, after all, been chosen as the ideal London third airport.

Did that really end the saga? Of course not! Autumn 1981 brought another enquiry, this time headed by Mr Graham Eyre QC, and held at Quendon Hall, just north of the airport. It devoured a vast amount of paper, used lots of money, wasted a lot of time and generated plenty of hot air before its leader went away to tackle the ascent of his mountain of evidence.

By now another hardy old event was gathering momentum, another recession, which was biting hard and resulting in route cutbacks and reduced season ITs. The end of Air Anglia's Stansted operation led to an overall cut in the airport's workforce. Nevertheless, confidence in the future was clear when terminal lounges were enlarged, and a restaurant and shop were added.

Late 1981 had seen the launch of an international service to Amsterdam. It involved a new operator, Air UK, created through the amalgamation of Air Anglia and three UK regional airlines. Its Head Quarters were at Norwich Airport, the second base being briefly at Blackpool. This private newcomer, the largest scheduled UK regional airline, which began trading on 1 January 1980, was, by the summer of 1982, running services from Stansted to Paris and Aberdeen. It took over a Brussels service from Jersey European Airways, which, in April 1982, had been granted a licence to begin a regular Stansted-Brussels service. IT summer charters increased, and in the summer of 1984 Dan Air joined in. General financial recovery in 1985 permitted the relaunch of more international flights, so additional Fokker F27s, leased F28s and BAC 111-400s came into Air UK use.

On 5 June 1983 Stansted had been the scene of an amazing event. A crowd estimated at 500,000 packed the area around to witness the arrival of a Boeing 747 carrying a mock-up of the American space shuttle. It is claimed that as a result of its call more than 4 million colour slides were taken, surely a record number at one event!

By then the M11 motorway linking London with the A14 was in use, providing easier road access to Stansted where car parking was cheap, the terminal was still improving and the staff were particularly welcoming. Air UK was still operating services to Paris and Aberdeen, HeavyLift ex-RAF Belfast freighters were transporting cargo worldwide and, in 1984, Air Atlantique was also operating DC-3s from here; GPO night flights were also calling.

The Eyre Report of December 1984 suggested expanding the airport to handle 15 million passengers a year, with 25 million a future target. Government soon approved a two-phase major development involving the airfield and the building of an entirely new terminal. Could such expansion come about without environmental desecration of a large area? Gatwick had little prospect of having a second runway, and there was no suggestion of a second runway at Stansted.

The expansion commenced in 1985 to increase Stansted's area to 2,300 acres, which made it a third larger than Gatwick. Government funding, around £400m, was to be channelled through BAA. Notable architect Sir Norman Foster was called upon to design a terminal covering 8 acres – roughly the size of Trafalgar Square – and able to handle 15 million passengers annually. A 121-panel roof would be supported by thirty-six girders positioned in groups to resemble trees and be their equivalent in height, some 15 metres. Baggage equipment to handle 3,600 items per hour was designed. There would be three rows of check-in desks, with arrivals and departures on the same floor level to avoid the use of escalators.

Passengers would board or disembark at satellite buildings, with space for more being allocated. To one satellite passengers would be conveyed over 2 minutes in an unmanned, tracked 'people mover' able to carry eighty and running on a continuous loop. When the new features opened Stansted was handling between 1 and 2 million passengers annually, a large proportion of them still involved with ITs and charters.

Incorporating plentiful glass, the white terminal structure rose boldly out of nowhere on Stansted's eastern fringe, and thus opposite existing passenger facilities. To reduce the impact of expansion, 250,000 trees would be planted, areas set aside for wildlife and 10% of the airport area landscaped. Only seven listed cottages and barns needed to be moved – for re-erection elsewhere. Construction of the new terminal commenced in 1988.

Passenger numbers gradually increased. In 1987 Air UK Leisure was launched using Boeing 737-400s, an all-charter subsidiary of Air UK with an HQ at Stansted. The same year KLM Royal Dutch Airlines, long-time partner of Air Anglia and subsequently of Air UK, acquired a 14.9% stake in Air UK, which, in 1987, began ordering BAe 146 aircraft. As that airliner's passenger capacity increased, so did orders, which by 1989 were for the dash-300 long version.

Main development at Stansted has been on the eastern side. In the foreground is Air UK BAe 146 G-UKHP. (via A J Wright)

Every major event – international, financial – rapidly disrupts airline activity, and recession in 1990 reduced travel, business and private. Then came the first Gulf conflict, which had very serious consequences for the airlines and Stansted. One was the collapse of the Air Europe/International Leisure Group. Another was the reduction in activity at both London Heathrow and Gatwick, which provided them with rare chances to offer flight slots even at desirable times at these much-preferred airports.

Stansted responded with the slogan 'Easy come, easy go'. It certainly would be easy to reach, easy to check-in, easy to leave, for a spur road from the M11 would lead to the terminal. A £4m railway link, via the nearby main line, would link not with preferred St Pancras but with Liverpool Street, despite its position away from central London. Liverpool Street station was forever crowded, so rail services between Cambridge and London King's Cross were enhanced to attract passengers to this other terminus. That allowed space for a 40-to-60-minute Stansted-Liverpool Street connection with a stop at Tottenham Hale to connect with London Underground's Victoria Line. In Stansted's terminal there was an easy baggage carousel with trolley and train platform and the so-called 'Stansted Flyer'. It was hoped that one day it would take only 30 minutes to reach London. Despite continuing local opposition, development of the entire project proceeded well.

On 15 March 1991 HM Queen Elizabeth II opened the terminal, from where scheduled services started three days later. Air UK soon moved its HQ and main operations base to Stansted, occupying pride of place. It undertook its own passenger handling, the airport terminal's total exceeding 400,000 in the first year. That was partly due to the introduction of six new routes and more frequent services. By summer 1991 Air UK, operating from Stansted to thirteen scheduled destinations, could call upon nine BAe 146s, thirteen Fokker F27s and two Short SD360s. Another five BAe 146s were expected. Hope was that busy European schedules, now to be year-round, might at last attract long-haul scheduled operators to use Stansted as a limited hub now that slots at Heathrow and Gatwick were once more full.

Air UK pair, Fokker F 100 'FH' and a BAe 146.

Among cities now linked with Stansted were Belfast, Dusseldorf, Frankfurt, Hamburg, Madrid, Milan, Munich and Zurich, but the main way ahead for Stansted was to be very different. In late 1991 Ryanair arrived on the scene and would grow to completely dominate the airport.

Formed by Christy Ryan, Club Tour operator Liam Lonergen and Tony Ryan of Guinness Peat Aviation, the now well-known Ryanair had a humble beginning. Deciding to challenge the monopoly of Aer Lingus and British Airways services between Britain and Ireland, it established a Cork-Gatwick service using a fifteen-seat Brazilian-built Embraer Bandeirante airliner. In 1986 the company opened a second route linking Dublin with Luton. That was only achieved with the help of Prime Minister Margaret Thatcher, for the Irish Government, which owned Aer Lingus, had objected. With only two aircraft and managing to convey 82,000 passengers in one year, Ryanair decided to expand its operation by opening further routes linking Ireland and Luton Airport. The latter could cope with little expansion, so late in 1991 Ryanair moved its main operations to Stansted, which appealed to it for several reasons. It was only 15 miles from the M25 London orbital motorway, which provided an easy link with South East England. Stansted had plentiful car parking spaces, 2,200 for short stay and 8,000 for long stay.

Ryanair was running at a loss. Chief Executive Michael O'Leary, given the task of making the airline profitable, travelled to the USA. He visited Southwest Airlines, which was operating a no-frills, low-fare, fast-turnaround, no-business-class, one-model-aircraft-type business. Ryanair would emulate the Americans.

EU de-regulation of airlines in 1992 gave an operating right between EU countries if one of those involved agreed. Ryanair, making maximum use of that rule, chose cheaper regional airports as destinations. Since Ryanair was providing increased business, it could drive hard bargains and very soon became Europe's largest low-cost carrier. At incredibly low fares it carried 2.25 million passengers in 1995, many of them from Stansted, and in 1997 became a public company. There was at this time another common sight at Stansted. Go Fly, with Barbara Cussini as CEO, had begun operations on 22 May 1995 and was a very busy B737 operator. Nevertheless, it was Ryanair that by the start of the new Millennium was dominating Stansted's traffic, although it was not alone at the airport.

With Ryanair remaining in that position, EasyJet, more associated with Luton, opened operations at Stansted on 31 May 1998 by despatching a flight to Rome. On 10 May 2002 EasyJet purchased Go Fly, the company fully merging with EasyJet in August 2002, by which time twenty-six destinations were being served. EasyJet was not intending to overtake Ryanair at Stansted – it was more a case of having to move to expand because of congestion at Luton.

Dominant in Stansted skies, Ryanair and Boeing 737-800s like EI-DCX (George Pennick).

Air UK's fortunes changed in 1999 when KLM became the sole shareholder. In 2000 the new company – renamed KLM uk – continued using BAe 146s, Fokker F50s and F100s, the latter being a Fokker F28 jet derivative with a more modern wing aerofoil section. With an all-up weight of 91,500lb, its fuselage was lengthened by nearly 19 feet to 115ft 10in. Able to carry 107 passengers, it was a relatively rare sight, except at Stansted. Powered by two Rolls-Royce Tay turbojets, its construction when compared with the smaller F28 featured increased use of composites.

Flying accidents at the airport have been few. The most spectacular involved a Boeing 747 of Korean Air Cargo, which, during the evening of 22 December 1991, crashed soon after take-off. Four died in the horrendous ensuing fire, after the aircraft came down by Hatfield Forest.

Stansted's longing for prestigious long-haul operators remained, but they were too well entrenched at Heathrow, a hub airport offering immediate transfer from long-haul to a wide array of short-haul destinations, UK internal and external. Heathrow and Gatwick both have plentiful, extensive, rapid and easy communications with central London and many other parts of the UK, prompting the question of why anyone would wish to undertake the longer journey to or from Stansted.

Nevertheless, several long-haul operators have tested its use. From May to September 2001 1990s Continental Airlines operated a Boeing 757-200 service to Newark, NJ, brought to an abrupt end by the criminal acts of 11 September 2001. The most successful long-haul operator has been El Al, using Stansted due to excessive demands on its Heathrow services. Incredibly tight security surrounded its operations, and also those of Israir Airlines. El Al moved to Luton in April 2009 and commenced services from there on 3 May.

In 2000 Ryanair passenger booking became completely 'on-line', although recently there has been change. In 2001 the company started establishing mainland Europe hubs, one at Charleroi and another at Frankfurt/Hahn, from where twenty-six Ryanair services were initiated. The company also concentrated on the use of one precise type of aircraft, the Boeing 737-800, which, in the new century, has very much become Stansted's aeroplane. Large orders were placed for the type, for delivery over an eight-year period.

On 6 February 2002 sanctuary was sought by hijackers aboard an Ariana Afghan Airlines Boeing 727 carrying 156 people. Tucked away in the south-eastern corner of the airfield, it sat at the preferred UK destination for hijackers requesting unlawful landing. The stand-off lasted four days, then all aboard safely left the aircraft. Apparently the hijackers had decided that this was a smart way to asylum in the UK, and some others aboard colluded with them. Incredibly, and surely deplorably, the highly illegal immigrants who wished to stay in Britain were officially welcomed.

Hardly surprising, in view of such extraordinary and unneighbourly activity on their doorsteps, in 2002 the 'Stop Stansted Expanding' (SSE) movement started in earnest. SSE's overall aim has been to contain the airport's development within tight, readily sustainable limits. To protect quality of life over a wide area, together with much local heritage, the movement fast gathered support among 100 local council outfits. By 2008 SSE had 6,000 members, whose greatest concern was that government would force change, including the building of a second runway and another terminal, possibilities that have come to dominate Stansted's possible future.

Ryanair expansion continued through 2003. By the end of the year it was recording its first loss, due mainly to competition. Nevertheless, Stansted's throughput increased, encouraging Ryanair in 2005 to want more Boeing 737s. Forecasters suggested the carrying of 34 million passengers a year, perhaps as many as 70 million by 2011. That was prior to huge increases in fuel costs and the international monetary collapse.

Ryanair was, of course, not alone at Stansted. A number of smaller airlines operated, and there were scheduled and charter services to Montreal, Toronto and Vancouver. Pakistan International Airlines opened a service in August 2006 running an Airbus A310 twice weekly to Karachi, and once a week to Islamabad. The EU banned all flights on 5 March 2007 for reasons of safety. The ban was lifted on 29 November 2007, but not until April 2009 were there briefly more flights. It was, incidentally, then that the Israeli Airline, El Al, announced its move to Luton Airport.

With passenger numbers high, on 28 April 2006 BAA approached Uttlesford District Council with a plan to increase the permitted number of aircraft movements to 264,000 annually and a removal of restrictions on passenger numbers. On 29 November 2006 the Council turned down the application, so BAA appealed. That resulted in yet another public enquiry, which took place from 30 May to 19 October 2007. In January 2008 recommendations were presented for scrutiny by two transitory and unlikely government 'experts'. In March 2008 BAA applied for permission to build a second runway, to open in 2015. Some eighteen listed buildings would need removal, and attractive countryside would be lost.

One thing was clear. No-frills operators were certainly attracting many passengers, private and business. In 2006 aircraft movements totalled 206,693, and 23,687,013 passengers passed through the airport, making the forecast 25 million realistic. In the first quarter of that year alone, passenger numbers had risen by 25% to 10.7 million, due particularly to the assertive business style of Ryanair. The total between October 2006 and October 2007 peaked at just over 24 million, but then reduction started. To keep profitable, Ryanair had, since 2005, been forced to raise the cost of flying. That came about not just through increased fares; in 2007 its passengers had to pay for check-in, no longer possible on-line.

It was during 2007 that Stansted at long last attracted one of the world's most prestigious mainstream transatlantic carriers, American Airlines. In October it began a daily service to J F Kennedy Airport, New York, and had in mind commencing a second service starting in April 2008, but instead it halted its Stansted venture on 2 July 2008. MAXjet operated some flights to Las Vegas, Los Angeles and Washington DC before being forced to cease operations on Christmas Eve 2007. EON Airlines, which served Dubai, filed for bankruptcy in April 2008 and ceased flying. The basic problem remained: long-haul services failed to attract sufficient trade away from Heathrow.

In 2008 Ryanair became Europe's largest airline by passenger numbers carried, and the world's largest in terms of internal destination passengers. The company, with 161 Boeing 737-800s all fitted with winglets, had on order another 138, with options on another 170. The company had, however, become tough, demanding, and faced complaints concerning hidden extras, deceptive advertising and poor cabin service – even for a no-frills operation.

In October 2008 twenty-nine passenger-carrying airlines were using Stansted, serving thirty-four countries and flying to more than 160 destinations. There were 120 check-in desks in the terminal and twelve ticket desks. Aircraft stands totalled sixty-five, thirty-seven being in multiples. Stansted was employing some 11,600 people. Aircraft movements were averaging around 182,000 a year, annual passengers numbers some 22.8 million. Stansted was at this time Britain's third busiest airport, 46th in the world. Ryanair, still by far the number one, was reaching ninety-eight destinations. Second by way of services, EasyJet was flying to twenty-seven, after which came Air Berlin with eight and Cyprus Turkish Airlines with six. EOS served Dubai, United Arab Emirates. Others operating included German Wings, WIZZ Air and Norwegian Air Shuttle. Since then the latter has moved to Gatwick, also now used by former Stansted resident, Air Malta. The most popular international destinations served were, in order, Dublin, Rome/Ciampino and Milan/Bergamo. In the UK they were Glasgow, Edinburgh and Prestwick. The most popular destination, overall, was Spanish territory.

Holiday charter operators numbered seventeen, busy among them being First Choice (becoming Thomson Airways on 1 May 2009), and Thomas Cook Airlines.

Ten cargo carriers were also using Stansted, which was handling about 203,000 tonnes of cargo annually. FedEx Express was serving eight destinations and the Boeing 747s of BA World Cargo flying to six. Regular internal flights were being made, together with others to Europe, the Far East and USA, operators including USP and Royal Jordanian. Titan Airways, Stansted-based for twenty years, had scheduled cargo services to Belfast, Edinburgh and Exeter, in addition to VIP passenger runs to Lourdes. Stansted was receiving many international private and business flights from around the world. Mohammed al Fayed keeps his helicopter and regional jet aircraft here, and military aircraft are sometimes to be seen, as well as aircraft wearing a wide range of exotic colours.

Airbus A.319 G-EZIG of easyJet early on 14 February, 2009.

Norwegian Air Shuttle Boeing 737 LN-KKW arriving for Tromso passengers on 14 February 2009.

A Stansted sparse long hauler, Air Asia Airbus A.340 (George Pennick).

What final effect the higher cost of fuel and chaotic international financial state will have is impossible to predict. In September 2008 Ryanair announced a reduction of 14% in flights during the coming winter season, lowering its total to around 1,600 a week and representing a reduction of around 900,000 passengers. World financial problems have undoubtedly hit Ryanair quite hard. A £5 charge was introduced on 1 May 2009 for on-line booking – or £20 at the airport. All booking would need to be online from October 2009, when all check-in desks would be closed. Luggage would then need to be left at a drop-in site. Around 130 destinations were still being served in the autumn of 2008.

During 2008 a 6,000sq m terminal extension for arrivals opened, and a sixth baggage reclaim belt came into use. Additional shops, opened in December 2008, showed courage in difficult times. On 11 March 2009 Air Asia introduced a Far East service using a leased Airbus A340, at which time it looked as if more approval might eventually be won for the government-permitted annual passenger number to rise to 35 million. A second runway at the time of writing remains in the very distant future.

Whatever happens, Stansted faces four inhibiting factors. It is further from London than Gatwick and Heathrow. The every-15-minutes rail journey to London Liverpool Street takes at least 40 minutes and costs £17 single and £26 return, which is not cheap. The other two major London airports are easily accessible, and by public transport plying from many directions. Stansted's local catchment area – not all that populous – is shared with the reasonably near, busy and popular Luton Airport. If one lives in East Anglia or Eastern England and needs a short haul to many destinations, Stansted is very accessible and avoids much dense traffic.

Throughout Stansted Airport's long life, never has there been a public viewing area, which is most unfortunate. Although something at last is to be provided, its position overlooking the 05 end of the runway nullifies its value. Also, this small feature is orientated to educational rather than recreational activity. Many fascinating aeroplanes, exciting to watch and a joy to harmlessly photograph, pass through, such as large, noisy and impressive ageing Antonov An-12s. There are several niches where one can harmlessly enjoy such sights. Perimeter security – indeed, all security – is tight, as it most certainly should be. The invasion of Stansted by protestors was utterly deplorable.

Main features (December 1944):
Runways: 243° 6,000ft x 150ft, 190°, 134°, concrete and tarmac. The present asphalt surfaced runway 05/23 has a length of 10,000ft. *Hangars:* four T2. *Hardstandings:* fifty-six circular. *Accommodation:* 417 officers, 2,241 enlisted men.

STEEPLE MORDEN, Cambridgeshire

52°03N/00°06W 168ft asl; TL302420. 2 miles N of A505, between Litlington and Steeple Morden village

Those living locally had it worked out. Since no hangars were visible they must be underground! Reality was that Steeple Morden began life as an Unbuilt Satellite, a glorified grass field supplemented by tents, a few huts and a perimeter track. When in late summer 1940, Wellington Is, Ias and Ics of No 11 Operational Training Unit Bassingbourn began flying from their satellite, one had only to 'disappear' from its normal dispersal squat to its home station to convince everyone that it had gone to earth! I know because I heard that tale many times and sometimes saw the vanishing Wimpey soon after – at Bassingbourn.

Steeple Morden was used for circuit flying and basic type conversion. Cross-country flying, bombing exercises, gunnery training along with other operational training was undertaken at the elaborate Permanent, parent station.

The foregoing beliefs did not fade easily, especially when in darkness German tourists arrived – very unconventionally. It was partly cloudy, a night when disorientation during a stressful flight would easily happen. Intruder activity was well underway in the area while night Blitz operations were causing Luftwaffe bombers to transit the region to their targets. On the night in question – 15/16 February 1941 – Birmingham was the main target. Among the participants was a Junkers Ju 88A-5 of III /KG 1, V4+GS, Werk Nr 6214. Quite new it was too. built by the parent firm Junkers Flugzeugbau at its main factory, Dessau, and with some parts from the Oranienburg Heinkel works. The Luftwaffe had accepted it on 11 November 1940.

As its crew headed home they became completely lost, believing they were over France. Actually, they were over Cambridgeshire and by then in bright moon-light. They switched on their landing light and when challenged by a Blenheim crew fired their signal cartridges then proceeded to land cross-wind over Steeple Morden's goose-neck flarepath and touched down on the far side of the field. Immediately, the aircraft's starboard undercarriage leg collapsed, the propeller, wing tip and engine cowling being damaged as the machine slewed across the grass. An Armadillo raced to the black Ju 88 and soon it was surrounded by a wide circle of RAF men. The crew in boiler suits dejectedly left the aircraft with the captain coming out last, Luger in hand. Several airmen rushed forward to grab it but instead he passed it to an officer. Only the aircraft's radio was of much interest; the airframe was too badly bent to fly again.

Meanwhile, 11 OTU flew on, and in 1942 supplied some of the force for the '1,000 bomber' raids. Some of the participants in the Cologne raid setting off from Steeple Morden.

After 11 OTU left Bassingbourn in September 1942 Steeple Morden fell quiet but only until mid-October. The first Americans had already moved in by 26 October when the 3rd US Photo Group arrived under Colonel Elliott Roosevelt's control. It was at this time that runways were quickly laid and hangars erected. Without knocking down a number of private houses enlargement of the landing ground was not really possible although an extension to the main run allowed a 3,200ft long concrete runway. After the US servicemen left for north-west Africa the RAF returned and between 13 January and 4 May 1943, Blenheim 1s of 17 OTU used the station until retirement. Then they were stored here.

In July 1943 the Americans returned, this time as the 355th Fighter Group flying P-47s. Operations began on 14 September 1943 with a fighter sweep over Belgium. Soon the Group soon switched to bomber escorts and by April 1944 had converted to flying P-51B Mustangs and later used P-51Ds and P-51Ks. The 355th's travels took the Group far – to distant Berlin, for instance, to Karlsruhe, Gelsenkirchen and Minden. But it was not just in fighter escort that they excelled, for the 355th was credited with the highest score of 8th AF Group of enemy aircraft destroyed during ground strafing.

P-51B-5-NA 43-6815 of the 358th FS, 355th FG.

With its aircraft armed with bombs the 355th also attacked airfields, locomotives, vehicles, radio stations and bridges. On D-Day they provided fighter cover for the Allied invasion later supporting the St-Lô break-out. Interdiction and escort duties continued to the end of the war, after which the Group left for Germany and joined the occupation force. As well as over 300 aircraft claimed in combat, the Group also laid claim to over 500 destroyed on the ground.

During their stay at Steeple Morden the 355th had some odd companions as well as those 17 OTU Blenheims which may well have been the last Mk 1s to have seen much active service. The Americans, ever ready to accept a good thing, had a Mosquito T III and one of the earliest to enter service. They also used for target towing a B-26 Marauder of ancient vintage. To allow the RAF to re-possess Debden the 4th Fighter Group spent four summer months at Steeple Morden.

After the USAAF left the station passed from one administrator to another until in March 1946 the decision was made that it had no future as an airfield and was then wholly abandoned. It closed on 1 September 1946 and was later sold for agricultural use. Apart from concrete areas the main item at the point where the P-47s and 51s used to cross the road to their dispersals is an imposing memorial.

Main features:

Runways: Steeple Morden for well over its first year was a grass field Unbuilt Satellite. When three runways were added they were shorter than normal viz: 220° 4,800ft x 150ft, 160° 3,300ft x 150ft and 280° 3,225ft x 150 ft and constructed of concrete and wood chips. *Hangars:* one T2 and nine Blister hangars. *Hardstandings:* eighty of concrete, for fighters. Accommodation (USAAF): 210 officers, 1,749 enlisted men.

STRADISHALL, Suffolk

52°08/00°30E 382ft asl; TL720515. By the A143, 7 miles NE Haverhill

'Gentlemen, we are at war. Your target for this first attack is – Berlin.' Pause, for gasps of astonishment. 'I need hardly add that it's going to be a difficult operation.' Luckily in September 1938 it never came to that, although incredibly Berlin really was the target chosen for Stradishall's Heyfords, and had the Munich crisis turned to war ... but the result is too awful to contemplate. Fortunately, Heyfords had been replaced before hostilities commenced.

Few stations can boast such a variety of uses as Stradishall. For over thirty years, and with barely a break, it was active and served in all home-based Commands except Army Co-operation. Many early photo-reconnaissance flights operated out of here and, continuing the 'spying' theme, 138 Squadron flew from here to drop agents.

Stradishall, although far from complete, opened on 3 February 1938 under Group Captain J H Herring DSO, MC. Nos IX Squadron with Heyford IIIs and '148' with Wellesleys began arriving on 10 March. Policy change soon resulted in the long range Wellesley's moving to Egypt and the Middle East leaving No 148 Squadron to take, in November 1938, the retrogressive step of rearming with Heyford IIIs while maintaining their monoplane skills by flying Ansons.

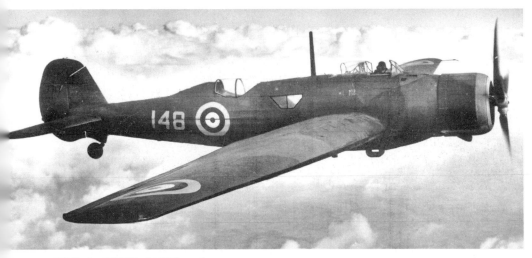

Wellesley K7747 of 148 Squadron.

In 1938 Stradishall joined that elite corps of aerodromes where metalled runways were added construction of a 3,000ft x 150ft strip starting late that year. True, Heyfords and runways do present a bizarre companionship, but they were intended for use by the new, exciting Wellington 1s with which No IX Squadron re-equipped in February 1939 and 148 Squadron the following month. On 15 July 1939 No IX moved out and was immediately replaced by 75 Squadron's Wellingtons and Ansons. These and 148 Squadron formed 3 Group Pool which trained and assembled crews to operate Wellingtons. They moved to Harwell on the outbreak of war.

On 9 September 1939, with the move complete, the station went to Care & Maintenance to the end of October 1939, then diversity set in. Stradishall re-opened to accommodate two specialised fighter squadrons, No 254 formed on 30 October and '236' formed the following day. Both received Blenheim If fighters, 254 leaving for Sutton Bridge on 9 December 1939 and '236' moving to Martlesham Heath the next day.

Stradishall's 3 Group bomber career resumed when the New Zealand Flight arrived on 15 January 1940. They left for Feltwell on 12 February. On 1 February 1941, 3 Group's training or towing Flight began its varied career and left for Newmarket on 21 May. It was the Wellington Ias of 214 (Federated Malay States) Squadron which began arriving on 8 February 1940 that was the main event, apart from a number of photo-reconnaissance sorties by Spitfires of No 3 PRU which used Stradishall as their advanced operating base. '214' came to be regarded as 'Stradishall's own' for they took part in many operations and stayed until 1 October 1942.

Stradishall in the early war years was home to Wellingtons of No 214 Squadron including T2476 reported missing from operations on 8 November 1940. (Imperial War Museum)

When No 15 OTU was established at Harwell by amalgamating Nos 75 and 148 ex-Stradishall squadrons a new '148' Squadron formed on 30 April 1940 at its former home only to disperse again on 23 May, possibly due to problems of establishment. No 150 Fairey Battle Squadron mauled in France began recuperation here on 6 June 1940 such being the chaos of withdrawal that it took two weeks to gather the survivors. They moved to Newton early July to join a new No 1 Group. Another squadron briefly associated with Stradishall was No 215 formed here on 9 December 1941 and passed through Bassingbourn in early January before proceeding overseas in February 1942 by which time much had happened.

For instance, Stradishall had its share of intruders the worst incident coming early in 1941 when bombs from a Ju 88 badly damaged a hangar. On 20 February two HEs cratered the main runway. Wellingtons were at this time being flown at night to the Middle East from here and Newmarket by ferry crews of 3 Group Training Flight, also known as the Reserve Squadron. At the end of April 1941 the Flight moved to Newmarket whose long run was ideal for fuel-packed overloaded bombers.

Another unit frequently using Stradishall was No 1419 Flight which centred its operational activities at Newmarket. They arrived at Stradishall on 9 October 1940 as 419 Flight and became 1419 Flight on 1 March 1941 and No 138 (Special Duties) Squadron on 25 August 1941. Its Whitley Vs were often seen on Stradishall's southern side dispersals. In November 1941 the squadron transferred most of their activities to Stradishall, their base for ninety days under Wing Commander Farley's command. During that period the Whitleys flew from here fifty sorties – to France, Poland, Holland, Norway and Czechoslovakia – before leaving for Tempsford in March 1942.

April 1942 saw No 214 Squadron convert to Stirling 1s, the last Wellington operation involving minelaying off Kiel on 29 April. Stirling operations commenced on 18 May and involved minelaying. On 27 June during a raid on Bremen N3751 flown by Sgt Frank Griggs was repeatedly attacked by fighters three of which were shot down, an amazing achievement. Badly damaged, the Stirling was skilfully belly landed at Stradishall. Main Force Stirling operations continued until 1 October 1942 when the squadron moved to Chedburgh which had opened as Stradishall's second satellite on 7 September.

Another facet in Stradishall's history came underway on 6 April 1942 when No 109 Squadron's HQ and 'C' Flight arrived. The remainder arrived later. Flying Wellington Ics from Stradishall they carried out radio reconnaissance duties and had the distinction of carrying out the first *Window* trials. On 4 July , 'B' Flight left for Gransden Lodge to become 1474 Flight. Head Quarters and the Wireless Development Flight remained at Stradishall where 109 Squadron was now re-organised on a two-Flight basis and held a mixture of Wellington Ics, IVs and VIs although apparently only the high-altitude Wellingtons were ever here from where, it is claimed, some reconnaissance operations were flown over Germany by one of them.

On 24 July an additional Flight equipped with six Mosquito IVs was formed then the squadron moved to Wyton to join the Pathfinders on 6 August 1942. The Wellington VIs, outclassed as flare droppers, had already left Stradishall.

Nudged out of Bourn by XV Squadron which was edged out of Wyton by the PFF, No 101 Squadron flying Wellington IIIs became Stradishall's next occupants but only briefly between 13 August and 30 September when they left to join 1 Group.

It was all change again when on 1 October 1942 No 1657 Conversion Unit formed replacing 214 Squadron. Opening at half strength of sixteen Stirling Is and a few Oxfords, it later doubled its strength and also made use of Shepherd's Grove from mid May 1944. Oxfords of 1521 BAT Flight arrived in autumn 1942 and stayed until 15 March 1943. Stradishall became the HQ station of 31 Operational Base on 26 April 1943, controlling Ridgewell (replaced by Wratting Common) and Chedburgh Sub-stations. Stradishall had been attacked by intruders more often than many stations, and on 22 October 1943 ten bombs and incendiaries fell on the camp damaging some buildings in this final raid. In a change of Command structure the station became HQ 73 Base on 1 November 1944. No 1657 CU disbanded on 15 December 1944.

On 17 December 1944 Stradishall rejoined 3 Group and became operationally active with the arrival of No 186 Squadron and their Lancaster IIIs here to the end of the war. They disbanded on 17 July 1945.

Stradishall passed to 47 Group and Transport Command on 1 August 1945, Nos 51 and 158 Squadrons flying Stirling CVs moving in during mid-August 1945. No 158 Squadron disbanded on 1 January 1946, but 51 Squadron continued flying Stirlings until March 1946. Their first York arrived on 16 January 1946, conversion taking place here and in June 1946 at Wratting Common while Stradishall's runways were resurfaced. The last Stirling left in April, route flying to the Far East using Yorks began on 1 July and before No 51 moved to Waterbeach between 14 and 18 August 1946.

Stradishall returned to 3 Group on 19 September 1946 by which time 35 Squadron flying Lancaster BI (FEs) were moving in from Graveley. No 115 Squadron, similarly equipped, joined them on the 27th also two other squadrons – Nos 149 and 207 – during November 1946. Lancasters remained until February 1949 when they moved to Mildenhall leaving Stradishall to pass to Care & Maintenance on 18 February.

On 27 April 1949 Stradishall's future was reviewed – it would become an advanced flying school. Within the GCI area it would train fighter pilots and others to work with the Army. By re-opening time on 6 July 1949 it had been transferred to Fighter Command. On 1 September No 226 Operational Conversion Unit reformed here to train all pilots for day fighter squadrons. No 226 took the entire output of Driffield's No 203 AFS, and also trained pilots for fighter reconnaissance squadrons. Used were Meteor 4s and 7s and assorted Spitfires – Mks 14, 16 and 18 – into the early 1950s. Vampire 5s

*Lancaster
B.1(FE) PA386
QN-Y of No 214
Squadron 1947.*

Meteor F4s like EE517 photographed at Stradishall equipped 226 OCU, along with Vampires.

were used until January 1951, Harvards for slightly longer. The start of 1950 saw a new plan within which Stradishall would become the base of Nos 19 and 41 intruder squadrons which would in 1951 equip with Meteor 8s. That fell by the wayside and 226 OCU remained busy here. In November 1950 the Meteor element of the OCU had an input of two thirty-four-pupil courses every four weeks taking two-month courses and the Vampire squadron ran two fourteen-pupil eight week courses.

To cope with the tasks 226 OCU in July 1951 had forty-six Meteor 4s. Aircraft types remained unchanged until Meteor PR9s replaced Spitfires in mid-1951. Tempest 5s and Beaufighter TT10s were briefly used for target towing, but Martinets bore the brunt of the task and were not withdrawn until early 1954. Mosquito TT35s had then taken over the role. Mid-1952 saw Meteor 8s became standard equipment supplemented by Meteor 7s. A few Oxfords served between 1949 and 1955, Vampire T11s from 1953 to1955. A Balliol, Tiger Moths and Mosquito T3s extended the assortment of types employed before No 226 OCU closed on 1 June 1955. Opened under 12 Group, the OCU had been a part of 81 Group since 18 February 1952 then passed to 11 then 12 Groups.

March 1955 saw it regain operational status for it was strategically well placed. To suit it for the new role a large ASP was built as an apron before the hangars, and ORPs were laid at each end of the main runway. Dispersal pans on the west and south-west areas were given blast wall protection. On 31 March No 125 Squadron reformed here with Meteor NF11s before re-equipping with Venom NF3s in January 1956. Their service was short, No 125 disbanding on 10 May 1957. Between 9 June and 18 July No 253 Squadron worked up with Venom NF2s then moved to Waterbeach. No 89 Squadron also reformed here on 15 December and used Venom night fighters.

Another night fighter squadron, No 152, was also Stradishall-based in the second half of 1956 using Meteor NF 12/14s. They returned with 263 Squadron on 18 August 1957 and left with them

Post-war Stradishall was a fighter station at one-time housing Venom night-fighters of No 89 Squadron.

With them were Meteor F8s (WF740 and WK893 depicted) of 245 Squadron.

on 8 July 1958. Longest-stay resident at this time was 89 Squadron which, in October 1957, converted to Javelin 2s and 6s. No 85 Squadron, similarly equipped, was based here between 30 November 1958 and 7 September 1959.

By then Stradishall was mainly a Short Range Day Fighter station, for No 1 Squadron's Hunter 6s arrived on 2 July 1958 and 54 Squadron joined them on 1 August 1958. Whilst here both converted to Hunter 9s, 1 Squadron leaving for Waterbeach on 7 November 1961 followed by 54 Squadron on the 21st.

Stradishall in 1960, and part of 12 Group since the autumn of 1959, hosted 208 Squadron rarely be seen as yet in the UK. Here from 1 April to 30 May, they were working up for overseas using Hunter 9s. Other Hunter squadrons also made use of Stradishall including 'Treble One' from 15 July to 13 September and 43 Squadron between 23 September and 13 October 1960.

The final stage in Stradishall's RAF history started on 1 December 1961 when it was transferred to Training Command and No 1 Air Navigation School moved in bringing Varsities and Meteor 7/14s. The latter served until the start of 1966, the first Dominie TIs arriving late 1965 to replace them. Dominies for training fast jet navigators and Varsities for heavier types remained in use until 27 August 1970 when 1 ANS left for Finningley. With that departure Stradishall's RAF days were over if not its notoriety.

Varsities like WF370 used for air navigation training were Stradishall's final RAF aircraft.

It figured in the news when used to accommodate Ugandan refugees fleeing from Amin's repression. Now, with its hangars gone, it is a forbidding place surrounded by high security fences for in July 1977 the site became HM Prison Highpoint. Its inmates have included the infamous Myra Hindley. Recently it has shown a kinder face – it is possible to hold a dinner party in the one-time Officers' Mess and in a rehabilitation exercise be waited on by some of the inmates. Change is certainly abounding.

Main features (December 1944):
Runways: 250° 6,000ft x 150ft, 320°, 040°, concrete. *Hangars:* five Type C, three T2. *Hardstandings:* thirty-six heavy bomber type. *Accommodation:* RAF: 184 officers, 659 SNCOs, 1,367 ORs; WAAF: 10 officers, 26 SNCOs, 498 ORs.

SUDBURY (ACTON), Suffolk

52°03N/00°45E 220ft asl; TL895435. NE of Sudbury town by B1115, W of Great Waldingfield. Layby-cum-gateway on roadside offers good view

Sudbury Town Hall carries a memorial plaque to the 8th AF which occupied this airfield for some twenty months. Sudbury was yet another temporary wartime bomber base of the usual type and often referred to as a Class A Airfield. Like so many it basically comprised three runways, two maintenance hangars and a variety of huts serving many purposes one of which was to accommodate around 2,800 personnel. Both T2 hangars, portions of perimeter tracks and some hardstandings still survive within an agricultural environment.

From late March 1944 to late August 1945 the 486th Bomb Group, 3rd Air Division, was based here. Although assigned to the 3rd Air Division, a B-17 organisation, they initially operated B-24H and J Liberators. Insufficient B-17s were available to equip the two Bomb Groups newly based at Sudbury and Lavenham so temporarily they operated Liberators. They were placed in the 92nd Combat Wing to operate closely together, which helped to ease tactical problems caused when aircraft of mixed types and characteristics operated within one formation.

Liege rail centre was the target when the 486th BG undertook their first combat venture on 7 May 1944. In the course of forty-six missions the B-24s bombed airfields, communications targets, V-weapons sites, gun batteries and participated in invasion support activities. After that they backed up the American advance across Europe. With the availability of B-17Gs much improved the B-24s flew their last sorties on 19 July then the 486th stood down to convert to 'Forts'. In less than a fortnight the Group was declared operationally ready and on 1 August the 92nd CW resumed operations with an attack on Tours airfield. Their first major mission – against Berlin – came on 6 August, then the Group's operations from Sudbury became mainly strategic in nature. Targets ranged widely and included marshalling yards at Stuttgart, Mainz and Cologne, airfields at Kassel and Munster, the docks at Kiel and Bremen, oil refineries at Merseburg and Hamburg and numerous factories. They also gave tactical support during the September airborne landings, during the Ardennes battle and for the Rhine crossing. B-17 missions totalled 142, the final venture taking place on 21 April 1945.

Sudbury had a short life as an active airfield, and after the Americans moved out in August 1945 it fell quiet. Its strategic position made it of potential use as a standby fighter station for which reason, like Lavenham, it was cared for on a low key basis with runways and perimeter track kept in reasonable condition along with the T2 hangars. In Plan G of 1951 its Standby status was confirmed to continue. On 13 November 1952 a decision was taken to develop it as a USAF base. Work was started, Sudbury being classified as a 'construction site' until October 1955. The work was never completed, the requirement lapsed and it was eventually released fully for civilian use between 1962 and 1964 following the V-Force rundown which led to further reductions in fighter defence.

Main features:
Runways: 250° 6,000ft x 150ft, 190°, 150°, tarmac on concrete. *Hangars:* two T2. *Hardstandings:* fifty spectacle type. *Accommodation:* 443 officers, 2,529 enlisted men.

Places of interest nearby:
Hedingham Castle features a Norman keep in fine condition seeing that it was built in the 1140s and is still owned by a descendent of the Earls of Oxford, original owners. Visited by Henry VII, Henry VIII and Elizabeth I, it is set in beautiful grounds containing woodland. Well worth visiting, its stands off the B1058 road between Sudbury and Hedingham. Close by is the Colne Valley Railway, which operates steam-hauled trains.

SUTTON BRIDGE, Lincolnshire

52°45N/00°12E 9ft asl; TF485205 9 miles W of King's Lynn, by A17

Travelling west from King's Lynn along the A17 a most unusual assortment and layout of huts and buildings used to came into view to the left immediately prior to crossing Sutton Bridge. They, and a large field, sufficed for a temporary aerodrome set on the low fenland alongside the major river Nene and not the best position for an aerodrome which, in 1940, was of supreme importance to the Nation. When I first saw it the slate roofed buildings were obviously permanent Married Quarters, but there did not appear to be any recognisable hangars, although there was a collection of temporary canvas shelters bordering the small landing ground. Actually those were Bessonneau hangars more at home with the RFC than the RAF although not entirely lost to the Service until the late 1970s. My initial siting having come on a Sunday, no aircraft were visible. There were a number of puttied airmen about for this was 1936.

Taking its name from the bridge alongside, an RAF landing ground used as an Armament Practice Camp opened in 1926. Fighter and light bomber squadrons of the RAF and Fleet Air Arm temporarily stayed in Spring and Summer carrying out gunnery and bombing training using ranges in The Wash. Sutton Bridge was used in this manner for ten years, the few buildings judged sufficient including tents for personnel and canvas hangars for aircraft. During this early period Sutton Bridge attracted Gloster biplanes, Furies, Hawker Hart and derivatives along with Bristol Bulldogs – all mainstream types of the period.

Come 1936 and it was all change. With fast increasing and more sophisticated operational training needs Sutton Bridge acquired permanent buildings and changed into being a full-time permanent Royal Air Force station administered by No 25 Group, Training Command. Married quarters were added, and newly established SHQ now administered No 3 Armament Training Camp which on 1 April 1938 was renamed No 3 Armament Training Station. It attracted front-line fighter squadrons and was the base for Westland Wallace target tugs resplendent in yellow and black stripes. When war started No 3 ATS moved to distant West Freugh.

September 1939 saw Sutton Bridge transferred to Fighter Command and established as a base for a Fighter Pilot Pool, forerunner of the wartime OTU scheme by which newly trained pilots underwent operational conversion training. This led on 30 October 1939 to the re-formation here of two 'new' squadrons, Nos 264 and 266, equipped initially with Battles for training only. The former – scheduled to be the first Defiant squadron – left in December 1939 to receive them at Martlesham. No 266 rearmed with Spitfire 1s in January 1940 and on 1 March 1940 also moved to Martlesham. Meanwhile No 254 Squadron flying Blenheim fighters had been in residence between 9 December 1939 and 28 January 1940. Brought from Stradishall to counter German mine layers and anti-shipping raiders, they were here until space for them became available at Bircham Newton.

A camouflaged Westland Wallace biplane in use at Sutton Bridge in June 1939. (Ron Clarke)

Probably on 6 March 1940, No 11 Group Fighter Pilot Pool, transformed itself here into No 6 OTU, one of three fighter OTUs then formed. Equipped with Hurricanes and Gladiators, Sutton Bridge OTU became vital to national survival for it was largely responsible for training Hurricane pilots during the Battle of Britain. At that time it was packed with aircraft, its establishment calling for fifty-three Hurricanes supplemented by a few Gladiators, Master 1s, Harvards and a communications Mentor.

Increased activity resulted in additional domestic temporary accommodation being erected in the nearby village. No 6 OTU was renamed No 56 OTU on 1 November 1940 and when No 81 Group formed at Sealand on 28 December 1940 to administer Fighter Command training No 56, in common with other fighter OTUs, then came under new management. Day fighter OTU courses holding twenty-five pupils were now lasting seven weeks, two courses running concurrently.

That pattern of training continued throughout 1941 with Hurricane Is and IIs forming the basic strength. Then came the Standardised Training Scheme which in March 1942 laid down a pattern calling for three courses each of thirty-two pupils per course at each Day OTU. Sutton Bridge could not cope with such numbers so on 29 March 1942 the OTU moved to Tealing, near Dundee.

When that change came about the station at once reverted to No 25 Group, Flying Training Command, and from Chelveston on 1 April 1942 the Central Gunnery School arrived. That unit offered courses for Gunnery Leaders and Pilot Gunnery Instructors, instruction involving air-to-air firing at towed targets and air-to-ground firing on the now very active Wash ranges. In the main the School relied upon Wellingtons, Hampdens and Spitfires while Henleys of No 1489 Flight provided the towed target facilities. Previously, from October 1941 to 13 April 1942, No 12 Group TT Flight's Lysanders had performed that task.

An all-yellow Hawker Henley L3260 in use at Sutton Bridge during 1939. As target-towers they served in wartime from stations in north Norfolk. (Ron Clarke)

On 22 February 1944 CGS moved to Catfoss and Sutton Bridge came under the control of No 21 Group, Flying Training Command. After a very brief spell as Newton's satellite, it was handed to Peterborough on 29 March 1944 becoming its satellite. Elements of No 7 (P) AFU brought along Oxfords in June 1944.

Sutton Bridge was now giving flying experience in the European environment to those trained in good weather overseas. With numbers of those decreasing, the unit was re-titled No 7 SFTS on 21 December 1944, and remained active here until April 1946 when a move was made to the Permanent Peacetime station at Kirton-in-Lindsey. Sutton Bridge always looked so small, yet it had played a vital part in the air war, but then so often places of historical importance do not convey impressions of their importance.

RAF occupancy was far from finished, maybe due to the presence of the pre-war married quarters. The hangars, too, were used from July 1954 by No 58 MU whose task was recovery and salvage of crashed aircraft. By then the wartime metal runways had long since been removed and the grass landing ground was in agricultural use.

On 1 November 1957 No 58 MU disbanded and the site had been mostly sold except for the married quarters useful for personnel serving on The Wash ranges. Remaining technical site buildings were gradually given over to agricultural use in what is a major farming area.

Main features:
Runways: For most of its use Sutton Bridge was a grass airfield, but mid-war saw the 3,450ft runway 080° laid using PSP and 2,400ft long runway 130° laid using Sommerfeld Tracking. There was also a NE/SW grass runway of 4,200ft. The landing ground was nevertheless rated grass only at all times with the river Nene as its somewhat disconcerting western boundary. *Hangars:* In December 1944 one ARS Type permanent, two Bellman, twelve 69ft Blister. *Hardstandings:* fourteen of tarmac laid on hard core. *Accommodation* (December 1944): RAF: 109 officers, 110 SNCOs, 1,266 ORs; WAAF: 6 officers, 12 SNCOs, 361 ORs.

Places of interest nearby:
King's Lynn has for 900 years been a maritime trade centre and has attractive buildings. Ships sail to Sutton Bridge quay and through to Wisbech. Castle Rising has a fine Norman Keep from which distant views can be enjoyed.

SWANNINGTON, Norfolk

52°44N/01°10E 135ft asl; TG141205. 1 mile N of Swannington, by the Brandiston Road, which encircles the site

Nowadays they would be called cruise missiles, although the 1944 German equivalent, the V-1 flying bomb, had neither the range nor the accuracy of its modern counterpart. Nevertheless, any cruise missile bombardment of the invasion force gathering in Britain during early 1944 could have posed a very serious threat to Allied victory. Fortunately the V-1 campaign started not on 1 January 1944 as intended, but after the Allies were already lodging in France.

Although anti-aircraft gunners and fighter pilots could readily locate V-1s in daylight they found it quite difficult to destroy them before they reached areas where serious damage and loss of life could be inflicted. Exhaust glare was very visible at night, but their flight speed usually approaching 400mph and low altitude run still made interception difficult. Mosquito XIX night fighters carrying narrow band centimetric radar could find and indeed catch them, but those were a precious commodity in June 1944. So serious was the night threat that Flights from the only two squadrons of these sophisticated night-fighters, based at Swannington, were detached to West Malling almost at the beginning of the flying-bomb assault, and within days of having started bomber support operations in 100 Group, and on 21 July both squadrons moved completely to Malling.

Flying-bombs came over in salvoes intended to swamp the defences. They had to be expected at any time of the night or day which meant maintaining costly standing patrols. Although shooting down a V-1 was far from easy, during July and August 1944 Swannington's 85 Squadron managed to destroy thirty and No 157 laid claim to another forty.

Construction of their three runway temporary wartime airfield home began on 3 November 1942, the station opening on 1 April 1944 in 100 Group. Arrival of the two squadrons, 85 and 157 at the start of May 1944 brought the airfield to life, and both possessed enviable night fighting credentials. No 85 had been led by Wing Commander John Cunningham and 157 Squadron was the first to operate Mosquito fighters. First to be equipped with Mosquito NF XIXs fitted with AI Mk X radar, the two squadrons introduced them to night operations on 5/6 June 1944, the night of the Normandy invasion. No 85 Squadron patrolled over the beach landing area while No 157 watched for responses at Dutch airfields. Not until 12/13 June was the first kill using a Mk XIX achieved and by Flight Lieutenant J G Benson of 157 Squadron who shot down a Ju 188 at Compiègne. No 85's first success followed on 14/15 June, a Ju 88 destroyed over Florennes.

Both squadrons – which returned to Swannington at the end of August 1944 – had experience of a new night phase, the launching of V-1s from He 111s. Their return to Swannington saw them, however, immediately resume their prescribed bomber support night role. As a result of that activity 85 Squadron was ultimately credited with forty-three kills, No 157 with twenty-eight. Before the war ended both squadrons rearmed with high flying Mosquito NF 30s. The squadrons flew their final operational sorties on 2/3 May 1945 when they provided high-level support during Bomber Command's last night raid, on Kiel.

No 85 Squadron left for Castle Camps on 27 June 1945 whereas No 157 Squadron stayed at Swannington, wound down and disbanded on 16 August. The station's 100 Group days ended on 30 September 1945.

Replacing them, HQ No 274 MU administered by 41 Group formed 1 October 1945 to store and reduce Mosquitoes here and at sub-stations – Little Snoring, North Creake and Oulton. Soon they were packed with Mosquitoes mainly ex-100 Group and all carrying the latest radar and looking quite exotic. Swannington closed to flying on 30 June 1947, disbandment of the MU came in November and the airfield site was sold for agricultural and semi-industrial use on 22 February 1957.

A narrow road encircling the site provides a view of the control tower which remains to the west of the north side industrial area. The best view of the airfield is across fields from the north where again the tower may be seen also some huts. On the west side the road crosses runway remnants and part of the perimeter track. This road also passes close to the surviving stop butts.

Main features:
Runways: 276° 6,000ft x 150ft, 320°, 230°, concrete. *Hangars:* two T2, one B1. *Hardstandings:* thirty-six spectacle type. *Accommodation:* RAF: 154 officers, 161 SNCOs, 1,055 ORs; WAAF: 10 officers, 12 SNCOs, 248 ORs.

SWANTON MORLEY, Norfolk

52°43N/00°58E 150ft asl; TG009185. NW of village

Swanton Morley was unusual having just one metal Type J hangar, immediate pre-war style buildings and was completed without metalled runways. The usual mix came because of a decision to complete it quickly and mainly for fighters. Instead it was mostly used by light bombers.

Building commenced in early 1939 and, since only one large 'K' hangar (changed to a Type 'J') was to be placed here, completion came fairly quickly, opening taking place in September 1940. On 31 October, 105 Squadron moved in bringing Blenheim IVs. They took a very active part in 2 Group's 1940-41 day and night bombing campaign and anti-shipping duties. It was from here that Wing Commander Hughie Edwards led a low level raid upon Bremen for which he was awarded the Victoria Cross. For three weeks in May 1941 they were away at Lossiemouth, between July and October in Malta, which readily allowed long-range Spitfire IIas of No 152 Squadron to utilise vacant space between 31 August and 1 December 1941.

The year's most prestigious event at the station came when, on 15 November, Geoffrey de Havilland Jr brought to 105 Squadron the first Mosquito bomber to enter RAF service. He provided a stunning aerobatic show amazing crews accustomed to the rather staid Blenheim. Such Mosquitoes were a rare commodity for months, only a handful reaching 105 Squadron before they moved to Horsham St Faith on 9 December 1941.

No 226 Squadron in the process of converting to Boston IIIs, replaced '105' during December. They were prematurely thrown into action during the 'Channel Dash' and it was on 8 March 1942 that their planned campaign began. Both Nos 88 and 226 Squadrons flew to Thorney Island and from there set out to deliver a low-level attack on Ford's Matford Works at Poissy near Paris. The six Bostons successfully bombed the factory, but Wing Commander Butler leading '226' either flew too low or was caught by the blast of exploding bombs, for his Boston soon crashed. Many *Circus* operations followed.

In August 226 Squadron operating from Thruxton laid smoke to screen the Dieppe landings, a precursor to the role Bostons played on D-Day.

Shortly before, an even more portentous event had taken place. Personnel of the USAAF's 15th Bomb Squadron (Light) had arrived at Swanton Morley, and by the end of June 1942 seemed ready to use some of 226's Bostons for operations. On the afternoon of 29 June four Americans climbed into a Boston at Swanton Morley then became the first of their nationals to carry out a bombing attack in Europe. On suitably chosen 4 July twelve Bostons, nine crewed by Americans with each section being led by experienced RAF personnel, set off to carry out low-level attacks on Dutch airfields. They took a pasting from enemy gunners during their highly eventful operation. Nevertheless, Americans were now on the scene and their numbers would soon increase.

Circus operations continued from Swanton Morley until poor weather arrived late in the year. Practices for the Eindhoven raid then occupied the Boston crews, twelve aircraft of 226 Squadron participating in that outstanding operation for the loss of one. Withdrawal of the Boston IIIs for north African service reduced operational capability until the Mk IIIA became available, but aircraft numbers increased here when Horsas arrived for storage. *Circus* and *Ramrod* operations were resumed and continued until 14 February 1944 when No 226 Squadron moved to Hartford Bridge. Its equipment had changed in mid-1943 when Mitchell IIs arrived allowing more Bostons to be released for use elsewhere. Employing Mitchells, 226 Squadron flew many daylight *Ramrods* against Continental targets including V-sites.

Others had shared Swanton Morley with the main occupants. Oxford-equipped No 1515 Blind Approach Training Flight formed here on 20 September 1941 and remained until November 1943. No 1508 BAT Flight came on 29 August 1943, became No 1508 (Gee Training) Flight on 1 March 1944 and, apart from a short time away, used Swanton Morley until June 1944. On 4 September 1943, 305 (Polish) Squadron had arrived to work up on Mitchells before leaving on 13 November to receive Mosquito FBVIs. Typhoons of 3 Squadron were also here between late November 1943 and February 1944. Apart from a team drawn from the glider support MU, No 228 MU was here from 4 October 1942 until 18 February 1943 and No 206 MU formed here on 26 June 1943 and remained until 21 August 1944.

In December 1943 No 2 Group's gunnery training flight, No 1482 B&G Flight arrived from Great Massingham bringing along Mitchells, Venturas and Martinets. On 1 April 1944 the Flight became the nucleus of 2 Group Support Unit whose task was to hold trained aircrew who could quickly replace any lost during the forthcoming invasion. No 2 GSU flew a variety of aircraft types – including Mosquito IIIs and Hurricanes for fighter attack training – and in September 1944 operated the six Ansons of No 2 Group Communications Flight. The unit moved to Fersfield in mid-December 1944.

Air support for the invasion of Europe by day was assured. Equivalent, effective night operations against the Wehrmacht were also needed. March 1944 saw Mitchells of 98 Squadron arrive at Swanton Morley to work out such tactics, initial trials taking place on 29/30 March over a road through the Stanford Battle Area. A day later 2 Group's 'great names' gathered at their nearby Bylaugh Hall head quarters to discuss the result of the trial. It was resolved that attacks would be made either against large targets lit by flares or by single Mosquitoes strafing roads, each crew being allocated a precise area to patrol and attacking every sign of enemy movement. On 25/26 April Swanton Morley was the base for a large-scale exercise as a result of which the plan was confirmed the plan was laid. Once the landing in Normandy had been made the trials were translated into operations, and until the end of the war the night interdictor work of Mosquitoes played a major part in the reduction of the Wehrmacht. In March-April No 98 Mitchell squadron and three flying Mosquitoes – 464, 487 and 613 – undertook night interdictor training here.

When 2 Group left in December 1944 the station switched to 100 Group whose Bomber Support Development Unit arrived on the 23rd. So important had radio warfare become that the BSDU was upgraded and became the Radio Warfare Establishment on 21 July 1945 and which moved into permanent post-war accommodation at Watton late September 1945. At Swanton Morley they had flown mainly Mosquitoes. The 100 Group Mosquito Servicing squadron was also to be found at Swanton Morley in early 1945, and the airfield's proximity to 100 Group HQ at Bylaugh meant that their Communications Flight formed on 9 February 1944 made use of the station until June 1945.

Being outclassed by many others as a front-line airfield November 1945 saw it pass to Flying Training Command and No 10 Air Navigation School arrived from Chipping *Warden* on 1 December 1945. They used mainly Wellington T10s also Ansons and Oxfords and moved out in September 1946. No 4 Radio School using Ansons and Proctors took their place on 5 December 1946 the unit becoming No 1 Air Signallers' School on 1 May 1951 which flew Anson 21s and Prentices. On 1 January 1955 the station passed from 27 Group to 23 Group and to 25 Group control on 1 January 1957. No 1 ASS became No 1 Air Electronics School on 1 April 1957 whose main equipment was the Anson T22. The School moved to Hullavington on 23 December 1957.

January 1958 saw the arrival from Winthorpe of the Central Servicing Development Establishment, whose experienced staff, mainly NCOs, developed the best methods of handling and servicing technical equipment. The Maintenance Data Centre moved in as a lodger during 1968. CSDE, the last major RAF unit based here, transferred to Wyton in 1995.

Swanton Morley being a grass field has long proved ideal for ATC gliding purposes undertaken by No 1 Gliding School and later by No 611 VGS until 1995. It has also been used by the Norfolk & Norwich Aero Club.

Closure day came on 6 September 1995, the Ensign being lowered as the Duxford Blenheim passed. Being one of the last pre-war airfields to be laid down, Swanton Morley displayed a mixture of the expansion period and hurried compromise demanded by war. Now in Army hands and called Robertson Barracks. The Light Dragoons, the Band of the Dragoon Guards and 12 Medical Squadron are based here.

Main features:
Grass runways: NE/SW 4,950ft, NNW/SSE 4,800ft, NW/SE 4,050ft. *Hangars:* one Type J, four T2, four Blister. *Hardstandings:* thirty-one frying pan. *Accommodation:* RAF: 157 officers, 422, 1,389 ORs; WAAF: 4 officers, 17 SNCOs, 369 ORs.

TEVERSHAM, Cambridgeshire – see CAMBRIDGE

*B-17G-1-BO
42-31049, an
early example,
being flown by
the 100th BG.*

THORPE ABBOTTS, Norfolk

52°22N/01°12E 165ft asl; TM180812. Turn off A143 at Thorpe Abbotts; by-road encircles airfield and joins perimeter track. Narrow roads lead to the airfield's excellent museum

Norfolk has a number of shrines – one of the very best is at Dickleburgh, near Thorpe Abbotts. By whichever route you arrive don't be put of by the need to negotiate narrow roads for they lead to something really excellent, the memorial to the 100th Bomb Group and the US 8th AF. Arrive during May and you might win the bonus of clusters of cowslips, hedgerows of wild roses and a splendid avenue of horse chestnut trees stylishly lining your final approach. Ample parking and picnic space, refreshments and visitor centre in a finely restored large wartime Nissen hut are welcoming features. Now you are ready to explore the tower which, like Framlingham's, has an additional vantage point from which to gaze across that one time 'field' thinking of B-17Fs and 'Gs of the 3rd Air Division's 100th Group whose 'D in a square' tail identity is presently perpetuated on Mildenhall's KC-135s. Exhibited in the tower are superb photographs, uniforms, decorations, equipment of past days, models all patiently cared for by a volunteer force. Please make a contribution to the upkeep of this splendid museum for entry is completely free – unlike the cost of upkeep.

Where, you may ask, is that 'shrine' to which the answer is 'all around you' for Thorpe Abbotts has always been a highly evocative place. The 100th, 'The Bloody Hundredth', repeatedly endured exceptionally high losses, 177 aircraft and all that implies. Expended bravery is highlighted by two DUCs awarded for courageous battles.

Base opening time came during April 1943 when the Americans took over this satellite of Horham. Although completed to the general wartime pattern, its landing ground was less usual being of a 'broad armed' L-shape and its longest runway stretched almost parallel with the northern leg of the perimeter track. From the tower this can be envisaged.

'The 100th', during June 1943, came from Podington after awaiting completion of their future base. Arriving on 9 June they flew their first mission (and lost three B-17s) on 25 June 1943. Their first major mission came on 17 August when, as part of the 3rd AD force, the 100th attacked Regensburg then carried on within the cavalcade making for North Africa thereby undertaking the first shuttle bombing mission and winning a Distinguished Unit Citation.

Between June 1943 and June 1944 the Group participated in many 3AD raids on strategic targets. An outstanding period came in March 1944, for on the 4th, 6th and 8th the 100th upon each date fought their way to Berlin for which they received their second Distinguished Unit Citation.

Support to the invasion and subsequent main events followed before oil targets in particular felt the effect of their bombs. The 100th helped pave the way for the capture of Brest and between October and December 1944 concentrated upon transport targets and then ground defences during the assault on the Siegfried Line. Dropping supplies to the French Resistance won them the Croix de Guerre with Palms for a duty performed between June and December 1944.

*Thorpe's control tower in early summer 1945, 351st BS B-17 on Hardstand 8.
(Capt Carl Thorkelson/100th BG Memorial Museum)*

Smoke trails stream spectacularly from falling target markers as B-17s of the 351st BS 100th BG from Thorpe Abbotts release their loads. (100th BG Memorial Museum)

B-17 23413 HARD LUCK of the 350th BS from Thorpe Abbotts flying a mission with newer B-17s of the 100th. The aircraft went missing in August 1944. (100th BG Memorial Museum)

During 306 missions flown from Thorpe Abbotts the 100th certainly suffered horrific losses before their last raid of 20 April 1945. The intention was to have the 100th as part of Occupation Force Germany. Instead, they gradually wound down here, the last personnel leaving in mid-December 1945. An RAF presence had been established in June 1945.

The site closed in April 1956 after the decision (probably taken in July 1948) that although in the Defended Area it had little Standby or strategic value. Official interest ceased in April 1956.

The control tower's state in the 1970s remained good enough for its preservation along with a few adjacent buildings. So, the late Mike Harvey and Ron Batley, keen to restore the tower as a memorial to the 100th, formed a small group who approached the land owner, Sir Rupert Mann. His response, 'What a good idea', was all that could be asked for and he granted a 999 year lease. Until recently the runways, some dispersal areas and the perimeter track were still visible but now only the main lines are discernible.

Main features:
Runways: 099° 6,600ft x 150ft, 350°, 043°, concrete topped with tarmac. *Hangars:* two T2. *Hardstandings:* fifty loop type, some of modified style. *Accommodation:* 421 officers, 2,473 enlisted men.

Places of interest nearby:
The 100th Bomb Group Memorial Museum is by Common Road, Dickleburgh reached by turning off the A140 to Thorpe Abbotts at Dickleburgh bypass seventeen miles south of Norwich. Alternatively, follow the A143 Scole-Bungay road two miles from Scole passing through the village of Billingford. The Museum (Tel: 01379 740708) is generously signposted. It is open at weekends and on Bank Holidays and Wednesdays in summer from 1000 hrs to 1700 hrs. During November, December and January it is closed.

Pulham St Mary airship station was near here. Occupying Home Farm and Lincolns Farm, it opened in February 1916. The first 'ship', a coastal reconnaissance blimp, arrived on 31 August 1916 and was soon followed by more. Their role was to seek German submarines off the East Coast, for which purpose the blimps operated from forward coastal sites. Airship armament trials were undertaken here, and in

1918 they included attempts to attach fighter aircraft to airships, from which they were launched for defensive purposes. German Zeppelins L64 and L71 came for post-war examination. The most famous airship tested at Pulham was the R33, which arrived from Howden, Yorkshire, on 2 February 1921. This was involved in fighter launch and retrieval trials. During a gale on 16 April 1925 R33 suffered serious damage to its nose, which collided with the mooring pylon. Flight Lieutenant R S Booth, 1st Officer, and his crew managed to fly the damaged airship to safety and, off the Dutch coast, rode out the storm. They brought the airship safely home next day and a new nose was fitted. On 21 April 1926 the airship *Norge* arrived from Italy for use by the Norwegian explorer Amundsen. On 12 May 1926 he flew the airship across the North Pole on his journey to Alaska.

In 1928 one of the station's two giant airship sheds was removed and taken to Cardington, where it was re-erected for use by the Royal Airship Works. The remaining hangar was, on 23 July 1940, hit by bombs from a Do 17. These created explosions that generated a fearsome and spooky moaning and groaning sound heard for miles around. No 53 MU Pulham Market (opened on 12 August 1940) functioned as an ammunition depot with sub-sites at Bungay, Earsham, Old Buckenham and Seething. It disbanded on 1 February 1958, and the site was sold on 1 August 1962. Parts of the Officers' Mess and a few other buildings survive.

TIBENHAM, Norfolk

52°27N/01°09W 178ft asl; TM145888. Off A140 N of Diss; turn left off B1134 then right for airfield

For seventeen months Tibenham – part of which was a landing ground in WWI – housed B-24Hs and 'J's of the 445th Bomb Group which arrived in November 1943 and returned to the USA during May-June 1945, after flying 282 mainly strategic bombing missions. Commanding the 703rd Bomb Squadron upon its arrival was the late Captain James Stewart.

Personnel of the 445th were not the first Americans at Tibenham. Some members of the 320th Bomb Group sojourned here in autumn 1942 awaiting a part in operation *Torch*. After they left, the base saw use for flying training, but not until the 44th arrived did it really come into play.

The 445th's first mission, the first from Tibenham, was a raid on Kiel carried out on 13 December 1943. Subsequently they bombed such varied targets as the synthetic oil depot at Lutzkendorf, a chemical factory at Ludwigshaven, Hamm's notorious marshalling yards, an airfield at Munich, underground oil stores at Ehmen and an ammunition centre at Duneburg. For their part in the attack on the Gotha aircraft factory on 24 February 1944 they received a Distinguished Unit Citation.

Participation in the pre-invasion attacks on France followed and operations were flown in support of the US Army on D-Day and during the St-Lô breakout. The Ardennes offensive was also supported. Tibenham's Liberators were particularly active on 24 March 1945 dropping food, medical supplies and ammunition to airborne forces at Wesel. Later that day they bombed the landing ground at Stormede. Leaflets were dropped on France in the summer of 1944 and fuel was ferried to advancing American forces. For their drops of supplies to the French Resistance between December 1943 and February 1945 the Group were collectively awarded the Croix de Guerre with Palm. Their final operation took place on 25 April 1945.

Tibenham's Group had one unwanted distinction, the highest casualty figure for any one operation in the 8th Air Force, when on 27 September 1944 they lost to fighter interception a staggering twenty-eight aircraft out of thirty-seven despatched.

The 445th BG officially moved out on 28 May 1945 and the RAF retrieved the station in July 1945. After a spell in Maintenance Command and allocation as a Standby station, part of the landing ground was sold off in 1952. Tibenham's main runway was lengthened in 1955 then the station was allocated for USAF use on 18 October 1956. A detachment from the 7536 Material Squadron (AMC) arrived on 20 October 1956 and stayed until 25 May 1957 when the unit disbanded and the airfield was returned to British control. It closed in March 1959. Runways and the perimeter track remain partially intact and the Norfolk Gliding Club has used the station since 1960.

Main features:
Runways: 211° 6,000ft x 150ft, 268°, 332°, tarmac and concrete. *Hangars:* two T2, *Hardstandings:* fifty frying pan and loop type. *Accommodation:* 421 officers, 2,473 ORs.

TUDDENHAM, Suffolk

52°18N/00°35E 65ft asl; TL760710. Turn off A11 at Barton Mills roundabout, airfield SE of village

You can't see the airfield for the trees and the gravel excavations which also make it hard to believe this was a bomber base active still at the dawn of the space age.

Building of Tuddenham to replace Lakenheath in the 3 Group Mildenhall Base structure was completed on 30 September 1943. Although opened on 1 October it was not fully operational until 31 December 1943.

First in came No 90 Squadron whose Stirling IIIs arrived from Wratting Common (West Wickham) on 13 October 1943. They first operated from here, laying mines, on 17/18 October. Much further minelaying was undertaken by the Stirlings which also undertook SOE drops from Tuddenham. Stirling Ills were replaced by Lancasters during May 1944, their first operation, against Dreux, taking place on 10 June. No 90 Squadron operated to the end of the war from here, by night and day, and against a variety of strategic and tactical battle targets. The latter included the June 1944 raid on Villers Bocage and others to assist a break-out from Caen. In September they participated in the reduction of Le Havre and in October the attack on West Kapelle. Raids on strategic targets included many directed at synthetic oil plants and the rail network of Germany. Throughout the final year of the war, Tuddenham's Lancasters were very busy.

On 5 October 1944 'C' Flight, 90 Squadron, was hived off to form the nucleus of 186 Squadron which, when complete, moved to Stradishall in December 1944. No 138 Squadron, no longer required for special duties at Tempsford, moved to Tuddenham on 9 March 1945 to reorganise as a 3 Group Lancaster squadron. They commenced bombing operations on 29 March 1945.

Both squadrons were retained in the interim post-war Air Force and re-equipped with brand new Lancaster B1 (FE)s which made them suitable for overseas service as well as in their maritime attack role. Two other squadrons, Nos 149 and 207 both similarly armed, left Methwold for Tuddenham in mid to late April 1946. All were by now at half squadron or cadre strength, so that Tuddenham held on average twenty-four Lancasters. Only briefly, though, because at the end of May 1946 No 138 moved to Wyton to re-equip with Lincolns.

The remaining three squadrons quit Tuddenham during November 1946 for their post-war permanent station, Stradishall. Tuddenham then closed to flying, but having had a brief post-war career, was retained as an Inactive Airfield supervised by Mildenhall for possible development as a bomber station.

In answer to the US Government's constant clamour for more airfields in Britain Tuddenham was on 30 June 1953 allocated for USAF use as a sub-station of North Pickenham. From 1 September 1953 it was occupied by a detachment of the 7559 Supply Squadron (Ammunition) and until that unit disbanded on 30 June 1958. Tuddenham was then returned to British control and late 1958 work began on building an enclave for three Thor IRBMs. On 22 July 1959 'C' Flight of 77 Squadron was renamed 107 Squadron which became effective at Tuddenham on 1 September 1959 and was fully operational and nuclear warhead armed by May 1960. The Thors were withdrawn from front line at midnight on 30 June 1963, and the squadron disbanded on 10 July 1963 after which the site was disposed of.

Main features:
Runways: 300° 6,000ft x 150ft, 067°, 186°, concrete. *Hangars:* two T2, one B1. *Hardstandings:* thirty-eight loop type. *Accommodation:* RAF: 116 officers, 290 SNCOs, 960 ORs; WAAF: 8 officers, 16 SNCOs, 260 ORs.

UPWOOD, Cambridgeshire

52°26N/00°08W 75ft asl; TL270845. Off B1096, 2 miles SW Ramsey

'I can't help crying, Mike', said a hardened ex-RAF soul as we took almost certainly our last look at Upwood. Its four dejected 'C' Type hangars still overlooked the Fens from their 'hilltop', two with their ends bricked in, a modification undertaken in connection with the huge USAF hospital established here and where provision was made to receive a vast number of casualties resulting from *Desert Storm*. The parade ground was still there and the water tower, along with a Sergeants' Mess more imposing than many. Materials used in constructing many of the buildings give Upwood a

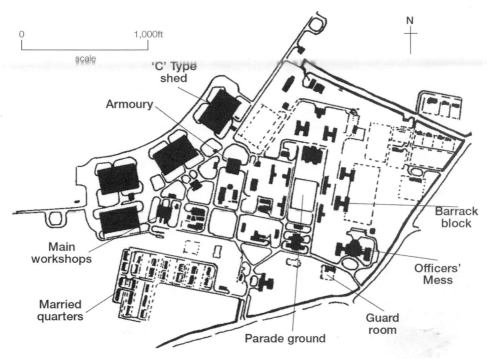

UPWOOD

Upwood – construction of which began in 1936 – was an early expansion station set on a Fenland isle. Although laid out as a five-hangar heavy bomber station, only four of the planned 'C' Type sheds were erected along the usual curved apron line following the landing ground shape while giving some measure of protection from air attack. Less usual was to position the main guardroom almost facing the Officers' Mess alongside of which was SHQ followed by the two-storey Sergeants' Mess affording accommodation for 105 SNCOs. Five barrack blocks included Type 'O' for three NCOs and sixty-eight airmen and 'R' for three NCOs and sixty-four airmen. Later thirteen barrack huts were built each for an NCO and twenty-four airmen. As initially completed the airmen's dining room was for 168 and was separate from the NAAFI building. Married quarters were on the western end of the site. Main stores and main workshops were in distinctive buildings with large doors, and the MT section utilised an eleven-bay shed. The engine test house was a feature not found at all stations of the period. On the apron sat the watch office and tower. Bomb stores were in the north-west corner of the flying ground. Maintaining the strict pecking order of those times three tennis court areas were available – one for Officers, one for SNCOs and one for other ranks.

grey look which makes it, so long after closure, a very sad looking place. Where the control tower stood there's just the flat base, and the landing ground has long since become agricultural territory. I could almost hear it begging me not to let it go, to find it a Blenheim or two or in desperation a Battle. I shall remember it as it used to be, a scene of intense Blenheim activity and with the Avro Tutor of Station Flight in the circuit.

Of course, this is not the only Upwood, there was a former one situated roughly in the north-west area of the 1940s airfield. It served as a night flying training camp to which, for example, No 191 (Night) Training Squadron came in July 1918 and disbanded on 26 June 1919.

Abandoned Guardroom at RAF Upwood in August 1999.

Officers' Mess, Upwood, became the Mathies NCO Academy USAF.

The one-time Sergeant's Mess, unusually next to the Officers' Mess and facing the Main Guardroom.

Barely had the grand expansion period aerodrome opened in January 1937 when it occasioned much interest for to Upwood came the first of the RAF's Fairey Battles. Although twice as fast as the Hawker Hind they replaced, the Battle's performance still left much to be desired. That was obvious as they flew about the area seeming to make leisurely progress and would almost float in to land. Their condition was due to them having been designed to be powered by the first Rolls-Royce Griffon engine based upon the engine used in the Supermarine Schneider Trophy winning seaplanes. When Rolls-Royce failed to deliver Fairey looked to their large, complex 2,000hp Prince engine but it might have been unsuitable. Instead they settled for the 1,200hp Merlin 1 which was insufficiently powerful for this quite large single-engined aeroplane.

Battles began joining No 63 Squadron at Upwood during May 1937. When '63' arrived on 3 March they were using Hinds and Audaxes. No 52 Squadron, which had flown in their Hinds a few days before 63 Squadron arrived, had to wait until the end of 1937 for their Battles.

The Battle's range was too short to enable it to attack Germany from Britain, and poor manoeuvrability linked with insufficient armament rendered it useless for ground-attack purposes. Only by operating from advanced bases in France could the Battles bomb Germany. Therefore when they stood at high readiness during to attack western Germany during the Munich crisis they also formed a mobile force ready for deployment to France. On the outbreak of war both 52 and 63 Squadrons had a non-mobilising role as training squadrons within 6 Group and promptly moved out of Upwood.

There they were replaced by Blenheim Is of 35 and 90 Squadrons supported by Ansons all providing operational training for 2 Group.

In April 1940 these were amalgamated becoming 17 OTU in 6 Group and from 15 June part of 7 Group which became 92 Group on 11 May 1942 and shared Blenheim bomber training for home and overseas squadrons with 13 OTU Bicester. Every day the sky around Upwood seemed full of the forty-eight Blenheim Is and IVs on nominal strength flying circuits or undertaking training sorties some to the bombing ranges off Holbeach. Circuit flying also took place at Warboys, the satellite between May 1941 and mid-1942. To late 1941 the Blenheim formed the backbone of the RAF at home and abroad. In a search for replacement early Douglas Bostons were briefly tried out here in 1941 and found inadequate for the war in Europe. Many who achieved fame in 2 Group and other Blenheim equipped organisations passed through Upwood, and sadly a large number flew very few sorties before being posted as missing.

Maybe the presence of No 1511 BAT Flight and its Oxfords between September 1941 and late April 1943 was partly responsible for it was at Upwood that the Woods brothers' developed Synthetic Night Flying using a Battle. For this, the pilot was masked and could only make out the take-off lane by the sodium flares placed along its sides. A Blenheim, Oxford and Anson were also involved in the trials. All types used by 17 OTU.

No 17 OTU disbanded at Upwood in mid-April 1943, moved out and quickly reformed as a Wellington OTU. Their movement allowed runway building to commence on 18 May 1943 with completion coming late October. Halifaxes and Lancasters of the PFF NTU made limited use of the station from mid-June 1943, but spent more time at Warboys due to the runway work. The station fully re-opened when the runways were completed on 31 December 1943.

At the start of February 1944 No 139 Squadron brought along its Canadian-built Mosquito XXs from Wyton and for night operations under 8 Group. Part of their fleet was fitted with *H2S* radar and 139 (Jamaica) Squadron carried out marking for other Mosquito bomber squadrons when they operated beyond the range of *Oboe*. From Upwood the squadron flew over 3,000 sorties.

The PFF NTU moved to Warboys in March 1944 making a swap which brought along the Lancasters of 156 Squadron Upwood-based until June 1945 and very actively engaged in the bomber offensive as marker and bombing aircraft of the Pathfinder Force.

No 156 Squadron moved to Wyton on 27 June 1945 and then No 105 Squadron took their place along with No 1409 Flight converting Upwood into an all-Mosquito marker station apart from a few Lincolns here for trials in the autumn. No 1409 Flight disbanded on 10 October 1945. When No 105 Squadron disbanded on 1 February 1946 No 139 Squadron joined 109 Squadron at Hemswell to form a new post-war Bomber Command marker team.

Upwood then passed to the control of Transport Command which, on 15 February repositioned No 102 Squadron here from Bassingbourn and on 1 March 1946 re-numbered it 53 Squadron. By then the new arrival's Liberators were joining in the repatriation of troops to India. March saw forty-three flights from Upwood bound for Mauripur and carrying 730 troops to India. Brought back were 811. Yet not until the end of the month had the squadron completed conversion to Liberators which next month allowed the despatch of thirty flights and the return home of 845 men.

Liberators had now to be purchased or cast aside under the sequel to the Lend Lease agreement. Therefore in late April the squadron commenced conversion to Yorks. During May repatriation flights using Liberators ended, the last Liberator returning to Upwood on 16 June 1946. The squadron disbanded on 25 June.

Like so many stations Upwood needed a thorough 'face-lift' after the war. After this was given No 7 Squadron arrived on 30 July 1946 allowing Mepal's closure. Its Lancaster BI (FE) aircraft were joined by others, 49 Squadron in July, and on 4 November by Nos 148 and 214 Squadrons which returned from Egypt.

During 1949 the three squadrons re-equipped with Lincoln IIs which saw overseas detachment and later took part in colonial policing operations in Malaya, Aden and Kenya dropping bombs in anger. Under Plan G Upwood was scheduled to become the main marker force base, the Lincolns moving out. Instead, 230 OCU at Scampton had to disband and make way for USAF B-29s there. Lincoln training still had to be undertaken and Upwood was the most obvious choice. There the Lincoln Conversion Flight was upgraded on 1 August 1953 to becoming No 230 OCU. Lincoln replacement resulted in the OCU reverting to being the Lincoln Conversion Flight on 1 February 1955 which moved to Hemswell on 9 January 1956 to support No 199 Squadron. Also operating from here between 27 March 1952 and 17 October 1955 was the Radar Reconnaissance Flight equipped with Lincolns. Decisions had to be made in the early 1950s as to which airfields should be much improved and runways lengthened for them to accept the V-bombers. Favour swung between Polebrook with the potential for an amazing 14,000ft runway and the expansion of Upwood. Eventually it was Wittering that was chosen for already it had a long runway and a large bomb dump nearby.

Lincoln WD131 of 7 Squadron. Upwood's hangars form the backdrop.

*Fairey Battle
K7650 of No 63
Squadron.*

To allow a fresh bomber force to form No 214 Squadron disbanded on 30 December 1954, No 148 on 1 July 1955 and No 7 on 1 January 1956, as each unit prepared itself for participation in the V-Force. No 49 Squadron had moved to Waddington on 25 June 1952.

In place of Upwood's Lincolns came squadrons of Canberra 2s to form the Upwood Wing established by first posting in 18 Squadron late May 1955 then as others were operationally ready No 61 Squadron late June 1955, 50 Squadron in January 1956 and 35 Squadron late June 1956.

In autumn 1956 Upwood's Canberra B2s took part in the Suez campaign. Eight of 18 Squadron and ten of 61 Squadron joined the Cyprus Bomber Wing, Nicosia, under the command of Upwood's Station Commander, Group Captain G C O Key. They operated on four nights as follows:

31 October/1 November:

Kabrit airfield – four of 18 Squadron as markers

Abu Sueir airfield – four of 18 Squadron as markers, two of 61 Squadron bombing – one aborted

Inchas airfield – five of 61 Squadron bombing

1/2 November:

Luxor airfield – one of 61 Squadron bombing

Fayid airfield – four of 18 Squadron marking, three of 61 Squadron bombing

Kasfareet airfield – four of 18 Squadron marked

2/3 November:

Luxor airfield – four of 61 Squadron bombed

Huckstep camp – two raids: first by four of 18 Squadron marking and, second, eight of 18 Squadron, four being markers

4/5 November:

Al Agani – four of 18 Squadron marking

As soon as the strength of the V-Force permitted the Canberra force began to be reduced. No 40 Squadron, which had arrived in October 1956, amalgamated with 50 Squadron on 15 December 1956. No 18 Squadron disbanded on 1 February 1957 and No 61 on 31 March 1958. Strength was somewhat restored when 21 Squadron flew in from Waddington in October 1958, but it disbanded on 15 January 1959. Flying at the station ceased on 11 September 1961.

Upwood then settled down as a training centre for clerical and accounts personnel. Then it became a store and dormitory for USAF Alconbury before a large wartime emergency hospital was built. In the 1990s the USAF has operated an important clinic here for servicemen and families.

A Lincoln of No 7 Squadron on a western dispersal at Upwood. (Eric Watts)

Closure and disposal of Upwood took place over a protracted period in the early 1990s. The Nene Valley Gliding Club uses a small part of the main runway.

Main features:
Runways: 058° 6,000ft x 150ft, 288° 4,800ft x 150ft, 194° 4,200ft x 150ft, concrete and tarmac. *Hangars:* four 11-bay Type C. *Hardstandings:* thirty-six heavy bomber loop type. *Accommodation:* One main domestic site and three groups of married quarters (December 1944): RAF: 201 officers, 510 SNCOs, 1,374 ORs; WAAF: 5 officers, 11 SNCOs, 320 ORs.

WADDINGTON, Lincolnshire

53°10N/00°31W 235ft asl; SK985645. S of Lincoln, between the A607and A15 roads

Waddington – home of the Vulcan? Probably, although it was here that the Lancaster joined the RAF. Maybe if you are old enough you will recall the relief as you stepped from a Lancaster after a frightening night raid, glimpsed Lincoln Cathedral and knew you had again made it. There will also be another group with more disturbing memories.

Around 1400 hrs on 27 October 1962 a U-2 spying upon Soviet weapons in Cuba was shot down producing a fearsome situation whereby the Western nuclear forces were placed at fifteen minutes readiness. Included were four of Waddington's Vulcans each loaded with an armed *Yellow Sun*, Britain's hydrogen bomb, eight of which were prepared for use by the V-Force which – being nearest to the USSR – would have been first to unleash these ghastly weapons. All through that Saturday afternoon the situation seemed likely to deteriorate and the standby stayed in place. Frantic negotiations were designed to give the Russian leader some means out of the impasse. Eventually he agreed to withdraw his IRBMs from Cuba and the *Yellow Suns* retired too. The world could breathe again, but it was the closest it had ever been to annihilation. For those then at Waddington and other V-force stations and aware of how serious it was, that must remain a sombre memory.

A visit to Waddington shows how favourably it is placed atop the Lincolnshire Heights, just south of Lincoln, and where the first aerodrome of that name opened in November 1916. Like so many others nearby it was a flying training station, base for 47 Reserve squadron controlled by Northern Group Command, York. As the war ebbed and flowed training stations changed titles, Waddington becoming No 48 Training Depot Station. The RFC's No 97 Squadron formed here on 1 December 1917 also as a training unit which, in January 1918, headed for a new home near Stonehenge. Among the aircraft they had operated were Armstrong-Whitworth FK8s, Avro 504s, Maurice Farman Shorthorns, DH4s, 6s, 9s and RE8s the presence of which is so hard to now visualise. Closure came in 1919.

Waddington retained its buildings throughout the post-war rundown. When RAF strength increased, it re-opened in October 1926 as the home of newly formed cadre strength Fairey Fawn light bomber No 503 (Bombing) Squadron. In 1929 their role change to a night bombing and they re-armed with Handley Page Hyderabads. In 1935 they reverted to day bomber, rearmed with Westland Wallaces. Part of the Special Reserve until 1 May 1936, they then became part of the Auxiliary Air Force as No 503 (County of Lincoln) Squadron.

Waddington – a non-split site – was completely rebuilt in the mid-1930s. 'C' Type Sheds replaced the General Service Sheds of the 1920s, there were many new buildings and a concrete apron skirted the Sheds and control tower. Single storey slate roofed huts were replaced by purpose designed buildings and much superior accommodation including married quarters single storey buildings and plentiful tiled roofs.

Operational expansion started when on 3 May 1937 No 50 (Bomber) Squadron reformed. They were followed on 18 May 1937 by No 110 (Bomber) Squadron and on 7 June by No 88 with personnel and aircraft hived off 110 Squadron. All were temporarily equipped with short-range Hawker Hind light bombers intended for Army support. June 1937 saw No 44 Squadron arrive after recently re-forming at Wyton and in July No 88 Squadron moved to Boscombe Down, Wiltshire. Bomber Command, backbone of the new air force, was fast expanding and in December 1937 No 44 received Blenheim Is with No 110 Squadron following suit next month. Both departed for Wattisham in May 1939. No 503 Squadron had disbanded on 1 November 1938 and become the nucleus of 616 (South Yorkshire) Squadron, Doncaster.

By the outbreak of war Hampdens had re-equipped Waddington's squadrons, No 44 in February 1939 and No 50 in December 1938. At 1835 hrs on 3 September 1939, nine Hampdens of No 44 Squadron were part of the force sent out too late to search for German warships off Helgoland. They later flew North Sea patrols, participated in the Scandinavian bombing campaign and in May 1940 began bombing targets in Germany.

Mid-1940 saw remnants of No 142 Squadron pass through on their way to Binbrook following their mauling in France, then in July No 50 Squadron moved out to Hatfield Woodhouse (re-named Lindholme in mid-August 1940).

On 1 November 1940 the second phase in the re-building of wartime Bomber Command began with the reforming of No 207 Squadron. They were to bring into service the most important new bomber, 1,000 examples of which were intended to serve. This was the twin-engined Avro Manchester. Very soon the first examples were exhibiting hosts of trivial faults – hardly surprising, for this was Avro's first bomber and most ambitious design so far. Nor was it long before Rolls-Royce Vulture engine failures were experienced and, even when flying moderately loaded, maintaining height on one engine was difficult. Expectation was that the Vulture would develop into a 2,000hp engine, but it never produced more than 1,760hp.

At Waddington the ill-starred Avro Manchester entered service, with No 207 Squadron. (BAe)

Rolls-Royce was devoting most attention to developing the Merlin and as early as June 1940 Avro suggested fitting four of those reliable but less powerful engines in the Manchester. Air Ministry and the Air Staff would not agree to that for reasons of cost and production upsets, but when they relented the Lancaster was the outcome. Meanwhile, Waddington's personnel persevered with the Manchesters. Six aircraft undertook intensive flying between November 1940 and January 1941 at which time two Manchesters were placed at Coleby for by 31 January thirteen were on strength. The first operation was flown on 24 February 1941, target a 'Hipper' class warship in Brest. Two nights later they ventured to Cologne. Next day a second Manchester squadron, No 97, with eight aircraft came alive and in March 1941 left for Coningsby.

Here, too, the magnificent Lancaster began its operational career like R5556, and with No 44 Squadron.

Through spring and summer 1941 No 207 coped with an errant bomber, heading for Berlin for the first time on 9 May. So bad was the type that on 4 July Manchesters were grounded and 207 switched to operating Hampdens. Manchester operations resumed on 7 August, then on 17 November No 207 left for Bottesford. By then No 44 had a brief taste of what was to come when in September BT308, the prototype Lancaster was briefly based at Waddington.

Before that happened No 420 (Snowy Owl) Squadron RCAF formed at Waddington on 19 December 1941 – equipped with Hampdens. But the highlight was the arrival, on Christmas Eve of three Lancasters for No 44 Squadron. No 420 Squadron who flew their first operational sorties on 21/22 January 1942, when five Hampdens were sent to bomb Emden, could only look on in envy. On 3 March 1942 the first two Lancaster operational sorties were flown from Waddington. Mines were laid in Kiel Bay. On 10/11 March 1944 Squadron flew the first two bombing raids, on Essen.

No 420 operated from Waddington until August 1942 when they moved to Skipton-on-Swale, Yorkshire, and from No 5 to No 4 Group, Bomber Command.

Lancasters were soon an impressive sight in eastern skies, but their existence was kept secret until 17 April 1942 when they carried out their courageous low-level, unescorted daylight attack on the MAN diesel works at Augsburg. Twelve Lancasters, six from Nos 44 and six of 97 (Straits Settlement) Squadron Woodhall Spa showed that even this fast, well defended bomber would need to operate in darkness for seven of the twelve Lancasters were shot down, four en route and three during the attack. Squadron Leader J D Nettleton of No 44 Squadron leading in R5508 was awarded the Victoria Cross. Build-up of the Lancaster force was so rapid that seventy-three took part in the Cologne 'thousand bomber raid' in May.

August 1942 saw IX Squadron from Honington replace No 420 and almost immediately re-equip with Lancasters. Both squadrons operated intensively. No IX moved to Bardney mid-April 1943 and No 44 Squadron left for Dunholme Lodge at the end of May. Waddington soon closed while three runways were constructed.

Re-opening came in November 1943 when the station greeted the Australian No 467 Squadron from Bottesford. They operated from Waddington to the end of the war. On 23 November 1943 a second Australian squadron, No 463, was created by renaming 'C' Flight No 467 Squadron. Both operated from Waddington to the end of hostilities. No 467 was the squadron that operated one of Bomber Command's most famous Lancasters, R5868 'S' Sugar, which completed 137 operational sorties, the second highest in Bomber Command. It can be seen at the RAF Museum, Hendon.

Air attacks on Waddington were relatively few, one of the most effective coming just before Lancasters were returning from Ladbergen on 4 March 1945. A Ju 88 started a fire in the bomb dump proving just how effective a sustained intruder campaign could have been. Operations from Waddington ended when the two squadrons bombed Tonsberg oil refinery in Norway.

Attention at once shifted to *Tiger Force* in which the Australians certainly would have played a part. In a shuffle No 467 Squadron moved to Metheringham in June and in July No 463 went to Skellingthorpe. Waddington was chosen as an early base for long range Lincolns. *Tiger Force* was not needed and the tempo of replacement slackened. No 50 Squadron returned on 25 January 1946 followed by No 61 Squadron from Sturgate on May 1946. Next in on 20 July came No 12 Squadron, all here to fly Lincolns. On 7 October No 57 Squadron arrived already using them. Often Waddington's Lincolns would be seen far from home as they undertook lengthy training flights overseas.

When in summer 1948 agreement was reached to place USAF B-29s temporarily at British bases space was made available at Waddington for one squadron. First in was the 372nd BS, 307 BG whose ten B-29s lodged here between July and November 1948. Dispersing the bombers for safety from air attack also gave them the chance of faster getaway. Between November 1948 and February 1949 the 341st BS, 97 BG was here and briefly four B-29s of the 374 Very Long Range Weather Squadron, 308 Recon Group. In February 1949 Sculthorpe's availability brought an end to this phase.

By 1952 the Lincoln era was clearly ending and in April No 57 Squadron moved to Coningsby. No 100 Squadron spent the period May to August at Shallufa, Egypt, and on returning found that, in July 1952, 49 Squadron and their Lincolns had arrived. The stay was brief for in August 1953 Nos 49, 61 and 100 left for Wittering.

Waddington had been selected for V-force use. Once cleared of aircraft the main 03/21 runway was extended to 9,000ft and widened to 200ft. On the south-east side of its eastern end was laid an ORP to accommodate four Vulcans placed on angled slots for fast getaway. New, stronger dispersal pans were built, interconnected allowing four Vulcans to depart fast in an emergency. Increased, improved accommodation for additional personnel was provided along with an imposing new operations block. Completed at the end of 1956, it had as companion a new electronics centre.

Waddington re-opened on 1 June 1955, again as a Master Diversion Airfield to where Nos 21 and 27 Squadrons flying Canberra B2s came and from Scampton. The Avro Vulcan, which made Waddington its ancestral home, had yet to come. Service trials of the Mk 1 were started by No 230 OCU in mid-1956 then on 21 May 1957 No 83 Squadron re-formed and became the first operational Vulcan squadron. Making way for the newcomers the Canberra squadrons disbanded, No 21 on 30 June 1957 and No 27 on 31 December 1957, by which time Vulcan crew training at 230 OCU was well underway.

On 10 August 1960, No 44 with such special Waddington association re-formed and equipped with Vulcans. No 83 on 10 October 1960 moved to Scampton for they were to become *Blue Steel* users. June 1961 saw 230 OCU depart for Finningley allowing No 101 into Waddington where a third Vulcan squadron was added when on 1 August 1961 No 50 Squadron re-formed. Bringing the strength to four squadrons, No IX arrived from Cyprus in January 1975 along with their Vulcan B2s. No 50 re-equipped with Vulcan B2s in late 1965, No 44 in late 1967 and No 101 soon after. Previously they had been using B Mk1As.

Their role had changed first to low-level penetration. After the deterrent in 1965 passed into naval hands they retained a nuclear capability but also trained in the use of more conventional bombs. It was the use of those in the Falklands conflict which brought Waddington's Vulcans into the public realm.

They were about to be retired when in April 1982 Argentina invaded the Falklands. On 13 April four Vulcans and five crews began flight training with an emphasis on AAR and dropping 1,000lb bombs. By 28 April they were ready to proceed to Ascension, the nearest British base to the remote Falkland Islands, and operation *Blackbuck* to deny the invaders use of the Port Stanley runway came underway.

Vulcan XA904 in Waddington's snow.

Squadron Leader John Reeves of 50 Squadron set off on the very long duration flight. Almost immediately he reported a cracked window making pressurisation impossible. XM607, a Vulcan of 101 Squadron flown by Flight Lieutenant Martin Withers and a crew of six, had also set out from Wideawake, Ascension. Now, accompanied by a fleet of Marham's Victor K2 tankers, they faced the awful prospect of a fifteen hour flight in cramped and partially dark conditions and with a staggering seventeen AAR sessions to cope with. Part of the approach would be at around 300ft, but the computer controlled bombing run would be from 10,000ft. At 0423 hrs on 1 May a stick of twenty 1,000lb iron bombs fell away. It was indeed an amazing venture, the bombs bursting across the runway in a defiant and morale boosting exercise. Five such operations by Waddington's Vulcans proved the value of the British invented in-flight refuelling to the extent that some of 50 Squadron's Vulcans were temporarily used as tanker aircraft. The Vulcan days were ending for they were large, vulnerable to the latest fighters and missiles and the force steadily wound down in favour of Tornados.

Following the departures of the Vulcans in the mid-1980s preparations began to give the station a new role. A huge hangar was built alongside an extensive concrete apron along the northern edge of the site, and to Waddington came seven Boeing E-3D Sentry early warning aircraft, adaptations of the Boeing 707-320B. The first arrived on 1 July 1991, the date when No 8 Squadron reformed to operate them. The RAF squadron, assigned to NATO Early Warning force, would carry out NATO given tasks. Nine crews each of seventeen members were allotted after passing through the Sentry Training Squadron, which became No 23 Squadron in April 1997. Three operational crews were later added in an Operations Flight. STF left 23 Squadron in 2005 to become part of No 54 (Reserve) Squadron. No 8 Squadron was re-established at six crews and No 23 at five. The pooled aircraft carried the markings of 8 Squadron on the port side, 23 on the starboard.

Sentries of No 8 Squadron carried out their first special operations from Trapani, Sicily, monitoring trade with Libya following the imposition of UN sanctions as a result of the 1990 Lockerbie atrocity. They also watched for Russian Bears prowling around the UKADR, first encountering one on 10 June 1990.

The UN arms embargo on the Balkans early in 1992 led to No 8 Squadron participating in operation *Maritime Monitor* flown over the Adriatic naval blockade. Trapani was again its operating base before it was switched to Aviano. From October 1992 the Sentries participated in operation *Sky Monitor*, which banned all military flights over Bosnia. By now the squadron was performing in an Airborne Warning & Control System (AWACS) and a second patrol orbit was introduced on 31 October 1992. Now the aircraft were over Hungarian territory and being assisted by a one-time unfriendly force. Satellite communications provided a direct link with the AW operations centre at Vicenzo, Italy. The Sentries provided airborne control of Combat Air Patrol, Close Air Support and AAR.

Waddington's Sentries again came into prominence during both Gulf conflicts. Since 2001 they have been involved with operation *Herrick*, the Afghan campaign. Additionally, they have been used to monitor situations linked with special events. Their AN/APY-2 radar, looking round and down, is carried above the fuselage in a large rotating disc, which monitors area air activity providing real-time pictures on monitors within the aircraft that can be relayed to ground stations through a data link, and to other airborne aircraft. *Yellow Gate* wing pods contain electronic surveillance equipment. From basic early warning activity the Sentries have become strike and in-flight refuelling co-ordinators. They also have limited maritime look-down ability.

Sentry ZH106 impressively sweeping in over the main road by Waddington.

When operational flying ceased at Wyton in the autumn of 1994 its three ELINT Nimrod R.1s and No 51 Squadron moved to Waddington making the station the main base of the UK's airborne electronic and intelligence surveillance force under No 1 Group, Air Command. Carrying a crew numbering up to twenty-four, the Nimrods seek enemy electronic and radar emissions to update information relating to systems and capabilities. These Nimrods – often away on detachment – played a part in the Falklands War, wearing, according to Argentine sources, Chilean Air Force roundels. These, too, have been active in the Balkans and over Iraq, and are at the time of writing involved in Afghanistan operations.

A further extension of Waddington's importance came with the re-formation of No 5 (Army Co-operation) Squadron on 1 April 2004 under control of No 2 Group. The squadron, which began assembling in September 2003, has a roll of more than 300 Army and RAF personnel – the Army element embraces eight badges – making it the RAF's largest. It operates five very high-flying Bombardier Sentinel R 1 Airborne Stand-off Radar (ASTOR) aircraft, the first of which arrived at Waddington on 6 June 2007. Their Intelligence, Surveillance, Target Acquisition & Reconnaissance role (ISTAR), using sensitive radar, is to monitor over a wide area troop movements and battlefield activity. Acquiring 3D images enables details of vehicles to be downloaded to ground centres, giving real-time data relating to the ground situation. To support the Sentinels, four Beech King Air 350 Shadow R1 aircraft have been added to squadron strength. The Sentinels are expected to be fully operational by 2011.

Sentinel R1 ZJ693 of No 5(AC) Squadron, November 2008.

Reformed here on 5 September 2005 was No 54 (Reserve) Squadron, its number awarded following disbandment of No 54 Squadron at Coltishall on 11 March 2005. The squadron, acting as the ISTAR OCU, trains crews for the three 'airborne platform' types used by Waddington's squadrons.

On 22 April 2008 another Reserve Squadron was formed at Waddington. Taking the title No 56 from the Tornado F3 squadron that disbanded then, it performs as the Test & Evaluation Squadron of the Air Warfare Centre. Through a number of Operational Evaluation Flights it will oversee development within the Sentry, Sentinel and all Nimrod fleets.

In the 1990s Waddington's south-eastern visiting aircraft dispersal area accommodated the UK and foreign air force fighters detached here to make use of BAE Systems' North Sea range facilities for electronic combat practice. In V-force days security at Waddington was very strong, whereas the intensive activity of the 1990s attracted so much interest among aviation enthusiasts that, as a good PR idea and because of heavy traffic on the A15 bringing danger, a large car park was built just south of the runway approach line. French Mirages, Swiss F-5s, Spaniards, an occasional E-2 Hawkeye – together with Tornados and Harriers – could all be seen close to the boundary fence. Changed operational scenarios and fiscal stringency have shunted those halcyon days to become cherished memories. Should the Red Arrows relocate at Waddington there will certainly be public interest..

Station ground protection of Waddington's expensive assets is in the hands of No 26 Squadron RAFR and Rapier FSC SAM organisation, supported by No 2503 (County of Lincoln) RAuxAF Squadron, formed at Scampton in 1979, which has been resident here since 1985. Staffed by regulars and reservists from within a 50-mile radius, these units are based on the station's eastern side, and were deployed for operation *Telic*. Their equipment comprises Land Rovers, 4-ton vehicles and devices for day and night perimeter protection.

Waddington is established as a four-Wing Station comprising Base Support Wing, Forward Support Wing, Operations Wing and, from 1 January 2007, No 34 EAW.

The station holds one other feature, perhaps portentously its most important, for here is found No 39 Squadron, the first RAF squadron to operate Unmanned Aerial Vehicles. In 2004 No 1115 Flight came into being at Creech AFB, Nevada, to work with the USAF and operate the unmanned MQ-1 Predator A. From their distant ground base Predators were controlled over Afghanistan. Their usefulness obvious, 2006 saw the RAF issue an Urgent OR for UAVs. Ordered were three MQ-9 Predator Bs, renamed Reaper by the British. The first example reached Kandahar, Afghanistan, in the autumn of 2007 and in November it was first flown in the hands of a reformed No 39 Squadron, still from Creech AFB. May 2008 saw the UAV cleared to carry AGM-114 laser-guided munitions and GBU-12 LG bombs. The Reaper's all-up weight is around 10,000lb, its duration around 20 hours. It carries a 3,000lb offensive load.

Operated by a team drawn from the three services, Reaper was introduced to operations as a reconnaissance platform. UAVs and UCVs have, beyond doubt, a major future role. In 2008 the RAF established a team of twelve, all non-pilots, to fly UAVs on a trial basis. All were given some piloting experience, but were not trained to 'wings level'. That UAVs will play an increasing part is certain. The replacement of the GR Tornado, could be a UAV. An Unarmed Combat Air System might well comprise a mixture of manned/unmanned combat craft. That would greatly reduce the cost of airframes, and certainly the cost of aircrew training. They would also nullify the need for huge, expensive airfields. Developments at Waddington may come to be seen as the basis for a very different air force. So, is it 'Goodbye, airfields?' No one can yet forecast for sure but the ultimate effect of the 2008 credit crisis will be fundamental.

Main features:
Runways: 212° 6,000ft x 150ft, 073°, 256°, concrete and tarmac. Runway 03/21(asphalt surfaced) extended to 9,000ft mid-1950s now has Rotary Hydraulic Arrester Gear. *Hangars:* five Type C. *Hardstandings:* thirty-six. *Accommodation:* RAF: 212 officers, 466 SNCOs, 1,407 ORs; WAAF: 13 officers, 15 SNCOs, 362 ORs.

WARBOYS, Cambridgeshire

52°23N/00°05W 100ft asl; TL300790. 7 miles NE of Huntingdon, off A141; airfield by road to W of village

Warboys had a surprisingly complex and comparatively lengthy history. Opened in summer 1940 as RLG for 17 OTU Upwood and in April 1941 reclassified as its Unbuilt Satellite due to the intensity of Blenheim crew training, it was upgraded to Class A standard survived to become an operational station during the Cold War.

Wyton's need for a satellite was just as important so when Alconbury was unavailable Wyton had priority use of Warboys which also spent awhile as Wyton's second satellite. Indeed, for a few weeks in autumn 1941 Stirlings of XV Squadron operated from Wyton and Warboys while runways were completed at Alconbury.

Warboys really came into its own when a new squadron, No 156, formed at Alconbury under Wyton's control in February 1942. On 5 August 1942 they began moving to Warboys thus making way for the Americans to have Alconbury. Quick was the change for on 9 August No 156 mounted its first operation from Warboys with Osnabrück as the target.

As part of the Pathfinder Force and flying Wellington IIIs the squadron's first operation under the new management took place on 18 August against Flensburg. There was drama at Warboys from the start for, moments after take-off, a flare ignited in Flight Sergeant Case's Wellington from which the remainder of the load was jettisoned five miles from the airfield. A more successful flare drop raid was directed at Frankfurt on 24 August, but two Wellingtons failed to return. Another loss came four nights later when Flight Lieutenant Gilmour flying X3728 was shot down during his 47th sortie. Near Essen on 1 September, Sergeant J M Hodgson's and another Wellington touched which tore the tail from his BJ757 in what must have been a terrifying experience. Even less fortunate was the crew of BJ617 for, during an attack on Saarbrucken on 19 September, they noticed sparks coming through the floor of their bomber. As the crew baled out, the pilot noticed that the fire was out. He risked staying aboard and landed his Wellington at West Malling.

A particularly grim night for the squadron was 5 October. On route to the target lightning struck BJ646 and about an hour later its port engine stopped. They turned back after jettisoning the flares then near the French coast the crew decided they must bale out. Just before he jumped the pilot noticed that the bomber was becoming controllable again, possibly due to the lightening of the aircraft's weight. He resumed his place and managed to scrape into Manston and belly-land his Wellington. Returning that night from Aachen another aircraft crashed, this time at Gestingthorpe and killing the pilot. Another came down at Somersham after the crew baled out.

Six times in November and December the squadron set off for Turin, an eight hour intensely cold journey over and among high mountains in pitch darkness in a twin-engined aeroplane. During one of these raids, on 20 November a Wellington was intercepted by a Fiat CR 42 biplane which the rear gunner claimed. Less fortunate was Sergeant R J Wallace during a raid on Stuttgart on 22 November. Persistently a night fighter attacked BK315 causing such serious damage that the sortie ended with a crash landing at Bradwell Bay.

Warboys based Wellingtons attempted 297 operational sorties in 1942 and fourteen aircraft failed to return. By the end of that year the Wellington was almost past its sell-by date where Main Force operations over Europe were concerned. The way ahead became clear when on the last day of 1942 three Lancaster Is arrived for squadron conversion. On 23 January 1943 the last Wellington raid from Warboys was despatched and against Lorient which was again the target when on 26 January Lancasters of No 156 Squadron first operated.

Thereafter they flew from Warboys within the Pathfinder Force making their first Berlin raid on 1 March 1943 and taking part in the highly successful Essen attack of 5 March. On 18 April the squadron's third Flight became operational.

Warboys had been raised from Built Satellite to Class A self accounting station status on 1 January 1943, and in between March and November of that year Oxfords of 1507 BAT Flight used the airfield. No 156 Squadron operated from here in the marker role as part of 8 Group with Main Force raids until March 1944 when it moved to Upwood.

During June 1943 the Pathfinder Force Navigation Training Unit reached Upwood, some of its Halifax IIs and Lancasters immediately moving to Warboys to make use of its concrete runways. As soon as metalled runways had been laid at Upwood No 156 Squadron swapped stations and on 5 March 1944 the PFF NTU moved all its Lancasters, Mosquitoes and Oxfords to Warboys the same day.

The training importance of Warboys was enhanced when on 1 March 1944 six Mosquito bombers overflew the station to herald the arrival of 1655 Mosquito Conversion Unit. This was the organisation responsible for crew training for Bomber Command's Mosquito squadrons. Bombing and navigation practice were undertaken using Oxford trainers. By the close of 1944 No 1655's Mosquito IVs had been supplemented with Canadian-built Mk XXs while crews were being taught to use *H2S* and *Oboe*. No 1655 MCU disbanded at the end of December 1944 when 16 OTU took on Mosquito bomber crew conversion. *H2S* and *Oboe* commitments passed to the PFF NTU by then flying some Mosquitoes acquired from 1655 MCU. That task continued at Warboys until the war ended.

No 571 Mosquito Squadron forced out of Oakington to make way for Transport Command Liberators moved to Warboys on 24 July 1945, wound down then disbanded on 28 September 1945. Most of the aircrew were posted to BAFO's 98 Squadron.

Warboys closed as an airfield in January 1946. For awhile it had a Standby classification then became an Agricultural Airfield with some areas remaining in government hands.

Its resurrection began in 1959 when a conclave was built for Bristol Bloodhound missiles to help defend V-bomber bases nearby. No 257 Squadron, part of No 151 Wing, North Luffenham, was on 1 July 1960 reformed here to operate them. That task continued until the squadron's disbandment on 31 December 1963.

Now cultivated land and Warboys Industrial Site, a T2, portions of one of the Warboys runways at the north end of the field and sections of the perimeter track remain. A few huts have also survived in the area of Warboys.

Main features:
Runways: 122° 6,000ft x 150ft, 179° 4,050ft x 150ft, 069° 4,200ft x 150ft, tarmac. *Hangars:* two T2, one B1. *Hardstandings:* thirty-six for heavy bombers. *Accommodation:* RAF: 256 officers, 245 SNCOs, 1,458 ORs; WAAF: 4 officers, 10 SNCOs, 277 ORs.

WATERBEACH, Cambridgeshire

52°16N/00°11E 17ft asl; TL495665. 6 miles NE Cambridge by the A10

If Waterbeach should, as threatened, change into a town site, how will I for one remember it? Will it be through drawings and a model of Wimpey 'LN-K' which sat by the junction of the village road and the A10? Will it be through the Stirlings ignominiously paddling, undercart bent, in the Roman ditch by the A10? Might it be through LL625 which took LN-Ks place and died one January 1944 night on a Berlin raid? Will it be through that amazing assortment of transport Liberators wearing coats of many colours? Could it come through seeing 56 Squadron's Meteors among the first sporting their colours?

Waterbeach is of the Fens, inseparably so. It sits by the edge of where the sea once swished, and close to ancient Denny Abbey. Maybe Hereward the Wake made his way through rushes once covering Waterbeach the land for which was requisitioned in 1939. There was strong opposition to that, for some of the finest agricultural land was being seized and now looks likely to be wasted forever if developers have their way.

During construction in the winter of 1940-41 the landing ground topped with fine Fen-style peat became a morass which, as any Fen dweller would expect, changed into a dust bowl once winter passed. Drainage became surprisingly good because a layer of sand and gravel rested close to the surface.

Waterbeach was designed before the war when the cost of aerodrome building was reduced by erecting buildings to lower specifications. Evidence of that is on camp everywhere. The two 'J' Type Sheds of metal and partially pre-fabricated were erected during 1940 when, to prevent German Ju 52 troop transports landing, the aerodrome surface was festooned with poles and trip wires. When on 30 December 1940 the Germans first called it was in a Dornier Do 17Z which delivered ten 50SC HEs while friends in a Do 215 strafed Cambridge generally 'snapping' all they could. The enemy returned on 3 February 1941 when a Dornier 17Z neatly supplied nine HEs, some along the face of the western hangar and others to damage the watch office and a runway – Waterbeach was completed with all three.

SHQ Waterbeach had opened on 11 January 1941 at which time a concrete track was being laid leading to dispersals set in an orchard to the south of the flying field and now overgrown by warehouses. Personnel accommodation to pre-war standards was good, and the runways were almost complete when, on the afternoon of 19 March 1941, Wellington Ics of 99 Squadron ceremoniously flew in from Newmarket Heath then dispersed on pans to the west and north of the perimeter track. There was plenty of the aforementioned mud to contend with for grass needed more time to take hold of the landing ground. By dusk on 19 March when 99 Squadron began setting out for Cologne clouds of dust were the problem. There was so much that only six crews could get away for the raid. Newmarket Heath again entertained 99 Squadron, operations not being attempted from Waterbeach until 30 March with an attack on Brest. Time and again Brest and its battle cruisers was to be the target for 99 Squadron, the Wimpeys being seen heading out in a stream to the south-west making the most of friendly territory as long as possible.

Berlin was first raided from Waterbeach on 9 April only three of seven crews listed as reaching the Big City. No 99 stood by to attack the Bismarck on 25 May and next day searched for the *Hipper*. Six Wellingtons were on 24 July among the large force that tackled Brest in daylight. By sheltering the *Scharnhorst* and *Gneisenau*, Brest attracted almost nightly treks from Waterbeach as 3 Group repeatedly tried without success to cripple the warships.

March 1941 saw 99 Squadron receive the first of the standard 3 Group allocation of three Merlin-engined Wellington IIs, 'LN-U, V and Z' each modified to carry a 4,000lb 'cookie', and first dropped (by W5400 and W5436) on 14/15 April 1941, during a Brest raid. Their higher engine output had resulted in them being chosen to carry larger bombs, but engine overheating problems and the need for modified tailplanes made them unpopular, and they were rated risky – until proven superior to the trusted Ics.

Several memorable accidents shook the area around in 1941. On 5 May 'J-Johnny' took off only to crash north-west of the airfield and produce a bright fire visible for many miles even though the bomb load did not explode. On 8 December 'Q-Queenie' set off for Aachen and when engine trouble started the crew turned back. On final approach their second engine cut and the Wellington, carrying a 4,000-pounder, crashed. All personnel on the station were ordered into the air-raid shelters. Five of the crew escaped from the burning aircraft before the large bomb exploded.

Berlin had again been the target on 7 November, two Wellingtons out of eight despatched failing to return. Three crews out of the other six were forced to abort for the weather embracing violent storms was very bad. That disastrous night brought the loss of thirty-three bombers.

Wellington II W5458 able to carry a 4,000 lb 'cookie' served with 99 Squadron between May and July 1941.

No 99 Squadron flew their last operation from Waterbeach, against Emden, on 14 January 1942. They had despatched 700 sorties during their stay and lost fifteen Wellingtons. Additional were those which for various reasons crashed. One was as a result of the crew suffering oxygen starvation at relatively high altitude and from which none recovered in time. No 99 squadron moved overseas during March 1942 by which time a new, memorable phase in the station's history was well underway.

On a grey November day in 1941 a Stirling circled the station, before its landing heralded the arrival of a type always to be associated with Waterbeach. Conversion training for 3 Group Stirling crews was soon on offer initially given by No 26 Conversion Flight and then through its larger derivative, No 1651 Conversion Unit, formed in January 1942.

For almost two years the Stirlings, for most of the time distinguishable by their absence of unit identity letters and strangely relying upon individual letters sometimes duplicated, droned around the circuit and often set off on cross country journeys. Closer scrutiny showed them to have usually been retired from front line service. Stirlings, initially hand made for a total of only 100 had been envisaged, were as a result very slowly introduced. Handling – particularly during take-off and landing – needed the right technique and a lot of practice. Ground accidents due to swing on take-off and during landing were common, but once the Stirling was safely airborne it was a delight to fly and could outmanoeuvre many other types. The view from its huge cockpit canopy was stunning, and the nose compartment was amazingly roomy. True, one had to bend a little when touring the very long fuselage at the end of which the lonely rear gunner found himself gently swaying. Overshooting Waterbeach to the west could result in the bomber catching its incredible undercarriage in the Roman drainage ditch along the Ely road. Many times in 1942-3 a Stirling was to be found literally ditched and looking sorry for itself. Not surprisingly, then, No 1651 CU worked through over 220 different Stirlings.

On 30/31 May 1942, 1651 CU took part in the Cologne 'Thousand Bomber' raid and again during the Essen operation. Not until late 1942 did unit strength reach the planned thirty-two aircraft by which time diversity of appearance and at last unit identity letters were in evidence. Backing the much enlarged Stirling force of 1943 able to field 100 aircraft raids, and supported by the output from three other Heavy Conversion Units, Stirlings remained at Waterbeach until November 1943.

In September 1943 the station became Head Quarters 33 Base for it was again to have an operational role. On 23 November 1943 the Main Party, 514 Squadron, arrived along with 1678 Conversion Flight, both armed with Lancaster IIs. Their dished bomb doors gave them the ability to accommodate two and even three 4,000lb bombs joined together. Generally, they delivered mixed loads comprising a 4,000-pounder and assorted incendiaries. It was soon very apparent that the Lancaster offered the station a chance to mount intensive operations and deliver very heavy punches.

No 514 Squadron's first operation from Waterbeach, flown on 25 November 1943, involved minelaying. Next night 514's part on The Battle of Berlin began, eight Lancasters setting off for the capital and one not returning. No 3 Group's Main Force activities occupied the squadron which, by the end of May 1944, had flown 754 sorties for the loss of eighteen Lancaster IIs. Four fell on the night of 30/31 May 1944 when the squadron raided Nuremberg and lost a fifth aircraft in a crash two miles from Waterbeach in what proved to be the squadron's worst night for losses. In the run-up to D-Day attacks were made on many transport targets followed by direct support for the Normandy invasion and attempts to blast a gap in German lines allowing the Army to break out of the lodgement area. Raids on V-1 targets and oil depots followed.

On 18 June 1944, 514 Squadron first despatched, to Montdidier, a Merlin-engined Lancaster, PB143-JI:B, for the squadron gradually changed to using the usual version. The first daylight operation, target Domleger, took place three days later.

King George VI and Queen Elizabeth held an investiture at Waterbeach on 5 July 1944 many awards for bravery being conferred. Lancaster Mk IIs undertook their final operational sorties on 23 September 1944. No 1678 Conversion Flight which supplied crews for the Mk IIs had disbanded after DS654 landed early on 12 June 1944. Although Hercules engines had conferred more power on the Lancaster their additional weight reduced all-round performance

No 514 Squadron fought a tough war to the bitter end, participating in raids on distant Dresden and Chemnitz in 1945. Their final bombing operation was delivered on 24 April, target Bad Oldesloe. The squadron had flown over 3,500 bombing sorties and another 126 during which food was dropped to the starving Dutch. Aircraft losses totalled forty-five. On 22 August 1945, 514 Squadron disbanded.

A spectacular change overtook Waterbeach on 12 September 1945 when No 47 Group Transport Command took control. Almost immediately Liberators of 59 and 220 Squadrons moved in from Ballykelly, and were soon operating marks 3, 5, 6 and 8 drawn from around the world – bombers, general reconnaissance examples and specially converted transport variants displaying an array of hues or left bare. Each squadron had sufficient personnel to crew thirty aircraft, their first task to assist in carrying 10,000 troops of the 52nd Division from Brussels to the Middle East during October's operation *Sketch*, and then airlift 10,000 Indian troops home from the Middle East. Phase Three involved bringing home 10,000 British personnel from India and the Far East. These were demanding, complex tasks, nine Liberators leaving Brussels daily, and with each squadron including those at Waterbeach having their prescribed route. Nos 59 and 220 flew the four-day journey from base to Brussels/Melsbroek then to Castel Benito, Shallufa, Lydda thence to Mauripur where '59' headed for Chakulia and '220' for Arkonam. Home-bound they came via Mauripur and Castel Benito where slip crews were placed. Each Liberator could carry twenty-six troops and 500lb of freight distributed throughout the aircraft.

Liberator C 8 by the A10 Ely road.

After the Brussels lift ended the Liberators from here and other Cambridgeshire bases flew direct to Castel Benito, Cairo West, Mauripur, Lydda and home via Castel Benito. If you served in the RAF at the time, you will certainly find those names – perhaps these places – unforgettable! The intensity of the operation soon began wearing down the aircrew. In one instance a crew flew for twenty-seven hours without a rest only to be ordered into the air after only six hours' break in India. Other complaints arose because troops persisted in crowding into the rear of the aircraft during landing which was highly dangerous. Although the flights were very uncomfortable it was only after a lot of persuasion that 'senior management' agreed to passengers having drinks and blankets during their flights. The official view was that nothing likely to permit serious diseases entering Britain should be tolerated. All involved were given a wide assortment of medication including malaria suppressant drugs for aircrew. It's difficult to link such goings on with Waterbeach of the 1940s!

Task completed, No 220 Squadron disbanded on 25 May 1946 and No 59 on 15 June. No 47 Group then positioned here No 51 Squadron which began arriving from Stradishall on 14 August 1946. This evolved into being a large squadron which from 18 November was re-organised into Route and Base Flights allowing trunk route operations carrying passengers and freight out of Lyneham to Cairo, Delhi and Singapore, and base training for York crews. No 51 at one time held thirty aircraft. About sixteen route flights were despatched monthly until 24 November 1947 when No 51 Squadron (by then at twenty UE) disbanded to reform as part of a new Long Range Force based at Abingdon to where the last York departed on 8 December.

Waterbeach in March 1947 little changed from wartime. Avro Yorks sit on the pans.

Events unfold very fast when flying. The main Waterbeach runway looked clear as we were approaching at four, three, two miles in misty weather. Flaps and undercarriage down and we had about a mile to touchdown when another York suddenly swung onto the runway. By the time it took to read this tale we were at the threshold and the other York was rolling.

With a lot of power applied K-King shook as if her rivets must pop as we flew low, above the other aircraft. I had never realised before how big a York could look from about fifty feet. By now we were racing towards Landbeach while fireworks were popping off as if we needed warning! Suddenly the captain pulled away to the right leaving the other aircraft scudding off low. After the pilot had settled himself we safely landed. Once '260' was home I watched as the captain took off his overalls then wrung out his damp shirt. Me? I was still shaking with fright!

Waterbeach (and sister station Oakington) then each became home for Dakotas of the 46 Group Medium Range Transport Force. On 8 December Dakotas of Nos 18, 53, 62 and 77 Squadrons each established at eight aircraft were assigned here. For much of the time they were route flying in Europe and the Near East then in July 1948 were sent to Germany to participate in the Berlin Airlift. No 18 Squadron returned in October 1949 and disbanded on 20 February 1950 which month saw the demise of 53 and 62 Squadrons. No 77 had disbanded in December 1949 all their places taken by No 24 (Commonwealth) Squadron which had arrived on 8 June 1949. Their task was transportation of VIPs and government personnel.

Transport Command's strength diminished in 1950, 24 Squadron leaving for Oakington by the end of February. Waterbeach's future had already been subject of much discussion.

Retaining Duxford as a fighter station had meant considerably updating it and building a metalled runway. Its two squadrons, 66/111 and 92, really needed a new home, also Middle Wallop's. Thorney Island was eventually brought into use but its runways were too short for Meteors. Waterbeach now entered the picture and, strategically well positioned, was chosen. On 1 March 1950 it entered Fighter Command as a replacement for Thorney Island. A jet fuel installation and suitably modified weapons stores were built, the runway was attended to and a variety of other changes converted it into a fighter station where, on 11 May 1950, Meteor F4s of Nos 56 and 63 Squadrons moved in.

Waterbeach showing the layout after modification in the early 1950s. ORPs can be seen at each end of the main runway, one ASP for each of two squadrons.

Within a few days the souring effect of the war in Korea led to increased US presence in Europe and in Britain. Among new arrivals were F-84Ds, escort fighters for B-29/50s. To help them quickly adjust to the British scene the USAF's 77th Squadron were on 22 August detached from Manston to Waterbeach for two weeks' intensive training, and were followed on 1 September by 79 Squadron. A long standing invitation for ten Swedish Air Force Vampires to visit Waterbeach brought a difficult situation, Sweden guarding her neutrality while enjoying association with RAF and USAF. So, the brief visit went ahead and also brought a Ju 86 to Waterbeach. The following month saw a few Danish Air Force Meteors based here for a part in exercise *Emperor*.

There can be no denying that the West seriously underestimated the speed with which the USSR would pose a major threat. Discovery that the Soviet aircraft industry was going ahead with radical designs, and worse still that their nuclear capability would soon be extremely threatening raised the spectre of very sudden attack. On 13 December 1950 squadrons at Waterbeach were informed that they would be involved in the Top Secret exercise *Fabulous*. For a prescribed week at a time, beginning on a Friday, each squadron would always have some aircraft operationally armed and fuelled and at readiness on the squadron dispersal. Standby aircrew would sit in aircraft cockpits awaiting instructions and others at Readiness would be fully kitted awaiting telephoned orders. Most specifically, no obstruction was to in any way prevent rapid scramble for action which would be given from Eastern Sector Operations Room and Head Quarters, Neatishead. Never before in peacetime had such drastic orders been issued to fighter squadrons. Expectation of an unprovoked Russian attack was now deemed high.

Ensuing decades were to see all home-based fighter squadrons (their UE increased from eight to sixteen) taking a turn throughout every twenty-four hours in all-weather alert states as prescribed under *Fabulous* or it successors, their QRA aircraft nestling between the reinforced concrete walls at protected dispersals built in 1953-4. Waterbeach for a time was the prime base to which all-weather fighter squadrons rotated taking their turn at *Fabulous*.

Into the mid-1950s Meteors equipped the squadrons using Waterbeach. They were placed fourth and fifth in the queue for the longer duration Meteor 8, received late in the year. Autumn 1951 saw the strength of these SRD squadrons increase to twenty-two UE dramatically raising the Command's overall strength to almost 1,000 fighters.

The first sign of major advancement came on a dreary day in February 1954 when Waterbeach received its first Supermarine Swift and Fighter Command its first swept wing fighter. Already much delayed – for the Attlee Government had wasted time by not pressing for its development – the Churchill post-war government in demanding haste found the newcomer not yet ready for service – except for political reasons. No 56 Squadron tried to make a success of the Swift but it was insufficiently armed, needed more power but worst of all there were serious accidents particularly because the Swift so easily tightened in high speed turns from which control and recovery were far from easy. No 56 Squadron persevered for the Swift 1 and 2 were the Air Force's preferred new fighter. All was to no avail in a saga costly in lives and money. To the chagrin of all, No 56 Squadron was fully re-equipped with Meteor 8s in March 1955 by which time the highly specialised very fast climb Sapphire-engined Hunter 5 with a role akin to that of the pre-war point-defence Hawker Fury, was almost available. It started equipping No 56 in May 1955. No 63 Squadron in November 1956 acquired the main stream Avon-engined Hunter 6.

Swifts of 56 Squadron on parade at Waterbeach in summer 1954.

Excess of T2 hangar space at Waterbeach enabled Marshall's Flying School to rent space where from 1950 repair and rebuild of damaged Vampires could take place with the added advantage of test flying them from a metalled runway. Marshall also completed at Waterbeach, and to a tight time scale, a batch of new Vampires for the Iraqi Air Force. Marshall flew both Vampire and Venoms from Waterbeach until the runway became available at Cambridge.

The Swift was not the only 'difficult' aeroplane with which RAF Waterbeach dealt. The other was the de Havilland Venom all-weather fighter. Britain's night fighter defences for years received scathing criticism because the Attlee Labour Government had failed to hasten a replacement for the Mosquito which became increasingly too heavy for the role. Eventually there came the hurriedly devised Meteor night fighter, a somewhat troubled machine. De Havilland, who lost their Vixen fighter-intruder scheme when the Javelin was approved, traded on their Mosquito reputation by first devising the two-seat Vampire and then a similarly modified Venom. So desperate was the night fighter situation that, with many reservations, the RAF accepted the Venom night fighter, and also the policy whereby two day fighter squadrons trained for high-speed getaway, and an all-weather

Hunter F5 S of 56 Squadron seen at Waterbeach in 1957.

Unusual visitor to Waterbeach in 1952, a Junkers Ju 86 of the Royal Swedish Air Force (Alan Wright).

fighter squadron joined them to form a Wing. A plan of June 1952 for Waterbeach provided for two SRD squadrons each at twenty-two UE and No 85 Squadron to be here with eight Meteor NF11s.

Instead, the policy led to No 253 Squadron reforming in April 1955 and becoming part of the Waterbeach Wing. Equipped with Venom night fighters No 253 had a short life and disbanded in August 1957 as part of the Fighter Command run-down. No 153 Squadron which replaced them in September was re-numbered 25 Squadron in June 1958 and continued to fly Meteor NF12/14 night-fighters. Then came No 63 Squadron's turn to disband, on 24 October 1958.

No 56 Squadron moved out in July 1959 and was immediately replaced by No 46 Squadron and their Javelin 2s here until May 1961. No 25 Squadron which remained until November 1961 had their Meteors replaced first in March 1959 by Javelin 7s and at the end of the year by Mk 9s. Crews for No 60 Javelin Squadron were trained at Waterbeach in early 1961 and left on 25 June to fly their Javelins to the Far East. No 64 Squadron's Javelin 9s replaced 46 Squadron and were at the station from 27 July 1961 until 13 July 1962.

A further major change came in January 1962 after Fighter Command was rundown to around 150 aircraft. Now No 38 Group, the tactical element of Transport Command, took over Waterbeach. January 1962 saw Hunter FGA 9s of Nos 1 and 54 Squadrons move in, their roles ground-attack and transport escort.

Their stay was short and on the afternoon of 8 August 1963 it fell to a Pakistani Air Force exchange pilot in Hunter XG264 of 54 Squadron to have the distinction of being last man home. He halted in front of my camera, stood up as best he could and saluted. That salute could well have been a tribute to all who had courageously flown from the station.

A probed Javelin FAW9 of 64 Squadron in a walled revetment at Waterbeach.

The last few moments of operational Waterbeach – Hunter FGA9s of 54 Squadron await the end on their ASP on 8 August 1963.

The Hunters left in the next few days for West Raynham, and with the runway in good state Varsities and Jetstreams from 5 FTS Oakington undertook 'touch and goes' until their withdrawal.

The Army took control after the RAF moved out and stationed No 39 Army Engineering Regiment and 12 Engineer Group (Air Support), at Waterbeach Barracks, which remains here. Detachments served during the Gulf conflict in the Balkans and Afghanistan.

At Waterbeach the runway remains along with many original buildings including the control tower. Army helicopters call and late in 1998 Hercules landed to see whether, if needed, they could readily move airfield building equipment.

The future of Waterbeach is uncertain. Government pressure to build more houses close to Cambridge whose infrastructure cannot cope with its present population led to the incredible idea of building a town on Waterbeach Road links to Cambridge have insufficient space even for current traffic volumes. Far better a return to the countryside.

Main features (December 1944):
Runways: 227° 6,000ft x 150ft, 099° 4,200ft x 150ft, 158° 3,900ft x 150ft, tarmac on concrete. *Hangars:* two 'J' Type, three T2, one B1. *Hardstandings:* thirty-six heavy bomber pans. *Accommodation:* RAF: 138 officers, 463 SNCOs, 1,773 ORs; WAAF: 14 officers, 16 SNCOs, 392 ORs.

Place of interest nearby:
Close is Denny Abbey founded in the 12th Century and used by Benedictine Monks, Knights Templar and, between about 1330 and 1530, by Franciscan Nuns. Impressive buildings remain – well worth a visit.

WATTISHAM, Suffolk

52°07N/00°57E; TM025510. Off B1078, 6 miles S of Needham Market

Memories of RAF Wattisham depend upon your age! I first encountered it unexpectedly in summer 1938 when my father took a wrong turning (easy in that area) and we found ourselves driving close to the first control tower which remains in place. From the 1960s cherished memories must be of the thrilling Lightning era and the summer time mounting from Wattisham of The Queen's Birthday Flypast when Lightnings of most squadrons participated. If you're younger then you'll think of Wattisham as the lair of the best Phantoms and if you were *extremely* lucky then you will never surely forget that magic moment when, airborne over Daventry, a group of us watched with delight Wing Commander Roger Spiller close upon the rear of our 'Herc' for a portrait of himself as much of 'T Tiger', the 74 Squadron Phantom now preserved at Duxford. For others, though, memories of Wattisham will be laced with terrible tragedies – and especially of the Blenheim days – which began as the war started.

Shortly before midnight on 3 September 1939 Wattisham was ordered to stand by for operations. Around 1500 hrs on 4 September ten Blenheims – five each of Nos 107 and 110 Squadrons – were despatched to attack German warships off Wilhelmshaven. The weather was very bad, the attack ineffectual unlike the cost for half the force did not return. The loss of four from 107 Squadron was a stunning, unbelievable start to the war for missing were very professional companions of long standing. Of the more fortunate participants a name which became well known was Kenneth Doran who led the raid and was awarded the DFC. Not all that long after he became a POW but the greatest tragedy came when he lost his life many years later in the Turkish Airways DC-10 crash in France.

Wattisham, a very refined pre-war station with four 'C' Type hangars and nestling in a superb Suffolk setting, opened in March 1939 and Wing Commander Oswald R Gayford DFC AFC (famous for his 1933 long-range record flight in the Fairey Monoplane) became Station Commander on 6 April 1939. On 1 April 1937 the Air Ministry had purchased some eleven acres of agricultural land from a Mr W Hunt which allowed construction to commence. Over the ensuing two years a further 450 acres were bought as a result of which Honeypot Farm, Red House Farm and White House Farm along with much of Crowcroft Farm were absorbed. Ten-Acre Wood was included within the new aerodrome boundary.

Blenheims of 107 Squadron had begun arriving at the end of April 1939 and 110's complement on 11 May, starting an association between famous residents. They formed No 83 Wing, part of the Second Echelon of the Advanced Air Striking Force. It was late September 1939 at a time when Hurricanes of Nos 17 and 504 were being daily detached to defend the station that Wing Commander Basil Embry arrived. He soon electrified the station with clever ideas and an array of ventures which attracted many similarly outstanding people like the much revered 'Attie' whose activities brought amazement and delight to so many. It was 'Attie' who concluded that the best way to attack a ship was from the rear, on the dubious basis that the crew would be looking where they were going! You can read his and other signatures on a ceiling panel preserved in Lavenham's delectable Swan Hotel.

Courage, which Basil Embry always displayed, was especially needed when the Blenheim squadrons were hurled into action in May 1940 incurring heavy losses. When he failed to return it was a terrible blow. How he spent his lonely hours escaping cannot be better told than in his biography *Mission Completed* (Methuen). Suffice it to say – he hid in a manure heap. Even better followed for, having escaped to England, he returned on 2 August 1940 to Stowmarket by train from which he climbed down onto the track and not the platform where his worshippers had gathered in force. A taxi took him back to Wattisham where he gleefully chastised his friends for not bothering to greet him sooner!

Those were terrible times as the remnants of 114 Squadron who passed through Wattisham in June 1940 could testify to. Both local Blenheim squadrons fought through the whole of 2 Group's brutal days. They experienced detachments to Lossiemouth, Manston and Malta, all connected with anti-shipping operations as hazardous, horrific and frightening as any operations during their entire war. For his courage in attempting to save the lives of the crew aboard a crashed aircraft in January 1941, Wing Commander Sinclair was awarded the George Cross, the highest decoration yet awarded to anyone serving at Wattisham. There were a number of air attacks on the station during one of which a barrack block received a direct hit which caused the upper floor to smash onto the ground floor with grievous casualties. On another occasion a shoal of difficult to deal with anti-personnel 'butterfly bombs' was sown across the landing ground. When incendiaries caused a major hangar fire some of Wattisham's personnel entered to retrieve burning Blenheims. The total of courage which Wattisham has known is simply tremendous.

No 107 Squadron moved to Great Massingham on 11 May 1941 but 110 stayed on until 17 March 1942 when a posting to the Far East came. Between March and May 1941 No 86 Squadron, Coastal Command, reinforced from here 2 Group's anti-shipping effort.

Wattisham's association with 2 Group was far from ended for No 226 Squadron had arrived in May 1941 flying Blenheims and stayed, except for detachments, until 9 December 1941 when they left for Swanton Morley. A depleted 18 Squadron – part was in Malta – replaced them, and No 18 stayed here until August 1942 by which time it was flying Blenheim Vd which they took to the Middle East. For the 'Thousand Plan' raids of 1942 No 13 Squadron, Army Co-operation Command, assisted from Wattisham in a night intruder role.

Unusual was the arrival on 9 February 1942 of the remnants of 236 Squadron flying Beaufighter Ics still under 16 Group control. They undertook maritime patrols, the highlight of their stay coming in May. The Germans always mounted a noon parade along the Champs Elysées in Paris – what better time to entertain and delight the inhabitants of that sad, beautiful city by 'tickling up' the occasion? Flight Lieutenant A K Gatwood and Sergeant G Fern volunteered 'for something' without knowing that they were to shoot up the parade and throw out a tricolour – when cloud was available for suitable protection.

They tried on 13 May but cloud ran out. Only on their fifth attempt, on 12 June, did the attack seem possible. They refuelled at Thorney Island and although cloud broke over the French coast they pressed on and at 1202 hrs flew over the Champs Elysées where no troops were to be seen. Had the enemy discovered the plan? Not to be entirely cheated, they hurled their tricolour over the Arc de Triomphe and sprayed discouragement into the Gestapo Head Quarters in the Ministry of Marine building. The only interception was provided by a crow which crashed into their starboard engine. Landing safely at Northolt they had performed in the best of Wattisham's traditions. On 7 July 1942 No 236 Squadron finally cleared for Oulton.

They were not alone for in September 1942 the RAF also vacated Wattisham, the Americans moved in and began laying runways and taxiways, but instead of using it as a bomber base as expected they established here the 4th Strategic Air Depot to carry out overall maintenance of all USAAF fighters in the UK for which reason an additional technical site was established in the southern corner of the airfield. Part of the 68th Observation Group, flying P-39Ds, was here between October and December 1942.

Wattisham resumed an operational career when on 15 May 1944 the 479th Fighter Group, 8th AF, arrived under the command of Col Kyle Riddle and the last Fighter Group to join the 8th AF. Flying P-38J Lightnings, they began their bomber escort and ground strafing activities on 26 May 1944. They gave cover until dusk to the Normandy invasion ships as they crossed The Channel on 5 June, then flew supporting sweeps over the armies and strafed targets of opportunity. For their attacks upon French airfields between 15 August and 5 September 1944 they received a Distinguished Unit Citation, a second being awarded after combats during the Munster raid of 26 September. The 479th had lost Col Kyle Riddle, their Commander, who was shot down in August. In his place came the famed Col Hubert Zemke who was shot down in October 1944. Riddle made his way back and uniquely took command here for a second time. During September 1944 the Group re-equipped with P-51Ds. Bomber escort and ground-attack missions continued to the end of the war and on 24 April 1945 the Group were credited with the last enemy aircraft to be shot down by the 8th Air Force during hostilities. Capt A F Jeffrey had also a special enemy aircraft to his credit for he had earlier been first to shoot down an Me 163 rocket fighter. After the USAAF left late in 1945 the RAF retrieved Wattisham which was placed on Care & Maintenance. In August 1946 Fighter Command took control of the station.

On 4 November 1946 No 266 Squadron arrived flying Meteor IIIs and was followed in mid-December by No 56 Squadron. Both left in mid-April 1947 because Wattisham's runways were deemed inadequate for jet aircraft. In their places at once came the RAF Publicity Unit and on 10 March 1947 the Air Ministry Servicing Development Unit whose trophies included the Martin Baker MB5 fighter. A detachment of 695 AAC (later No 34) Squadron using Spitfires, Martinets and Oxfords used the station between May 1946 and July 1950.

Plan F of 21 January 1948 directed that four long-range fighter squadrons equipped with Hornets should be based here. When in October 1949 the construction of 2,000 yard concrete runway was approved a review of the site concluded that not only were the buildings were in good state, Wattisham was also ideally positioned for use as an interceptor fighter station – near to, but not on the coast. The change of use was approved along with its use as the Metropolitan Sector Commander's base sufficiently near to the Sector Operations Centre at Trimley. Intention was to move two Meteor squadrons here from inadequate Thorney Island after runway completion. A policy change in January 1950 directed that Nos 257 and 263 would instead move here from Horsham, confirmation coming in March on the expectation that Wattisham's runway would be completed in September 1950.

Building of a new main runway was completed on time and on 27 October 1950 Nos 257 and 263 Squadron began moving here from Horsham St Faith, instead of the Thorney Island squadrons which were nudged out earlier to Waterbeach. Both newcomers were flying Meteor 4s and the first task almost immediately taken was to re-arm them with Meteor 8s and raise them both from cadre to full squadron strength of sixteen UE by which method the fighter force was being doubled. A further increase approved within Plan H of late 1951 raised their establishment to twenty-two aircraft each. Wattisham was also scheduled now to have a night fighter squadron, No 85 being the initial choice. By June 1952 the latter had instead become 'A' Squadron equipped with twelve Vampire NF 10s and which never materialised. Instead Plan K of January 1954 required Wattisham to have two short range day (SRD) fighter squadrons with Rattlesden as their Standby airfield, supplemented soon by a Meteor NF squadrons. That emerged as No 152 Squadron reformed here on 30 June 1954 completing the Wattisham Wing and flying a mixture of Meteor NF12s and 14s with differing radar and indeed flying characteristics. Apart from normal interception tasks those were also here to attack enemy fast patrol boats venturing to the coast.

Meteor F8 WF755 'B' of No 263 Squadron on the ASP at Wattisham in 1954. Squadron markings repeated on the engine nacelle.

Development of Wattisham was discussed on 30 April 1953 and plans were drawn up for walled revetments. Wattisham figured largely in the ORP/ASP idea and telescramble. In 1955 it was decided the main runway was to be of LCN45 type like Coltishall

No 257 Squadron hit the headlines in November 1954 when they became the first to receive 'the vulnerable point defence specialist' Sapphire-powered Hunter F2. No 263 received theirs the following year. In August 1956 they were replaced by F.Mk 6s because Armstrong-Siddeley who made the Sapphire engine had ceased aero-engine work.

In 1957 with the V-force fully functioning, and the missile threat ever increasing, cutbacks in fighter strength came into play. No 257 Squadron disbanded on 31 March 1957, No 152 left for Stradishall on 28 August 1957 and No 263 followed them to their new base the following day. The Hunters had previously been detached to Wymeswold to allow Wattisham to be prepared for English Electric Lightnings.

Before those arrived No 111 Squadron which formed 'The Black Arrows' aerobatic team arrived in style on 18 June 1958 and flew many displays whilst based here, among them the twenty-two aircraft formation spectacular at the SBAC Display. No 41 Squadron began moving in with Javelin FAW4s and 5s at the end of June 1958 and in 1960 became the first Javelin FAW8 squadron.

Javelin FAW 8 XH971 'A' of 41 Squadron on the ASP at Wattisham, October 1960.

In January 1961 Lightning Ias began to gradually replace No 56 Squadron's Hunter 6s which had arrived on 10 July 1959 from Waterbeach. That heralded a lengthy association between Wattisham and what was so obviously the most spectacular interceptor fighter the West possessed. Nevertheless it was a complex, demanding aeroplane throughout its career. Come April and 'Treble One' Squadron was also receiving Lightning Ias. No 56 fielded a team, 'The Firebirds', but the Lightning was not suitable for team display.

At the end of 1964 No 111 Squadron began to receive Lighting F3s, No 56 starting conversion early in 1965. In January 1967 No 56 moved to Cyprus and on 10 May 1967 No 29 Squadron replaced them and received Lightning F3s. With 111 Squadron they saw out the Lightning era. Nos 29 and 111 Squadrons were removed after elements of the squadrons re-equipped with Phantoms at Coningsby.

No other fighter could provide the fast, furious, and immensely thrilling experience of standing by Wattisham's runway when a stream of Lightnings landed. XP753 Y here is returning from a visit to Buckingham Palace to see The Queen.

When in February 1976 No 23 Squadron moved in they brought along Wattisham's first Phantoms, FGR2 interceptors with which they were re-equipped in December 1975. No 56 Squadron returned on 8 July 1976 with more Phantom FGR2s. No 23 Squadron vacated Wattisham in March 1983 for involvement in the Falklands. They were replaced by 'C' Flight, 25 Squadron equipped with Bloodhound IIs which were enclaved on the airfield's east side. Not until October 1984 did a fighter replacement come in the form of No 74 Squadron and its ex-US Navy F-4J Phantoms. No 56 and 74 Battle Flight maintained five minute QRA South standbys for

Wattisham's enhanced control tower, June 1990.

twenty-four hours a day on every day from the two special 'hangars' close to the pre-war control tower. No longer was Wattisham providing for the defence of London, its sphere of operations now extended over the entire UKADR with Phantoms being scrambled to investigate any intruders within that region with the assistance, if needed, of AAR.

After the Cold War ended first it was No 56 Squadron which disbanded. No 74 continued functioning from the dispersed HASs in the extreme NW corner of the airfield. For No 74 Squadron's Phantom days ended with a farewell fly-past on 1 October 1992. Fixed-wing RAF operations ended at Wattisham on 31 October 1992 by which time there was already a Phantom graveyard at the station.

There was some consideration as to what purpose Wattisham could now serve, an elaborate and well equipped base far from any sizeable population centre. What better than for it to remain an active airfield? In July 1993 the station was handed over to 3 Regiment, Army Air Corps. The last Phantom was airlifted by Chinook to Neatishead there to serve as a gate guardian. RAF presence had not entirely ceased for the QRA sheds were in July 1994 occupied by two Sea King HARs of B Flight, 22 Squadron tended by fifty RAF personnel overall parented by Honington and able to help with AAC survival training but only after much discussion as to who and from where should search and rescue often of civilians be funded and provided. The Sea Kings would operate on the front Dungeness-The Wash.

The Army newcomers were very soon heard and seen widely over East Anglia, the loud bellow of the Phantoms being replaced by the buzzing, clattering helicopters. Wattisham soon had the biggest concentration of Army Air Corps aircraft in the UK once 4 Regiment had arrived.

Wattisham's helicopters were available to support military operations world-wide, detachments being placed in Bosnia and Northern Ireland. Training was partly carried out in Canada and Belize while the Regiments were made available to take part in Rapid Reaction Force training by day and night. In 1995, 3 Regiment was deployed to Croatia to operate within the UN Protection Force in Bosnia. Each Regiment has three flying squadrons, a workshop and an HQ Squadron.

On 1 July 1995 Michael Portillo, then The Secretary of State for Defence, announced that the Westland 'Longbow' Apache attack helicopter had been chosen for the AAC. As a result two custom-built hangars for Apaches were soon being erected at Wattisham. In all sixty-seven Apaches were acquired for the three combat regiments with delivery to be completed in 2003.

In September 1996 there were forty-one Lynx Mks 7/9 and twenty Gazelles held by the two regiments, part of 24 Airmobile Brigade with HQ at Colchester, out of some eighty helicopters on the base at the time. 3 Regiment embraced 653, 662 and 663 AAC Squadrons, 4 Regiment having 654, 659 and 669 Squadrons. 4 Regiment had placed a detachment from 659 Squadron in Bosnia assisting in overseeing democratic elections along with a detachment of 71 Aircraft Workshop and 7 Battalion, Royal Electrical & Mechanical Engineers. Specialist support was also given by the 132 Avn Support Unit, Royal Logistics Corps.

Wattisham is now very much 'barracks' and no longer a 'station'. Swarms of Army helicopters have made use of it, like these Lynx.

Not as elegant as a Lightning, but highly efficient, the brutish looking Apache Longbow ZJ182 at Wattisham 23 July 2005 (George Pennick).

During the last decade Wattisham has become the base of the Army's attack helicopter, the Augusta Westland AH Mk 1 Apache Longbow, which since 2006 has been operational in Afghanistan. The British version of the Apache is powered by the Rolls-Royce RTM322, providing 25% more power than is available in the US version. It can operate at greater height, which is very useful in hot areas, and can do so above AAA and RPGs. It always has mast-mounted radar in place, and a defensive aids system detects radar intercepts and missile threats.

At Wattisham the squadrons work on a four-month cycle, embracing deployment, recuperation phase, continuation training and boost to high readiness. Crews train part of the time in Arizona using local firing ranges. A set target is to hold thirty-two of the total sixty-seven Apaches at 'theatre standard' to back up at all times the eight deployed to Afghanistan as part of the Joint Helicopter Force (Afghanistan). Despite the sand and grit, constant problems, the Apaches operate by day and night flying intelligence gathering missions, and carry out planned or quick response sorties directed precisely against Taliban venturers. Apache can carry seventy-six 2.3in rockets, 1,200 rounds of 30mm and sixteen Hellfire missiles together with highly sophisticated aiming capability, which makes it a highly potent attack helicopter.

Apache ground handling, maintenance and flying training is undertaken at Wattisham by Aviation Training International Ltd, a joint venture between AugustaWestland and Boeing, in 1998 awarded a twenty-year contract

The choice of seventy-year-old Wattisham as the main Apache base gives it a fairly secure future. The quite large helicopter, 57ft 6in long with a 48ft-diameter rotor disc, resulted in the construction of a large custom-built servicing hall. Within, Urgent Operational Requirement (UOR) modifications by service and civilian technicians are undertaken, such as fitting the specially protected external fuel tank to make room in the fuselage for additional ammunition. A longer-range target acquisition system has been fitted.

Embracing 1,072 acres, Wattisham is home to up to 3,000 Army personnel and civilians for whom 600 married quarters are locally available. Around 300 heavy vehicles and 200 Land Rovers on site indicate the extent of the Army presence, which is supplemented by a sizeable contingent of civilians in Headquarters, the fire service, Air Traffic and other services.

Peacetime in the 21st century sees all battlefield helicopter units administered by the Joint Helicopter Command, within which is the Army Air Corps. Comprising eight regiments together with independent squadrons and Flights, some two-thirds of its 2,000 personnel are non-commissioned officers. RAF support helicopter squadrons form part of the Air Manoeuvre Force within 16 Air Assault Brigade, which includes two battalions of the Parachute Regiment based at Colchester.

During 2007 the Army Air Corps was reorganised, the Apache force being concentrated in Nos 3 and 4 Regiments, each having three Apache squadrons assigned. Previously there had been three Regiments each with two squadrons, both armed with eight Apaches, and a Support Squadron holding eight Lynx utility helicopters, the Mk 7 fitted with skids or the Mk 9 with wheels. Gazelle helicopters, also serving as support aircraft, were about to be phased out, their intended replacement the still-awaited Battlefield Light Utility Helicopter.

The late years of the Cold War included plans to compensate for Soviet armoured vehicles trying to penetrate a weak spot in the NATO front line, then racing ahead to prevent a second NATO defensive line forming. A responsive attack helicopter and A-10 force was formed to 'take out' such an action. The Westland Scout armed with SS11 wire-guided missiles was the first British Army combat helicopter chosen for the task. In the 1980s the role passed to the Lynx armed with TOW. Carrying twice the offensive load, it could fire them from 1,000 metres, giving the force enhanced capability.

For 2003 operation *Telic*, the AAC contribution included Wattisham's No 3 Regiment's Lynx squadrons and two RAF Pumas of the Support Helicopter Force. They combined to make a battle group, together with 16 AA Brigade, later supplemented with the 7th Armoured Brigade and operating over an area of 6,000 sq km.

The Lynx lost its combat role in 2004, and in April No 656 Squadron at Wattisham commenced training to operate the Apache AH Mk 1. Conversion was completed in October. In June 2005 No 656 became fully operational within 4 Regiment, and by early 2007 both 3 and 4 Regiments, Wattisham-based, held their full complement of twenty-four Apaches. On 31 August 2007 the Apaches of 9 Regiment moved to Wattisham, for it was more cost-effective to have them all at one base. Both Lynx squadrons, Nos 659 and 669, moved from Wattisham to Dishforth.

No 9 Regiment, comprising Nos 656, 664 and 672 Squadrons based at Dishforth, had been the first to equip with Apaches. It was followed by No 3 Regiment (653, 662 and 663 Squadrons), then by No 4 (654, 659 and 669 Squadrons), all Wattisham-based.

Wattisham became the dedicated service centre for Apache, holding central servicing expertise, and the following year it became the Apache Hub as well as the base for all front-line Apache attack helicopter operations. Full technical back-up to the entire Apache force was now provided from here.

During 2008 No 4 Regiment replaced No 3 at Kandahar, Afghanistan. There it faced not only small arms fire and SAMs, but also high temperatures, high-altitude operational zones and dust, all of which makes high demands upon servicing. Deployment was for one year, during which personnel served for three-month periods.

Also based at Wattisham in 2008 was the 7th Air Assault Battalion, REME, a worldwide front-line helicopter repair organisation, No 132 Aviation Supply Unit Royal Logistics Corps, and an RAF Brigade Parachute Section. The latter is not the only RAF occupant. Quartered within the QRA Sheds, once housing fighters at advanced readiness, reside a pair of Westland Sea King HAR 3/A air-sea rescue helicopters of 'B' Flight 22 Squadron. Their rescue area extends far along the east coast and out to sea. How much longer they will remain seems always uncertain.

On Sundays between April and October Wattisham's museum is open to public view, portraying the station's glorious past and the current activities of Britain's brave and very fine Army – still the world's best.

Main features:
Runways: 060° 6,000ft x 150ft, 110°, 350°, concrete and tarmac. *Hangars:* four C Type, four T2. *Hardstandings:* fifty-two spectacle type, nineteen frying pan type. *Accommodation:* 190 officers, 1,519 enlisted men.

'Get on, parade!' Phantoms on Wattisham's ASP August 1990 await a part in the Battle of Britain flypast.

During the 1950s a large ASP was built and ORPs were laid at each end on the southern side of the 05/23 7,537ft main runway. This was fitted with Type B Barrier and BAK-12(j) RHAG. Protected dispersals were built in the south-west and north-west areas of the airfield. HASs were constructed in the north-west area in the early 1980s sufficient for two fighter squadrons. Two alert sheds were built in the south-east corner of the airfield and now house 22 Squadron's detachment.

WATTON, Norfolk

52°33N/00°51E 190ft asl; TL945000. E of Watton town by B1108

Watton's claim to fame stems from the years when it was a 2 Group station. So much outstanding courage was shown by so many that it would be invidious to single out any one. Twice the station encountered crippling losses, the first when 82 Squadron attacked enemy formations near Gembloux in May 1940 and were all but wiped out. The second came even more spectacularly in August 1940 when again the squadron was ambushed, this time during a high-level raid on Aalborg airfield, Denmark. Only one of the dozen Blenheims returned effectively wiping out '82'. Not for long, though, for within a few days The Earl of Bandon, one of those truly great 2 Group people of whom there were so many, had the show on the road again. Through those bad days of 1940 Watton sustained an appalling casualty rate, yet fought on through the dark winter nights. Then the slaughter began anew during murderous, lunatic and often unrewarding anti-shipping raids of 1941. Losses continued mounting when Watton's Blenheims were fielded as bait for enemy fighters during *Circus* operations, and when they took part in August's incredible low-level daylight raid on Cologne's power stations. What applied to Watton at this time was of course equally so at the satellite, Bodney. My book *2 Group* (Crécy Publishing 1974, 1992) recalls many of the operations during that period.

Watton, an impressive Permanent Station of typical pre-war pseudo Georgian style, opened at the start of 1939. Four 'C' Type Aircraft Sheds, tall brick water tower, assorted domestic and technical buildings and still standing, were erected on the north side of an unusual fan-shaped landing ground later much extended.

First in was 34 Squadron and their Blenheims which arrived late February 1939 and followed a few days later by 21 Squadron. Both had a hard workup period until August 1939 when 34 Squadron left for the Far East. No 82 Squadron replaced them in late August and by now both units were flying Blenheim IVs whose first operations – photographing enemy airfields – were flown on 27 September 1939.

Blenheim 1s of No 21 Squadron seen here at Watton.

In March 1940 the satellite at Bodney came into use for both squadrons. Although operations were usually from the parent station, Unbuilt Bodney was used more than most satellites both squadrons alternating their stays at the two airfield.

No 21 Squadron moved to Lossiemouth during the invasion scare period to watch for enemy shipping off the Scottish coast. They returned to Watton late October. Whilst they were away 105 Squadron had taken their place after reforming following their mauling as a Fairey Battle squadron in France and now part of 2 Group flying Blenheims and operating by day against Continental targets. No 18 Squadron were also briefly here, a station that the enemy was always showing an interest in.

On days when clouds hung low in 1941 East Anglian airfields were subject to sudden enemy attack by raiders dipping out of the overcast, often undetected by radar. One such day was 18 February, when an He 111 operating over Norfolk attacked Watton. Response was fast, the weapons which engaged the bomber being of the Parachute and Cable variety (PAC) installed at many East Anglian airfields.

PAC had a touch of Captain Mainwaring and his Army about them for they were fired as a salvo from a group of tubes acutely angled in the ground in groups each set pointing in the same direction. From them a miniature aerial minefield could be released comprising parachutes from each of which dangled a cable and a grenade. PAC was designed mainly to deal with dive-bombers and low fliers and this time Heinkel 111H-3 A1+CM W Nr. 3349 of 4./KG53, The Condor Legion, which fluttered bang into the bizarre concoction. One cable penetrated the port wing cutting through to the main spar then severing the port aileron control rod. Another sliced in near the port wing tip while a third slammed into the starboard wing ensnaring its controls. All was clear to see after the raider crashed near Ovington, Norfolk, one of the few credited to PAC and probably the only one to fall to the weapon in East Anglia.

For the 2 Group Blenheim squadrons cloud-cover day raids, night Main Force attacks and fighter-escorted day raids occupied them in 1941, but the anti-shipping campaign was increasingly their prime employment – and not only off British shores.

In May 1941, 21 Squadron was detached to operate from Malta against Mediterranean shipping. July found them using Manston as a base for *Channel Stop* and in September they carried out raids on Norwegian coastal shipping, again from Lossiemouth. In December it was once more to Malta for more punishment and then to North Africa for a touch of desert war.

Meanwhile 82 Squadron had been hurled against shipping too and, apart from a spell in Malta in May-June 1941, used Watton as their base for daylight operations throughout 1941. As if they had not been punished enough No 82 left Watton in March 1942 to reinforce the RAF in the Far East. Throughout 1941 Blenheims had been flying overseas from the station after their preparation at Watton.

Another aspect of the station's 1941 career deserves mention, for it was here that 90 Squadron reformed on 7 May to operate Boeing B-17C Fortress Is, although they flew from Bodney and not the parent station. Three Blind Approach Training Flights operated under 2 Group and one of these, No 1508 flying Blenheim Is and Oxfords was Watton-based, from 20 December 1941 to 19 January 1942.

No 2 Group's tenure which had seen such unspeakable horror, supreme courage and sacrifice ended in January 1942. Curious were the replacements, over 150 Master II trainers of 17 (P) AFU formed on January 29 in 21 Group and surrounded, in mid-Anglia, by operational bases. No 17 (P) AFU Watton trained pilots following their elementary courses usually overseas. Here they experienced flying in a very different environment. The Unit left Watton and Bodney in May 1943 for Calveley.

It was then that the 3rd Strategic Air Depot, USAAF took over the station. Watton's sole 2,000 yard runway was now laid, just the one because of the unusual shaped landing ground set relatively close to Watton town. The new Depot complex known as Neaton situated on the southern side of the airfield had the job of maintaining the 2nd Air Division's B-24 fleet.

On 22 April 1944 the 802nd Reconnaissance Group (Photo) moved in. B-17s and B-24s equipped its 652nd BS(H) while the 653rd BS(L) and 654 BS(SP) flew Mosquito PR XVIs. The Group was re-designated 25th Bomb Group (Recon) on 9 August 1944.

The 802nd had formed to provide material to help crews identify targets from *H2X* radar equipment carried in 8th AF bombers, which allowed bombing through clouds. The 653rd BS concentrated upon weather reconnaissance over enemy territory prior to bombing operations. Also using Mosquito PR XVIs fitted with *H2X* radar, the 654 BS also flew lone sorties to many targets in Europe. A K24 camera was used to photograph images from the radar screen secured during a steady and often hazardous daylight *Gee*-guided and dead-reckoning run-in to a target. Bomber crews operating above cloud could use those photographs to compare with radar-produced images presented on the Plan Position Indicator in their bomber during target run-in. Clear returns on radar were not all that easy to secure, but lakes and buildings could usually be identified, providing a good idea of the position for bomb release.

Mosquito NF 30 NT276 joined the BSDU 2 March 1945 and the RWE 11 August 1945 before the formation of CSE with whom it served until November 1946.

The Americans left in summer 1945, the RAF resuming control of Watton on 27 September when the Radio Warfare Establishment moved in and which became the Central Signals Establishment on 1 September 1946 and remained here until disbandment on 1 July 1965.

This organisation was responsible for the development of radio and radar warfare for the RAF and generally looked after the introduction of ECM apparatus and navigational aids, etc. For this purpose it was later re-organised into three squadrons. No 192 operated Canberras, Washingtons and Comets for radio and radar reconnaissance flights around the perimeter of the Warsaw Pact countries and in other 'sensitive' regions of the world after using for similar purposes Lincolns and

Lincoln WD132 'C' of CSE.

Mosquitoes in the period 1953-5. No 527 was a calibration unit which worked with defence radar stations using Canberras; and No 116 equipped with Varsities checked on navigational aids having earlier relied upon Ansons and Mosquitoes. Additionally, Development Squadron flew Varsities in 'A' Flight and some of the last RAF Lincolns in 'B' Flight. For investigating Soviet radar and general electronic and other activity the Lincolns were fitted with considerably modified *H2S* which could look sideways and not just vertically.

Major changes took place on 21 August 1958 when 192 Squadron became No 51, '527' changed into No 245 and '116' altered to No 115, the latter two squadrons with a very different role moving to Tangmere in September 1958. The Development Squadron became No 151 and, in November 1958, 90 Group which had administered the station was upgraded and became Signals Command, testifying to the importance of Watton's 'snooping activity'. One of their earliest tasks had involved the electronic jamming of aerials and future methods of jamming bomber equipment. Try as they could they found it was impossible to defeat *Window*.

In 1962 a CIA detachment stationed all-black unmarked U-2s here in connection with the High Altitude Sampling Programme which monitored Soviet nuclear tests at Novaya Zemlya. In March 1962 the SAM Operational Training School opened and trained Bloodhound operators until January 1964.

Further change resulting from contraction September 1963 brought Nos 245 and 115 Squadrons back and '245' became 98 Squadron on 1 October. No 51 Squadron which moved to Wyton in March 1963 also then transferred to Bomber Command.

For much of the 1950s the Royal Navy also had a squadron very busily developing specialised radio and radar, test flying it in Gannets and Sea Venoms.

On 9 April 1969 No 115 Squadron by then flying Varsities and Argosy E1s moved to Cottesmore. On 17 April 1969 No 98 Squadron and their Canberra B2s and E15s joined them. The RAF had by no means left Watton for Eastern Radar remained for a number of years. Watton's proximity to the Army's Stanford Battle Area ensures that helicopters call from time to time at a landing ground on the eastern side of Watton. Such activity takes place against a large, extensive non-active camp bisected by the main road to Norwich beside which some of the one-time married quarters are in civilian hands. The close proximity of the station to the town is unusual.

Main features (December 1944):
Runway: 110° 6,000ft x 150ft concrete; two grass runs of 4,200ft and 4,800ft.
Hangars: four Type C, two B1, three T2, three Blister. *Hardstandings:* forty-one loop type, twelve 'frying pan'. *Accommodation:* 190 officers, 1,519 enlisted men.

WELLINGORE, Lincolnshire

54°04N/00°31W 250ft asl; SK988545. Situated E of A607 main Lincoln-Grantham road, just S of village of Wellingore

Drive north from the flat fenland of southern Lincolnshire and one quite quickly reaches an undulating, attractive plateau which, since the RFC was born has harboured landing grounds. Among them have been Waddington, Leadenham and Scopwick. Another was at Cranwell and much developed. When flying in this area dramatically increased in the 1930s several additional sites nearby were acquired for use as relief landing grounds. One called Welbourn situated on Wellingore Heath – just south of the village – began to be used by Cranwell between 1937 and June 1940. In September it became classified as a Relief Landing Ground for the use of Digby.

That attracted a detachment of 46 Squadron Hurricanes, others including Blenheims and Beaufighters of No 29 Squadron. December 1940 brought along Hurricanes of No 402 (Canadian) Squadron. Although based at Digby, these squadrons made use of the landing ground by now renamed Wellingore for training and night activity as well as for purposes of dispersal and until June 1941.

The airfield was used as an RLG for Oxfords of No 11 SFTS between 29 September 1941 and mid-October 1941 when the unit departed. Digby resumed control and fighter squadrons returned. First in, on 20 October, was No 412 Squadron equipped with Spitfires which remained until 30 April 1942 when they left for Martlesham Heath. Then came No 154 Squadron which arrived on 1 September accompanied by No 81 Squadron also flying Spitfire Vs. Both left on 30 October for their part in the north-west Africa invasion, operation *Torch*.

More squadrons made use of Wellingore generally for only a few weeks. One was No 288 Squadron dispersed from Digby on 5 December 1942 and bringing along Hurricanes, Defiants and Oxfords. No 288 returned to its parent station, Digby, on 18 January 1943. Mustang 1s of No 613 Squadron were here between 29 March and 28 May while participating in exercise *Spartan*. They were at once replaced by Spitfires of No 416 (Canadian) Squadron which remained until 6 June when they moved to Merston, Sussex for a spell in the front line which lasted until 19 September 1943 when they rejoined the Digby Wing and were again placed at Wellingore until 1 October 1943 when they rejoined Digby.

On 31 December 1943, No 439 (Canadian) Squadron equipped with Hawker Hurricane Mk IVs formed at Wellingore. This had originated as a Canadian army co-operation training squadron now preparing for a part in the Allied invasion of Europe. They moved to Ayr, Scotland, on 7 January 1944. On 12 February No 402 returned now armed with Spitfire Mk Vs. They were the last fighter squadron to use Wellingore and left on 29 April 1944. No 17 SFTS then used the airfield between 2 April 1944 and 1 May 1945 as their RLG.

Wellingore was then transferred to Technical Training Command and became the satellite for the Radio School, Cranwell until closure in 1945.

Throughout its life, Wellingore remained what amounted to an un-built, grass surfaced unlit satellite airfield with primitive facilities mainly on the western side. Evidence of some shelters and a hangar survives visible from the road to the west of landing ground.

Main features:
Runways: NE/SW 3,300ft, WNW/ESE 3,150ft, PAB stripping being applied to these grass runways in 1944. Unlit. *Hangars:* seven Over Blisters, one EO Blister. *Hardstandings:* six hardened sites for twin-engined aircraft. *Accommodation* (RAF): 28 officers, 50 SNCOs, 561 ORs.

WENDLING, Norfolk

52°41N/00°50E 250ft asl; TF925150. 2 miles N of A47(T) at Wendling

While there is little left of Wendling airfield, its position cannot easily be missed for by the roadside has been built an impressive large memorial garden and monument to those who served here. Built in 1942 as a wartime temporary bomber base, Wendling had the usual three runway, two T2 hangar layout with dispersed domestic accommodation around the village of Beeston.

Wendling was the home of the 392nd Bomb Group, fourth Liberator Group to join the 8th Air Force and the first to be fully equipped with nose-turreted B-24Hs. These began to arrive in Britain, albeit in small numbers, in August 1943 at the time the 392nd moved into Wendling. Commencing operations on 9 September 1943, they flew 7,060 sorties during 285 missions from this base and within the 14th Combat Wing which included the Groups at Shipdham and North Pickenham.

Targets were as for other 2nd Division Groups, although the 392nd arrived too late for participation in Middle East ventures. For their participation in the attack on an aircraft factory at Gotha on 24 February 1944 they received a Distinguished Unit Citation. The Group's operations included an attack on municipal targets in Berlin, a tank factory at Kassel, oil refinery at Gelsenkirchen, steel plant at Brunswick, marshalling yards at Osnabrück and later the railway viaduct at Bielefeld which was eventually brought down by 22,000lb bombs dropped by Lancasters of 617 Squadron.

B-24H-1-FO 42-7521 POOP DECK PAPPY of the 392nd BG seen at Wendling. Evident is the
red surround to the national identity, a feature not very often clearly photographed.
(390th BG Museum)

Coastal defences and choke points were bombed on D-Day and the Group assisted at St-Lô
and in the Ardennes battle. They also took part in the airborne support operations at Nijmegen
and during the Rhine crossing. After their final bombing raid flown on 24 April 1945 the 392nd
dropped food to the Dutch.

The Group left Wendling in June 1945, and the station was returned to the RAF on 25 June. It
was selected to be a Standby Airfield. A USAF radio relay site between 30 June 1960 and 15 April
1964, it was occupied by a detachment of the 2145 Communications Squadron (AFCS) from 1962
to 15 April 1964. It was not eventually closed until November 1964. Broiler houses of Bernard
Matthews's turkey empire line some parts of the one-time runways.

Main features:
Runways: 260° 6,000ft x 150ft, 010°, 130°, concrete with wood chip and protective
surface coating. *Hangars:* two T2. *Hardstandings:* fifty pan-type, concrete.
Accommodation: 421 officers, 2,473 enlisted men.

WESTLEY, Suffolk

52°14N/00°41E 200ft asl; TM835645. On W outskirts of Bury St Edmunds

Visit the site of this small airfield immediately west of Bury and all you find is an airfield gate and
a large housing estate where Westley used to be. Small, insignificant, it might have played a
major part in thwarting a German invasion of Britain.

Built in 1938, the aerodrome initially had two small hangars and served as home for the West
Suffolk Aero Club which acquired two attractive and seemingly very modern cream and red painted
Taylorcraft Plus C high wing monoplanes. Our wartime Austers were derived from the design. Too
small for incorporation in the Civil Air Guard Scheme, and RAFVR use, only club and private
flying were practised. When war came the aerodrome closed.

Bury St Edmunds was a garrison town, close proximity of the local barracks certainly
influencing Westley's future. Increased activity came soon after France fell, the RAF having made
little use of Westley so far. During summer 1940 Lysanders and armed Tiger Moths visited the
airfield but major use started on 30 September 1940 when No 268 Squadron reformed here.
Generating the squadron meant joining 'A' Flight of No 2 Squadron with 'B' Flight 26 Squadron
which provided the necessary Lysanders. Their immediate role was to co-operate with the many
Army units in the vicinity and share in patrolling the East Anglian coast at dusk and dawn seeking
German raiding parties which would have created great havoc ashore.

At the start of 1941 Army Co-operation Command pressed for faster, less vulnerable aircraft, and
the failure of the American Curtiss Tomahawk to meet the requirements for a front-line fighter led to
its being chosen for the new task of fighter-reconnaissance within Army Co-operation Command.
That raised another problem for the Tomahawk needed a longer run than was available at Westley
and other bases. So, as soon as Snailwell was ready, 268 Squadron moved there on 1 April 1941 and
to convert. Their place was taken in mid-April by Lysanders of 241 Squadron which had made the

then long journey from Inverness. They stayed only until 1 July 1941 when they transferred to Bottisham. That left the small airfield vacant for such army communications aircraft that needed it.

On 21 August 1942 a new phase was initiated when No 652 (AOP) Squadron arrived flying Tiger Moths. Re-equipment came in late 1942 when some of the first Auster AOP 1s were supplied. Westley – ideal for Austers – saw other squadrons train here in 1943. For all their ruggedness, they were also very light aeroplanes as a Stirling pilot from Ridgewell proved. Making a very low pass over Westley, the bomber's slipstream overturned an Auster!

A stream of Auster AOP squadrons passed through until the summer of 1944 before they were operationally deployed. Regular flying then ended at Westley.

Parented by Snailwell since 1941, Westley joined Technical Training Command. When the Parent became the Belgian Training School, Westley provided limited accommodation for personnel before being sold for civilian use in 1947. Prior to that No 103 Gliding School formed in October 1943 for the TAC functioned until December 1943 flying Dagling and Cadet gliders while 89 MU which handled assorted equipment was here from May 1944 to closure on 31 March 1946.

Main features:

Grass area runs: NE/SW 700 yards, E/W 550 yards, NW/SE 500 yards, N/S 670 yards all with no possible extensions. Hangar: One measuring 37ft x 42ft. *Hardstandings:* nil, aircraft picketed. *Accommodation:* Officers and SNCOs in requisitioned homes or lodging off camp, provision for 93 ORs.

WEST RAYNHAM, Norfolk

52°47N/00°44E 244ft asl; TF850245. 2 miles from village, off A1065

Like Marham, West Raynham was built amid farmland. High hedgerows concealing it extremely well achieve that because of neglect for the one time flagship of Fighter Command presents a very sad image. The impressive, extensive 'Bloodhound kennels' still cover a large area, and the runways remain. As with so many such places, who has a need for a large, well-built imposing expansion period airfield set far from any population centre or industrial base?

West Raynham opened in 1939. First in were Blenheims of 101 Squadron which arrived in May 1939, but despite its front line situation West Raynham was at first deprived of an active operational career for, at the start of the war, it became for 2 Group a second training pool. No 76 Squadron briefly here from 30 April 1940 never acquired the expected Hampdens with which the re-equipment committee wanted to re-arm 2 Group. Instead, it disbanded on 20 May 1940.

Like the modern tourist the Luftwaffe too appeared to have difficulty in finding West Raynham and proved it on 22 May 1940. A He 111 dropped a stick of bombs to the south in one of the first attempted attacks on an East Anglian airfield.

A trio of Blenheim IVs of 101 Squadron in summer 1940.

No 139 Squadron came in on 30 May 1940 to re-establish themselves after their mauling in France. They left for Horsham St Faith on 10 June and then No 101 Squadron reverted to front line service. They began operational flying on 4 July 1940 by which time a wide assortment of aircraft were on the station. No 2 Group Target Towing Flight, formed on 22 February 1940, had absorbed some of 101 Squadron's assorted items including a Battle target-tower, Blenheim Is and IVs, and an Avro Tutor.

On 12 June 1940, 18 Squadron reformed with Blenheim IVs and stayed until 9 September 1940 then moved to the Unbuilt Satellite at Great Massingham which became their permanent and gradually improved home. During autumn and winter 1940 No 101 Squadron participated actively in 2 Group's campaign. Following detachment to Manston for anti-shipping operations during April-May 1941, No 101 was re-armed with Wellington Ics, and flew a few sorties using them while still a part of 2 Group and before moving to Oakington on 6 July 1941. Air Ministry was still eager to have more longer range squadrons and to replace Blenheims in Bomber Command with more modern types.

In May-June 1941 West Raynham had served as Head Quarters for the RAF Fortress 1 Squadron, No 90, although the aircraft used Massingham. No 1420 Flight which flew special reconnaissance using Blenheim IVs arrived on 20 July 1941 and disbanded here in November.

No 101 Squadron was replaced on 6 July 1941 by another Blenheim squadron, No 114, which operated from West Raynham until August 1942. They then re-equipped with Blenheim Vds (commonly called Bisleys) before setting out for North Africa on 13 November 1942. In August 1942 No 18 Squadron returned from Massingham and, also using Blenheim Vds – which were for a few weeks an unusual yet common sight over East Anglia – emigrated to North Africa late October 1942. Among their pilots was the celebrated Wing Commander H G Malcolm VC. In May 1942, 614 Squadron's Blenheim IVs on detachment carried out intruder sorties from West Raynham in support of the '1,000-bomber' raids, a portentous act.

Lysander target towers had, in 1941, replaced the Battles in 2 Group TT Flight which, on 1 January 1942, became 1482 Bombing & Gunnery Flight (sometimes called Bomber and Gunnery Flight). Subsequently they flew Blenheim IVs, Boston IIIs and Defiant target tugs from West Raynham. In November 1942 four Martinets replaced the Defiants; a Blenheim V flight was formed and the unit acquired their first Ventura.

No 180 Squadron formed at West Raynham on 13 September 1942, their Mitchells being stationed at Great Massingham to where No 1482 Flight moved on 19 May 1943, and soon after the arrival of No 342 (Free French) Boston Squadron on 7 April 1943. That squadron moved to Sculthorpe on 5 May 1943 and West Raynham was now free of aircraft which allowed the construction of three runways which took place between 17 May and 15 November 1943. No 1482 Flight returned and made use of grass runways from 17 September. In December 1943 their Hurricanes and Mitchells were posted to Swanton Morley because a major change had come about.

On 1 December 1943 the station was transferred from 2 Group to 100 Bomber Support Group. That brought in No 141 Squadron on 4 December and No 239 on 10 December 1943, both soon taking a very active part in bomber support operations and using Mosquitoes to the end of the war. No 141 Squadron left for Little Snoring on 3 July 1945 and 239 was disbanded on 10 July 1945.

West Raynham's most influential days started with the movement here, between October and December 1945, of the Central Fighter Establishment (CFE) from Tangmere. With them came a wide assortment of aircraft used by a variety of units within the Establishment. Its role can be summarised as exploration, exploitation and example. Fighter aircraft were tried to gain the maximum Service value from them, tactical uses best suited to each type were devised and personnel with leadership qualities were trained to obtain the best returns from the high investment in aircraft and airman.

At West Raynham telescramble was developed, used in conjunction with aircraft on operational readiness platforms. 'Snake', the airborne combat flight technique was devised and trials were undertaken to gather aircraft quickly within each Sector for massed assaults on bomber formations at speed well out to sea. Dual runway operations were devised for trials at Duxford. Fighter duration employing AAR was explored, and so were recovery after combat techniques because aircraft might have to land far away from base.

There were a number of distinct units within CFE. The Air Fighting Development Squadron watched over tactical development of the Meteor F4, F8 and night fighters. Vampires, Venoms, the Swift, Hunter and finally the Lightning, although AFDS flew the latter from Coltishall. The Day

Spitfire LF 14e RM704, part of the CFE force photographed in 1946. (Sqn Ldr G R S McKay)

Fighter Leader School used Meteor 4s then 8s and in March 1958 evolved into the Day Fighter Combat School and later Fighter Leader School. Eventually it changed first into No 122 (Reserve) Squadron and then into No 63(R) Squadron which left for Binbrook in late autumn 1962. The Night Fighter Leader School (NFLS) initially flew Mosquito 36s and later Meteor 11s and 14s. In July 1950 it became the All Weather FLS and in March 1958 the AWFCS which changed into No 219(R) Squadron flying Javelins. From the Night Fighter Development Unit came the Night Fighter Development Wing which changed into the All Weather Wing and then the All Weather Development Squadron in 1951 which ultimately was No 176(R) Squadron. Reserve squadron numbers were allocated for use in wartime although some were used. Complicated name changes reflected tactical alterations from day and night fighting to all-weather operations ultimately combined in the Lightning. Exploration of early warning techniques resulted in the use of a Hamilcar glider which looked most strange among the fighters.

The Fighter Command Instrument Training Squadron moved to West Raynham in February 1950 successively flying Oxfords, Mosquito 3s and Mk 7s before becoming part of CFE in December 1952. Working alongside CFE was Nos 746 Squadron which carried out night fighting trials using Hellcats and Fireflies. They became part of 787 Squadron in January 1946, the latter operating Gannets and Avengers later. These were a later edition of the original Naval Air Fighting Development Unit.

Gradually CFE was reduced in size. In 1959 it absorbed the Fighter Weapons School and AFDS and AWDS moved to Coltishall leaving the bright-spined Hunters of DFCS, and the AWFCS, at Raynham. Those closed in 1962 leaving only the two elements at Coltishall to proceeded to Binbrook in October 1962.

Javelin F(AW) 1 XA623 of the All Weather Development Squadron seen at West Raynham.

Air Commodore E G L Millington CBE DFC heads the CFE team at the time of transfer from West Raynham to Binbrook. (Bruce Robertson Archives)

West Raynham had resumed an operational role in August 1960 when Javelin 8s of 85 Squadron arrived and were based here until disbandment on 31 March 1963. Next day the Fighter Command Target Facilities Squadron here flying Canberra T11s was renumbered 85 Squadron, and moved to Binbrook on 25 April 1963.

West Raynham then passed to 38 Group and when Waterbeach closed to flying in August 1963 accepted its two Hunter squadrons, Nos 1 and 54 flying FGA 9s which arrived in mid-August. It was from West Raynham that a pilot of No 1 Squadron was flying in April 1968 when he mounted his own 50th anniversary tribute to the Royal Air Force by flying between the spans of Tower Bridge. Feelings at the time were right behind him, although his action was hazardous. Harold Wilson's Labour government had handled some vicious defence cuts most clumsily and lacked the sense to heal running sores by agreeing to mount a special event in recognition of the birthday.

Hunters of CFE by Raynham's tower.

Between September 1965 and September 1970 No 41 Squadron's Bloodhound IIs were a skyline sight. In the 1980s more in the hands of No 85 Squadron pointing East were a constant reminder of the real threat from the Warsaw Pact. Based here between 1975 and 1988 was the Bloodhound Mobile Support Unit which closed when No 85 Squadron disbanded. The Bloodhound Is had an action radius of around seventy miles whereas the Mk II had almost doubled that reach. The Hunter left in July 1969. During their stay they had, between October 1964 and November 1965, had for companions the Kestrel Evaluation Squadron here to evaluate the revolutionary concept which was a lead in to the Harrier.

Two Canberra target facilities squadrons moved in, No 85 on 28 January 1972 and No 100 which reformed on 1 February 1972. No 85 disbanded on 19 December 1975 and No 100 moved to Marham. On 1 August 1972 No 45 Squadron reformed with Hunter FGA9s to provide a training force within 38 Group. They proceeded to Wittering on 29 September 1972. West Raynham then closed to flying, but remained an important station for Bloodhound Mk II missiles of 85 Squadron were based here in an enclave on the eastern side of the flying ground. No 85 disbanded, West Raynham wound down, the RAF ensign was lowered for the last time on 1 July . Part of the domestic site has been sold for private dwelling.

Main features (December 1944):
Runways (only two): 040° 6,000ft x 150ft, 100°, concrete and tarmac. *Hangars:* four C Type. *Hardstandings:* thirty-six heavy bomber type. *Accommodation:* RAF: 156 officers, 144 SNCOs, 1,364 ORs; WAAF: 12 officers, 24 SNCOs, 324 ORs. During the mid-1950s two large ASPs were built forming an apron flanking flying control, An ORP was laid at each end of the main runway. Technical sites were behind the hangars and on the south-east side of the airfield which was not a split site.

WETHERSFIELD, Essex

51°58N/00°30E 315ft asl; TL720335. On B1053 SE of Finchingfield

'We've had the OK from HQ USAFE', said the Base Commander. 'The Captain here will be flying you.' We journeyed to the helicopter in the inevitable giant limousine, yet the Piasecki was only a stone's throw away. Kitted out we wandered over to the banana-shaped object. 'I think I should tell you that we've never flown one of these before in such a strong wind', said the pilot. 'There is quite a chance that when we start a gust could cause the main rotor to crash onto the cabin roof. It could be sticky.' Then he added, 'If we have an engine failure – and there have been some – then the helicopter will drop tail first, and you will hear the rotor blades break on impact. Best sit up front for the whole journey. You're still keen to come aren't you?'

You bet I was, a flight in an H-21 would never become one of be life's most common experiences for anyone. In the event all went well, and we carried out fire fighting training before returning at almost no forward speed in a 24-knot headwind.

But the day many more will ever recall was that when the Americans introduced the F-100, the Super Sabre. Ancient 16mm poor quality colour films, chit-chat about approach patterns and noise, a Yankee brunch and all the usual US razzmatazz preceded a stunning show by The Skyblazers, by far the best US team ever seen in Europe and whose low-level crossovers above the crowd were – wow!

And surely, no recollections of Wethersfield's other super show days could be complete without mention of that wonder machine, the Starfighter, billed as 'The Missile with a Man in it'. But what became more memorable? Machine, or man standing by the prow of his mount in stetson and cowboy rig complete with gleaming silvery spurs, a truly fabulous, incredible sight before he headed off into the wild blue yonder – presumably towards Roswell to deal with the aliens.

Professionals will doubtless have more action-packed memories of Wethersfield – the alarming 'all-out' then 'all-in' alerts, the mass scrambles, the Mk VII 'nukes' hung only on Thunderstreaks and Super Sabres after give away curved external racks were fitted. What disturbing moments that combination produced. Whether any ever fell off we may never know – or even want to know! Why worry, you have survived – so far.

Wethersfield announced as completed on 30 June 1943 seemed an unlikely place for such goings on. Although largely complete by December 1942 as a satellite for Ridgewell, it saw relatively little use probably because the USAAF did not disperse its bombers arriving as it did when German air attacks

A-20G 5H-B of the 668th BS, 416th BG (USAF).

were few. It opened as a self accounting RAF station within Bomber Command in January 1944, and passed to the US 9th AF which took up residence on 1 February positioning the 416th Bomb Group and its A-20G and H Havocs here. Clear-nosed leadships led formations usually eighteen-strong and linked with the other two A-20 Groups within *Rodeos* when they began tactical daylight bombing on 4 March 1944 during the pre-invasion period and the assault on V-weapon sites in France.

Once a large foothold in France was secured the 416th was based beyond effective operational range so in September 1944 it quit Wethersfield for Melun/Villeroche, south of Paris and from where the 'famous' Cambridge Do 217M-1 set out.

Transfer began during the immediate run-up to the September airborne venture became complete on the 25th, intention being that upon its completion RAF airborne squadrons would advance to stations vacated in East Anglia by the 9th AF. Instead, it was delayed until Albemarles were replaced and Stirling squadrons recovered from their terrible mauling during operation *Market Garden*.

Transfer of 38 Group Stirlings to Wethersfield began on 9 October 1944, but it was incomplete until November by which time the Stirling GT IVs of Nos 196 and 299 Squadrons were in place. Supply drops to Resistance forces soon commenced, interspersed with much daylight glider tug training. Within a few weeks serious drainage problems plagued the airfield so much that the squadrons moved to Shepherd's Grove in two stages during the last week of January 1945. During this period the station was under the control of Fighter Command like others in the area where substitutions were involved.

Once conditions permitted 9th Air Force C-47s – lighter than Stirlings – moved in briefly for a share in the Rhine Crossing operation of 24 March 1945. All carrying paratroops, no less than eighty-one C-47s – Dakotas to us – set forth to release the 6th Airborne Division into battle. Task completed the Americans left, Wethersfield quietened and Transport Command pondered the future. That turned out to involve the Operational & Refresher Training Unit which in October 1945 brought along Halifaxes and a Flight of Stirlings. On 19 October 1945 No 1677 Target Towing Flight slotted in and stayed until disbandment on 25 January 1946. O & RTU became No 1385 Heavy Transport Support Conversion Unit on 1 April 1946, relinquished Stirlings and remained until July 1946 when SHQ Wethersfield closed. The station passed to Care & Maintenance and in January 1947 was declared a Standby uncommitted station.

To officials Wethersfield held a major post-war attraction – it was situated well away from many anti-noise civilians. In wartime the populace did not complain about noise and was more than happy with the trade and 'entertainments' that airfields brought.

In September 1950, when the Americans were pressing for permanent fighter bases in Britain, Wethersfield soon became a firm choice. The airfield, with the usual three runways-two T2s – and fifty spectacle-type hardstandings had, after four neglectful years, fallen into poor state. With basic accommodation still only Nissen huts from wartime days, 16 April 1951 saw Fighter Command take control and investigation began into upgrading the base. On 30 June 1951 it was allocated to the USAF for use under Plan *Galloper*. Only the main 6,000ft runway would be lengthened and by 1,000ft at either end which meant acquiring agricultural land and closing a public road at the east end. Modern runway lighting required cable ducts along its edges and by taxiways. Much stronger hardstandings – eventually forty-two – would be able to accommodate eighty-four fighter-bombers, another four stands being modified into a maintenance platform. A new, but standard 'R' Type 70,000 gallon bulk fuel store, fed by underground piping, would replace the existing one and be supplemented later by a 60,000 gallon store.

On 24 August 1951 Wethersfield passed to Third Air Force control, the first US occupants being a Det. 1780th AACS which came on 24 November 1951. The British and US agreed that a 153-pupil RAF Flying Training School using sixty-five Harvards could, if necessary, make interim use of the base from March 1952. School staff would number 773, pilot training taking place alongside the base rebuilding programme. That included erecting Armseal or Quonset pre-fabricated huts and some US Butler buildings. The extent of the work was very considerable for it included resurfacing 4,000 square yards of existing roads and laying 900 feet of 18ft wide new roads. A 10ft high 3,500ft long chain link fence with three-strand barbed wire topping would initially surround the base and help protect eighteen earth revetments housing weapons including nuclear types.

With the Cold War intensifying the Americans returned in strength. On 1 December 1951 the base was attached to the 49th Air Division who designated it operational from 12 February 1952. The 20th FBG which began moving in from Langley, VA, on 22 May followed on 1 June by two squadrons nominally of fifty Republic F-84G Thunderjet fighter-bombers which came via Labrador and Iceland. Wing HQ began functioning at Wethersfield on 31 May, each of its three squadrons (55 blue, 77 red and 79 yellow based at Woodbridge) having a T-33A continuation trainer. A tactical force under USAFE, they were from 31 May 1952 controlled by the 49th Air Division. Overall control passed to HQ 3rd AD on 5 June 1952.

They trained in dive and general fighter bombing in the UK, European fine weather countries and in north Africa. On 8 February 1955 the 20th Fighter-Bomber Group became the 20th Fighter-Bomber Wing. A more evident change came when in June 1955 they began converting to F-84F Thunderstreak fighter-bombers started replacing ageing F-84Gs. The other very obvious feature of the swept-wing new-comers was the multiplicity of stores they readily carried – including core-less 'nuclear' weapons when training.

F-84F Thunderstreak of the 55th TFS 20th TFW Wethersfield.

Next came the spectacular 'Century Fighter', the noisy re-heat F-100D Super Sabres. Invitations to learn about them flooded the area, for the local population had awoken to jet noise and worse was now to come. In an extensive publicity stunt they brought seemingly everyone to have a good look at the aircraft and, after amazingly limited medical checks, flew a few unwise souls some of whom had never even flown before and whose introduction to flight was in supersonic fighters. One to whom I spoke, a local important person, had clearly been petrified and probably never regained his former political posturing!

The Americans explained that run-up pens would be shielded by trees from nearby delightful Finchingfield. Harmless 'after burners' would indeed roar, and they were sorry that their flight plan – the best they could achieve – might cause some annoyance. Noticing that climb out took them over Cambridge I told them they had at least one satisfied customer. Mine, though, was a lone voice.

F-100Ds on Wethersfield's maintenance area O-53655 nearest, in June 1966.

F-100D and 100F Super Sabres began re-arming the 20th in June 1957 and the unit was renamed the 20th Tactical Fighter Wing on 8 July 1958. Thereafter the USAF's Wethersfield annual Armed Forces Days attracted huge crowds, the many splendid shows passing into aviation folklore.

The 23rd Helicopter Squadron (Detachment), 322 AD, had four medical role Piasecki H-21Bs here from November 1956 until late 1957, replaced later by the 40th ARRW (Det.12) using HH-43F Husky helicopters with intermeshing rotors and used for rescue and 'fire suppression'.

On 1 July 1961, because of the latest Berlin crisis, the 20th was passed to 17th AF control and returned to 3rd AF on 1 September 1963. Constant modifications were made to the base and in 1967 extra accommodation was built. The F-100s camouflaged from 1966 were becoming dated by 1970 and when the 20th began re-arming with F-111Es in September 1970 they did so at Upper Heyford better equipped and sited more protectively from air attack. On 1 April 1970 the 66th Combat Support Group took over Wethersfield from where the 55th TFS departed on 1 May and the 77th on 1 June 1970 upon which day HQ 20th TFW also left.

Wethersfield became a Dual Operating Base redesignated a Standby Operating Base (for Alconbury's 10th TRW) on 28 July 1970 (and throughout known as RAF Wethersfield) and prepared to host dual-based CONUS units. The 66th CSG was reduced to being the 66th CSS on 1 October 1970.

Between May and August 1975 five U-2C (upgraded to U-2F standard) *Pave Onyx* aircraft of the 349th SRS, 100 SRW, flew missions from here. On 31 July 1976 the 66th was replaced and Wethersfield became Operation Location A (OLA), 10th Tactical Reconnaissance Wing, RAF Wethersfield and on 1 August 1976 was renamed Detachment 1, 10th TRW, RAF Wethersfield. During 1977 assigned military strength fell from 138 men to 9. In 1977 RAF Phantoms from Wattisham were detached here while their runway was being attended to. The 819th CES (HR) arrived from McConnell AFB on 8 April 1979 along with the 819th Red Horse Engineering Squadron.

Det.1 of the 17th TRW early in 1984 was established at Wethersfield to support Alconbury but the runway state was too poor to permit that. Instead the 7119th AB Support Flight watched over US activity and the 2166th Communications Squadron.

USAF tenancy ended in Spring 1991 after which Wethersfield became and remains a depot for the MoD Police.

Main features (December 1944):
Runways: 290° 6,000ft x 150ft, 330°, 040°, concrete. *Hangars:* two T2.
Hardstandings: fifty. *Accommodation:* RAF: 207 officers, 473 SNCOs, 1,360 ORs;
WAAF 10 officers, 7 SNCOs, 371 ORs.

Places of interest nearby:
Attractive Finchingfield should not be missed. Hedingham Castle has fine grounds and a superb keep dating from 1140. The Colne Valley steam railway operates from near Castle Hedingham.

WEYBOURNE, Norfolk

52°57N/01°10E 70ft asl; TG010437. Off A149, 3 miles W of Sheringham

What constitutes an airfield? Is it a site where aircraft land and take off? Although Weybourne fitted that description much of the flying was unconventional.

Summer 1936 saw anti-aircraft gunners at the No 5 Heavy AA Division Practice Camp begin using new ranges on the north Norfolk coast for firing at targets towed by Westland Wallace biplanes flying from Bircham Newton. Firing practice continued, including the use of US Skysweep cannon from Stiffkey Marshes, into the mid-1950s.

Weybourne, though, was special for there was built a catapult launcher from which radio-controlled Queen Bee targets could be released and guided out to sea. After the gunners had tried to shoot them down, disable them or engage with proximity fused shells, the aircraft could either be brought down in the sea – upon the sea if they were of the floatplane variety – or landed in a field close by for further use.

Queen Bee N-1846 ready for catapult launch from Weybourne. (Bruce Robertson Archives)

Such activities began at Weybourne after 'X' Flight, No 1 Anti-Aircraft Co-operation Unit, arrived on 16 May 1939. First launch of a Queen Bee took place on 6 June 1939 and subsequently many repeats followed although not without moments of concern. N1846 was launched on 29 June, damaged by gunfire, landed on the sea, repaired and hit by 3.7in anti-aircraft fire on 2 August as a result of which it sank.

The Flight left Weybourne just after the war started and then more conventional firing training directed at towed sleeve or banner targets took place from the AA camp.

A second period of Queen Bee activity commenced in January 1941 with the formation at Weybourne of 'T' Flight, a Pilot-less Aircraft Flight of 1 AACU. A salvage boat was assigned followed in February by a seaplane tender. The first catapult launch took place on 8 April 1941, when the Queen Bee flew out to sea and was not heard of again. Exercises undertaken on 22 April were more successful and resulted in a Queen Bee landing on the beach after being hit. A steady release of targets and shoots then ensued.

Considerable excitement came on 6 June 1941 when the Prime Minister and a large distinguished company arrived to watch a demonstration of 'Z' battery firing. The principle under which the batteries operated was for a salvo of rockets to be fired in such a manner as to produce a box barrage with the target being caught in the centre. As intended the rockets roared away, Queen Bee V4797 ran into a salvo of 160 UP rockets, then landed unscathed on the sea and was retrieved by the salvage boat SS *Radstock*. There was not time for a repeat performance. What thoughts passed through Sir Winston's mind seem nowhere to have been discovered, but he did have a sense of humour!

Subsequent training with UP weapons was more successful, but more often than not what brought total success was the loss of an aerial sometimes shot away causing control of the target to be lost.

On 18 June 1941 another demonstration of rocket power was held for the Prime Minister. After no less than forty-five minutes of firing a near burst put a Queen Bee out of control and it spun into the sea. A repeat demonstration of the weapons resulted in no hits so the Queen Bee was finished off by Bofors fire.

Landing the Queen Bees on a prepared grass area close to the RA camp was also far from easy because they had often sustained damage. On 23 August after ninety-one rounds of fire had managed to damage a Queen Bee it was landed on the strip only to head on through a hedge and into an adjacent meadow. 'T' Flight was disbanded on 29 April 1942 and the aircraft side of activity ceased at Weybourne, although AA gunners used the off-shore range for more than a decade, firing against towed targets. 'Z' rocket firing practice was also undertaken by the shore at Heacham where Home Guard AA units undertook practice live firing.

Place of interest nearby:
The Muckleburgh Collection of military equipment, radar, memorabilia, photographs etc is near the AA firing site.

WITCHFORD, Cambridgeshire

52°22N/00°14E 45ft asl; TL520780. 2 miles S of Ely W of A10, also visible S from A142

For hundreds of years the isles of the Fens have provided sanctuary and succour. In times past, when floods came, local people fled to protecting high ground and the Isle of Ely upon which Witchford partly stands. Helping the needy was something Witchford's fliers also achieved.

In late autumn 1944 the Dutch, seeing the Allies advancing, decided to give them special support, and railway workers in the north of Holland went on strike. By way of retaliation the Germans flooded large areas, effectively cutting off the region of Holland which had virtually revolted. Food supplies ran low, and the Germans thought they could starve the Dutch into submission. Starve them they did, to the extent that the Netherlanders scoured their fields for bulbs safe to eat and were forced to consume their pets in order to remain alive.

The Allies had their hands full with offensive action, but by February 1945 felt bound to do something about aiding the Dutch. What could be done? Food would have to be delivered, but how could that be achieved? It would need to be air dropped in daylight which was clearly a hazardous venture.

To explore what would be involved a Lancaster crew of 115 Squadron, Witchford was detached to Netheravon, there to conduct trials in which food packed in bags in Small Bomb Containers was dropped from low level. That was not as easy as it might sound for the food sacks repeatedly burst upon impact until the delivery aircraft flew very low to drop the load successfully.

On 6 April 1945 practise dropping of food supplies, thought also likely to be needed by our POWs, was shown to VIPs at Witchford. Next day the technique using HK798 was demonstrated to Bomber Command officers gathered at Lacey Green. Displayed was the delivery of six SBCs each carrying 1,245lb of food, one fifth the possible load. Witchford hosted Marshal of the RAF Lord Trenchard who came to tea on 19 April and saw a Lancaster dropping food supplies. Preparations were now going ahead for what became operation *Manna* in which Bomber Command heavies and some from the US 8th AF would deliver supplies once the bombing campaign seemed completed.

No 115 Squadron flew their final wartime bombing raid, against Bad Oldeslö, on 24 April 1945 and on the 29th food drops to the Netherlanders began. Each Lancaster carried five packs of provisions, 115's eight Lancasters delivering 59,551lb of food. In clear weather apart from April showers the Lancasters thundered low over huge crowds watching in Den Haag. So grateful for salvation were they that it seemed as if the entire city was in the streets celebrating. Yet for all involved there were moments of sorrow when many sacks burst open upon impact. As they crashed onto the ground flour dispersed in clouds but so desperate were some people that they seized handfuls of the 'manna' and immediately swallowed it. The small size of the drop areas caused congestion for the fliers some of whom had to drop from greater heights than planned. Food supplies drifted into target indicator flares and quite large fires resulted and that was distressing to all.

The following day, 30 April, the Lancaster crews tried again, among them twenty of 115 Squadron. This time the DZ was near Rotterdam, and too many sacks slumped in drainage ditches. Others, as they fell, smashed into the desperate crowds and caused serious injuries. Others waiting in carts and lorries seized all the supplies that they could. One of the most distressing moments came when a target indicator dropped from a Mosquito hit a house which, within seconds, was engulfed by fire. No 115 Squadron participated in six more drops the last on 8 May, deliveries including sweets for children and tobacco for their elders whose appeals had been seen in huge white letters on roof tops. As soon as *Manna* was completed, and like so many other squadrons of Bomber Command, 115's Lancasters on 9 May joined in operation *Exodus*, the bringing home of POWs from French airfields.

Manna brought unforgettable sights to Eastern skies. My recollection is of hundreds of Lancasters – much of Bomber Command's strength – flying truly at little above roof top height, something seen only at this time. On 7 May almost the whole of 1 Group and others flew at no higher than 200ft over Cambridge, the gaggle so lengthy that the lead aircraft were returning just as the tail end was heading out! It was as if the Command was mounting a fantastic victory fly-past now that the slaughter was all but over. For Witchford that also meant that its end was drawing nigh.

Another of those awfully muddy typically wartime bomber airfields, it was just a collection of two 'T' Hangars, a 'B1', three runways and assorted concrete, metal or wooden huts. Building it on the side of the Isle of Ely, its surface sloping considerably, led to various drainage problems.

The station opened on 1 June 1943 as an un-built satellite in 3 Group. Although complete by 1 August, it was not declared fully open until 31 August 1943 by which time it was in operational use. No 196 Squadron began moving in on 9 July 1943, was being transferred from 1 Group and taken off operations on 14 July. Their eighteen Wellington Xs were all there by 19 July then on 22 July No 196 received their first two Stirling IIIs. With establishment of sixteen plus four, they met on 24 August and despatched their first operation, mining, on 26 August and Witchford's first bombing raid, against Mönchengladbach, was launched on 30 August. Next night they attacked Berlin, took part in the Mont Lucon raid of 15 September and the following night bombed Modane. Other targets attacked included Frankfurt, Hanover, Kassel and Mannheim. Mines were also placed in enemy waters.

Between 25 August 1943 and 1 September 1945 Witchford was part of 33 Base Waterbeach. A second Witchford-based Stirling III squadron, No 513, began forming on 15 September 1943. It took on charge its first two aircraft ex-75 Squadron. Mepal, on 21 October and had eleven by 27 October. Withdrawal of Stirlings from bombing operations had been decided upon on 31 July but Lancasters losses and production output extended the Stirling's career. Another policy leader was to use them as glider tugs which resulted in No 196 Squadron flying its last operation from Witchford on 10 November and re-locating at Leicester East after briefly joining 93 Group before switching to No 38 Group, Transport Command on 18 November and after operating on twenty-nine nights from Witchford. No 513 Squadron on 27 November 1943 saw all its Stirlings withdrawn from strength before any operations were flown. Three days later all squadron personnel were posted to Chedburgh where a new No 1653 Conversion Unit was forming. No 513 Squadron was officially closed on 24 December.

On 24 November Lancaster IIs of 115 Squadron, the first to fully equip with Hercules-engined Lancasters, began arriving from Little Snoring. On 26/27 November the squadron despatched twelve aircraft to Berlin. One failed to return and another with serious flak damage forced landed on return. On 28 November a third or 'C' Flight was added to the squadron raising its strength from twenty to thirty aircraft. Mk IIs served until May 1944 by which time Merlin-engined Lancaster Is and IIIs had largely replaced them, conversion taking place while the squadron continued to operate intensively. Berlin, the Ruhr, the railways on the mainland of north-west Europe softening-up for the Normandy invasion, participation in all those operations took place. One memorable night was 18 April 1944 when, as the bombers were returning from Rouen, an Me 410 joined the circuit and shot down two Lancasters (LL667-R and LL967-J) which were circling prior to landing.

On 1 October 1944 No 195 Squadron reformed here and was armed with sixteen Lancaster Is plus four Lancaster IIIs some crews being posted in from 115 Squadron. The first operation by '195' took place on 26 October with Leverküsen as target. Ten raids involving over 130 sorties were flown, the last to Homberg on 8 November. On 13 November No 195 moved to West Wratting there replacing No 1651 CU.

During its tenure at Witchford No 115 Squadron despatched 4,601 sorties during 218 operations from which forty-three Lancasters failed to return. Bombs dropped included 8,000lb HC weapons produced by joining 4,000-pounders and for which aircraft were specially modified, HK698-IL:A of 'C' Flight being one example. On 20 December 1943 six aircraft each dropped one of these large weapons on Frankfurt. Some No 195 Squadron aircraft had the same capability, three of them (HK587, HK679 and HK686) each delivering an 8,000-pounder to Homberg on 2 November 1944.

No 115 bade farewell to Witchford towards the end of August 1945 and began re-establishing itself at Graveley on 10 September 1945 although it was not fully functioning there until the end of that month. That had left Witchford winding down. Closure came in March 1946.

In September 1950 Wyton assumed responsibility for what was now 'Inactive Station Witchford' soon to be transferred to the Ministry of Agriculture. Nevertheless February 1951 saw its status confirmed as a Standby Airfield within Plan G. Although the landing ground and some buildings were being used for agricultural purposes the B1 hangar was allocated to the USAF on 1 June 1950 and designated Ely Ration Depot. Between 10 April 1952 and 9 August 1952 it was manned by a Detachment 7558 Supply Squadron Depot and then returned to the UK. The hangar remains, modified and in good condition in civilian hands. Little else marks the one-time airfield, apart from a converted hangar, a few huts and two gate posts marking an entrance from the A10(T) road.

Main features:
Runways: 100° 2,000 x 50 yards, 160°, 220°, all concrete. *Hangars:* two T2, one B1. *Hardstandings:* thirty-six concrete. *Accommodation:* RAF: 125 officers, 345 SNCOs, 1,032 ORs; WAAF 2 officers, 6 SNCOs, 222 ORs.

Places of interest nearby:
RAF Witchford Museum, assembled by Barry Aldridge, can be found in the offices of Grovemere Holdings on the old airfield business site. Ely Cathedral, the heart of the small city, stands on a site where in 673 St Etheldreda founded a monastery. Work on the magnificent Romanesque cathedral started in 1081 and was completed in 1189. During the 1939-45 war it served as a welcoming homing sight for many aircrew and now is a prominent sighting for US citizens approaching RAF Mildenhall. Inside may be found the Memorial Books for Nos 2, 3, 8 and 100 Groups RAF which rest below stained glass windows recalling the Groups and their aircraft. The cannon on the green outside was used at Sebastopol in the Crimean War, and nearby is the one-time home of Oliver Cromwell.

Beyond Ely on the Littleport Road was the famous RAF Hospital to which a large number of RAF personnel injured in battle or unwell came for treatment. In appearance it had all the graciousness of a pre-war expansion period permanent RAF station. Opened in 1940, its last RAF patient was discharged on 7 July 1992. The RAF began leaving on 31 July, and its tenancy ended in December 1992 when the NHS moved in to operate the hospital as a 'community health resource'. Hope was that as The Princess of Wales Hospital, it would provide for Ely and the surrounding area but the magic word 'funding' brought general disappointment and sadly has much reduced its value.

WOODBRIDGE, Suffolk

52°05N/01°24E 94ft asl; TM330487. S of B1084, S of Bentwaters

Woodbridge clearly doesn't want to be divorced from flying! That's not surprising when one considers all that it has witnessed. Take for example the story of Flying Officer R F Limbert and crew who were among twenty-nine flying Lancasters of 514 Squadron from Waterbeach, and which set off at midday on 15 November 1944 to bomb the Hösch Benzin works at Dortmund. Aboard LM288 was a 4,000lb 'Cookie', fifteen 500-pounders and flares. Flak on the run-in to Dortmund was quite heavy, but it was not this that soon brought alarm.

Above them were other Lancasters and, at the moment of bomb release, LM288 alias 'C Charlie' was directly below one of these other aircraft. A falling 500-pounder smashed into their port outer engine and another rammed against the port inner badly damaging it. Another penetrated the fuselage beside the main spar and yet another hit the starboard outer engine. Their own bombs released they made for home, and miraculously scraped in at Woodbridge.

Bringing damaged bombers safely home, and particularly at night, had been a great problem. Many crashed because their crews became lost, or the aircraft ran out of fuel or had severe battle damage. Usually they were told to land at any aerodrome able to receive them, but many airfields were unable to accept them at short notice, or had unsuitable runways. As a result of the great increases in night bomber activity in 1942 came the decision to construct three huge runways at Carnaby, Manston and Woodbridge and all able to accept aircraft in trouble.

All three wide runways were sited close to the East Coast to allow crippled bombers to land immediately after crossing the coastline. Each strip was 9,000ft long and 750ft wide. At either end was an overshoot 1,500ft long giving the runway a total length of 12,000ft. Each runway was laterally divided into three lanes. The southern lane lined with green lights at night and white by day was the emergency lane into which any aircraft could land without first contacting flying control. The centre lane was lined by white lights at night, the northern by yellow. By day the lines of lights clearly defined the three sections of the runway. The airfield lighting system comprised contact and Drem lights on the runway, with funnel and approach lights on the circuit.

FIDO was installed at all three bases. Investigation into fog dispersal by petrol burning from a long line of jets by the runway edge had much increased during 1942. It was found that, after entering the fog zone and descending to 100ft, touchdown then became virtually visual. The main burner lines for the runway lighting began 250 yards from the touchdown end of the runway which was sealed from fog intrusion by a cross line of burners. FIDO installed at fifteen airfields became operational in November 1943. Woodbridge opened on 1 September 1943, the runway was declared completed on 15 September and it opened for business on 15 November 1943, its usefulness at once apparent for thirty-six aircraft landed there in the next two weeks, one needing 9,000ft of runway and 600ft of overshoot.

The site chosen was almost ideal because it was nearly fog free and had no obstructions for miles. But it was in the middle of a forest owned by the Forestry Commission and before construction could commence more than a million small trees had to be cleared, which much displeased the local population. Construction began in July 1942 and when completed the runway was 3,000ft longer than normal runways and five times wider. It covered 159 acres.

Woodbridge received its first emergency landing on 18 July 1943, long before it opened – a B-17 short of fuel. This was the first of 4,120 emergency landings made to the end of June 1945. A fateful incident on 17 December 1943 led to the realisation that the runway approach lighting was inadequate. Five Halifaxes were diverted here and haze was at 300ft so that the pilots could not see any lights. None of the aircraft had beam approach equipment and the direction finder could not home them in. One crew landed, but the others crashed in the vicinity with the cost of thirteen lives. By the end of April 1944 sodium and incandescent lights had been installed on the south side of the runway to within a mile of the coast at Orford.

Over sixty aircraft were handled in January 1944 and seventy-two the next month, of which forty-eight were USAAF aircraft. FIDO began to be installed in February 1944. In March 130 landings were made, followed by 159 in April. These totals increased steadily, June 1944 being a busy month when, for the first time, the station came under enemy attack. Several bombs fell close on 28 June, the nearest being 300 yards from the FIDO fuel store tanks containing over a million gallons of petrol. Flying-bombs also penetrated the area and a sharp eyed controller thinking one to be an aircraft tried homing it with his Aldis Lamp. Luckily he was unsuccessful.

Incidents came fast at Woodbridge. In the early hours of 22 June a Lancaster damaged by fighters and with 11,000lb of bombs aboard touched down in the green lane. On landing it swerved and came to rest on the south side of the amber lane. Personnel were warned away because a B-17 was landing on the green lane. This swerved and cut the Lancaster in half. Since the green lane was free another Lancaster was allowed to land, and in doing so its undercarriage collapsed and the bomber slid to a halt blocking the lane. The controller was about to close the runway until wreckage could be cleared when yet another Lancaster requested an emergency landing. The pilot had so little fuel when landing that he passed low over the wreckage, illuminated by searchlights, touching down beyond the debris. This all took place within a mere thirteen minutes.

The early hours of 13 July 1944 were equally memorable. An aircraft landed and when ground crew arrived they found it was German. The occupants on realising their error were trying to destroy the aircraft when an NCO wrenched open a door beneath the aircraft and the pilot fell out. There was a struggle and then the other two occupants surrendered. Interrogation revealed they had been on a flight from Holland to Berlin and, with little fuel left, landed unaware of their position.

Their aircraft, a fairly new Ju 88G night fighter, was no mean prize for it carried the latest German *Liechtenstein* SN-2 radar which was proving very effective against RAF bombers. The Ju 88 was flown to Farnborough where its radar was examined. As a result Bomber Command used a revised system against SN-2 during the Kiel raid of 23 July 1944.

The 1,000th emergency landing at Woodbridge came in August. One of the most spectacular arrivals then was a B-17 with a 16ft hole in the belly under the spar and another 6-8ft hole in the fuselage side. More than 50 per cent of the starboard mainplane was missing, and all due to heavy calibre flak. It was a write-off, but many arrivals were repaired then flown out.

October 1944 found the station a quagmire due to the heavy rain. Much water rested on the runway and the drainage system could barely cope with it. Many of the 306 landings were aided by FIDO. The first fatal accident during November occurred when a Lancaster flew into the runway. By the end of 1944, 2,719 aircraft had made use of Woodbridge, 570 aircrew had been treated in station sick quarters and records were forever being broken. In 2½ hours on a January day 950 diverted aircrew arrived, but activity lessened when better weather came.

The station was closed on 19 March 1945 for five days when two Halifax squadrons towed in sixty-eight Hamilcar and Horsa gliders. Sixty combinations then took part in the Rhine crossing assault, operation *Varsity*, but for various reasons only thirty-eight Hamilcars and eleven Horsas landed in the designated areas.

As an extensively damaged Halifax approached on 9 April 1945, one of the crew was seen to be dangling beneath. The mid-upper gunner had in fact fallen through the floor and his parachute harness was caught in the rear of the shattered bomb bay. Apart from 3½ hours suffering terribly from exposure he was uninjured, although his oxygen mask and goggles scraped the runway surface as the bomber landed. By the end of June 1945 4,120 landings had been made, an outstanding contribution to the war effort. Post-war the station remained in use, with only 244 landings in one year.

The proximity of Woodbridge to Martlesham Heath, virtually an RAE outpost, led to its use for experimental work including the dropping of 'Tallboy' and 'Grand Slam' bombs at Orfordness by Lancasters of the BBU flying from Woodbridge and formed in summer 1944 with Halifaxes and a Mosquito. The Blind Landing Experimental Unit also worked from here as well as Martlesham.

On 15 May 1946 the maiden flight of the DH 108 Swallow tail-less jet took place here, but by then Woodbridge was a shadow of its former self although experimental work at Martlesham had been transferred there. Woodbridge was abandoned by the RAF on 15 March 1948 being surplus to need although the site was retained and used by the Ministry of Supply.

RAF interest was resumed on 26 May 1952 when Fighter Command took control from Maintenance Command leaving the MoS as a lodger. The USAF gained administrative control of Woodbridge on 5 June 1952 and it became the home of the 79th Bomber Squadron of the 20th Bomber Wing flying F-84Gs and later F-84Fs, and from 1957 F-100s. A new squadron operations block was constructed in 1953, a new fire station in 1956 and base housing which was brought fully into use in April 1957. These dwellings were built by the UK Government in a deal by which tobacco was accepted in payment, so that the scheme quickly became known as 'Tobacco Housing'.

Operational control of Woodbridge was taken over by the 81st TFW Bentwaters and at the same time, 8 July 1958, it became twinned then and prepared to receive another squadron, although facilities were none too adequate. In December, the runway ends were resurfaced and turn-offs placed at the 3,000ft and 6,000ft intervals and in January 1959 the 78th Tactical Fighter Squadron moved in from Shepherd's Grove. At the time they were converting from F-84Fs to F-101s, and arrived from Shepherd's Grove. F-4C Phantoms for the 81st TFW touched down at Woodbridge on 2 March 1966, and the 78th TFS received their first F-4D on 23 April 1969 and were fully re-armed by July.

F-84G Thunderjet of the 79th FBS, Woodbridge, seen at Bentwaters in May 1955.

F-86D 52-0055 of the 406th FIW arrives at Woodbridge from weapons training at Tripoli, 18 May 1957. (Alan J Wright)

In November 1969 the 79th TFS moved to Upper Heyford. In their place during December 1968 and January 1970 came the 67th Aerospace Rescue & Recovery Squadron from Moron AFB in Spain. They brought in HC-130N and 'P' Hercules and HH-3E Jolly Green Giant helicopters all of which were a familiar sight over the ensuing years.

Late 1977 saw the establishment of an F-4E 'Pave Strike' modification line, but more dramatic was the local change from F-4s to A-10As. As part of the 81st TFW's expansion scheme to provide more space for four A-10 squadrons, the 91st TFS moved from Bentwaters to Woodbridge in 1978. The 92nd TFS became effective with A-10s on 24 August 1979 and the 78th TFS on 3 June 1979. The 116th FS had become the 78th (red) years before.

The next major change came on 3 June 1988 when the 21 Special Operations Squadron was activated here, controlled by the 39 SOW at Hurlburt Field and to operate the ex-601 TCW HH-53Cs and HH-53Js. The same day the 67th ARRS became the 67 SOG, part of the 39 SOW. The combined SOG then moved to Alconbury.

On 15 May 1992 the 78th TFS stood down, followed by the 91st TFS on 28 August. In the middle of that month aircraft movements ceased apart from a few transport flights connected with the collection of equipment.

HC-130H 14866 of the type based at Woodbridge in the 1960s.

F-4D 65-702 of the 78th TFS, 81st TFW on the Woodbridge runway in 1970.
(P Offen via George Pennick)

A common sight in the Woodbridge area, an Apache Longbow from Wattisham.

After a break of two years flying resumed at Woodbridge. Army helicopters – Lynx and Gazelle – used a small part of the base for flying training. Autumn 1998 saw it used as the starting point for a large scale helicopter exercise. Much of the housing is now occupied by Army personnel and families and much new building has taken place.

In Rendlesham Forest near the east gate of Woodbridge on 26 December 1980 a strange light was seen which supposedly landed amongst the trees and scorched its touchdown area. Nothing was then seen on local radar, nor when the spectacle returned later that day. Many years later it was stated that the reported 'UFO' was a beam of light from Orfordness lighthouse which the USAF admitted chasing. Most UFO sightings can be shown to have no 'ET' origin – except for a few which defy simple explanation.

Main features:

Sole emergency runway: 270° 9,000ft x 750ft with 1,500ft grass overruns at each end. Sand-mix and bitumen. Mk II Drem lighting. *Hangars:* one B1, one Blister. *Hardstandings:* eight loops each able to accommodate fifteen large aircraft. *Accommodation:* 18 officers, 47 SNCOs, 520 ORs.

Post-war alterations included T2 hangars at the eastern area of the site and a narrowed, shortened runway. Much new building has occurred.

WOODHALL SPA, Lincolnshire

53°08/00°11W 45ft asl; TF210615. 2 miles E of Woodhall Spa by B1192 Coningsby road

Set amid the small, attractive town of Woodhall Spa stands a bold wall, its concave face shaped like that of a dam. This is an impressive memorial to one of the RAF's most famous squadrons, No 617, The Dam Busters, immortalised by Paul Brickhill in his book, and in the subsequent film accompanied by a magnificent melody from Eric Coates. Carved into panels within the wall is an all too extensive listing of the fallen. Without a call at the memorial and an allowance of time for contemplation, respect and maybe personal memories of Bomber Command in 5 Group territory, a look at what little remains of Woodhall Spa would be incomplete.

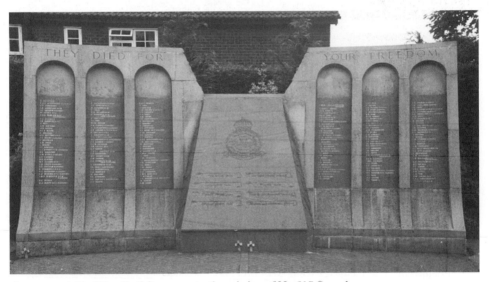

Apt memorial in Woodhall Spa town to the missing of No 617 Squadron.

That airfield, launch pad for what came to make 5 Group so very special, lies to the south by the road to Coningsby within whose 54 Base command Woodhall was placed. Looking at the site now it may even be hard to believe that so many hallowed names passed through its gateway, that earth shaking events were launched from what looks to be a very inconsequential place. The RAF has not entirely left because RAF Coningsby Golf Club flourishes here along with an engine test facility both of which share the site with Butterly Aggregates, a ready-mix concrete business. Great events in history so often are found to have occurred in most unlikely places.

From the commencement of construction in 1941 on what was then a largely wooded area – some of which was retained to provide cover and indeed remains – the intention was to quickly complete a station which could accommodate nearby Coningsby's established strength while runways were laid at that important base. Then, Woodhall Spa with runways laid, would quickly become a Built Satellite and soon achieve upgrading to Class A temporary bomber base standard.

Lancaster B1(Special) PD119 YZ-J of 617 Squadron modified to carry a 22,000 lb 'Grand Slam' bomb.

As Coningsby's satellite, Woodhall Spa opened in February 1942 and entered elitist No 5 Group, Bomber Command. On 1 March 1942 No 97 Squadron – which in January 1942 had become the second to fly Lancasters – started the move from Coningsby. Only six weeks later half a dozen Lancasters of the squadron led by Squadron Leader Sherwood set off during the afternoon of 17 April and joined six more from Waddington to carry out a low-level deep penetration raid on the Maschinen Augsburg-und-Nuremburg (MAN) diesel-engine factory at Augsburg in Bavaria. Flying low the Lancaster was fast, well defended, but seen in retrospect it was clearly too much to expect even of one of the finest designs of all time that such an operation could be launched without losses. Which ever route they took German fighters would pounce and AA gunners would have easy targets. They flew at 500ft to south of Paris, enemy fighters starting to attack just after they crossed into France and only eight Lancasters dropped their 1,000lb bombs which seriously damaged the factory although it was soon repaired. Of the dozen Lancasters seven were shot down.

No 97 Squadron equipped with Lancaster Mks I and III, remained at Woodhall Spa until 17 April 1943. From there they took part in the 1,000 bomber raids on Cologne, Essen and Bremen, the dusk raid on Le Creusot during which ninety-four Lancasters took part and bombed the target every four seconds and Bomber Command's first daylight attack on Italy when the target was Milan. No 97 Squadron contributed much to the increasing power of Bomber Command and after a heroic year the squadron moved to Bourn on loan for a year to No 8 (PFF) Group to bolster in the main its back-up force.

By the time of 97's departure Woodhall Spa was fully developed and to replace No 97 a new Lancaster squadron, No 619, formed here on 18 April 1943 around a three-crew nucleus drawn from 97 Squadron. They first operated on 11 June and thereafter participated in many Main Force raids before moving to Coningsby on 10 January 1944.

At the same time No 617 Squadron moved from Coningsby to Woodhall Spa. There they remained until June 1945 using The Petwood Hotel, requisitioned in the village, as their Officers' Mess. It was from Woodhall Spa that Group Captain Leonard Cheshire, then a Wing Commander, and ultimately holder of the Victoria Cross, Distinguished Service Order and Distinguished Flying Cross, along with Wing Commander Micky Martin DSO and Bar DFC and two Bars AFC carried out a variety of ideas to improve target marking accuracy which led to the use of the *spotfire* released onto the target during a shallow dive.

During such activities the Lancaster was vulnerable, so trials were flown using two Mosquitoes acquired after some controversy from the PFF. Proving their worth resulted in a request for more and led to the transfer here on 15 April 1944 of No 627 Squadron and their Mosquito IVs. These were of the low-level bomber type lighter and more manoeuvrable than the heavier *Oboe*-equipped Mk IXs successfully spearheading Bomber Command Main Force raids led by the PFF.

With skill and much courage Cheshire used the Mosquito to accurately place special markers on precise targets particularly during the D-Day run-up period. On 5/6 June as the vast Allied invasion fleet crossed the English Channel 617 Squadron carried out operation *Taxable*. Two consecutive waves each of eight Lancasters set out from Woodhall Spa to drop *Window* and simulate, with perfect timing and the aid of some small ships, a 'spoof' large convoy of ships to mislead the enemy's judgement of the likely landing area. It proved to be a highly effective ruse and as the 'convoy' closed in German coastal artillery began firing huge shells – at nothing. The little ships had already headed for home.

Wing Commander Cheshire's Victoria Cross was awarded during August 1944. Usually this highest award is given for a particular act of gallantry. Cheshire won his for innumerable acts of courage, over four years and particularly for his low-level marking activities which included an extremely dangerous marking session over Munich's roof tops.

Forever associated with '617' will be Wing Commander Guy Gibson. Soon after the dams raid he was taken off operations. Always keen to return, he volunteered to act as Master Bomber. Flying a Mosquito of No 627 Squadron he set out from Woodhall Spa for Rheydt on 19/20 September 1944. What happened after the marking phase remains uncertain but it is known that Guy Gibson and his navigator, Squadron Leader Warwick, made for home at low-level. They may have encountered AA fire for a farmer claimed that he saw flames in the aircraft's cockpit moments before it crashed and was then burnt out. Before any Germans reached the scene local people removed the identity tags from the bodies of the crew to ensure that their dependants could be informed. When it was discovered who the two men were the 'dog tags' were withheld from the Germans. Buried with unknown identities their names were added later.

It was from Woodhall Spa that No 617 Squadron in June 1944 set out to drop for the first time operationally the Barnes Wallis designed 12,000lb Tallboy Deep Penetration (DP) weapons with the intent of halting traffic through the Saumur railway tunnel. On 14 March 1945 from Woodhall Lancaster PD112 'S' flown by Squadron Leader C C Calder the first operational drop took place of a 22,000lb 'Grand Slam' DP bomb intended, through an earthquake effect, to wreck the high Bielefeld rail viaduct. No 617 Squadron's ultimate operation flown on 25 April 1945 allowed them to leave calling cards on Hitler's Berchtesgaden eyrie.

Woodhall Spa soon became a kitting-out centre for *Tiger Force* personnel but the end of the war stopped that and the end of the airfield began indecently soon for, on 15 June, No 617 Squadron moved to Waddington to work-up for the Far East. On 1 October No 627, which had been using mainly Canadian-built Mosquito B XXs and XXVs and B XVIs, was re-numbered 109 Squadron and, fully equipped with Mosquito XVIs, left for Wickenby on 19 October 1945. Woodhall Spa's flying days ceased but the site remained in government hands and 95 MU stored bombs here.

During 1960 work started on building a security fenced enclave enclosing the facilities needed to operate a Bloodhound Mk II squadron. On 2 November 1964 No 112 Squadron reformed to operate sixteen of the missiles, and remained at Woodhall Spa until October 1967 when the squadron left for Cyprus.

Site reactivation resulted in renewed use as Coningsby's out-station where jet engines for Tornados were overhauled and test run. Part of the former airfield including a 'T2' hangar and surrounding buildings were also used for sundry purposes by RAF Coningsby. Into the 1990s the presence remained. The only very visible item is a white, red and black insignificant sign proclaiming 'RAF WOODHALL SPA'. You can easily miss it.

Main features (December 1944):
Runways: 240° 2,000 yards x 50 yards, 180°, 300°, concrete. *Hangars:* two T2, one B1. *Hardstandings:* thirty-six concrete. *Accommodation:* RAF only: 167 officers, 205 SNCOs, 681 ORs.

Places of interest nearby:
Apart from the 617 memorials, Thorpe Camp Visitor Centre is by the B1191 south of the airfield on part of No 1 Communal Site built in 1940 and which included messes, NAAFI and Airmen's Dining Hall. The Visitor Centre is devoted to RAF Woodhall Spa and civilian life in WWII.

Petwood Hotel, gracious wartime Officers' Mess for Woodhall Spa and now almost a 617 Squadron 'shrine'.

Well worth a call – better still a stay, which I'm sure you will think is quite a treat – is the excellent Petwood Hotel, Woodhall's wartime Officers' Mess. Upon its walls hang a host of paintings mainly of 617 Squadron Lancasters. There are items of memorabilia to be seen, and a splendid room (with bar) wholly devoted to 617 Squadron. By the car park are remains of an Upkeep weapon. The grounds are superb, and very extensive. Petwood Hotel (tel: 01526 352411), a few minutes away from ever-active Coningsby, is an ideal base from which to view the many historical places in Lincolnshire. Call on a special day and you are bound to meet very interesting people!

WOOLFOX LODGE, Rutland

52°42N/00°34W 345ft asl; SK133960. Approximately 6 miles NW of Stamford, adjacent to A1 S of Stretton junction

That the Cold War was reality was only too evident when in the early 1960 collections of supersonic Bloodhound Mk 1 ram-jet missiles bred in security-protected enclosures and pointed easterly constantly awaiting the launch command. Their purpose at Woolfox was to help defend the V-force Victors at Cottesmore.

Woolfox Lodge, a typical temporary wartime two-hangar three-runway well dispersed airfield existed alongside the A1 just south of Stretton junction. Initially it existed as an Unbuilt Satellite which, from 13 December 1940, began service as 14 OTU Cottesmore's RLG. Hampdens and Wellingtons of No 14 OTU made use of the landing ground until August 1941. Then came improvements and by October Woolfox had become a satellite of North Luffenham, a No 5 Group station from where No 61 Squadron and its Manchesters moved in during the month. They commenced Lancaster conversion during April 1942 and moved to Syerston the following month.

Their place was briefly filled – between 1 July and early August – by 3 Group's No 1429 (Czechoslovak) Operational Training Flight which moved in from East Wretham and trained crews to operate Wellington Ics.

On 15 October 1942 the airfield closed for full upgrade into a Built Satellite which converted it into Class A status and meant concrete runways of operational standard, additional domestic and technical accommodation and a general 'facelift'.

On 1 June 1943 the airfield re-opened and within the first week of the month newly formed No 1665 Heavy Conversion Unit arrived from Waterbeach with Stirling Is and IIIs. Airfields used by OTUs, HCUs and other training organisations were usually renamed to incorporate the airfield name following the unit title. That resulted in 'No 1665 HCU Woolfox Lodge' and now an independent accounting station status. Stirlings, of which the established strength was thirty-two, were unforgiving bombers if their handling was not as demanded. In consequence the accident rate was quite high. During autumn of 1943 thirty-two Horsa gliders were towed to and released over the airfield for storage. After being maintained by No 2 HGMU Snailwell they were moved to their operational bases in Southern England during March 1944. At the end of 1943 demand for Stirling bomber crews fell while an increasing number was needed to man Stirling IV glider tugs of 38 Group. As a result No 1665 HCU moved with its Stirlings to Tilstock, Shropshire, on 29 January 1944.

Further improvements at Woolfox included installation of sodium light funnels on the approaches to two runways. That work complete, Stirling III bombers of No 218 (Gold Coast) Squadron moved in on 7 March 1944 and resumed night operations on 9 April when they attacked Lille marshalling yards. Other operations included mining and supply dropping supplies to the French Resistance. Lancaster conversion began in July, strength and type of aircraft for No 218 Squadron at the end of that month standing at ten Stirling Mk IIIs, six Lancaster Mk Is and three Mk IIIs.

Stirling IIIs of No 218 Squadron flying from Woolfox in the summer of 1944.

The last 218 Squadron Stirling operation flown from Woolfox Lodge, a daylight attack on V-1 facilities at Mont Candon, south of Dieppe, was flown on 2 August 1944, all six participants of No 218 Squadron returning safely. By 4 August No 218 Squadron had left Woolfox Lodge for Methwold.

Departure of the squadron ended the station's wartime operational service. A Flight from No 3 LFS Feltwell made use of Woolfox during August for circuit handling of Lancasters and which ended when they returned to Feltwell on the 28th. Woolfox Lodge was then reduced to care and maintenance. Runway resurfacing followed, and the airfield was transferred to the US 9thAF on 1 September 1944.

Through September and into October the station was occupied by the 9th TCCSU and the 62nd Station Complement Squadron. It returned to No 7 Group, RAF Bomber Command, on 20 October 1944 and became a sub-station of North Luffenham.

From 10 November 1944 until disbandment on 13 July 1945 Woolfox Lodge was the home of No 1651 HCU which left Wratting Common when that station was switched to operational flying as part of Stradishall Base. Now '1651' came within North Luffenham Base structure. At the time of arrival '1651' were still using Stirling Mk IIIs, conversion to Lancaster Mk/III taking place in February 1945.

They were joined by Lancaster I/IIIs of No 1654 HCU forced out of Wigsley because it was running down. The unit disbanded on 1 September 1945, No 1651 having done so on 13 July 1945.

Since 1 August 1945 – when Woolfox was transferred from Bomber Command to Maintenance Command and became a satellite of North Witham – it had been held under care & maintenance and was subsequently used by 259 MU until 29 April 1946.

Resurrection for flying followed after transfer to Flying Training Command in September 1948. Then the airfield became available for use as an RLG by No 7 FTS Cottesmore. From May 1951 their Harvard T2Bs and in 1953 Balliol T2s made use of the airfield until it was reduced to Inactive status in April 1954 but retained for future use.

That came about when an entirely new phase started in 1959. A special enclave roughly in the airfield's centre soon contained launch pads with associated technical and domestic facilities because Woolfox Lodge had been chosen as a Bloodhound Mk 1 defensive missile site. On 1 February 1960 as part of 151 Wing, North Luffenham, No 62 (SAM) Squadron formed here and remained in place as a V-Force defender until disbanded on 30 September 1964.

The station reverted to C & M, was again reclassified Inactive from 6 January 1965 and finally disposed of on 4 November 1966. It retains the look of an airfield, but few buildings remain.

Main features (December 1944):
Runways: 149° 5,550ft x 150ft, 035°, 086°, tarmac. *Hangars:* four T2, one B1.
Hardstandings: fifty mixed heavy bomber type. *Accommodation:* RAF: 108 officers, 262 SNCOs, 779 ORs; WAAF: 7 officers, 6 SNCOs, 239 ORs.

WORMINGFORD, Essex

51°56N/00°47E 220ft asl; TL920308. 1 mile SE of village

Once seen and never forgotten, my first glimpse of the strange looking P-38 Lightning came on 5 August 1942. Exaggerated stories of technical wizardry, capability – and woe – preceded the twin-boomed wonder long before one reached Britain for the P-38 was a demanding aeroplane. Most useful for patrol and escort, a Lockheed test pilot later related how he was not keen carrying out high-G manoeuvres in a P-38. From Wormingford the 55th Fighter Group operated some of the last in the 8th AF.

With triple runways, two T2s and dispersed domestic sites, Wormingford was prepared during 1943 for the US 9th Air Force whose 362nd Fighter Group – Thunderbolt equipped – opened 'the shop' in November 1943, and first operated on 8 February 1944 escorting Liberators bombing a Pas de Calais V-1 site. The 362nd concentrated on bomber escorts before responding to policy with a mid-April 1944 move to Headcorn. Replacement at Wormingford came in the form of Lockheed P-38J Lightnings of the 55th Fighter Group.

Prominent during operations from Nuthampstead, they had moved out making way for B-17s of the 398th Bomb Group. Initially operated over France in August 1942 by the 4th FG, the P-38 was first taken into mainstream combat by the 55th. By the time they reached Wormingford the use of the P-38s as fighter-bombers was under review. Although not ideal for low-level strafing or fast combat needing tight turning circles, P-38s could operate like A-20s – in formation led by a 'drop

P-47D 275587 of the 379th FS, 362nd FG.

P-38J CL-P of the 338th FS, 55th FG (USAF).

snoot' P-38 and thereby make very useful shallow dive attacks of a tactical nature during escort missions. Possibly their best contribution came after 1600 hrs on 5 June 1944 when relays of P-38s began drawing upon their good duration to be largely responsible for providing daylight protection for the entire Allied fleet heading south from the Isle of Wight for Normandy.

Obsolescent by June the 55th began replacing the P-38s with P-51Ds which could do all and more than the Lightning. Low-level operations continued, the Group giving general support during the St-Lô break-out. For its bomber escort duties and strafing of airfields, the 55th was awarded a Distinguished Unit Citation.

The 55th supported the September Allied airborne operations, was active during the winter Ardennes offensive and received a second Distinguished Unit Citation for extensive low-level attacks on communications during February 1945 immediately prior to operation Clarion. As the Allies crossed the Rhine Wormingford's P-51s were strafing locomotives, trucks, and oil targets near Wesel. Their last mission came on 21 April 1945.

On 22 July the 55th left Wormingford for Kaufbüren. No 160 Staging Post was established here in November 1945 to assist with links to Norway and closed in March 1946. Then the base was taken over by RAF Training and Technical Training Commands and occupied until January 1947. In summer 1948 it was declared to be of no development value despite its geographical position. Light civil aircraft later flew from what remained after the site was sold for agricultural use in the early 1960s. Wormingford is now home for a flourishing gliding club.

Main features:
Runways: 270° 6,000ft x 150ft, 230°, 330°, concrete and tarmac surfacing.
Hangars: two T2. *Hardstandings:* fifty loop type. *Accommodation:* 421 officers, 2,473 enlisted men.

WRATTING COMMON, Cambridgeshire

52°07N/00°24E; TL645510. By B1052, 2½ miles from Balsham

Astride the East Anglian heights sits Wratting Common, a typical three-runway wartime temporary bomber airfield opened on 3 May 1943. Essential tasks were performed here, with rather less glamour than at some airfields in the area although the flying was no less intense, often more hazardous.

General re-organisation of Stirling squadrons in 31 Base run by Stradishall resulted in 90 Squadron moving here on 31 May 1943 from Ridgewell when this station was known as West Wickham, and at the height of the Stirling bomber's career. Horsa gliders also arrived for storage. Although the airfield was not declared officially as complete until 1 August, No 90 commenced operations from the airfield by despatching on 3/4 June ten aircraft on a *Deodar* mining operation. The Battle of the Ruhr was at this time being fiercely waged and 90 Squadron's targets included Krefeld, Mülheim and Wuppertal. They also took part in the gruesome destruction of Hamburg in July, and fifteen crews operating from West Wickham and without loss participated in the August Peenemunde raid. 'C' Flight of the squadron had become operational on 8 August 1943. Twice that month they attacked distant Turin and suddenly 'West Wickham' disappeared. The station's name having caused confusion with a similarly named RAF station was, on 21 August 1943, changed to Wratting Common thereby adopting the name of an area a little to the north of the airfield. Operations by the Stirlings continued, increasingly with less frequency and until mid-October when 90 Squadron moved out to Tuddenham.

No 1651 Conversion Unit replaced 90 Squadron at Wratting Common on 21 November 1943 and the station's name changed again for to be precise its designation now became 'No 1651 Heavy Conversion Unit, RAF Wratting Common (32 Base)'. Previously No 1651 CU had been administered by No 7 Group and very briefly Wratting Common as 73 Base. OTUs and CUs replaced SHQs at all training stations which were suitably re-titled. Wratting Common now became part of the second clutch of No 3 Group stations.

Stirling training was in all ways costly, many accidents occurring at Wratting and mainly as a result of handling problems during take-off or landing. Training involved converting crews (trained at OTUs where they had learnt to operate twin-engined aircraft) onto four-engined bombers. As well as local activity there was much cross-country flying by day and night. The Ladder Plan, whereby in phases 3 Group squadrons would re-arm with Lancaster Is and IIIs was introduced in November 1943. Once a crew had completed the 1651 CU course they now proceeded to No 3 Lancaster Finishing School, RAF Feltwell. As soon as the supply of Lancasters permitted it No 1651 Conversion Unit moved, on 10 November 1944, to Woolfox Lodge where it forsook its Stirlings for Lancasters.

For Wratting Common the final main switch occurred on 13 November 1944 when No 195 moved in from Witchford. It commenced operations on 16 November 1944 when twelve Lancasters were despatched for the raid on Heinsburg. Equipped with thirty Lancasters, the squadron's operations followed 3 Group's pattern including a concentrated effort against oil targets. Thus Nordstern, Castrup-Rauxel and Wanne Eickel all figured prominently in battle orders, along with many other well known German strategic target areas including Munich, Duisburg, Dortmund and Kiel. The squadron took part in the famous raid on Dresden upon which nineteen crews bombed each unloading a 4,000-pounder and an incendiary load. However, a more eventful operation for '195' had taken place on 12 December 1944.

Lancaster of 195 Squadron making a Manna drop May 1945 (Gerrit Zwanenburg).

Witten was the target for eighteen crews of the squadron within a force of escorted Lancasters. It was a misty day and, near the target area a gaggle of German fighters suddenly zoomed upwards through the protecting fighter screen to attack 195's bombers. In the sudden confusion, jettisoned bombs from NG186 narrowly missed two Lancasters while enemy fighters penetrated to 195's leading formation which was broken apart, a rare event. Flying Officer D Bale (NG351) corkscrewed away and jettisoned his bombs. His rear turret was hit by cannon fire, also his No 2 port fuel tank so he landed at B60 in Belgium. PB139 attacked by fighters also corkscrewed to safety as the others scattered. Three Lancasters (HK697, PB112 and RB196) were shot down and a gunner aboard PB790 claimed an attacking Bf 109. Among the enemy fighters were several Me 410s. The torture was far from over because before the squadron reached Wratting Common fog had descended there forcing eleven crews to land away from base.

The final bombing operation by 195 Squadron was against railway installations at Bad Oldeslö, and took place on 24 April. No 195 Squadron flew 1,367 bombing sorties from Wratting Common during the course of seventy-nine operations in which 6,144.6 tons of bombs were dropped. After the bombing campaign ceased the squadron flew eight *Manna* drops to the Dutch then participated in operation *Exodus* which involved bringing released POWs to Tangmere and Westcott.

No 195 squadron disbanded on 14 August 1945. For a while the station then housed some of the personnel needed for Stradishall's transport operations, and Stirling Vs called. Oxfords of 1552 RAT Flight flew from the airfield in April 1946, at which time a ground school functioned here to assist 51 Squadron's conversion to Avro Yorks. No 116 Sub-Site, 273 MU was here between 20 July 1946 and 15 September 1947, and the station also housed displaced persons. A long line of conifers now strides across the one-time airfield whose presence is marked with a memorial, a few huts, two T2 and one B1 Type hangars. Although rated surplus to need in July 1948 it was held as a Standby Airfield under Plan G but largely returned to agricultural use by the early 1950s. Its remnants now ring to the sound of farm implements and commercial vehicles.

Main features:
Runways: 308° 6,000ft x 150ft, 252°, 197°, concrete and wooden chip surfaces. *Hangars:* four T2, one B1. *Hardstandings:* thirty-six concrete. *Accommodation:* RAF: 164 officers, 609 SNCOs, 1,352 ORs; WAAF: 6 officers, 12 SNCOs, 330 ORs.

WYTON, Cambridgeshire

52°21/00°06W 131ft asl; TL285741. 4 miles NE of Huntingdon, by the junction of A141/B1090

Wyton – home of the Blenheim for, soon after re-opening in 1936, the first of those RAF bombers 'faster than the (biplane) fighters' to enter service did so at Wyton. Furthermore, it was a 139 Squadron Blenheim, N6125 which, moments after war was declared, made the first Bomber Command operational sortie, to photograph the German fleet in the Schillig Roads. Had a Mosquito of 128 Squadron landed three minutes later on 3 May 1945 Wyton instead of Downham Market would have received Bomber Command's final wartime operational landing.

Wyton will always be remembered for its Bristol Blenheim days because few aeroplanes arrive amid the euphoria which courted it, this bomber supposedly able to outpace existing fighters. That was not so and the initial arrival on 19 March 1937 was overshadowed by misfortune when the aircraft ended its career with a ground loop.

The station in 1942 became linked with the Mosquito. From here in December No 109 Squadron's Mosquitoes first tried out *Oboe*, the blind bombing radio system which transformed the effectiveness of The Battle of the Ruhr. Six Mosquitoes of 109 Squadron on 5 March 1943 successfully marked Essen's Krupp works for a devastating attack.

From Wyton Wing Commander J H Searby, the first Master Bomber, operated. His task was to control the attack on the V-weapons research establishment at Peenemunde. Wyton's influence on history was considerable.

It has a long, highly important history, the present aerodrome swallowing the small field where, in 1910, a local crowd watched in awe as a newfangled contraption called an aeroplane landed, after a short hop, on a prepared gravel patch. During the First World War a procession of RFC men learned to use a wide variety of aircraft types at what became Wyton aerodrome. On 1 October 1916 No 4 Training Depot Station had opened and remained until closure on 2 September 1918. Other organisations formed here included Nos 31 and 34 (ex-Reserve) Squadrons during 1917. Americans also trained at Wyton.

Between the wars, Alan Cobham's *Circus* made use of the field. When building of the new aerodrome started at the end of 1935 the imposing 'C' Type Sheds were erected on the southern side, the entire station being on one site. Personnel and a few communications aircraft moved in during July 1936 even before the hangars were ready, such was the desperate pace of rearmament. When No 139 Squadron re-formed on 3 September 1936 an attempt was made to house their Hinds in an aged wooden shed whose roof sagged so much that once opened the doors could not be closed again. Their Hinds had to be picketed out until the new No 1 Hangar opened in November.

Wyton's other squadron, No 114, reformed on 1 December as winter rain reduced much of the flying field to mud apart from the area where the original landing ground was sited. Old flying grounds, albeit small, were carefully selected.

On 1 March 1937 Wyton passed to 2 Group and the Blenheims arrived. Short-nosed Blenheim 1s were replaced with Mk IVs having a superior navigation station and with them both squadrons went to war. They flew few sorties before moving to France in late November 1939 and in an exchange which brought Battles of XV and 40 Squadrons to Wyton for Blenheim conversion.

An expected return to France did not come, both squadrons being at Wyton when the Germans launched their Blitzkrieg in May 1940. Harshness of battle was immediately in evidence when 40 Squadron attacked targets in the Netherlands. Appalling casualty lists opened, the Blenheim's limitations on facing Bf 109s being hammered home on 12 May when half of XV Squadron failed to return. After a few days the squadron was back in business and soon, daily, in vics of three, twelve Blenheims in a formation, they could be seen heading for terrifying action all to no avail.

After France collapsed both squadrons using Alconbury for dispersal operated in a day bomber and reconnaissance role relying on cloud cover, often dangerously flying solo, occasionally in formation. Late May 1940 saw the tattered remnants of 57 Squadron – all but wiped out in France – re-assemble at Wyton. Re-equipped with Blenheims they were on 24 June detached to Lossiemouth as an anti-invasion measure, and for raids on bomber airfields in Scandinavia. When the squadron returned to Wyton on 29 October 1940 the station's 2 Group Blenheim days were nearly over.

On 1 November 1940 Wyton and its three squadrons were transferred to 3 Group and re-equipped with Wellington 1cs because the Blenheim was unsuitable for the strategic night offensive. No 57 Squadron moved to Feltwell on 20 November and 40 Squadron to Alconbury on 2 February 1941. Early 1941 brought No 4 Blind Approach Training Flight to Wyton where it became 1504 BAT Flight before moving to Graveley on 5 August 1942.

January 1941 took on greater importance when Short Brothers established here a working party to support the Stirling's entry into 3 Group. During March 1941 XV Squadron began equipping with the new four-engined bomber and was declared back in the front line on 10 April. When XV Squadron took the new type into action they did so in style – target, Berlin.

For many months the Stirling force, small in strength, carried out night raids. In July holding eleven aircraft of which just over half were serviceable XV Squadron tried to sink the *Scharnhorst* at La Pallice and at the end of the year raided Brest in daylight. These sorties received plentiful publicity but had little effect. XV Squadron carried out several *Trinity* radio-controlled night raids, but effective equipment was a year away.

The second MacRoberts Reply, Stirling LS-F of XV Squadron, at Wyton in 1942.

Stirlings usually operated from Wyton, training being undertaken at Alconbury. Many who flew in the very sturdy, manoeuvrable bomber thought highly of it and rated the Lancaster as a tinny contraption! The main problem with the Stirling was its low operating ceiling.

Wyton experienced its next major change in August 1942 with the birth of 3 Group's Pathfinder Force. The Stirlings moved to Bourn and, on 15 August, Lancasters of 83 Squadron loaned from 5 Group came to replace them and operate in a target marking back-up role. Ensuing months saw them improve their accuracy and attack concentration while helping to develop tactics leading to the use of target indicators in place of flare bundles. No 83 Squadron were at Wyton until 20 April when they returned to Coningsby. They left behind at Wyton No 1499 (Bombing) Gunnery Flight, formed on 31 March 1943 for 8 Group use and equipped with Martinets. A policy change saw the unit move to Ipswich in mid-June 1943.

Mosquito IVs, five of which with three Wellington Ics came with 109 Squadron from Stradishall in early September 1942, were now very busy flown. Intention had been for '109'to operate thirteen Wellington VIs and a Lancaster, but the Mosquitoes were far more reliable and ideally fast for the marker role. Under the watchful eye of Air Commodore Don Bennett they had worked up *Oboe* blind bombing techniques. In June 1943, when 2 Group was shoved into Fighter Command, side-lined 139 Squadron carrying out night nuisance raiding changed places with No 109. No 105 became the second *Oboe* squadron at Marham. No 139 Squadron flew small scale and very effective nuisance raids before leaving Wyton in February 1944.

In January 1944 No 1409 Meteorological Reconnaissance Flight brought along seven Mosquitoes from Oakington for gathering weather data. On 15 September 1944 No 128 Squadron re-formed at Wyton and equipped with twenty Mosquito XVIs, became part of the Light Night Striking Force. No 163 Squadron reformed here with twenty Mosquito XVIs on 25 January 1945 and disbanded on 19 August that year.

Wyton's peacetime phase began with the arrival of 156 Squadron from Warboys. Although they disbanded on 25 September 1945 there were fifty-eight Lancasters at Wyton late December, thirty of them assigned to XV Squadron. No 1688 BDT Flight with six Martinets arrived on 19 March 1946, disbanded in November.

After a general post-war clear-up 3 Group moved a quartet of bomber squadrons in, after 3 Group Modification and Support Unit, recently established, had left for Mildenhall on 7 August 1946. Lancasters of Nos XV and 44 Squadron came first, with 90 and 138 Squadrons following during November. Lincoln IIs replaced their Lancasters then the squadrons flew overseas exercises *Sunray* and *Sunbronze*. Anti-shipping techniques were practised and in October 1947 No XV Squadron involved in Project 'Ruby' dropped 12,000lb 'Tallboys' on concrete structures on the German coast. In December 1947 establishment stood at six Mk II (IIIG) per squadron, but there were only eighteen Lincolns on the station.

Nos 90 and 138 Squadron disbanded on 1 September 1950 and more space became available when No XV Squadron departed in November 1950 departed and No 44 in January 1951. All had left to rearm with Washingtons. Perchance they had made space for the arrival, on 11 September, of dispersed B-50Ds of the 330th Bomb Squadron, 93rd Bomb Group, USAF soon replaced by B-50Ds of the 340th Squadron, 97th Bomb Group. They in turn left and B-29s of the 509th Bomb Group took their places. May 1951 brought their replacements, KB-29Ps of the 2nd ARS and B-50Ds of the 20th Bomb Squadron, 2nd Bomb Group. Later that year it was the turn of the 33rd

RF370 LS-A of Wyton-based XV Squadron was unusual in that it had 'dished' bomb doors to allow carrying large weapons.

*Lincoln B2 LS-E
RF395 September
1950. (John Rawlings)*

Bomb Squadron before No 22 Bomb Wing did their tour of duty. Between 11 December 1950 and 16 May 1951 the 7514 Air Support Squadron (USAFE) was based at Wyton while the RAF Technical Training Command Communications Flight, here since 6 November 1945, was the sole RAF flying unit. It disbanded on 1 April 1964.

Wyton in 1952 saw great changes for it had been selected for development into the strategic reconnaissance centre replacing Benson which was unsuitable for the V-force aircraft element. Wyton's main runway was lengthened to over 9,000ft causing closure of the St Ives-Ramsey road, and at the end of the year, the PRU began moving in from Benson. Bomber Command's last Lancaster squadron, No 82, along with Mosquito PR34s and a few Meteor PR10s supplemented by more Mosquito PR34s of Nos 58, 540 and 541 Squadrons, arrived early in 1953 and soon were called to photograph serious East Coast floods recorded on over 20,000 negatives. Canberra PR3s replaced the Mosquitoes first in 540 Squadron which later used PR7s able to reach 50,000ft. June 1953 saw three Canberras of 540 Squadron rushing newsreels of the Queen's coronation to Canada. In October a Wyton PR3, WE139, won the high speed section of the London to New Zealand Air Race.

No 1323 Flight re-formed on 20 October 1953 from the 2nd TAF Tactical Development Unit upon arriving at Wyton. Joining 3 Group, they used four Canberra B2s, holding two more in reserve. Detached to Laverton in March 1954, they returned to Wyton in June 1954 after air sampling.

No 542 Squadron re-formed with Canberra PR3s in May 1954 and joined the high level day and night photographic reconnaissance and survey force sending detachments overseas. Diminishing need and high cost caused No 542 Squadron to disband in October 1955. At Wyton No 1323 Radar Reconnaissance Flight, operating Lincolns and Canberras as airborne listening posts became a new 542 Squadron on 1 November 1955 which moved to Weston Zoyland on 15 December 1955 to carry out air sampling over the UK in preparation for the 1956 nuclear weapon trials in Australia. In place of 540 Squadron and the RRF came No 543 Squadron to operate PR Valiants which were arriving at Wyton by mid-November 1955.

*Lincoln RE319-A of
the Radar
Reconnaissance
Flight in 1955.*

At the end of 1 March 1956 No 540 Squadron disbanded, followed by No 82 on 1 September. A detachment of 58 Squadron's Canberra PR7s was then preparing for operation *Musketeer*, the Suez event which was cost them an aircraft shot down by a Syrian Air Force Meteor.

No 237 OCU, specialising in reconnaissance training, moved into Wyton during October 1956. In January 1958 their role was taken over by Bassingbourn's OCU. A section of 100 Squadron flying Canberra PR7s was attached to 58 Squadron in July 1957 prior to taking part in the 1957-8 nuclear weapon tests on Christmas Island. Victors arrived in 1958 for a newly established Radar Reconnaissance Flight disbanded on 1 September 1961.

Primarily a strategic reconnaissance centre, Wyton was also involved in large-scale surveys and mapping tasks for which the Valiants were ideal. In 1960 Canberras of 58 Squadron photographed 200,000 square miles of East African territory, and Valiants carried out a full-scale survey of Thailand. Individual Canberras and Valiants also undertook smaller specialised tasks including photographing the Serangah Game Reserve, Tanganyika, for a scientific assessment of the migration pattern and size of zebra and wildebeest herds. They also took high-level horizon-to-horizon pictures of cloud formations for comparison with those obtained by the US Tiros satellite.

Valiant B(PR)1K WZ391 of 543 Squadron spectacularly banking on the approach to Wyton, September 1962.

Work upon the Bloodhounds protecting Wyton.

Early 1961 found 543 Squadron surveying from 40,000 feet the island of Tristan da Cunha. Later the same year they carried out a photo assessment of hurricane damage caused to British Honduras, while a detachment of 58 Squadron Canberras reinforced the MEAF during the Kuwait crisis.

Closure of Watton resulted in the arrival of 51 Squadron in March 1963. That proved to be a turning point in the station's activity since the newcomer with Canberras and Comet R2s was an electronic intelligence gathering squadron rather than primarily a photo reconnaissance unit.

The first Victor SR2 arrived in May 1965 for 543 Squadron which had long awaited this sophisticated replacement for the Valiant. That year the squadron was to photograph Saddleworth Moor in the hunt for the Moors Murderers victims, and in 1967 kept watch over oil pollution from the *Torrey Canyon*.

Lone high-level reconnaissance aircraft having become vulnerable particularly to guided weapons, 58 Squadron switched to a low-level PR role before disbandment on 30 September 1970. No 39 which operated Canberra PR7s (until 1972) and PR9s at once took their place. Additional to survey tasks they undertook low-level PR and shipping reconnaissance. With emphasis on electronic intelligence gathering ever increasing, the Electronic Warfare and Avionics Unit arrived at Wyton to design and install special equipment.

Canberras being serviced in a Wyton hangar.

Canberra T17 EN WJ981 on Wyton's apron.

In 1971, 51 Squadron received their first Nimrod R1. After being suitably equipped, the type made its first operational flight on 3 May 1974. One of their Comet R2s was retired to Duxford, another to Strathallan and, on 3 April 1975, 543 Squadron's last Victor SR2 (XL193) vacated Wyton. In 1976, 51 Squadron gave up their last Canberra, a B6 (WT305).

Wyton's affair with the Canberra was far from over for in August 1975 No 360 Squadron jointly manned by the RAF and RN took up station with their T17 electronic warfare trainers employed to give shore and ship based defensive radar operators opportunities to practice their skills. Their emblem was a Druce moth, the only type able to transmit a bat's signal to protect itself.

Nimrod R1 XW666 of 51 Squadron landing at the end of a 'probing sortie'.

A total of twenty-four Canberra B2s were converted to T.Mk 17 standard, six being further modified into T.17As, which carried extra underwing communications jammers.

More Canberras arrived on 3 October 1978. From Malta, they were PR7s of 13 Squadron, and they concentrated upon low-level night photography. No 39 Squadron was by now equipped with Infra-red Line Scan for use during night operations.

No 26 Squadron Wyton-based since 3 February 1969 and using Basset and Devon light transports wound down during February 1976 and officially disbanded on 1 April. Its aircraft and crews became part of No 207 Squadron Detached Flight for use by RAF Support Command.

Positioning remaining RAF Canberras at Wyton to ease technical support followed the disbandment of 13 Squadron on 1 January 1982, and led to No 100 Squadron (which received 13 Squadron's Canberra PR 7s and absorbed target-towing No 7 Squadron) moving in during January 1982. No 100 Squadron provided target facilities for Tornado F3 crews of No 229 OCU, Coningsby. Canberra B2s performed as 'silent' targets for them, whereas PR 7s and E 15s served for radar station calibration purposes. The Canberra TT18s – two of which were placed on detachment at RAF Akrotiri, Cyprus – wore distinctive yellow and black striped undersurfaces, and could tow a banner target attached to the end of a 900ft line to allow for safe air-to-air firing. Affording target practice for Rapier SAM units, one dart-shaped Rushton target carried beneath each wing could be trailed for between 3 and 5 miles behind the aircraft. On 29 July 1982, No 231 OCU, merely a Flight of Canberra B2s and T4s, arrived from Marham.

Wyton, whose electronic intelligence gathering Nimrods worked over a wide area and in contrasting climes, secretly became involved in the April 1982 South Atlantic conflict.

Disbandment of 39 Squadron on 28 May 1982 made way for the re-forming on 1 June of No 1 Photographic Reconnaissance Unit, which received 3+2 Canberra PR 9s fitted with Avon 206 engines. One of their roles was medium-level photo-survey using three F95 cameras, and for military and civilian agencies including the Ordnance Survey.

April 1983 saw the arrival of HQ 25 Squadron whose 'B' Flight was sited on the northern side of the airfield station along with Bloodhound 2 ram-jet guided weapons here until the end of the Cold War.

More than forty RAF Canberras were concentrated at Wyton by 1982, where they remained into the 1990s. No 231 OCU ran five thirteen-week courses embracing fifty-five hours of flying and thirty-one sorties involving general handling and low flying. It was equipped with seven Canberra T4s and two reserve examples, together with a B Mk 2(T) navigation trainer. The T4s' lives reached around 7,000 flying hours and 20,000 landings. Out of No 231 OCU on 15 December 1990 came the Canberra Standardisation and Training Flight, which returned to 231 OCU on 13 May 1991. When 231 OCU disbanded on 23 April 1993 it had been flying Canberras for forty-one years, peaking at an establishment of sixty instructors serving in separate bomber and PR streams.

On 6 September 1991 No 100 Squadron received its first Hawk T.Mk 1, ultimate strength reaching six Mk 1s and six T.Mk 1As. With Canberra replacement completed on 1 January 1992, the squadron was declared Hawk effective on 7 January. Although more agile and economical than Canberras, their endurance was far less and they were unable to tow a Rushton target.

100 Squadron couple – Canberra TT18 WJ682 C-U formates with Hawk XX247 C-M. (British Aerospace)

Additional to the squadrons, which in the mid-1980s between them held almost fifty Canberras, there were other units on the station including the Electronic Warfare Engineering & Training Unit, which came from Watton on 25 January 1971 and became the Electronic Warfare & Avionics Unit in September 1976; as the Electronic Warfare Operations & Support Unit, it was involved in the design and development of communications equipment for aircraft, and participated in the Falklands campaign. EW&OS moved out to join the Air Warfare Centre on 1 October 1993. Also at Wyton were the Joint School of Photographic Interpretation and No 1 Air Survey Liaison Section, Royal Engineers.

The last flight of a Canberra B2 (WJ631) took place from Wyton on 7 July 1992. On 31 October 1994 Wyton's wind down was prominently to be seen when No 360 Squadron, the RAF's youngest, disbanded. The eight remaining Canberra T17/17As were to be scrapped here. Making its last sortie on this day was Canberra WD955 (which became forty years old on 15 November 1991), the front-line aeroplane which joined the Service in 1951 and had the longest career of any such RAF aircraft. No, you will not find it in the RAF Museum where it should be, a grateful Ministry sold it to Norway sending it on its way via Marham and in great secrecy. The 'final' departure from Wyton by an operational aircraft was made by a Nimrod R1 one Sunday afternoon to very privately mark its 'closure' to flying.

In April 1994 RAF Brampton (never a flying station) was amalgamated with Wyton, the pair becoming 'RAF Brampton Wyton', making it pertinent to recall Brampton's history here.

On 1 September 1941 a new organisation, No 8 (Light Day Bomber) Group, formed with its HQ in requisitioned Brampton Park Grange. A role change led to its disbandment on 28 January 1942, its place being taken by a new organisation still bearing the 8 Group title whose task was to substitute USAAF units for British on UK airfields.

Canberra T17A WJ630 of 360 Squadron taxiing out for take-off at Wyton.

On 15 August 1942 the Pathfinder Force HQ opened at Wyton and on 8 January 1943 became a new No 8 (PF) Group, whose HQ moved to Castle Hill House in Huntingdon on 15 May 1943. There it remained until disbandment on 15 December 1945, the building later becoming a base for local government offices.

Brampton Park Grange was requisitioned for use by the USAAF in the spring of 1942. HQ 1st Air Division, USAAF, became effective in the Grange Hotel on 15 June 1942, and 1st Bombardment Wing HQ was activated here on 19 August 1942. HQ 8th AF 1st Air Division took over Brampton, remaining there until September 1945, when they moved to Alconbury. The Americans vacated Brampton in 1946.

Retained for RAF use, the decision was taken in 1955 to make it a permanent station. A new building completed on site by 1957 housed the Central Reconnaissance Establishment (CRE), re-formed in 3 Group on 12 January 1957 to mastermind PR operations. Alongside was the Joint Air Reconnaissance Intelligence Centre (JARIC), and both had originated within CPE Medmenham. CRE disbanded on 1 October 1970 but JARIC remained, a vitally important organisation within the Western photographic, imaging and intelligence community.

When in 1968 Flying Training Command and Technical Training Command merged, they moved into another new building at Brampton, which later housed HQ Training Command. HQ Air Training Corps, which arrived from White Waltham in October 1968, stayed at Brampton until moving to Newton in 1975.

The large training HQ building was, on 23/24 October 1985, completely destroyed by fire. A replacement, completed on 24 February 1988, was opened by HRH The Duke of Gloucester on 7 June 1988.

In April 1994 Support Command became HQ Logistics Command, at which time RAF Wyton ceased to be an independent station and became part of RAF Brampton.

Further service contraction resulted in the October 1999 disbandment of HQ Logistic Command. It was replaced by the Defence Logistics Organisation, which occupied offices at Wyton. The combined station passed under the control of HQ Personnel & Training Command.

In 2001 Henlow and RAF Stanbridge joined Brampton Wyton, Stanbridge remaining the home of the RAF's main computer system, monitoring logistics throughout the world. Having Henlow in the fold brought in the RAF Centre for Aviation Medicine, Tactical Provost Wing, Assistant Directorate Engineering and a department of the Defence Communications Services Agency.

On 1 April 2007 Personnel & Training Command amalgamated and came under the control of High Wycombe's HQ Air Command. At the same time the Defence Logistics Organisation merged with the Defence Procurement Agency to form Defence Equipment and Support. Brampton now accommodated support facilities for a range of defence agencies.

In July 2008 a Ministry of Defence Estate Development Plan was revealed outlining the establishment of a network of fewer but larger defence sites across the UK. Brampton became allocated for disposal in 2012, apart from retained MoD housing.

In April 2004 a completely new look for Wyton was revealed. Over a four-year period a £150m extensive rebuild of the station would now convert it into a key UK intelligence gathering centre. Demolition of 1930s-style brick accommodation blocks was already under way, their replacements being four entirely new accommodation blocks and messing facilities. RAF Wyton's future thus looks assured. Around 1,100 defence intelligence employees will move in by 2013, together with 500 other staff. HQ Intelligence Gathering Group will arrive from Feltham, Middlesex, others moving in being the National Imagery Exploitation Centre, JARIC and No 42 Engineer Regiment (Geographic) from near Newbury and Germany, all to undertake a wide range of intelligence gathering activities.

Regular flying had resumed at Wyton in October 1999 when the civilian Bombardier Service Division – which took on the Light Aircraft Flying Task PFI contract, and operated and owned Grob 115E Tutors – arrived at Wyton to make this the first station using that type. Initially they equipped No 2 Squadron, No 1 EFTS. In July 2003 that became No 2 EFTS, which, in 2006, was redesignated No 57 (Reserve) Squadron Elementary Flying Training School Wyton, one of four reserve squadrons manned by Service QFIs and which are elements of No 1 EFTS, whose HQ is at Cranwell. Positioning the squadrons away from busy Cranwell makes better use of airspace. No 57 (R) Squadron has seventeen civilian-owned and operated Tutors also used by Cambridge University Air Squadron, University of London Air Squadron and No 5 Air Experience Flight. The latter and the CUAS moved here from Cambridge Airport in 1990.

Also at Wyton is the base and support organisation of the Cambridgeshire Police Force helicopter, and facilities for standby of a BK-117 helicopter operated by the East Anglian Air Ambulance organisation, whose HQ is at Norwich.

Main features (December 1944):
Runways: 093° 6,000ft x 150ft, 057°, 340°, concrete. *Hangars:* four Type C. *Hardstandings:* thirty-six for heavy bombers. *Accommodation:* RAF: 252 officers, 301 SNCOs, 1,740 ORs; WAAF: 8 officers, 14 SNCOs, 406 ORs.

Point of special interest:
Thanks particularly to the initiative of Squadron Leader Gavin Sugden and colleagues, 27 June 1998 saw the first Pathfinder March, a forty-six mile journey in tended to be completed in twenty-four hours. It starts and ends at Wyton, and takes in Gravely-Oakington-Warboys using a marked route. Of the 200-plus sponsored walkers who started out on the first one an amazing ninety completed it in the given time and some in an even shorter time. Put it on your list for next June!

With their turbojets, electronic imaging, computer wizardry, global positioning and astonishing skills in managing them, Wyton and Brampton's personnel at the forefront of science and technology surely provide an ideal ending for our review. Looking back upon the most amazing century of all time it is a wonder we managed without the aeroplane and aerodromes!

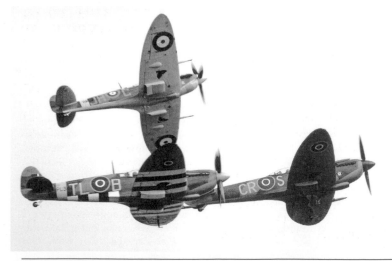

Form and sound supreme were combined in the all-British Spitfire, the most beautiful military aircraft of all time. It was reliant upon the Rolls-Royce Merlin, the finest piston engine of them all.

Index

Personalities: Civilian

RAF Maintenance Units

RAF and other military miscellaneous organisations/units/ Army Air Corps

Army AOP Squadrons

RAF Squadrons

USAAF/USAF Squadrons

USAF Wings continued…

The Action Stations Revisited Series

Volume 1 Eastern England
9780859791458

Volume 2 Central England and the London Area
9780947554941

Volume 3 South East England
9780859791106

Volume 4 South West England
9780859791212

Volume 5 Wales and the Midlands
9780859791113

Volume 6 Northern England and Yorkshire
9780859791120

Volume 7 North East England, Scotland and
Northern Ireland
9780859791441

Published by Crécy Publishing Ltd
1a Ringway Trading Estate
Shadowmoss Rd
Manchester M22 5LH
www.crecy.co.uk

SAMURAI WARLORDS

Hajikano leads the Takeda army to Odawara

This plate reproduces a dramatic moment during the Takeda army's advance against the Hōjō family in 1569. As the army under Takeda Shingen (shown here wearing a red *jinbaori* surcoat) moved against the Hōjō's fortress of Odawara, their progress was halted by the swollen waters of the Sasaogawa river. One of Shingen's junior commanders,

Hajikano Masatsugu, who bore the rank of *ashigaru-taishō* (general of foot-soldiers), volunteered for the dangerous task of assessing the depth of the raging river. He rode his horse into the water and, having first tested the depth with the shaft of his spear, rode on until for a brief moment only the *sashimono* flag on the back of his armour was visible above the surface. The design on the banner was one of the playing pieces in the Japanese board game of *shōgi*,

representing a spear, which in *shōgi* can only move forward, and not retreat. Hajikano put this to Shingen as a reason for his confidence in advancing.

Hajikano Masatsugu is drawn according to his description in the account of the incident in the *Kōyō Gunkan*. The flags among the Takeda army are those of the two subordinate commanders who attended Shingen on this occasion, Naitō Masatoyo and Baba Nobuharu.

STEPHEN TURNBULL

SAMURAI WARLORDS
The Book of the Daimyō

Illustrated by James Field

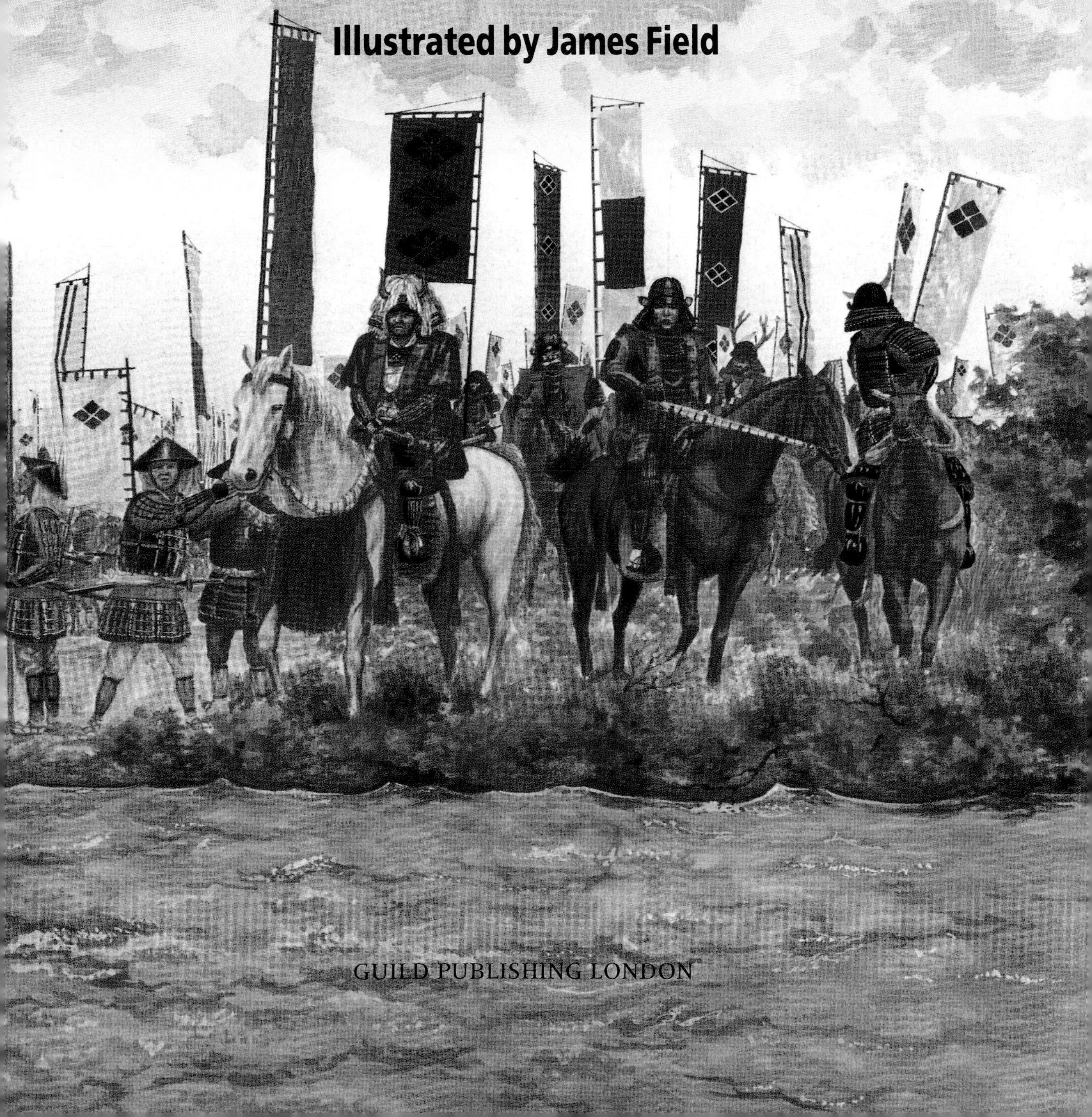

GUILD PUBLISHING LONDON

To Katy Turnbull

Contents

Introduction

The samurai were the military élite of old Japan, and the daimyō, the 'Samurai Warlords', were the élite of the samurai. This book is therefore about the *'crème de la crème'* of the samurai class — the samurai who succeeded first as warriors, and went on to found petty kingdoms of their own, which they defended with armies of samurai who owed allegiance to them and to none other. From these original warlords grew great dynasties of daimyō, who enjoyed a symbiotic existence with the central government of the Shōgun until all were swept away in the upheavals of the 1850s which gave birth to modern Japan.

There is a popular theory, nowadays, that one reason the Japanese are so successful in the modern world is that they give to their company, and to their country, that same loyalty which once they gave to the daimyō. In the pages that follow we shall see of what that fierce loyalty consisted.

Unlike any of the present author's previous books on the samurai, this work is not arranged chronologically, but as a series of chapters, each of which examines in depth a particular role which the daimyō was required to play. We shall see him as a warrior, as a commander and as a focus for that legendary loyalty which still amazes one even today. We shall examine his other demanding duties as the founder of a dynasty, as the keeper of the peace and as the patron of the arts. To be a daimyō was a demanding life, and the demands did not stop with the warlord's death, for he then entered on a new and strange role as spiritual guardian of the family, to be honoured, and, if necessary, bloodily revenged.

In a sense, this book is about two very different types of people, the *sengoku-daimyō*, the warlords of the Sengoku Period, or the 'Age of War' (which is roughly the same as the sixteenth century AD), and the daimyō of the Edo Period, the three centuries that followed, which were marked by the almost total absence of war. The lives of these two groups were very different but closely related, because it was the experience of life in the Age of War, or at the very least the tradition passed on from their ancestors, that prepared the later daimyō to survive the different demands of the Age of Peace. It is this thread of tradition of self-sacrifice, of the needs of the group, of identification with a leader, that tells us so much about Japan today.

This book is based entirely upon Japanese sources, and therefore could not have been written without the help and support of many people. First mention, as ever, must go to Mrs Nahoko Kitajima for her assistance, especially during the preparation for my study tour in 1986. I would like to thank the staff of the Oriental Collections at the British Library, particularly Mrs Yu-Ying Brown, for guiding me through the valuable source materials I have used here. Once again it has been a pleasure to work with James Field, and to see my ideas and notes translated into his splendid paintings. The colour photographs are all my own, but I would like to thank several people for allowing me to photograph the black-and-white material that

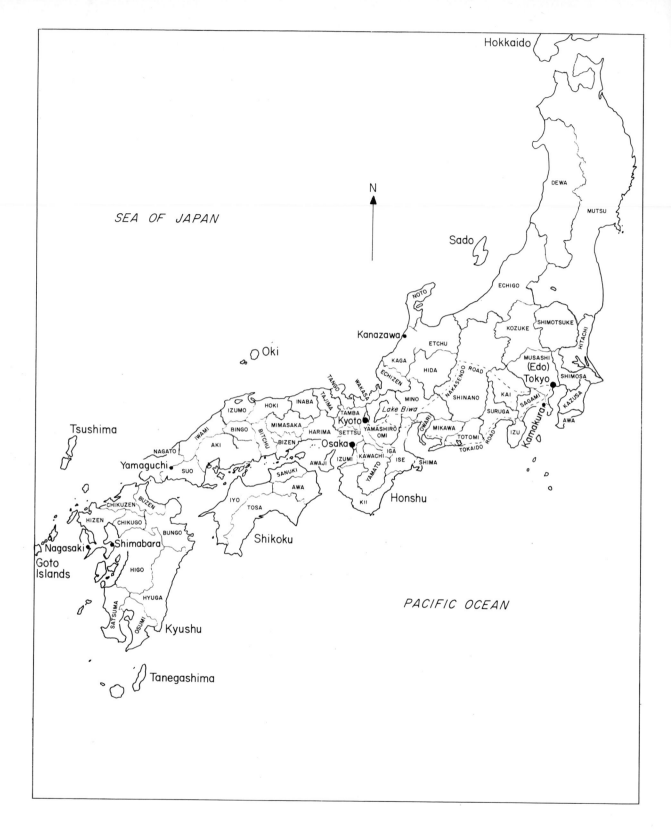

has provided the fine detail of the past. In particular, I am indebted to Dunstan Gladthorpe for supplying photographs from the pages of his copies of the *Hōjō Godai-ki* and the *Ehon Taikō-ki*.

My greatest thanks are, of course, to my dear wife Jo, and my three *wakamusha*, Alex, Richard and Katy. They have now endured nine books, and without them, nothing would happen.

Stephen Turnbull
Leeds 1988

11

Daimyō – The Warlords of Japan

Hōjō Sōun leads his followers into Izu

Hōjō Sōun's most decisive move was his invasion of Izu, an operation nominally carried out to avenge the murder of the former *shugo* of the province. It resulted in the allegiance to Sōun of the former retainers of Izu, and Sōun's establishment as a daimyō. In this illustration, taken from an eighteenth-century wood-block-printed edition of the *Hōjō Godai-ki*, Sōun used his war-fan to signal to his men in a charge. One of his samurai lunges at an enemy with a barbed rake.

In 1491 a 60-year-old samurai, who, the chronicles tell us, had 'clear eyesight, good hearing and all his own teeth', invaded the province of Izu and started a revolution.

The man's name was Ise Shinkuro Nagauji, better known to posterity as Hōjō Sōun, and known to the eastern provinces as the first 'Samurai Warlord'. The eventual success of his conquests, and his ability to control them and pass them on to his descendants, marked him out as a new breed of samurai leader, and he was to become famous for his military skill, his political cunning, and his religious faith. He was also to become legendary for his longevity. He was certainly no wild young samurai warrior when he invaded Izu, and he still had another 27 years of active life ahead of him.

Hōjō Sōun called himself a *daimyō*, a word which, when literally trans-

lated means 'great name'. 'Warlord' is an English word which conveniently encompasses in its associations everything that made the daimyō what they were. The revolution Hōjō Sōun caused in Izu, which gave him the territory for his own, brought to that particular area of Japan the notion of *gekokujō*, 'the low overcome the high', the savage principle of opportunistic rebellion sweeping away the old order, which was to characterise sixteenth-century Japan, and set the pattern whereby other 'great names' could be made in other parts of Japan, until by the third quarter of the sixteenth century these daimyō warlords controlled huge territories as independent princes.

The Hōjō family, whom we shall examine in some detail in this chapter, are prime examples of the daimyō of the Sengoku Period, the 'Age of War', which is roughly coterminous with the sixteenth century AD. In the chapters which follow, we shall note various aspects of the role of the daimyō of the 'Age of War', and compare them with those of the 'Age of Peace' which followed.

The rise of the samurai

The part of Japan where the Hōjō established themselves was known as the Kantō, a word which means 'east of the barrier'. The barrier in question was an ancient toll-barrier in the Hakone Mountains, although the mountains themselves were as secure and forbidding a barrier as any that the hand of man could provide. The deeply wooded Hakone Mountains, which

The Hakone Mountains
The proud Hōjō family, the archetypal daimyō of the Sengoku Period, relied as much on the natural defences provided by the Hakone Mountains as on their numerous castles. This view is taken looking across terraced rice fields at the time of the transplanting of rice seedlings in May.

The Samurai
The samurai were the élite of old
Japan, and the daimyō were the élite
of the samurai. This actor from the
Toei-Uzumasa Film Studios in Kyōto
is dressed in the costume of the
samurai retainer of a daimyō of the
Edo Period, with the characteristic
two swords. He wears a loose jacket,
called a *haori*, and on his feet are
wooden *geta*.

are foothills to the crowning glory of the gigantic Mount Fuji, provided an obstacle to east–west communications until the present century, allowing the inhabitants of the fertile Kantō plain, with its ready access to the sea, to develop relatively unhindered by political and military changes in the more sophisticated western provinces. Civilisation came from the west, from the capital city of Nara, until AD 794 when it was replaced by Kyōto, also in the west.

The Kantō, by contrast, bred warriors. From the Kantō had come the samurai warriors of the Minamoto clan in the twelfth century, who had fought the western Taira clan in a fierce civil war from 1180 to 1185, which had ended with the Taira destroyed in a naval battle so bloody that the seas had turned red. The Taira had ruled from Kyōto, marrying successive daughters into the imperial family and making their own family the dominant line of government. The victorious Minamoto needed no political chicanery. It was military force that had put them in a position of power, so it was by military force that they would rule. The Emperor was condemned to being a shadowy living god. Real power lay with the possessor of the title of *Shōgun* which the Minamoto leader was granted by the powerless Emperor – 'commander-in-chief for the suppression of barbarians'.

The first Shōgun, Minamoto Yoritomo, chose to base himself at Kamakura, in the heart of the Kantō, past the barrier and far from Kyōto. But even the mighty Minamoto were not to last forever, and in 1333 the old imperial capital became also the Shōgun's capital when the founder of a new dynasty, the Ashikaga, moved his seat of government westwards. The Ashikaga dynasty, too, began its own curve of triumph and decline, frustrated by the problems of controlling a disparate country where communications were difficult and centuries of warfare had bred distrust and resilience among their subjects.

The Ashikaga Shōgun's rule in the provinces was devolved through men called the *shugo* and the *jitō*. The *jitō* were the civil arm of local government, and the *shugo* the military. The Nambokuchō civil wars of 1330 to 1392 greatly weakened the authority of the *jitō* until, by the beginning of the fifteenth century, the *shugo* stood alone as the Shōgun's deputy and military governor. Many were related by blood to the Ashikaga. Others were appointed for no better reason than that they were the strongest samurai in the province and thus more likely to command respect. It was useful for the Ashikaga Shōgun to have someone they could rely on, and gradually the *shugo* acquired more devolved powers.

The centre collapses

As long as the Ashikaga stayed in control there was no problem of stability, and when the fifteenth century began the Ashikaga were at the height of their powers. Ashikaga Yoshimitsu had built a pavilion coated with gold, and had entertained princes and ambassadors, and now his successors looked as if they would lift the dynasty to greater heights. Then one by one, the blows came. In 1441 the sixth Ashikaga Shōgun, Yoshinori, was murdered. He was succeeded by an 8-year-old son, who died two years later, to be followed by his younger brother Yoshimasa. Yoshimasa, in fact, reigned as Shōgun for 30 years, and witnessed the gradual seeping away of all Shōgunal authority. Power passed into the hands of the *shugo*; but theirs

The Battle of Minatogawa
This section of a painted scroll at the Nampian Kannon-ji at Kawachi-Nagano (reproduced here by kind permission of the Chief Priest) depicts the last battle fought by the hero, Kusunoki Masashige. In the background, troops of the Hosokawa clan are landed from boats, an action which cut Kusunoki off from assistance, and led to his death by suicide. It was the defeat of the Kusunoki that paved the way for the establishment of the Ashikaga dynasty of Shōguns.

was an ordered world, traditionally controlled from the centre, and the centre, in the shape of Kyōto and the artistic and sensitive Shōgun, kept pulling them in. So they clung to Kyōto, to their mansions and their gardens, and to the Ashikaga grandees who made a great show of 'carrying on as normal'. Meanwhile their own authority in the provinces began to slip away, until in 1467, in an act of reckless disregard for political reality, the *shugo* once more gathered in Kyōto, but this time it was to fight a war amongst their own kind.

The Ōnin War, which had Kyōto as its first battlefield, dragged on for ten years, during which the fighting spread to the provinces and the *shugo* families fought each other to extinction. Others rushed to fill the gaps their deaths had caused, persons who knew nothing of the Shōgun's commissions and poetry parties in Kyōto. These 'new men' were peasant farmers, or oil sellers, or blacksmiths, men who realised that only military force was now needed. They would gather round them a handful of like-minded souls who were good fighters, and build a secure stockade on a hill, from where they could defend their rice fields. No tax-collector would be coming from Kyōto. No message would arrive from the Shōgun requesting them to chastise rebels on his behalf. Now was the time to build one's own kingdom and make a name for oneself, to make oneself a 'big name' – a daimyō.

That was where most of the daimyō came from. Some *shugo* families did

17

survive and themselves became daimyō, but they tended either to be remote from Kyōto, or to have received the commission of *shugo* as an act of desperation on the part of the Shōgun. In the majority of cases, daimyō were created by *gekokujō*-style usurpation. Existing *shugo* were murdered by their subjects. Brothers, fathers even, were deposed. Daughters were traded like horses to secure alliances, as the territories grew from one hilltop fortress to two, then three, surrounding a fertile valley. Then a neighbour's lands were seized, and the area doubled, and so it grew. The map of Japan began to resemble the playing-board for a game of *go*, where the protagonists begin with an empty board. One by one spaces are surrounded and captured, then themselves are swallowed within another growing territory, until at the end of the game there are no spaces left to occupy, and there is only one winner.

Hōjō – the exemplary daimyō

The end of the game was over a century away when Hōjō Sōun led his samurai into Izu. Over the next four generations of the family, the Hōjō illustrated all of the aspects of daimyō rule which are discussed in the following chapters, the foremost of which was the ability to wage war.

The first point to note about the Hōjō was their comparatively humble origin. The Hōjō did not originate in the Kantō. Hōjō Sōun was very probably the son of a minor official of the Ashikaga Shōgun, based in Kyōto. He was born in 1432 and was educated by the monks of the Daitoku-ji, and was therefore 35 years old when the old capital was torn apart by the long and terrible Ōnin War. Sōun managed to leave Kyōto and the devastation the Ōnin War had caused sometime around 1469. He had with him a band of six loyal samurai, and took up a position with Imagawa Yoshitada, who had married Sōun's sister, and held the post of *shugo* of Suruga province. In 1476 Imagawa Yoshitada was killed in battle, and a succession dispute arose among the Imagawa retainers. Sōun, who was perceived as a well-educated and disinterested party, acted as chief mediator between the factions, and secured the succession for his nephew, Imagawa Ujichika. The grateful Ujichika rewarded his uncle with the castle of Kōkokuji, and Sōun's band of loyal samurai started to grow.

The need to build a retainer band was a vital characteristic of the daimyō. The small band of followers which Sōun had brought with him from Kyōto grew into an army as Sōun developed the means to feed them, and the success to attract them to him. These were the men he led into Izu, the most important turning-point in his career. It is also a classic illustration of *gekokujō*. Sooner or later every successful daimyō had to strike, and strike hard to establish himself as somehow superior to the competition, and to intervene in a succession dispute in a neighbouring family was an ideal technique. The *shugo* of Izu was of the Ashikaga family, one Masatomo, and when he died his son, known only by his boy's name of Chachamaru, succeeded to the post by murdering his mother and his elder brother. The old retainers of Izu were horrified at the act and turned against him. Hōjō Sōun, watching from the neighbouring province, resolved to avenge the father. He crossed the provincial border and attacked, forcing the treacherous Chachamaru to commit suicide. All the retainers of the former *shugo* gladly submitted to the honourable Sōun, and by their acclamation Izu was his.

Odawara castle
Odawara castle became the capital of the Hōjō territories when it was captured by Hōjō Sōun in 1518, and stayed in their possession until 1590, in spite of numerous attacks by the Takeda and the Uesugi. The present keep is a modern reconstruction.

Sōun had therefore moved on from the ownership of one castle, given by the Imagawa, to controlling a whole province, with no grant from a Shōgun, or commission from the emperor. It is about this time that he changed his name to Hōjō. There had been a famous Hōjō family centuries before. Sōun had no connection with them, of course, but the name had a certain ring to it, and in the climate that was developing in Japan at the time, surnames, like provinces, were there for the taking.

Four years later, he cast his eyes eastwards along the sea coast and sided with one of the quarrelsome branches of the doomed Uesugi family. This further piece of opportunism won him the strategic castle of Odawara, soon to become the Hōjō capital, and gave him a secure base in western Sagami. In 1512 he captured the old Shōgunal capital of Kamakura, and then completed the conquest of Sagami province in 1518 with the defeat

---

Building a Castle

This scene represents the building of a castle round about the year 1600. Two officials examine the plans, while a surveyor checks the line of building. In the background a final stone is levered into place around the massive earth core, while the wooden beams that will form the skeleton of the keep begin to take on the shape of the finished building.

The building of castles was one of the most important steps in establishing the *daimyō* of the Sengoku Period as the most important powers in their particular areas. Whereas earlier castles had been fortresses made of wood and earth that clung to the natural topography of mountains, or were concealed among meandering watercourses, the new castles had all their defences built in to their design, and much stone was used in their construction. Their location was chosen on the basis of the control it offered over lines of communication through their provinces, regardless of any natural defensive aspect. Toyotomi Hideyoshi appreciated the power of a large and well-garrisoned castle, and took steps to restrict their proliferation among potential rivals. Castle-building was further controlled under the Tokugawa.

Many of the Japanese castles that have survived to this day, such as Himeji and Hikone, were started during the Sengoku Period.

of the Miura family at Arai in 1518 – a battle famous for the defiant act of suicide by the Miura family's heir, who is supposed to have cut his own head off.

Ujitsuna and Ujiyasu carry the flag

The following year Hōjō Sōun died at the age of 87, a man who had sprung from nowhere, who had witnessed the Ōnin War and its destruction of the *shugo*, and had gone on to become daimyō of two provinces. He had, in fact, retired from the position of daimyō the previous year to allow his son Ujitsuna to begin his rule while he still had his father to help him. The succession of a series of eldest sons was one of the Hōjō dynasty's great strengths, which stands in marked contrast to the unhappy experience of

Hōjō Ujitsuna
Ujitsuna was Sōun's son and heir, and continued the process of conquest of the Kantō which his father had begun. He defeated the Uesugi at Edo, the Satomi at Kōnodai, and established the temple of Sōun-ji in his father's memory.

other families we shall discuss in a later chapter. Although less colourful a character than his father, Ujitsuna was to continue the process of conquest and consolidation that Sōun had begun.

The vital factor in the continuity of the operation was the loyalty of the family retainers. Soon after his father's death, Ujitsuna founded the temple of Sōun-ji in Sōun's memory, which impressed the old retainers considerably, and they showed their faith in Sōun's heir by fighting valiantly for him when he expanded the Hōjō domain further into the Kantō by defeating the Uesugi at their castle of Edo in 1524. This village at the mouth of the Sumida River, which is now the city of Tōkyō, was the key to Musashi province, which Ujitsuna confirmed by defeating the combined forces of Satomi Yoshitaka and Ashikaga Yoshiaki at the Battle of Kōnodai in 1538.

To some extent, Ujitsuna had a much more difficult task than his father. Sōun, admittedly, had had the uphill job of establishing himself from nowhere; but by the time Ujitsuna was in command, there was much less opportunity for *gekokujō*. Ujitsuna's enemies were daimyō like himself, not decaying *shugo*. Apart from the odd opportunistic assassination and the dubious activities of *ninja*, issues had to be settled by warfare. Ujitsuna, therefore, concentrated heavily on building up his army, and establishing an efficient system of military obligation, which is discussed in detail in the following chapter. He also established laws, and made sure that within the Hōjō domain it was Hōjō law that mattered. But the daimyō was still first and foremost a military leader, and Ujitsuna saw it as his duty to lead his samurai personally into battle.

The Sōun-ji
It was vitally important for Hōjō Ujitsuna to retain the loyal service of his late father's old followers, and one way in which he did it was to found this temple, the Sōun-ji, at Yumoto, near Odawara. It lies at the foot of the Hakone Mountains, on the course of the old Tōkaidō road, and has recently been re-roofed.

Like his father before him, Ujitsuna groomed his son Ujiyasu for his eventual succession. Also like Sōun, Ujitsuna left behind a set of House Laws to guide future generations. In one section he warns: 'After winning a great victory, a haughty heart, disdain for the enemy, and incautious actions often follow. Avoid this. There have been many families in the past destroyed in this manner.'

Ujitsuna died in 1541. The third daimyō, Hōjō Ujiyasu, continued the conquests of his predecessors until, by 1560, when he retired in favour of his son Ujimasa, the Hōjō controlled most of the Kantō region.

Ujiyasu was Sōun reborn. To defend the Kantō from the north, his father had established a series of forts along the Sumidagawa, and in defending one of these, Kawagoe, Ujiyasu won his most celebrated victory in 1545. The Battle of Kawagoe has a special place in samurai history in that it was fought at night, which alone pays tribute to Ujiyasu's skills in handling troops. In 1564 Ujiyasu again demonstrated his skills as a general in a remarkable 're-run' of his father's battle at Kōnodai in 1538. In the second Battle of Kōnodai, Hōjō Ujiyasu, son of the previous victor, defeated Satomi Yoshihiro, son of the daimyō formerly vanquished.

Hōjō Ujiyasu
Hōjō Ujiyasu (1515–70) was the grandson of the founder of the family, Hōjō Sōun, and the descendant most like his illustrious predecessor. He led the celebrated night attack on the besieging forces of the Uesugi at Kawagoe in 1545, which was held for the Hōjō by his adopted brother Hōjō Tsunanari, and won the second Battle of Kōnodai in 1564. It was Ujiyasu who led the family to its greatest heights of achievement, in spite of competition from other powerful daimyō, such as Takeda Shingen.

The second Battle of Kōnodai (1564)
Kōnodai, on the edge of what is now Tōkyō Bay, saw two battles between two generations of the Hōjō family and the Satomi. In both, the Hōjō were victorious. In this vigorous illustration from the *Hōjō Godai-ki*, the Hōjō samurai use their swords and spear to deadly effect against the Satomi soldiers.

The territories meet

At this point a new dimension entered into the Hōjō's plans. The smaller daimyō of the Kantō had now been squeezed into extinction, or had submitted as vassals of the Hōjō. Ujiyasu now had to face the threat from other

24

Takeda Shingen
The greatest rival to the Hōjō's domination of the Kantō was Takeda Shingen, who had built his own territory in much the same way as they had. The collision between the Hōjō and the Takeda marks a new phase in the history of daimyō confrontation. Smaller daimyō had been squeezed out, and rivalry became a contest between large-scale daimyō who controlled huge armies. This contemporary painting of Shingen is in the Preservation Hall of Nagashino castle, and is reproduced here by kind permission of the Horai-cho local government office. He is wearing a red *jinbaori* (surcoat), a monk's *kesa* (scarf), and his helmet is covered by a horsehair plume.

successful families whose own territories bordered the Kantō, and who had built their own multi-provincial domains in much the same way as the Hōjō. The history of the next two decades became one of a series of fights, alliances and treaties between the three power-blocs of Hōjō Ujiyasu, Takeda Shingen and Uesugi Kenshin.

The latter two names were every bit as formidable as the Hōjō, but fortunately spent a great deal of time fighting each other at five successive 'Battles of Kawanakajima', so that their incursions against the Hōjō took the form of minor raids. We will refer to the Takeda and Uesugi many times in the pages to come. Both were innovative in their strategy and tactics, and the fact that they were so evenly balanced made most of their contests indecisive, leading a later generation of historians to dub their Kawanakajima encounters 'mock battles'. In fact they were no more mock battles than any of the encounters of the Sengoku Period, and the fourth Battle of Kawanakajima in 1561 (described by the present author in '*Battles of the Samurai*') had one of the highest percentage casualties of any battle in which samurai engaged.

Consequently, grand strategy became the most important martial art. It was strategy that took into account all the military necessities of knowing when to attack, where and with what, as well as less glamorous considerations, such as the making and breaking of alliances and treaties. There was still territory to be won by the giving of battle, but the prize changed from the winning of one castle, or even half a province, to securing control of two or three provinces at one stroke. The skilled strategist thus took a long-term view of warfare, conducting operations by outstretching the enemy

25

The daimyō's castle
The symbol of the daimyō's power was the castle. It acted as a centre of the economic life of his territory, and provided defence in times of war. In this photograph, we are looking from within the castle walls to the battlements of Kanazawa castle.

army and then cutting his lines of supply and communication. Thus the mark of a good daimyō was that he could field an army of well-trained samurai, who had received a reasonable amount of military training, without denuding his fields of agricultural workers. So prolonged, and so intense, were these 'little wars' that every available man was needed. It is at this stage of Japanese history that *ashigaru* (foot-soldiers) began to emerge as an important factor, but still only as a separate unit under well-disciplined samurai, as illustrated by the Takeda army in the *Kōyō Gunkan*:

Ashigaru taishō shū *(units):*
Yokota Juro'e 30 horsemen, 100 ashigaru
Hara Yozaemon 10 horsemen 50 ashigaru

Different areas of Japan called for their own tactical skills. The Takeda, for instance, carried out most of their offensive campaigns on the flatlands of Echigo and the Kantō, and accordingly developed a powerful cavalry arm, able to strike swiftly and heavily. They used cavalry as mounted spearmen, and the days of the élite mounted archer were seen no more. The spears could be carried as lances, or used for cutting from the saddle, the horseman leaning forward in his stirrups. A long-bladed *naginata* (glaive) could also be very effective in a charge.

26

The armour of the samurai also changed. No longer was it carried to the battlefield in a box and donned for combat; with long-drawn-out battles ranging over a wide area, the samurai had now to live and sleep in their armour. Thus, for example, whereas earlier armour had numerous silk cords holding it together, in the new conditions of warfare these collected lice, sweat and dirt, and complicated designs were abandoned. Samurai were still encouraged to emulate their ancestors, but the successful general in these warlike times thought not in terms of samurai but of samurai armies, and no individual glory, no noble deed, was to come in the way of the serious business of winning battles. Needless to say, old traditions died hard, and there are numerous instances of glory-seeking samurai all but ruining a carefully planned campaign in their pursuit of honour. The invasion of Korea in 1592 developed into a race between two rivals to see whose army could enter the capital first, and the preliminary campaign to the great Battle of Sekigahara in 1600 nearly collapsed when two generals each insisted on leading the assault on a vital castle.

The nemesis of Nobunaga

The bow, the original samurai prestige weapon, was relegated to specially trained *ashigaru*, who were most useful as sharpshooters. As for the majority of lower-rank soldiers, they acted as foot spearmen, or formed the numerous corps armed with the most devastating addition to the samurai arsenal – firearms. Firearms were introduced to Japan by the Portuguese in 1542, and were eagerly adopted. While supplies were still limited, they were prized as samurai weaponry; but as the nimbler swordsmiths converted their trade to that of a gunsmith, vast quantities were produced, and squadrons of *ashigaru* trained in their use. It was the ideal *ashigaru* weapon, as the minimum of training was needed to enable it to be fired with all the accuracy of which it was capable.

27

There were, no doubt, some daimyō to whom this comparatively crude weapon came to be looked on as inappropriate for a samurai. The gun, after all, equalised the lowest and the highest by demanding no greater strength, control or daring than it took to pull the firing mechanism or load a bullet. To a noble samurai it represented the encroachment of barbarian culture into that most traditional of all Japanese social arenas: the battlefield. It defiled both the possesser and the victim, who was thereby deprived of an honourable death. But daimyō who believed in these views tended to be either very rare, or dead. In practice, wars had to be won, and no major daimyō would dare to be without large numbers of firearms.

All that divided the daimyō on the question of firearms was the way in which they were used, and Hōjō Ujiyasu did not live to see the ultimate proof of their worth. He died in 1571, and four years later some sound military thinking, rather than social considerations, led Oda Nobunaga to his famous decision to line up three ranks of matchlockmen at Nagashino. The Takeda and the Hōjō had kept the *ashigaru* to the rear, or in small units under individual commanders, where their guns were less effective. Nobunaga's volley firing, on a large enough scale, tended to ensure that someone would at least hit something. The result was the destruction of the Takeda cavalry on a colossal scale, and a revolution in daimyō thinking.

It also established Oda Nobunaga as the first of the 'super-daimyō', who had begun to acquire some of the former Shōgun's notional powers. But for the Hōjō, the visible result of the lessons of Nagashino was an investment in the defensive architecture of their castles and the natural walls of the surrounding mountains. The destruction of the Takeda, which took until 1582, and the unexpected death of Uesugi Kenshin in 1578, which was followed by a succession dispute, both served to give the Hōjō tranquil borders. Following the family tradition, Ujimasa retired in 1577, leaving his son Ujinao with a false sense of security. From within their kingdom

Hōjō Ujimasa (1538–1590)
Ujimasa was the eldest son of Hōjō Ujiyasu and took part in all his father's campaigns. The turmoil in the rival families of Uesugi and Takeda gave Ujimasa a false sense of security, which was to be totally eclipsed in 1590 when Odawara fell to Hideyoshi's army.

of the Kantō they heard of Nobunaga's murder in 1582, and the take-over by one of his former *ashigaru*, Toyotomi Hideyoshi. Then they began to hear of Hideyoshi's conquest of western Honshū, his taking of Shikoku island, the astounding conquest of the vast southern island of Kyūshū, and by the time they had grown used to the idea that Japan had a new Shōgun in everything but name, an army of 200,000 men was encamped around Odawara castle.

The new daimyō

Here, in 1590, the story of the Hōjō as daimyō came to an end. The siege was long, but largely bloodless, and ended with Hideyoshi ordering the suicide of Ujimasa and the exile of Ujinao. The Hōjō territories were given to Hideyoshi's ally, Tokugawa Ieyasu, but within ten years their vanquisher was to die, leaving an infant to inherit, and with the Battle of Sekigahara in 1600 the great game of *go* was won, and Japan was covered with the playing-pieces of one daimyō – the Tokugawa.

All the existing daimyō had already submitted to Hideyoshi. Now they were forced to submit to the Tokugawa, and to their relief were allowed to keep their heads on their shoulders. In his wisdom, Tokugawa Ieyasu recognised the skills and systems by which these warlords had built up and governed their territories. Their petty kingdoms had been managed well, as we shall see in the chapters that follow, and Ieyasu saw the possibility of using the existing structures as part of his new domain, which was the whole of Japan. So the former warlords became the 'local government' of the dynasty he founded. The Japanese expression is the *baku-han* system,

A daimyō's procession
One of the subtler ways by which the Tokugawa Shōguns sought to control the daimyō was by the *sankin-kōtai*, or 'Alternate Attendance' system. This required the daimyō to leave their families in Edo, the Shōgun's capital, and alternate their own residence between Edo and their own *han* each year. The roads of Japan, therefore, witnessed a succession of gorgeous parades. These daimyō followers are from a scroll depicting such a procession, in the Hōsei-Nikō Kenshōkan, at Nagoya, and are reproduced here by kind permission of the curator.

which combined within it the best of centralised government through the Shōgun's *bakufu*, and the local duties of the daimyō's territory, or *han*. The price the daimyō had to pay was to be severed from their traditional provinces and to be settled elsewhere in Japan, where they had no local loyalties that could spark a rebellion. The first few years of the seventeenth century thus saw a colossal act of moving house. The *fudai-daimyō*, the traditional supporters of the Tokugawa, were given the provinces that controlled the most vital lines of communication. The *tozama-daimyō*, the 'outer lords' who had submitted after Sekigahara, or whose loyalty was felt to be less than total, were given domains far from their roots and far from one another.

The *baku-han* was a successful system that lasted until the Meiji Restoration and the establishment of modern Japan in the mid-nineteenth century. The Tokugawa family supplied a dynasty of fifteen Shōguns over two and a half centuries, supported by the descendants of the original daimyō warlords. We shall see in the pages that follow how they coped with the various demands made on them by peace and war to maintain the continued benevolent rule, under the Shōgun, of the daimyō, the 'Samurai Warlords'.

Focus of Loyalty

Throughout samurai history, whether in peace or in war, the daimyō had one outstanding role to play — to be the leader, to act as focus for loyalty, as through him the family, the clan and the domain were personified. A writer of the Edo Period put it succinctly: 'The relation of parent and child is limited to this life on earth; that between husband and wife continues into the after-life; that between lord and retainer continues into the life after that again.'

This vital loyalty took various expressions, many of which we will examine in the chapters that follow: self-sacrifice in battle, thorough and unspectacular management of a *han's* finances, following-in-death by the bizarre and wasteful act of suicide known as *junshi*, revenge for a beloved dead master, or total loyalty to a family in spite of a dishonourable heir whose conduct betrays the good name of his ancestors. But many of these expressions belonged solely to times of peace. In the Sengoku Period, loyalty required a mixture of the unspectacular and the dramatic, none more so than the total commitment to a defeated daimyō to restore the family fortunes. There is no better illustration of this than the 'Samurai of the Crescent Moon' — Yamanaka Shika-no-suke Yukimori.

The Samurai of the Crescent Moon

The name of Yamanaka Shika-no-suke Yukimori is one almost totally unknown outside Japan, and as the personification of samurai loyalty to a daimyō he deserves to be better known. Yamanaka Shika-no-suke risked his life for the restoration of the Amako family of Izumo Province, to whom the Yamanaka were related. He fought his first battle at the age of 13, when he took an enemy head, and met a tragic death at the age of 34, but by far the most famous episode occurred at the time of the destruction of the Amako family, when he is said to have prayed to the new moon (the 'three-day' crescent moon as the Japanese call it). He had been born on the fifteenth day of the eighth lunar month of 1545, the day of the most brilliant harvest moon, and believed himself to be a heavenly child of the moon. 'Burden me with the seven troubles and eight pains,' he prayed, a Buddhist prayer inviting the gods to place the suffering of the Amako family upon his shoulders.

The Amako had claimed hegemony over the Chūgoku, the southwestern extremity of the main Japanese island of Honshū, at the time of Tsunehisa (1458–1541), but their sway declined over subsequent generations, until they were opposed by the up-and-coming Mōri Motonari (1497–1571) during the rule as daimyō of Amako Yoshihisa. There were many battles with the Mōri in which Yamanaka took part, and at the Battle of Shiraga Yamanaka Shika-no-suke led 200 mounted samurai, and carried out daring tactics of withdrawing calmly then returning to the fray up to

A samurai in formal dress
A daimyō's loyal retainer served him in times of peace as well as war. Here we see a samurai in his formal attire of *kami-shimo*, which consisted of a winged jacket (the *kataginu*) with matching *hakama* (trousers) over a *kimono*, as depicted by an actor at the Toei-Uzumasa Film Studios in Kyōto.

Yamanaka Shika-no-suke
This print by Kuniyoshi depicts Yamanaka Shika-no-suke praying before the crescent moon when he made his vow to restore the fortunes of the Amako family: a vow that ended with his own death. For this reason, Shika-no-suke is one of the paragons of samurai fidelity, though, sadly, he is little known outside Japan.

seven times, against a large army that was running them hard. His military fame was utterly without question, but was not enough to prevent the Amako's castle of Toda-Gassan being captured by Mōri Motonari. The defeated daimyō Yoshihisa retired from the life of a samurai to become a monk, and lived until about 1610, but his loyal retainer was not giving up so easily. He gave his famous prayer to the crescent moon, and from this moment on, in exile, Shika-no-suke's fight began to complete the restoration of the honourable family.

33

As Yamanaka was only a clan vassal, it was vital for him to work through existing members of the Amako family. The most senior member of the family was a certain Katsuhisa (Yoshihisa's father's first cousin), who had long since been a monk at the Tōfukuji in Kyōto. Yamanaka contacted him and persuaded him to return to lay-life and bring together the remnants of the Amako. With Yamanaka as his military commander, they could now plan the restoration of the Amako territory. Yamanaka sensibly realised that it would be a mistake to attempt the recapture of Toda-Gassan castle. Instead he conducted guerrilla operations against the Mōri in various places. On one raid he was captured by Kikkawa Motoharu, but managed to trick his way out of the trap. In 1578 he went to Kyōto to seek alliance with the most powerful daimyō in Japan, Oda Nobunaga, and appealed to him for the restoration of the Amako.

At that time the Mōri and the Oda clans were in a head-on collision. The Mōri had been supporting the fanatical monks of the Ikkō-ikki against Nobunaga, ferrying in guns to their fortress at Ōsaka. To take on the Mōri on their home ground was a difficult proposition for Nobunaga, as they controlled most of the shipping in the Inland Sea, which could cut off any army advancing overland. To have an ally in the Mōri heartland was an attractive proposition, and Oda Nobunaga's general, Toyotomi Hideyoshi, was already in the process of capturing Kōzuki castle in Harima province. Once it was secured, Nobunaga allotted it to Amako Katsuhisa and Yamanaka Shika-no-suke, who were immediately besieged by the Mōri with a great army of 30,000 men.

Detail from the Ōsaka Screen
In this detail from a painted screen, in the Hōsei-Nikō Kenshōkan in Nagoya, depicting the siege of Ōsaka castle in 1615, we see a mounted samurai advancing into the attack. He is wearing a white *horō* on his back.

34

At the time Hideyoshi had a Mōri general confined in his castle of Miki, and, hearing of the danger to the Amako, detached half his army to relieve them. But he was overridden, and received an order from Nobunaga to abandon Kōzuki castle to its fate. There were, apparently, more important strategic considerations than the fate of the Amako. Hideyoshi brought back the troops as they were. The Amako army was isolated and surrendered without the least resistance to the Mōri general, and Katsuhisa committed suicide. By this final act, the Amako were destroyed and obliterated. The loyal Shika-no-suke was taken prisoner and murdered in cold blood while under escort on the road at Takahashi in Bitchū province.

What are we to make of the story of Yamanaka? It is a strange tale of a daimyō's retainer having faith in the fortunes of a doomed family even when the daimyō himself had renounced the struggle. That Yamanaka eventually failed makes his efforts even more tragic, and so much more like the classic heroic failure, whose pattern we find throughout samurai history. There is a marked contrast here between Yamanaka and, say, the retainers of Takeda Katsuyori, hundreds of whom pledged service to Tokugawa Ieyasu when he was defeated in 1582. Yamanaka Shika-no-suke, with his stubborn adherence to samurai honour and the demands of loyalty, has a special place in the history of Japan.

The practical obligations of loyalty

Samurai history is dotted with similar examples of loyalty to a daimyō to the point of death, where a warlord's wishes were carried out in spite of extreme personal suffering. The above account shows this side of the nature of loyalty – the behaviour of the loyal retainer acting essentially as an individual; but the daimyō could not command a kingdom of individuals. There was more to being a samurai than fighting fiercely and loyally in battle. There had to be organisation, delegation of command, and discipline

35

on the battlefield. In times of peace there had to be efficient administration, and a means for converting peace-time samurai into soldiers. The umbrella under which this happened was the *kashindan*, or retainer band, which was mentioned in the context of Hōjō Sōun. The samurai who served a daimyō in a *kashindan* were vassals in a highly developed feudal system. They held lands granted to them by the daimyō, in return for which they would fight his wars. As war was mercifully not a continual process, their services were 'retained', hence the word 'retainer' (in Japanese *kashin* or *kerai*).

Although the definition of a retainer could be made with precision, during the sixteenth century there was a considerable ambiguity and diversity about what constituted samurai status. The popular use of the term today, which usually embraces all Japanese warriors, was truer in the sixteenth century than it was at any other time in Japanese history, before or after. The overriding factor was the enormous increase in the numbers of men who called themselves samurai because they bore arms. Even though there was a great social difference between, say, the son of a daimyō, who had a horse, splendid armour and servants, and a minor part-time samurai from a village, each was part of the same system, which had as its primary function the aim of delineating the military obligation of each and every retainer. So, when war came, each retainer not only supplied devoted individual service, as in the example of Yamanaka above, but also supplied other men and equipment in proportion to the amount of income he received from his landholdings. There were two ways of expressing this in-

Rice fields and mountains
The basis of any daimyō's wealth was the yield of his rice fields, and this view, taken from the summit of Shizu-ga-dake in Shiga prefecture, shows how every bit of available flat land can be pressed into service.

Cooking rice for the army
We are reminded of the mundanities of command by this fascinating illustration from the *Ehon Taikō-ki*. A huge cauldron bubbles away, cooking rice for Hideyoshi's army, while sweating foot-soldiers poke the fire and unload straw bales.

come. The first was in terms of *koku*, which was the rice yield of the fields (one *koku* was 180.4 litres of dry measure, the amount that would theoretically feed one man for one year). Alternatively, as in the case of the Hōjō retainers, in *kanmon*, which was the cash equivalent. The resulting obligation was called the retainer's *yakudaka*.

The daimyō compiled registers of *yakudaka*. In the Hōjō's 1559 register (see Appendix I), the *Odawara-shū shoryō yakuchō*, the units (*shū*), which would make up the army in wartime, are delineated either geographically (for example, Izu-*shū* and Edo-*shū*) or according to a very broad functional definition (for example, *go-umawari-shū*, 'bodyguard', and *ashigaru-shū*, 'foot-soldiers'). There were also separate categories for the Hōjō relatives (*gokamon*) and allies (*takoku-shu*). There are several very good examples of the ratios of obligation used for *yakudaka*, which are missing from the Hōjō example. Asakawa's study of the Iriki family of Kyūshū quotes the muster of troops by the Shimazu daimyō when they attacked Takabaru castle in 1576. A 30 *koku* samurai had to supply personal service, plus one other; a 60 *koku* man added another follower, and so on up to 300 *koku*, who served personally, attended by ten other samurai. When Hideyoshi invaded Korea in 1592, the daimyō nearest to the embarkation port in Kyūshū had to supply six men per 100 *koku*, with lesser proportions from more distant supporters. The Jesuit François Caron, writing at the end of the Sengoku Period, noted that:

each of them must, proportionably, entertain a select company of Souldiers, always in readiness for the Emperor; so that he who hath a thousand koku *yearly, must bring into the field, when ever he is in command, twenty Souldiers & two Horse-Men.*

Thus the Lord of Hirado, who hath 60,000 koku *a year, must entertain, as he easily may, one thousand two hundred Foot, and one hundred and twenty Horse, besides Servants, Slaves, and what more is necessary for the Train.*

37

(The 'Lord of Hirado' at the time was the daimyō Matsuura Shigenobu 1549–1614.)

Such mobilisation orders could only work if the daimyō had the ability to survey his retainers' lands accurately and assess their value of income. As the sixteenth century progressed, the means for doing this became more sophisticated, and a daimyō acquired a very detailed knowledge of the location and extent of his retainers' holdings. It also gave the daimyō two additional powerful tools in ruling his domain. First, the *kandaka* meant that the retainer's relationship to the daimyō could be expressed in terms of income, rather than the mere possession of land. Great income meant great responsibilities, and the appointment to prestigious positions, such as *jōshu*, keepers of castles, and *bugyō*, magistrates.

Second, it made it much easier for a daimyō to transfer retainers from

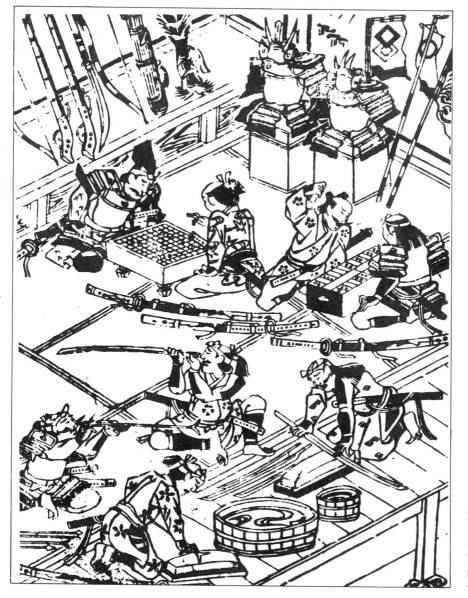

Samurai resting in the castle
This unusual illustration from the *Hōjō Godai-ki* shows samurai polishing swords, playing *go*, and *sugoroku* (backgammon). One man is inspecting an arrow, while in the background sit their suits of armour and various weapons.

Hamamatsu castle
Hamamatsu castle covered a strategic section of the Tōkaidō road, and was owned by a succession of daimyō through the Edo Period as the Tokugawa Shōguns moved them from one fief to another. It had its most celebrated taste of action in 1572, when Takeda Shingen advanced on Hamamatsu and fought the Tokugawa at the Battle of Mikata-ga-Hara.

one set of lands to another. In particular it meant that a retainer's holdings could be split up geographically while still ensuring the same income. This reduced the risks of rebellion by retainers, as the lands, and therefore the people who worked them, were not a contiguous whole. It is also worth noting that retainers who were granted castles were given ones far away from their traditional territories. This, of course, was more pronouncedly so in the case of conquered enemies who had grudgingly pledged service.

To some extent, this anticipated the physical separation of the samurai from the land which was to be the hallmark of the Tokugawa class system. The retainers of all classes now identified themselves more and more with the daimyō, and less and less with the land they farmed. A relationship of dependancy developed as the retainer came to rely on daimyō authority to help him collect taxes from his lands. The relationship between a retainer and a daimyō thus gradually changed from one of independence and local identification to one of dependence and association with a great name. This was fine as long as the daimyō kept winning, but as the Takeda were to show dramatically in 1582, when a daimyō sneezed, the retainers caught a cold.

The élite retainers

Within every *kashindan* were an élite, a select group of senior retainers, called usually *karō* (elders). There are many surviving records of retainer bands in the sixteenth century, most of which are arranged in similar ways under these élite persons. Our source for the Takeda is the list of retainers in the *Kōyō Gunkan*, which is itself based upon two earlier registers of Takeda retainers, one of 1567, which contains 235 names, and the other of 1582, which lists 895 surviving members of the Takeda *kashindan* who pledged service to Tokugawa Ieyasu following the destruction of Takeda Katsuyori by the combined armies of Oda and Tokugawa.

The Takeda *kashindan* consisted largely of three parts:

1   In the first place we have the *jikishindan*, or direct retainer band, who were divided into the *go-shinrui-shū* (relatives), the *go-fudai karō-shū*, the 'elders', and the leaders of the separate *ashigaru-shū*, the *ashigaru-taishō*.
2   The second main grouping was the *sempo-shū*, the unit for the surviving retainers of the many daimyō conquered by the Takeda, such as the Sanada family of Shinano.
3   The final section was the *kuni-shū*, the regional *bushi-dan* from the Takeda lands, who ranged down to village samurai.

Takeda Shingen was the leader of this 'Ever-victorious, invincible, Kōshu Warband', as he called it, of which the élite core were the hand-picked leaders, magnificent in action, of whom 24 brave and fierce individuals became well known as the 'Twenty-Four Generals'. The *Kōyō Gunkan* records Shingen's criteria for a good general, which laid as much stress on peace-time work as on the field of battle: 'Concerning honouring the exploits of great generals, first, (they must be) persons of judgement, second, (they carry out) punishments in the province, third, they achieve great victories in battle, we honour their fame in these three.'

The 'Twenty-Four Generals' is, in fact, not a contemporary term, but one invented later. The Japanese as a race seem peculiarly fond of numerical categories, and the 'Takeda Twenty-Four Generals' is a popular concept from stories and illustrations. The selection of the 24 relates to their popu-

The Takeda 'Twenty-Four Generals' Every daimyō had an élite corps of senior retainers. In the case of the Takeda family, the élite were the so-called 'Twenty-Four Generals'. The term is not contemporary, and different illustrations depict different individuals. This scroll is in the Memorial Hall on the site of Nagashino castle.

larity with the masses in the Edo Period, and we see them in the portraits included in three painted scrolls of the Twenty-Four Generals, on which there are various faces of generals. The commander-in-chief Shingen is painted in the top centre, and 24 individuals are arranged to left and right in two rows. The 24 generals join Shingen and Katsuyori, and Shingen's younger brothers Nobukado and Nobushige are shown in various ways.

I have examined these scrolls carefully, and discovered that there are, in fact, 33 individuals represented. Furthermore, some of the greatest names in the Takeda hierarchy are not included at all. One example is Hajikano Dene'mon Masatsugu, an *ashigaru-taishō*, or general of *ashigaru*, a demanding post, who added his own unique chapter to the Takeda legend, when in 1569 Takeda Shingen led his army against the Hōjō. On approaching Odawara, the Takeda army was met by a swollen river. Shingen ordered his army to stop while the depth was tested, and Hajikano volunteered for this dangerous task. He drove his horse into the angry waters and began to swim it across. So deep was the river that at one time all that could be seen of Hajikano was the *sashimono* banner on his back, which bore a design of a playing piece from the Japanese board game of *shōgi*. Hajikano's piece was the spear, which in *shōgi* can only move forwards, a reason he put forward to Shingen for his confidence in advancing!

Another strange omission is Morozumi Bungo-no-kami Masakiyo. Masakiyo is said to have been the youngest son of Takeda Nobumasa, and was therefore Shingen's great-uncle. He is believed to have been 81 years old at the time of his death at the fourth Battle of Kawanakajima, and held the rank of *ashigaru-taishō*. Shingen had, in fact, made this old general *honjin-hatamoto*, 'headquarters-samurai', for the battle, a comparatively safe position, but the headquarters was attacked in a surprise charge by Uesugi Kenshin. The old general drew his sword, plunged into the enemy and was killed. Shingen bitterly regretted his death, and Morozumi is one of only three Takeda generals to be buried at Kawanakajima.

Other names surprise one by their inclusion. Anayama Baisetsu and Oyamada Nobushige are included but, after years of service to Shingen, these two later betrayed his son Takeda Katsuyori. Nevertheless, the concept of the 'Twenty-Four Generals' remains a popular one, and they can

---

A daimyō in command

The great warlord Uesugi Kenshin sits with his generals to receive a message from a wounded scout. As Kenshin was a Buddhist monk he wears the traditional white headcowl. Behind him fly the three banners that always indicated his presence: the red rising sun on blue which was the treasure of the Uesugi house; the elaborate version of the character for 'dragon', which was always raised on the battlefield as his army went into an attack; and on

the viewer's right the character *bi*, the first syllable in the name of Bishamon-ten, under whose divine protection Kenshin lived, which was flown at his headquarters on a battlefield.

His generals, accompanied by retainers carrying their personal banners, sit beside him. From left to right, they are as follows: Shimojō Saneyori (white ring on red), who was in the forward division at the fourth Battle of Kawanakajima in 1561; Takanashi Masayori (chequerboard); Nakajō Fujikashi,

who received a personal commendation from Kenshin for his action at Kawanakajima, has the red flag with white designs; Honjō Shigenaga has the bold character *jō*; and Suda Chikamitsu, also of the forward division, has the gold swastika.

The wounded samurai bears the Uesugi *mon* of love-birds on his *sashimono*, which identifies him as a retainer of a member of Uesugi Kenshin's family, or of someone regarded as equivalent to a family member.

be found represented at the festivals held every year in the area around Kōfu, Shingen's old capital. Many others of the famous daimyō of the age had their 'number of generals'. Tokugawa Ieyasu had 16, Uesugi Kenshin either 14, 17 or 28, depending on which version you read.

One factor that was common to the generals on both sides, as indeed it was to many powerful daimyō retainers of the period, was the giving of honorific titles. In addition to their surname and given name, they tended to be known as 'Feudal Lord of...'. The surprising thing about these titles, which appear in Japanese as '...no kami' is that they frequently refer to territories not actually owned by the clan in question, and often hundreds of miles away. Shingen's great-uncle, Morozumi Masakiyo, was 'Bungo no kami', the nominal feudal lord of Bungo province on the island of Kyūshū, over a thousand miles to the west, and which probably none of the Takeda had ever visited. Other titles reflect nearby territories controlled by other daimyō which the retainer's overlord coveted. Baba Nobuharu, one of the most skilled to the 'Twenty-Four Generals', was Mino no kami, Mino province being a possible future gain for the Takeda as part of an advance on Kyōto. At one time, there were living no less than three prominent samurai all bearing the identical title of 'Suruga no kami'. One was Katō Nobukuni, a general of the Takeda who had responsibility for the teaching of archery; another was an Uesugi general, Usa Sadayuki, the truce-bearer

The 'Twenty-Four Generals' at Shimobe
Every May, the Takeda 'Twenty-Four Generals' are brought to life in the *Shingen-kō* Festival at Shimobe, in Yamanashi prefecture. The character on the far end of the line is Yamamoto Kansuke, easily recognisable by his buffalo-horn helmet. The 'generals'' names are painted on their *sashimono* banners, which would not have been done in the sixteenth century.

after Kawanakajima, and the third was a retainer of the Mōri daimyō in the west of Japan – Kikkawa Motoharu. None had any direct connection with Suruga province, which was actually owned by the Hōjō.

In spite of all the honorific titles, feudal obligation and rewards, not all lord-vassal arrangements succeeded, even among the élite. There were, in fact, some spectacular failures, such as Sasa Narimasa (1539–88). He was one of Hideyoshi's most senior retainers, granted a fief of 100,000 *koku* in Etchu province, but when Hideyoshi was opposed by Oda Nobuo in 1584, Narimasa backed Nobuo, and was chastised by his former comrade, Maeda Toshiie. Hideyoshi dealt with Narimasa with the great generosity that was his hallmark, and transferred him to a new fief in far-off Higo province in Kyūshū in 1587, giving Narimasa then following warning as he did so:

1   *To the 53 local magnates the same fief as before is to be granted.*
2   *No land survey shall be made for three years.*
3   *Due precaution is to be taken never to embarrass farmers.*
4   *Due precaution is always to be taken that no insurrection shall take place.*
5   *No charge shall be made upon farmers for the contribution to the public works to be carried out at Ōsaka.*

The above are strictly and carefully to be observed.

Unfortunately Sasa Narimasa betrayed the trust Hideyoshi put in him, and was 'invited' to commit suicide.

The lord's horse
Two samurai attendants wait with the lord's horse outside the *maku*, the curtained enclosure used to screen the field headquarters of a daimyō. The *mon* on the *maku* is the chrysanthemum-on-the-water design of Kusunoki Masashige. This is a further section from the scroll of Kusunoki's career owned by the Nampian Kannon-ji at Kawachi-Nagano, and is reproduced here by kind permission of the Chief Priest.

The call to arms

With a call to arms, the *kashindan*, with its detailed records of obligation, was transformed from a paper army into a fighting force. An example relating to the year 1557 has been preserved in the archives of the Uesugi family. It is in the form of a highly detailed letter, which is not surprising considering that the man who is being summoned is Irobe Katsunaga, Kenshin's *gun-bugyō*, a rank equivalent to Chief of Staff. He lists the disturbances attributed to Takeda Harunobu (Takeda Shingen) and warns Katsunaga of the dangers to the province of Shingen's belligerence:

Concerning the disturbances among the various families of Shinano and the Takeda of Kai in the year before last, it is the honourable opinion of Imagawa Yoshimoto of Sumpu that things must have calmed down. However, since this time, Takeda Harunobu's example of government has been corrupt and bad. However, through the will of the gods and from the kind offices of Yoshimoto, I, Kagetora have very patiently avoided any interference. Now, Harunobu has recently set out for war and it is a fact that he has torn to pieces the retainers of the Ochiai family of Shinano and Katsurayama castle has fallen. Accordingly, he has moved into the so-called Shimazu and Ogura territories for the time being....My army will be turned in this direction and I, Kagetora will set out for war and meet them half way. In spite of snowstorms or any sort of difficulty we will set out for war by day or night. I have waited fervently. If our family's allies in Shinano can be destroyed then even the defences of Echigo will not be safe. Now that things have come to such a pass, assemble your pre-eminent army and be diligent in loyalty, there is honourable work to be done at this time.

With respects
Kenshin,
1557, 2nd month, 16th day

A celebratory banquet
In this page from the *Ehon Taikō-ki*, a group of senior retainers feast after a victory. Their food is served to them on lacquered trays, and the *saké* is flowing freely!

46

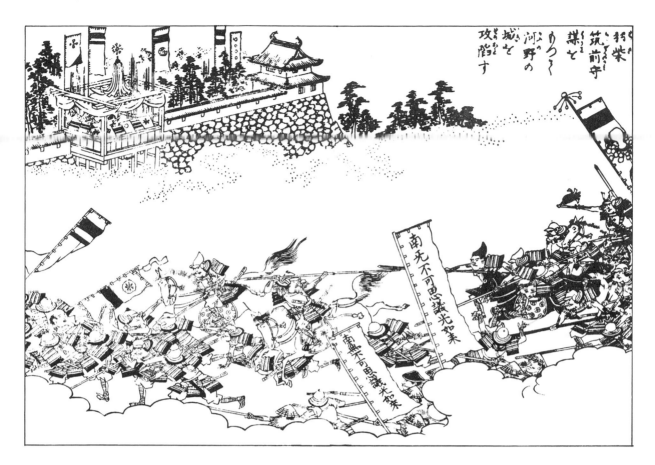

Hideyoshi attacks a castle
Here the *Ehon Taikō-ki* shows
Hideyoshi's troops neutralising an
opportunistic attack by the defenders
of a castle, identified by the caption
as Kawano.

Needless to say, less important retainers received a less imposing call to arms and, in the case of the part-time samurai of the countryside, a general proclamation would suffice. The well-known example from about 1560 of the call to arms against Uesugi Kenshin by Hōjō Ujimasa (though sealed by his retired father Ujiyasu as the young daimyō was off campaigning) has sometimes been ridiculed as evidence of his lack of concern for the quality of his troops. In contrast, it shows the universality of the definition of samurai referred to above, and his willingness to reward any who serve him well:

1   All men, including those of the samurai class in this country district, are ordered to come and be registered on the 20th day of this month. They are to bring with them a gun, spear, or any kind of weapon, if they happen to possess one, without fearing to get into trouble.
2   If it is known afterwards that even one man in this district concealed himself and did not respond to the call, such man, no matter whether he is a bugyō *or a peasant, is to be beheaded.*
3   All men from 15 to 70 years of age are ordered to come; not even a monkey tamer will be let off.
4   Men to be permitted to remain in the village are those whose ages are above 70 years, or under 15 years, and too young to be used as messengers, but the others are all ordered to come.
5   It will be good for the men to prepare for the call by polishing their spears

47

and preparing small paper flags to be taken with them. Those who are fitted to be messengers, and desire to do that service, will be so permitted.

6 All the men covered by this order are to come to Katsukui on the 4th day and register before the lord's deputy and then return home. . .if the appointed day happens to be rainy they are to come the first day the weather is settled. Men must arrive at the appointed place properly armed with anything they happen to possess, and those who do not possess a bow, a spear or any sort of regular weapon are to bring even hoes or sickles.

7 This regulation is generally applicable, and even Buddhist priests who desire to do their duty for their native province are ordered to come.

It is ordered to pay strict attention to the implications of the above seven articles, and if there be anyone who disregards this ordinance and neglects his duty, such a one is to be severely punished; while the man who is careful and eager to be loyal to his lord will be rewarded with the grant that is reasonable and suitable to him.

By such means, the sixteenth-century warlord assembled his army. The obligation of loyalty was fulfilled in part. It could now be tested on the battlefield.

Commander-in-Chief

When the samurai clan went to war, the daimyō's role became that of transforming this retainer band with its patterns of loyalty into an efficient fighting unit on the battlefield. The daimyō thereupon assumed the demanding role of commander-in-chief of the domainal army.

Setting off to war

Setting out for war
This picture from the *Ehon Taikō-ki* shows the meticulous preparations made when an army set out for war. Armour is removed from boxes, bamboo flagpoles are threaded through the banners and, in the left foreground, an attendant fixes a samurai's *sashimono* into place on the back of his armour.

Once the troops had been assembled, the actual process of setting out for war was attended by much ceremony, whether it was for a long campaign, or as a farewell ritual immediately prior to the start of a battle. There are copious records of the form these rituals took, which have provided the basis for the re-enactments of such ceremonies in the former castle towns of noted daimyō. I am well acquainted with two of these – the Uesugi *Butei shiki* at Yonezawa, which re-enacts the departure ceremony of Uesugi Kenshin, and the *Shingen-kō matsuri* at Kōfu, which is part of a number of

commemorative events for Takeda Shingen. (I have also had the unique privilege of being invited to play the part of Shingen's general, Baba Nobuharu, at the latter celebration in 1986.)

In ancient times, according to Japanese legend, a battle would customarily begin with a blood-offering to the gods of war in the form of a human sacrifice, either a captured prisoner or a condemned criminal, though there does not appear to be any written evidence for such practices continuing beyond the eighth century AD, and certainly during the time of the samurai the blood-sacrifice is confined to the offering of severed heads after the battle, rather than an actual sacrifice beforehand. Nevertheless, the need for prayers to the gods of war, of whom the most important was Hachiman-dai-Bosatsu, the deified spirit of the Emperor Ōjin (201–312) and tutelary deity of the Minamoto clan, permeates much of the ritual surrounding departure for war and victory ceremonies.

The ceremony of departure was centred around the practical need for a review of troops. With his army drawn up ready to march off, the daimyō would sit, surrounded by his generals in a semicircle, against the backdrop of the *maku*, the large curtains used to screen the headquarters position from view. In the case of Uesugi Kenshin, who was a Buddhist monk, this would have been preceded by his praying for victory within the shrine of the Buddhist deity Bishamon-ten inside Kasuga-yama castle. Only then would Kenshin go out into the courtyard to take his seat with his generals.

Four Generals at the Nagashino Festival
A general's military costume was often embellished by the wearing of a surcoat, called a *jinbaori*. The four men here are taking part in the annual Nagashino Festival.

There he would partake of the traditional farewell meal, served to him with great dignity. There were three dishes, *kachi-guri* (dried chestnuts – probably included for no reason other than the literal translation of the characters used is 'victory chestnuts'), *kombu* (kelp – a basic ingredient in Japanese cooking) and prepared *awabi* (abalone), all three of which were regarded as bringing good fortune. He would also drink *saké* (rice wine), served within three cups, one inside the other. The number three was also regarded as bringing good luck from the divinations of yin and yang geomancy, and the three cups represented heaven, earth and man.

When the army was ready to move off, an attendant would tie the commander's sword round his waist, then his quiver of arrows (rarely encountered in the Sengoku Period) after which the daimyō would stand up, take his signalling fan and receive the shouts of his assembled troops. There were various ways of doing this, but there are two shouts in common – the first being 'Ei!' (Glory!), to which there is given the response 'Ō!' (Yes!). In the *Shingen-kō-matsuri*, the man playing the part of Shingen's *gun-bugyō*, Yamamoto Kansuke, orders the other generals to raise their swords, and calls, 'Ei! Ei! Ō!', to which the generals reply, 'Ei! Ei! Ō!'. In the Uesugi version, it is 'Kenshin' himself who calls 'Ei! Ei!', and his generals reply, 'Ō! Ō!' repeated twice. This shout was also given at the end of a successful battle. (There is a splendid example in Kurosawa's film *Ran*.)

Traditionally, the general would then mount his horse, put on his helmet, and the flags would be raised. Just before the procession moved off, a Shinto priest would bless the army with the chanting of *sutras*. Uesugi Kenshin would also re-dedicate to Hachiman the 'Hachiman-bow' which was a treasure of the Uesugi. After this, Kenshin would mount his horse, surrounded by his three banners: the Bishamon-ten, a red rising sun on blue (a gift from an emperor), and the 'warring dragon' flag, which led a charge by the Uesugi samurai.

Organisation on a battlefield

Armies were controlled on the battlefield using a range of visible and audible signalling methods. Of the latter, the most important were the *taiko*, the big war-drums and the *horagai*, the conch-shell trumpet. War-drums varied in size from the very large specimens mounted in the open-work towers of castles, to ones carried in a frame on a man's back. In the eighth chapter of the *Hōjō Go-dai ki*, we read: 'The *horagai* was blown when a battle plan was put into disorder. Similarly on hearing the voice of the *taiko* the soldiers would regroup...'

In another section of the *Hōjō Go-dai ki*, we hear of the use Hōjō Sōun made of a *yamabushi* who was adept at playing the *horagai*:

The soldiers obeyed the commands of the horagai, *and those proclaimed by the* taiko. *There was a* yamabushi *called Gakuzenbo of Ōyama in Sagami [province]. He took the Buddhist name of Satsuma, and possessed a large* horagai. *This* yamabushi *was especially skilled in blowing the* horagai. *It could be heard for a distance of 50 chō [about six miles!]. When Hōjō Sōun set out to war this* yamabushi *came from the Ōyama temple. He was [made] a* hatamoto *and blew the* horagai. *It is said that his descendants blow the* horagai *to this day.*

Horagai were also used for time-keeping.

The use of flags to identify and control units of troops was based on a very sophisticated use of heraldry. Prior to the sixteenth century, heraldry in Japan had not gone much further than the straightforward identification of an army. Now it became the means for subdividing and controlling an army, made necessary by the need to control large bodies of troops. My study of the army of the Shimazu shows how the troops fielded by the Shimazu grew from 3,000 in 1411 through 5,000 in 1484, to an estimate of possibly 115,000 at the siege of Minamata in 1576. Even during the straightened circumstances forced upon them by Hideyoshi's defeat of them in 1578, they were still able to supply 10,600 warriors for the Winter Campaign of Ōsaka in 1614. Complex manoeuvring of such numbers, such as the early morning clash during the fourth Battle of Kawanakajima (1561) between the Takeda (16,000) and the Uesugi (13,000) also presupposes quite sophisticated methods of troop recognition and signalling, in addition to well-rehearsed drill and discipline. Also, armour was becoming uniform in style, and the gradual introduction of armour protection for the face, which within the century was to develop into a complete mask, made the need for quick identification more pressing than ever. The response to this was a considerable development of the use and design of flags, notably in three forms: the *nobori*, the *uma-jirushi*, and the *sashimono*.

The *nobori* is the familiar form of long vertical flag, supported along the

一足不去忠佐文

top edge, which can be seen everywhere in Japan today, from shops to temples. Its military use seems to be well established by the third quarter of the sixteenth century, and several contemporary painted screens show a great profusion of *nobori*, many of which have *mon* (family badges).

The *uma-jirushi*, literally 'horse insignia', was introduced to distinguish the person of a general, which was the function of the European 'standard'. According to regulations introduced early in the Edo Period, a daimyō with an income of 1,300 *koku* or over was entitled to a *ko-* (small) *uma-jirushi*, held by one man, while those with 6,000 *koku* and over could have an *ō-uma-jirushi*, which required two or three people to hold it. A samurai 'standard-bearer' would either have the *uma-jirushi* seated in a leather pocket at the front of his belt, or strapped into a frame on his back. In the case of the *ō-uma jirushi* the other two men would hold on to separate tethering cords.

The *uma-jirushi* did not always take the form of a flag. Several three-dimensional objects were used, such as a large red umbrella by Oda Nobunaga, and the *sen nari hisago* or 'thousand gourd standard' of Toyotomi Hideyoshi. Of the flag versions, one well-known example is Uesugi Kenshin's red sun disc on dark blue. The flowing *hata-jirushi*, popular in earlier centuries, continued to be used in armies, and in the case of Katō Kiyomasa (1562–1611) served as his *uma-jirushi* in the form of a long white banner with the Nichiren motto *Namu myōhō renge kyō*, which is preserved in the Hommyō-ji in Kumamoto.

The sashimono

The real innovation in heraldic display in the sixteenth century was not in the use of large flags but in the introduction of a personal banner for the

The sashimono of Tadano Samon
See overleaf for the account of how this particular *sashimono* inspired a comrade in the heat of battle.

Detail from the Ōsaka Screen, showing sashimono
The *sashimono* was the most important addition to Japanese heraldry during the sixteenth century. It consisted of an identifying device, usually a flag, fixed to the back of a suit of armour. This picture is from the painted screen of the siege of Ōsaka in the Hōsei-Nikō Kenshōkan at Nagoya.

individual called the *sashimono*, and worn on the back, its shaft slotting into a specially constructed carrier. Two cords ran under the armpits from the *sashimono* shaft to two rings on the front of the armour, to help hold the flag in place. *Sashimono* sometimes bore the *mon* of the commander, though there were many exceptions, as we shall see, and some cases where the *sashimono* was not actually a flag at all but a three-dimensional object.

Two examples of the use of *sashimono* appear in the chronicle *Meiryō Kohan*: 'At the time of the Ōsaka campaign there was a retainer of Kii Raisen called Yabe Tora no suke, of great strength with a *sashimono* of length two *ken* [12 feet!], and a long sword over three *shaku* [3 feet].'

The second extract shows how a striking *sashimono* could inspire a comrade:

There was a retainer of Satake Yoshinobu called Tadano Samon. He was expert in the ways of horse and bow, spear and sword, and furthermore became a samurai of great bravery and strength.... At the time when this Samon went to the battlefield he wore a large sashimono. *The* sashimono *was a* nobori *of white cotton cloth on which was written in large characters, 'hitoashi-fu ko Tadano Samon' [Tadano Samon who will not take one step backwards]. There was once a time when the Sasaki army were defeated in battle. One of their common soldiers had lost heart and retreated, but when he was about to drink water from a stream by the road-side, he saw the great* sashimono *where it had fallen into the water. He saw the characters on it, and regretted that he had retreated. This mere footsoldier hurried back and charged into the midst of the great army of the enemy. He fought with*

Battle across a river
At the signal given by a bursting rocket, samurai ford a river into battle, under the covering fire of their arquebusiers. (From the *Ehon Taikō-ki*.)

Smashing an aqueduct
A reliable water supply was vital to the defenders of a castle. In this illustration from the *Ehon Taikō-ki*, the besiegers of Chōko-ji castle are attempting to smash the aqueduct, having driven off the guards. It was the destruction of the aqueduct that led to Shibata Katsuie's final, desperate charge into the midst of the enemy. (See *Battles of the Samurai* by this author.)

great desperation and took three helmeted heads. . . . He ended his career with 200 koku.

The best evidence of the role heraldry could play on a battlefield is the Hōjō army under Hōjō Ujiyasu in about the year 1559. The *shū* units in the 1559 register, referred to in the previous chapter, are largely preserved on the field of battle, with great use being made of the heraldic *sashimono*.

Ujiyasu's army consisted of two major parts, the first being the troops supplied by his well-established and loyal family retainers, the 28 *roshō*. Of these the 20 *shōshō*, 'captains', formed the first rank, while behind them were the 8 *karō*, 'elders', five units of which were identified by the use of different coloured *sashimono*, and therefore called the *go-shiki sonae*, or 'five colour regiments'. Thus Hōjō Tsunanari (1515–87), the victor of the Night Battle of Kawagoe, led men with yellow flags on their backs; Hōjō Tsunataka wore red; Tominaga Masaie (who is recorded as the keeper of Edo castle in 1564) wore blue; Kasawara was white; and Tame, black.

It is almost certain that each of these coloured flags would bear in addition the Hōjō *mon* of the *mitsu uroku*, the fish-scale design, which is depicted on a red *sashimono* preserved in the Kanagawa Prefectural Art Museum in Yokohama. There is also a reference to black *sashimono* ('*sashimono* should be black and new') in a military ordinance issued by Hōjō Ujikuni (1541–97) in 1574.

The most fascinating use of heraldry in the Hōjō army is, however, found in the core of the army, the *go-hatamoto* 48 *banshō*. The 48 *banshō*, 'captains', were under Ujiyasu's direct command, and were divided into 6 companies of 7 *banshō*, and one of 6. Each *banshō* commanded 20 men, and every unit was distinguished by a single *kana* on his *sashimono*. The interesting point about this arrangement is that the seven units were grouped in accordance with the *i-ro-ha* syllabary. The *i-ro-ha* is a poem which contains every one of the phonetic *hiragana*, and is traditionally used as a way of teaching Japanese children their alphabet, so that the order was:

– *i, ro, ha, ni, ho, he, to*
– *chi, ri, nu, ru, o, wa, ka,*
– *yo, ta, re, so, tsu, ne, na*
– *ra, mu, u, i, no, o, ku,*
– *ya, ma, ke, fu, ko, e, te*
– *a, sa, ki, yu, me, n,*
– *mi, shi, e, hi, mo, se, su*

This meant that the *sashimono* of Ujiyasu's army spelled out a poem, which roughly translated, means 'Colours are fragrant, but they fade away. In this world of ours none lasts forever. Today cross the high mountain of life's illusion, and there will be no more shallow dreaming, no more drunkenness.' Among this group we know that a certain retainer called Nanjō Gemba-no-suke, along with his own men, wore the character 'u' on his *sashimono*.

There are few details regarding the heraldry of the other units, though one may assume that the allies (the *takoku-shū*) displayed their own *mon*. The *ashigaru-shū*, who were little regarded at this time, were kept in a homogeneous unit under reliable command, probably with little identification.

Heraldry and the Takeda

Hōjō Ujiyasu frequently found himself in arms against his belligerent neighbour Takeda Shingen, and there is considerable evidence of the use of heraldry by this renowned commander. The most important flag was a large *nobori*, preserved today in the Takeda Museum at the Erin-ji at Enzan (Yamanashi-ken), bearing in gold characters on blue the motto 'Swift as the wind, silent as the forest, fierce as a fire, steady as a mountain'. Other flags included what is now the oldest surviving 'rising sun' flag in Japan. He also had two long red *nobori* bearing Buddhist prayers, and a personal flag with three Takeda *mon* with 'flowery' edges.

Shingen also used heraldic devices to differentiate the various units of his army in a similar fashion to that of the Hōjō. Instead of the Hōjō use of colour and *kana*, the various units of the Takeda are distinguished by the flags of their commanders. There is little use of the Takeda *mon*, or indeed of any device resembling a *mon*. Instead there is a predominant use of bold design and colour. Two examples from the *go-shinrui-shu* are Takeda Nobutoyo, who used a black flag bearing a white sun's disc (Nobutoyo was the son of Shingen's younger brother Nobushige, who was killed during the fourth Battle of Kawanakajima in 1561, where it is believed he used the same flag), and Ichijō Nobutatsu, another of Shingen's brothers,

The flags of the Hōjō army, 1559
These are the *hiragana* characters used on the *sashimono* of the Hōjō army. (See text for full description.)

いろはにほへと
ちりぬるをわか
よたれそつねな
らむうゐのおく
やまけふこえて
あさきゆめみし
　　ゑひもせす

who had a flag divided horizontally into two halves, white on top and red underneath. From the *go-fudai karō-shū*, we find Baba Nobuharu, killed during the pursuit from Nagashino in 1575, whose flag was a black zigzag on white. All are displayed at the Takeda festivals (see pages 154–5).

Takeda Shingen's arch-rival, Uesugi Kenshin, is less fortunate in his present-day commemoration. Of his 'Twenty-Eight Generals' who are personified at the annual re-enactment, nine of the families died out during the Edo Period, and are therefore not recorded in the illustrated register of 1841, which the organisers of the *Butei-shiki* have used to reconstruct the

---

Kakizaki leads the charge of the Uesugi samurai

This plate illustrates the pivotal moment during the fourth Battle of Kawanakajima in 1561. The Takeda army had crossed the river in secret during the night, expecting the Uesugi army to come fleeing across their front after a dawn raid by a Takeda unit on their camp. In fact, the reverse happened. Guessing Takeda Shingen's plan, his rival Uesugi Kenshin had similarly transferred his army by night. As dawn broke, the Uesugi samurai pounced upon the Takeda flanks in a devastating charge.

The Uesugi vanguard was led by Kakizaki Kageie, whose *uma-jirushi* (personal standard) bore a large golden grasshopper, and whose samurai wore a *sashimono* charged with the unlikely sounding device of a giant radish! To their rear are the flags of Shimazu Norihisa (the same black cross as the better-known family of Shimazu in Kyushu), whose samurai accompanied Kakizaki in the charge, and in the distance appear the flags of two minor Uesugi retainers, Ōishi (star pattern) and Nozokito.

To the rear of the Takeda lines is the flag of Hara Toratane, whose position close to Shingen's headquarters meant that his soldiers received the brunt of the charge. The *ashigaru* in the foreground bear the Takeda *mon* on black, indicating that they follow a family member, namely Takeda Nobushige, Shingen's brother, who was killed during the battle. Note how the spearman carries his sword blade downwards, it being the only practical way for it to be carried if it is thrust through the belt and the wearer has to use a spear. (The author is indebted to Messrs. Bottomley and Hopson for this point of detail.)

flags used in the re-enactment of the departure for war of their favourite son. The 1841 register is extrapolated backwards to a register of 1575, which, unlike the Takeda list, gives no indication itself of flags, but has the additional advantage that it lists the weapon types to be supplied by each unit (see Appendix II). As they are heterogeneous collections, it is reasonable to assume that the Uesugi army, like the Takeda, fought in units under the banner of the commander. This is supported by the notes and illustrations which the festival committee kindly supplied to me. Once again, there is a minimal use of actual *mon*. Two of the most remarkable designs are recorded for Kakizaki Izumi-no-kami Kageie, leader of the Uesugi vanguard at the fourth Battle of Kawanakajima in 1561, who used a personal *uma-jirushi* of a golden grasshopper on a blue field, while his followers had red *sashimono* charged with a white *daikon*, the giant radish!

Heraldry and specialised units

In the three examples above, there seems to have been little use made of heraldry to indicate differing functions, other than the broad categories of *ashigaru, go-umawari-shū*, etc.; not that this is surprising, because the battle-field organisation of the time, being based on registers such as the Hōjō 1559 survey, relied on retainers supplying their own troops and fighting loyally for the daimyō. The one exception is the use of *sashimono* to distinguish the *tsukai-ban*, or messengers, whose role was a vital one in warfare. The Tokugawa *tsukai-ban* used a *sashimono* bearing the character *go* (the figure 5), and the Takeda *tsukai-ban* bore a centipede. The colours are variously described as being black on white, white on black, black on red, gold on black and gold on blue. The chronicle *Musha Monogatari* tells us a good story about the Takeda *tsukai-ban* which is interesting in that it illustrates the meticulous regulations in a daimyō's army, and also the refreshing discovery that samurai could have a sense of humour!

Takeda Shingen instructs one of his tsukai-ban
The *tsukai-ban*, or messengers, were a vital arm of any daimyō's army. Here Takeda Shingen instructs one of his messengers, who has a centipede on his *sashimono*, at the second Battle of Kawanakajima, also known as the Battle of the Saigawa. (See *Battles of the Samurai* by this author.) This version is from a wood-block print in the author's collection.

Among the honourable [followers] of Takeda Shingen-kō, were the twelve o-tsukai ban. Their sashimono *were white flags with a black centipede. However, among them was a person called Hajikano Den'emon who wore a white flag without a centipede. Shingen-kō inspected them and questioned him why he did not have the same white flag* sashimono *as everybody else in the* tsukai-ban. *Shingen-kō got angry when someone disobeyed orders, and Den'emon had disobeyed military regulations. Den'emon showed a one sun [2.5 cm/1 in long] centipede that had attached itself to the loop of the sashimono under his armpit. Said Den'emon, if I attach it in place of the other centipede, I shall mingle with the other warriors, as it is like the others. Shingen-kō began to laugh.'*

This is the same Hajikano Den'emon Masatsugu whose use of a different *sashimono* design was described in the previous chapter.

The use of messengers and scouts was the most reliable way in which orders were transmitted and the units of an army controlled from the daimyō's headquarters. In the *Kōyō Gunkan*, we read that 'Sixty horsemen and one on foot from the samurai retainers of Itagaki were sent out as *o-mono miso* [scouts], but seeing no enemy approaching in the vicinity they returned....' Membership of a *tsukai-ban* was highly regarded, as is indicated in the chronicle *Tosenkigyō*:

There was a retainer of the Echizen-Shōshō Tadanao called Hara Hayato Sadatane. He was originally a retainer of Takeda Shingen, but following the downfall of Takeda Katsuyori the Shōshō Tadanao, hearing at second hand of the fame of his

Warrior wearing a horō
The *horō* is surely the most impractical addition to a suit of armour ever devised. It consisted of a cloak on a bamboo frame, which took the place of the *sashimono* on the back of armour. It was often worn as an identifying device by messengers.

military exploits, engaged him [as a member of] the kuro-horō shu *[the 'black* horō *unit']. He served diligently as an army messenger.*

Note how the brave samurai is appointed to a responsible position, and that Tadanao's messengers were distinguished by wearing a black *horō*. The *horō* was a cloak-like bag, worn on the back of the armour, which was often stiffened with a basketwork cage, surely the most impractical item of military equipment ever devised, though even *sashimono* must have been a hindrance in the heat of battle. In fact, the painted screen in Hikone castle, depicting the Summer Campaign of Ōsaka, shows an *ashigaru* patiently holding a samurai's *sashimono* while the latter delivers the *coup de grâce*. Oda Nobunaga's retainer band included his own *go-umawari-shū*, which was divided into two parts: the red *aka horo-shū* and the *kuro horo-shū*.

The use of heraldry to distinguish such units presupposes a growing specialism of weaponry or tactics within a samurai army, and this was indeed slowly happening. The change from organisation based on feudal service to a more 'professional' army was a gradual development during the final quarter of the sixteenth century. Great impetus was given by Oda Nobunaga's victory of Nagashino in 1575, which owed a great deal to his use of *ashigaru* firing arquebuses against the advancing Takeda cavalry. This implies a considerable degree of discipline and shows how the use of *ashigaru* had developed. Their position at the very front of Nobunaga's army, rather than at the rear as in the case of Hōjō Ujiyasu's standard battle plan, is a striking difference. As his career progressed, Nobunaga became one of the first daimyō to issue his *ashigaru* with a simple, standard suit of armour, and there are many illustrations showing these *okegawa-dō*, and the lampshade-like *jingasa* helmets, emblazoned with *mon*, which became the typical *ashigaru* armour of the period.

One of the Takeda generals, Obu Toramasa, somewhat anticipated this future development in heraldry by dressing all his soldiers in uniformly coloured armour: a bright-red lacquer. Records tell us that this was common to all ranks, and included horse-harness and the *sashimono*, which bore a white crescent moon. Obu Toramasa's troops were known as the 'red regiment', thereby providing circumstantial evidence that the troops provided by such a retainer fought as one group under that general. They 'exploded on the enemy like a ball of fire', according to the *Kōyō Gunkan*. This was later adopted by his younger brother, Yamagata Masakage, and subsequently copied at the suggestion of Tokugawa Ieyasu by one of his chief retainers, Ii Naomasa (1561–1602). His 'red-devils', as they came to be known, are depicted on the painted screen of the Summer Campaign of Ōsaka, which is in the Ii Art Museum in Hikone. Incidentally, Yamagata Masakage was killed at Nagashino in 1575, and his troops wore a black *sashimono*.

The rituals of victory

Even more ceremony surrounded the celebration of victory than attended the setting out to war. After a battle, the victorious daimyō would reward his loyal followers. Great honour was attached to having taken the first head, though as mounted troops were able to return their trophies more quickly than foot-soldiers, the claims often had to be revised at a later

Samurai with arquebus
The introduction, by the Portuguese, of firearms in 1542, was a major turning-point in the history of Japanese warfare. All daimyō used firearms, but few realised how effective they could be if employed in large quantities. This was demonstrated at the Battle of Nagashino in 1575, which is commemorated every year by the festival shown here, where reproduction arquebuses are fired from the site of the keep of Nagashino castle. The gunner is wearing full samurai armour.

The Hōjō take Fukane
The taking of Fukane castle by the Hōjō army was attended by appalling savagery. The heads were cut off all the defending garrison, and displayed. This illustration from the *Hōjō Godai-ki* reminds us of the often savage and bitter nature of samurai warfare.

stage. There is, therefore, no shortage of written source material relating to brave exploits and head-taking in particular. One *kanjō* (letter of commendation) from Uesugi Kenshin and dated 1561, is addressed to Nakajō Echizen-no-kami Fujikashi, who died in 1568, praising his behaviour at the fourth Battle of Kawanakajima.

We departed on the tenth day of the ninth month, and at the time when we gave battle to Takeda Harunobu at Kawanakajima in Shinano, he was a person unparalleled in the earnestness of his efforts. It is a fact that relatives, retainers and even reserve troops, a large number of whom were killed in battle, were inspired to loyal military service. Even thought the rebels sent a thousand horsemen into the attack we won a great victory, an event that will give us satisfaction for many years to come. Futhermore, there was also much glory gained. These loyal exploits will certainly never be forgotten by the descendants of Uesugi Kagetora. We admire

*his military exploits all the more set beside the great importance of his loyalty,
which is not surpassed by anyone.*

A general account of the army's exploits was also valuable, as in the following fragment from the *Kōyō Gunkan*:

*Concerning the exploits of the samurai retainers of Takeda Shingen, in the first
place the spearmen met, [earning] fame for their lances, and renown when the
same ones grappled with and pulled down horsemen. We also praise the second
rank of spearmen.*

Most of the ritual surrounding a victory celebration concerned the bizarre
practice of head inspection, which we will discuss later, but for a retainer,

or an ally, alive and victorious, there were other more welcome privileges, as we read in the chronicle *Yamamoto Toyohisa-shiki*, which refers to the Ōsaka Campaign:

That night twenty-three heads were taken. At dawn on the seventeenth day twenty-four men were summoned before Hideyori . . . and received rewards of gold. One man called Kimura Kizaemon who had suffered a wound was given surgery.

Most daimyō appreciated the effects of hot-spring bathing for treating wounds, and general recuperation after a battle. The actual location of these hot springs was kept secret, as a wounded daimyō would be at his most vulnerable to an assassin. Takeda Shingen had three secret springs, one of which, at Shimobe in the mountains of Yamanashi prefecture, celebrates Shingen's use of its healing waters in an annual festival. The care Shingen took of his wounded is confirmed by the records of the Erin-ji. Four months before one of his five battles at Kawanakajima, he requested the monks to be ready to provide rest and recuperation facilities for the wounded.

The battle having been fought and won, the trophies taken and examined, the part-time samurai of the territory could now return to their fields, until by the end of the sixteenth century even this would stop, and even these lowly samurai would be warriors and nothing else, having no function in life other than to serve their warlord with loyalty and devotion in peace and war.

The wounded general at the healing spring
The beneficial effects of hot springs have long been known to the Japanese, and every daimyō had his own 'secret springs' where he could recuperate safely from wounds. Takeda Shingen had a secret spring at Shimobe, and his use of the healing waters is commemorated annually by a festival, where local people dress up as Shingen and his 'Twenty-Four Generals'. The man in the foreground represents Shingen himself, and wears a mock bandage.

The Cultured Warlord

It is sometimes difficult, when scanning the pages of the war chronicles of the sixteenth century, to appreciate that the samurai, and a daimyō in particular, was regarded as the supreme aesthete and the arbiter of good taste. How could the hand that wielded the bloody sword so readily caress the delicate surface of a tea bowl? This apparent dichotomy between the utterly barbarous and the utterly beautiful is one of the most difficult concepts to understand in the life of the samurai.

It is tempting to discern a certain national trait, an innate ability that comes simply with being Japanese, to translate the most functional of objects into works of art, even to weaponry and instruments of death. That most deadly of weapons, the Japanese sword, is well recognised as having an outstanding beauty of its own. Somehow the samurai appreciated that perfection of form and perfection of function went hand in hand, and that perfection of form required a commensurate elegance of behaviour that complemented the elegance of the surroundings. There is no doubt that the families of daimyō, if not all samurai, were trained as extensively

A musical interlude
Seated on an improbably dramatic crag, the great general Toyotomi Hideyoshi listens to music while contemplating the siege of a castle. As well as a drum and flute, he is entertained by two men playing the *shō*, an ancient Japanese form of 'Pan's Pipes'.

in matters of literature and aesthetics as they were in the arts of war. More than one daimyō likened the literary and the martial arts as being the two wheels of a carriage.

Patronage of the arts was one aspect of the daimyō life that we were not able to identify in the turbulent world of the Hōjō family, but the 'super-daimyō' of the latter part of the sixteenth century, of whom Oda Nobunaga and Toyotomi Hideyoshi are the outstanding examples, were also considerable patrons of the arts. They employed artists to paint the screens that divided room from room in their palaces, and commissioned potters to produce vessels for the tea ceremony. Their tastes reflected their wealth, enabling them to share in peaceful luxury when not fighting. It is to Hideyoshi that we owe the elevation of the tea ceremony to an art form. The tea ceremony consists of an aesthetic exercise performed around the simple pleasure of sharing tea with friends. It is at once ritualistic and artistic. It involves the aesthetic appreciation of the tea bowl from which the tea is drunk, the flower arrangement and the vase which complement it, and the overall design of the tea house and the garden. A rare tea bowl could be more welcome to a daimyō than a fine sword, and was frequently much more difficult to acquire.

Nobunaga was also a patron of the *Nō* theatre, and is recorded as having chanted some choruses from the *Nō* play *Atsumori* before setting off to the Battle of Okehazama. *Nō*, like tea and the contemplation of a cleverly designed garden, brought serenity in much the same way as did the practices of the meditative Zen sect of Buddhism, to which many samurai were attracted because of its inner tranquility. But the appreciation of taste gave

Tea house of the Gyokusen-En, Kanazawa
The performance of the tea ceremony was one of the highest expressions of taste enjoyed by the cultivated warlord. This is a side view of the exquisite tea house of the Gyokusen-En, a garden in Kanazawa.

the cultivated warrior more than a serene and a composed mind, however useful that may have proved on the battlefield or in conference. It was also the means that sorted the accomplished man from the common, that proclaimed a subtle ostentation that may sometimes have teetered on the edge of vulgarity, but never quite managed to slip off. This cultivation, this refinement, was the mark of true aristocracy, and was part and parcel of being a daimyō, of being an élite among the élite.

The fortress of beauty

All the wealth of Japanese art and architecture that has survived to our day – and there is a great deal of it – points to the fierce warrior as patron of the arts, exercising the remarkable skill, noted above, of being able to transform the functional into the beautiful. Take, for example, the development of the Japanese castle. There is no more beautiful example of military structure in the entire world, and yet these graceful buildings, which soar above sweeping stone walls, evolved largely through savage military necessity. A castle of the early sixteenth century, such as would have been known to an early daimyō like Hōjō Sōun, was either a *yamashiro*, 'mountain castle' or a *hirajiro*, 'castle on the plain'. In each case, the style of architecture, if such a term is applicable, was entirely subservient to the need for defence, and the construction of the means of defence depended entirely upon the fortress's location, and would follow the lines of strength. A *hirajiro* would make use of a river or a swamp. A *yamashiro* would make use of rocky crags, concealing trees, and the slope of the ground. I have visited the recently excavated site of Odani, the *yamashiro* of the Asai family, burnt by Nobunaga in 1573. The buildings of Odani were spread across two hills joined in a saddle, and there is good visibility from every level. Only on the top is there an expanse of level ground, where Asai Nagamasa had his great hall.

One influence of Nobunaga's victory at Nagashino in 1575 was the beginning of what was almost a defensive mentality among the daimyō,

The site of Odani castle
This overgrown patch of land on the top of the wooded hill of Odani was the site of the main hall of the *yamashiro* of the Asai family. A few stones are all that is left of the fortifications, which were burned down by Oda Nobunaga in 1573. Odani has recently been excavated.

leading to the establishment of the huge fortresses we see today. For the first time stone was used in their construction, the labour being assessed by and supplied to the daimyō in much the same way as he obtained military service from among his subjects. But the spate of castle building, which Japan witnessed from 1580 to about 1615, was only partly connected to the introduction and effective use of firearms. As domains grew, the careful balance between agricultural and military needs could be solved by a strict division of labour between military men and farmers, and it was the achievement of very powerful daimyō, such as Oda Nobunaga, to produce a corps of professional soldiers. The new castles, many of which survive to this day, were built as the economic centre of the territory. They were also built very large, so that, if necessary, the entire standing army of the daimyō could be sheltered within the vast encircling walls.

Nobunaga's own castle of Azuchi was the first, and the greatest, of this new trend. It was built to control Kyōto, but it was not built there, but on a rocky plateau overlooking Lake Biwa. Where Nobunaga's creation differed, even from its contemporaries, was in the lavish decoration that was applied to it, so that this great step forward in castle design intimidated as much by its appearance inside and out, as by its strong walls and its armaments. Sadly, Azuchi castle is no longer with us. When Nobunaga was murdered in 1582, Azuchi proved no more impregnable to excited looters and arsonists than any other castle that had suddenly lost its leader, and it was burned to the ground.

Several other castles have survived and, if one disregards those that have been rebuilt in ferroconcrete in the last 20 years, there is a wealth of material for study. Inuyama, which floats on a wooded hill above the

Inuyama castle
Inuyama castle, which seems to float over the Kisogawa, enjoys one of the loveliest settings of all Japanese castles. It is also one of the best preserved, and is unique in being the sole remaining Japanese castle still under private ownership.

Kisogawa, is a very fine example. It is the only castle in Japan still in private hands, and its owners, the Naruse family, have cared for it since it was given to their ancestor, the daimyō Naruse Masanari, whose father Naruse Masakazu (1538–1620) had fought for Ieyasu. The site received its first defences in 1440 as a *yamashiro*, for which it was ideally suited, and the present tower-keep dates from 1600, replacing an earlier one which suffered when Inuyama was taken during Ieyasu's Komaki campaign in 1584.

Although from the outside the keep appears to have three storeys, in reality there are four. The uppermost storey commands an extensive view from the balcony that surrounds it, but the first storey holds the most interest. The daimyō's 'audience chamber' is built into the centre of the room. It is of modest dimensions, and fitted with sliding doors at the rear, through which samurai could come to the lord's aid at speed. The wooden floor which entirely surrounds it is 3 m (10 ft) wide and called the *musha-bashiri*, the 'warriors' run'. The other floors share the same austere design of plain, dark wood; the floors being connected one to another via alarmingly steep staircases.

Interior of Inuyama castle
The daimyō's private quarters at Inuyama are surrounded by a highly polished wooden corridor, called the *musha-bashiri*, or 'warrior's run'. To the rear of the room are sliding doors, behind which armed guards could be concealed.

The castle town – a world in miniature

As the sixteenth century gave way to the seventeenth, the castle, standing alone, surrounded by bare ground, itself gave way to the castle town, the *jōkamachi*. The castle towns symbolised in their design the feudal hierarchy which the daimyō had created for themselves and their retainers. They

were ordered places which, by their physical layout, made a statement about the classes within society, and the nature of the cultivated daimyō.

Edo castle, the seat of the Shōgun, was surrounded by the residences occupied by the daimyō on their annual visits, the *yashiki,* which we shall study in more detail later. The daimyō's own castle towns back in the provinces were simply miniature versions of Edo. Around their castles, where the family, and some senior retainers lived, were the homes of the other retainers, their distance from the castle walls being in roughly indirect proportion to their rank. The higher retainers, the *karō,* were placed just outside the keep, within the castle walls proper; the lower were outside the walls, protected perhaps by a moat, or an earthen wall. Completely walled cities on the European model were unknown. Between the two groups of samurai retainers lay the quarters of the favoured merchants

A home of a retainer in Nagamachi, Kanazawa
The narrow streets of the Nagamachi quarter of Kanazawa disclose the tiny courtyard of a former samurai's dwelling. Stepping stones lead to the door from the more formal granite paving.

Garden of the Toyokawa Inari Shrine

This charming garden, within the extensive grounds of the Inari Shrine at Toyokawa, shows many of the classic features of the Japanese garden, a miniature landscape with which every warlord would be familiar. *Koi* swim in the pond, which has its edge set off with tightly clipped box bushes. An ornamental pagoda balances the background.

and artisans, most, if not all, of whom would be engaged in trading and producing the goods that were in demand from the samurai class. Outside the ring of lower samurai lay a quarter of temples and shrines, whose buildings acted as an outer defence cordon, and from where the roads could be sealed off and guarded. From the edge of the castle town began the fields of the farmers, who grew the rice to support those within the jōkamachi's boundaries.

The city of Kanazawa is one of the best examples of such a layout. Owing to its position far from the Pacific coast, Kanazawa was spared the bombing of the last war which destroyed the layout of nearly every other city of comparable size, and it is possible to walk round Kanazawa today, as I did in 1986, and appreciate at first hand the effort of town planning that went into its original design. Kanazawa was the territory of the Maeda family, whose founder was Hideyoshi's general, Maeda Toshiie (1538–99).

Their castle town is built on a high plain between the Sai and the Asano Rivers. At its centre are the remains of the old castle, whose outer walls now house the university. Only the huge Ishikawa gate and tower remind one of its martial past, but even these remains are considerable. Across the road from the gate is the Kenrokuen, which is now a public park but which until 1871 was the private garden of the Maeda daimyō. The Kenrokuen is one of the best examples in Japan of the formal landscaped garden, but its most eloquent tribute to the civil engineering skills of the day lie in the way in which its lakes and waterfalls are fed with water. Water is in fact channelled from a distance of 10 km (6 miles) away, where the Saigawa is tapped, a system that was built in 1632 and is still functioning perfectly.

The best surviving examples of the retainers' residences are found in the quarter called Nagamachi. Here are quiet courtyards and tiny gardens surrounded by mud and plaster walls roofed with tiles. Of the merchants' quarters, little remains except the names, such as Ishibikichō, 'stone-cutters' quarter' and Daikumachi, 'carpenters' quarter'. To reach the temple areas, you have to cross one of the rivers – a forceful reminder of how the religious buildings were deliberately situated as the outer lines of defence.

It is possible, having seen Kanazawa, to imagine how Edo must have looked to the early European visitors before fire, earthquake and war took their toll of the Shōgun's capital, the bustling city that became Tōkyō. How fascinating it must have been to have looked with the eyes of someone such as Thomas McClatchie, who recorded his impressions of the soon-to-be-destroyed daimyō mansions of Edo for the members of the Asiatic Society of Japan in December 1878:

In passing through the streets of the city of Yedo, and most especially in what is commonly termed the 'official quarter' lying inside the Castle moats, the attention of the visitor is particularly attracted by long continuous buildings lining the roadway on either side. These present towards the street an almost unbroken frontage, save where a few large gateways, composed of heavy timbers strengthened with iron clamps, interpose to relieve the monotony of the general style of architecture. The buildings mostly stand upon low stone foundations, surrounded by small ditches; the windows are barred, and the general aspect gloomy in the extreme. They often differ widely as regards size, shape, mode of ornamentation etc.; but there is yet manifest a general likeness, there are still noticeable many common attributes which at once serve to stamp them, to the observant eye, as structures of one and the same type. These are the nagaya, or barracks, for retainers, which formed the outer defences of the yashiki or fortified mansions wherein dwelt the feudal nobles of Japan until the era of the recent Revolution in this country; and though now in many cases deserted, ruined and fallen into decay, time was when they played a conspicuous and honoured part in connection with the pomp and grandeur of the old feudal system which received its death blow only a half score years prior to the present date.

McClatchie's article goes on to list how the amount of land available for the *yashiki* depended upon the income of the daimyō, as did the size and design of the building he might raise upon it. The rules are precise:

Kokushū daimyō – gate either detached, or else built into the nagaya; two small side gates or posterns, one on either side, immediately adjoining it; two porters' lodges, situated just behind the posterns, built on stone foundations jutting out into the roadway for about three or four feet, and furnished with barred windows; roofs of lodges convex, formed of two slopes descending from a central roof ridge protruding at right angles from the wail of the nagaya.

The outer wall of the Sanada mansion
The Sanada mansion gives us a good idea of the appearance of the daimyō's *yashiki* in Edo, none of which have survived. The outer wall is surrounded by a gutter, and windows project from the sides of the gateway.

There is nothing left in Tōkyō now, or even in Kanazawa, that gives us any indication of the appearance of these *yashiki*, which because of their associations are among the most important buildings of Edo Japan, but McClatchie's descriptions, and extant sketches of the buildings, are uncannily similar to a group of buildings in Matsushiro, a town in the mountainous Yamanashi prefecture. Matsushiro was the site of Takeda Shingen's Kaizu castle, of which the stone base alone remains, and was the fief

granted to the son of the Sanada, Nobuyuki, who served the Tokugawa. The complex of buildings which contain the Sanada mansion, its clan school and a fine garden, have survived almost perfectly, owing to their remoteness. Matsushiro is a sleepy little place a few kilometres from the city of Nagano, but has recently seen an influx of tourists, drawn there by a very successful television series called *Sanada Taiheiki*, which told the story of the division of the Sanada family referred to in a later chapter. The outer wall of the complex must be as near to the appearance of a *nagaya* as one can find, and in fact bears remarkable similarities to the actual *nagaya* depicted in a photograph of the Satsuma daimyō's *yashiki* in Edo, which was burned in 1868.

Further delights await visitors inside the grounds, as there is revealed to their eyes the perfect example of a daimyō's mansion, complete with landscaped garden. The nearby Sanada museum, with its rich collection of the daimyō's personal possessions, completes a unique time capsule of the Edo daimyō.

The journey of pride

The *yashiki* was a very private place, unsuited to ostentation or the flaunting of wealth, but nowhere was the pride and the good taste of a daimyō more on public display than when he travelled along the great highways of Japan to visit the Shōgun. The *yashiki* of Edo may have belonged to the daimyō, but he was only able to live in it one year out of two, the alternate year being spent back in his castle town. This *sankin kōtai*, the 'Alternate Attendance' system, was the most unusual, and the most successful, of all the means the Tokugawa *bakufu* were to devise for reducing the risk of rebellion from the warlords. In essence, the *sankin kōtai* was no more than kidnapping on a colossal scale, because the rule was that the daimyō's wife and children lived in the *yashiki* of Edo, while the daimyō himself alternated his residence between his fief and the capital. That was one aspect of it. The other was that the muster lists, which in times of war had regulated a daimyō's feudal oligations in terms of the supply of men and equipment for war, were continued into peace-time by prescribing the size and equipment of the retinue which the daimyō would be expected to have accompany him on his alternating trips. As stipends were fixed, and there were no fresh lands to conquer, the cost of the *sankin kōtai* kept the daimyō in a state of genteel poverty, and probably constant worry.

Certain daimyō with particular defence responsibilities were allowed a reduced commitment. The Sō daimyō on the island of Tsushima, which lies between Japan and Korea, only had to reside in Edo for four months in every two years. A similar concession applied to the little-known but strategically vital daimyō of the Matsumae family on the northernmost island of Hokkaido. In the early nineteenth century there were fears of expansion by Russia on to Japan's northern territories, and there was a tentative Russian incursion on to Matsumae's territory in 1807.

For other daimyō, the likelihood of any conflict was a remote possibility, but they still had to march at the head of a huge army, gorgeously dressed and ready for battle, either from their *han* to Edo or back again, once every 12 months. When the procession of the Maeda daimyō, the richest in Japan after the Tokugawa (their income was a staggering 1,250,000 *koku*),

The mansion of the Sanada daimyō
The azaleas bloom in the garden of the mansion of the Sanada family at Matsushīro, an outstanding expression of the aesthetic side of the daimyō's life. We are looking from the garden to the main set of rooms which comprise the mansion.

left Kanazawa in the years of the mid-seventeenth century, it consisted of no less than 4,000 samurai, but within a century the sheer financial burden forced a reduction in numbers to 1,500. There is a pathetic note in the account books of the Inaba daimyō referring to additional expenses encountered in 1852 after being overtaken by darkness in the Hakone Mountains. The daimyō suddenly found himself compelled to purchase 8,863 candles and 350 pine torches, as well as hiring extra porters and lantern bearers.

But if the *sankin kōtai* was a burden to the daimyō, it proved otherwise to his retainers. There was the prospect of a long, but not unpleasant journey, much of which, for most daimyō, would be along well-trodden highways. The two main roads linking Edo with Kyōto were Tōkaidō, which followed the Pacific coast, and the Nakasendō, which wended its way through the mountainous interior. As early as 1604, three decades before the *sankin kōtai* was introduced, a system of post-stations was introduced along the Tōkaidō, and by 1633 and efficient post-horse and courier system was completed, and reduced the travelling time for the 480-km (300-mile) journey from Nihombashi in Edo to Sanjobashi in Kyōto to a mere ten days. By frequent changes of horses, couriers could make the journey in three days. Needless to say, a daimyō's procession was conducted at a much more leisurely pace, making good use of the *Tōkaido Gojusan tsugi*, the 'Fifty-three stations of the Tokaido' made familiar from the prints of Hiroshige. (The Nakasendō had 69 post-stations.)

Each of the 53 post-stations acquired its own personality. Each had some famous site or historical association, such as an exceptionally long bridge, a hot spring or a dangerous river. Some towns were famous for their local delicacies, others for their inns, their girls and their porters. The porters, the *kumosuke*, were available for hire to carry baggage or palanquins. Whatever the weather these 'tough guys' wore only a loincloth. They were notorious for their rude songs, their drinking and their gambling!

To a daimyō's retainer, the annual march was not a risky voyage into the unknown, but a familiar journey repeated year after year, and with details familiar even to those who had never set foot along its length. Numerous wood-block prints and popular literature painted a picture of the great road for any who cared to enjoy it at second hand. There is very little left of the original Tōkaidō today, as Hiroshige's road has disappeared under railway lines and motorways, but, here and there, there are small sections, now no more than footpaths, which the determined traveller can find. I walked along such a short stretch near Yumoto, on the way into the Hakone Mountains in Odawara, and within seconds modern Japan disappeared from sight and from hearing. The traveller on the mountainous Nakasendō is more fortunate, and can walk a full 8-km (5-mile) stretch of the old road which once echoed to the feet of samurai. The path lies between the villages of Tsumago and Magome, high in the wooded mountains above the Kisogawa. Both villages, now bypassed by a modern road, are exceptionally well preserved by consent of the inhabitants, and give you the most vivid glimpse of old Japan available anywhere in that country today.

Street in Edo
A corner of the film set at the Toei Uzumasa Film Studios in Kyōto, showing a typical street of the Edo Period.

Elegant pleasures

One of the main attractions of the bustling city of Edo will be discussed in a later chapter, when we look at the notorious pleasure quarter of Yoshiwara. But there were other more seemly pleasures of which the daimyō and his family might partake during their sojourn in the capital. Where their appreciation of the arts differed from that enjoyed by their ancestors of the sixteenth century, who had invited artists and performers into their castles,

Garden of the post-station at Tsumago
This view is taken from within the main room of the post-station at Tsumago, looking out on to a simple, yet totally effective, Japanese garden. The ground cover is of moss, and the view is attractively framed by a split bamboo fence.

Masks for the Nō theatre
The *Nō* was the classical theatre of Japan, and the form of theatrical art that members of the samurai class were expected to patronise, unlike the vulgar *kabuki*. *Nō* actors wore masks, and a selection are shown here in this backstage photograph, which the author was kindly allowed to record.

was that the daimyō of the Edo Period could not claim much credit for patronage. The most notable cultural flourishing of the age occurred during the era-name of Genroku, which lasted from 1688 to 1703, and its impetus came largely from the newly wealthy merchant classes. The samurai class, and the daimyō in particular, may have pretended that the *chōnin* (townsfolk) were vulgar, of disreputable origin and with poor tastes, but by 1700 they had a century of tradition behind them, the wealth to enjoy artistic pleasures, and the confidence to commission them. So the culture which the daimyō enjoyed was one into which he was drawn, and which derived from a prosperous bourgeoisie devoted to amusement. The expression they used for it, *ukiyo*, the 'floating world', was a very telling one.

Hand in hand with the growth of *ukiyo* expression, 'samurai culture' went into something of a decline. There was little advance in architecture, probably because, as we noted above, the Shōgun's *bakufu* made rules for the size and shape of just about everything. Classical poetry all but disappeared, unable to compete for interest beside the vitality of the *ukiyo*.

The kabuki *theatre*

The year is 1713, and the renowned *kabuki* actor Ichikawa Danjurō II makes his dramatic entrance along the *hanamichi* as the hero Sukeroku during one of the first performances of the play *Sukeroku Yukari no Edo Zakura*. He wears a black *kimono* bearing the Sukeroku *mon*, while his *obi* bears in addition the actor's (Danjurō's) own family *mon*, a precedent followed by every actor in the role to this day. Sukeroku is an *otokodate*, a 'chivalrous fellow'. He is brave, charming and resourceful — all qualities that the townspeople looked for in a hero. In his

characterisation of the flamboyant Sukeroku, Danjurō even went so far as to wear a head-band and socks dyed with a certain indigo dye which, because of the huge cost of obtaining it from China, only the Shōgun himself was accustomed to using.

On the stage the ladies of the town await their hero's arrival. The villain Ikyū is not so pleased to see him! Two members of the audience squabble while their companions watch the actor's every move.

The *kabuki* theatre provided the townspeople of Edo with the ideal vehicle for examining the morals

and behaviour of the samurai class. Several of the most popular plays were based on actual incidents in history, often ones that had occurred very recently. Family feuds, such as those within the Data and Maeda families, were included in the repertoire, although names and characters were always changed, and the plot elaborated almost beyond recognition. *Meiboku Sendai Hagi*, for example, which is based on the Date feud, includes a villain who can change himself into a giant rat! *Kabuki* was banned by the Shōgunate on several occasions, but its popularity ensured its survival.

The last bastion of true samurai aesthetics was the *Nō* theatre, which continued under daimyō patronage. The *chōnin* had their own theatrical art-form, the flamboyant *kabuki*, which attracted the samurai in droves. *Kabuki* was banned, totally ineffectively, on six occasions, and always bounced back owing to public demand and the willingness of the authorities to turn a blind eye. Its rewriting of recent history and current events, both elements of which were absent from the *Nō*, appealed to the samurai every bit as much as it did to the *chōnin*. Much use was made in the *kabuki* of general incidents which would have been familiar to the samurai, either from their actual experience, or from the traditions in which they were educated. For example, the play *Ōmi Genji Senjin Yakata*, first performed in 1769, contains a famous scene of a head inspection. *Mekura Nagaye Ume ga Kagatobi* re-enacts a real-life quarrel that occurred in Edo between fire-fighters employed by the Maeda daimyō and the official Edo fire brigade. The other great theatrical art of the age was the *bunraku* puppet theatre, where each large doll was manipulated by three men, producing the most amazingly lifelike effects. The *bunraku* was regarded as even safer than the *kabuki* for satire and the riskier sort of plot, and several *kabuki* plays began life as dramas written for the puppets.

The *Nō*, by contrast, took all its plots from ancient legend. The first Tokugawa Shōgun, Ieyasu, had been a great patron of the *Nō*. He had invited leading companies to Edo castle, and *Nō* performances were a regular part of important State functions. Some of his descendants took part in *Nō* themselves, which certainly kept them away from *kabuki*, and then in 1700 the arch-moralist of the day, Arai Hakuseki, in a severe attack of pomposity, pronounced even this most stately and restrained of theatrical forms to be deleterious to morality and a danger to the State. At a Shōgunal banquet in 1711, ancient music was substituted for the *Nō*, and from that time on the *Nō* lost much of its official prestige and the larger part of its samurai popularity. The tea ceremony went much the same way, degenerating into an empty ritual, far too complicated for the *chōnin*, and unable to compete with other delights awaiting the samurai.

Perhaps the fate of *Nō* holds the key to understanding the apparent paradox. During the Sengoku Period, there was a genuine need for the reassurance of nobility against the evidence of his own barbarism that the daimyō accumulated. Aesthetics gave reassurance. It soaked up the reality of their deeds in the same way as the spiked board and the cosmetics transformed a ghastly severed head into an object for neutral contemplation. Without the cultivation of art, and gardens, and theatre, the samurai would have gone mad. Then, when wars had ceased, the samurai class had nothing to prove to anyone. Their social position was firmly established and, apart from a few rare exceptions, they did not kill. Instead, they were stultified within a stagnant culture, from which the new merchant classes, with none of their inhibitions, were to liberate them.

However, as we noted earlier, to the first daimyō there was no paradox. The two aspects of the samurai life not only could coexist, they had to coexist. One could not be a successful daimyō without both, as Hōjō Sōun wrote in the last words of his 'Twenty-One Articles':

It is not necessary here to write about the arts of peace and war . . . for to pursue these is a matter of course. From of old, the rule has been, 'Practise the arts of peace on the left hand, and the arts of the war on the right'. Mastery of both is required.

An actor performing kagura
Kagura is a form of dance-drama which was the forerunner of the *Nō*. Performances are quite rare nowadays, but a particularly fine rendering is given annually by the villagers of Shimobe in Yamanashi prefecture, as part of their annual festival. The *kagura* is performed on a stage at the Kumano Shrine in the village. This photograph was taken at the 1986 performance.

Notwithstanding the fact that the Hōjō had little time for practising purely aesthetic pleasures for their own sake, and that their emphasis on the arts of peace concentrated almost totally on good government, there is no better summary of the duties in peace and war of the cultivated warlord of Japan.

The Keeper of the Peace

During the Edo Period, one of the most important duties delegated to a daimyō, as part of the *baku-han* system, was the keeping of the peace and the administration of justice within the *han*. In this, the daimyō would find the reality of the streets of his castle town to be very different from the theoretical world of ordered and cultivated society which was the ideal. He would often find himself faced with a fire-trap of a city, where subservience to samurai was a myth, and where his own men would find

The daimyō presides
This page from the *Hōjō Godai-ki* neatly illustrates the daimyō's social position, as he receives gifts from his retainers. The daimyō sits on an elevated dais, while those lower squat on the *tatami*.

themselves in opposition to well-organised gangs of swordsmen every bit as well trained as well armed, and who owed equally firm allegiance to their own variety of Japanese warlord.

In theory, at any rate, this was a situation that could not possibly exist, because according to law, to established precedent and to a century of tradition, members of the samurai class were the only people allowed to carry swords. It was the wearing of swords that defined a samurai, as his privilege and his right. A series of edicts, beginning with Hideyoshi's famous 'Sword Hunt' of 1587, had set this trend in motion, and had theoretically disarmed all but the samurai class. In practice, swords, and other weapons, were readily obtainable and well used, sometimes by criminals, otherwise by desperate gangs of lower-class citizens upholding their rights and their lives against the abuse of power by samurai.

The samurai police

It was a very unusual daimyō, however, who failed to recognise the reality of life in Tokugawa Japan, and every daimyō was helped in his peace-keeping role by a well-developed police force. In common with many other institutions of Tokugawa Japan, the nature of the *baku-han* system allowed a successful system for the Shōgun's direct retainers in Edo to become the norm for the whole of Japan, and by 1631 the organisation of policing in Edo was replicated on a smaller scale in every *han* in the country.

As a daimyō spent much of his time travelling to and from Edo, he would delegate a major degree of responsibility within his own castle towns to magistrates, known as the *machi-bugyō*, who combined within their role

The seat of the Shōgun
In the Shōgō-In in Kyōto, this ornate audience chamber is preserved, with its characteristic raised dais.

the functions of chief of police, city mayor and presiding judge. In Edo there were two *machi-bugyō*, the need for two being similar to that which produced the system of two consuls in ancient Rome – each one kept an eye on the other! These two *machi-bugyō* worked a 'shift' system of one month on-duty, one month off-duty, though as the duties became more onerous in the expanding cities, particularly Edo, the 'off-duty month' became no more than a welcome quiet time for writing reports and seeing to other essential paperwork.

The Edo *machi-bugyō* had daily liaison with the Shōgun's senior councillors in Edo castle, which alone indicates the high status of the position. Even though the post of *machi-bugyō* was earmarked for comparatively lowly retainers of 500 *koku*, it carried an additional allowance of an extra 3,000 *koku*, and a court rank equivalent to that of some daimyō.

Under each of the two *machi-bugyō* were the *yoriki*, or assistant magistrates. There were 50 *yoriki* in all in Edo, 25 under each *machi-bugyo*. They were chosen from the Shōgun's direct retainers who had an income of 200 *koku*, and, in the case of the Edo *yoriki*, the appointment became hereditary within certain families, the position of *yoriki* passing from father to son. This resulted in a 'police force' that was very familiar with its territory, but also one that became very much a caste unto itself, living in a social limbo between the townspeople whose lives they controlled, and the samurai of the castle. The latter would have nothing to do with them because of the ancient Shintō fear of pollution from people who had a connection with death, as the *yoriki* had with the execution of criminals. In fact, the *yoriki* did not actually carry out executions; that was left to the outcast *hinin*, the 'non-humans', but the mere association with such practices, and their own fierce pride, kept the *yoriki* apart. The proud *yoriki* would wear a full samurai costume of the wide *hakama* trousers and the *haori* jacket, and wore the two swords of the samurai. They had a reputation for smartness in appearance, particularly in their hair-styles.

Serving under the *yoriki* were the *dōshin*, who played the role of the policeman 'on the beat'. They wore tight-fitting trousers rather than *hakama* and only carried one sword, though they were regarded as being of samurai status. In Edo, there were 120 *dōshin* under each *machi-bugyō*, and they were instantly recognisable by a distinctive side-arm that was a badge of office and a vital defensive weapon. This was the *jitte*, a steel rod fitted with a handle, and with one or two hooks along the edge of the 'blade'. Its purpose was to catch a sword stroke so that a felon could be taken alive.

The *dōshin*, accompanied by several assistants from among the townsfolk, who ranged from public-spirited citizens to paid informers, thus maintained the visible 'police-presence' on the streets of the castle towns, the *yoriki* being called to the scene of an arrest only if the situation warranted it. In this case, the *yoriki*, dressed in light body armour, would supervise affairs from horseback, with a spear kept as a last resort. The emphasis was always on taking the prisoner alive, which was no mean feat should the felon be an accomplished swordsman, as we shall see later in this chapter. Japanese ingenuity, however, allowed for the obvious danger and, in addition to the *jitte*, the *dōshin* were armed with a range of fierce-looking hooked and barbed spears, which kept the swordsman at bay, pinned him into a corner, or could usefully entangle items of clothing as he tried to escape. The determination of a cornered criminal was legendary, and many would sell their freedom as dearly as a samurai would sell his life.

86

The main street of Tsumago
The miraculously preserved main
street of the village of Tsumago gives
the best illustration of a village street
from the Edo Period. It lies on the
old Nakasendō road, which linked
Kyōto and Edo (now Tōkyō) along
the alternative mountain route.

Once the man was cornered and disarmed, he was rapidly tied up, and
there existed a whole specialist area of 'martial arts' techniques for quickly
and securely roping suspects. There is a famous wood-block print by Kuniyoshi depicting the arrest of a criminal by *dōshin*, which James Field has
used for his picture on page 88, that brings the whole process of justice
vividly to life. It is an illustration to a scene from a popular novel, first
published in 1814. The hero, Inuzuka Shino Moritaka, takes to the roof of
the Hōryūkaku temple to avoid arrest by the *dōshin*. There are several
versions of the scene, where Moritaka seizes one unfortunate *dōshin* by
putting his arm round his neck, as his companions thrust their *jitte* at him,
and blow whistles, while their more nervous companions wait below with
bamboo ladders, ropes and sleeve entanglers.

Making an arrest

This plate is based on a vivid
woodblock print by Kuniyoshi
depicting the arrest of a criminal by
dōshin. It is an illustration to a
popular novel entitled *Nansō Satomi
Hakkenden* by Takizawa Bakin
(1767–1848). The plot of the novel
concerns with the exploits of eight
brothers, one of whom, Inuzuka
Shino Moritaka, ends up on the roof
of the Hōryūkaku temple. He is
pursued by *dōshin* armed with *jitte*,
the peculiar 'sword-catchers', and
other devices designed to facilitate
arrest. They are dressed in typical
fashion, with fitted trousers rather
than *hakama*, thus freeing their legs
for such exploits as climbing roofs.

The popular image of the
wandering lone samurai owes much
to the activities of the criminal
element in Edo society. The same is
also true of the martial arts, which
are often regarded as the preserve of
the ruling samurai class. In fact
many martial arts techniques owe
their development to farmers and
townsmen, deprived of the right to
carry weapons, who turned to the
use of simple weapons and bare
hands to defend themselves against
any abuse of power by their betters.
(See *The Lone Samurai* by the present
author for a detailed consideration of
these points.)

The resulting punishments which the *machi-bugyō* had in their power to dispense ranged in severity up to death – including crucifixion, for such crimes as murder. For a samurai, the death penalty could, on occasions, be carried out by the convicted man himself in the honourable act of suicide, called *seppuku*. In certain cases, the execution of a condemned criminal could be a means of testing the quality of a sword blade – making a more realistic alternative to the more usual *tameshigiri* performed on a corpse. There is the story told of one such condemned man who went to his end with remarkable coolness, telling the sword tester that if he had been fore-warned that this was how he was to die he would have swallowed some large stones to damage the samurai's precious blade. A much lighter punishment was exile, which had been used for centuries in Japan as a way of dealing with offences of a political nature.

The great benefit of the *dōshin* system lay in its capacity for crime prevention. To the *dōshin's* local knowledge was added a topographical system that divided Edo into tightly controllable *machi*, or wards. This arose from the original design of the city, which was deliberately intended to make an approach to Edo castle difficult for an attacker. Like other big cities, the castle was surrounded by mazes of streets where the *chōnin* (townspeople) lived, and each *machi* was physically separated from others either by canals, walls or fences. It was thus a simple matter to control movement from one *machi* to another by means of gates which were fastened at night, and anyone passing through had to have appropriate authorisation.

Corporal punishment
A swift punishment for offenders from the lower social orders was a sound thrashing. Here, in an illustration to *Miyabu gaikotsu tobaka-shi*, the felon is held down securely while he receives his punishment under the watchful eye of the *yoriki*.

The brave otokodate

If areas of a city, such as Edo, could be sealed off from outside, they could also be well defended from within, and it is not surprising to hear of the development of organisations of townspeople to provide protection against

House in Tsumago
One of the many houses of Tsumago which convey the feeling of a past age. The wooden slats filter the bright sunlight from the dusty street.

rivals, or against samurai who neglected their code of conduct. Against the *hatamoto-yakko*, or samurai gangs, there developed the *machi-yakko*. They became very well organised in the Edo Period, and their leaders, styled *otokodate*, became famous. The word *otokodate*, 'chivalrous fellows', implies the resistance to authority by those of lower class. In fact, some of the great *otokodate* were originally of the samurai class and had become *rōnin* for various reasons, and moved to find employment in distant towns. One such was Banzuin Chōbe'e, 'Father' of the *otokodate* of Edo.

Banzuin Chōbe'e was originally from Higo province in Kyūshū, and was a retainer of the Terazawa clan of Shimabara, the scene of the great Christian upheaval of 1638, known as the Shimabara Rebellion. Following the suppression of the revolt, he felt Kyūshū as a *rōnin* and went to Edo, where his talents were soon put to use. He became a *warimoto*, an agent who acted as a go-between for acquiring labourers. Once established in Edo, Chōbe'e took the name of Banzuin, which was the area where he lived, and set himself up as a 'Godfather' of *warimoto* who acted particularly as agents for supplying carriers and other labourers to daimyō undertaking their annual pilgrimage to Edo to pay respects to the Shōgun. Chōbe'e received 10 per cent of the labourers' earnings as commission, and in return provided for them in times of sickness. Banzuin Chōbe'e, therefore, came to exert the same authority over his followers as a daimyō did over his samurai, which came in very useful when the townspeople were oppressed by the samurai *hatamoto-yakko*.

In the enforced idleness of the Edo Period, boredom and poverty turned many samurai into criminals. Groups with names such as the *Shiratsuka-*

Retainer's house in Nagamachi, Kanazawa
In contrast to the simple houses of Tsumago, this town house in Kanazawa reflects the type of architecture that would have been enjoyed by the retainers of the Maeda daimyō of Kanazawa. This house, in the Nagamachi quarter, is one of the best known in the city.

gumi and *Jingi-gumi* formed and caused violence. The city people 'hated them like scorpions', according to one Japanese historian, and their unreasonableness against the townspeople became proverbial. Because such violence and perverseness among the samurai could not be crushed by the townspeople alone, former *rōnin*, such as Chōbe'e, became the natural nucleus for opposition. As their confidence grew, the *otokodate* of the *machi-yakko* began to walk openly in the streets in defiance of rules forbidding them swords. At the same time, they developed the art of combat with other weapons, such as the the long, 2-m (6-ft) staff, or *bō*, and the shorter 1.5-m (4-ft) long *jō*. They also became accomplished in the art of the *tantō* (dagger), which could be concealed under clothes, and the defensive use of implements such as the *tessen*, the iron war-fan.

Greatness has its penalties. Chōbe'e's fame was considerable, which brought him into direct opposition to the boss of the powerful *hatamoto-yakko* called the *Jingi-gumi*, one Mizuno Jūrōzaemon. Jūrōzaemon was of senior samurai rank, worth 2,500 *koku*, and had the reputation for being something of a dandy (the Japanese term is *datemono*) dressing in the finest clothes.

One day, according to a popular tale, it was rumoured that Chōbe'e was in the vicinity of Yoshiwara, where Jūrōzaemon's party was meeting. Jūrōzaemon desired some iced *soba* noodles and, as Chōbe'e was in a *soba* shop, he proposed, after some ritualistic bragging, that Chōbe'e should buy him some *soba*, knowing already that the shop had sold out of *soba* and did not have a steamer. It was a neat way of humiliating Chōbe'e, but, nothing daunted, Chōbe'e went downstairs and gave one of his followers a considerable sum of money, and ordered him to buy up all the cold *soba* that was available, which the *machi-yakko* members proceeded to dump unceremoniously in front of Jūrōzaemon. As the huge pile grew, Jūrōzaemon realised that he could not get the better of Chōbe'e and retired with considerable loss of face.

Not long afterwards, one of Chōbe'e's followers, called Iida no Nibe'e, caught three of Jūrōzaemon's men making unreasonable demands of a drunken townsman. He set on them and threw them into a ditch. This increased Jūrōzaemon's bad feelings for Chōbe'e, and resolved him to invite Chōbe'e into a trap. The treacherous means whereby Mizuno Jūrōzaemon planned to dispose of Banzuin Chōbe'e, and the latter's willingness to walk into the trap for the sake of his honour, forms the basis of the greatest of all legends of the brave *otokodate*. It is quoted as an example of how the honour of a townsman could be every bit as noble as that of a samurai. In fact, Chōbe'e's determination to carry out the inevitable drama reminds one of the decision of Kusunoki Masashige to fight the Battle of Minatogawa because it was the wish of the Emperor, even though he knew the situation to be hopeless.

The evil Jūrōzaemon invited Chōbe'e to come to his house for a drinking party as a way of saying 'thank-you' for the gift of *soba*. Chōbe'e guessed that it was a trap, but went along nonetheless. He was attacked by two of Jūrōzaemon's men as he entered, whom he defeated, but before they began to drink together Jūrōzaemon invited Chōbe'e to take a bath, a common enough courtesy to a visitor. Once Chōbe'e was in the bath-house, Jūrōzaemon's men began to stoke the boiler to raise the temperature of the hot tub and scald him to death. As the hot steam rose, Chōbe'e tried to break out, but Jūrōzaemon had locked the door. With his

The murder of Banzuin Chōbe'e
Banzuin Chōbe'e is the great hero of the *otokodate* of Edo, both from his championing the cause of the townspeople against unruly samurai, and his violent death in a bath-house, where he was treacherously murdered by Mizuno Jurozaemon, his great rival from the samurai.

rival cornered within, Jūrōzaemon's men thrust spears at him through the partition. One spear pierced his leg and broke off at the shaft. Chōbe'e had no weapons on him and was surrounded by about ten spears. One then struck him a mortal blow under the ribs and the pitiful Chōbe'e, a spear through his chest, ended his days in a bath-house, in a manner every bit as noble as the samurai he had once been.

The unofficial daimyō

Crime was by no means confined to Edo, nor was the capital the only place where non-samurai ruled as petty daimyō over their criminal or lower-class kingdoms. The eight provinces of the Kantō plain, the large area of flat land that nowadays accommodates metropolitan Tōkyō, Yokohama and the Chiba peninsula, and extends northwards towards Nikkō and the Pacific coast, acted as a cradle for the criminal element towards the end of the eighteenth century, when crime was on the decline in Edo itself. Hoodlums were rampant in the Kantō provinces, because police power was dispersed in the complexity of Crown land, daimyō land and *hatamoto* land. The *yakuza* (gangsters) gathered there for making money. Kōzuke in particular was a centre of *yakuza* activity.

The nature of the locality of Kōzuke had made it a centre of textile manufacturing, and it was also well known throughout the whole country

A gambling den
The provision of gambling places was one of the main reasons for the growth of criminal gangs in the Edo Period. Here, in an illustration from *Tsūjin san kyoku-shi*, a group of men settle themselves for a session, refreshed by tea and tobacco.

94

for its hot springs. In earlier days, the recuperative qualities of hot springs were privileges known only to the upper reaches of the samurai class, as we noted earlier in connection with the treatment of wounded, but as the Edo Period wore on, the wealthier among the merchants, who already knew the value of hot baths, gained access to these pleasures. The taking of baths in 'spa-towns', where the mineral waters had healing properties, thus became a popular way of relaxing, as it is today for all Japanese, and hot spring resorts vied with each other in the quality of their mineral waters and the range of comforts and entertainments they could provide. The spas of Kōzuke were convenient places where the textile wholesalers and healing-spring guests could resort for relaxation and amusement, and one pastime appealed above all others – gambling.

The provision of gambling dens promised immense profit for those willing to take a risk and, as they were operating in a very shadowy area of legality, it is not surprising that controlling gambling became an activity for

A fight in a gambling den
This lively sketch from *Miyabu gaikotsu tobaka-shi* depicts the violent end to a gambling session. Coins fly everywhere, and a dagger is drawn in anger.

organised crime. The gangs acquired territories in which their law held sway, much the same as the Sengoku warbands had developed into daimyō territories. The leaders of these gangs acquired the airs of daimyō themselves. Some of these gang leaders, especially those of samurai origin, acquired such a reputation for swordsmanship and command that they were employed by the civil authorities to teach swordsmanship to samurai.

At that time, the great swordsmen of the day, who were not hereditary samurai retainers of daimyō could be divided into two types: those who worked for the existing authority, hiring to them their swords and their skills, and those who by choice or by pressure of circumstances lived outside the law as outlaws. The outstanding example of the former was a man called Ōmaeda Eigorō. He comes over as something of a 'Godfather' figure, like Edo's Banzuin Chōbe'e, attracting to his side many of the young men who were to make their names in the criminal world of the Kantō provinces. Like the samurai, these bosses worked on a well-established hierarchical model of a 'father-figure' at the top, to whom followers held allegiance.

Ōmaeda Eigorō was a native of Kōzuke province, and killed his first man at the age of 16, a person called Kugo no Shōhachi. He went on to become a dependable and charismatic leader who influenced a generation of swordsmen, yet he was always careful to operate within the law. He was certainly not a murderer, unlike some of his disciples, and did not needlessly start quarrels. The *han* authorities found him very useful, and were ready to co-operate with him to gain some share of the enormous influence he exerted. His service to the civil authorities was as reliable as any samurai of the Sengoku Period, and he deserved his leader's stipend. His duties included teaching swordfighting, as he was a fencing master of the Nenryū *dōjō*.

A later example of another successful 'unofficial daimyō' is Shimizu no Jirochō, who acquired the title of the 'First Boss of the Tōkai'. Like Ōmaeda Eigorō, he built his territory on gambling, and developed his remarkable leadership skills through evading the numerous traps set for him by *yoriki* and rivals alike, until he achieved a quasi-official position within his own province. He died in 1893, his life having encompassed the final days of the Japanese warlords, most of whom he outlived.

The Battle of the Tonegawa Dry-River-bed
Iioka no Sukegorō and Sasagawa no Shigezō were two rival gang-bosses in Shimōsa. Their feud exploded into violence in 1844, in an encounter on the dry river-bed of the Tonegawa. Blades flashed in the moonlight in a battle as fierce as many of the skirmishes of the Sengoku Period. (From a wood-block print in the author's collection.)

The outlaws

On the opposite side of the coin from Ōmaeda Eigorō and Shimizu Jirochō, both of whom either co-operated with the authorities, or learned how to handle them, stood characters such as Kunisada Chūji (1809−50). Chūji never sold out to the samurai, and his exploits in resisting authority, retold in numerous plays and novels, made him something of a 'Robin Hood' of Japan. He was certainly a popular subject for fiction, and the romantic gloss of works such as *'Yagi bushi'* disguising the unattractive reality of a long catalogue of extortion and murder for which he was finally arrested and crucified in 1850 at the age of 41.

Kunisada Chūji's criminal acts may have caused great problems to the civil authorities of the day, but at least his expressions of rivalry were on an individual level. Two other 'pupils' of Ōmaeda Eigorō collided on a much larger scale, one of which produced a virtual battle that brought back echoes of the samurai wars of the Sengoku Period. It happened in another of the Kanto provinces where crime flourished – Shimōsa. Shimōsa bordered the Pacific Ocean, and the fishing industry predominated, exerting a similar economic influence as the textiles of Kōzuke. The fishing industry of Shimōsa was centred around the port town of Chōshi, at the mouth of the Tonegawa with its huge flat river-bed. Around Chōshi, two leaders had their spheres of influence. Their names were Iioka no Sukegorō and Sasagawa no Shigezō. Neither was a samurai, and their surnames merely refer to their localities, as the possessive adjective 'no' indicates. Sukegorō was based in the present-day town of Iioka, and Shingezō held authority in Tōshō by the Sasagawa.

Iioka was a prosperous fishing port on the coast. Tōshō was also a bustling river port, 19 km (12 miles) away on the Tonegawa. Sukegorō is referred to in a Japanese account of his life as a 'sumo delinquent' (!), and a vagrant, at one time employed by Iioka no Amimoto as a fisherman. In course of time, he pledged loyalty to a gang leader, called Chōshi no Gorozō, from whom he received an enormous stipend, and whose territory he inherited.

In contrast to Sukegorō, Shigezō was born and raised in a large farming family of the area. His sphere of influence was handed over from a leader called Shibajuku no Bunkichi of Hitachi. Sukegorō was, in general, the senior of the two rivals, and Shingezō also looked up to Sukegorō but gradually, as their spheres of influence grew, respect gave way to wariness. Their territories grew rapidly during the early 1840s, and eventually the two spheres of influence reached their limits. Both men were of equal standing. Sasagawa no Shingezō acted first, and like his contemporary Kunisada Chūji, hatched a plot to murder Iioka no Sukegorō. However, Sukegorō got to hear of the plot and acted first, attempting to destroy his

rival on a grand and dramatic scale by carrying out a night raid on the Sasagawa headquarters on the south bank of the Tonegawa in the ninth month of 1844. The sight of this frenzied mass swordfight by moonlight has inspired some fine wood-block prints, and one particular work of literature, *Tempō Suikoden*.

By all accounts the raid was a ferocious affair, with all the hallmarks of a medieval battle. It even had its fallen hero, in this case a certain Hirate Miki who was the *yojimbō*, or bodyguard, to the Sasagawa family. Hirate Miki is the popular person in the narrative of *Tempō Suikoden* who 'makes the blood flow at the Tonegawa dry riverbed'. Hirate Miki made a dramatic fight to the death as the samurai blades flashed in the moonlight. The overall purpose of the raid failed when they did not succeed in capturing Shigezō. This action is known to the world as the 'quarrel in the dry riverbed of the great Tonegawa'. Perhaps by virtue of it being so inconclusive, the battle set both sides at odds, until matters were resolved three years later when assassins from the Iioka side murdered Shigezō. This was a murder so underhand that even their own side did not admire the action, but it brought peace to the area.

Fire-fighting in Edo
The prevention and control of fires was one of the daimyō's most solemn obligations. For a daimyō to allow a fire to start in his own *yashiki* was an act of gross negligence. Here a daimyō's retainer, dressed in a fire-cloak and helmet, supervises operations.

The 'Battle of the Firemen'

The other demanding area of a daimyō's civil authority was the prevention and control of fires. Nowhere was this need more pressing than in Edo itself, and there was a considerable responsibility placed upon the daimyō owners of *yashiki*. If a daimyō allowed a fire to start within his *yashiki*, he was punished by a number of days confinement to his *yashiki*, but if the fire had not spread to other mansions, the punishment might not be carried out. Certain *yashiki* belonging to daimyō above 10,000 *koku* were allowed to have a look-out tower, the *hinomi*. The *hinomi* had mounted on it a bell and a striking-beam. Between 1704 and 1711, when orders were issued for the formation of fire brigades in Edo, the newly appointed commanders of the brigades, of *hatamoto* rank, were given leave to build *hinomi* 9 m (30 ft) high. There is the record of a certain Matsudaira samurai who 'having been charged, in the year 1810, with certain duties as to fires, he for the first time hung up a bell and a striking-beam, and during his term of office made use of the same'. Fire was of course an ever-present hazard in a city built largely of wood, and would spread so rapidly through it that if a fire started near Edo gaol, the prisoners were released on parole, with heavy fines if they did not return once the fire had been brought under control.

During the 250 years of the Edo Period, there were twenty large fires and three large earthquakes in the capital. In the fire of 1657, half the city was destroyed and over 100,000 people lost their lives. In 1772, half the city was again lost, and in 1806 nearly all the retainers' *yashiki* were swept

An earthquake
Earthquakes have always been a fact of life for the Japanese. Three major earthquakes hit Edo during the two and a half centuries of the Tokugawa. This rather poor-quality illustration from the *Gempei Seisu-ki* shows the effects of a tremor, which brings buildings crashing to the ground. The startled citizens run for cover.

away. The fire brigades were organised in a similar way to the *yoriki* and the *dōshin* who kept order in the city. They wore protective clothing made of leather and heavy cotton, and helmets similar to 'battledress' helmets, but with a cloak attached at the rear which buttoned under the chin. Cutting fire-breaks was the most effective means of controlling a blaze, and there are a number of exuberant wood-block prints which depict the firemen in action, using hooks to pull burning shingles off roofs (thatch was forbidden, for obvious reasons), and carrying buckets. Standing his ground, in the most visible position he dare occupy, is to be found the squad's standard-bearer. During the 1760s, water pumps were introduced and, with increased training, many potentially dangerous fires were averted.

There was, however, intense rivalry between the *hikeshi,* the fire brigades, which on one occasion erupted into serious violence. The greatest jealousy occurred between the members of the Edo *machi-hikeshi,* the 'city fire brigade', and the *daimyō hikeshi,* the brigades maintained by the individual daimyō in the city. The rivalry, which has great echoes of the violence between the *hatamoto-yakko* and the *machi-yakko,* probably had similar social origins, and the leader of the Edo *machi-hikeshi,* Shimmon no Tatsugorō, had the popularity and the airs of Banzuin Chōbe'e. He lived from 1800 until 1876, a time when memories of previous conflagrations made the citizens very frightened of the danger of fire, and ready to greet a successful fire-chief as the nineteenth-century equivalent of a conquering daimyō.

Tatsugorō's collision with the *daimyō hikeshi* took place with the fire brigade of the Arima daimyō of Chikugo. One night, Tatsugoro's *machi-*

The 'Battle of the Firemen'
One of the most extraordinary conflicts to have taken place in the streets of Edo was the battle between firemen of the Edo citizenry, the *machi-hikeshi,* and firemen of the Arima daimyō. At the end of the brief but violent argument, 18 men lay dead.

A water garden
A harassed daimyō, beset by the many duties which required his attention, would refresh his spirit by the contemplation of a garden, such as this beautiful example at a Zen temple in Okazaki.

hikeshi arrived at the scene of a fire to find the Arima brigade's standard flying over the scene. Tempers exploded, and the scene of the fire became one of carnage as the two groups of firemen attacked one another with their short swords and their fire-axes. By the time order had been restored, 18 men lay dead, a death toll higher than many of the celebrated vengeance feuds that scarred contemporary Japan. Tatsugorō took full responsibility for the lack of control among his men, and surrendered himself to the *machi-bugyō*. His resulting banishment was only temporary, and he was to end his life as personal retainer to the last of the Tokugawa Shōguns, Yoshinobu, during the civil war of the Meiji Restoration. He accompanied the doomed Shōgun during his flight from the imperial forces, and eventually died peacefully at the age of 75, as honoured as any warlord.

This was the world outside the samurai class which the daimyō was required to control, a world occupied by corrupt samurai, hereditary policemen, proud firemen, gambling bosses and bitter gangland feuds. The Edo Period may not have been scarred by the wars of the Sengoku era, but it can hardly be called an age of peace.

Sex and the Samurai

The great houses of daimyō of the Edo Period came into being by various means. Some were won, like the Hōjō, and then, unlike the Hōjō, were retained. Others were increased in the great shake-up after Sekigahara, or were created daimyō by the Tokugawa Shōgun. Yet, whichever way the houses were created, all shared the same desire – to found a dynasty that would carry the family name forward into the future, a noble name forged in the heat of battle, and made even nobler in the wisdom and virtue of successive generations of good government in peace-time. That was the ideal to which they all aspired, but the reality was to be that the maintenance of an honourable name was every bit as difficult in the age of peace as it had been in war. In wartime, daimyō houses could be wiped out in dramatic battles, but peace placed its own demands on behaviour, and sometimes these were more difficult to cope with. As well as the external pressures from administration and the suppression of crime, so much depended upon internal personal factors, upon the daimyō himself, upon his wife and concubines, and upon the quality of those who came after him.

A doll for the Boys' Festival
This display, set out in the living quarters of a temple in Kawachi-Nagano, for 'Boys' Festival Day' illustrates the value still placed on Japan's samurai past, and also reminds us that Japanese aesthetics are not always governed by restraint.

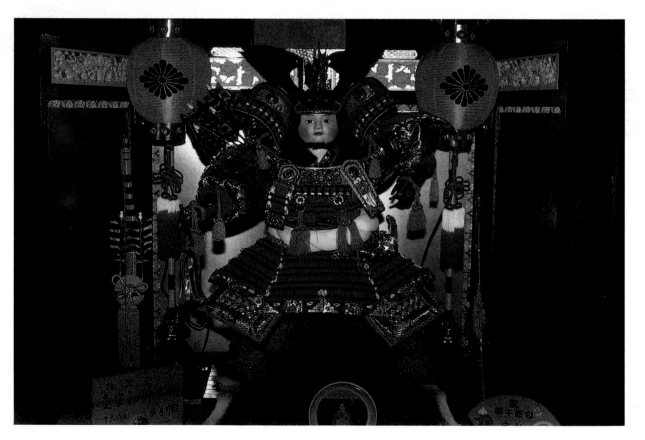

Ladies of the samurai class
Two actresses from the Toei-
Uzumasa Film Studios in Kyōto pose
for the camera. They are wearing
kimono, and their wigs are
characteristic of the hair-styles of the
eighteenth century.

Women and the daimyō

*The relation of parent and child is limited to this life on earth; that between
husband and wife continues into the after-life; that between lord and retainer
continues into the life after that again.*

This pious statement was quoted earlier as an illustration of the firm bond
of loyalty between daimyō and vassal. We may now turn it on its head and
examine its implications for the role of women in samurai society.

Women occupy a shadowy position in accounts of the Sengoku Period.
When a woman comes into prominence, she is frequently cast either as an
out-and-out villain or as a mere token, a pawn in a daimyō's game of
power. There is no equivalent in the Sengoku Period for the only 'female
warrior' in the whole of samurai history – Tomoe Gozen, wife of the Minamoto general Kiso Yoshinaka, who fought beside her husband in the campaigns of the Gempei War and met her death with him in 1184. Nor is
there any woman remotely approaching the status of Masako, widow of
the first Shōgun Minamoto Yoritomo, whom history presents as a bitter
schemer, determined to destroy the Minamoto succession in favour of her
own clan, the Hōjō.

In contrast, the daimyō of the Sengoku Period tended to use women as
chattels, as objects who were useful for acquiring power through the de-

vice of *seiryaku kekkon*, the political marriage. So useful was marriage as a weapon that the making of political marriages was specifically banned on the rise to power of the Shōgun Tokugawa Ieyasu. In my *Samurai Warriors*, there is a description of the incredibly complex web of marriage alliances that linked the families of Takeda, Hōjō and Imagawa in the mid-sixteenth century; but it is to the more powerful daimyō that we must look to see how cynically marriage, or rather divorce, could be manipulated for political ends.

When Oda Nobunaga made his alliance with Tokugawa Ieyasu in 1561, following the Battle of Okehazama, he married his daughter to Ieyasu's son Nobuyasu. The girl fully understood that she was expected to act as a spy on her new family, which she did very successfully, and informed Nobunaga about a plot to kill him and replace him with Nobuyasu. The plot had been hatched, apparently, by her new mother-in-law. As the alliance with Nobunaga was very important to him, Tokugawa Ieyasu showed his good faith to Nobunaga by putting to death his son Nobuyasu and also his scheming wife.

Such channels of information could also be used for false intelligence. Oda Nobunaga was himself married to the daughter of his rival, Saitō Dōsan (1494–1556), and told his wife, quite falsely, that he was plotting with some of Dōsan's senior retainers to have Dōsan murdered. His wife dutifully conveyed the message to Dōsan, who obligingly put to death some of his most loyal men, greatly weakening his position against

A raid on a house
The women of a household flee in terror as a castle falls, and the enemy samurai gain access to their living quarters.

Nobunaga. It is not surprising that the wisdom of the age, enshrined in documents such as the *kakun*, or 'house-laws' of the daimyō, contained references to the dangers of trusting a woman, of which the most telling is one attributed to Takeda Shingen: 'Even when husband and wife are alone together, he should never forget his dagger.'

But no example of the political manipulation of women can quite compare with Nobunaga's use of his sister O-ichi, and her daughters. She was first married to Shibata Katsuie, Nobunaga's most senior retainer, but Nobunaga desperately needed a marriage alliance with the Asai family of Ōmi, so O-ichi was divorced from Katsuie and married to Asai Nagamasa, the heir of the family, in 1568. The alliance did not hold, and Nobunaga went to war against the Asai clan in 1570. When Nobunaga burned Nagamasa's castle of Odani in 1573, Nagamasa and his father committed suicide, having first returned O-ichi and her three daughters to Nobunaga. Nobunaga thereupon made O-ichi remarry her former husband, Shibata Katsuie.

In 1582, Nobunaga was murdered, and Shibata Katsuie led the opposition to a take-over of Nobunaga's domains by another of his generals, Toyotomi Hideyoshi. After his defeat at Shizugatake in 1583, Katsuie was besieged in his castle by Hideyoshi and he committed suicide, along with O-ichi. The daughters were again spared, and the victor, Hideyoshi, took the eldest as his wife.

This girl led the most unbelievably tragic life. She had already seen her father, mother and stepfather commit suicide and then be consumed by flames in blazing castles, and so much more was in store for her. As the Lady Yodo-gimi, the title she acquired on her marriage to the future dictator of Japan, she bore him a son, Hideyori, who was to inherit the whole of Japan as his kingdom at the age of 5, when Hideyoshi died in madness. Hideyori's succession was disputed by the newly victorious Shōgun Tokugawa Ieyasu, and in 1615 his heavy cannon bombarded Ōsaka castle, where the desperate Hideyori had taken refuge with his army, accompanied by the Lady Yodo-gimi. As Ōsaka castle fell, she too committed suicide, along with her son, as another Japanese fortress blazed around her.

The faithful wife

Nevertheless, in spite of being used in so many cynical ways, a wife was expected to show the same loyalty to her husband as he would towards his

---

A family commits suicide

The reader may recognise the inspiration for this plate as being the dramatic scene in Kurosawa's film *Ran*, where the defeated warlord's family commit suicide in the blazing castle keep. A samurai wife was expected to show loyalty to her husband every bit as great as the loyalty he showed towards his lord. Hence such an act of mass suicide.

Two women are stabbing each other at the same moment, while in the background a man commits *seppuku*, assisted by a faithful retainer.

An understanding of the various motivations possible behind a decision to commit suicide is fundamental to an appreciation of *bushidō*, the code of conduct and honour of a samurai. The act of suicide could simply be one way of making a dramatic protest against

the conduct of one's lord. Alternatively it provided a means of 'wiping the slate clean' when one had failed, thus dying with honour. There are many examples of this from the battlefields of the sixteenth century. In the case of the family in this plate, the suicide is motivated by a desire to accompany the defeated lord in death, and serve no other master.

warlord. 'A woman has no specific daimyō,' said a moral tome of the period, 'she looks on her husband as her lord', a neat summary of the actual status of woman in feudal society. On the question of adultery, there was one rule for a man, and another for a woman. The 'house-laws' of the Tokugawa family made the right of a husband to kill an adulterous wife and her partner into a duty every bit as solemn as the duty of vengeance for a slain master.

There was, however, no such thing as adultery on the part of a husband, provided that another man's wife was not involved. The taking of concubines was no more than a means of ensuring that a daimyō house would produce a son to inherit, and the more concubines, the greater the chances of success. One daimyō, Mito Mitsukuni, of a branch family of the Tokugawa, who was known for his virtue, had assigned his inheritance to his brother's son, and, although he kept many concubines, obliged each one to undergo abortion lest the production of an heir should imperil his nephew's chances. Even in less extreme cases than this, the concubine was vastly inferior to the wife in a feudal household, having a rank of no more than a servant. Not that an unmarried daughter was much better off. She hardly ranked as a relative within the blood-line, her only function being to marry and beget children for her husband.

The lowest point to which samurai society brought women was the selling into prostitution of daughters and sisters, often from impoverished farming families. Although this practice was virtually unknown and for-

bidden in the Kamakura Period, which ended in 1333, the urbanisation of the Edo Period, and deteriorating agricultural conditions, ensured a growing demand and a steady supply. The story of the revenge of the sisters Miyagino and Shinobu, recounted later in this book, has as its background the selling of daughters into the brothels of Edo.

The Tokugawa Shōguns took a very pragmatic view of prostitution, much as they did towards the *kabuki* theatre, that it was a necessary evil but needed regulating lest it get out of hand. It, therefore, set up 'pleasure quarters' in the great cities, of which the best known was Yoshiwara in Edo. The name, literally, meant 'the plain of the reeds', but had a pun in its pronunciation which made it also sound like 'lucky field', not that the district itself had much luck. It was founded in 1617, and suffered four disastrous fires during the following two decades. The inhabitants of Yoshiwara: the girls, the pimps, the brothel-keepers and the clients, form the raw material of half the romantic literature, the plays and the wood-block prints of the Edo Period. A man taking his pleasure in Yoshiwara could, if he chose, bankrupt himself with the highest-ranking girls – the *tayū*, each of whom had the right to refuse any customer she did not fancy – or merely enjoy a little 'window-shopping' along the narrow streets, where the girls of lower grades would sit behind wooden slatted grills on the ground floor of the houses.

Kōsaka Danjō, the lover of Shingen
In a predominantly male society, homosexual attachments could be stronger than those of marriage. Kosaka Danjō Masanobu was the lover of Takeda Shingen, and his constant companion. His prompt action at the fourth Battle of Kawanakajima in 1561 almost certainly saved the Takeda from annihilation. This photograph is of actor Hiroaki Murakami, who played the part of Danjō in the 1988 television series, 'Takeda Shingen', and is reproduced by kind permission of NHK Television.

Comrade loves of the samurai

It is impossible to leave the subject of the personal relationships of the samurai class without some reference to the practice of homosexuality. Indeed, the attachment of men for men could in many cases far surpass the love of women, though bisexuality was as common as homosexuality. Takeda Shingen, for example, who produced many children through wives and concubines, had a particular attachment for his retainer, Kōsaka Danjō Masanobu. The devoted Masanobu became one of his most trusted, and most skilled, military commanders, and was instrumental in saving Shingen from defeat at the cataclysmic fourth Battle of Kawanakajima in 1561. It was, however, left to a novelist from the merchant class, Ihara Saikaku, who was born in 1642, to put into words the homosexual nature of much of samurai society. His writings, tongue in cheek as they were for many observations of his supposed betters in the world of Edo Japan, tease the samurai, as in one preface when he writes, 'Our eyes are soiled by the soft haunches and scarlet petticoats of women. These female beauties are good for nothing save to give pleasure to old men in lands where there is not a good-looking boy.'

Such attachments were not merely tolerated, they were encouraged, in what was predominantly a male society, as being conducive to comradeship and self-sacrifice on the battlefield. A young boy, taken into the service of a daimyō as a page, could almost expect to be used as an object of sexual gratification. For some retainers, to be the favoured page of a member of the lord's family was a gateway to further advancement. Others were forced to manipulate this position when a patron's interest waned, as in the case of Ōtsuki Denzo, whose success caused a split within the Maeda family.

Popular history, as represented particularly by the plays of the *kabuki*

A boy of the samurai class
This young actor from the Toei-Uzumasa Film Studios is dressed in simple fashion. His hair is tied back in a queue, without the shaven front portion which would later denote his entry into manhood.

大月傳蕚

theatre, has not dealt kindly with Ōtsuki Denzō. Of all the villains who enter the stage in a family feud, he is the epitome of treachery – the Japanese equivalent, one may say, of Shakespeare's caricature of Richard III. Denzō was born the son of an insignificant retainer of the Kaga-han, called Ōtsuki Shichiemon, and when he was 14, on account of his good looks, he was summoned by Maeda Yoshinori, and employed as his page with a considerable stipend of 2 ryō of gold. Denzō became very well acquainted with Yoshinori, being a very handsome youth, and the affection Yoshinori showered on him rivalled that given to the favourite children of the family.

Realising his good fortune, Denzō aimed at the chance of a successful career in the administration of the *han*. However, Denzō had not been born into the family's line, and it was made clear to him that he would be most unlikely to succeed to a position of responsibility once Yoshinori's homo-

Kanazawa castle
Kanazawa castle was the seat of the Maeda daimyō, and the scene of the epic feud between Ōtsuki Denzō and Maeda Naomi, immortalised, and much embellished, in the 'soap operas' of the *kabuki* theatre. The outer wall and gateway are all that remain of the castle, which is now the site of Kanazawa University.

sexual preference for him began to wane. In fact, he rose to a high position within the family, and the mere existence of the stories that have grown up about Denzō's machinations tell us a great deal about the jealousies that could be aroused within a family.

According to the 'treachery' theory, Denzō devised a cunning, but very risky, plot. He stole a poisonous plant from the *han* medicinal herb garden, and poured it into Yoshinori's bowl of soup. At the very instant when Yoshinori was about to put it into his mouth, Denzō shouted 'My lord! Wait a moment' and, making it appear he was loyal, drank from the bowl. As soon as he had the taste of poison in his mouth, he vomited copiously and fell in convulsions. Yoshinori was enormously impressed by Denzō's acute awareness of danger and his outstanding loyalty, and promptly increased his stipend by 1000 *koku,* and appointed him to a senior rank. He became entrusted with Yoshinori's personal affairs, acting as a go-between for his feudal lord with beautiful women, and even though these stories are embellished, they give a good indication of the services a retainer was expected to perform for a daimyō, particularly an idle one.

Denzō's greatest coup came in procuring for Yoshinori, as a concubine, a celebrated beauty called O-tei. She was Yoshinori's second concubine, and inevitably provided a rival to his existing paramour, O-kiku, a situation exacerbated when both became pregnant at the same time. Eventually both gave birth, O-kiku producing Yoshinori's second son, O-tei his third. In reality, though, O-tei was to insist, her son had been born two days

113

earlier, while the other child's birth was the first to be notified. This had serious consequences for them both, because should Yoshinori's eldest son meet with an early death, then the third son would rank as subject to the heir. Ōtsuki Denzō took up her case.

Soon after, Yoshinori took a new concubine. O-tei was distraught, and entered into a plot with Denzō to have Yoshinori and his heir murdered, as a result of which Denzō would have undisputed power within the clan. The story goes on to relate how Yoshinori is ambushed while returning from Edo on the *sankin kōtai* visit, and stabbed as his horse is crossing a flooded river. His heir, Munetoki, is poisoned, and the servant girl, who is made a convenient scapegoat, meets a horrible end in a pit full of snakes, one of the most bizarre scenes in all the *kabuki* repertoire! Denzō is eventually found out and exiled to a distant place, where he commits suicide.

Historical reality is much more sober, but in its way far more tragic. Denzō did succeed to a high position within the Maeda family as a result of Yoshinori's attachment to him, and it is true that on Yoshinori's death, which was from natural causes, he was exiled to Gokayama in Etchū province and killed himself in 1745. Why should this have come about?

Needless to say the other retainers, and the family members in particular, were violently jealous of Denzō, in particular a certain Maeda Tosa-no-kami Naomi, who was a pillar of society, and his branch of the Maeda family counted as first among the eight families of Kaga. Naomi, who had a burning sense of duty towards great affairs of the family, was an exemplary player at power politics. History also tells us that Maeda Yoshinori was not a careless ruler, nor was Ōtsuki Denzō a bad, scheming person, but one who stimulated and enforced economy among the retainers, and raised funds by borrowing gold from Ōsaka merchants. He handled difficult economic affairs of the *han*, not by oppression, but from a position of wisdom and strength. Yet the whole affair shows how fragile such a position could be. Once Yoshinori was gone, Denzō could be removed by jealous family members. To a daimyō, family blood was thicker than water, and, inevitably, as a counter to Denzō's personification of evil in the *kabuki*, the indignant Maeda Naomi is presented as a shining example of the loyal samurai.

The servant girl in the pit of snakes
This illustration, which is taken from a nineteenth-century, wood-block-printed book cover, summarises the *kabuki* plot as the 'soap opera' of its day. The scene, rarely performed nowadays, is the bizarre climax of a play based loosely on the events of the Maeda family feud.

The divided sword

The universal acceptance of concubines may have ensured the birth of an heir, but numerous offspring could lead to rivalry within a family as bitter as the mistrust between Maeda Naomi and the outsider Denzō. Yet even though the wars of medieval Japan were civil wars, there are very few examples of families being split over allegiance in wartime, such as happened during the English Civil War. Such a split did in fact happen to the Sanada family, which greatly imperilled their future; yet it was the loyalty between them, and their recognition of samurai duty, that saved the Sanada as a daimyō family.

The Sanada were a family of Shinano province. The first to bear the name, Yukitaka, submitted to Takeda Shingen when he invaded Shinano. He went on to serve him together with his elder son, Nobutsuna, who was killed in 1575 at Nagashino. His younger son, Masayuki (1544–1608), inherited his father's position and, on the ruin of the Takeda with the death

Interior of the Sanada mansion
The simplicity of the Japanese domestic interior was a common thread that united all classes. From the simplest home to a grand house such as this, the Sanada mansion in Matsushiro, the straw *tatami* mats and the unpainted wood were characteristic of a deep and meaningful unity.

of Katsuyori in 1582, he was one of many Takeda retainers who were made to submit to Tokugawa Ieyasu. Masayuki grew to have little love for the Tokugawa. As a result of Masayuki's submission to Ieyasu, his elder son, Nobuyuki (1566–1658), was taken as a hostage to Hamamatsu, and eventually married the daughter of Ieyasu's great captain, Honda Tadakatsu; but Ieyasu went much further in his demands on the Sanada, and in 1586 tried to strip him of his territory to give to the Hōjō. So Masayuki rebelled, in spite of his son's presence with Ieyasu. The Tokugawa army advanced on Ueda and laid siege to the castle, but a truce was patched up, owing to the intervention of Hideyoshi.

When war came again in 1600, Masayuki instructed his son Nobuyuki to join Ieyasu, as that was where his duty lay. For Masayuki, and the other celebrated member of the family, Yukimura (1570–1615), their duty lay in opposing the rise of the Tokugawa. (Their emotional parting has long been a favourite theme for Japanese artists.) Ueda castle was strategically situated on the Tokugawa's most vital line of communication – the Nakasendō road, and as it had already withstood one siege by the Tokugawa army, Masayuki no doubt thought it could withstand another. The Sanada family, thereupon, contributed to the Sekigahara campaign by delaying the progress westwards of Ieyasu's son, Tokugawa Hidetada, which they did so successfully that the siege of Ueda in 1600 is regarded as one of the three classic sieges of Japanese history when the defenders were

115

not defeated. A huge army was kept from Sekigahara, and had it not been for the attendant treachery on the field, their tactics may well have tipped the balance against the Tokugawa.

After Sekigahara, Masayuki and Yukimura were captured by the Tokugawa and faced almost certain death, but Nobuyuki interceded on their behalf and the sentences were commuted to exile. Nobuyuki was granted the castle of Ueda. Masayuki died in exile in 1608, and Yukimura returned from exile in 1614 to join the army that opposed Ieyasu once again from within the walls of Ōsaka castle. Here he was one of the most skilled of the defenders, and was finally killed in the Battle of Tennōji in 1615.

There seem to have been no bitter feelings from Masayuki to his son or vice versa. Each followed his duty as they saw it, and Nobuyuki carried on the family line, which to all of them was what really mattered. Through him the Sanada continued and prospered, and in 1622 he was transferred to Matsushiro, where they established the magnificent mansion which exists to this day.

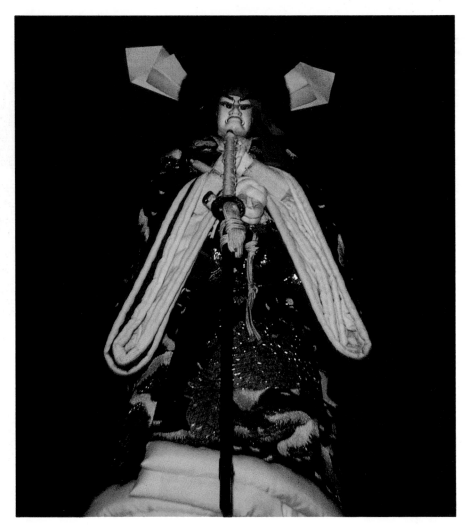

A puppet from the Bunraku theatre
Like the *kabuki*, the plays of the puppet theatre would take their plots from contemporary events, such as family feuds. In fact the puppet plays tended to be more daring in their attempts at satire.

The Date family feud

The split within the Sanada family, mutually agreed by all parties as being in keeping with samurai honour and duty, is as nothing compared to the mighty rifts torn through the fabric of family loyalty in other great families, and there are several examples of daimyō families brought to the brink of ruin by corruption and feuding within their own blood-relatives. Unfortunately, as we have seen in the illustration of the Maeda family dispute, in the majority of cases, the facts behind these family feuds have been obscured by the treatment they received at the hands of novelists and dramatists, who used real-life stories of weakness and disaster among the rich and powerful as material for the 'soap operas' of their day. An excellent example is the near-disastrous rift within the Date family, daimyō of Sendai. The truth of the conflict is interesting enough as an example of the decline of loyalty and filial values, but the resulting story has been expanded out of all proportion.

Date Masamune (1566–1636) was one of the noblest daimyō to make the transition between Sengoku warlord and Edo daimyō, and the internal discord of the Date family arose entirely from the immorality of his grandson, the third generation daimyō Tsunamune. He devoted himself entirely to pleasure, with daily attendance in the red-light district of Yoshiwara. He was eventually condemned by the *bakufu*, an unusual and

A scene from **kabuki**
A wood-block print depicting a squabble between women of a daimyō's household. The scene is taken from the *kabuki* play *Meiboku Sendai Hagi*, which dramatises the events of the Date family feud.

very serious step for the Government to take, and as a punishment was made to underwrite the expense of the extension to the moat of Edo castle in 1660, an enormous civil-engineering project. But long before matters came to this pass, his retainers forced him to take early retirement in favour of his heir Kamechiyo (the future Tsunamura), who was still in his infancy.

The 2-year-old Kamechiyo's guardians were to be Date Hyōbu Mune-katsu and Tamura Ukyō. Hyōbu was the tenth son of the *han* founder, Date Masamune, and Ukyō was Tsunamune's illegitimate elder brother. But Hyōbu Munekatsu was ambitious, and by and by clawed his way to abso-lute power, shielded from criticism by his relationship, through his son's marriage, to a powerful *bakufu* official. He dismissed senior retainers who opposed him, and promoted his particular favourite, a man called Harada Kai. Tamura Ukyō was gradually squeezed out of any control over the affairs of the *han*. In the 10 years of Hyōbu's office as guardian, he man-aged 120 retainers, and during that time had ordered 17 of them to commit suicide.

The story of the Date family feud forms the basis of the *kabuki* play *Meiboku Sendai Hagi*, which begins to diverge from reality at the point when Date Hyōbu is believed to have been plotting to murder the young heir, Kamechiyo, so that he could take over the domain. The child's nurse, Masaoka, tries to protect the boy by retiring to an inner room on the pretext of the child's illness. Two 'villains', acting on behalf of Date Hyōbu, bring cakes as gifts for the supposed invalid. The cakes are, of course(!) poisoned, and as a fine gesture of loyalty toward an infant lord, Masaoka's own son takes one to test it for poison. To avoid discovery of the fact that the cakes are poisoned, one of the villains stabs the boy to death.

In reality, the show-down with Hyōbu came from the person who was the next most powerful man in the family – one Date Aki Muneshige. The confrontation between Hyōbu and Aki made the Date feud grow more and more violent. Aki lodged a complaint with the *bakufu*, although he had little firm evidence on which to base his argument. Was there any more to the affair than Hyōbu's apparent incorrect treatment of land distribution? Aki stuck his neck out, and exposed fully Hyōbu's evil deeds and immoral acts as he saw them, accusations that forced the *bakufu* to intervene. The resulting investigation of Hyōbu's conduct and management took place in 1671 on neutral ground, at the residence of Sakai Ude-no-kami, the *tairō*, or chief retainer of the family, and therefore the most influential man outside the actual family.

Four people were questioned in turn about Date Hyōbu Munekatsu's conduct: Date Aki Muneshige, the retainers Shibata Geki and Yoshiuchi Shima, and Harada Kai. The accounts of the first three agreed totally, while Harada Kai's version differed wildly. Suddenly the investigation reached an unexpected climax when the enraged Harada Kai drew a short *wakizashi* sword and attacked Muneshige. Muneshige sustained two sword strokes and was severely wounded. The two other witnesses, Geki and Shima, chased after Harada and wounded him. Harada Kai was panting for breath, then lost his head completely and slashed indiscriminately at Geki and another retainer, called Haraya Yoshihiro, wounding them so badly that they died that evening.

But this sudden eruption into violence marked the end of the Date feud. Date Hyōbu Munekatsu's defence collapsed, and punishment was swift.

Harada Kai, villain of the Date feud
Harada Kai is the real-life villain
of the feud within the Date family
of Sendai. Here he is shown
brandishing a blood stained knife at
the residence of Sakai Ude-no-kami,
where his fellow conspirator, Date
Hyōbu, was impeached by the
bakufu for mismanagement of the
han.

The young heir, Tsunamura, was judged to have played no part in the upheaval of the *han*, and to have been powerless to prevent it on account of his youth. The *han* was, therefore, spared the confiscation by the *bakufu* of its wealth, which totalled 620,000 *koku*. As for Date Hyōbu Munekatsu, he was deprived of his stipend of 30,000 *koku*, and placed in the custody of the *han*. He was reduced to an insignificant rank, and died eight years later, in 1679, at the age of 51.

In the *kabuki* plays, Date Hyōbu Munekatsu and Harada Kai are the villains, while Date Aki Muneshige is presented as the finest of loyal family

119

members. However, this is in itself something of an exaggeration to make the play interesting. In reality, there was always factional strife among the loyal retainers of a large *han*, and to paint the combatants so clearly black or white is an oversimplification. The murderous outburst by Harada Kai, however, did actually happen, and is such a dramatic touch that one wonders why *Meiboku Sendai Hagi* has to be embellished so much, as, for example, in one scene when a sorcerer is introduced who changes magically into a rat!

A samurai youth
A youth of the samurai class, showing the characteristic samurai pigtail and the half-shaven head, as modelled by an actor from the Toei-Uzumasa Film Studios in Kyōto.

The Kuroda feud

As a final illustration, let us examine the feud within the Kuroda family, which has received little embellishment. In this case, the dying lord, the great Kuroda Nagamasa (1568–1623), veteran of many battles including the invasion of Korea, hesitated before making his son Tadayuki his successor. There was much immorality in Tadayuki, Nagamasa reasoned, and he relied on his trusted *tairō*, Kuriyama Daizen, to remonstrate with him, even at the risk of his life. Nagamasa handed Daizen his famous helmet with water-buffalo horns and said, 'If Tadayuki gets foolish, put this helmet on and admonish him yourself.'

   Legend says that Tadayuki had a favourite, Kurahashi Shudayu, whom he had originally procured as his personal retainer, and Tadayuki's

120

debauchery continued in spite of Daizen's remonstrations against him. Shudayu, another bisexual, procured a beautiful girl called O-hide no kata for Tadayuki, who was carrying Shudayu's child in her womb, through whom he was planning to usurp the family. However, evil did not prosper and O-hide no kata was killed by a retainer. In disgust, the *tairō* Daizen left the service of Tadayuki and lodged a complaint with the *bakufu*. Daizen had Tadayuki placed in the temporary custody of the Nambu clan and Kurahashi Shudayu was exiled to Toishima. The *bakufu* recognised the loyal service to the Tokugawa of the previous head Nagamasa, and maintained intact the territory of the Kuroda, to which Tadayuki was later restored.

That is the tradition, but how much is true? There was a show-down between the two men, Tadayuki and Daizen, and the model of Shudayu is said to be a person called Kuraya Sodayu, who existed as Tadayuki's professional flatterer, but the Kuroda feud is just one more story of a fight between a stupid ruler and a stubborn old retainer, a feature common enough to the turbulent world of the warlords of Japan.

Death and the Daimyō

The nearness of death, and the awareness of the nature of the spirit world, was an omnipresent factor in the life of the warlord. We have noted twice already that the relationship between daimyō and retainer was regarded as extending beyond death, and that terrible gap between life and death was one that every samurai had to be willing to cross. If loyalty meant anything, it had to include dying for one's lord. Many years after wars had ceased, a samurai of the Nabeshima daimyō was to put this principle into words: 'The Way of the Samurai,' he wrote, 'is found in death.'

The supreme sacrifice

The 'way of the Samurai' was found in death, and this death could be brought about by an enemy sword, spear or bow, or even a gun – the means did not matter as long as the death was honourable, and for a death to be honourable it had to come about as a result of loyal service to one's lord.

Suicide on the battlefield
The daimyō's loyal samurai hold off the enemy while their master commits *seppuku*.

The loyal exploits of Sengoku Hidehisa
Death in battle was the ultimate expression of a warrior's loyalty, and on occasions was actively sought, but such self-sacrifice did not always lead to the daimyō's advantage. Here the hero Sengoku Hidehisa (1551–1614) performs valiantly, in a companion scroll to that depicted on the cover of *Battles of the Samurai* by this author. (Ueda castle museum)

In times of war, the achievement of such a death was prized as the ultimate proof of loyalty, and on occasions death could actively be sought for its own sake. There is a very fine dividing line between accepting the likelihood of death in reckless battle and actively seeking it out, which was effectively to commit suicide. An appreciation of the place of suicide in the concept of the loyal samurai warrior is essential for understanding the many acts of seemingly wasteful self-destruction we read of in the old war chronicles. What motivated this apparent eagerness for extinction, and how could destroying oneself ever be seen as loyal behaviour?

There were occasions when suicide was regarded as appropriate because of failure, and the samurai would commit *sokotsu-shi,* or 'expiatory suicide', the very act itself wiping the slate clean. Such a decision could be spontaneous and dramatic, like the action of the veteran warrior Yamamoto Kansuke at the fourth Battle of Kawanakajima in 1561. As Takeda Shingen's *gun-bugyō*, he had devised 'Operation Woodpecker', by which the Takeda were to surprise the Uesugi army. Realising his bold strategy had failed, Kansuke took his spear and plunged into the midst of the enemy army, committing suicide to make amends for his error. Minutes after Kansuke's suicide, he was joined in death by Morozumi Masakiyo, Shingen's 87-year-old great-uncle mentioned earlier. To Morozumi, a dramatic suicide was a way of dying honourably when faced with what he interpreted as certain defeat. In his case, there was no sense of personal failure, merely the culmination of loyalty in joining Shingen in his coming death. The tragedy of both these deaths is that their interpretations of the certainty of the destruction of the Takeda very soon proved incorrect. Reinforcements arrived, the army rallied, and a defeat was turned into

123

victory. Yet two experienced generals had been lost, both of whom would have served Shingen better by staying alive.

The motivation behind suicide is much less well appreciated than the means whereby it was carried out, which was usually the well-known act of *seppuku*. (If the two characters which make up the work *seppuku* are reversed, it produces *hara-kiri*, the word more familiar to Western ears.) *Seppuku*, which has been much described and much discussed, was a particularly painful act of suicide in that the samurai himself released his spirit from its seat in the abdomen by a swift and deep cut with his dagger. The rite was somewhat modified in later years to allow the presence of a second, who cut off the victim's head at the moment of agony.

The committing of *seppuku* was not always a voluntary activity. It could be allowed as an honourable alternative to execution for a condemned criminal of the samurai class, and we also noted earlier how Sasa Narimasa was 'invited' to commit suicide by Hideyoshi following his disastrous

Seppuku *on the battlefield*
This page from the *Hōjō Godai-ki* shows the act of *seppuku*, or ritual suicide, at its most poignant and dramatic – the mass suicide of a defeated army. One warrior receives the blessing of a second to cut off his head. Others discard their armour for the classic act of *hara-kiri*, while one throws himself on to his sword.

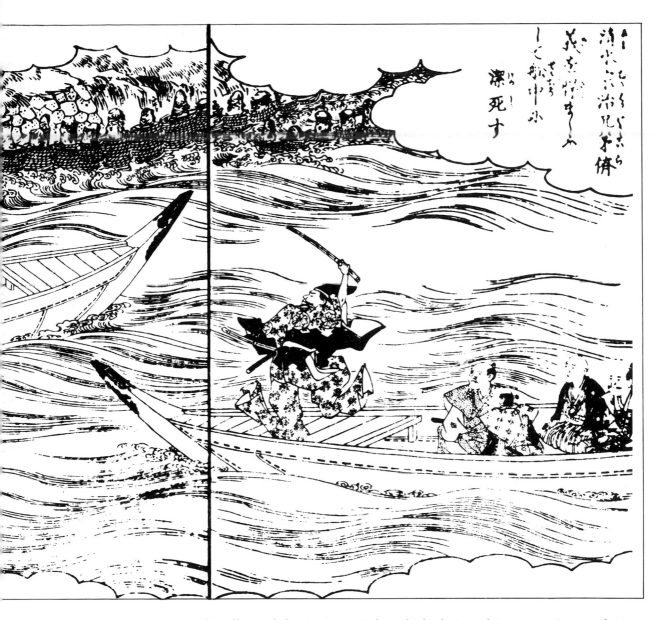

深死す

The suicide of Shimizu Muneharu
One of the most dramatic acts of suicide in samurai history was that of the defender of Takamatsu castle, Shimizu Muneharu, who took a boat out into the artificial lake created by Hideyoshi's siege operations, and committed *seppuku* in front of the besieging army.

handling of the territory Hideyoshi had given him. Sometimes a daimyō was called upon to perform *seppuku* as the basis of peace negotiations, the idea being that the surrender of a castle could be accepted without further bloodshed, providing that the current daimyō committed suicide. This would so weaken the defeated clan that resistance would effectively cease. Toyotomi Hideyoshi used an enemy's suicide in this way on several occasions, of which the most dramatic, in that it effectively ended a dynasty of daimyō forever, is what happened when the Hōjō were defeated at Odawara in 1590. Hideyoshi insisted on the suicide of the retired daimyō, Hōjō Ujimasa, and the exile of his son Ujinao. With one sweep of a sword, the most powerful daimyō family in the east ceased to exist, and disappeared from history.

Alternatively, the victor could be satisfied with the death of his enemy's

125

retainer, which would be most effective if the subordinate was in charge of the castle he was besieging. There are several examples of this from Hideyoshi's earlier campaigns on behalf of Oda Nobunaga. The most theatrical occurred when Hideyoshi besieged Takamatsu castle in 1582. It was a long siege, and only looked like being successful when Hideyoshi diverted a river to make a lake, which gradually began to flood the castle. Unfortunately it was during these operations that Hideyoshi received the dramatic news of the murder of Nobunaga, and knew that he had to abandon Takamatsu rapidly before any other of Nobunaga's generals found out and became his avengers instead. He hurriedly drew up peace terms with Mōri Terumoto, which included the clause that the valiant defender of Takamatsu, Shimizu Muneharu, should commit suicide. Shimizu Muneharu was determined to go to his death as dramatically as he had lived, and took a boat out into the middle of the artificial lake. When he was satisfied that Hideyoshi's men were taking careful note of what he was doing, he committed *seppuku*.

Sometimes such a suicide provided an honourable end only after extreme privations. Tottori castle, in Inaba province, held out for an incredible 200 days before it surrendered to Hideyoshi in 1581. Its commander, Kikkawa Tsuneie, inspired his men to this long resistance even though they were reduced to eating grass and dead horses. Tsuneie's suicide letter to his son survives to this day. It reads:

We have endured for over two hundred days. We now have no provisions left. It is my belief that by giving up my life I will help my garrison. There is nothing greater than the honour of our family. I wish our soldiers to hear of the circumstances of my death.

His suicide, along with that of two others, was the condition of surrender.

Another reason for committing suicide was the making of a protest. This is known as *kanshi*. Examples of this are rare, but it profoundly affected one of the greatest daimyō of the Sengoku Period. Oda Nobunaga inherited his father's domains at the age of 15 and, although he was a brave warrior, showed little interest in the administration of his territory. One of his best retainers, Hirade Kiyohide, tried in vain to persuade him to mend his ways, and when the young Nobunaga showed no inclination to listen to him, Kiyohide put all his feelings into a letter to his lord, and committed *seppuku* in protest. Nobunaga was greatly moved, and changed his ways for the better, with, of course, considerable consequences for the history of Japan.

Following in death

To return briefly to Shimizu Muneharu and his *seppuku* in the middle of the lake, there is a related anecdote which illustrates the one reason for committing suicide which did not meet with universal approval. This was the practice of *junshi*, or 'following in death'. In Muneharu's case, the loyal retainer actually preceded his lord in death, because Muneharu was invited to the man's room in Takamatsu castle the evening before his own suicide was due to take place. There his loyal retainer explained that, to re-assure his master about the ease with which *seppuku* could be performed, he had himself committed suicide, and, pulling aside his robe, showed

秀吉の神祭
大宮父子か
害心を識て
殺さーむ

The execution of prisoners
One reason for the continuing
tradition of *seppuku* was the fact that
prisoners were invariably executed.
The other alternative, to become a
vassal of the victor, was often less
palatable.

Muneharu his severed abdomen. Muneharu was touched by the gesture,
and acted as his retainer's second to bring the act to a speedy and less
painful conclusion.

As noted above, there was a fine line between *junshi* and merely
continuing a desperate fight. In the confusion of a battlefield, the circumstances of a retainer's death could never be clearly established. But when
death from natural causes during times of peace provoked the performance
of *junshi*, whereby a loyal retainer committed suicide to show that he could
serve none other than his departed lord, it could only be regarded as utterly
wasteful. During the Sengoku Period, such an act may have been approved
of, and indeed some retainers did have little left to live for, but in times of
peace *junshi* was a deliberate, premeditated and unnecessary act, noble,
perhaps, in its sentiments, but scarcely helpful in maintaining the stability
of a dynasty.

In the early Edo Period, as many as 20 leading retainers of an individual
daimyō were known to have committed *junshi* on the deaths of their lords.
For this reason, strong condemnation was made of *junshi*. A better way to
serve one's departed lord, the *bakufu* argued, was to render equally loyal
service to his heir. But *junshi* was firmly engrained in the Japanese mentality. It had been abolished originally by an imperial decree in the year AD
3 (!), yet still the tradition persisted, and as noted above, reached its peak in
the Sengoku Period. A strong condemnation of it is found in the so-called
'Legacy of Ieyasu', the 'house-laws' left by the first Tokugawa Shōgun in

127

1616, but at the death of his grandson, the third Tokugawa Shōgun Iemitsu in 1651, five of the leading retainers of the Tokugawa committed *junshi*, a remarkable gesture against the law they themselves had formulated. A further attempt to ban it was introduced by the *bakufu* in 1663, and included the statement:

In the event that a lord had a presentiment that a certain vassal is liable to immolate himself, he should admonish him strongly against it during his lifetime. If he fails to do so, it shall be counted as his fault. His heir will not escape appropriate punishment.

Five years later, an instance of *junshi* occurred among the retainers of the recently deceased daimyō of the house of Okudaira, but little action was taken against the family because of the great service the Okudaira had rendered to the Tokugawa in previous years. (Their ancestor had been the defender of Nagashino castle at the time of the famous battle there.) The family of the actual performer of *junshi* was not so fortunate. His two sons were ordered to commit *seppuku*, and his two sons-in-law, one of whom was of the Okudaira family, were exiled.

Other daimyō finally took note, and from the mid-seventeenth century onwards, the practice of *junshi* effectively ceased, until it came dramatically to the attention of modern Japan in 1912. On the eve of the funeral of Emperor Meiji, General Nogi and his wife committed *seppuku*. Nogi had commanded troops in the Sino-Japanese War of 1894–95, and led the battle to take Port Arthur in the Russo-Japanese War of 1904–05. It was an

A Buddhist priest at prayer
A Buddhist priest of the Shingon sect kneels in prayer at the temple of Fudō-ji, on the site of the Battle of Kurikara.

act that astounded his contemporaries because of the bizarre disloyalty to the Emperor's wishes that the illegal act implied. It was also sobering evidence that the samurai spirit lived on in the Japan of the twentieth century.

The death of an enemy

In the Sengoku Period, the death of one's enemy was the aim, and the natural consequence, of the practice of war. Nevertheless, the recognition of an enemy death became surrounded by considerable ritual, of which the most bizarre, to Western eyes, were the practices surrounding the collection and inspection of heads. This is a feature found throughout samurai history, and was the surviving element of the ancient practice of sacrifice to the gods of war mentioned in a previous chapter. The heads would be washed, the hair combed, and the resulting trophy made presentable by cosmetics – all tasks performed with great delicacy by the women of the daimyō's court. The heads would then be mounted on a spiked wooden board, with labels for identification. If the ceremony were to be held with no time for this preparation, the heads could be presented on an opened war-fan, or on a paper handkerchief. Some leaves from a tree were recommended to soak up any dripping blood. The daimyō would sit in similar state to the one he had enjoyed when he had presided over the departure ceremony, and one by one the heads would be brought before him for comment. If a daimyō were otherwise engaged, the head ceremony could be delegated to a trusted subordinate, as in the *Hōjō Go-daiki*:

It is Nakayama Shurisuke that Hōjō Ujitsuna favours with [the right] to raise the flags and sit on the camp-stool at Kōnodai. This is a person who is known for his traditional virtues of military lore and loyalty by which he has destroyed enemies, carrying out strategy in numerous battles, and at the same time he is a samurai official. This person will be bugyō *for head inspection. He will record the relative importance of loyalties, and examine the details of contests when the heads were taken.*

Of course, not all the hundreds of heads taken during a battle were saved. The *Gunyōki* quotes the following document:

Tembun 2nd year (1533) 7th month, 6th day at the Hour of the Monkey. The list for [the Battle of] Ōyama. These are the heads that were taken:

Item: one head:	*Maekawa Zaemon*
taken by	*Kinichi Danjōshū and Shōshu Uemon*
Item: one head:	*no given name known*
taken by	*a* chūgen *[called] Genroku*
Item: one head:	*Arakami Jirozaemon*
taken by	*Nagao Gagaku Sukeshu and Masuda Danjochu*

The number of heads taken and discarded is not known.

One little-known feature of the head-inspection routine was that certain expressions on the faces of the deceased were supposed to be unlucky, and others lucky, namely:

1 *Eyes looking towards heaven – unlucky (and particularly disliked by the Takeda family).*

2 *Eyes looking towards the earth – generally lucky.*

3 *Eyes looking towards the head's left – lucky in enemies.*

4 *Eyes looking towards the right – lucky in allies.*

5 *Eyes closed – lucky, 'a head of tranquillity'.*

6 *One eye closed, gnashing teeth, etc. – unlucky.*

The mention of the heads of allies above refers to the practice of sending back to an enemy the heads of their noble dead.

A special privilege was reserved for the head of a defeated enemy general or a daimyō. It would be brought before the daimyō by two men, not just one, and, after the victorious army had given the shout of victory, the general would ceremoniously eat the same three dishes of which he had partaken before setting out, but with a difference – the head of the defeated general was allowed to share the *saké*. In a grisly ritual, some *kombu* (dried seaweed) was placed in the head's mouth, and *saké* poured on to it, with much dignity, from a long-handled cup.

As may be imagined, the expression on the face of a dead daimyō was very closely examined, as the chronicle *Ō-monogatari* tells us of the occasion when Oda Nobunaga viewed the head of his bitter enemy, Takeda Katsuyori, in 1582:

Oda Nobunaga views the heads
One of Oda Nobunaga's retainers is overcome by emotion as he contemplates the severed head of an enemy, during one of Nobunaga's head-viewing ceremonies following a victory.

When Oda Nobunaga inspected the head of Takeda Katsuyori the right eye was

130

closed and the left eye was enlivened with a scowl. Nobunaga was moved to sympathy at the sight of the dead head of the powerful general, and it is recorded that all concerned agreed that Nobunaga may have been victorious in battle, but had been defeated by Katsuyori's head.

The Japanese spirit world

The attitude of a samurai towards his own death, and that of his family, lord and enemy, was deeply coloured by his beliefs regarding the world of the spirits of the dead, to which the act of dying committed him. The religious beliefs of the Japanese relating to death and dying are not easy for non-Japanese to appreciate, as was brought home to the world's media in 1985 when the then Japanese Prime Minister Nakasone made an official visit to the Yasukuni Shrine in Tōkyō on 15 August, the fortieth anniversary of the end of World War II. There was considerable protest from overseas, particularly from the Chinese, who pointed out that war

The Mimakude Shrine
The Mimakude Shrine, where are enshrined the spirits of the Kusunoki family, is typical of thousands of such Shintō shrines throughout Japan. Note the characteristic *torii* gateway.

criminals, such as General Tōjō, were enshrined there. Analogies were drawn with President Reagan's equally unpopular visit to the West German military ceremony at Bitburg, where the remains of SS troops were buried. But there the resemblance ended. Bitburg contained human remains, while Yasukuni contained nothing at all – and there we have the key to understanding the notion of the Japanese spirit world.

A Shintō shrine, like Yasukuni, is neither a burial ground, nor is it simply a place of worship, like a Christian church, a synagogue or a mosque. It is also a spirit house, a gathering place for the spirits of the dead enshrined there. Since ancient times, the Japanese have believed that the spirit lives on after the death of a body, returning from time to time to the land of the living. The season of cherry blossoms is one of these times, when the *tama* (spirits) flock to the cherry-tree-covered hills of Yoshino. The midsummer festival of *Bon* is another occasion on which the spirits of the dead are welcomed back from the mountains or other sacred places where they live. In many parts of Japan, lanterns are floated on water to light the spirits' way home. In this Shintō scheme, the worlds of the dead and the living are coterminous. The spirits of the dead are always close at hand, and the theme of communication between the living and the dead is a strong theme running through Japanese tradition.

Shintō is, of course, not the only religion of Japan but, being so thor-

A Buddhist grave
A large stone *sotoba* marks the site of a Buddhist grave, where the cremated remains of a samurai are buried. Buddhism teaches that the soul is reborn after death in a state of reincarnation.

132

The Buddha of mercy and the vengeful judge
Two aspects of Buddhist cosmology are illustrated here. On one hand there is the beatific figure of the healing Buddha, Amida, who waits to welcome souls into his Western Paradise. On the other is one of the fierce judges of the underworld, whose judgement will decide into which of the states of transmigration the reincarnated soul will be born.

oughly grounded in traditional beliefs and folk practices, it has managed to absorb much of other religions within its own world view, so that even though the influence of Buddhism (introduced during the sixth century AD) encouraged the custom of preserving the ashes of the dead in family graves, the spirit has always been regarded as more important than the body. In most aspects of religious life, Shintō and Buddhism can be regarded as totally intermingled until the Separation Edict of 1868, which sought to make Shintō an 'Established Church'.

Sharing this acceptance of two apparently contradictory religions, the samurai believed that, 33 years after death, a person's spirit moved from

133

the Buddhist temple where he or she was buried to a shrine, an idea totally contrary to the Buddhist doctrine of reincarnation, which saw the spirit existing in limbo, waiting to be reborn, and we read comments made to a dying samurai like, 'May you be reborn in bliss'.

This process of rebirth was not without its hazards. Where a spirit ended up depended on the person's actions during his life, and no one else's prayers made the slightest difference. There was a very strong belief in judgement during the sixteenth century. People believed that the Ten Kings of the Underworld, in Buddhist cosmology, passed judgement on each person's spirit after death. Seven days after death, the spirit was judged by King Shinkō; seven days later it was judged by King Shokō, and so on every seventh day until on the forty-ninth day, seven weeks after death, the verdict was handed down and the spirit was reborn in one of the six realms of transmigration – hell, the realm of Hungry Ghosts, the realm of the Beasts, the realm of the Asuras, or Titans, the human realm, or heaven. Above these six realms were the four states of enlightenment leading to final Buddhahood – the *sravaka*, the *prateya-buddha*, the *bodhissatva*, and finally, the completely enlightened *nirvana*. The spirit's individual 'case' was reviewed after a hundred days, a year, and three years. During the Tokugawa Period, the Buddhist memorial period for the dead was stretched from 3 years to 7, 13 and 17 years, until, finally, 33 years was accepted as the time of trial.

Shintō shrines were the homes for these spirits, and it is noticeable from old chronicles that the daimyō of the Sengoku Period would honour the fallen impartially, enshrining the spirits of friend and enemy alike. The act of enshrinement was very important, because it was believed that any-

The temple of Daitsu-ji, Nagahama
The Daitsu-ji is a large Buddhist foundation at Nagahama. Buddhism and Shintō are the two major religions of Japan, and have much in common. We are looking at the *hondō*, or main hall.

Parade of yamabushi
Yamabushi from the Shōgō-In in Kyōto march to their *goma* ritual.

one who had died unjustly or by violence, including on the battlefield, would become a *onryō*, or 'angry ghost', and haunt the living and cause misfortune. Even peaceful spirits at death could change their nature and become malevolent if neglected during the 33-year period. The samurai had a vivid concept of the nature of these unruly spirits. They saw the spirit right after death as having 'sharp edges'. If you enshrined it, it slowly lost its rough edges until it was 'as smooth as marble'. After the period of 33 years, these featureless spirits then gathered into one collective spirit – the 'god of the village'. Presumably the spirit of the war criminal General Tōjō is now 'as smooth as marble', owing to the safeguards of enshrining it

---

Yamabushi

This plate is an attempt to reconstruct the appearance of the members of the Shugendō sect, the *yamabushi*, as they would have appeared in the sixteenth century. They are on pilgrimage in the Yoshino mountains and are paying homage before a statue of Fudō. Fudō is always represented with a fierce expression and surrounded by flames. In his right hand he holds a sword to strike down demons, and in his left he holds a rope with which to bind them. The *yamabushi* themselves look unkempt, which is supported by contemporary descriptions of them, but they wear their traditional skull-cap and carry staffs. These, with the details of the robe, symbolise various aspects of Buddhist doctrine.

Successive pilgrimages such as these, which included performing rituals of prayer and fasting at anciently defined sites, were a form of initiation into the mysteries of Shugendō. *Yamabushi* were therefore regarded as the possessors of mystical powers. They were believed to be able to cast out demons, to talk to animals and to overcome fire. The sect was suppressed at the end of the nineteenth century, but has since undergone a revival, and annual pilgrimages are now undertaken.

135

correctly in 1978, 33 years after his death? Seen in this light, the existence of Yasukuni Shrine is not a glorification of the past, but a safeguard for the future.

However, a different Buddhist view of death was provided by the 'mass movement' Amidist sects that developed during the thirteenth century. According to the sect called Jōdo Shinshū, on death the believer's spirit left the world immediately for Amida's paradise, which explains the fanaticism of the *ikki* armies of the Sengoku Period, who vanquished daimyō forces, secure in their belief that death in battle ensured instant heaven. But even though such beliefs about the dead appear contradictory, they were regarded as complementary, and were firmly rooted in Japanese tradition. For example, the spirit of Taira Masakado, who was killed in AD 940, is enshrined in the Kanda Myōjin shrine in Tōkyō. Masakado was a rebel against the Emperor, and during the Meiji Period, when the institution of the Emperor was being strengthened against the memory of the overthrown Shōgun, it was decided to move Masakado's spirit from the main shrine to a subshrine. When this was done, local people refused to go to the main shrine, and boycotted its annual festival, the reason being, apparently, that it was wisest to keep an unruly spirit pacified, and that if Masakado's spirit was deprived of its proper shrine, then it would start causing trouble again.

Nagahama castle
A modern reconstruction of the keep of Nagahama castle, which was originally built for Toyotomi Hideyoshi.

The **yamabushi** *light the sacred bonfire*
The climax of the *yamabushi*'s *goma* is the lighting of a huge bonfire in the centre of the courtyard. Strips of wood, containing petitions, are flung into the billowing white smoke that ensues.

Communication with the spirit world

Although the living had a duty to perform to the recently dead, there were benefits to be gained from the departed spirits, who could pass the barrier between our world and theirs. The Japanese medium, or *miko,* allowed the spirit to possess his or her body, and transmitted messages to the living. Closely related to the *miko* was the notion of the ascetic who acquired special powers, the best known of whom were the *yamabushi,* the followers of the religious sect of Shugendō. *Yamabushi* means 'he who lies in the mountains', and the term has often been applied erroneously to the armies of warrior monks who plagued Kyōto during the twelfth century. Yoshitsune's companion, the warrior monk Benkei, disguised himself and his companions as *yamabushi* to avoid detection during their flight from Yoritomo's vengeance in 1185.

The figure of the wild-looking, wandering *yamabushi* is one that crops up regularly in Japanese art and literature, and we noted earlier how Hōjō Sōun recruited a *yamabushi* as his *horagai* blower. A *yamabushi* was endowed with magical powers, acquired as a result of fasting, onerous climbs of sacred mountains, and various ascetic exercises, such as standing naked under waterfalls. The initiate was believed to have the power to cast out demons, to talk to animals, and to overcome fire. By the recitation of prayers, *yamabushi* could overcome and exorcise any *onryō,* the above-mentioned 'angry ghosts', that were causing trouble in a locality.

The *yamabushi* thus reflected a blending of the Buddhist, Shintō and animistic traditions which were outlined above. To a *yamabushi,* a mountain was not just the abode of the *kami* (the gods of Shintō): it was a Buddhist mandala – a sacred space separated from ordinary space and time. His climb was a spiritual journey as well as a physical one, and the disciple passed symbolically through the ten worlds of transmigration. Each of these states was negotiated by means of a rite, the ordeal representing hell being vividly described during the sixteenth century by a former *yamabushi* who had become a Christian. The ritual, called *gōhyō,* or 'weighing one's karma', consisted of the disciple being tied and seated on a beam projecting over a cliff, with a large rock as a counterweight. In this terrifying position, he was required to confess his sins to his fellow *yamabushi.* If he confessed all, his karma was lightened. If he refused, he would be tipped off into the valley below. The rite of the Hungry Ghosts, which followed, was fasting; of the Beasts: abstinence from water; and of the Asuras: *sumō* wrestling. Following the final rite for heaven, a sacred dance, the climber received a form of baptism, confirming his powers as a *yamabushi.*

The rituals of the *yamabushi* lasted, with little change, right through the time of the samurai, but with some reduction in the severity of the disciplines. Shugendō all but ceased to exist with the Meiji Restoration, but has since been revived, and I was privileged to join some modern *yamabushi* on an ascent of their holy Mount Ōmine in 1986.

There are numerous references in war chronicles to daimyō consulting *yamabushi,* and more orthodox priests. It was, in fact, quite common for daimyō of the Sengoku Period to become monks while continuing the profession of warlord. Takeda Shingen and Uesugi Kenshin are the prime examples, and their banners with Buddhist prayers were among their most treasured possessions. Other daimyō took a more sceptical view of religion.

'Fearing neither gods nor Buddhas' is a frequent phrase used to describe such iconoclasts, as in the legend of 'Hideyoshi's Bridge':

On the sacred mountain of Kōya-san, where lie the mausoleums of numerous daimyō, there are three bridges on the road that leads to the tomb of the saint Kōbō Daishi. According to tradition, the third bridge cannot be crossed by anyone whose morals are unacceptable to Kōbō Daishi, and a sinful person could not proceed further. After Hideyoshi had risen to the highest position in the Empire he made a ceremonial pilgrimage to the tomb of Kōbō Daishi. Knowing that during his career he had committed many acts of violence, Hideyoshi went to the third bridge the night before and made a trial crossing. Nothing happened, and relieved of the anxiety that he would be publicly embarrassed Hideyoshi returned to the bridge the following day and marched over it in a grand and contemptuous manner.

The Duty of Vengeance

If the loyalty due from a retainer to his daimyō was tremendous in life, it became all the more so after his death. But whereas *junshi* remained condemned for the larger part of samurai history, there was an entirely opposite requirement for revenge. Should one's lord die as a result of murder or other foul play, then a retainer's revenge was his by right. In fact, it went far beyond a right: it was a solemn duty, both sanctioned and practised at the highest levels of the samurai class.

The rules of vengeance

The notion of vengeance is inseparable from the ideals of the noble samurai. To the samurai, a man who took revenge was a man of honour; while he who shrank from this obligation was beneath contempt: a person to be despised more than the villain who had performed the original deed for which vengeance was sought. Such sentiments appear throughout samurai history, from the revenge of the Soga brothers at the time of the first Shōgun Minamoto Yoritomo in the twelfth century, to the classic epic of the Forty-Seven Rōnin (recounted in detail by me in *Samurai Warriors*).

The story of the Forty-Seven Rōnin, although the best-known outside Japan of any story of revenge, is not typical. The details, briefly stated, are that Lord Asano was required to commit *seppuku* as punishment for the crime of drawing a weapon within the Shōgun's palace, and wounding the

The revenge of the Soga brothers
The duty of revenge was found throughout samurai history, as illustrated by this wood-block print from the author's collection, which depicts the revenge of the Soga brothers during the twelfth century.

The Forty-Seven Rōnin
In this detail from one of many prints produced on the subject of the Loyal Retainers of Ako, the avenging rōnin engage the retainers of Kira in a fierce swordfight.

official who has been taunting him. His retainers, who survived him, hatched an elaborate plot of revenge in complete secrecy, turning to drunkenness and debauchery as a cloak for their intentions,which were achieved in a spectacular raid. Having taken the head of their lord's 'judicial murderer', they surrendered to the authorities, and committed suicide.

There are, in fact, very few examples in Japanese history of the murder of a daimyō and his subsequent avenging. Indeed, the Forty-Seven Rōnin is the only example of revenge being carried out in peace-time at such an elevated social level. This uniqueness probably accounts, to some extent, for the enduring popularity of the tale. It is also atypical in the secrecy with which the deed was carried out, which thereby put the avengers outside the law, and in the resulting condemnation by the authorities. The point illustrated by the Forty-Seven Rōnin is that, although revenge was central

---

The Forty-Seven Rōnin

The exploit of the Forty-Seven loyal retainers of Ako is vividly brought to life by this plate. They have arrived outside the gate of Kira's mansion. A dog is silenced for the split second before the enormous mallet crashes against the timbers of the gate. Their leader, Ōishi Yoshio, despatches men to the rear of the house.

Ōishi Yoshio was a pupil of the *bushidō* theorist Yamaga Sokō, and this expression of the loyalty to one's master due from a samurai is the best known practical illustration of *bushidō* in Japanese history. Yet even this famous raid was not without its critics. Yamamoto Tsunetomo, the author of *Hagakure*, a classic of *bushidō* writing which begins with the words 'The Way of the Samurai is found in death', praised the act of revenge on the grounds that it was the conduct to be expected, but went on to question the means whereby it was carried out. Yamamoto Tsunetomo was an adherent of the Wang Yang Ming school of Confucian philosophy, which taught that knowledge should always be accompanied by action, action that was swift and immediate. The revenge of the Forty-Seven Rōnin had been long in the planning, and Tsunetomo expressed surprise that it took so long for them to act. Dramatic acts of revenge were what appealed to men of such opinions, not a calculated and secretive plot such as that of the gallant Forty-Seven.

to the samurai philosophy, it must not be presumed that in carrying out revenge, a man was entirely free to do as he liked. Certainly, by the eighteenth century, the procedure of revenge was very clearly recognised.

If a deed was committed which required avenging, the avenger was required first to present a complaint to the daimyō, from whom he would get authorisation to search for and slay the enemy. This authorisation would be in the form of a letter certifying his identity, and indicating the name of his own *han* and the purpose of his search. After this, if everything had been carried out in perfect order, the particular way in which he slew his enemy was of no consequence, providing it was not attended by public disorder. Once the deed was done, the avenger was required to report immediately to the nearest authorities and explain the circumstances of his revenge. He would be interrogated on the details by the *machi-bugyō*, and asked the name of his family and of his *han*. He would then be required to present satisfactory proof that he had in fact been authorised to carry out the deed. Once his revenge was acknowledged as accomplished according to the rules, he was released from custody and walked away a free man, as in the account of the vengeance of the great swordsman, Miyamoto Musashi:

Miyamoto having encountered his enemy on the way, struck him and killed him. Having revenged himself in that manner, he narrated what he had done to the

Swearing vengeance before the lord's head
Retainers of a dead lord kneel in reverence before his severed head, swearing vengeance on his killer. Vengeance was the samurai's privilege and solemn duty.

The Mountains of Iga
The misty Mountains of Iga shelter
the town of Iga-Ueno, scene of the
Igagoe Vendetta.

daimyō of the province, who instead of blaming him, congratulated him and sent him back in security to his lord's territory.

The duty of vengeance received its solemnest expression in the collection of laws and recommendations referred to as the 'Legacy of Ieyasu', attributed to the first Tokugawa Shōgun, who died in 1616. The section dealing with revenge is a later addition, but sums up beautifully the requirements of the vendetta:

In what is concerning the revenge to be exercised against the man who killed your father or lord, it is expressly written by Confucius that you and your enemy cannot live together under the same heaven.

In consequence of that, the man who has an act of revenge to do must first notify it to the Court of Criminal Justice, which must neither prevent him from accomplishing his desire, nor obstruct him in its execution. Whatever be the case, it is prohibited to kill his enemy by raising troubles or in a riot.

The individual who revenges himself without notifying it to the Court of Criminal Justice, must be considered as a wolf, and his punishment or pardon will depend on the circumstances.

The Igagoe Vendetta

Even though revenge for the death of a daimyō is a very rare event, there are, however, many examples where a daimyō was intimately concerned

147

with a blood feud among his own retainers. The best example of this is the Igagoe Vendetta, which we shall study in some detail, because of the illustration it provides of the legal requirements surrounding the vendetta which we have outlined above.

The city of Ueno lies about 97 km (60 miles) due east of Ōsaka, among the wooded mountains of Mie prefecture. It is commonly called 'Iga-Ueno' (Iga being the name of the pre-modern province of which Ueno was the provincial capital) to distinguish it from the better-known Ueno, which is a district of metropolitan Tōkyō. Nowadays, Iga-Ueno is a mecca for tourists interested in the famous *ninja,* bands of whom had their headquarters in these remote valleys; but this is a modern phenomenon, and for centuries Iga-Ueno was known for a very different reason: as the site of one of the most dramatic acts of vengeance in Japanese history – the Igagoe Vendetta.

The Igagoe Vendetta has its origin in the incident when a certain Watanabe Gendayū was murdered by Kawai Matagorō, a retainer of the Okayama *han.* The Okayama *han,* which was under the control of the Ikeda family, had for some time been troubled by dissension among the samurai retainers, and between the retainers and the daimyō. The murder of Gendayū, which was in a sense the culmination of these troubles, happened on the night of the lively *Bon Odori* festival in 1630 in Okayama, the castle town which was the *han* capital, hundreds of kilometres from Iga-Ueno on the shores of the Inland Sea. That night, Matagorō, accompanied by some companions, was visiting Kazuma, a retainer of his comrades. Kazuma's younger brother, Gendayū who was keeping him company, was absent at that precise moment. Somehow a brawl developed. Matagorō and his associates mortally wounded Gendayū and took flight. Gendayū died very shortly afterwards, while Kawai Matagorō ran away from Okayama and went to Edo.

At this point in the story, we note the involvement of the daimyō. Watanabe Kazuma, who now had the responsibility of avenging his brother, was only 16 years old, and at first seems to have hoped that the Ikeda daimyō would bring Matagorō to justice on his behalf. But relations within the *han* had become so strained that Matagorō was safe in Edo, where a comrade, called Andō Jiemon, eagerly sheltered him. Even the daimyō himself, Ikeda Tadao (1602–32), could not enter unannounced, but hoped that, by employing various stratagems, he could capture Kawai Matagorō, who had caused him a great deal of trouble in the past. A raid was, in fact, carried out, but was seriously bungled. The attackers overcame Andō Jiemon but let Matagorō escape.

Before long, Ikeda Tadao died of a disease, smarting from the humiliation caused him by this public evidence of dissension among the retainers. Such was his tenacity of purpose that his dying wish is supposed to have been: 'For my memorial service, above everything else offer on my behalf the head of Kawai Matagorō.' His younger brother, Ikeda Teruzumi (1603–63), took to heart his elder brother's dying wishes, and relations among the retainers, some of whom openly supported Matagorō, increasingly took a dangerous turn. The be-all and end-all was the existence of Watanabe Kazuma, who sought revenge, and whose unfulfilled desires acted as a goad.

Eventually, the *bakufu* stepped in and officially ordered the exile of Kawai Matagorō. As it was the Shōgun's orders, a samurai had to submit, and by this preserve the honour of the Okayama *han.* This was Kazuma's

opportunity. He was now 18 years old and able to save his own honour as
well as that of the Okayama *han*, so he applied to the Ikeda family for
discharge and, with official approval, began to search everywhere for
Kawai Matagorō.

Kazuma left the service of the Ikeda family in the ninth month of 1832.
At the end of much hardship and long journeying, he located Kawai
Matagorō, in the eleventh month of 1834, in the neighbourhood of Iga-
Ueno. By now Watanabe Kazuma had been joined in his revenge by his

149

sister's husband, Araki Mata'emon, one of the foremost swordsmen of the day. We know that Araki Mata'emon was a swordsman of the celebrated school of fighting called the 'Yagyū Shinkage-ryū' and had been taught by Yagyū Mitsuyoshi. He served the Matsudaira family of Yamato-Koriyama and gave instruction in *kenjutsu*, and seems to have combined good intelligence with swordfighting skill, as related by an anecdote about Mata'emon fighting a swordsman called Yamada Shinryūkan. This Shinryūkan's favourite weapon was the *kusari-gama*, which consisted of a very sharp sickle, to the handle of which was attached a long weighted chain. The skill in using the *kusari-gama* was to whirl the chain at high speed, thus either keeping a swordsman at bay or entrapping his sword. The weight could also be spun to catch the opponent's leg and pull him over. When faced by this weapon, Araki Mata'emon enticed his enemy into a bamboo grove, where the *kusari-gama* could not be used effectively, and overcame him.

Sometime during the period of Kazuma's quest for revenge, Araki Mata'emon took his leave of the Matsudaira *han*, and volunteered his services as his brother-in-law's 'second'. The alliance caused great consternation among Matagorō and his followers, for one of their number had once been defeated by Mata'emon in a fencing match.

On the seventh day of the eleventh month of 1834, Watanabe Kazuma,

The Kagiya crossroads at Iga-Ueno
The scene of the Igagoe Vendetta is marked nowadays by this stone at the Kagiya crossroads in Iga-Ueno.

150

Araki Mata'emon and two others waited for Kawai Matagorō's faction in Iga-Ueno. They had been reliably informed that Kawai Matagorō was *en route* from Ōsaka to Ise, a journey that would take them through Iga-Ueno. That morning the road was frozen. At the Hour of the Dragon (8 am), Mata'emon and followers entered a shop belonging to a certain Yorozu Yakiemon at the Kagiya Crossroads in Iga-Ueno, and waited for Matagorō's party to arrive along the road from Ōsaka. One man of their party stood guard. The time passed very slowly. Apparently Matagorō's uncle, Kawai Jinzaemon, complained of a chill, and their pace had slackened, so they entered Iga town later than Mata'emon had anticipated.

In one of several novels written about the incident, Mata'emon's guard whispers 'They have come!', keeping his voice as low as possible. Mata'emon and his followers leave the shop and line up at the crossroads; then in a gesture towards samurai honour, Mata'emon returns alone to the shop to settle the account of one *sen*. No doubt this incident is included to show the great swordsman's attention to the mundane, and to demonstrate his desire not to be troubled by money during such a great affair. It is also a fact that by this gesture of honesty towards his host, thereby disregarding the chance of being killed within the next few minutes, he would show himself as a samurai who was a defender of the law. This was of crucial importance. The whole of the vendetta had to be carried out according to the spirit and the letter of the law.

The Igagoe Vendetta
A vigorous wood-block print depicting the vengeance of Watanabe Kazuma at Iga-Ueno.

The six-hour blood feud

The law prevailed right through the conflict that followed. Mata'emon first struck the old Jinzaemon, and also killed the followers who were surrounding Matagorō. (The story as it has grown puts the number slain by Mata'emon at 36). But Mata'emon had decided that he did not intend to kill Matagorō. Kazuma was the one to do that, as the law demanded, so Mata'emon pushed Matagorō to Kazuma's side. He himself patiently joined his companions and did not invite them to join in. The Igagoe Vendetta was, in essence, a duel between Kazuma and Matagorō, and nothing must inconvenience it, nor must there be unnecessary deaths.

The duel between Kazuma and Matagorō continued for six hours until the Hour of the Ram (2 pm). Both became so weakened in mind and body that they could not even see their opponent. Nevertheless Mata'emon did not intervene. In a hoarse voice, he encouraged Kazuma, and at one point was able to head off Matagorō from scaping. Discipline was also maintained by Matagorō's side, who had supported him during his exile. There was an equal need for their side to be seen to be behaving according to the law and the dictates of samurai honour. If Matagorō behaved in accordance with the wishes of the Emperor, he might regain the daimyō authority following a victory. So he made a desperate effort. Much more than samurai honour was at stake.

By now the sun was sinking in the west, and the area around the Kagiya crossroads was dotted with corpses, and only Kazuma and Matagorō's

The Erin-ji
The temple of repose of Takeda Shingen, one of the greatest of the Warlords of Japan, as seen from its magnificent garden.

violence could be heard. But a resolution of the combat was not far away. Kazuma hit home on Matagorō, and just before Matagorō responded, Kazuma's sword cut the artery in Matagorō's left arm. Half of Matagorō's body was dyed with blood, and as he fell Kazuma dealt him a decisive and final blow to the neck.

To the bitter end, the law had priority, and the duel at the Kagiya crossroads became famous as a legal duel, ending as it had begun. Mata'-emon and the others carried out the appropriate procedures afterwards, and surrendered themselves to the local Tōdō *han*. They had fulfilled the legal requirements to the very end. There was no riot, and Mata'emon and the others had not killed people indiscriminately. Their operation had been conducted within the limits laid down by law.

The Kameyama Vengeance

One important aspect of the Igagoe Vendetta is that the revenge killing was actually carried out by the immediate kin of the murdered man. Should this prove impossible – the passage of time, for example, preventing such an act from taking place – then the duty of revenge passed from that man to his son, and on, theoretically, until the final generation, when revenge could be gained. The outstanding example of this is the Kameyama Vendetta, which, unlike the Forty-Seven Rōnin and the Igagoe Vendetta, is virtually unknown outside Japan.

On the morning of the ninth day of the fifth month of 1701, beneath the

---

The flags of the Takeda family

In this plate are shown the flags of Takeda Shingen and those of his 'Twenty-Four Generals' of which details have survived.

They include the large standards of the Takeda family, passed from father to son (which are described in the text), the centipede flag of the messengers, Shingen's personal *uma-jirushi* of three 'flowery-edged' *mon*, and the flag with three *mon* which identified Shingen's personal retainers.

The blue flags of Anayama Baisetsu (d. 1582) (drawn to scale) illustrate the range of flags available to one of Shingen's generals. As Anayama is in the *shinrui-shū*, i.e. the 'relatives', the large *sashimono* worn by his mounted samurai and the smaller one worn by those on foot bear the Takeda *mon*. The long *nobori* and *uma-jirushi*, however, have the same coloured ground, but an individual device. The same would apply to the others of the 'Twenty-Four Generals' illustrated here who were family members, namely the two Takedas. Itagaki and

Ichijō. With the others we may assume that the device that appears on the *uma-jirushi* appears also on the *sashimono* and the *nobori*.

The other flags are the personal *uma-jirushi* of the 'Twenty-Four Generals'. As noted in the text, the term is not a contemporary one, nor were they all active over the same period. In some cases the colours of the flags are controversial. Reading from left to right:

Top row: Kōsaka Danjō Masanobu, Omari Torayasu (killed at Ueda, 1548), Takeda Nobukado (brother of Shingen; design also shown as black on white), Takeda Nobushige (killed at Kawanakajima 1561) and also his son Nobutoyo, Yamamoto Kansuke (killed at Kawanakajima 1561)

Second row: Tada Mitsuyori (d. 1563), Tsuchiya Masatsugu (killed at Nagashino 1575), Obu Toramasa ('red regiment', executed 1565), Obata Toramori (d. 1561), Okiyama Nobutomo (killed 1575)

Third row: Oyamada Nobushige, Sanada Yukitaka (d. 1574), Yokota

Takatoshi (killed 1550), Saigusa Moritomo (killed at Nagashino 1575), Ōbata Masamori (son of Toramori, d. 1582)

Fourth row: Ichijō Nobutatsu (Shingen's brother), Itagaki Nobukata (killed at Ueda 1548), Anayama Baisetsu, Hara Masatane (killed at Nagashino 1575), Sanada Nobutsuna (son of Yukitaka, killed at Nagashino 1575)

Fifth row: Yamagata Masakage (brother of Obu Toramasa, who inherited the 'red regiment', killed at Nagashino 1575), Naitō Masatoyo (killed at Nagashino 1575), Baba Nobuharu (killed at Nagashino 1575; alternative design has flag black on white, as shown in frontispiece, Hara Toratane (died 1564)

Not illustrated here are the flags of Takeda Katsuyori, Shingen's heir, who had two *uma-jirushi*, each bearing the character *ō* meaning 'great', one white on black, the other reversed, and Morozumi Masakiyo. whose flag was light blue with the family *mon*.

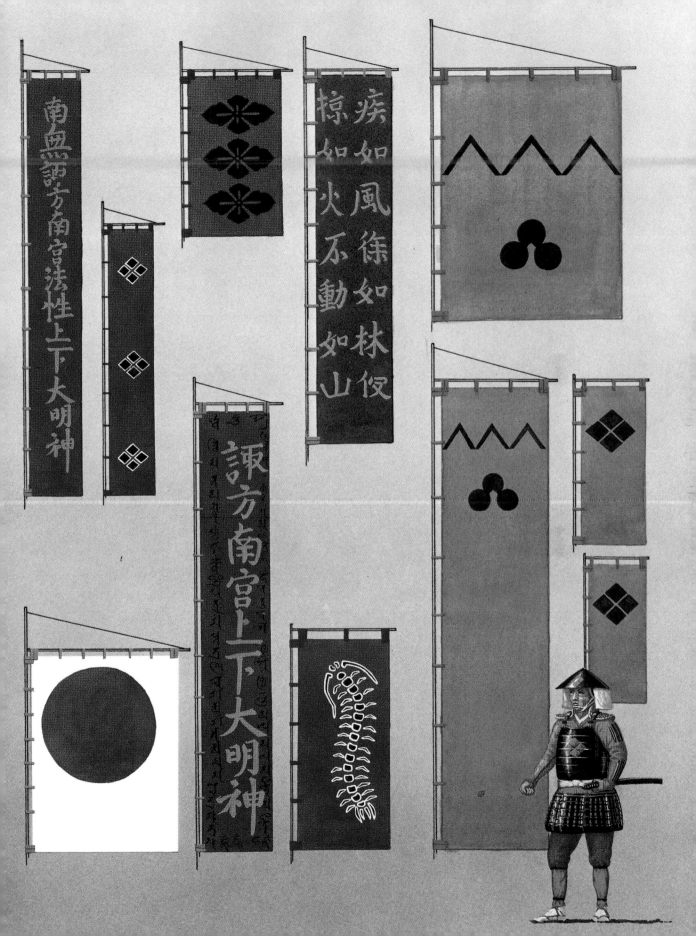

Ishigaki gate inside Kameyama castle, Akabori Sui-no-suke, a retainer of Itagaki Shigefuyu, the keeper of Kameyama castle, was heading for guard duty when his attendant heard the voices of two men, and a sword stroke was brought down from his forehead to his neck. As he fell, the two men gave him a finishing stroke. After this, they tied a message by a cord to Sui-no-suke's *hakama*, and departed calmly, the deed having been accomplished. Some retainers of the Kameyama *han* spotted them and chased after them, but the two men got away. According to the message, the two men who murdered Akabori Sui-no-suke were Morihei, a sandal bearer, and Hanemon, an attendant, and it became clear that they had killed the man who had killed their father. They had carried out this vengeance, they wrote, in accordance with the traditions of the samurai class, and after a wait of an amazing 28 years!

Their late father, one Ishii Uemon, was a samurai who received a stipend of 250 *koku* as a retainer of the keeper of Komoro castle, in Shinano. On the twenty-ninth day of the third month of 1662, his overlord agreed that he should become the warden of Ōsaka castle, and he moved to Ōsaka together with his four sons. This Uemon was a friend of a *rōnin* from Otsu in Ōmi province, called Akabori Yugen, and he was asked if Yugen's adopted son, Gengoemon, might come and study in Ōsaka. Uemon gave his whole-

Journey on the Nakasendō
To seek vengeance, a samurai would wander for years along the roads of Japan in search of his quarry.

156

hearted consent, and summoned Gengoemon to Ōsaka, on the understanding that he applied himself diligently to the martial arts.

However, this Gengoemon was an arrogant young man, and showed little progress in skill when he began instruction in spear fighting with the assembled pupils. On being reprimanded by Ishii, Gengoemon got very angry and challenged him to a contest. Ishii Uemon reluctantly agreed to a contest with wooden swords, but Gengoemon used a real spear, yet was easily defeated. As a result, Gengoemon lost face with his fellow pupils and, when the opportunity presented itself, he murdered Uemon and fled.

Uemon's son, Hyōemon, was 18 years old at the time, and personal retainer to the daimyō Munetoshi. That night he was on guard duty, and on learning of his father's death he applied for leave of absence, and set off in search of revenge. However, the enemy was nowhere to be seen. A long search began, and that winter Hyōemon killed Gengoemon's father Akabori Yūgen in Otsu, hoping thereby that Gengoemon would make an appearance; but he did not turn up. That act made Gengoemon also thirst for revenge for *his* father, and he tracked down Hyōemon to a bath house. Gengoemon attacked him suddenly from behind. Hyōemon drew his sword at the same time and thrust for his thigh, but a deep wound from the first swordstroke led to his death.

The defence of Chihaya castle
One of the most celebrated acts of defiance in samurai history was the defence of Chihaya castle by Kusunoki Masashige and his tiny army. In this section from a painted scroll, owned by the Nampian Kannon-ji at Kawachi-Nagano, the defenders set fire to a bridge.

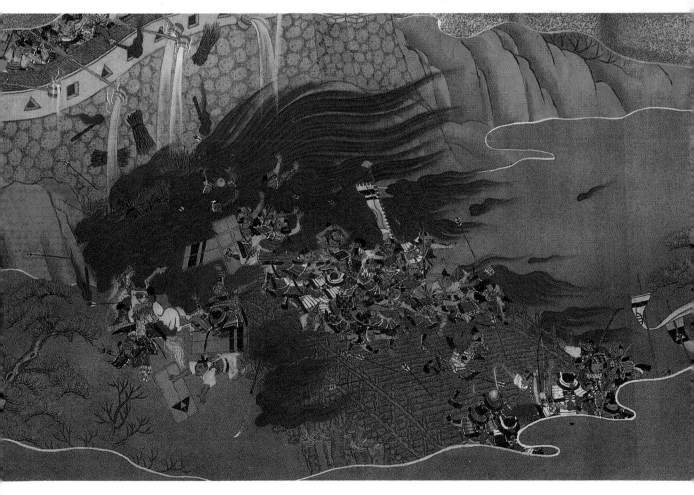

Thereupon, the duty of revenge passed to his younger brother, and Uemon's second son, Hikoshichiro, set out on a quest for vengeance, but ill luck led to his early death. Two young children were left, who were being cared for by a relative called Aki. The third son, Genzō, was 6, and the fourth son, Hanzō, only 3. Gengoemon felt a sense of relief because the remaining sons were just young children, but a relative who was a retainer of Itagaki, the keeper of Kameyama castle, nevertheless recommended vigilance, and proposed that he should enter the service of the Itagaki. Gengoemon was given a stipend of 150 *koku*, and changed his name to Akabori.

Through Aki, Genzō and Hanzō nurtured their desire for revenge, and through him also heard of their enemy's change of name and that he had become a retainer at Kameyama. Genzō was not yet 14, but wanting to comply with the wishes of his family, he sent Aki on a quest for revenge. He came to Kameyama and sighted Sui-no-suke, but there was no way to sneak into the castle, and he spent an ineffective day. In 1688, the youngest son, Hanzō, became 17, and the brothers felt confident enough to take matters into their own hands. Leaving Aki behind, the two went to Edo, and studied the comings and goings of the Itagaki clan on the *sankin-kōtai*, disguised as pedlars. Then they got the chance to serve Hirai Zaiemon, a senior retainer of the Itagaki daimyō. At the time, when Zaiemon was to accompany his overlord on the *sankin-kōtai*, the two Ishii brothers went along as *chūgen*. No sooner had they begun to rejoice on being able to enter the castle than Zaiemon unfortunately died a natural death, and they saw their enemy departing for Edo, while they were unable to prevent it. However, their lowly service had at least brought them within the circle of the Itagaki retainers. Genzō changed his name to Morihei, and Hanzō to Hanemon, and impressed the *bugyō* by their soberness. Soon they grew to have the confidence of the castle family. The two frequently met and talked about their revenge, and as fellow retainers they kept watch on their enemy, Akabori Sui-no-suke.

Then came the day of realising their ambition. In the morning of the ninth day of the fifth month of 1701, at the Hour of the Dragon, 8 am, Akabori Sui-no-suke was making his way under the Ishigaki gate, accompanied by his sandal bearer. The brothers came up from behind and shouted simultaneously, 'We are the sons of Ishii Uemon, Genzō and Hanzō, and you are our father's enemy Akabori Gengoemon. Fair Play!' They cut him from forehead to neck. Sui-no-suke unsheathed at the same time, but the wound was too severe, and he fell. Sui-no-suke's sandal bearer fled. The two brothers tied the message to his *hakama*, fled from Kameyama and wrote a letter to their family, expressing satisfaction at the outcome. Then they went to Edo via the Nakasendō, and reported to the *machi-bugyō*, but neither received any punishment for their deed. Instead, because of the talent they had shown, they were enlisted by Aoyama Tadashige, keeper of Hamamatsu castle in Tōtōmi, and were each given a stipend of 250 *koku*.

The Revenge of the Daughters

Let us conclude this account of the duty of vengeance by noting that its requirements were by no means confined to the male line of a family. Once again, the most celebrated example is practically unknown outside Japan.

A woman's revenge
The duty of revenge was not
confined to the male line of a family.
On occasions, as shown by this
illustration from the *Ehon-Taikō-ki*, a
woman could revenge her lord in
dramatic fashion.

The courtyard of the Keitoku-In
The site of the passing of the last of
the Takeda warlords, Katsuyori, the
Keitoku-In shows many
characteristics of the styles of
dwellings with which the daimyō
would have been familiar.

159

This is the vengeance of the two daughters, Miyagino and Shinobu. Popular accounts of this affair exist in many versions. The *kabuki* play *Gotai eiki shiro ishi banashi* is the result of the joint work of three persons, and, like most *kabuki* plays, is much embellished, particularly with romantic detail.

The factual basis of the story concerns a samurai, called Shiga Daishichi, who was on the run because of a misdemeanor and hid in a paddy-field in a village near Shiro-ishi-banashi, in Mutsu. By chance, he was observed by a farmer, Yomosaku, who had been transplanting rice seedlings, and in his surprise Shiga Daishichi panicked and killed the farmer. Yomosaku had two daughters, the eldest of whom, Miyagino, had (according to the more romantic versions of the tale) been engaged to be married, but through poverty had been sold into prostitution and become a *tayū*, a courtesan of the highest status in Yoshiwara, in Edo. The younger daughter, Shinobu, intending to tell her elder sister about her father's death, went to Edo from far away, and, not being familiar with the topography, she was helped by a person at the Kaminari gate of Asakusa. By chance, he was the master, Muneteru of the Okurosha, where Miyagino was employed. Shinobu was taken by Muneteru to the Okurosha, where she was teased by the girls for her naïve provincialism. Her Mutsu accent revealed her to her sister, so the girls met, and Shinobu recounted their father's untimely last moments.

In the *kabuki* play, she says: 'The man who did it has been captured by our uncle the village headman.' Miyagino, too, when she knew of her father's death, said: 'Such an event brings my tears, . . .let us pray that our requests be granted...' The audience expresses sympathy at this scene, one of the great tear-jerkers of the *kabuki* stage. At all events, the two daughters, Miyagino and Shinobu, secretly slipped away from Yoshiwara in order to seek revenge for their father's death, and began to study the martial arts under the guidance of Miyagino's samurai fiancé. They were eager in their pursuit of knowledge, and the result was the vengeance on their father's enemy, Shiga Daishichi, in 1649.

The girls were determined to carry out the revenge themselves. When the time was ripe, they went through the formalities of asking their daimyō overlord for authorisation to avenge the death of their father. There was, in this case, no need for a long search for the enemy, as he had remained in the daimyō's service. The lord accordingly ordered him to be brought before him, and, according to the popular accounts, the girls set on him there and then. Miyagino was armed with a *naginata*, the long curve-bladed polearm which by the Edo Period had become the traditional weapon for women. Shinobu wielded a *kusari-gama*, the sharpened sickle to which was attached a long weighted chain. With the aid of the chain, Shiga Daishichi's sword was rendered ineffectual, and the other sister finished him off with her *naginata*.

This remarkable duel, carried out in front of the approving daimyō and his senior retainers, has proved a popular theme for wood-block prints. In the *kabuki* play *Shiro-ishi-banashi*, Miyagino is freed from servitude as a courtesan and is united with her fiancé, and lives happily ever after.

Exposure of heads
Wax dummies at the Toei-Uzumasa Film Studios remind us of the surest proof of a samurai's loyal service: to bring back the severed head of his enemy.

The end of vengeance

The above examples serve to illustrate how the notion and duty of revenge

160

Vengeance
This crude fragment from a *kawaraban*, or broadsheet, depicts a revenge killing, probably that of Miyagino and Shinobu. *Kawaraban* were the forerunners of modern Japanese newspapers, and often featured vendettas in their accounts of contemporary life.

was a feature of samurai culture from the earliest times. The Meiji Restoration dealt the death-blow to the tradition of samurai revenge, as it was to do to so many aspects of the warrior tradition. The imperial decree forbidding revenge was issued in February 1873, and went as follows:

Assassination being absolutely prohibited by the law of the Empire, the Government's duty is to punish any individual who kills another.

According to ancient habits, it was an obligation on a son or a younger brother to revenge a father or elder brother, nevertheless, personal interest must not lead one to transgress the law and despise the public powers by revenging himself. Whoever so acts cannot be pardoned, the more especially because in that case it is impossible to know who is in the right and who in the wrong. Therefore from this day, no one shall have the right to avenge or pass judgement for himself. If unfortunately someone has done wrong towards a member of your family, take your complaint and explanations to the authorities, but do not follow the ancient custom, or you will be punished according to law.

There were many more decrees to come: the abolition of the wearing of the pigtail, the restriction of the wearing of swords to the armed forces, and soon the actual abolition of the name and class of samurai itself; but of all the new laws that took Japan into the modern world, none so eloquently reversed the duties of a previous age, and set at nothing the values of the 'Warlords of Japan'.

APPENDIX I
The 1559 Hōjō Register

The typical daimyō's retainer band was commonly divided into three main parts, namely: family members and relatives (which might include others regarded as equivalent to family because of a long and close relationship); *fudai*, the hereditary retainers of the family; and 'outsiders', either the surviving retainers of conquered enemies, the inhabitants of newly gifted lands or simply newcomers whose loyalty had yet to be tested. Allied families were usually placed in this category. There is often a separate unit for the daimyō's bodyguard, but its members tended to be recruited from the *fudai*.

The balance of evidence seems to be that only the troops furnished by the 'family members' category bore the family *mon* on their *sashimono*. The *fudai* and allies fought under the flag of their commander, and the daimyō's bodyguard and messengers usually had their own distinctive appearance.

The Hōjō register, the *Odawara-shū shōryō yakuchō*, listed the military

The Hōjō bodyguard
A samurai wearing the *sashimono* of the personal guard to the head of the family.

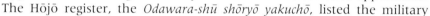

The personal standards of the Hōjō family (not to scale)
Upper left: the Hōjō *mon* in black on a very large white banner of *shihō* type (horizontal dimension exceeds vertical), used by Hōjō Ujiyasu; *right*: a long inscription (practically untranslatable!) in black on white, used by Hōjō Ujimasa; *lower left*: 'hachiman' in black on pale yellow, used by Hōjō Tsunanari.

162

The character mu
The character *mu*, which means 'nothing', is a popular device in Japanese heraldry. It appears within a black ring on the *uma-jirushi* of Sengoku Hidehisa (1551–1614), and here as the *uma-jirushi* of Hōjō Ujinao (1562–1591). According to Takahashi, an identical banner was used as a *sashimono* by Uesugi Kenshin up to about 1555. He presented it to Usa Sadayuki, his general in charge of the messenger unit, following one of the Battles of Kawanakajima (probably the second, in 1555).

obligation of the retainers of the Hōjō in 1559, under the third daimyō Hōjō Ujiyasu. There would also be a sizeable contribution to the army from the daimyō lands, which were not registered. Each of the retainers counted below would have had to supply men in accordance with the current compilation, which gives roughly 10,000 men. (The notes are the present author's observation.)

Unit Name	Notes, and prominent members	No. of retainers
Gokamon	('relatives', inc. heir Ujimasa, 2nd son Ujiteru, 3rd son Ujikuni)	17
Go-umawari-shū	('the daimyō's bodyguard')	94
Takoku-shū	('allies')	28

Units identified by geographical location —

Tamanawa-shū	(inc. Hōjō Tsunanari, Ujiyasu's adopted brother)	18
Miura-shū	(inc. Ujiyasu's 4th son Hōjō Ujimitsu)	32
Kotsuke-shū	(inc. Ujiyasu's 5th son Ujihide, adopted by the Uesugi in 1563)	29
Tsukui-shū	(inc. Naitō family)	57
Izu-shū	(inc. Kasawara family)	29
Matsuyama-shū	(inc. Kano family)	15
Edo-shū	(inc. Toyama family)	103
Odawara-shū	(inc. Matsuda family)	34

Other units

Ashigaru-shū		20
Temple land		28
Shrine land		13
Shokunin-shū	(craftsmen)	26
Total retainers listed		560

APPENDIX II
The 1575 Uesugi Register

This list is particularly interesting as, in addition to similar information to that for the Hōjō in Appendix I, it shows the various weapons to be supplied. The totals, from 39 names of retainers (simply classified as *ichimon*, family; *fudai*, inner retainers; and *kuni-shū*, country units) are as follows:

Mounted samurai	600
Foot-soldiers	
Spearmen	4,899
Flag bearers	402
Arquebuses	360
Reserves (inc. servants etc.)	610
Grand total:	6,871

The fine detail shows how the above proportions of one mounted to ten foot-soldiers are maintained throughout the army. As examples, for the family (*ichimon*) and family equivalent (*kakushō*), they appear as:

Name	Spears	Reserve	Arquebuses	Flags	Horsemen	Total
Uesugi Kagekatsu	250	40	20	25	40	375
Nagao Kagetori	106	15	10	10	15	156
Nagao Kagenobu	54	10	4	5	8	81
Sambonji Sadanaga	50	10	2	3	6	71
Kamijō Masashige	63	15	2	6	10	96
Murakami Kunikiyo	170	20	25	15	20	250
From among the eleven fudai *families*						
Matsumoto	101	15	13	13	16	158
Honjō	150	30	15	15	30	240
Yamayoshi	235	40	20	30	52	377
Naoe	200	30	20	20	35	305

Name	Spears	Reserve	Arquebuses	Flags	Horsemen	Total
From the kunishū, *well-known names are:*						
Nakajō	80	20	10	15	15	140
Irobe	160	20	12	15	20	227
Takemata	67	10	5	6	10	98
Kakizaki	180	30	15	15	20	260
Saitō	153	20	10	12	18	213
Shibata	135	20	10	12	17	194
Yasuda	60	15	5	5	10	95
Shimojō	32	10	2	3	5	52
Shimazu	58	10	6	7	10	91

The proportions and the overall numbers are very similar to an earlier, but less detailed, Uesugi Register of 1559. Combining this with contemporary accounts of the Fourth Battle of Kawanakajima it is possible to reconstruct the divisions of the Uesugi army at this encounter. (See my *Battles of the Samurai* for a detailed account of the fighting).

Forward troops
Vanguard: Kakizaki, Shibata, Shimazu
Second rank: Suibara, Takemata, Saitō
Third rank: Suda, Matsumoto, Shimojō

Headquarters troops
Takanashi, Ōgawa, Ayukawa, Inoue, Murakami, Watauchi
Irobe (*gun-bugyō*), Usa (messengers)

Flanks
Right: Yamayoshi, Shibata, Kaji
Left: Nagao, Yasuda, Honjō

Rear-guard
Nakajō, Koshi, Ozaki

Support
Amakazu (who held the ford at Amenomiya), Naoe (supplies)

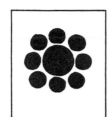
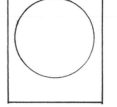

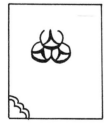

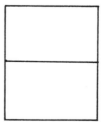

The personal standards of the Uesugi generals
Depicted here are the remaining known designs of flags used by Uesugi Kenshin's generals which are not shown elsewhere in the plates in this book. All are in black and white except where noted. Reading from left to right:
Top row: Suibara (white on red), Saitō, Takemata, Matsumoto
Second row: Nagao (dark blue on white), Yasuda, Usa, Irobe (red on white)
Third row: Yamayoshi (red disc, black inscription), Ayukawa, Inoue, Amakasu
Fourth row: Naoe, Nakajō (retainers' *sashimono*), Murakami, Sambonji (white over red)

166

APPENDIX III
Takeda Shingen

The following list is taken from the *Kōyō Gunkan*, showing the obligation to the Takeda Shingen by family, hereditary retainers and newly acquired vassals:

Name	No. of horsemen	Name	No. of horsemen
Family members			
Takeda Nobutoyo (son of Nobushige)	200	Ōyamada Nobushige	250
		Amari	100
Takeda Nobukado (brother of Shingen)	80	Kurihara	100
		Imafuku	70
Takeda Katsuyori (heir)	200	Tsuchiya	100
		Akiyama	50
Ichijō Nobutatsu (brother of Shingen)	200	Hara Masatane	120
		Ōyamada Bitchu no kami	70
Takeda Nobuzane (brother of Shingen, killed at Nagashino)	15	Atobe	300
		Others (four names in total)	255
Takeda Zaemon (cousin of Shingen)	100		
Nishina	100	*Ashigaru taishō*	
Mochizuki	60	30 names, commanding 255 horsemen, 785 *ashigaru* in all	
Katsurayama	120		
Itagaki Nobukata (killed at Ueda, 1548)	120	*Semposhū* (by province)	
Kiso	200	Shinano (includes Sanada family)	2020
Anayama Baisetsu	200		
		East Kozuke	1035
Fudai		Suruga	430
		Totomi	320
Baba	120	Hida	150
Naitō	250	Etchu	170
Yamagata	300	Musashi	180
Kōsaka	450		

Navy (41 ships, no numbers of crew given)

Shingen is also said to have had a bodyguard of 6,373, though whether these were drawn from the above or were his direct retainers is difficult to say. It seems a very large figure, even for such an important daimyō.

APPENDIX IV
Hashiba Hideyoshi

In 1573, following the defeat of the Asai family, Hashiba (later Toyotomi) Hideyoshi achieved a certain degree of independence from Oda Nobunaga by being granted in fief the castle of Nagahama. The details of his troops and their heraldry are interesting in providing a 'snapshot' of the future *Taikō* at one stage of his rise to glory. Unfortunately there are no numbers or weaponry given.

His *uma-jirushi* was a single golden gourd. Takahashi Ken'ichi, in his book *Hata Sashimono*, devotes several pages to a discussion of whether or not Hideyoshi ever did adopt the famous 'thousand-gourd standard', and notes that as late as 1575 only one gourd is to be seen. (This is on the famous painted screen of the Battle of Nagashino.)

His retainer band organisation follows the pattern common to many daimyō. There are the *ichimon-shū* (relatives), the *fudai-shū* and the *shinzan-shū* (literally 'newcomers'). This latter group is divided geographically by province, giving the Omi, Mino and Owari-*shū*, and includes such names as Ishida Mitsunari (Omi) and Yamauchi Kazutoyo (Owari).

The *fudai-shū* included a seven-man contingent who formed Hideyoshi's personal bodyguard known as the 'yellow *horō-shū*'. (Compare Nobunaga's use of black and red *horō* in his army.) Their numbers were later raised to 22.

Hideyoshi's messengers, 29 in all, were distinguished by an identical gold-coloured flag (see illustration).

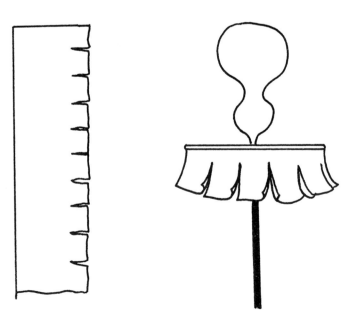

Hideyoshi's flags
These sketches illustrate the golden gourd standard, with its golden flag, and the style of flag used as a *sashimono* by Hideyoshi's messengers.

168

APPENDIX V
The Ii 'Red Devils'

The troops of Ii Naomasa and his son Naotaka, the most loyal of the Tokugawa *fudai*, formed an important part of the Tokugawa army at Sekigahara and at Ōsaka, and provide the most striking illustration of a *fudai* contingent adopting its own distinctive colours. The *Iika Gumpō*, quoted by Takahashi, gives the full regulations for the appearance of this army, to a degree of detail that is quite unique. Takahashi gives no date for the document, but it probably dates from the early seventeenth century.

Item, the standard is a 5-shaku [1 shaku = 1 foot] length of four widths of silk. On a red ground, the mon, *which is the character 'i' in gold in the centre. The pole is lacquered black.*

*Item, personal large banner [*nobori?*] is two widths of silk, 1 jō [9 feet] long. The* mon *on red ground. By invitation, on a 7-shaku length, on a red ground, the characters 'Hachiman Dai Bosatsu' in white. The pole is lacquered black.*

Item, the uma-jirushi *is a gold fly-catcher, with a black-lacquered pole.*

Item, mounted samurai, on a 5-shaku length of two widths of silk, on a red ground the surname written in gold.

Item, retainers' personal flags the same, excepting that by invitation the family mon *in white on a red ground.*

Item, ashigaru's back-flags, three, each of one width of silk, 5 shaku long, immediate ashigaru a red field with no mon, *retainers the* mon *of the family of birth in white.*

Item, armour, harness, saddle and stirrups to be red, with the exception that retainers may display in gold the mon *of their family of birth.*

Note how much the heraldry adopted depends on the nature of the relationship, such as being a retainer or a warrior directly commanded by the lord. The regulations fit almost exactly with the figures depicted on the painted screen depicting the Ii army at Ōsaka. Using a rule of thumb of two mounted and twenty foot-soldiers per 1,000 koku the Ii contingent at Ōsaka would have consisted of about 20 and 200 men respectively, plus their own followers. On the screen appear the 19 mounted samurai, of whom 9 wear red *horō*. There are 123 samurai on foot, mostly armed with long spears. Nearly all have inscriptions in gold, which must be the surnames referred to above, though one or two have *mon*. There are 50 *ashigaru*, of whom 19 have arquebuses.

BIBLIOGRAPHY

Ackroyd, Joyce, 'Women in Feudal Japan', *Transactions of the Japan Society of London*, 1957.

Asakawa, Kan'ichi, *The Documents of Iriki*, Yale University Press, 1929.

Baba, Ichiro, *Heike Monogatari Emaki*, Taiyō special edition, winter 1975, Heibonsha, Tōkyō, 1975.

Birt, Michael P., 'Warring States: A study of the Go-Hōjō daimyō and domain, 1491–1590, Ph.D. thesis, Princeton, 1983.

Birt, Michael P., 'Samurai in Passage: The Transformation of the Sixteenth Century Kantō', *Journal of Japanese Studies*, Vol. 11, No. 1, 1985.

Caron, François, *A True Description of the Mighty Kingdoms of Japan and Siam*, C.R.Boxer, London, 1935.

Inoue, Toshio, *Kenshin to Shingen: Nihon Rekishi shinshō*, Tōkyō, 1977.

Kobayashi, Keiichiro, *Kawanakajima no tatakai*, Nagano, 1985.

Kōsaka Danjō (attributed to), *Kōyō Gunkan*, in *Sengoku shiryō-shū*, series 1, Vols. 3–5.

Kuwada Tadachika (editor), *Sengoku Bushō no shōkan*, Tōkyō, 1968.

Kyūan, Rōjin, *Uma-jirushi*, Edo, 1655.

Matsumoto, Tamotsu, *Kassen Enki Emaki. Taiyō Classics and Picture Scroll Series IV*, Heibonsha, Tōkyō, 1979.

Miura Jōshin (attributed to) 'Hōjō Godaiki', in *Hōjō Shiryō-sōshō*, series 2, Vol. 1.

Nakamura, Shinju, 'Taiheiki', illustrated in *Taiyō Monthly*, 178, February 1978.

Sachiya H., and Yamamoto, S., 'Kūki to shite no Yasukuni', *Shokun*, April 1986.

Sadler, A.L., 'Heike Monogatari', *Transactions of the Asiatic Society of Japan*, Vol. 46, No. 49, Yokohama, 1918 and 1921.

Sasama, Yoshihiko, *Buke senjin sahō shūsei*, Tōkyō, 1968.

Sugiyama, Hiroshi, *Hōjō Sōun*, Odawara, 1976.

Sugiyama, Hiroshi, *Sengoku daimyō (Nihon no Rekishi 11)*, Chuo Koronsha, Tokyo, 1971.

Sugiyama, Kyushiro, 'Yasukuni no kiso chishiki jūhachi', *Shokun*, April 1986.

Takahashi, Ken'ichi, *Hata Sashimono*, Akida Shōten, Tōkyō, 1965.

Takahashi, Ken'ichi, *Daimyō-ke no kamon*, Akida Shōten, Tōkyō, 1974.

Takahashi, Ken'ichi, *Kamon, hatamoto, hachiman-ki*, Akida Shōten, Tōkyō, 1976.

Takahashi, Masato, *Buke no jirushi*, Iwasaki Bijutsusha, Tōkyō, 1979.

Turnbull, S.R., *The Samurai – A Military History*, Osprey, London, 1977, reprinted 1988.

Turnbull, S.R., *Samurai Armies 1550–1615*, Osprey, London, 1979.

Turnbull, S.R., *Warlords of Japan*, Sampson Low Library of the Past, 1979.

Turnbull, S.R., *The Mongols*, Osprey, London, 1980.

Turnbull, S.R., *The Book of the Samurai*, Arms and Armour Press, London, 1982.

Turnbull, S.R., *The Book of the Medieval Knight*, Arms and Armour Press, London, 1985.

Turnbull, S.R., *Samurai Warriors*, Blandford Press, London, 1987.

Turnbull, S.R., *Battles of the Samurai*, Arms and Armour Press, London, 1987.

Turnbull, S.R., *The Lone Samurai*, in preparation.

Turnbull, S.R., 'Shorthand of the Samurai – the Use of Heraldry in the Armies of Sixteenth Century Japan', *Proceedings of the Japan Society*, London, 1989.

Turnbull, S.R., *The Ninja*, in preparation.

Yoshida, Taiyo, *Kamon kakei jiten*, Shōbunsha, Tōkyō, 1979.

Index